EIGHT OF T

SURREY'S GLORY Y]
by TREVOR

LIMITED NUMBERED EDITION
This is one of only 200 specially bound, hand-numbered copies

Number 30 of 200

To Trevor

With best wishes and many thanks for your support

from Trevor Jones

EIGHT OF THE BEST

SURREY'S GLORY YEARS 1996-2003

TREVOR JONES

Sporting Declarations Books

www.sportingdeclarations.co.uk

PO Box 882, Sutton, Surrey, SM2 5AW

First published in 2005 by Sporting Declarations Books

© Trevor Jones 2005

All rights reserved. No part of this publication may be reproduced, stored in a retrieval system, or transmitted, in any form or by any means, electronic, mechanical, photocopying, recording or otherwise, without the prior written permission of the publishers

ISBN 0 9535307 7 9

Cover Photographs

FRONT - TOP:
Surrey celebrate their 1999 County Championship triumph
(PA/Empics)

FRONT - BOTTOM LEFT:
Chris Lewis and Alec Stewart with the AXA Equity & Law League trophy (1996)
(PA/Empics)

FRONT - BOTTOM MIDDLE:
The Surrey team on the outfield at Lord's after winning the Benson & Hedges Cup (2001)
(Empics/Surrey CCC)

FRONT - BOTTOM RIGHT:
Adam Hollioake and his team celebrate their Twenty20 Cup triumph at Trent Bridge (2003)
(Empics/Surrey CCC)

BACK:
The players savour their 2002 County Championship success at The Oval
(Empics/Surrey CCC)

Typesetting and design by Trevor Jones

Printed and bound in Great Britain by MPG Books, Victoria Square, Bodmin, Cornwall, PL31 1EB

Contents

1	Up With the Greats	4
2	An Unhappy Anniversary	7
3	1996 - Ending The Drought	10
4	1997 - Consoled By Gold	38
5	1998 - Shattered Dreams	63
6	1999 - The Dream Fulfilled	91
7	2000 - Doubling Up With Delight	121
8	2001 - A Mixed Return	156
9	2002 - From Tragedy To Triumph	182
10	2003 - Two In Blue	222
11	2004 And Beyond	265
12	Team Statistics - Surrey Versus The Rest	267
13	Player Statistics	278
	Successes And Failures - Surrey Players	
	Successes And Failures - Opposition Players	
	National Service	
14	Eight Of The Best	325
	Matches	
	Championship Batting & Bowling	
	Limited-Overs Batting & Bowling	
	Catches	
15	Keys To Success	338
16	Nobody Loves A Winner	341
17	Doing It The Right Way	345
	Acknowledgements/Sponsor-Subscribers	348

1 Up With The Greats

Since county cricket became formally organised in this country in 1890, Surrey's successes have tended to come in blocks. The club enjoyed an immediate golden age as the County Championship title was captured six times in the first ten years of its existence (1890-1892, 1894, 1895 and 1899), and another highly successful period followed in the 1950s with the famous seven-year run of triumphs from 1952 to 1958, after the 1950 title had been shared with Lancashire. There were also isolated Championship successes in 1914 and 1971, before the club once again struck gold as the twentieth century drew to a close. Having claimed limited-overs trophies in 1996 and 1997, their 1999 Championship triumph confirmed that Surrey were once again a force to be reckoned with.

Until 1963, when the 65-overs-a-side Gillette Cup was introduced, the UK's only first-class cricket competition was the County Championship. The only way to become recognised as a 'great' side, therefore, was to string together a run of winning seasons. Apart from Surrey, with their two aforementioned glorious sequences, Lancashire (from 1926 to 1928) and Yorkshire (1900-1902, 1922-1925, 1931-1933 and 1937-1946) were the only sides to register three or more consecutive titles before the advent of one-day cricket gave the counties an expanded range of silverware to aim at. Although Yorkshire managed to complete another Championship hat-trick (1966-1968) after the introduction of the Gillette Cup, no team was able to achieve the County Championship-Gillette Cup double until 1977, when Middlesex shared the Championship title with Kent and beat Glamorgan at Lord's in the one-day final. By this time, however, the counties were chasing four trophies every summer, since the Sunday League had come into being in 1969 and the Benson & Hedges Cup had arrived on the scene in 1972.

The chances of going down in history as one of the great sides has therefore increased with the addition of all this extra silverware, though the County Championship remains the competition that the vast majority of players and supporters most want to win at the start of every season. This is because it represents the purest and most demanding test of cricketing ability.

How then is greatness to be judged since the introduction of one-day cricket? Personally, I would only classify a team as 'great' if they have achieved success in both Championship and limited-overs cricket over a period of at least five seasons. I would, therefore, immediately discount the claims of three brilliant one-day sides from the past forty years. Lancashire, who were the first side to achieve a double of any sort in 1970 when they won the Gillette Cup and the John Player Sunday League, were a supreme force as they won five one-day titles in the four years from 1969-1972, and they repeated this level of success by claiming six more limited-overs crowns in the five-year period between 1995 and 1999. Somerset were, similarly, the champion one-day team from 1979 to 1983 as they won five competitions, while Gloucestershire have ruled the limited-overs roost in more recent times with the capture of five of the six available cups in 1999 and 2000. None of these teams were able to capture the Championship title that would have secured the seal of greatness, however, and it is interesting to note that both Somerset and Gloucestershire have still yet to win county cricket's most prestigious competition, while Lancashire haven't been County Champions since they shared the 1950 title with Surrey.

Having cast aside these fine limited-overs teams, with the greatest of respect for their achievements, an analysis of the trophy winners since 1972, when four competitions per season became the norm, reveals that there have been a number of sides worthy of the 'great' tag.

WINNERS OF MAJOR DOMESTIC TROPHIES 1972-2003

Year	County Championship	Sun/Nat League	GC/NWT/ C&G	Benson & Hedges Cup	Twenty20 Cup
1972	Warwickshire	**Kent**	Lancashire	**Leicestershire**	
1973	Hampshire	**Kent**	Gloucestershire	**Kent**	
1974	Worcestershire	**Leicestershire**	Kent	Surrey	
1975	**Leicestershire**	Hampshire	Lancashire	**Leicestershire**	
1976	Middlesex	**Kent**	Northamptonshire	**Kent**	
1977	**Kent**/Middlesex	**Leicestershire**	Middlesex	Gloucestershire	
1978	**Kent**	Hampshire	Sussex	**Kent**	
1979	**Essex**	**Somerset**	**Somerset**	**Essex**	
1980	**Middlesex**	Warwickshire	**Middlesex**	Northamptonshire	
1981	Nottinghamshire	**Essex**	Derbyshire	**Somerset**	
1982	**Middlesex**	Sussex	Surrey	**Somerset**	
1983	**Essex**	Yorkshire	**Somerset**	**Middlesex**	
1984	**Essex**	**Essex**	**Middlesex**	Lancashire	
1985	**Middlesex**	**Essex**	**Essex**	Leicestershire	
1986	**Essex**	Hampshire	Sussex	**Middlesex**	
1987	**Nottinghamshire**	**Worcestershire**	**Nottinghamshire**	Yorkshire	
1988	**Worcestershire**	**Worcestershire**	Middlesex	Hampshire	
1989	**Worcestershire**	Lancashire	Warwickshire	**Nottinghamshire**	
1990	Middlesex	Derbyshire	Lancashire	Lancashire	
1991	Essex	**Nottinghamshire**	Hampshire	**Worcestershire**	
1992	Essex	Middlesex	Northamptonshire	Hampshire	
1993	Middlesex	Glamorgan	**Warwickshire**	Derbyshire	
1994	**Warwickshire**	**Warwickshire**	Worcestershire	**Warwickshire**	
1995	**Warwickshire**	Kent	**Warwickshire**	Lancashire	
1996	Leicestershire	**Surrey**	Lancashire	**Lancashire**	
1997	Glamorgan	Warwickshire	Essex	**Surrey**	
1998	Leicestershire	**Lancashire**	**Lancashire**	Essex	
1999	**Surrey**	**Lancashire**	**Gloucestershire**	**Gloucestershire**	
2000	**Surrey**	**Gloucestershire**	**Gloucestershire**	**Gloucestershire**	
2001	Yorkshire	Kent	Somerset	**Surrey**	
2002	**Surrey**	Glamorgan	Yorkshire	Warwickshire	
2003	Sussex	**Surrey**	**Gloucestershire**		**Surrey**

I have split the table with dividing lines that mark some surprisingly distinct periods of dominance enjoyed by one or more counties. It is interesting to note that no county club has managed two sustained spells of success during the modern era, though it should be pointed out that Middlesex won no fewer than fourteen trophies (seven Championships, seven limited-overs) in the eighteen seasons from 1976 to 1993 inclusive. It is also noticeable that two or three powerful sides have often co-existed and enjoyed successful eras of almost identical lengths.

Between 1972 and 1978, Kent and Leicestershire - who were the first-ever winners of a Championship/limited-overs double in 1975 - won fourteen of the twenty-eight titles on offer. Then, during the eight-year period from 1979 to 1986, Essex, Middlesex and the one-day kings of that time, Somerset, captured no fewer than twenty-one of the thirty-two cups that were up for grabs, while Worcestershire and Nottinghamshire were the dominant forces between 1987 and 1991 as they snapped up nine out of twenty available trophies. Warwickshire then took over single-handedly for three seasons, during which time they claimed their glorious treble in 1994 and followed up with a double in 1995, before Surrey gradually became the most powerful force in the land alongside the one-day specialists, Lancashire and Gloucestershire. With Surrey winning eight varied 'majors', and the two limited-overs champions securing eleven crowns between them, we witnessed a similar kind of domination to that enjoyed by Essex, Middlesex and Somerset from 1979-1986, with the three new leading sides winning nineteen out of thirty-two titles between 1996 and 2003. It is worth noting that Lancashire were unfortunate to finish as runners-up in the Championship on no fewer than four occasions (1998, 1999, 2000 and 2003) during this period, thereby only just failing to qualify as a truly great side.

THE MODERN 'GREAT' SIDES AND THEIR PERIODS OF DOMINANCE					
Period	County	Total Trophies	No. Of Seasons	Championship Titles	Ltd Overs Titles*
1972-1978	Kent	9	7	2	7
1972-1977	Leicestershire	5	6	1	4
1979-1986	Essex	9	8	4	5
1980-1986	Middlesex	7	7	3	4
1987-1991	Worcestershire	5	5	2	3
1987-1991	Nottinghamshire	4	5	1	3
1993-1997	Warwickshire	7	5	2	5
1996-2003	Surrey	8	8	3	5

* Includes only major titles, i.e. Gillette Cup, Nat West Trophy, Cheltenham & Gloucester Trophy, Benson & Hedges Cup, Sunday League, National League Division One, Twenty20 Cup.

If the true test of a side's excellence is the ability to win all the available competitions over a sustained period of time then Surrey fall short of some of the other great teams listed above because they failed to win the premier limited-overs cup competition (Gillette Cup/Nat West Trophy/C&G Trophy) during their spell at the top of the tree. The introduction of the Twenty20 Cup in place of the Benson & Hedges Cup in 2003 did, however, enable them to accomplish something that none of the other counties had the opportunity to achieve. Their victory in the inaugural Twenty20 tournament meant that they had won competitions of five different durations - the County Championship (four days); the Benson & Hedges Cup (50 overs-per-side in both 1997 and 2001); the National League (45 overs-per-side in 2003), the Sunday League (40 overs-per-side in 1996) and the Twenty20 Cup (20 overs-per-side).

2 An Unhappy Anniversary

It is amazing how often triumph comes forth from adversity, especially in the world of sport, and Surrey's renaissance during the closing years of the twentieth century is certainly a good example of this. Although the club was not quite at its lowest ebb, it would be fair to say that The Oval was not the happiest of places in the period leading up to the start of Surrey's glory years in 1996.

Everyone had hoped that 1995, the club's 150th anniversary season, might produce some inspiration and silverware to end a twelve-year drought that extended back to the 1982 Nat West Trophy triumph over Warwickshire. Only Gloucestershire and Kent could match Surrey's barren run as the campaign got under way.

By the end of a miserable summer for the men from London SE11, things were worse still - Kent had broken their losing streak by claiming the Sunday League title, while Surrey had endured a dismal season, finishing twelfth in the County Championship and ninth in the 40-over competition after suffering early exits in both of the one-day knockout cups.

Having started the campaign with two wins from their first three Championship matches, a run of five defeats and two draws from their next seven games saw the team slump to the bottom of the table by 10th July, leaving the Nat West Trophy second-round contest against Middlesex at The Oval two days later as the club's last remaining chance of glory with two months of the season still to play. An ignominious 79-run defeat in this match turned out, predictably enough, to be the final straw for many members, a large number of whom were soon signing a petition - calling for a Special General Meeting (SGM) - organised by the Surrey Action Group (SAG). The SAG was formed in 1993 by a group of members who were concerned by the direction the club was taking under the stewardship of the newly appointed Chief Executive, Glyn Woodman, and it had gathered a good deal of support during the intervening period. Although the team's struggles had sparked more widespread interest in forcing an SGM, it was clear that there were just as many problems off the field as there were on it. Apart from the fact that the club was not in good financial shape - having announced a loss of £350,000 for 1995 - The Oval had become a joyless, undemocratic place. The Cricket Committee, chaired by the former Surrey stalwart Arnold Long, had been scrapped, while a five-man Executive Board, chaired by Woodman, was wielding far too much power for the liking of many people close to, and around, the club. In the eyes of many supporters, commerce seemed to have become more important than cricket.

The team's results improved only marginally in the latter stages of the summer, which made it easier for the SAG to collect 400 signatures, thereby compelling the club to call an SGM for 5th October. Changes were already under way, however, as the season drew to a close. Although he had not been targeted by the SAG, and wished to emphasise that his departure had nothing to do with the crisis engulfing the club, the chairman, Brian Downing, resigned at an emergency committee meeting on the final day of the season. Downing, 62, a Surrey committee member for twenty-eight years and a tireless worker in the fields of marketing and finance, stated that he felt "the time was right for a younger man, a man with new zest" to replace him as chairman. That man turned out to be Michael Soper, a 50-year-old businessman who had been involved with the club for a number of years, and had been a member of the Marketing, Cricket and General committees.

While the storm clouds had been gathering, it was to the club's credit that they had at least instigated a management and procedure review under the chairmanship of Sir Peter Imbert, the former Metropolitan Police commissioner, though the members still had numerous areas of concern. For example, it was hugely ironic that the mailing informing members of the SGM outlined the committee's reasons for rejecting the Surrey Action Group's motion calling for greater democracy in decision-making yet failed to list any grounds for supporting it! This was in line with the way the club was being run at the time. The annual committee election ballot papers provided another example of the absence of true democracy - although any member could be nominated to serve on the committee, certain candidates were marked with an asterisk as being 'recommended for election' by the club.

It was not all doom and gloom as the SGM approached, however, since Surrey were able to announce the signing of Chris Lewis, the mercurial England all-rounder, on a two-year contract, following his highly acrimonious split with Nottinghamshire, which had resulted in the Midlands county cancelling his contract in July. With Lewis's season having been wrecked by a hip injury that restricted him to just a couple of outings in the Benson & Hedges Cup, Surrey sensibly stipulated that he would have to prove he had regained full fitness before the contract was confirmed.

If the announcement of this significant new signing was a ploy to sweeten the members ahead of the SGM on 5th October it failed to work. Although proxy votes saved the committee from an embarrassing defeat, securing an overall 1,043 to 746 'victory' for them, the vote in the Banqueting Suite produced a 338-39 outcome in favour of the Surrey Action Group's motion. The debate was, at times, stormy and prompted Mike Soper to admit that he had been "staggered and humbled by the depth of feeling." Then, promising the assembled members that he would digest what had been said and take the appropriate action, he declared: "If we don't listen to what's been said then we will be bloody fools."

Further changes were inevitable after the SGM, and the first of these saw Graeme Clinton - the Surrey coach since November 1993 when Geoff Arnold had been unceremoniously sacked by Woodman - leaving the club 'by mutual consent'. This wasn't unexpected given the team's two disappointing campaigns since Clinton's appointment, and it didn't take long for the club to reveal Dave Gilbert, the former Australian seam bowler, as their new Cricket Manager. Although he wouldn't turn thirty-five until late December, Gilbert, whose playing career had been curtailed by back problems, had been Manager of the Young Australia side that had toured England in the summer and was already highly regarded - particularly for his man-management skills - by the Australian Cricket Board. He had, however, narrowly missed out on landing the role of Head Coach at Queensland and then New South Wales during the previous eighteen months, allowing Surrey to move in with the offer of a two-year deal. Having played in the Surrey Championship for Old Emanuel in 1988, Gilbert was well known to Vic Dodds, a stalwart of that club, who was to become the chairman of the Cricket Committee upon its reinstatement in December. Dodds liked the fact that Gilbert was young and very competitive, and felt that the Australian would fit in well with the playing staff at The Oval. He was proved to be correct in that assessment and the appointment turned out to be a masterstroke.

At around the same time, it was announced that the 24-year-old Adam Hollioake had been appointed as the club's first official vice-captain since Alec Stewart was handed that role in 1991 prior to his accession to the captaincy. The Melbourne-born all-rounder had certainly been an impressive leader of the side during the second half of 1995 while standing in for the injured Stewart, and clearly had the charisma and strength of personality for the job. With Stewart missing so many matches because of his England commitments, there was even a school of thinking that said the club should have taken the plunge and handed Hollioake the job on a permanent basis, in the interest of continuity if nothing else.

The final - and arguably most significant - departure of 1995 then came in December when Glyn Woodman resigned from the post of Chief Executive, claiming that his position had become untenable. The recently completed Imbert report was said to recommend that his role should be restricted to business affairs, with many of his reforms being abandoned and some of his decisions reversed. Paul Sheldon, who had successfully organised the club's 150th anniversary celebrations, was named as Woodman's successor, while the new chairman stated that he felt this would mark the end of the revolution that had taken place at The Oval since the end of the season. "There are not many people left to change," cracked Mike Soper, before adding "I am not a revolutionary. I just want to bring the fun back for everyone in the club and make us the acceptable face of cricket." Time alone would tell whether or not he could succeed in that aim.

3 1996: Ending The Drought

In addition to a new Cricket Manager, Surrey went into the 1996 pre-season period with three new players in their ranks - Chris Lewis, the 28-year-old England all-rounder; Richard Pearson, 24, an off-spinner who had been unable to break into an Essex side that boasted a fine spin attack in Peter Such and John Childs; and Brian MacMillan, the South African all-rounder, aged 32, who had signed a two-year deal as the county's overseas player, taking over from the veteran Australian paceman, Carl Rackemann, who had replaced the injured Waqar Younis at very short notice in 1995 and had bowled manfully without making a major impact.

The squad looked much stronger for the addition of the two all-rounders plus a more experienced spinner to take some of the workload off the shoulders of the promising 20-year-old slow left-armer, Richard Nowell, and there was a sense of optimism in Surrey circles until the McMillan signing suddenly ran into serious trouble. The South African had looked to be a fine replacement for the county's first-choice overseas star, Waqar, who was unavailable because Pakistan were touring England, but with the new campaign just three weeks away he was forced to pull out of the deal following pressure from Ali Bacher, the Managing Director of the United Cricket Board of South Africa. Bacher was concerned that one of his nation's key players, who had a history of back and knee injuries, would be unable to cope with the strain of county cricket and would, consequently, end up suffering from 'burn out' at a time when South Africa faced a heavy international schedule. This represented a terrible blow to Surrey's prospects and continued the run of misfortune with overseas players that had plagued the club since Waqar had terrorised opposition batsmen throughout the 1991 campaign. With McMillan having already signed his contract, Surrey had every right to feel aggrieved and the UCB of South Africa eventually admitted that they had been wrong to let the deal progress that far, paying a four-figure sum in compensation as well as offering their apologies. This was little compensation for the fact that, yet again, Surrey were left searching for an overseas player with the new season just a matter of days away.

Numerous alternatives were mentioned in the press before the club announced the signing of Brendon Julian, the 25-year-old bowling all-rounder from Western Australia who had made his first two Test appearances, as well as his one-day international debut, against England in 1993. Having added four further Test caps and another ODI cap to his collection in the meantime, the left-arm paceman and hard-hitting right-handed batsman looked to be a pretty good replacement for McMillan and came highly recommended by Dave Gilbert and Alec Stewart, both of whom knew him well. One advantage Julian had over the South African was the fact that he would add much needed variety to an attack that had been sorely lacking in that respect in recent times. Already handicapped by the absence of a match-winning spinner, Surrey's attack in 1995 had consisted largely of a group of rather similar right-arm fast-medium seamers, which made life a lot easier for opposition batsmen, especially once they were well set. Julian's presence would give them something different to think about, while his all-round excellence in the field and undoubted ability as a stroke-playing batsman gave him the look of a player who would thrive in both forms of the game.

As the season dawned, with Chris Lewis having managed to prove his fitness, it was clear that the new Manager had a talented collection of players at his disposal, though that had been the case on numerous occasions during the previous three decades when precious little silverware had ended up in the trophy cabinet at The Oval. The losing culture seemed to be deeply ingrained and it was patently obvious that Surrey needed to win a trophy of some kind in order to unleash the full potential of the squad. Gilbert was sure to bring a fresh and vibrant approach to the club, however, and had made his mark immediately with the widely publicised demolition of the wall in the dressing room that separated the capped and uncapped players. This, quite rightly, was seen as an anachronism that did nothing to encourage unity within the team. Optimism at the start of a new season had rarely been more justified.

The first two Benson & Hedges Cup fixtures that opened the campaign certainly suggested that everyone was right to feel confident as Surrey came out on top in two high-scoring contests at The Oval. After Alec Stewart's marvellous 151-ball knock of 160 enabled his team to total 333-6 and record a 59-run win over Hampshire, despite an excellent 123 from Robin Smith that underpinned the visitors' reply, Gloucestershire were beaten by three wickets in an exciting match after compiling 307-4 from their fifty overs. An impressive unbeaten 137 by the 22-year-old Rob Cunliffe ultimately counted for nothing in this game as Ali Brown's quick-fire eighty-two enabled Surrey to scorch to 134-1 from their first fifteen overs and then ease home with seven balls to spare, with Mark Butcher, batting at eight, and Chris Lewis, at nine, together at the crease. This demonstrated the team's massive potential in the limited-overs form of the game, since Butcher, Lewis, Brendon Julian and Adam Hollioake were all rightly regarded as three-in-one cricketers in this particular line-up.

The County Championship and Sunday League campaigns didn't get off to such a promising start, however, as Somerset provided formidable opposition on their home patch at The County Ground, Taunton. The drawn four-day game was dominated by the bat, with two men in particular enjoying the placid pitch - Peter Bowler contributed a fine 207 to Somerset's total of 558, which also contained a frightening tally of seventy-nine extras, while Adam Hollioake became the first Surrey batsman to score two centuries in a Championship match since Alan Butcher achieved the feat in 1984. Hollioake's first-innings 128 had rescued his side from the depths of 55-4 on the first day after Kevin Shine (6-95) had run amok with the new ball, and he then followed up with an unbeaten 117 second time around as he and Graham Thorpe (100 not out) led Surrey to safety at 410-4 with an unbroken fifth-wicket stand of 196 on the final day.

There had been no escape act in the Sunday League game the previous day, however, as Simon Ecclestone had blitzed the Surrey attack in powering his way to 130 from 112 balls in a 40-over Somerset total of 285-4. Alec Stewart, well supported by Thorpe and Adam Hollioake, compiled a fine 101 in reply but, as the overs started to run out, a collapse from 181-3 to 232 all out saw the hosts emerge with a comfortable 53-run victory.

Fortunately, a return to Benson & Hedges Cup action swiftly restored confidence to the ranks as Sussex were thrashed by nine wickets at Hove. Although the home side's final total of 208 represented a good recovery from 76-6 it was still nowhere near good enough to test Ali Brown (117 not out) and Alec Stewart (61 not out) who rushed their side to victory with almost fifteen overs to spare. Qualification for the quarter-finals was confirmed by this triumph, though the team still faced one more group match against Ireland the following week.

Before their trip across the Irish Sea, Surrey had to face Kent at The Oval in both league competitions. The Championship match started well for the home side with Kent struggling to 92-5 after winning the toss and only reaching 225 thanks to middle-order contributions of forty-five from Graham Cowdrey and fifty-one from Mark Ealham.

Surrey then built up a valuable first-innings lead of 135 by the end of the second day, thanks largely to Mark Butcher, who guided his team through choppy waters early on with a mature ninety-four, and then Chris Lewis (61) and Brendon Julian (74), who provided lower-order ballast after a slump to 206-6.

The bulk of Surrey's advantage was then wiped out by an opening stand of ninety-three by David Fulton (59) and Matthew Fleming (56) before Lewis (3-81), Pearson (3-84) and Martin Bicknell (3-79) hit back to reduce the visitors to 161-5 and then, half an hour into the final morning, 261-8. Spirited ninth-wicket resistance from Martin McCague (63 not out) and Min Patel (26), who added eighty-nine precious runs while eating up thirty-five overs, put Kent back in the match, however, and by the time Pearson dismissed the last batsman, Tim Wren, the visitors had reached a total of 361, leaving Surrey to chase 227 from a minimum of forty-five overs. This was soon looking unlikely as McCague picked up four prime early wickets, and when the spinners removed Adam Hollioake and Lewis with the score at eighty-one, Kent were suddenly the side who were pressing for victory. Luckily for Surrey, Julian (41 not out) and Mark Butcher (35 not out) kept cool heads to bat out time at 160-6 and salvage a draw from a match their side really should have won.

Had the last day of the Championship game not turned sour for Surrey they would have been celebrating two wins in two days, since they had earned their first Sunday League victory the previous day, routing their local rivals by 150 runs. The home side's imposing total of 307-5 was based around scintillating knocks by David Ward, who scored a rapid 112, and Ali Brown, whose eighty-four dominated a sizzling opening partnership of 127 in a mere eighteen overs. The likes of Stewart and Thorpe didn't even need to put their pads on as Lewis, Julian and Adam Hollioake were promoted up the order to create further mayhem, before the bowlers set to work on dismantling the Kent innings. Two early wickets for Martin Bicknell quickly put the skids under the visitors' reply, allowing Julian (3-38) and Adam Hollioake (4-34) to slice through the middle and lower order, leaving Kent all out for 157 in just 26.5 overs. The 18-year-old Ben Hollioake made his debut in this game and, since both Bicknells were also in the team, this was the first instance of a county fielding two sets of brothers in the same side since 1957 when Surrey included the Bedsers and the Pratts in their team against Oxford University.

After emerging from their final Benson & Hedges Cup group fixture with a comfortable five-wicket win over Ireland, Surrey spent five very damp, if not totally unrewarding, days in Gloucester.

The visitors' team was much changed from the Kent match owing to the absence of Alec Stewart, Graham Thorpe, Ali Brown and Chris Lewis, who were all included in England's Texaco Trophy ODI squad to face India. Lewis's early season form following his move to Surrey had earned him an instant recall to the national set-up, while Brown, who ended up scoring a match-winning century at Old Trafford in his third match, was another who was rewarded for making a bright start to the summer. The reshuffled Surrey line-up, captained by Adam Hollioake, saw Jason Ratcliffe, Nadeem Shahid, David Ward and Joey Benjamin making their first Championship appearance of the summer, though they all spent quite a lot of time in the pavilion during the rain-affected first three days of the game. In the available playing time Gloucestershire, inspired by Tim Hancock's 116, posted 373, despite the best efforts of Brendon Julian (5-97) who recorded a maiden five-wicket haul for Surrey, before the visitors declared their first innings closed at 228-6, immediately after avoiding the follow-on. This set up the prospect of an interesting final day, though, as was generally the case at this time, the Sunday League game now intruded on the Championship contest.

With the ground very wet underfoot and the weather still unsettled, the limited-overs fixture ended up being reduced to fifteen-overs-per-side, with Surrey being put into bat when Courtney Walsh won the toss for Gloucestershire. Although the visitors soon slumped to 23-3, the West Indian fast bowler was regretting his decision by the end of the innings as Darren Bicknell (51), Shahid (38) and Ratcliffe (18 not out) propelled their side to a magnificent total of 138-5. Walsh himself ended with the almost unbelievable figures of 3-0-51-0 and his team never looked like challenging Surrey's total as they collapsed to 66 all out. The Gloucestershire wickets were evenly shared around, though Julian, who bowled just eight legitimate deliveries, ended with figures of 3-5. The big Australian had already shown himself to be rather inconsistent with the ball in one-day cricket, delivering a liberal sprinkling of no-balls and wides to go with genuine wicket-taking deliveries, and this short spell neatly summed up his early performances, with two wides being more than balanced by the dismissal of three batsman - all clean bowled!

Returning to Championship mode the next day, Gloucestershire scored 163-2 from thirty-two overs before leaving Surrey two sessions to make 309, which they were always unlikely to do after losing their first two wickets with just thirty on the board. Although Mark Butcher and Adam Hollioake recorded half-centuries to steady the ship with a third-wicket partnership of eighty-four, Walsh (3-52) and Martyn Ball (3-40) put the visitors under pressure again late in the game, before Martin Bicknell and Richard Pearson blocked out the closing overs to secure their side's third successive draw at 174-8.

Having won six of their seven one-day games thus far, Surrey - with a full-strength side at their disposal again - went into their Benson & Hedges Cup quarter-final against Yorkshire at The Oval two days later as fairly firm favourites. This counted for nothing, though, as the home side struggled with the bat after being put in by David Byas. Although six men reached twenty, only Ali Brown (40) and Graham Thorpe (41) got as far as forty against keen Yorkshire bowling and fielding, led by the promising young fast bowler, Chris Silverwood (3-41), and a final total of 229 all out looked some way below par. Any hopes that Surrey's seamers might get their side out of a tight corner were then rapidly dashed as Byas and the promising young opening batsman Michael Vaughan tore into Martin Bicknell and Chris Lewis while posting an opening stand of ninety-four. After Vaughan fell to Benjamin for thirty-six, the Australian one-day maestro, Michael Bevan, strode to the crease and helped his skipper hasten Surrey's demise by nine wickets with nearly thirteen overs to spare. Bevan ended with an unbeaten sixty-five, while Byas, whose driving to all parts of the ground had been quite majestic, finished on 116 not out from just 103 balls and deservedly won the Gold Award as man of the match.

Surrey needed to get this setback out of their system quickly, though they would have wanted more than one day's rest before Derbyshire, who had made a solid start to the season under the captaincy of Dean Jones, arrived at The Oval for the Championship and Sunday League encounters. After being put in to bat, Surrey amassed an impressive total of 477 at almost four runs per over, thanks largely to an excellent knock of 185 by Graham Thorpe and half-centuries from Mark Butcher, Adam Hollioake and Alec Stewart. Stewart, incidentally, was not keeping wicket for his county in Championship matches, allowing the up-and-coming former Kent gloveman, Graham Kersey, to fill that role.

Undaunted by their hosts' imposing score, Derbyshire replied confidently, with four of their own men - Kim Barnett, Jones, John Owen and Colin Wells - passing the fifty mark as they ran up a total of 469 at a similarly good tempo.

As the bat continued to dominate the ball, Surrey then knocked up 345-3 at over five an over, courtesy of four further individual half-centuries, before leaving themselves sixty-five overs in which to pull off an unlikely victory on what was clearly still a very good pitch.

Some superb bowling by Martin Bicknell, who took 5-17 in nine overs before he was forced off the field by a groin strain, looked to have given the home team a great chance, however, as Derbyshire crumpled to 124-8 with the tea interval imminent. At this point the combative Dominic Cork, always one to relish a scrap, was joined at the wicket by Colin Wells, who could barely walk after damaging ligaments in his foot while batting in the first innings. Rather than face the return trip to the pavilion for tea five minutes later, Wells remained out in the middle during the break, reposing on a chair provided for him by a kindly steward, and then continued to defy the bowlers upon the resumption while Derbyshire waited for their last man, Paul Aldred, to return from a trip to hospital for x-rays on an arm injured earlier in the day by a drive from Ali Brown. Luckily for the visitors, Aldred was back at the ground and padded up by the time Brendon Julian (3-93) finally dismissed Wells with twenty-three overs left for play, thereby reviving hopes of a first Championship victory of the season for the home side. The brave Aldred and the determined Cork had other ideas, however, and gamely held out for the draw at 246-9, with Cork finishing unbeaten on eighty-two after a fine battling effort.

Fortunately, the Sunday League fixture that had split days three and four of the Championship game had provided Surrey with a welcome 50-run win that pushed them up amongst the early leaders. Victory in this match had looked far from certain when the home county crashed to 16-4 in the face of some good new-ball bowling by Cork (2-19) and Kevin Dean (1-19), and it was only a magnificent unbeaten 112 by Alec Stewart, with excellent support from Nadeem Shahid (47) and Brendon Julian (41) that enabled Surrey to reach 221-6 from their forty overs.

In reply, Derbyshire were going along quite nicely at 88-2 until Ben Hollioake, who had maintained his place in the Sunday League side since his debut against Kent, entered the attack to rip the heart out of the innings with a brilliant spell of 8-1-10-5 that sent the visitors nose-diving to 111-9. The gap between the two sides was eventually reduced to fifty runs, however, by some entertaining hitting from Devon Malcolm, who made a career-best score of forty-two before being bowled by Richard Pearson.

The team now headed up to Middlesbrough to face a Yorkshire side that had made a decent start in the Championship by securing victories over Glamorgan and Durham. Surrey badly needed to break their duck in the premier domestic competition in order to keep in touch with the early leaders, Kent, who already had three wins under their belt and a total of eighty-one points in the bank compared to the thirty-eight so far gathered in by Dave Gilbert's men. The gap would have been a lot smaller had Surrey been able to force victory against their local rivals a few weeks previously, and it was a matter of some concern that Derbyshire had been able to replicate Kent's escape act. It appeared to indicate that the team still lacked a bowler of real penetration at crucial times.

For the match at Acklam Park, the visitors - shorn of Alec Stewart, whose pregnant wife was ill; Graham Thorpe and Chris Lewis, who were playing for England against India; and the injured Martin Bicknell - gave a first-class debut to Ben Hollioake, who certainly deserved his call-up after his match-winning bowling in the Sunday League win over Derbyshire. The youngster made a good start, too, picking up the wickets of Bevan, White, Blakey and Hartley at a cost of seventy-four runs, though a very fluent knock of 135 by Michael Vaughan ensured that Yorkshire put up a reasonable total of 305 after winning the toss.

Surrey's reply, on a pitch that was already offering encouragement to the spinners, was a real disappointment, as only Darren Bicknell, with fifty-two, got past thirty in a total of 197. Vaughan, a capable off-spinner, returned 4-62, while the slow left-armer, Richard Stemp, conceded just forty-four runs from twenty-six overs while removing Mark Butcher and the hard-hitting triumvirate of Adam Hollioake, Ali Brown and David Ward.

Having already enjoyed a fantastic match, Vaughan then went out and notched another ninety-one runs, sharing in a 170-run stand for the second-wicket with Michael Bevan that really ground Surrey into the Middlesbrough dirt. Bevan went on to compile an unbeaten 160 out of a final total of 387 as the visitors' seam attack and their principal spinner, Richard Pearson, struggled to make any impact. Worryingly for Surrey, Pearson (1-80) was outbowled by both Darren Bicknell, who claimed 2-29 with his left-arm spin, and Mark Butcher, who picked up 3-49 with some unexpected off-breaks, as Adam Hollioake was forced to try some of his more occasional bowlers on the turning surface.

The target of 496 to win was always going to be beyond Surrey, though Butcher batted extremely well to make 112 and ensure that the team wasn't totally humiliated. No one else scored more than thirty-one, however, as the England discard Darren Gough (5-36) rounded off an easy 221-run victory with a fiery burst on the final morning of the game, taking his county to the top of the table in the process.

This defeat compounded the misery suffered by Surrey the previous day when the Sunday League game, which had seen everyone decamp to Headingley, resulted in a crushing eight-wicket win for the Tykes. Routed for a miserable total of 90 by Yorkshire's seam attack, the only bright spot for the visitors was another encouraging bowling performance by Ben Hollioake as Vaughan (25 not out) and Bevan (37 not out) swept their side to victory with more than fourteen overs to spare.

With his team out of the Benson & Hedges Cup and already trailing the leaders by forty-nine points in the Championship, Dave Gilbert must have been a rather worried man as he and his men travelled back to The Oval to take on a Leicestershire side that had made an average start in the Sunday League but were unbeaten in the Championship, having won two and drawn three of their five games to date.

That unblemished record looked very much under threat during the first two days of the match as a Surrey team lacking only Brendon Julian took full advantage of Alec Stewart winning the toss to total 452. This fine tally was largely thanks to Mark Butcher's 120 - his second successive Championship century - and Graham Thorpe's 154, while off-spinner Adrian Pierson toiled manfully for the visitors to return 6-158.

Joey Benjamin, standing in for Julian, then took four early wickets to put Leicestershire in deep trouble at 65-5 before Aftab Habib (77 not out) and Paul Nixon (66) launched a recovery that saw them reach the halfway stage of the contest at 222-6. Darren Bicknell, who had claimed Nixon's scalp in the final over of day two, then removed Habib for seventy-nine first thing the next morning to raise hopes of Surrey enforcing the follow-on or, at the very least, securing a substantial first-innings lead. The home side hadn't bargained for the efforts of the Leicestershire tail, however, and the game was back in the balance by the time the elder Bicknell (3-50), who had been brought back into the attack almost in desperation, bowled Alan Mullally for a career-best sixty-eight. The visitors' left-arm seamer had exactly doubled his previous personal best and, aided by contributions of fifty-one from Gordon Parsons and thirty-three from Adrian Pierson, had lifted their total to 411.

Phil Simmons, the West Indian all-rounder, then continued Leicestershire's comeback by claiming the scalps of Bicknell, Thorpe and the out-of-form Brown, to send Surrey sliding to 54-4 before Butcher (66) managed to revive his side with his eighth score of fifty-plus in his twelfth Championship innings of the summer. The left-handed opener, who had been awarded his county cap the previous day, had played an important role in levelling up the match as the teams 'broke up' for the Sunday League game with Surrey leading by 145 runs with five second-innings wickets standing.

Any thoughts that the rigours of the forty-overs-a-side contest might leave the players fatigued for the vital last day of the Championship fixture were soon forgotten as Leicestershire were brushed aside in the shortest Sunday League game ever recorded. It lasted just one hour fifty-three minutes, during which time 26.3 overs were bowled and Surrey won by ten wickets. The hosts required just twenty-two overs to dismiss the Foxes for forty-eight, with extras contributing the top score of twelve, no batsman making more than eight, and just one boundary being hit in anger. Chris Lewis (3-13), Martin Bicknell (3-16), Joey Benjamin (2-10) and Brendon Julian (2-7, including a wide, two no-balls and two batsmen clean bowled!) all contributed to Leicestershire's stunning downfall before Ali Brown (30 from 15 balls) and Darren Bicknell (15 from 12) knocked off the required runs in just 4.3 overs to send everyone home for an early tea. This was the visitors' second successive defeat in the league, though the previous week's four-wicket setback had come in rather different style. On that occasion the Foxes had amassed a county record 311-4, with openers Vince Wells and Phil Simmons - who had both recorded a duck against Surrey - putting on 228 for the first wicket!

Although this victory had moved Dave Gilbert's team up into fourth place in the Sunday League table behind Kent, Middlesex and Northamptonshire - the leaders, who were still boasting a one-hundred percent record after six games - a first County Championship win of the season was what everyone at The Oval most wanted... and the chances of it coming in the game that was about to be completed looked fairly remote.

With the pitch still playing very well, Surrey's first task was to avoid defeat, which they achieved comfortably enough thanks to some steady batting by Chris Lewis (36), Graham Kersey (59 not out), and Adam Hollioake (37 not out). By the time Alec Stewart felt able to declare at 242-6, with a lead of 283, there were only fifty-six overs left in the match, however, and a draw looked the most likely result. Leicestershire wickets fell at regular intervals during the afternoon, though, and as the game entered the last sixteen overs the visitors found themselves six down and in danger of defeat. Darren Bicknell, called upon to bowl after a disappointing spell from the ineffective Pearson, then unseated Paul Nixon for the second time in the match, allowing Chris Lewis (5-25) to run through the tail, clean bowling each of the Foxes' first-innings batting heroes, Parsons, Pierson and Mullally, to secure an unlikely victory with thirty-four balls remaining.

Boosted by these two triumphs, Surrey now had to travel north again to Stockton-on-Tees to play a struggling Durham outfit whose only win so far had come against the Minor Counties in the Benson & Hedges Cup.

Belying this miserable sequence of results, the home side made a good start to the Championship game against a visiting team shorn, once again, of Stewart, Thorpe and Lewis, with the West Indian Test opener Sherwin Campbell (69) and Stewart Hutton (47) putting on 130 for the first wicket. In typical Durham style, however, a collapse set in, with Martin Bicknell and Richard Pearson (3-103) making the initial breakthroughs before Joey Benjamin (4-69) scythed through the lower-middle order with a spell of 4 for 3 in sixteen balls to reduce the home team to 244-8. Totally unexpected resistance then came from the former Surrey wicketkeeper David Ligertwood (56) and Simon Brown (60) who put together a stand of 127 before Durham were finally bowled out for 377. Disappointingly for the visitors, the innings contained no fewer than fifty-eight extras, including eighteen no-balls costing two runs apiece, though Graham Kersey at least had reason to feel pleased, having become the thirteenth Surrey keeper to claim six catches in an innings.

Although the performance in the field had been below par, there was nothing wrong with Surrey's early batting as Mark Butcher (160) scorched to his third Championship century in his past four innings during an opening stand of 245 with the previously out of touch Darren Bicknell (106). With Jason Ratcliffe (51) helping Bicknell add a further hundred runs for the second wicket, the visitors were strongly placed at 345-1 before an astonishing collapse saw the last nine wickets fall for just ninety-five runs.

Fortunately for Surrey, their 63-run first-innings advantage was soon looking more than adequate as Durham flopped to 81-5 against some much improved bowling. Ligertwood (44) again resisted stoutly but the Championship strugglers could only muster 203 in their second knock and Surrey were left to score 141 for victory on the final day.

The Sunday League match now intervened, as ever, and gave David Ward a chance to show that he was still a devastating force with the willow in one-day cricket even though he was unable to secure a place in the county's Championship line-up.

Surrey had progressed to 181-4 after thirty-five overs, with Ward's contribution being forty-four from 40 balls, when the Banstead C.C. batsman really cut loose, blasting eight sixes - including four in succession off Phil Bainbridge - and two fours in the space of four overs. Having completed his fifty from 42 deliveries he suddenly had a 55-ball century to his name and, supported by an equally aggressive Adam Hollioake, had advanced the total by eighty runs in just four overs. Although Ward was out two balls later for 108, his sensational innings had pushed the final total up to 268-8, virtually snuffing out any hopes Durham had of putting together a successful run chase. The home side battled gamely, in fact, but no one was able to play a long innings as their reply eventually petered out at 209 in the thirty-sixth over, giving Surrey a 59-run victory that allowed them to move level with Kent in third place in the Sunday League table.

An advance to sixth in the Championship - albeit still thirty-one points behind the leaders, Kent - was then secured the following day as the expected win in the four-day match was achieved by eight wickets, with Jason Ratcliffe (68 not out) and Nadeem Shahid (52 not out) steering Surrey home after the 19-year-old Steven Lugsden had disposed of Bicknell and Butcher early on.

With their hosts having now recorded four successive wins, Holland couldn't have been relishing their trip to The Oval for a first round Nat West Trophy contest on 25th June. Predictably enough, Surrey dominated from start to finish after Alec Stewart won the toss, with the skipper himself, Mark Butcher and Ali Brown all recording half-centuries in a commanding 60-over total of 346 all out. Despite the fact that they were without Martin Bicknell and Chris Lewis, the home side had no trouble in dismissing the Dutch for 187, with Brendon Julian, who was still struggling badly with no-balls and wides, returning figures of 3-48, and Tony Pigott, the second eleven captain-coach, taking 2-22 on what turned out to be his final appearance in county cricket at the age of thirty-eight.

With their passage to the next round of their bogey competition safely secured, Surrey returned to action just two days later against Essex at Southchurch Park, Southend, where a placid pitch offered slow turn to the spinners. The visitors made good use of winning the toss by piling up a total of 476-8 declared, with Graham Thorpe (143) notching his fourth Championship century of the season and Adam Hollioake (128) compiling his third during a fourth-wicket partnership of 201. When Essex slipped from 131-0 to 134-3 in the closing overs of the second day, Surrey harboured hopes of victory, but Graham Gooch (149) and Stuart Law (125) quickly condemned the game to a draw with a 232-run stand on day three. At stumps, Essex were 425-8, with Richard Pearson (5-142) having earned some reward for forty-six overs of honest toil against his former team.

The Sunday League fixture that preceded the final day of what already looked to be a dead match provided rather more excitement, though not the result Surrey wanted. After electing to take first use of the pitch, Essex were given a 203-run start by fine knocks from Darren Robinson (80) and Stuart Law (110 from 95 balls), and though they lost their way late in the innings against the impressive Chris Lewis (2-28) and Adam Hollioake (2-43), they still ended up posting an imposing total of 278-8. In reply, Surrey started well through Darren Bicknell (46) and Ali Brown (41) before Peter Such (3-53) swept away the dangerous middle-order of Alec Stewart, Adam Hollioake and David Ward, leaving Nadeem Shahid (37) and Chris Lewis (44 not out) chasing a lost cause as the visitors closed twenty-seven runs short at 251-7.

Surrey's fruitless five days by the sea ended with the inevitable County Championship draw on the Monday, with a violent afternoon storm being welcomed by just about everyone but Mark Butcher, who was stranded fifteen runs shy of a hundred as the game was abandoned with the score standing at 167-2. Despite failing to win either of the games against Essex, Surrey maintained sixth place in the Championship and third in the Sunday League, though they now trailed the new leaders, Middlesex, by six points in the forty-overs competition.

As luck would have it, the two London-based rivals were to go head-to-head at The Oval over the course of the next five days. After Middlesex had won the toss and elected to bat, the Championship match quickly started to flow in Surrey's favour once Mark Ramprakash went for eighty, following stands of 126 with Mike Gatting (52) and fifty with John Carr. Martin

Bicknell, with 5-54, and Brendon Julian, who took 4-63, raced through a flimsy lower order to send Middlesex crashing from 192-3 to 232 all out, with the only disappointment from the home side's point of view being the shocking contribution of forty-two runs to the total courtesy of twenty-one no-balls.

An opening stand of eighty-five by Darren Bicknell and Mark Butcher, followed by the second half-century of Ali Brown's stuttering season and a 90-run fifth-wicket alliance between Jason Ratcliffe and Adam Hollioake (84), then put Surrey in a powerful position at 296-4 before Phil Tufnell (5-56) led a Middlesex comeback that saw the last six wickets tumble for the addition of just seventy runs. The hosts' 134-run lead still looked as if it might be sufficient, though, when Joey Benjamin removed Weekes and Pooley with just sixteen on the board and at close of play on Saturday the men from Lord's trailed by ninety-one runs with eight wickets standing.

The big Sunday League clash that interrupted the Championship match at this point turned out to be something of a damp squib, though Surrey weren't complaining. After being put in to bat under heavy cloud cover, Middlesex never threatened to get to grips with the bowling as they lost wickets at regular intervals and ended up being dismissed for 131 - including twenty-one wides - with almost seven overs of their allocation unused. Fortunately for the hosts, overhead conditions gradually improved during their reply, allowing Darren Bicknell (52 not out) to see his side through to a comfortable victory by eight wickets with 11.2 overs in hand.

This win moved Surrey into a share of second place in the table, the top of which was becoming very congested with just six points covering the top seven sides.

SUNDAY LEAGUE - TOP OF THE TABLE AT 7TH JULY					
	P	W	L	A	PTS
Middlesex	9	6	2	1	26
Northamptonshire	8	6	2	0	24
Kent	9	6	3	0	24
Surrey	9	6	3	0	24
Warwickshire	9	5	4	0	20
Yorkshire	9	5	4	0	20
Worcestershire	8	4	2	2	20

The Sunday League win had put Surrey in fine spirits as they attempted to complete the one-day/four-day double over their north London-based rivals the following day. Ramprakash and Gatting, the not out batsmen, were clearly key scalps for the men from SE11 to capture, so the early loss of the former to Julian represented a body blow to Middlesex. Although Gatting managed to resist long enough to record his second half-century of the game, Surrey were scenting a maximum-points victory once he fell to Bicknell for fifty-three with his side still three runs in arrears. The lower-order did show a little more fight than they had in the first knock, but Bicknell (4-57) and Julian (3-54) eventually proved too good for them again, leaving the visitors all out for 194 shortly after extras had registered the second half-century of the innings. Although Dave Gilbert would have been concerned that his team had gifted Middlesex no fewer than ninety-eight of the 426 runs they scored in the match, Surrey were soon pocketing twenty-four points - and advancing to fourth place in the table - by knocking off the required sixty-one runs for the loss of three wickets.

It was much to Surrey's credit that both victories against Middlesex had come with the county fielding their so-called weakened side, since their England players - Stewart, Thorpe and Lewis - had been taking part in the third Test against India at Trent Bridge.

COUNTY CHAMPIONSHIP - TOP OF THE TABLE AT 8TH JULY					
	P	W	D	L	PTS
Kent	9	5	4	0	145
Yorkshire	9	5	2	2	140
Leicestershire	8	4	3	1	129
Surrey	9	3	5	1	124
Warwickshire	9	4	2	3	120

The draw for the second round of the Nat West Trophy had provided Surrey with an extremely difficult task - a trip to Edgbaston to take on the holders, Warwickshire, who had suddenly hit form in the Sunday League with four successive wins and were now, like Surrey, well placed in both leagues.

A tough assignment then became harder still when the Bears won the toss and put their visitors in to bat in bowler-friendly conditions on an overcast morning. Fortunately for Surrey, the in-form Mark Butcher (33) and Graham Thorpe saw off the dangerous combination of Shaun Pollock and Tim Munton after the early loss of their skipper for ten, and when conditions improved after lunch Thorpe pressed on positively to an excellent ninety-six with ideal assistance from Ali Brown (34) and Adam Hollioake (57 from 53 balls). Consequently, Surrey racked up an impressive 291-7 from their sixty overs and the pressure of chasing at almost five an over clearly got to the Warwickshire batsmen. With Chris Lewis (3-33), Brendon Julian (2-23) and Adam Hollioake (2-28) producing particularly good spells, Nick Knight (68) was the only batsman to pass thirty as the home side were dismissed for 203 inside fifty-two overs. After an all-round performance that Dave Gilbert rightly hailed as "outstanding", it was becoming apparent that Surrey were going to be genuine contenders for silverware come the end of the season.

This feeling was further underlined just four days later when the team thrashed Worcestershire at The Oval in the Sunday League and as a consequence, with Kent and Middlesex both losing and Northamptonshire not playing, moved to the top of the table. Having been put in by Alec Stewart, Worcestershire's innings was one long struggle against Surrey's six-man seam attack, with no batsman making any impact at all - nine made it to double figures but no one reached twenty-four - and the wickets being shared around amongst the bowlers. The only cloud on Surrey's horizon as they dismissed their visitors for 175 was a £660 fine and the deduction of two overs from their reply because of their dilatory over rate.

A brief shower then caused some confusion over what Surrey's revised target should be, though this turned out to be a complete irrelevance as Ali Brown powered his way to fifty-five from just 39 balls. Although this was only his third half-century in all cricket since his one-day international hundred against India on 27th May he looked to be in decent enough form as he ensured his side would have no problems in reaching their target of 157 from thirty-four overs. Adam Hollioake (47 not out) struck four sixes in hustling the home county to victory by eight wickets with ten overs to spare, before the news of results from elsewhere in the country confirmed the significance of the result.

SUNDAY LEAGUE - TOP OF THE TABLE AT 14TH JULY					
	P	W	L	A	PTS
Surrey	10	7	3	0	28
Middlesex	10	6	3	1	26
Northamptonshire	8	6	2	0	24
Kent	10	6	4	0	24

Buoyed by their rise to the top of the Sunday League table, Surrey went into the annual Guildford festival in high spirits, with Sussex their opponents in both the four-day and one-day fixtures. The south coast county were comfortably placed in both leagues, though there were strong rumours of dressing room discontent, as well as whispers during the festival linking Ian Salisbury with a possible move to Surrey in the winter. Although Richard Pearson had contributed usefully in the Sunday League, his lack of penetration in the Championship remained a worry, so the prospect of the England leg-spinner moving to The Oval was most exciting. Surrey fans certainly got to see plenty of overs from their potential close-season signing as the home side rattled up 411 in their first innings, with Mark Butcher (57), Alec Stewart (74) and Graham Thorpe (66) all making fifties before a dramatic collapse from 251-2 to 320-9 was followed by a most valuable last-wicket stand of ninety-one between Graham Kersey (68 not out) and Pearson (a career-best 37).

The Sussex reply then followed a similar pattern, with Neil Lenham (51) and his beleaguered skipper Allan Wells (81) taking the score to 124-1 before Chris Lewis produced a breathtaking catch at cover point to remove Lenham, allowing Brendon Julian (4-41) to rip through the middle-order and send the visitors tumbling to 175-7. A semblance of order was then restored by an 83-run partnership between Salisbury (62) and Paul Jarvis until Stewart pulled off a masterstroke by turning to his part-time slow left-armer, Darren Bicknell, in place of the struggling Pearson. Fully justifying his captain's faith in him, Bicknell took just three overs to wipe out the tail with career-best figures of 3-7, thereby securing a lead of 146 for his team.

With two days left to play, Surrey now set out to establish a winning position and, thanks to fine knocks by Thorpe (130, his fifth Championship ton of the summer) and Stewart (80), they were in a position to declare at 304-6 half-an-hour after tea.

Although Sussex lost just one wicket in knocking sixty off their 451 target before the close, they soon slumped to 95-5 on the final morning as Pearson captured his first two scalps of the contest. The visitors then showed some backbone at last as Bill Athey (91) combined with Peter Moores in a superb stand of 164, which was only ended when Darren Bicknell again entered the fray to bowl the former England batsman via his pads. Moores continued to bat beautifully, reaching 119 not out before he finally ran out of partners, with two wickets falling to run outs and the last two to Darren Bicknell, who ended with the amazing figures of 3-41 in the innings and 6-48 in a match that Surrey ultimately won by 135 runs during the final session.

Having recorded four maximum points wins in their last five games, it was no surprise to see that Surrey had advanced to third place in the table once this round of matches had been completed.

COUNTY CHAMPIONSHIP - TOP OF THE TABLE AT 22ND JULY					
	P	W	D	L	PTS
Yorkshire	10	6	2	2	164
Leicestershire	9	5	3	1	149
Surrey	10	4	5	1	148
Kent	9	5	4	0	145
Derbyshire	9	4	3	2	131

Surrey's Championship joy turned to Sunday League disappointment the following day, however, as their mid-table visitors exacted swift revenge with a 75-run triumph. The home team started well, with Joey Benjamin and Adam Hollioake claiming two wickets apiece as Sussex stumbled to 71-5, before Martin Speight and Ian Salisbury combined superbly to regain the initiative for their side by adding 137 runs in nineteen overs. After Salisbury's departure to an unusually expensive Martin Bicknell for forty-two, and Speight's demise for a wonderfully inventive 117 from just 96 balls, Paul Jarvis (43) piled further misery upon Surrey in taking the total up to a commanding 281.

Even on the small, fast-scoring Woodbridge Road ground this represented a tall order for the league leaders and the loss of Brown and Stewart early on further damaged their prospects. Adam Hollioake, who had claimed 5-44 during the maelstrom of the Sussex innings, batted magnificently in plundering seventy-four runs from just 50 balls, but he received scant support from his colleagues as Vasbert Drakes (4-50) hit the stumps four times to condemn Surrey to defeat with seven overs remaining unused. Despite this setback, Dave Gilbert's team retained a share of the lead in the table, with Northamptonshire, Warwickshire and Yorkshire - who had recorded two wins in the past week - also now on twenty-eight points. This was becoming a very closely contested league.

Southampton was Surrey's next port of call for matches against a Hampshire side who were having an average season and were, therefore, the sort of opponents that Surrey had to beat if they were to claim some silverware come the end of the summer.

The County Championship game started on the Thursday, with Hampshire making the early running by compiling 332-7 on the opening day, thanks to half-centuries from John Stephenson (61), Paul Terry (57) and Robin Smith (54).

Martin Bicknell (4-64) finished as Surrey's most successful bowler when the home side were bowled out for 359 the following morning, then his elder brother scored forty-eight in partnership with Mark Butcher (58) to put the visitors into a promising position at 124-1. The rest of the batting contributed relatively little, however, with the exception of Adam Hollioake, who played a captain's innings of eighty-three in the absence of Alec Stewart, on duty for England in the first Test against Pakistan. Consequently, Surrey fell twenty-eight runs short of their hosts' total on a good wicket as the second day drew to a close.

Hopes of a positive conclusion to the match were then dented by a wet Saturday that saw half the day's allocation of overs lost as Hampshire extended their lead by 150 runs for the loss of four wickets, including John Stephenson (62) for his second half-century of the contest. It appeared that some collusion between the captains would represent the only hope of a competitive last day on the Monday.

The Sunday League clash that preceded the conclusion of the Championship fixture saw Surrey fritter away a fine start once again after they had been invited to bat by John Stephenson. Mark Butcher (57), included in the 40-overs team for the first time since the opening game of the season, and a typically positive Ali Brown (51 from 46 balls) enabled the visitors to reach 130-1 before Stephenson and Paul Whitaker worked their way through the rest of the batting to return identical figures of 3-44. A final total of 222-9 was certainly a disappointment and it began to look inadequate as Robin Smith (30) and Winston Benjamin, who scored thirty from 24 balls after being promoted to number four in the order, put their side well ahead of the required run rate at 101-2. Adam Hollioake disposed of both in quick succession, however, sparking off a slide to 130-7 that put Surrey in control of the match. Although a 55-run stand between Kevan James and Adrian Aymes briefly raised the hosts' hopes of a comeback, the visiting skipper eventually returned to the fray to seal a 23-run victory and finish with figures of 4-38.

With Northamptonshire's game at Worcester being abandoned, Surrey's win put them two points clear at the head of the table, though there was still a very long way to go to beat their previous best Sunday League finish of third in 1993.

SUNDAY LEAGUE - TOP OF THE TABLE AT 28TH JULY					
	P	W	L	T	A	PTS
Surrey	12	8	4	0	0	32
Northamptonshire	11	7	3	0	1	30
Yorkshire	12	7	5	0	0	28
Kent	11	6	4	1	0	26
Middlesex	11	6	4	0	1	26
Warwickshire	11	6	4	0	1	26
Worcestershire	11	5	3	0	3	26

The chances of Surrey recording a Championship victory on the Monday had looked fairly remote when rain lopped off the first forty minutes of the final day's play, but fortunately it didn't deter John Stephenson from opening up the game upon the resumption - declaring his side's second innings closed at 301-4, he set Surrey a predictably stiff target of 330 in a minimum of fifty-four overs.

Although Mark Butcher provided a good base for his side with his second fifty of the game after Darren Bicknell had gone for twenty-six, he departed in the midst of a collapse to 119-4 that also saw the loss of Jason Ratcliffe (26) and Ali Brown, first ball, to a blinding catch by Paul Terry off Rajesh Maru. Nadeem Shahid and Adam Hollioake thus came together with Hampshire very much on top but, adopting an admirably positive approach, they eschewed any thoughts of settling for a draw and launched into the bowling with gusto. Almost before the hosts knew it, the initiative had switched hands again, with both men racing to centuries at better than a run a ball during a stand of 195 in just twenty-eight overs. Although Shahid perished for 101 with his side on the brink of a thrilling victory, Hollioake was still there on 104 when Brendon Julian smashed Stephenson for the decisive boundary with five balls remaining, earning his adopted county a share of the leadership of the Championship in the process.

COUNTY CHAMPIONSHIP - TOP OF THE TABLE AT 29TH JULY				
	P	W	D	L	PTS
Leicestershire	10	6	3	1	171
Surrey	11	5	5	1	171
Yorkshire	11	6	2	3	170
Kent	10	5	5	0	156
Essex	10	4	4	2	140
Derbyshire	10	4	4	2	139

With the team now well placed to mount a challenge in both leagues, it was time for a return to cup action as Somerset visited The Oval for a quarter-final Nat West Trophy tie. Although Surrey went into the game as the bookmakers' favourites, their four previous encounters with the cidermen in the 60-overs competition had all ended in defeat, so there was clearly a score to settle as Alec Stewart won the toss and put his opponents in to bat.

The home side's opening bowlers, Martin Bicknell (2-38) and Joey Benjamin (2-35), both started tightly - with the latter also claiming the wicket of Mark Lathwell for nine - before Peter Bowler and Simon Ecclestone, who each scored fifty-two, began to regain the initiative for Somerset. From a high point of 117-1, a total in the region of 280 looked more than likely, but Brendon Julian (4-46) and the returning Bicknell had other ideas as they engineered a collapse from which the visitors never recovered. Although a final total of 225 all out appeared, initially, to be inadequate, especially given Surrey's powerful batting line-up, this opinion was soon in need of reassessment as the hosts slumped to 34-3, with Darren Bicknell and Graham

Thorpe both victims of an excellent burst from Andy Caddick, and Alec Stewart needlessly run out. It was fortunate for Surrey that Mark Butcher had kept his cool throughout this traumatic early period and, with a typically positive Ali Brown (41) taking on the principal role, the home team's fourth-wicket pair took advantage of some fairly innocuous back-up bowling to put their side back on course for victory. As the light deteriorated and drizzle began to fall, Caddick returned to have Brown very well taken by Rob Turner down the legside to end a vital stand of eighty-three before play was suspended at 126-4, leaving Surrey needing another hundred runs the next day.

It was very much in the home county's favour that the dangerous Caddick had just two overs left to bowl when play resumed, and once he had been seen off with final figures of 3-34, Surrey stormed home by five wickets with seven overs to spare. Although Butcher (91) missed out on his century when he was stumped off a legside wide, Adam Hollioake was 45 not out as his team booked their berth in the semi-final.

Surrey's reward for this victory was a week off, during which time the top of the Championship table became more congested following victories for Derbyshire and Essex. Fortunately, however, Yorkshire were beaten by Sussex at Eastbourne after holding a first-innings lead of ninety-two, Leicestershire were held to an unexpected draw by struggling Northamptonshire, and Kent suffered their first defeat of the campaign at the hands of Worcestershire. These results left Leicestershire top, with 180 points from eleven games; Yorkshire second, with 177 from twelve; and Surrey third, with 171 from eleven. It was obvious, therefore, that momentum had to be maintained as Dave Gilbert's men undertook a trip to the seaside to take on Lancashire at Southport.

After a delayed start, due to damp areas around the square, Surrey were put in on a recently relaid pitch that turned out to be somewhat 'sporty' in its behaviour. A number of batsmen found themselves undone by the bounce, or lack of it, as the visitors, led by Brendon Julian's hard-hitting forty-one, posted an acceptable total of 211 in the face of steady seam bowling from Ian Austin (4-46) and Peter Martin (4-59). Predictably enough, Lancashire found the going equally difficult when they replied, losing four wickets to Martin Bicknell before closing the first day on 128-5.

In the presence of the former Surrey groundsman, Harry Brind, now the TCCB's Inspector Of Pitches, the match swung very much in the visitors' favour the next morning as Martin Bicknell (5-48) claimed his fiftieth wicket of the season before Joey Benjamin (4-38) produced a spell of 4-2 to send the home side crashing to 145 all out.

Lancashire - fearing a points deduction for the state of the pitch - must then have had very mixed feelings as Darren Bicknell (42) and Mark Butcher (66) launched Surrey's second knock with a quick-fire stand of ninety-six. Although they were badly hampered by injuries to their first-innings bowling heroes, the home side managed to hit back through the part-time medium pace of Jason Gallian, reducing Surrey to 159-5 and restoring some balance to the contest as the pitch began to ease a little, before a fine knock of sixty-six by Nadeem Shahid and an astonishing effort by Julian just as rapidly tilted the scales back in Surrey's favour. Having survived a boundary 'catch' that was incorrectly ruled illegal by umpire John Holder - realising that his momentum was going to carry him over the rope as he completed the catch, Nick Speak had tossed the ball to his team-mate, Stephen Titchard - Julian rushed to a magnificent maiden first-class century from 109 balls before the second day's play drew to a close with the visitors on 366-6.

Although the Aussie all-rounder departed for 119 - including seven sixes and fourteen fours - early on the third morning of the game, Surrey were already leading by 432 runs, and by the time they were dismissed for 442, with Gallian returning a career-best 6-115, Lancashire required 509 to win.

Ignoring the fact that they were facing mission impossible, the hosts started well, thanks to half-centuries from Gallian and Titchard that enabled them to reach 174-1, but Surrey were not to be denied as Julian (5-99) claimed five of the last six wickets to crown his excellent match and seal a 140-run victory.

The impact of this victory was somewhat reduced as Derbyshire, Essex and Kent also recorded wins in this round of matches, though it was sufficient to regain top spot for Surrey, as Glamorgan managed to hang on for a draw against Leicestershire. Yorkshire slipped to sixth after sitting out this round of matches, and only seven points now separated the top five teams.

COUNTY CHAMPIONSHIP - TOP OF THE TABLE AT 12TH AUGUST					
	P	W	D	L	PTS
Surrey	12	6	5	1	192
Leicestershire	12	6	5	1	191
Essex	12	6	4	2	188
Derbyshire	12	6	4	2	185
Kent	12	6	5	1	185

With the Championship fixture having finished a day early, the players had a day's break before their next big match, the Sunday League game at Old Trafford. Going in to this game, Dave Gilbert's men sat in second place in the table, having lost top spot to Northamptonshire during their week of inactivity before the trip to Southport.

After winning the toss and electing to bat, Surrey found runs hard to come by for the greater part of their innings, with only Ali Brown, who struck a purposeful thirty-five at the top of the order, and Nadeem Shahid, who compiled a responsible fifty-eight from number four in the line-up, getting to grips with some typically tight one-day bowling from their hosts. Although Glen Chapple (3-29) and Richard Green (1-30) returned fine figures, handy late twenties from the Hollioakes and Brendon Julian lifted the total to 202-7, which was at least respectable.

When Lancashire replied, the visitors were boosted by the early run out of Jason Gallian before Joey Benjamin won lbw verdicts against Mike Watkinson and Neil Fairbrother to peg the red rose county back to 41-3 just as rain brought about a break in play.

With four overs lost, the hosts faced a revised target of 182 in 36 overs, but soon ran into major problems as Martin Bicknell (3-25) decimated the middle-order - from a position of 69-3, where they were still very much in contention, Lancashire collapsed to a hopeless 94-7. The Hollioake brothers then ensured there would be no dramatic recovery, with Adam claiming two wickets and Ben one as the home team - dismissed for 128 in 31.3 overs - surrendered the four points to a Surrey side who consequently moved back to the top of the league, courtesy of Kent's victory over Northamptonshire at Northampton.

SUNDAY LEAGUE - TOP OF THE TABLE AT 11TH AUGUST					
	P	W	L	T	A	PTS
Surrey	13	9	4	0	0	36
Northamptonshire	13	8	4	0	1	34
Nottinghamshire	12	8	4	0	0	32
Yorkshire	13	8	5	0	0	32

The position in the Sunday League couldn't have been much tighter, especially as Nottinghamshire - Surrey's next opponents in the competition - had also moved into the picture with a run of four straight wins. Two other contenders, Northamptonshire and Warwickshire, were also to come on Surrey's fixture list, so there were some very important games to play in the closing weeks of the season.

Also in that category was the Nat West Trophy semi-final against Essex at The Oval, which was scheduled to take place just two days after the Sunday League match at Old Trafford, giving the players precious little recovery time. The situation was even worse for the four England players involved in the match - Stewart, Thorpe, Lewis and Nasser Hussain - since they came into this important county contest straight from the tedious drawn second Test against Pakistan at Headingley.

Fatigue didn't appear to be a major problem for Stewart, however, as he anchored the Surrey innings quite superbly to add another century to the 170 he had scored in the Test. Unfortunately, the big guns of the middle-order failed to fire at the other end and it took an explosive 29-ball innings of forty-five by Chris Lewis late in the day to ensure that his skipper's undefeated 125 was not wasted as Surrey posted a final total of 275-5.

Although the capture of two early Essex wickets then put the home side in the driving seat, it also brought Stuart Law to the crease to join Graham Gooch... and, as a result, the tide started to turn. The Australian promptly tore into the bowling of Lewis, Brendon Julian and Joey Benjamin, scoring fifty-three from just 44 balls to put his side in a fine position before Benjamin had him caught on the midwicket boundary. Gooch eventually went for fifty with the total on 175, but Surrey were unable to regain control as they lost their discipline in the field, conceding no fewer than forty-seven extras - including twenty-three wides and fifteen no-balls - as Ronnie Irani (52 not out) and Robert Rollins (26 not out) saw their side home with four wickets and almost as many overs in hand. In addition to missing out on a Lord's final and the chance of a treble-winning season, Surrey were fined £4,620 for being seven overs behind schedule when the match ended. It was inevitable that the team's problems with over-rates, wides and no-balls would catch up with them one day, but it was extremely disappointing that it should happen in a cup semi-final.

The team now had an eight-day break before their next matches in the Championship and the Sunday League, against Nottinghamshire at Trent Bridge, and during that time Derbyshire and Kent took advantage of the fact that none of the three sides above them were in action by leapfrogging their way into the top two places in the Championship table.

COUNTY CHAMPIONSHIP - TOP OF THE TABLE AT 19TH AUGUST				
	P	W	D	L	PTS
Derbyshire	13	7	4	2	208
Kent	13	7	5	1	206
Surrey	12	6	5	1	192
Leicestershire	12	6	5	1	191
Essex	12	6	4	2	188

The head of the Sunday League table meanwhile became even more crowded with contenders as Nottinghamshire, Yorkshire, Warwickshire and Worcestershire all recorded wins, though Surrey maintained a share of the leadership on thirty-six points.

SUNDAY LEAGUE - TOP OF THE TABLE AT 18TH AUGUST					
	P	W	L	T	A	PTS
Nottinghamshire	13	9	4	0	0	36
Surrey	13	9	4	0	0	36
Yorkshire	14	9	5	0	0	36
Northamptonshire	13	8	4	0	1	34
Warwickshire	13	8	4	0	1	34
Worcestershire	13	7	3	0	3	34

With both leagues so tightly contested it was clear that Surrey couldn't afford any more poor performances if they were to keep alive their hopes of pulling off the double. Some things were beyond their control, however, as they discovered when dreadful weather in Nottingham caused immense frustration over the course of the next five days at Trent Bridge.

Following a wretched opening day in the Championship match, during which the home side piled up 393-6, thanks to some indifferent Surrey bowling and fine centuries by Graeme Archer (143) and Mathew Dowman (107), rain held sway for almost four days.

With the whole of day two having been lost to the inclement weather, Nottinghamshire progressed to 446-9 (Julian 4-104) before declaring on a rain-interrupted third day that saw Surrey close on 128-4 with Ali Brown unbeaten on fifty-six. Clearly it was going to take collusion between the captains, Paul Johnson and Adam Hollioake, on the Monday if this game was to be brought back to life.

The miserable weather then continued throughout the next day, wiping out the keenly anticipated top-of-the-table Sunday League clash and allowing Yorkshire, who beat Lancashire at Headingley, to jump to the top of the table.

SUNDAY LEAGUE - TOP OF THE TABLE AT 25TH AUGUST						
	P	W	L	T	A	PTS
Yorkshire	15	10	5	0	0	40
Northamptonshire	14	9	4	0	1	38
Surrey	14	9	4	0	1	38
Warwickshire	14	9	4	0	1	38
Nottinghamshire	14	9	4	0	1	38

A disastrously wet Sunday was then followed by another depressingly damp day that put paid to the Championship match. After the loss of the whole of the morning session to the weather, followed by a declaration apiece, Surrey set out to chase 319 to win but after reaching 53-0 from the first thirteen overs the rains returned yet again to put everyone out of their misery.

Although rain was widespread throughout the country during this round of matches, Essex managed to find enough time to thrash Gloucestershire at Colchester and, consequently, claim a share of the leadership with Kent, who had played an extra game.

COUNTY CHAMPIONSHIP - TOP OF THE TABLE AT 26TH AUGUST					
	P	W	D	L	PTS
Essex	13	7	4	2	212
Kent	14	7	6	1	212
Derbyshire	13	7	4	2	208
Leicestershire	13	6	6	1	202
Surrey	13	6	6	1	199
Yorkshire	14	6	3	5	192

With so many sides in the running for the Championship title it seemed imperative for Surrey to win their next match, against Warwickshire at The Oval, if they were to keep up with the rest of the pack.

They were again required to field their 'weakened' team, however, since the game clashed with England's series of three one-day internationals against Pakistan. While Adam Hollioake had been called up for the first time to join Alec Stewart and Graham Thorpe in the national squad, Chris Lewis had been omitted on disciplinary grounds after turning up forty minutes late for practice before the fourth day of the final Test Match at The Oval, which had resulted in a nine-wicket defeat for the host nation. Subsequently, the TCCB asked Surrey to 'suspend' Lewis from their two matches against Warwickshire but failed to get the response they had hoped for - in the absence of both Stewart and Holioake, Surrey not only selected Lewis they also made him captain! This seemed entirely reasonable since the mercurial all-rounder's offence was England-related and not an issue for the county.

Having performed his first task to perfection by winning the toss, Lewis put Warwickshire in to bat and proceeded to play as if he had a point to prove, snapping up two early wickets as the reigning county champions stumbled to 27-4. He then added two further scalps to his collection later in the innings to return figures of 4-45 as Warwickshire totalled 195, with 101 of these runs coming from a seventh-wicket stand between Keith Piper (45) and Ashley Giles (50) before Brendon Julian (4-66) ruthlessly disposed of the tail.

Mark Butcher (70) and Darren Bicknell (55) then built upon this great start by compiling a 135-run stand for the first wicket that gave Surrey a chance to amass a match-winning total during the second day's play. Although Ali Brown - whose disappointing county form since scoring a century in England's last one-day international had led to his omission from the current squad - was forced to bat at number ten because of a damaged finger, the title challengers still managed to pile up an intimidating total of 468, thanks to half-centuries from Jason Ratcliffe, Graham Kersey, who each made sixty-three, and the stand-in skipper, Lewis, who fell just six runs short of three figures.

Facing a first-innings deficit of 273, Warwickshire - badly missing their own England man, Nick Knight, and the injured Shaun Pollock - crumbled dismally from 32-0 to 109 all out, with Joey Benjamin (4-17) removing the top four batsmen, and Martin Bicknell (4-38) slicing through the lower order with assistance from Ben Hollioake (2-22) to secure an emphatic triumph by an innings and 164 runs.

With four of the other five title contenders also winning their game, Surrey's victory only moved them one place up the table at the end of this round of matches, though the effect of Essex's defeat at the hands of Yorkshire - they slid from first to fifth - underlined how important it was to keep on winning at this stage of the campaign.

COUNTY CHAMPIONSHIP - TOP OF THE TABLE AT 2ND SEPTEMBER					
	P	W	D	L	PTS
Kent	15	8	6	1	233
Derbyshire	14	8	4	2	232
Leicestershire	14	7	6	1	224
Surrey	14	7	6	1	223
Essex	14	7	4	3	220
Yorkshire	15	7	3	5	214

Having disposed of Warwickshire inside three days, Surrey were able to go into the following day's all-important Sunday League clash against their title-chasing rivals safe in the knowledge that the County Championship points were already in the bag. This was certainly a bonus for Dave Gilbert's men, who made a great start to the match as Joey Benjamin (3-33) claimed two wickets to follow up early strikes by Chris Lewis and Brendon Julian, leaving the Bears in deep trouble at 43-4. Dougie Brown then pulled things around for Warwickshire, compiling a solid sixty-six and leading the way in an 80-run partnership with Michael Burns (29) before Richard Pearson (3-33) struck three important late blows to stymie the visitors' progress. The Bears eventually mustered 185 before being bowled out in the final over, though they were given a boost during the tea interval when it was revealed that Surrey were to be docked three overs from their reply, and fined yet again, because of a slow over rate.

Although Ali Brown departed early in the hosts' reply, stands of sixty between Mark Butcher (48) and Darren Bicknell (21), and forty-two between Butcher and Nadeem Shahid (43) put Surrey in charge at 121-2 before the loss of two quick wickets pushed the door ajar for Warwickshire. Shahid and Chris Lewis (26 from 26 balls) then appeared to have secured victory with a steadying partnership of forty-seven until nerves began to show late in the match. A clatter of wickets, two of which fell to the combative Brown (3-28), saw Surrey dip from 169-4 to 173-7 before Julian hit a mighty six over the distant midwicket boundary in the penultimate over to bring some relief to a sizeable Oval crowd. Although the Australian was taken at third man in the final over, Martin Bicknell kept his head to pick off the last two runs with two balls to spare, thereby keeping his team in the hunt for the title and eliminating Warwickshire from the race.

With the Bears being the only side in the top six to lose, it was pretty much 'as you were' at the top of the table with just two rounds of matches to be played. Two of the remaining fixtures - Surrey versus Northamptonshire in a week's time, and Yorkshire against Nottinghamshire on the final Sunday of the summer - appeared to be the key games as the Sunday League season moved towards a thrilling climax.

SUNDAY LEAGUE - TOP OF THE TABLE AT 1ST SEPTEMBER						
	P	W	L	T	A	PTS
Yorkshire	16	11	5	0	0	44
Northamptonshire	15	10	4	0	1	42
Nottinghamshire	15	10	4	0	1	42
Surrey	15	10	4	0	1	42
Somerset	15	9	5	0	1	38
Warwickshire	15	9	5	0	1	38

While the other three counties were able to concentrate all their efforts on the 40-overs competition, Surrey had another fish to fry as they attempted to maintain their challenge for a first County Championship title since 1971.

Northamptonshire, who languished near the foot of the table, were the next team that had to be vanquished if Dave Gilbert's side were to remain in the hunt, and one wondered how motivated they would be ahead of the crucial Sunday League match.

Any thoughts that they might take things easy were soon dispelled, however, as they reduced a full-strength Surrey team to 147-6 on a pitch offering enough assistance to the seam bowlers for the home side to omit Richard Pearson. Fortunately, this selection lengthened the batting, allowing Brendon Julian to enter the fray at number eight and join Adam Hollioake in a partnership that ultimately proved decisive in the context of the match. Matching one another stroke for stroke, these two pulverised the visitors' attack as they added 181 for the seventh wicket in forty overs, each completing a superb century as the bowlers wilted. Hollioake finally departed for 129, his fifth Championship ton of the campaign, while Julian reached 117 before being dismissed by the visitors' most effective bowler, Paul Taylor (4-87), towards the end of the first day's play.

By the end of the second day, Surrey were in complete control of the match and seemingly on course for a straightforward victory. Having advanced their overnight score of 378-9 to 395 all out, the home side claimed three early wickets through the efforts of Martin Bicknell and Chris Lewis before Julian worked his way through the middle order with a three-wicket burst that left the innings in tatters at 95-6. Northamptonshire were then rallied by David Ripley (55) and Jeremy Snape (36 not out), who took their side to 231-7 with a determined 87-run partnership that was only ended by another three-wicket salvo from the returning Julian. Finishing with a career-best 6-37 to add to his century, the West Australian terminated the visitors' innings at 235, allowing Surrey to extend their 160-run lead by eighty-two before the close of play after electing not to enforce the follow-on. Julian wasn't the only member of the home county to have reason to celebrate at the end of the day, however, since Graham Kersey was awarded his first eleven cap. It was richly deserved as he had continued to make great progress with both bat and gloves throughout the season.

Although they were already in a powerful position, Surrey faltered early on the third morning as Curtly Ambrose (4-55) bagged three scalps to peg them back to 127-5. Adam Holioake - who led the team for the rest of the game while Alec Stewart was absent for the birth of his daughter - stood firm on his twenty-fifth birthday, though, ushering his side towards a total of 298 and falling just two runs short of his second century of the match. Had he reached three figures he would have become only the third Surrey batsman, after Hobbs and Hayward, to record twin centuries in two matches in the same season, having taken two tons off Somerset at Taunton back in May.

Chasing a theoretical 459 to win, Northamptonshire recovered from the early loss of Alec Swann to reach 104-1 before Lewis (3-65) followed Julian's first-innings example, producing a three-wicket burst that ripped out the middle order and gave Surrey a chance of a three-day win. Although David Capel (48) and Tony Penberthy ensured that their team made it through to the close at 173-6, the visitors didn't delay their hosts for too long on the final morning. After Ripley was forced to retire hurt with a damaged finger, Julian crowned his highly impressive match by taking two of the remaining wickets as Surrey completed a 225-run triumph.

Having failed to record a County Championship victory until mid-June, the team had now won eight of their last ten matches in the competition, with five of these wins coming in games that clashed with international fixtures. Since all the leading sides had played fifteen matches at this stage, the position at the top of the table was much clearer, with just seven points between leaders Leicestershire - who had just beaten Nottinghamshire at Trent Bridge - and fourth placed Essex, conquerors of Warwickshire at Edgbaston. Third-placed Derbyshire had lost a little ground after Somerset had hung on for a draw at the end of a high scoring match at Taunton but were still very much in contention.

COUNTY CHAMPIONSHIP - TOP OF THE TABLE AT 6TH SEPTEMBER					
	P	W	D	L	PTS
Leicestershire	15	8	6	1	248
Surrey	15	8	6	1	247
Derbyshire	15	8	5	2	242
Essex	15	8	4	3	241

The next match was another potential Sunday League 'eliminator' contest at The Oval. Both Northamptonshire and Surrey knew that defeat could spell the end of their title dreams as the visitors got away to a poor start after being inserted by Alec Stewart. At 18-2, Rob Bailey's side were clearly in trouble, though the home county had already suffered a scare of their own with Chris Lewis having been forced off the field for treatment after damaging an ankle while celebrating his dismissal of Richard Montgomerie with his second delivery.

Fortunately for Surrey, he eventually returned to the fray and pulled off an astonishing catch - one-handed, diving full length to his right - at short third man to remove the dangerous Mal Loye, who had put his side back into the match at 101-2 with a fine half-century. Thereafter, it became the David Capel and Adam Holioake show as Capel blasted the bowling all around the park, while Hollioake (5-58) picked up wickets at regular intervals after Tony Penberthy had helped his team-mate advance the score to a threatening 191-3. Once Capel had been run out in the final over for a magnificent 112 from just 88 balls, Hollioake bowled Curtly Ambrose to register his 36th Sunday League victim of the season, thereby establishing a new record for the competition.

Having been left to chase 235 to win from their forty overs if they were to maintain their title challenge, Surrey made a shocking start, with Mark Butcher, Graham Thorpe and Alec Stewart all departing before the total had reached forty. Despite losing Adam Hollioake with the score advanced to seventy-eight, Ali Brown played with great fluency, unleashing some glorious strokes in racing to forty-nine from a mere 37 balls before becoming the victim of an awful umpiring decision that put Northamptonshire firmly back in the driving seat. A large home crowd was fearing the worst, in fact, as Chris Lewis walked out to join Nadeem Shahid in the middle with Surrey on 100-5, needing 135 to win from just eighteen overs. This pair adopted a positive approach against the medium-pace of Kevin Curran and an injured Capel, however, and put their side right back into contention, only for John Emburey to claim Shahid lbw for a feisty forty-one (32 balls) with Surrey still seventy-six runs short of victory. It was already looking likely that we would have another nail-biting finish on our hands, though Lewis continued to play a superb hand even after losing another partner when Brendon Julian departed for a quick-fire sixteen with the total on 189. Surrey couldn't afford any more mistakes at this stage, and everyone knew that Martin Bicknell and Lewis would probably have to score the bulk of the remaining runs since only Richard Pearson and Joey Benjamin were left to bat. With supporters of both sides barely able to watch amidst growing tension, the eighth-wicket pair used all their experience to guide their side to within five runs of victory with five balls remaining... at which point Lewis, having made a splendid sixty-three from just 47 balls, holed out at extra cover to put the contest back in the balance again.

The next three deliveries then yielded three runs, leaving Bicknell to score two from the final ball, with everyone in the ground on the edge of their seat. Luckily for the batsman, Curran's attempted leg-stump yorker turned out to be a half-volley that Bicknell gleefully thumped to the boundary at wide long-on to seal victory for Surrey and keep their title hopes very much alive. A triumphant Bicknell sprinted back to the dressing room where he was greeted by his equally elated team-mates as the club's members and supporters cheered ecstatically.

Although Nottinghamshire had beaten Leicestershire at Trent Bridge, Surrey had a far superior net run rate, which would decide the destiny of the title if two sides were to finish equal on points. Consequently, the result of Nottinghamshire's game against Yorkshire at Scarborough would be irrelevant provided that Surrey won their match against Glamorgan at Sophia Gardens. The club was just one victory away from claiming its first trophy since 1982.

SUNDAY LEAGUE - TOP OF THE TABLE AT 8TH SEPTEMBER						
	P	W	L	T	A	PTS	NRR
Surrey	16	11	4	0	1	46	16.12
Nottinghamshire	16	11	4	0	1	46	9.09
Yorkshire	16	11	5	0	0	44	12.87

There was, however, the small matter of a vital Championship fixture to play before Surrey could tilt at elusive glory, and hopes of pulling off the double were raised in the early stages of the game when Glamorgan's prolific opening batsmen, Steve James and Huw Morris, fell to consecutive deliveries from Martin Bicknell and Chris Lewis with just fourteen runs on the board. With the Cardiff pitch proving very flat, life thereafter became much tougher for the bowlers as David Hemp (47), Matthew Maynard (82) and Adrian Dale (90) put the hosts back on track, enabling them to reach 364 before they were finally bowled out early on day two. This was no better than a par score in the circumstances, and the six bowlers amongst whom the Glamorgan wickets had been evenly distributed could feel satisfied with their efforts, even though they had slipped back into some of their bad old ways by conceding forty-six extras.

In reply, Surrey were stuttering somewhat at 102-3 before they manoeuvred themselves into a promising position at 273-4 by the end of the second day, thanks to Graham Thorpe (77), Nadeem Shahid (66 not out) and Adam Hollioake (45 not out). With the scoring rate having been kept in check all day by the Glamorgan spinners, the visitors needed to press on during day three, however, especially as Leicestershire had piled extra pressure on their rivals by annihilating Durham inside two days at the Riverside.

Rising to the occasion, Surrey's lower middle-order did indeed accelerate their side's scoring the following morning after the early loss of Shahid (79) and Hollioake (51). Putting bat to ball most purposefully, Chris Lewis (57), Brendon Julian (41) and Martin Bicknell (59 not out from 44 balls) added 198 runs from just thirty-seven overs during the first session, allowing Alec Stewart to declare at 471-9, with his side holding a 107-run advantage.

Although the day's middle session also belonged to Surrey as they captured three wickets with Glamorgan still in arrears, Steve James and Tony Cottey held sway after tea as the bowlers toiled fruitlessly and the total grew steadily to 218 by the close. There was clearly much work to be done on Monday if the Championship challenge was to be maintained.

Before then, glory beckoned in the Sunday League. With Nottinghamshire needing to beat Yorkshire by something like 300 runs at Scarborough if they were to match Surrey's net run rate, victory would enable Dave Gilbert's men to secure the club's first title in fourteen years. Consequently, a large crowd, swollen by an impressive number of travelling supporters, had gathered at Sophia Gardens.

Upon winning the toss Alec Stewart asked Glamorgan to bat and it wasn't long before this decision was paying dividends, as the hosts lost Adrian Dale, David Hemp and Alistair Dalton before reaching fifty. Steve James (43) and Tony Cottey (41) breathed some life back into the innings, however, during a partnership of forty-nine for the fourth wicket before Richard Pearson (2-33) struck two vital blows for the visitors, bowling James behind his legs and then holding a simple catch off his own bowling to eradicate the threat of Matthew Maynard. Now in pole position, Surrey were soon tightening their grip on the match, and the league title, as Adam Hollioake (3-28) dismissed Cottey, Ottis Gibson and Robert Croft to snuff out any chance of a Glamorgan recovery and improve his new Sunday League record to thirty-nine wickets. As the home team's overs finally ran out - with all the visiting bowlers having done a fine job - their total stood at 159-9 and Surrey stood on the verge of that long-awaited triumph.

With their side requiring exactly four runs per over, Mark Butcher (30) and Ali Brown (41) gave Surrey a perfect springboard to victory, taking toll of some early looseness from Steve Watkin and the disaffected Gibson - who had just been told that he was surplus to requirements for 1997 - to compile an opening partnership of eighty-two from just 12.3 overs before Butcher fell to Croft. Although Brown followed his colleague back to the pavilion soon afterwards with the total advanced to ninety, his team already had one hand on the trophy, allowing Stewart (41 not out) and Graham Thorpe (28) to put together a fairly sedate but match-clinching stand of sixty-seven as the Surrey fans celebrated noisily around the ground. Just three runs were required for victory when Thorpe fell to a catch at midwicket off Cottey's occasional off-spin, which left Nadeem Shahid to stride to the wicket and smite the winning boundary that sparked further revelry.

As fourteen years of famine came to a joyful and emotional end with the Sunday League trophy being presented to a beaming Alec Stewart on the dressing room balcony, the gloomy

150th anniversary season seemed a distant memory… and the revolution and upheaval that had resulted from those dark and desperate days seemed all the more worthwhile. For the supporters and officials of Surrey the celebrations were to last all night long, but the players had another big day ahead of them. If they could win tomorrow then there would still be a chance of winning the most important trophy of all, the County Championship. If the players could go on to capture that title then today's celebrations would certainly be put in the shade by those that would follow!

	SUNDAY LEAGUE TABLE 1996							
		P	Pts	W	L	T	A	NRR
1	Surrey	17	50	12	4	0	1	16.31
2	Nottinghamshire	17	50	12	4	0	1	9.20
3	Yorkshire	17	44	11	6	0	0	11.47
4	Warwickshire	17	42	10	6	0	1	4.88
5	Somerset	17	42	10	6	0	1	1.14
6	Northamptonshire	17	42	10	6	0	1	0.42
7	Middlesex	17	38	9	7	0	1	-0.92
8	Worcestershire	17	38	8	6	0	3	1.88
9	Lancashire	17	36	9	8	0	0	-0.16
10	Kent	17	34	8	8	1	0	-7.65
11	Derbyshire	17	34	7	7	1	2	4.35
12	Leicestershire	17	34	7	7	0	3	0.10
13	Glamorgan	17	32	7	8	0	2	2.73
14	Sussex	17	28	6	9	0	2	-11.57
15	Hampshire	17	22	4	10	0	3	-6.22
16	Gloucestershire	17	22	4	10	0	3	-8.19
17	Essex	17	18	4	12	0	1	-3.57
18	Durham	17	6	1	15	0	1	-15.37

In order to gain the victory they required, Surrey badly needed to make a couple of early breakthroughs on the final morning of the Championship match but, unfortunately, they couldn't even manage one as James and Cottey continued to defy the visitors' attack, taking their partnership to 168 before Nadeem Shahid (3-96), purveying his leg-breaks to good effect, removed Cottey for eighty-three. Although the occasional wrist-spinner then proceeded to unseat James (131) twenty-four runs later, with the total at 286, Surrey's prospects of winning the match by dismissing their hosts were already pretty dim. As Richard Pearson (1-88) struggled to make any real impact on the dry and dusty surface, Shahid's excellent effort brought him a third wicket when Adrian Dale was caught behind for eleven at 311-6, before Adrian Shaw (74) and Robert Croft (38) combined to ensure stalemate. The Glamorgan skipper, Matthew Maynard, owed Surrey nothing in terms of a declaration to set up a run chase and probably felt that his own team had no chance of victory in any case, given the strength and depth of his opponents' batting and the unresponsive nature of the pitch. As a result, the innings meandered on, with Stewart himself taking a turn with the ball, before Maynard finally declared at 442-9, setting the visitors a theoretical 336 to win in a minimum of 37 overs.

In a forlorn attempt to chase this most unlikely target, Stewart shuffled his batting order, sending Brendon Julian in to open with Mark Butcher, and then promoting Adam Hollioake and Chris Lewis to numbers three and four after Julian had gone immediately for nought and Butcher had departed for nine. Although Lewis played a fine aggressive innings of forty and Hollioake gave it his best shot by making eighty-five from just 70 balls, the challenge facing Surrey was always beyond them and, after a clatter of wickets saw the score dip from 154-4 to

171-7, they were eventually left to try and bat out time against Robert Croft (3-49) and Dean Cosker. Fortunately for the visitors, the revised batting order had left this task in the capable hands of Darren Bicknell, batting at number six, and Nadeem Shahid, batting at nine, and they had no real difficulties in repelling Glamorgan's late bid for victory and securing the three points for the draw.

It had been an undeniably good round of matches for Leicestershire, who now required just a draw against Middlesex at Grace Road to secure the Championship title. While Surrey were being thwarted in Cardiff, the man on Surrey's wish-list, Ian Salisbury (8-75), had sent Essex spinning to defeat at Chelmsford, while Derbyshire had lost to Warwickshire at Derby after getting themselves into a match-winning position. Kent had meanwhile moved to within a point of Surrey and kept their title hopes flickering by claiming the last eight Hampshire wickets for just seven runs to snatch a sensational victory from the jaws of defeat at Canterbury... but the smart money was now very much on Leicestershire.

COUNTY CHAMPIONSHIP - TOP OF THE TABLE AT 16TH SEPTEMBER					
	P	W	D	L	PTS
Leicestershire	16	9	6	1	272
Surrey	16	8	7	1	258
Kent	16	9	6	1	257
Essex	16	8	4	4	249
Derbyshire	16	8	5	3	247

Surrey's lingering hopes of overturning Leicestershire's significant advantage were then dealt a crushing blow when the first day of their final Championship match, against Worcestershire at The Oval, was washed out by rain. This loss of time was crucial, especially as Dave Gilbert's men needed to obtain maximum bonus points from the match. To further dampen Surrey's spirits, the Foxes enjoyed better luck with the weather in Leicester and had a most profitable first day against Middlesex, dismissing their visitors for just 190 and then reaching 36-1 in reply.

The second days of the two contests then pretty much decided matters, with the start of play in London SE11 delayed until 1.10pm. After capturing the first three Worcestershire wickets for thirty-two, they were then further frustrated by a stand of 102 between Tom Moody (60) and Reuben Spiring (30) that endured until stumps were drawn, while Leicestershire were extending their first innings to 381-8 and taking a firm hold on their match at Grace Road.

Since it now looked almost impossible for James Whitaker's side to lose their match, Surrey knew the game was up as day three began at The Oval. Consequently, the decision was taken to pursue second place prize money by setting up a last-day run chase. Alec Stewart therefore forfeited his team's first innings - confirming Leicestershire as champions - as soon as Worcestershire had been bowled out for 362, whereupon the visitors plodded to 61-1 before setting Surrey 424 to win at around four runs per over. An already tough task was then made all the more difficult when Mark Butcher fell before the close of play, leaving the home side up against it at 15-1.

Things then went from bad to worse for the hosts on the final morning as they collapsed to 108-7 before respectability was restored by Darren Bicknell, who went on to carry his bat for 129, and Brendon Julian, who scored eighty at almost a run a ball during an eighth-wicket partnership of 141 and was subsequently awarded his county cap. As Surrey eventually subsided to a 124-run defeat, Leicestershire claimed a well deserved first Championship crown since their initial triumph of 1975 by completing victory over Middlesex by an innings and 74 runs. Results elsewhere left Surrey in third place, their best finish in the blue riband event for a decade and a fine achievement at the end of an incredible season. Dave Gilbert's men could also gain a degree of satisfaction from being the only side to beat the new County Champions. History had therefore repeated itself, since the only defeat Leicestershire had suffered on their way to the 1975 title was also at the hands of Surrey at The Oval.

	COUNTY CHAMPIONSHIP TABLE 1996	P	Pts	W	D	L	Bat	Bwl
1	Leicestershire	17	296	10	6	1	57	61
2	Derbyshire	17	269	9	5	3	52	58
3	Surrey	17	262	8	7	2	49	64
4	Kent	17	261	9	6	2	47	52
5	Essex	17	255	8	4	5	58	57
6	Yorkshire	17	248	8	4	5	50	58
7	Worcestershire	17	222	6	7	4	45	60
8	Warwickshire	17	218	7	4	6	39	55
9	Middlesex	17	213	7	4	6	30	59
10	Glamorgan	17	207	6	6	5	50	43
11	Somerset	17	197	5	6	6	38	61
12	Sussex	17	196	6	2	9	36	58
13	Gloucestershire	17	177	5	5	7	23	59
14	Hampshire	17	166	3	7	7	41	56
15	Lancashire	17	160	2	9	6	49	52
16	Northamptonshire	17	159	3	6	8	36	57
17	Nottinghamshire	17	131	1	7	9	42	52
18	Durham	17	97	0	5	12	22	60

Although Surrey could have been celebrating a double- or treble-winning campaign had they not made such a slow start to their season, everyone was delighted that the club's trophy drought had been brought to an end with the capture of the Sunday League title. Dave Gilbert had certainly done a fine job in his first year, and there was now a real sense of optimism at The Oval. The players were clearly all pulling in the same direction, which hadn't always been the case in the past, and it seemed almost inevitable that Surrey would go on to win further trophies in the years to come.

Although the county had never previously been a force to be reckoned with in the Sunday League, the team's success in this competition hadn't been a huge surprise, given that they'd had a number of three-in-one all-rounders at their disposal. Chris Lewis, Brendon Julian and Adam Hollioake were all extremely capable with the bat, the ball and in the field, while the young Ben Hollioake had shown considerable promise in all three areas. With these players in the side, the batting line-up was always long, strong and powerful - five men scored their runs at better than a run a ball - while the captain also had plenty of bowling options. The side had been consistently excellent in the field, since it always contained a number of sensational performers who were capable of pulling off match-turning catches and run outs. Surrey's only real Achilles heel had been a slight lack of discipline in the bowling. Although they both compensated for their indiscretions by being aggressive wicket-taking performers, Lewis and Julian had been particularly prone to conceding no-balls and wides, which for a lesser side could have been very costly. This profligacy with extras had been a major factor in only one significant defeat - at the hands of Essex in the Nat West Trophy semi-final - though it had resulted in some tight finishes in Sunday League games after overs had been deducted from Surrey's allocation.

The capture of the County Championship title was the obvious goal for this rejuvenated Surrey squad in 1997. Although everyone at the club was pleased with third place in the premier competition, there was a feeling that the side could have claimed a first crown since 1971 had the team been stronger in the spin department. It was an acknowledged fact that the county champions often turned out to be the team with the best slow bowlers and, though he always gave of his best, Richard Pearson had not looked like a match-winning spinner. On the pitches that offered encouragement he had been regularly upstaged by Darren Bicknell, while on the flat decks he lacked the guile, variety and strength of spin to worry county batsmen. It was little wonder then that Ian Salisbury, the Sussex and England leg-spinner, was being hotly pursued by Surrey as the south coast county went into meltdown, with rumours of a mass exodus of players putting some big names on the market. If the club could sign Salisbury, or another top-class spinner, they would be set up for a realistic assault on the Championship title, since the batting, wicketkeeping and seam-bowling departments were all looking in good shape.

At the end of the summer the county bade a fond farewell to the 35-year-old David Ward, who was now seen as surplus to requirements, despite having shown on occasions that he was still capable of playing explosive match-winning innings in the limited-overs form of the game.

1996 SEASON SUMMARY					
COMPETITION	P	W	D/A	L	POSITION/PROGRESS
County Championship	17	8	7	2	3rd
Sunday League	17	12	1	4	1st
Nat West Trophy	4	3	0	1	Semi-final
Benson & Hedges Cup	5	4	0	1	Quarter-final
TOTAL	43	27	8	8	1 Trophy

1996 RESULTS SUMMARY				
28/4	HAMPSHIRE	OVAL	BHC	WON by 59 runs
30/4	GLOUCESTERSHIRE	OVAL	BHC	WON by 3 wickets
2/5	Somerset	Taunton	CC	Match Drawn
5/5	Somerset	Taunton	SL	LOST by 53 runs
7/5	Sussex	Hove	BHC	WON by 9 wickets
9/5	KENT	OVAL	CC	Match Drawn
12/5	KENT	OVAL	SL	WON by 150 runs
14/5	Ireland	Eglinton	BHC	WON by 5 wickets
23/5	Gloucestershire	Gloucester	CC	Match Drawn
26/5	Gloucestershire	Gloucester	SL	WON by 72 runs
28/5	YORKSHIRE	OVAL	BHCqf	LOST by 9 wickets
30/5	DERBYSHIRE	OVAL	CC	Match Drawn
2/6	DERBYSHIRE	OVAL	SL	WON by 50 runs
6/6	Yorkshire	Middlesbrough	CC	LOST by 221 runs
9/6	Yorkshire	Headingley	SL	LOST by 8 wickets
13/6	LEICESTERSHIRE	OVAL	CC	WON by 108 runs
16/6	LEICESTERSHIRE	OVAL	SL	WON by 10 wickets
20/6	Durham	Stockton	CC	WON by 8 wickets
23/6	Durham	Stockton	SL	WON by 59 runs
25/6	HOLLAND	OVAL	NWT	WON by 159 runs
27/6	Essex	Southend	CC	Match Drawn
30/6	Essex	Southend	SL	LOST by 27 runs
4/7	MIDDLESEX	OVAL	CC	WON by 7 wickets

Date	Opponent	Venue	Comp	Result
7/7	MIDDLESEX	OVAL	SL	WON by 8 wickets
10/7	Warwickshire	Edgbaston	NWT	WON by 88 runs
14/7	WORCESTERSHIRE	OVAL	SL	WON on faster scoring rate
17/7	SUSSEX	GUILDFORD	CC	WON by 135 runs
21/7	SUSSEX	GUILDFORD	SL	LOST by 75 runs
25/7	Hampshire	Southampton	CC	WON by 5 wickets
28/7	Hampshire	Southampton	SL	WON by 23 runs
30/7	SOMERSET	OVAL	NWT	WON by 5 wickets
7/8	Lancashire	Southport	CC	WON by 140 runs
11/8	Lancashire	Old Trafford	SL	WON on faster scoring rate
13/8	ESSEX	OVAL	NWT	LOST by 4 wickets
22/8	Nottinghamshire	Trent Bridge	CC	Match Drawn
25/8	Nottinghamshire	Trent Bridge	SL	Match Abandoned
29/8	WARWICKSHIRE	OVAL	CC	WON by an inns & 164 runs
1/9	WARWICKSHIRE	OVAL	SL	WON by 2 wickets
3/9	NORTHANTS	OVAL	CC	WON by 225 runs
8/9	NORTHANTS	OVAL	SL	WON by 2 wickets
12/9	Glamorgan	Cardiff	CC	Match Drawn
15/9	Glamorgan	Cardiff	SL	WON by 7 wickets
19/9	WORCESTERSHIRE	OVAL	CC	LOST by 124 runs

COUNTY CHAMPIONSHIP BATTING AVERAGES 1996

	M	I	NO	Runs	HS	Ave	100	50	c	st
G.P. Thorpe	9	17	2	1044	185	69.60	5	4	10	-
A.J. Hollioake	16	28	6	1521	129	69.13	5	8	18	-
M.A. Butcher	17	32	3	1540	160	53.10	3	13	21	-
C.C. Lewis	8	13	1	442	94	36.83	-	3	13	-
B.P. Julian	16	23	2	759	119	36.14	2	3	9	-
D.J. Bicknell	17	31	3	969	129*	34.60	2	3	9	-
N. Shahid	10	17	3	448	101	32.00	1	3	5	-
J.D. Ratcliffe	8	14	1	403	68*	31.00	-	3	6	-
A.J. Stewart	9	16	1	434	80	28.93	-	3	10	-
R.M. Pearson	14	14	9	142	37	28.40	-	-	3	-
M.P. Bicknell	16	18	5	333	59*	25.61	-	1	2	-
G.J. Kersey	15	20	4	402	68*	25.12	-	3	45	1
A.D. Brown	14	22	2	361	57	18.05	-	3	14	-
J.E. Benjamin	13	14	6	141	38*	17.62	-	-	1	-

Qualification: 8 innings

COUNTY CHAMPIONSHIP BOWLING AVERAGES 1996

	O	M	Runs	W	Ave	BB	10wm	5wi
D.J. Bicknell	124.2	21	368	16	23.00	3-7	-	-
M.P. Bicknell	568.1	146	1633	66	24.74	5-17	-	3
B.P. Julian	447.4	86	1762	61	28.88	6-37	-	3
J.E. Benjamin	375.3	83	1217	39	31.20	4-17	-	-
C.C. Lewis	260.4	50	889	27	32.92	5-25	-	1
R.M. Pearson	475.0	101	1509	31	48.67	5-142	-	1
A.J. Hollioake	226.0	44	764	12	63.66	3-80	-	-

Qualification: 100 overs, 10 wickets

LIMITED-OVERS BATTING AVERAGES 1996

	M	I	NO	Runs	HS	Ave	100	50	c	st
A.J. Stewart	18	16	4	778	160	64.83	4	3	22	2
C.C. Lewis	15	11	5	289	63	48.16	-	1	7	-
A.D. Brown	24	24	2	943	117*	42.86	1	6	5	-
M.A. Butcher	13	12	2	404	91	40.40	-	3	4	-
G.P. Thorpe	15	12	1	369	96	33.54	-	1	12	-
N. Shahid	13	12	1	352	58	32.00	-	1	4	-
D.J. Bicknell	19	18	4	441	52*	31.50	-	2	7	-
A.J. Hollioake	24	20	2	492	74	27.33	-	2	6	-
D.M. Ward	18	17	1	433	112	27.06	2	-	11	-
B.P. Julian	24	16	3	233	41	17.92	-	-	11	-
R.M. Pearson	23	7	5	35	12*	17.50	-	-	2	-
M.P. Bicknell	24	10	6	69	22	17.25	-	-	3	-
B.C. Hollioake	13	8	2	70	22*	11.66	-	-	7	-

Qualification: 6 innings

LIMITED-OVERS BOWLING AVERAGES 1996

	O	M	Runs	W	Ave	BB	4wi	RPO
A.J. Hollioake	150.5	3	767	48	15.97	5-44	5	5.08
C.C. Lewis	115.1	9	462	25	18.48	3-13	-	4.01
J.E. Benjamin	133.3	10	534	24	22.25	3-33	-	4.03
B.C. Hollioake	69.4	5	318	14	22.71	5-10	1	4.56
B.P. Julian	160.0	5	839	33	25.42	4-46	1	5.24
M.P. Bicknell	189.0	16	848	31	27.35	3-16	-	4.48
R.M. Pearson	143.4	2	762	18	42.33	3-33	-	5.30

Qualification: 40 overs, 10 wickets

4 1997: Consoled By Gold

Just as it appeared that Surrey's fortunes were on an upward curve, with their team capable of achieving further success, the club received a devastating blow with the tragic death of Graham Kersey on New Year's Day, following a serious car collision in Brisbane, Australia on Christmas Eve. In common with the team he represented with pride and skill, the 25-year-old wicketkeeper - voted Player Of The Year in 1995 - was making great progress and looked sure to be Surrey's stumper for years to come, allowing Alec Stewart to concentrate on his batting when playing for the county in Championship matches. As everyone at the club grieved, Stewart spoke for all who knew Kersey when he described his late team-mate as "without doubt the most popular man on the staff - a true players' player", while Paul Sheldon concluded that "as a very dear friend to the club and the wider world of cricket... he will be immeasurably missed." It was the most awful start to a new year.

Although the 1996-97 close season period was quiet by the standards of the previous year there were, nevertheless, a number of changes, both within the club and at national level.

With Waqar Younis having signed for Glamorgan as Ottis Gibson's replacement, Surrey had been forced to revise their plans to re-sign the Pakistani pace ace after Brendon Julian's one-year deal expired. This wasn't a huge problem, however, since Julian had performed so well that Surrey were happy to offer him a new contract as their overseas player for 1997. The Australian would be playing under a new full-time captain, though, since Adam Hollioake had taken over the reins on a permanent basis from Alec Stewart, who had been given the title of Honorary Club Captain. This was, presumably, to make it clear that Stewart had been 'stood down' only because his England commitments meant that he was frequently unavailable to the county. The new captain would also have Ian Salisbury at his disposal, after the Sussex and England leg-spinner, who turned twenty-seven in January, had made the widely predicted move to The Oval to add more bite to a spin attack that had clearly been inadequate in 1996.

There had also been a change on the coaching side of the club, with Keith Medlycott, the county's former left-arm spinner, taking charge of the second eleven following Tony Pigott's departure to Sussex, where he had taken the Chief Executive's job after the county had undergone a Surrey-style revolution. Medlycott, 31, had moved into coaching/management in South Africa after his playing career fell apart, and had enjoyed great success with the Northern Transvaal side, leading them to their first ever trophy in his first season with the club.

The Surrey team was also to undergo a change of name in 1997, with the moniker 'Surrey Lions' to be adopted for all Sunday League matches. Further attempts to jazz up the matches in that competition and, hopefully, attract more young fans, were to include the introduction of short bursts of music to herald boundaries, landmarks and the entrance of batsmen; a match compere/announcer, and various other 'family entertainments'. Additionally, Surrey planned to stage the first competitive floodlit match in Great Britain, with the game against Nottinghamshire on the evening of Thursday 26th June to be played out under temporary lights brought in specially for the occasion.

On a wider scale, 1997 was to see the start of the phasing out of what had been dubbed 'the Sunday sandwich' - the situation where the Sunday League game was often slotted in after the first three days of the four-day County Championship match. Although this set-up was unpopular with the players and highly unsatisfactory in many ways, it was clearly going to reduce the amount of cricket that spectators attending on a Saturday would be likely to see, which had possible longer-term implications for the domestic game.

Finally, the newly devised Duckworth-Lewis system was to be used for the first time in rain-affected limited-overs matches, which had, in the past, almost always resulted in victory for the side batting second. This was because their revised target was based on the first team's run rate and made no allowance for the fact that it was easier for the chasing side to pursue a total over a reduced number of overs with all ten wickets still at their disposal. Although it appeared to be rather complex, the scientific algorithm-based Duckworth-Lewis system, based on statistics from past matches, was sure to make for a much fairer contest.

With the start of the season just over a week away Surrey's bad luck with overseas players resurfaced as Brendon Julian was selected in Australia's Ashes squad. It presented the county with a sadly familiar situation, though they came up with a novel solution this time after much consideration... they would do without an overseas registration at the start of the campaign and see how things developed as the summer unfolded. This was a praiseworthy and brave decision, especially as international call-ups were bound to affect the make up of the side throughout the season.

As in 1996, Dave Gilbert's team started their campaigns in the Championship and Sunday League with matches against Somerset, though this time it was Surrey's turn to play host.

The four-day fixture was preceded by a minute's silence in memory of both Graham Kersey and the Middlesex and England legend Denis Compton, who had passed away that very morning at the age of 78.

Somerset then proceeded to dominate the first two days of the contest after winning the toss and electing to bat, running up a total of 463 and reducing Surrey to a miserable 172-7 in reply. The visitors' impressive score was built around an undefeated innings of 136 from Richard Harden, half-centuries by Mark Lathwell, Peter Bowler and the debutant off-spinner Steve Herzberg, plus a world record-breaking 86-run contribution from extras (52 no-balls, 8 wides, 10 byes and 16 leg-byes). While the obvious lack of discipline in much of the bowling was rather worrying, the performance with the bat was even more disappointing, as an opening stand of ninety-four by Darren Bicknell (48) and Mark Butcher (46) was wasted by an experienced middle order that was all too easily despatched by Graham Rose (3-35).

Facing a damaging defeat, Surrey were extremely fortunate that only an hour's play was possible due to rain on day three, during which time the home county progressed to 209-8, while the whole of the final day was washed out, much to Somerset's disappointment.

Thankfully, the reigning Sunday League champions managed a slightly better display as they began the defence of their title the following day, scraping home by three wickets after getting themselves into all sorts of trouble while chasing 181 to win.

The Somerset innings turned out to be a colourless affair after they had been asked to bat by Adam Hollioake, with Harden (53) playing the only knock of any substance and the wickets being evenly spread amongst Surrey's six bowlers. Rose and Andy Caddick then reduced their hosts to 69-5 after twenty-one overs before Nadeem Shahid and Chris Lewis restored balance to the contest with a sixth-wicket stand of fifty-one in twelve overs. Although the loss of Shahid and Ben Hollioake in quick succession then made Somerset hot favourites again, Lewis found an outstanding ally in Ian Salisbury, who played a sensible supporting role while his colleague went for his strokes and managed to level the scores with one ball left to bowl. With excited spectators poised on the edge of their seats the match ended in slightly anti-climactic fashion as Michael Burns delivered a legside wide to hand Surrey a three-wicket victory that was no more than the excellent Lewis (68 from 64 balls) deserved for his efforts.

Buoyed by this last-gasp triumph, the team's attentions now turned to the Benson & Hedges Cup campaign, which started with Kent's visit to The Oval. This turned out to be a quite amazing contest, full of twists and turns, that went right down to the wire.

Surrey's innings started explosively through Brown, Stewart (51) and Ben Hollioake, whose combined efforts brought up the hundred in the twelfth over before a kamikaze approach against some fine bowling from Matthew Fleming (5-54) and Paul Strang (2-27) resulted in a swift decline from 108-1 to 135-6. Graham Thorpe (47) and Adam Hollioake then steadied the listing ship with a stand of fifty-six, allowing Chris Lewis to add late impetus and take the total up to 257.

The home fans' fears that this score might not be good enough in fine batting conditions looked justified as Matt Walker (56) and Trevor Ward (42) saw their side through to 134-1 before top-class bowling from Ian Salisbury and Joey Benjamin (3-48) brought the wickets of both men in quick succession to revive Surrey's hopes of victory. Another vital partnership of ninety-six between Allan Wells (40) and a typically positive Graham Cowdrey (47) set Kent up for their final surge, however, and, though a degree of panic set in late in the day, Ealham held his nerve at the last. Although the visitors only needed two to win from the final delivery of the match from Ben Hollioake, Ealham sealed victory in style by hoisting the ball high over midwicket for six.

Surrey now needed to get back on course quickly as they travelled to Bristol to take on Gloucestershire. Curiously, this match closely followed the course of the corresponding Benson & Hedges encounter between the two counties played exactly a year ago to the day, with Rob Cunliffe scoring a century - 113 on this occasion out of a total of 280-7 - but ending up on the losing side as Surrey chased down a difficult target with three wickets in hand. Ali Brown, who had scored eighty-two in the 1996 match, this time made sixty-six from 61 balls in laying the foundations for the visitors' success in partnership with Ben Hollioake (69), while Adam Hollioake (43) and the expert 'finisher' Chris Lewis (35 not out) united after something of a mid-innings wobble to enable their side to scramble home with four balls to spare.

After three tense finishes in succession, Surrey fans were finally able to relax as British Universities provided their side's next opposition at The Oval. Although the visiting team included a large number of players who would go on to play regular county cricket, they could only muster 198 in their innings, thanks almost exclusively to Will House (93) and James Ford (38), who added eighty-eight for the fifth wicket. Surrey's almost inevitable victory came inside twenty-six overs by six wickets after Alec Stewart (86 not out) and Ali Brown (47) had launched their side's reply with a partnership of ninety-eight in eleven overs.

A Sunday League fixture against Kent at Canterbury now interrupted the Benson & Hedges qualifying campaign and presented Surrey with an early opportunity to avenge the last-ball defeat they had suffered at The Oval. After rain had reduced the contest to 25-overs-per-side, Kent posted an impressive 193-8, with Graham Cowdrey playing a muscular knock of eighty-two from a mere 46 balls to put Kent in the driving seat. The visiting bowlers had performed well until Cowdrey entered the fray at 90-4 to smite seven fours and five sixes, three of which came in the space of five balls during Adam Hollioake's final over. Although the Surrey skipper emerged with Sunday best figures of 5-38, his side faced a major task if they were to win the match, especially once Alec Stewart was bowled by Alan Igglesden for seven. Ali Brown (52) and Graham Thorpe (33) did their best to keep up with the run rate during a second-wicket stand of sixty-six, but the visitors' charge was eventually halted by Dean Headley, who produced a decisive spell of 4-27 to secure a 12-run victory for his side.

With the games continuing to come thick and fast, the vanquished Surrey team travelled to Southampton to face a struggling Hampshire outfit in a Benson & Hedges qualifying match the next day. Having won the toss, Adam Hollioake elected to bat and then watched his men slump to 22-4 against John Stephenson's interesting choice of opening bowlers, Simon Renshaw, a 23-year-old swing bowler, and the veteran left-arm spinner, Raj Maru. Fortunately for Surrey, Nadeem Shahid (52) and the skipper himself (80) - century-making heroes of the previous season's County Championship victory on this ground - managed to retrieve the situation during a partnership of 138, before Renshaw returned to double his haul of wickets and finish with 6-25, the best figures by a Hampshire bowler in the Benson & Hedges Cup.

Although they had lost all five of their previous one-day games, the hosts must have felt that they had a fair chance of success as they set out to chase 229 for victory, even though conditions were offering some assistance to the bowlers. Their hopes were soon in tatters, however, as Jason Laney, Matthew Hayden and Shaun Udal - promoted to number three to act as a pinch-hitter - all fell to Martin Bicknell (3-20) during an excellent opening spell by the Surrey swing king that left them reeling at 23-5. Unable to emulate their visitors' powers of recovery, Hampshire's miserable start to the season continued as Joey Benjamin (4-19) wiped away the lower middle-order with the minimum of fuss, leaving them all out for 63, some 165 runs short of their target.

With a demanding schedule of six limited-overs matches in eight days now completed, Surrey's players were able to put their feet up for three days… though only one of these was a scheduled day off.

After making their way north from Southampton to Derby, rain prevented any play on the first two days of the County Championship match against Derbyshire at the County Ground, leaving little prospect of a result being obtained when the game finally got under way on the third morning. Electing to bat on a difficult pitch, Surrey were soon in trouble at 16-3, but eventually recovered to post a total of 267, thanks largely to the efforts of Graham Thorpe (83) and Martin Bicknell (74), who added seventy-four for the eighth wicket. Although Bicknell then went on to claim two quick scalps when Derbyshire replied, they were comfortably placed on 113-2 at stumps.

Any hopes that the captains might have harboured of conjuring up a contrived final-day finish were dashed when day four turned out to be as grey and unpleasant as the first two had been. Derbyshire managed to take their score up to 158-3 in the first fifty minutes of the morning before rain, followed by a small-scale tornado, brought about a merciful abandonment.

Surrey hadn't seen the last of the Derby rain, however, as the Sunday League match also fell victim to the weather, thereby bringing a thoroughly depressing five days to a close.

This abandonment at least allowed Surrey to beat a swift retreat to The Oval for the following day's final Benson & Hedges qualifying game against Sussex, with a place in the quarter-finals beckoning for Adam Hollioake's men if they could win the match.

They certainly started well after being put in to bat, with the now established one-day opening combination of Alec Stewart (72) and Ali Brown (40) taking full advantage of Peter Moores' surprising decision to give the new ball to his leg-spinner, Amer Khan (1-70). This pair's stand of 101 inside seventeen overs gave Surrey an excellent platform and allowed Graham Thorpe (78) and Mark Butcher (48) to accumulate runs steadily during a 112-run third-wicket partnership that heaped further misery on the visitors. Although Paul Jarvis bowled well at the death to pick up 4-60, the home side still managed to rack up an imposing total of 310-8 in their fifty overs.

Sussex were not about to surrender tamely, however, especially after getting away to a great start through Keith Greenfield (44) and Rajesh Rao (61), whose opening stand was worth ninety-three. Neil Taylor (67) and Mark Newell (60) then both struck out at a run a ball to put their side in with a fine chance of victory at 268-3 before Ian Salisbury (4-53) rapidly changed the course of the match with a stunning spell of bowling. The former Sussex leg-spinner captured four wickets in six balls, clean bowling Newell, Bill Athey and Nicky Phillips before claiming Khan lbw as the visitors slumped to 283-9. Jarvis briefly revived his team's hopes in the penultimate over by taking fourteen runs from three Ben Hollioake deliveries before Ali Brown ran out Mark Robinson to seal an 11-run victory and a quarter-final berth.

A return to County Championship action two days later brought Surrey back down to earth with a bump, as Gloucestershire routed them for just 115, their lowest total at The Oval since 1988. Some woeful batting was fully exploited by the visitors' four seamers, led by Shaun Young (4-26) and Mike Smith (3-35), and by the end of day one Gloucestershire led by seventy-five runs with five wickets in hand.

Jack Russell (59) and Tim Hancock (49) then added a crucial eighty-one runs for the seventh wicket the following morning, before Smith and Lawrence further embarrassed their hosts during a last-wicket stand of thirty-nine that boosted the total to 371. In what had been a dismal game for Surrey thus far, there was at least one bright spot as the 19-year-old Alex Tudor finished with career-best bowling figures of 6-101. Trailing by 256 on first innings, the home county were soon in trouble again, ending a rain shortened second day on 59-3, with Darren Bicknell, Mark Butcher and Alec Stewart all back in the pavilion.

A determined Graham Thorpe (81), assisted first by Nadeem Shahid and then by Jason Ratcliffe, restored some pride to the Surrey performance on day three, but eight wickets were down by the time the home county moved into the lead. Once Mark Alleyne (6-64) had efficiently lopped off the tail to finish the innings at 269, Gloucestershire strolled to a nine-wicket victory with four sessions of the match remaining to become the surprise early leaders of the Championship.

After their unscheduled rest day both sides returned to The Oval for the Sunday League match, with Surrey keen to atone for their poor display in the Championship encounter. The early signs were promising, too, as Martin Bicknell (3-24) justified his skipper's decision to insert Gloucestershire by removing Nick Trainor, Shaun Young and the former Oval favourite Monte Lynch during a fine opening burst. Rob Cunliffe (42) proved to be a thorn in Surrey's side once again, however, as he staved off a total collapse before departing at 87-5, then Mark Alleyne took charge, compiling a most welcome fifty-eight that enabled his side to total 176-9.

In reply, the home side lost Ali Brown for a duck, and then stuttered along unconvincingly, keeping wickets intact but failing to keep up with the required run rate. As the overs began to run out, Nadeem Shahid (34 not out) and Adam Hollioake (30) managed to press the accelerator just in time, allowing Surrey to scramble a last-ball single that earned a tense five-wicket victory from a rather featureless game that only really caught fire in the latter stages. This win gave Dave Gilbert's team ten points from their first four matches in defence of their title, placing them just behind a cluster of teams on twelve points.

Having already endured five damp days in Derby, Surrey were confronted by similar conditions in Leicester, where the first day of the next Championship match was a complete washout. Since the game coincided with England's Texaco Trophy series against Australia, Surrey were some way below full strength, with Alec Stewart, Graham Thorpe, Adam Hollioake and Ben Hollioake, who had been given an early chance to demonstrate his talents on the bigger stage, all missing. They were also lacking Ian Salisbury, who had been absent from the side since damaging his principal spinning finger in the Benson & Hedges Cup match against Sussex. With so many absentees, opportunities were granted to Ali Brown, who had been controversially omitted from the four-day line-up thus far, Jason Ratcliffe, Richard Pearson and James Knott - the son of England legend, Alan - who had made three one-day appearances earlier in the season to allow Stewart to rest a badly bruised finger.

In the absence of Hollioake senior, Chris Lewis skippered the visitors against his old team and lost the toss on the second morning, condemning his new side to a difficult day with the bat. Although Mark Butcher (59) was the only man to reach fifty, most of his middle-order colleagues got a start before falling to the off-breaks of Adrian Pierson (4-47) as Surrey made their way to 235-8 by the close of play.

Martin Bicknell (34 not out) was then largely responsible for pushing his side's total up to 278 the next day before David Millns (4-64) claimed the last wicket, allowing Darren Maddy and Vince Wells (56) to launch the Leicestershire reply with a partnership of 131. Although Surrey worked their way back into the contest by snaring five wickets in fifteen overs during the afternoon, they let things slip again in the later stages of the day, as Maddy (103) completed a fine century on his 23rd birthday and Paul Nixon notched a quick fifty that enabled the hosts to gain a 27-run lead by stumps.

Ultimately, the loss of the first day's play saved Surrey from defeat as they limped to a draw on day four. Although Lewis (4-64) tidied up the Foxes' tail rapidly to keep his team's first-innings deficit to sixty-two, the visitors were three down before they cleared the arrears and only managed to grind their way to the safety of 116-5 thanks to dogged knocks by Brown (40) and the stand-in skipper himself (47 not out).

While Surrey had been playing out this turgid draw, their England men had been propelling the host nation to an unexpected and unassailable 2-0 lead in the Texaco Trophy series -Graham Thorpe (75 not out) and Adam Hollioake (2-22 and 66 not out) had seen England to a six-wicket win in the first game at Headingley, while Alec Stewart (40) and Hollioake senior (53 not out) had both played important roles in repeating the margin of success two days later at The Oval. With the series sewn up, the England selectors decided that Ben Hollioake, at the age of 19 years 195 days, should make his debut in the final match of the series at Lord's. This game coincided with Surrey's Sunday League fixture at Grace Road... and both produced an amazing innings.

At Lord's, Ben Hollioake blasted the full might of the Australian attack to all parts of the ground in scoring sixty-three from just 48 balls, eleven of which he hit for four and one of which, from Shane Warne, sailed away for six. Graham Thorpe's unbeaten forty-five then built on Hollioake junior's stunning knock from number three in the order to enable England to complete a hat-trick of six-wicket victories.

Meanwhile, at Grace Road, Ali Brown was the man who produced something sensational as Surrey secured a five-wicket win over Leicestershire. Put in to bat by Chris Lewis, the Foxes started well with a 75-run opening partnership between Neil Johnson (40) and Vince Wells (39) before Joey Benjamin (2-40) and Ian Salisbury, who claimed 3-56 on his return to action, chipped away at the Leicestershire line-up to peg their hosts back to 187-7. Jon Dakin's hard-hitting unbeaten forty-one - including nineteen from Salisbury's final over - undid much of this good work, however, and allowed his side to total 234-7 from their forty overs.

Given their severely depleted batting line-up, which saw Salisbury listed at number seven, Surrey's victory target looked rather distant as they began their reply after tea. With Mark Butcher (16), Jason Ratcliffe (7), Nadeem Shahid (0) and Ian Ward (1) all dismissed cheaply, you would have expected Surrey to be in dire straits, but by this time there were actually 139 runs on the board, ninety-eight of them to Ali Brown, who was batting on an entirely different plane to everybody else in the match. After completing his century from just 76 balls, Brown lost Lewis at 175-5 before finding a perfect ally in Salisbury (23 not out) to see his team home with five wickets and twenty balls in hand. By beating his club record Sunday League score of 142 not out and finishing with an amazing 157 runs to his credit from only 117 balls, Brown had sent a clear reminder to the England selectors that just 363 days had passed since he had been a century-making hero against India in a Texaco Trophy match at Old Trafford. Equally, Surrey's win had given notice to all the other counties that the champions wouldn't be giving up their title without a fight. They were now sitting in third place in the nascent league table.

LEADING POSITIONS:- Essex P4, Pts 16; Lancs P4, Pts 16; Surrey P5, Pts 14

With all their England players - including Ben Hollioake, who had become the darling of the media and the talk of the town since his fine debut at Lord's - back in a much changed line-up, Surrey now travelled to Chelmsford for a Benson & Hedges Cup quarter-final against Essex, who were unbeaten in all competitions thus far.

By asking their hosts to bat and then removing the dangerous trio of Paul Prichard, Stuart Law and Graham Gooch with just thirty-seven runs on the board, Surrey put themselves in a position of strength which they rarely looked like relinquishing, even while Nasser Hussain (52) and Ronnie

Irani (38) were adding seventy-one runs for the fourth wicket. The men who had given the visitors such a good start, Martin Bicknell (3-40) and Chris Lewis (3-51), then returned to the attack and, combining with Adam Hollioake (2-6), finished off the Essex innings twenty-five balls ahead of schedule for 214 despite the best efforts of Paul Grayson, who was left stranded on forty-nine.

The early loss of Alec Stewart and Ben Hollioake set Surrey back on their heels briefly but while the in-form Ali Brown was in residence the Essex total never looked likely to be big enough. By the time Brown fell to Grayson for seventy-one after facing 78 balls, the visitors needed just eighty more runs, most of which were knocked off by Graham Thorpe (73) and Mark Butcher (41 not out) as Surrey cruised in by six wickets with seven overs to spare.

Having participated in fifteen matches, of varying durations, in just over a month, Surrey now had a week off before Essex were due at The Oval for fixtures in both the County Championship and the Sunday League. During this break the team slipped to the bottom of the Championship table, a situation that could not have been envisaged at the start of the season when many good judges had been tipping Surrey to win the title. With England calls sure to hit hard during the six Test series against Australia, the club therefore elected to reverse the decision to do without an overseas player, signing the richly talented 20-year-old Pakistani off-spinner, Saqlain Mushtaq, who had been such a success on his country's tour of England in 1996. Although he hadn't played in any of the three Tests, Saqlain had captured twenty-nine wickets at 15.72 runs apiece in the first-class matches against county opposition, frequently baffling batsmen with a 'mystery ball' that behaved like a leg-break. Since Ian Salisbury was still struggling with his damaged finger, and Richard Pearson had again proved ineffective during the leg-spinner's enforced absence, this looked to be an eminently sensible signing.

Unfortunately for Surrey, Saqlain didn't arrive in time to play in the Championship match against Essex at The Oval, while Alec Stewart, Graham Thorpe, Mark Butcher - who made his Test debut - and Adam Hollioake - who ended up as twelfth man - were involved with England at Edgbaston. To add to the county's woes, Martin Bicknell was absent with a neck injury.

After Chris Lewis lost the toss, his charges found a promising start, which saw four good wickets - Gooch, Grayson, Stuart Law and Irani - down for 103, negated by the much less celebrated Darren Robinson (98) and Stephen Peters (33), who doubled the score before being parted. A decent Surrey fightback that reduced Essex to 239-7 was then wasted as the visitors' tail wagged vigorously to take them up to 347 all out just before stumps on day one.

One of the successful tailenders, Ashley Cowan, then starred with the ball on the second morning, snapping up three wickets in his opening burst as Surrey slumped to 36-4. Fortunately for the hosts they were then rescued by a splendid 109 from Ali Brown - his first Championship ton since August 1995 - and forty from Lewis before Cowan returned to complete figures of 5-58 and spark a terminal subsidence to 280 all out.

After extending their advantage to 107 by the close of day two, Essex put the game beyond the home side's reach on the third day as Gooch (56) and Grayson (105) played the principal roles in taking their side to 197-2. Although Surrey eventually hit back through Ian Salisbury (3-79) and Ben Hollioake (3-53) to dismiss the visitors for 302, the chances of their below-strength batting line-up scoring 370 to win were slim indeed, especially as they knew that Brown would be unable to bat after sustaining a nasty hand injury during his innings. The loss of two wickets for seventy before the close confirmed Essex's status as hot favourites.

Resistance on day four came principally from Jason Ratcliffe, who scored fifty-three from 170 balls, and Ben Hollioake (72), who gave further notice of his talent while compiling his maiden first-class half-century, before Essex claimed their expected victory, by 147 runs, at 3pm. It was of little consolation to Surrey that their six bonus points had moved them one place up the

Championship table to seventeenth, though it would be wrong to be too hard on a side that had been shorn of five of its best players.

At least Dave Gilbert had a stronger side for the Sunday League match, with Adam Hollioake and Martin Bicknell back in his line-up, and the newly arrived Saqlain Mushtaq making his debut. This was offset by the loss of the injured Brown, though a new opening pair of Ratcliffe (69) and Ian Ward (31) saw their side off to a good start after Graham Gooch had won the toss for Essex. Sadly for Surrey, only one other batsman - Adam Hollioake, with thirty-nine - reached double figures as that man Cowan (4-36) and the spinners, Peter Such and Paul Grayson, induced a headlong collapse from 139-2 to 176 all out. With the hosts' innings having twice been interrupted by rain that had consequently reduced the match to a 35-overs-per-side affair, the Duckworth-Lewis system came into play and decreed that Essex would now have to score 184, rather than 177, for victory.

Things seemed to be going Surrey's way when excellent catches by Martin Bicknell and Nadeem Shahid left the visitors struggling slightly at 97-4, but an unbroken stand of eighty-eight in twelve overs by Ronnie Irani (32 not out) and Danny Law (55 not out from just 41 balls) rapidly turned the tide and allowed Essex to sail home with seven balls to spare.

This was fast becoming a very trying season for Dave Gilbert and his team, and everyone at The Oval was in need of a boost in order to get the campaign back on track. It was hoped that the Benson & Hedges Cup semi-final against Leicestershire at The Oval, offering the prospect of a big match at Lord's, would provide the sort of tonic that everyone was looking for.

With England players and injured parties restored to their team, Surrey were put in to bat by James Whitaker and made a very shaky start by losing Ali Brown and Ben Hollioake to Alan Mullally in the opening overs. Alec Stewart (87) and Graham Thorpe (79), who had just made an excellent 138 in the Test victory over Australia at Edgbaston, soon restored order, however, during a third-wicket stand of 158 in thirty-two overs. As a result, Surrey gradually assumed complete control on an excellent pitch, eventually posting 308-8, thanks to Adam Hollioake's murderous sixty-three from 40 balls and other brief-but-bright acts of violence from the men in the lower middle-order.

Martin Bicknell (4-41) then went to work on the Leicestershire top-order, dismissing Maddy, Whitaker, Habib and Wells to send the visitors into a tailspin at 68-6 and book Surrey's place in the July 12th final. Although there was clearly no way back for the Foxes from this position, Paul Nixon (53) and Tim Mason (30) did manage to save a little face for their side with a ninth-wicket partnership of seventy-five that prolonged the innings until the forty-sixth over and reduced the final margin of defeat to 130 runs. As the players and supporters celebrated Surrey's first win in a cup semi-final since 1991, when they went on to lose to Hampshire in the Nat West Trophy final, everyone was hoping that this victory could prove to be the turning point of the season.

Yorkshire, who had made a decent start to the campaign, were to be Surrey's next opponents in both four-day and one-day formats at The Oval. Although the home side were without the resting Graham Thorpe they were able to give a Championship debut to Saqlain Mushtaq and took the early honours after Adam Hollioake had won the toss and elected to bat. A solid opening partnership between the in-form Jason Ratcliffe (45) and Mark Butcher (43) prefaced two century-plus stands between Alec Stewart and the Hollioakes, with Ben (53) notching his second successive half-century and Adam plundering sixty-nine runs from 72 balls before becoming the fifth man out at 366. Stewart, who was in fine touch and struck the ball beautifully in registering his first Championship ton since June 1995, accelerated away as the bowlers began to flag and completed a superb 231-ball double-century with a hooked boundary from the penultimate ball of the opening day.

On day two, Surrey converted their overnight 426-6 into 549 all out as Stewart advanced to 271 not out, which, apart from being a personal career-best, also represented the highest individual score made against Yorkshire to date in the twentieth century and the best tally by a wicketkeeper in a Championship match since Les Ames scored 295 for Kent versus Gloucestershire in 1933. Requiring 400 to save the follow-on on a pitch that offered turn to the spinners, Yorkshire were indebted to Martyn Moxon (57), David Byas (59) and Darren Lehmann (61 not out) as they reached 226-4 in reply by the close, though Saqlain's three wickets during a long spell had given them notice that they still had much work to do if they were to stave off defeat.

With Lehmann completing his century before falling immediately afterwards to Ian Salisbury, and Richard Blakey resisting stubbornly Yorkshire looked likely to avoid the follow-on until Adam Hollioake brought himself into the attack to flatten the tail and equal his career-best bowling figures (coincidentally, against Yorkshire at The Oval in 1995) with a spell of 4-22 in 29 balls. Even though the visitors trailed by 162, the Surrey skipper decided against inviting them to bat again on the dusting pitch, preferring to try and bat them out of the match. This plan went somewhat awry, however, as attempts to put quick runs on the board led to Surrey being bowled out for 153 in 46.1 overs, with Chris Silverwood (5-49) and Richard Stemp (3-44) the principal destroyers. With Yorkshire, needing 316 to win, closing on 19-0 there was all to play for on day four, which followed the Sunday League game.

This now rare instance of the 'Sunday sandwich' had a tasty filling for Surrey, as they revived their prospects of retaining their title with a five-wicket win that owed much to the efforts of four players. Martin Bicknell (3-27) and Joey Benjamin (0-22) produced exemplary eight-over spells with the ball as Yorkshire totalled 198-9 (Lehmann 56), before Graham Thorpe, with an excellent unbeaten hundred, and Ben Hollioake (39 not out) rescued their side from the depths of 96-5 and secured victory with nine balls to spare.

SUNDAY LEAGUE - TOP OF THE TABLE AT 15TH JUNE					
	P	W	L	T	A	PTS
Essex	7	6	1	0	0	24
Lancashire	7	6	1	0	0	24
Kent	7	5	2	0	0	20
Surrey	7	4	2	0	1	18
Somerset	8	4	3	0	1	18

Sadly, we were denied an exciting climax to the incomplete four-day fixture as rain arrived the next day to ruin Surrey's chances of recording their first victory of the campaign. Although the impressive Darren Lehmann - undefeated on fifty-seven when the match was abandoned as a draw - might have had other ideas, the hosts looked on course to win, since Yorkshire had struggled to 115-4 after losing three wickets to Martin Bicknell at the start of the day.

Rain was yet again a problem for Surrey in their next Championship match at New Road, Worcester. After a full first day, which saw the visitors amass 382-7 despite being without their England men, only thirty-five overs were possible on day two, while the last couple of days were completely devoid of action as the dismal weather took hold. Surrey's final total of 452-9 declared was based around two fine centuries, one by Jason Ratcliffe (135), which was his first for Surrey and a career-best to boot, and the other by Ali Brown (121), who reached three figures from just 107 balls. Brown's effort was especially creditable since it transpired that he had been playing with a broken hand since the Championship match against Essex. Before the match succumbed to the weather, Worcestershire replied with 81-1 after losing Tim Curtis to the first ball of their innings from Martin Bicknell.

A hugely forgettable Championship encounter was then followed by a Sunday League match that saw Surrey slip to a damaging defeat. Put in to bat on the pitch used for the four-day game, they were reduced to a desperate 36-7, and then 59-8, as Gavin Haynes (4-13) got the ball to zip around on a surface that had been sweating under the covers for two-and-a-half days. Martin Bicknell, with a Sunday League best of 57 not out, and Saqlain Mushtaq (29) pulled off something of a rescue act with a stand of eighty-three but the visitors' final total of 149 was never likely to be enough as the pitch eased. There was just a glimmer of hope for Surrey when their seamers removed Tom Moody, Vikram Solanki and Graeme Hick with the total just past fifty, but Haynes (47) and Reuben Spiring (43) then came together to see their side home with almost nine overs in hand.

With league success in both forms of the game already looking pretty unlikely, the two cups appeared to represent Surrey's only chance of a trophy, giving added importance to the next match, a first round Nat West Trophy tie against Durham at The Oval.

Invited to bat in conditions that assisted the seamers early on, the visitors soon lost Jonathan Lewis and Nick Speak to Martin Bicknell and Chris Lewis respectively, but were put back on course by John Morris (75) and David Boon (57) during a third-wicket stand of 117. Ian Salisbury then regained the initiative for Surrey with a fine spell of 3-36 before Michael Foster's unbeaten fifty-seven from 40 balls allowed Durham to finish on a respectable 247-7 from their sixty overs.

Although Mark Butcher went for a duck when the home county replied, some woeful new-ball bowling allowed Jason Ratcliffe (39) and Alec Stewart (90 not out) to raise the hundred in the twentieth over and make the rest of the run chase something of a formality. While Stewart held his end up, Ali Brown (44) and Adam Hollioake (34) ensured that Surrey romped to an easy victory by five wickets with eleven overs unused.

The keenly anticipated floodlit Sunday League match against the Nottinghamshire Outlaws - as they were to be dubbed for this game - was next up for the Surrey Lions on Thursday 26th June. An immense amount of time and effort had been put into organising, marketing and arranging sponsorship for a ground-breaking fixture which was expected to draw a large crowd to The Oval, so it was extremely disappointing for all concerned when prolonged heavy rain resulted in the famous old Test ground being flooded rather than lit on the day of the match. There was never any chance of the game getting under way, so for the second successive year Surrey and Nottinghamshire failed to get on to the park for their Sunday League contest... and the champions had, through no fault of their own, dropped another two points. To add to the club's frustration, Warwickshire drew a crowd of 15,174 to Edgbaston when their floodlit match against Somerset became the first such fixture played in Great Britain on 23rd July.

Of more immediate concern, however, was the continuing rain and the appalling state of the turf around the edges of the ground after the temporary floodlight pylons and supports had been transported from the sodden outfield - it was obvious that the huge muddy patches left behind would take a lot of time and effort to repair. As we came towards the end of the UK's wettest June of the twentieth century, the ground was so saturated that the first day's play in the Championship match against Nottinghamshire was actually called off before 9am, while the second day's play was abandoned three hours later, some twenty-three hours before it was due to start!

When the game finally got under way on its third scheduled day, Surrey were soon struggling at 21-4 against the 18-year-old Paul Franks (4-47) after Adam Hollioake - captaining the side in place of Alec Stewart, whose wife was ill - had surprisingly opted to bat. Ali Brown (27), Ben Hollioake (44) and Chris Lewis (48) managed to stop the rot, however, and enabled their side to pick up a batting point before declaring at 201-9. Nottinghamshire then dawdled to 73-1 by the close after Lewis had gleefully captured the early wicket of Tim Robinson, who had apparently become the England all-rounder's principal adversary during his unhappy spell at Trent Bridge.

The game appeared to be going nowhere at this stage, but an immediate declaration by Robinson on the fourth morning, followed by a Surrey closure at 123-6, breathed life into the contest and left the visitors to chase 252 to win from a minimum of fifty-nine overs. This appeared to be a good deal from the hosts' point of view, especially once Lewis had again disposed of Robinson early in the piece, and Bicknell had unseated Matthew Dowman with the score on forty-eight. The match still looked to be heading for a draw, however, until the spinners started to rattle through the Nottinghamshire line-up after tea. Although there were isolated periods of resistance, none of them lasted long enough for the visitors as Salisbury eventually earned Surrey their first Championship victory of the season by having Mark Bowen well taken at the wicket by James Knott from the first ball of the final over. The combination of Salisbury (18.1-11-19-6) and Saqlain (26-13-34-2) had proved irresistible as Nottinghamshire had been bowled out for 120 and it promised much for the future.

The new Surrey spin twins were unable to show what they could do in the next match, however, as the seemingly incessant rain affected the Championship game against Warwickshire at Edgbaston, leaving the pitch damp at the start of play. Put in by Nick Knight, the visitors - lacking their three England Test men, the injured Ben Hollioake, and the out-of-favour Darren Bicknell and Nadeem Shahid - mustered 193 runs during a first innings that bridged the first two rain-affected days. This, in fact, represented a reasonable effort in conditions that were very much to the liking of Graeme Welch (4-62) and Allan Donald (4-64).

When Warwickshire replied the Surrey fielders proceeded to drop a host of catches, allowing their hosts to recover from a three-wicket burst by Martin Bicknell (4-96) that had left them reeling at 55-4. All three Bears' batsmen who passed fifty - Trevor Penney (99), Dougie Brown (66) and Neil Smith (69 not out) - were given extra lives and, consequently, the home side were able to build a 113-run advantage during the second half of day two and the first half of day three.

Surrey were then bundled out for 144 by Donald, who proved he had recovered from recent back problems by returning 6-55, including a burst of 5-18 during an eight-over spell that sent the visitors plummeting from 87-1 to 107-8. Jason Ratcliffe resisted stoutly during a fine battling knock of fifty-nine against his old county, but Surrey still looked likely to suffer an innings defeat until Ian Salisbury contributed twenty-four from number nine in the order.

Requiring just thirty-two runs to complete their victory, Warwickshire found their efforts to finish the match before the end of day three thwarted by Bicknell (3-24) and Lewis (2-9), who reduced them to 8-3 and then 21-4. This unexpected clatter of wickets forced them to return the next morning, when they duly claimed their win despite the loss of Brown to Bicknell.

With his team having dropped back to fourteenth in the table after this heavy defeat, Dave Gilbert was not a happy man, putting the total number of chances missed by his side at eight and saying "It was unprofessional and everyone should feel embarrassed. The whole thing became contagious and we became panic-stricken about our catching. If we had been more disciplined we would have won." The Surrey Manager was also disappointed that neither Gregor Kennis nor Ian Ward, the younger batsmen who had been selected ahead of Bicknell senior and Shahid, had taken their chance, while James Knott was struggling with both bat and gloves. As a result, there were changes for the Sunday League game, with Darren Bicknell returning to the side after making 244 in a second eleven fixture, and Jonathan Batty, Oxford University's wicketkeeper in 1996, taking over behind the stumps.

These changes failed to improve Surrey's fortunes, however, as they went down to a comprehensive 48-run defeat that was not even as close as the final margin suggested. Although Joey Benjamin and Chris Lewis (2-38) impressed with the ball as Warwickshire stumbled to 62-3, Dominic Ostler (58), David Hemp (46 from 46 balls) and Graeme Welch (32 not out from 17 balls) eventually took control and powered their team on to an impressive total of 231-6, despite the excellent efforts of Saqlain Mushtaq (2-34). In reply, the Lions lost two wickets to run outs in crumbling to 35-4, and they continued to dip towards defeat at 103-7 despite Adam Hollioake's 34-ball knock of fifty. The lower order accumulated another eighty runs while batting out the rest of the overs but it was an exercise in futility as Surrey's hopes of retaining their title took a potentially fatal body blow.

The next week therefore took on an even more important look for the team, since the second-round Nat West Trophy clash with Nottinghamshire at The Oval was to be followed by the Benson & Hedges Cup final against Kent. If success was not forthcoming in one of the knockout competitions then the 1997 season was likely to go down in Surrey's history as a very disappointing one, and the momentum gained by the 1996 Sunday League triumph would be lost.

Nottinghamshire had looked to be a pretty average one-day side throughout the summer to date, so their visit to The Oval appeared to provide Surrey with a reasonably safe passage into the third round. This certainly looked to be the case as they slipped to 10-3 against Martin Bicknell (2-28) and Chris Lewis after being asked to bat on a used pitch that would clearly allow the home county to exploit their massive advantage in the spin bowling department. Although Ian Salisbury (2-32) and Saqlain Mushtaq (3-30) did indeed find the surface receptive to their spin, it also provided constant inconsistent bounce to trouble batsmen throughout the match. The visitors' New Zealand international all-rounder, Nathan Astle (56), who was dropped at second slip off Bicknell before he had scored, was the only man to look even remotely comfortable as Nottinghamshire struggled to 176 before being bowled out in 55.1 overs.

With Surrey's batting line-up boosted by the return of Stewart, Butcher and Thorpe - who had all played in the third Test, which England had lost by 268 runs - the victory target didn't seem too demanding, despite the tricky nature of the pitch. The early loss of Jason Ratcliffe was a disappointment but was soon forgotten as Butcher (35) and Stewart (26) took the total to seventy-two in the twenty-first over, at which point Surrey looked to be in control of the game. At 80-4, with all three England men back in the pavilion, the situation wasn't so rosy, however, and from that moment on every single run had to be eked out against keen Nottinghamshire bowling and fielding. No batsman was able to establish himself and the seamers simply throttled the life out of their hosts, who subsided from 100-4 to 132-9 in the face of naggingly accurate bowling from Mark Bowen (3-38), Chris Tolley (3-21) and man-of-the-match Astle (10-5-12-1). Although Bicknell and Saqlain bravely added twenty-two for the last wicket, Evans eventually bowled Bicknell in the fifty-sixth over to seal a stunning Nottinghamshire victory by twenty-two runs and provide Surrey's likely Benson & Hedges Cup final team with a stern lesson just three days ahead of the big match. Adam Hollioake later described the defeat as "my most disappointing loss here", but promised that it wouldn't affect morale for the impending final.

The big day at Lord's was, of course, a re-run of the opening group match, in which Kent had beaten Surrey when Mark Ealham hit Ben Hollioake's final ball of the match for six. The teams therefore appeared to be evenly matched... and Dave Gilbert's men had a score to settle. While Kent fielded the same eleven that they had put out at The Oval in April, Surrey had undoubtedly been strengthened by the arrival of Saqlain Mushtaq, and his inclusion in place of Joey Benjamin, along with the substitution of Jason Ratcliffe for Nadeem Shahid, were the only two changes in the line-up they announced at the toss, which was won by Steve Marsh.

After they had elected to bat, Kent were soon struggling, thanks to Surrey's trusted new-ball pairing of Chris Lewis and Martin Bicknell who removed Matthew Fleming, Matt Walker and Allan Wells with just twenty-three runs on the board. Although a subdued Trevor Ward then helped to stabilise the innings with Nigel Llong (42) before falling to Adam Hollioake with the total advanced to sixty-eight, Kent never really managed to get a grip on the game, despite the best efforts of Mark Ealham (52). Every time a partnership looked like developing Surrey would capture a wicket, with the returning Lewis's yorking of the potentially dangerous Graham Cowdrey proving to be a particularly devastating blow to Kent's prospects. As the innings came to a close at 212-9, the bowlers could reflect on a job well done, with all bar Ben Hollioake having picked up a wicket and no one having yielded more than forty runs, while Adam Hollioake had marshalled his troops expertly, making timely and intelligent bowling changes to stymie his opponents' progress.

As Surrey began their reply on a gloriously sunny afternoon with the pitch playing really well, the hop county's total looked undeniably below par, though they were given an immediate fillip when Ali Brown crashed Martin McCague to cover point, where he was well caught by Fleming. This brought Ben Hollioake to the crease to join Alec Stewart, and the 19-year-old was soon demonstrating once again how much he relished the big stage by reeling off some glorious strokes. As a result, the game quickly began to flow in Surrey's favour, with Paul Strang, the Zimbabwean leg-spinner, the only Kent bowler able to exert any pressure or control. Kent's medium-pacers certainly posed no threat to Hollioake as he cruised to his half-century in fifty balls and led his team to the seemingly impregnable position of 120-1 at the halfway stage of their reply. With the vastly experienced Stewart sensibly allowing his young partner to dominate proceedings there was no way back for Matthew Fleming's men, and it was no real consolation to them when Hollioake fell two runs short of what would have been a splendid century with the total on 161. Having driven his 114th ball to mid-on, the talented youngster departed to a standing ovation from the Lord's crowd, with his reputation further enhanced and his side assured of victory.

Unruffled by his team-mate's departure, Stewart soon completed his own half-century, from 89 balls, before ushering his team towards the finishing line in the company of Graham Thorpe. The honorary club captain was undefeated on seventy-five as he secured Surrey's second trophy in two years with five overs to spare and eight wickets in hand, sparking off the same kind of celebrations as we had witnessed in Cardiff ten months previously. While Kent tried to come to terms with their sixth successive defeat in a Lord's final - four of them in this competition - Adam Hollioake was dedicating his team's triumph to the memory of their great friend and team-mate, Graham Kersey, who was still very much missed by everyone at the club. It was wonderful that they had won the gold Benson & Hedges trophy in his honour, especially as success was looking unlikely in the two league competitions.

BENSON & HEDGES CUP FINAL 1997
KENT v SURREY at Lord's

Saturday 12th July   Surrey won by 8 wickets

Kent won the toss and elected to bat   Umpires:- George Sharp & David Shepherd

KENT

Fall Of Wkt	Batsman	How	Out	Score	Balls	4s	6s
2-15	M.V. Fleming	lbw	b Lewis	7	7	1	-
1=15	M.J. Walker		b Bicknell	6	12	1	-
4-68	T.R. Ward	lbw	b A.J. Hollioake	15	40	2	-
3-23	A.P. Wells	lbw	b Bicknell	5	15	1	-
5-106	N.J. Llong	c Butcher	b Saqlain	42	65	5	-
8-194	M.A. Ealham	c Brown	b Lewis	52	88	4	-
6-135	G.R. Cowdrey		b Lewis	8	20	1	-
7-170	P.A. Strang		b Salisbury	23	25	2	-
	S.A. Marsh *+	Not	Out	24	23	1	-
9-198	M.J. McCague	c Thorpe	b Saqlain	0	3	-	-
	D.W. Headley	Not	Out	3	3	-	-
	Extras	(1b, 7lb, 17w, 2nb)		27			
	TOTAL	(50 overs)	(for 9 wkts)	**212**			

Bowler	O	M	R	W	NB	Wd
Bicknell	8	0	33	2	1	6
Lewis	10	3	39	3	-	2
A.J. Hollioake	7	0	31	1	-	2
B.C. Hollioake	6	0	28	0	-	2
Saqlain	9	1	33	2	-	1
Salisbury	10	0	40	1	-	1

SURREY

Fall Of Wkt	Batsman	How	Out	Score	Balls	4s	6s
1-2	A.D. Brown	c Fleming	b McCague	2	4	-	-
	A.J. Stewart +	Not	Out	75	125	7	-
2-161	B.C. Hollioake	c Strang	b Ealham	98	112	14	-
	G.P. Thorpe	Not	Out	17	32	-	-
	A.J. Hollioake *	did not bat					
	M.A. Butcher	did not bat					
	C.C. Lewis	did not bat					
	J.D. Ratcliffe	did not bat					
	M.P. Bicknell	did not bat					
	I.D.K. Salisbury	did not bat					
	Saqlain Mushtaq	did not bat					
	Extras	(11lb, 6w, 6nb)		23			
	TOTAL	(45 overs)	(for 2 wkts)	215			

Bowler	O	M	R	W	NB	Wd
McCague	8	0	45	1	3	1
Headley	10	0	53	0	-	-
Fleming	7	1	29	0	-	1
Ealham	6	0	31	1	-	3
Strang	10	1	31	0	-	1
Llong	4	0	15	0	-	-

Gold Award Winner - Ben Hollioake

Having had three days to bask in the glow of their success, Surrey were back to the bread and butter of league action with matches against Hampshire at Guildford. The visitors had endured a difficult campaign thus far and had failed to make an impression in any competition, so they could have done without losing the toss and being belted all around the Woodbridge Road ground on day one of the Championship match. Although no one reached three figures, five men passed fifty - Stewart (98), Thorpe (84), Adam Hollioake (75), Butcher (69) and Lewis (66 not out) - as Surrey rattled up 457-9, which was only their third total in excess of three-hundred in their tenth Championship match of the summer.

After Lewis (76) and Alex Tudor (35 not out) had extended their team's score to 477 on the second morning, the bowlers faced the prospect of trying to dismiss the Hampshire batsmen on a good pitch. The excellence of the surface was demonstrated by Jason Laney (41) and Matthew Hayden (58), who managed to put on seventy-six for the first wicket before the former fell to Ben Hollioake and the latter was bowled by Martin Bicknell when thirty-five runs short of becoming the first man to a thousand first-class runs in what had been a very wet summer. The rest of the visitors' batting was rather patchy, however, with only Adrian Aymes (45) reaching thirty as an overnight position of 200-5 crumbled away to 303 all out in the face of fine bowling by Bicknell (4-88) and Ian Salisbury (3-83) on the third morning.

Asked to follow on, 174 runs in arrears, Hampshire then crashed to 24-5 as Bicknell produced a magnificent opening spell that saw him claim four wickets for three runs - including Hayden for a duck - in his first five overs. The younger brigade, in the form of Tudor and Ben Hollioake, then claimed a wicket apiece to reduce the visitors to the hopeless position of 71-7 before a battling partnership of 123 for the eighth wicket between Aymes and Simon Renshaw (56) helped Hampshire take the game into day four.

Leading by just fifty-three runs with two wickets standing, the visitors were, predictably, unable to extend the contest much further on the final morning - Stuart Milburn was soon run out and James Bovill became a fifth victim for Bicknell (5-34) when he edged to Mark Butcher, who had taken over behind the stumps late in Hampshire's first innings after Stewart had been hit above the eye by a Salisbury delivery that deflected off a batsman's pad. Poor Adie Aymes was left stranded on ninety-six after his second impressively defiant knock of a match that the hosts duly won by nine wickets before lunch.

Attention now switched to the televised Sunday League match, which was to feature a record-breaking innings from Ali Brown in front of a packed Woodbridge Road crowd.

Having invited Surrey to bat, John Stephenson was soon wondering whether he'd made the right decision as Brown set off like a rocket, blasting Cardigan Connor (8-0-81-0) and Simon Renshaw all around the park in reaching fifty from just twenty balls, three of which had disappeared for six and five of which had been hammered for four. The efforts of the batsmen at the other end quickly became irrelevant as Brown proceeded to race to a 56-ball century (six sixes, nine fours), after taking a particular liking to the seam bowling of James Bovill (7-0-73-0). Although he took advantage of a short boundary on the Dapdune Wharf side of the ground, every shot seemed to come out of the middle of Brown's bat as he sailed on to reach 150 (10 sixes, 12 fours) from the eighty-fourth delivery he faced and soon overtook Graham Gooch's 176 against Glamorgan at Southend in 1983 to claim the record for the highest individual score ever recorded in the Sunday League. By a strange coincidence, Gooch had announced his imminent retirement earlier in the day.

Everyone in the ground, and watching on television, was now wondering if Brown could achieve the seemingly impossible feat of reaching two-hundred as the overs started to run out. Having got this far, Brown wasn't about to disappoint his audience, duly arriving at the magical milestone from his 118th ball to earn congratulations from his generous opponents as well as a rousing standing ovation from all the spectators around the ground. When he departed to a catch by Stephenson off Renshaw from the next delivery he faced, at the start of the last over, he had 203 to his name. His fantastic knock had included eleven sixes and nineteen fours and fallen just four runs short of exceeding the highest score recorded in a limited-overs game in the UK, Alvin Kallicharran's 206 for Warwickshire against Oxfordshire in the Nat West Trophy in 1984. Thanks to Brown's heroics, Surrey's final total of 344-5 looked absolutely untouchable.

This did indeed turn out to be the case, though Hampshire put up a brave fight after their two biggest hopes, Matt Hayden and Robin Smith, had fallen cheaply. After Jason Laney (47) and Will Kendall (34) had averted the possibility of the visitors suffering total humiliation, Shaun Udal struck out boldly to record a career-best Sunday League score of seventy-eight from 56 balls before becoming the first of three victims for Ben Hollioake. Hampshire were eventually bowled out for 276, sixty-eight runs short of Surrey's total, but the most important figure of an astonishing afternoon's cricket was 203.

After the match, Brown admitted that he had been targeting the Sunday League record, saying "I sat down during the winter to look at the records, so I was fully aware of what I had to beat. Indeed, I said to our coach, Dave Gilbert, at the start of the season that it was possible to score 200 in the Sunday League, given the right conditions. They were certainly to my liking today. The occasional ball did keep low but, generally, the pitch was true and the ball came on to the bat with pace. That is bound to help anyone with a positive approach and, fortunately for me, things came off today."

After the excitement of Brown's record-breaking innings at Woodbridge Road, everyone decamped to Northampton for the County Championship and Sunday League fixtures against a mid-table Northamptonshire side.

On the first morning of the four-day match Adam Hollioake did his side a considerable service by winning the toss and deciding that his weakened team - without Stewart, Thorpe, Butcher and Saqlain because of international commitments - should bat on what looked to be a very flat pitch. Darren Bicknell, who had finally been recalled to the side after an absence of five Championship matches, took full advantage with a typical innings of 162, while the in-form Ali Brown did likewise in rattling up an unbeaten 170 that spanned the first two days and enabled his skipper - who had himself contributed eighty-one to the Surrey cause - to declare at 581-7 after just 140 overs. The rest of a rain-curtailed second day saw the home side prospering to the tune of 154-1, with Russell Warren (56 not out) and Alan Fordham (69 not out) steadying the ship after the early loss of David Roberts to Chris Lewis.

Fears that this game was going nowhere fast were then confirmed on day three when an early Northamptonshire collapse from 164-1 to 199-5 proved to be nothing more than a temporary blip for the hosts. By adding 123 for the sixth wicket, Tony Penberthy (96) and Jeremy Snape (52) extricated their side from the hole they had dug for themselves and put the match firmly on course for stalemate. Although Lewis (4-82) eventually polished off the innings at 401, allowing Hollioake to enforce the follow-on, Warren and Roberts saw the home team safely through to stumps at 48-0.

The final day then turned out to be as uninspiring as everyone had expected, with Surrey's capture of two early wickets being followed by the loss of almost two hours to rain. This ended the game as a contest, with Fordham (82 not out) and Rob Bailey (62 not out) left to bat out time against the bowling of Jason Ratcliffe, Ali Brown and Jonathan Batty on his Championship debut. Batty's selection as wicketkeeper for this match suggested that he had now moved ahead of James Knott in the pecking order as Alec Stewart's deputy.

Desperate for a win to keep their Sunday season alive, the following day's 40-over contest started badly for Surrey, with Darren Bicknell and Ali Brown both falling cheaply to Mohammad Akram in the opening stages. Ben Hollioake (40) then helped Jason Ratcliffe (82) restore equilibrium to the contest during a third-wicket stand of eighty-three but, after the reigning champions had reached a high point of 157-3, Akram (4-19) returned to end Ratcliffe's impressive innings and restrict the Lions to a disappointing 206-7 from their allotted overs.

Northamptonshire's reply then began with a 104-run opening partnership between Alan Fordham (43) and Tony Penberthy (81 not out) that went a long way towards deciding the outcome of the game. Saqlain Mushtaq did his utmost to bring his team back into the match by taking 3-31, but the rest of the bowlers were unable to emulate his excellence as the hosts cruised home by five wickets with nine balls in hand.

Although it appeared that Surrey had waved goodbye to their Sunday League crown at Northampton, they still harboured hopes of mounting a dramatic late challenge as they made the short trip across the Thames to take on Middlesex in their next fixture a week later. On a thoroughly miserable afternoon, the champions' flickering hopes were extinguished, however, as they limped to 74-7 from twenty-three overs before rain put an end to the match and left the London-based rivals with two points apiece.

A return to County Championship action with a home game against struggling Durham now gave Dave Gilbert's team a golden opportunity to get back on the winning trail, though it would have to be done with a much changed line-up. With England having been humbled by an innings and 61 runs in the fourth Test at Headingley while Surrey were playing at Northampton, the selectors had made dramatic changes to the national side. This mini revolution had seen Mark Butcher being dropped, while the Hollioake brothers had both been selected in the hope that they could repeat their Texaco Trophy heroics. At 19 years 269 days, Ben became England's youngest Test debutant since Brian Close had played against New Zealand at the age of 18 years 149 days in 1949.

With Ben and Adam away at Trent Bridge, becoming the fifth set of brothers to play in a Test for England, Chris Lewis was left to skipper the Surrey side again, while the 19-year-old left-arm spinner, Rupesh Amin, made his debut in place of the injured Ian Salisbury.

After a rain-affected first day had seen the hosts compile 164-2, John Wood (4-73) and Michael Foster (3-52) led a Durham fightback that resulted in a Surrey slump from 215-2 to 266-8 once the overnight batsmen, Jason Ratcliffe and Ian Ward, had departed for seventy-six and fifty-six respectively. Saqlain Mushtaq (41 not out) and Joey Benjamin (35) were therefore forced to carry out some valuable remedial work before Chris Lewis was able to declare with Surrey's final batting bonus point in the bag at 350-9. The two lower-order batting heroes then got amongst the wickets as the north-east county finished the day in peril at 120-6.

Durham's fate appeared to be sealed on the third morning when Saqlain (5-17) and Bicknell (3-37) ran through the tail in next to no time, dismissing the visitors for 136 and forcing them to follow on 214 runs in arrears. The Championship stragglers put up far greater resistance second time around, however, with the middle-order trio of John Morris (53), David Boon (34) and Martin Speight (51) batting particularly well against testing spin bowling from Saqlain and Amin on a pitch that was now offering significant assistance. There was always a feeling that a collapse could be just around the corner, though, and so it proved as Joey Benjamin returned to the attack to remove Speight and allow the spinners to engineer a slide from 209-3 to 241-7 before stumps were drawn.

Amin (3-58) and Saqlain - who finished with 5-111 to become the first Surrey bowler to take ten wickets in a match since Tony Pigott in May 1995 - then wrapped up the innings for the addition of a further thirty-one runs the next morning, leaving the hosts to coast to a nine-wicket victory just before lunch. From a position where they had no spin attack to speak of, Surrey suddenly seemed to have the best hand of spinners in the land, and the progress of the two young twirlers in this game didn't augur well for the careers of Richard Pearson and Richard Nowell.

It was seam rather than spin that damaged Durham in the following day's Sunday League match, as Surrey maintained their 100% record against the county who had joined the first-class ranks in 1992. Martin Bicknell claimed 4-28 as the visitors - sustained largely by Michael Roseberry's unbeaten fifty-five - made their way to a total of 189-9, which looked unlikely to test Surrey even when Ali Brown was out for eight with just twenty on the board. Mark Butcher, who scored eighty-one, and Darren Bicknell, with an unbeaten forty-nine from number four in the order, ensured that no further problems were encountered as the four points were secured by a margin of seven wickets with nine balls to spare. With just three matches left to play, Surrey had lifted themselves to equal sixth place in the table, but they were an irretrievable ten points behind leaders Warwickshire and eight adrift of second-placed Kent, who also had a game in hand. The Lions were about to be dethroned.

A few days later, with England having gone 3-1 down in the Ashes series following a 264-run defeat at Trent Bridge, Surrey were back to full strength - Alec Stewart and Ian Salisbury excepted - as they returned to Lord's for a County Championship fixture against a Middlesex side who were in a decent position to challenge for the title.

Although they had come off second-best in the vast majority of matches against their London rivals at Lord's in the recent past - and had failed to register a Championship win there since 1984 - Surrey got away to a good start when Ben Hollioake (3-23) removed Jason Pooley and Jacques Kallis soon after entering the fray as the visitors' first-change bowler. Mike Gatting (54) and Owais Shah (44) managed to steady the ship, however, and then manoeuvred Middlesex into a fine position at 142-2 before the visitors hit back in style after lunch through the efforts of Saqlain Mushtaq (5-50). The Pakistani spin sensation's mesmerising spell of 5-2, which included the first hat-trick by a Surrey bowler since Sylvester Clarke performed the feat against Essex at Colchester in 1987, sent the home side crashing to 162-9 and changed the course of the match. Although Middlesex recovered marginally to 205 all out, thanks to a spirited innings from Angus Fraser, their visitors had replied with 123-2 by the close and were looking well placed to build on their defeat of Durham.

Day two then saw a very respectable home attack, including Fraser, Richard Johnson, Jacques Kallis and Phil Tufnell, put to the sword by Surrey's fast-scoring middle-order batsmen. After Mark Butcher departed for seventy-nine at 168-3, Adam Hollioake took centre stage with a magnificent career-best knock of 182 that knocked the stuffing out of the bowlers and put his team in a position of immense power. Stands of 150 for the fourth wicket with Brown (70) and 143 for the fifth wicket with brother Ben - who once again enjoyed batting at Lord's during a career-best first-class innings of seventy-six - enabled the south London-based county to declare at 531-9 and then dispose of Kallis for nine before time was called at 24-1.

Having trailed by a daunting 302 runs at the start of day three, Middlesex managed to reach 67-1 before the loss of nightwatchman Richard Johnson to a run out prefaced a crucial period of play during which Saqlain snapped up the crucial wickets of Gatting and Ramprakash before the total had reached three figures. Thereafter no one, with the honourable exception of Jason Pooley (72), was able to resist for long against the Surrey spinners as Middlesex slowly subsided to 201 all out and defeat by an innings and 125 runs. While Rupesh Amin (2-55) had again shown promise, Saqlain (5-66) had stolen the show with a fourth successive five-wicket haul that also completed his second consecutive ten-wicket match.

Surrey's back-to-back victories had elevated them to fifth place in the Championship table and suggested that a late surge could yet give them a shot at the title come September.

COUNTY CHAMPIONSHIP - TOP OF THE TABLE AT 18TH AUGUST				
	P	W	D	L	PTS
Gloucestershire	13	6	4	3	181
Kent	12	6	2	4	171
Glamorgan	12	5	5	2	165
Worcestershire	12	4	7	1	159
Surrey	13	4	6	3	153

The team now had to sit tight for a week, as they were not involved in the next round of Championship matches, which clashed with the Oval Test. Ben Hollioake was rather harshly omitted from the England side for this match, while Mark Butcher was recalled and the host nation gained a consolation victory as Australia won the series 3-2.

With a full squad now available to Dave Gilbert for the rest of the season, Surrey headed down to Hove for what looked likely to be two relatively easy games against Sussex. Still reeling from the departure of so many key players at the end of 1996, the south coast county were languishing at the bottom of both leagues, having earned just twelve points in the Sunday League and lost six of their previous seven Championship matches.

The 40-overs fixture preceded the four-day game, since it was to be played under floodlights. Around 4,000 spectators were drawn to the County Ground by the novelty factor, though they didn't see much of a match as Sussex posted a wholly inadequate 151 after electing to bat first. Rajesh Rao, with fifty-eight, was the only batsman to reach twenty, while Chris Lewis took three late wickets to finish with 4-21 for the Lions. Although the visitors lost three wickets in progressing from sixty to ninety, they were never in any danger of defeat and sailed home with five wickets and 10.3 overs in hand.

And things got no better for Sussex when the Championship game got under way the next day - after they had won the toss and elected to bat their opponents dominated the match from start to finish. With Chris Lewis (5-42) and Martin Bicknell (3-53) shooting out the top five batsmen for 0, 0, 3, 1 and 5, the hosts required help from extras to reach 23-5, and only made it to 102-7 at the end of a rain-curtailed opening day thanks to a battling unbeaten twenty-eight from their beleaguered captain, Peter Moores.

Day two saw the hosts fired out for 137 before Surrey rattled up 400-7 in just seventy-five overs and then declared. With unsettled weather being forecast, it made perfect sense to get on with the game as rapidly as possible, and Graham Thorpe (106 not out), Adam Hollioake (87 from 57 balls) and Mark Butcher (61) certainly didn't hang around as they battered an inexperienced attack into submission. Surrey's declaration then paid dividends as Ian Salisbury, pressed into action along with Saqlain Mushtaq because of poor light, took four wickets before stumps were drawn with Sussex in dire straits at 20-4.

Slightly more determined batting by the home side extended the game beyond lunch on the third day, with Moores (31) and Jamie Carpenter (33) sharing Sussex's only half-century stand of a ludicrously one-sided match before the visitors sealed their expected victory by an innings and 101 runs. Salisbury, who had captured his 500th first-class wicket earlier in the contest, finished with 5-66 in the second innings as Surrey's fifth win in their last seven Championship matches moved them within twenty points of the joint leaders of the table, Glamorgan and Kent, both of whom had yet to play Dave Gilbert's team.

COUNTY CHAMPIONSHIP - TOP OF THE TABLE AT 31ST AUGUST				
	P	W	D	L	PTS
Kent	14	6	4	4	197
Glamorgan	14	6	6	2	197
Gloucestershire	14	6	4	4	187
Yorkshire	14	5	7	2	180
Middlesex	14	6	4	4	178
Surrey	14	5	6	3	177

The next match, against Glamorgan at The Oval, was therefore vitally important since it had the potential to throw the title race wide open. It was clear, however, that Surrey would need to win all of their final three games if they were to overhaul the current leading sides.

Unfortunately, by the end of the first day it was already looking unlikely that they could clear the first of the three hurdles ahead of them. Having elected to bat, Surrey - lacking the injured Chris Lewis - kept losing wickets at regular intervals as they stumbled and stuttered to 204 all out, with Ali Brown's sixty being the only innings of substance in the face of impressive bowling led by Darren Thomas (3-36) and Robert Croft (3-54). The Glamorgan captain, Matthew Maynard, then raced to an undefeated fifty-six as the Welshmen capitalised on their fine fielding performance by reaching 133-2 by the close.

The prognosis certainly didn't look good for Surrey as the overnight pair of Maynard (76) and Adrian Dale (72) extended their third-wicket partnership to 122 on a rain-affected second day that saw the visitors building a potentially decisive lead. Although Ben Holioake (3-91) did his best to bring his side back into contention by capturing three middle-order scalps, including Croft for fifty-three, Glamorgan reached the halfway point of the contest with 363-7 on the board, a lead of 159.

The Welsh county's first-innings advantage was then extended to 234 by Darren Thomas's unbeaten seventy-five on the third morning, before the visiting bowlers set their side on the path to victory by reducing Surrey to 32-3. At this stage the hosts appeared to be in a hopeless position, but Graham Thorpe got his head down and forged successive partnerships of 63, 120 and 49 with Ali Brown (41), Adam Hollioake (65) and Ben Hollioake (31) respectively while compiling a marvellous century that kept his side in the match. By the time stumps were drawn, the England left-hander had 140 runs to his name and his seventh-wicket stand with Saqlain Mushtaq had added another sixty runs to the total, leaving Surrey ninety runs to the good with four wickets still standing.

Although Saqlain didn't last long on the final day, Thorpe continued to defy the Glamorgan bowlers, finding another steadfast ally in Martin Bicknell (53), who kept him company during a vital stand of 110 in thirty-three overs that opened up the possibility of Surrey being able to complete an amazing turnaround in the game. The hosts decided against declaring and setting their visitors an inviting target, however, batting on beyond Thorpe's dismissal for a quite brilliant

222 out of 451-8 until Bicknell's demise brought the innings to a close at 487. This left the Welsh side forty-six overs in which to chase 254 to win, but they soon gave up on the challenge and the match fizzled out into a tame draw at 107-3.

With Kent having crushed Gloucestershire at Canterbury, Surrey's outside chance of the title had gone, leaving a frustrated Dave Gilbert to vent his spleen at his title-chasing opponents. "It was outrageous they should give up so early. It had the makings of a great game," he railed, before adding a further mischievous comment that caused consternation at Lord's. "If they are going to play like that they can't expect too many favours from us when we play Kent in the final game," said the furious Surrey manager. Whilst it was easy to understand his frustration, it was clearly Glamorgan's prerogative to spurn the run-chase, especially as Adam Hollioake had chosen to bat on until the final Surrey wicket fell, rather than set a tempting target. It appeared that the visitors were more concerned about Surrey moving into Championship contention than they were about keeping pace with Kent, which seemed a rather negative way of thinking, but Matthew Maynard, their captain, and Duncan Fletcher, their coach, were perfectly within their rights to adopt that approach if they so wished.

COUNTY CHAMPIONSHIP - TOP OF THE TABLE AT 5TH SEPTEMBER					
	P	W	D	L	PTS
Kent	15	7	4	4	220
Glamorgan	15	6	7	2	208
Yorkshire	15	6	7	2	202
Gloucestershire	15	6	4	5	193
Warwickshire	15	6	7	2	188
Middlesex	15	6	5	4	186
Surrey	15	5	7	3	185

When the two sides clashed again two days later in the Sunday League, Matthew Maynard used his bat to express his displeasure at (a) having missed a good chance to win the Championship fixture, and (b) Dave Gilbert's post-match comments. There certainly appeared to be a great deal of anger in his approach as he thrashed some lacklustre Surrey bowling around The Oval during a quite amazing innings of 132 from just 75 balls that enabled his side to total 242-8. The Lions had the last laugh, however, as belligerent knocks from Ali Brown (64), Adam Hollioake (63) and Jason Ratcliffe (54) carried them through to a two-wicket victory despite the best efforts of Owen Parkin (4-54).

There then followed a quite horrendous performance against Lancashire at The Oval in the penultimate County Championship game of the season. Shorn of the services of Graham Thorpe (rested), Chris Lewis (injured) and Saqlain Mushtaq (on duty with Pakistan in Toronto), a Surrey team that was clearly dispirited by the failure of another belated Championship charge conceded 459-4 on the first day, including a record-breaking opening stand of 259 between Mike Atherton (149) and Nathan Wood (155).

After Neil Fairbrother (112 not out) had become a third Lancastrian century-maker, the visitors declared on 592-4 after just 135 overs and went on to dismiss Surrey for 270 on the third morning. This represented a dismal effort by the home side, since Darren Bicknell (74) and Mark Butcher (49) had given their team a 103-run start, while Alec Stewart had contributed seventy-three.

Following on, 322 runs in arrears, the second innings then closely mirrored the first - a promising position of 173-3, established by Butcher (52), Jason Ratcliffe (90) and Ali Brown (47), was followed by a desperate collapse to 267 all out as Gary Keedy claimed career-best figures of 6-79 to complete a match return of 10-173 and secure victory for the visitors inside three days.

Surrey were at least able to redeem themselves slightly with a five-wicket triumph in their final Sunday League match of the summer. Lancashire's 206-8, which was based around an 80-run partnership for the fourth wicket between Neil Fairbrother (54) and Graham Lloyd (41), proved insufficient to prevent the Benson & Hedges Cup heroes, Alec Stewart (67 not out) and Ben Hollioake (61), from setting up a comfortable victory after Ian Austin (3-25) had taken two early wickets.

	SUNDAY LEAGUE TABLE 1997						
		P	Pts	W	L	T	A	NRR
1	Warwickshire	17	52	13	4	0	0	14.14
2	Kent	17	50	12	4	0	1	7.70
3	Lancashire	17	46	10	4	1	2	1.89
4	Leicestershire	17	42	9	5	1	2	7.11
5	Surrey	17	42	9	5	0	3	1.06
6	Somerset	17	40	9	6	0	2	4.31
7	Essex	17	40	9	6	1	1	-2.38
8	Worcestershire	17	38	8	6	1	2	6.87
9	Northamptonshire	17	38	8	6	0	3	2.78
10	Yorkshire	17	36	8	7	1	1	5.24
11	Gloucestershire	17	36	7	6	0	4	1.01
12	Nottinghamshire	17	34	7	7	0	3	-0.19
13	Glamorgan	17	26	5	9	0	3	-4.01
14	Derbyshire	17	24	4	9	0	4	-3.04
15	Hampshire	17	22	5	11	0	1	-4.73
16	Middlesex	17	20	3	10	1	3	-8.28
17	Durham	17	14	3	13	0	1	-12.27
18	Sussex	17	12	2	13	0	2	-16.72

With Glamorgan having moved back to the top of the table, one point ahead of Kent, during the penultimate round of matches, Surrey travelled to Canterbury for their last game of the season with their line-up and performance clearly under scrutiny following Dave Gilbert's comments after the draw with the Welsh county. Upon arriving at the St. Lawrence ground, the visitors, lacking Adam Hollioake, Graham Thorpe, Saqlain Mushtaq and Martin Bicknell - all for perfectly legitimate reasons - were confronted by a grassy under-prepared track that was clearly designed to produce a positive result. Kent were clearly hoping that Glamorgan might be held to a draw at Taunton while they themselves were putting Surrey to the sword at Canterbury.

Unsurprisingly put in to bat after Alec Stewart had lost a potentially decisive toss, Surrey were bundled out for 124 in just twenty-seven overs, with Mark Butcher (38) and Chris Lewis (27) the only men to register a score of any magnitude against a five-man seam attack led by Julian Thompson (4-33). In reply, the home side progressed to 217-9 by the close, with all of their batsmen bar Mark Ealham (52) and Allan Wells (48) struggling, despite signs that the pitch might be easing.

Although it took just nine deliveries of the second morning for Ben Hollioake (4-54) to finish off Kent's innings with just three runs added to the overnight total, the hosts still looked well placed when Surrey slipped to 69-2 in their second knock. With the ECB's pitch inspection team present at the ground, Darren Bicknell and Alec Stewart then constructed a partnership that made a points deduction for the Championship contenders highly unlikely. Taking advantage of a surface that had certainly mellowed, they added 219 runs for the third-wicket before Bicknell was bowled by Ben Phillips at the end of a day shorn of thirty-five overs by bad light. By this time, the tall left-hander had 130 against his name, while Stewart, who had blazed his way to a magnificent century from just ninety deliveries, was unbeaten on 122.

It was good news all round for Kent on the third morning of the match. After the announcement that the county's only 'punishment' for the state of the pitch on the first day was a ten-point suspended penalty, Surrey collapsed dramatically against Phillips (3-58) and Thompson (3-112), losing their last seven wickets for just eighty-three runs in little over an hour-and-a-half. Stewart, last out for a superb 170, could probably not believe what he had witnessed at the other end as the visitors' position of strength crumbled away to leave Kent a target of 276 to win.

Although they struggled against Mark Butcher, who added figures of 3-26 to the 3-24 he had claimed in their first innings, the Championship chasers rarely looked in trouble as David Fulton's fine 110 ushered them towards a victory that was eventually sealed, with five wickets in hand, by Matthew Fleming (41 not out). Kent were top of the table for just fifteen minutes, however, before Glamorgan clinched a ten-wicket triumph at Taunton to claim their first County Championship title since 1969 and leave Fleming's team runners-up in three of the season's four competitions.

	COUNTY CHAMPIONSHIP TABLE 1997							
		P	Pts	W	D	L	Bat	Bwl
1	Glamorgan	17	256	8	7	2	50	57
2	Kent	17	252	8	5	4	44	60
3	Worcestershire	17	228	6	8	3	49	54
4	Warwickshire	17	219	7	8	2	32	51
=	Middlesex	17	219	7	6	4	33	56
6	Yorkshire	17	215	6	8	3	41	54
7	Gloucestershire	17	206	6	5	6	35	60
8	Surrey	17	192	5	7	5	39	52
=	Essex	17	192	5	6	6	39	55
10	Leicestershire	17	191	4	12	1	37	54
11	Lancashire	17	186	5	6	6	34	54
12	Somerset	17	183	3	11	3	38	64
13	Nottinghamshire	17	175	4	10	3	26	55
14	Hampshire	17	158	3	9	5	42	41
15	Northamptonshire	17	156	3	9	5	33	48
16	Derbyshire	17	141	2	6	9	32	59
17	Durham	17	131	2	7	8	22	56
18	Sussex	17	115	1	6	10	24	57

As the season drew to a close it was announced - much to everyone's disappointment - that Dave Gilbert had decided to reject the offer of a new contract, stating that he wanted to move into cricket administration after five years as a coach. It was sad to see him departing so soon after getting the team back on track and winning trophies but it seemed likely that his legacy would be a lasting one, with further silverware sure to follow now that a talented squad of players had tasted success.

Putting to one side the capture of the Benson & Hedges Cup, the season had, as a whole, seen more lows than highs, with the Championship campaign only gaining some mometum when it was too late, the retention of the Sunday League title never looking likely, and the Nat West Trophy performance against Nottinghamshire best forgotten. The tragic loss of Graham Kersey at the start of the year must have been a factor in the sluggish start to the campaign, however, as it was sure to have had a profound effect on the players who had spent so much time with him over the past four summers since his move from Kent.

On the plus side, the emergence of Ben Hollioake had excited everyone, while Saqlain Mushtaq looked to be another fantastic young talent who would be a great asset to the club if he could be signed on a long-term basis. Saqlain's spin partnership with Ian Salisbury - who had been dogged by a couple of unfortunate injuries - promised much for the future, while Rupesh Amin also looked to have a good career ahead of him, having impressed many a good judge on his appearances for the first team. With such riches in the spin department all of a sudden, it was no surprise that the two Richards, Pearson and Nowell, were not retained on the staff.

The biggest post-season disappointment for the club came when Chris Lewis decided to return to his first county, Leicestershire, who had offered him a lucrative five-year deal and a future shot at the captaincy on a permanent basis. Although he had rarely excelled in the County Championship, the England all-rounder would be badly missed in the limited-overs form of the game, where he had proved to be a very valuable member of the Surrey team.

1997 SEASON SUMMARY

COMPETITION	P	W	D/A	L	POSITION/PROGRESS
County Championship	17	5	7	5	8th
Sunday League	17	9	3	5	5th
Nat West Trophy	2	1	0	1	2nd Round
Benson & Hedges Cup	8	7	0	1	Winners
TOTAL	44	22	10	12	1 Trophy

1997 RESULTS SUMMARY

23/4	SOMERSET	OVAL	CC	Match Drawn
27/4	SOMERSET	OVAL	SL	WON by 3 wickets
28/4	KENT	OVAL	BHC	LOST by 4 wickets
30/4	Gloucestershire	Bristol	BHC	WON by 3 wickets
2/5	BRITISH UNIVERSITIES	OVAL	BHC	WON by 6 wickets
4/5	Kent	Canterbury	SL	LOST by 12 runs
5/5	Hampshire	Southampton	BHC	WON by 165 runs
7/5	Derbyshire	Derby	CC	Match Drawn
11/5	Derbyshire	Derby	SL	Match Abandoned
12/5	SUSSEX	OVAL	BHC	WON by 11 runs
14/5	GLOUCESTERSHIRE	OVAL	CC	LOST by 9 wickets
18/5	GLOUCESTERSHIRE	OVAL	SL	WON by 5 wickets
21/5	Leicestershire	Leicester	CC	Match Drawn
25/5	Leicestershire	Leicester	SL	WON by 5 wickets
27/5	Essex	Chelmsford	BHCqf	WON by 6 wickets
4/6	ESSEX	OVAL	CC	LOST by 147 runs
8/6	ESSEX	OVAL	SL	LOST by 6 wickets
10/6	LEICESTERSHIRE	OVAL	BHCsf	WON by 130 runs
12/6	YORKSHIRE	OVAL	CC	Match Drawn
15/6	YORKSHIRE	OVAL	SL	WON by 5 wickets
18/6	Worcestershire	Worcester	CC	Match Drawn
22/6	Worcestershire	Worcester	SL	LOST by 7 wickets
24/6	DURHAM	OVAL	NWT	WON by 5 wickets
26/6	NOTTINGHAMSHIRE	OVAL	SL	Match Abandoned
27/6	NOTTINGHAMSHIRE	OVAL	CC	WON by 131 runs
2/7	Warwickshire	Edgbaston	CC	LOST by 5 wickets

Date	Opponent	Venue	Comp	Result
6/7	Warwickshire	Edgbaston	SL	LOST by 48 runs
9/7	NOTTINGHAMSHIRE	OVAL	NWT	LOST by 22 runs
12/7	KENT	LORD'S	BHCf	WON by 8 wickets
16/7	HAMPSHIRE	GUILDFORD	CC	WON by 9 wickets
20/7	HAMPSHIRE	GUILDFORD	SL	WON by 6 wickets
23/7	Northamptonshire	Northampton	CC	Match Drawn
27/7	Northamptonshire	Northampton	SL	LOST by 5 wickets
3/8	Middlesex	Lord's	SL	Match Abandoned
6/8	DURHAM	OVAL	CC	WON by 9 wickets
10/8	DURHAM	OVAL	SL	WON by 7 wickets
15/8	Middlesex	Lord's	CC	WON by an inns & 125 runs
27/8	Sussex	Hove	SL	WON by 5 wickets
28/8	Sussex	Hove	CC	WON by an inns & 101 runs
2/9	GLAMORGAN	OVAL	CC	Match Drawn
7/9	GLAMORGAN	OVAL	SL	WON by 2 wickets
10/9	LANCASHIRE	OVAL	CC	LOST by an inns & 55 runs
14/9	LANCASHIRE	OVAL	SL	WON by 5 wickets
18/9	Kent	Canterbury	CC	LOST by 5 wickets

COUNTY CHAMPIONSHIP BATTING AVERAGES 1997

	M	I	NO	Runs	HS	Ave	100	50	c	st
G.P. Thorpe	8	12	2	707	222	70.70	2	3	9	-
A.J. Stewart	9	14	1	726	271*	55.84	2	2	16	-
A.D. Brown	14	21	1	848	170*	42.40	3	2	11	-
D.J. Bicknell	9	15	0	594	162	39.60	2	1	1	-
A.J. Hollioake	13	19	0	731	182	38.47	1	5	10	-
J.D. Ratcliffe	15	26	2	759	135	31.62	1	4	3	-
M.A. Butcher	13	22	1	659	79	31.38	-	5	19	-
B.C. Hollioake	12	19	0	483	76	25.42	-	3	10	-
Saqlain Mushtaq	8	10	4	149	41*	24.83	-	-	2	-
C.C. Lewis	13	19	2	389	76	22.88	-	1	10	-
A.J. Tudor	8	11	6	109	35*	21.80	-	-	-	-
M.P. Bicknell	15	20	5	305	74	20.33	-	2	8	-
J.A. Knott	5	9	3	118	27*	19.66	-	-	8	1
N. Shahid	7	11	0	198	34	18.00	-	-	4	-
J.E. Benjamin	11	15	6	152	35	16.88	-	-	-	-
I.D.K. Salisbury	13	17	2	159	30*	10.60	-	-	7	-

Qualification: 8 innings

COUNTY CHAMPIONSHIP BOWLING AVERAGES 1997

	O	M	Runs	W	Ave	BB	10wm	5wi
Saqlain Mushtaq	254.5	75	617	32	19.28	5-17	2	4
M.P. Bicknell	385.2	94	1174	44	26.68	5-34	-	1
C.C. Lewis	291.4	66	970	33	29.39	5-42	-	1
A.J. Hollioake	108.4	19	388	13	29.84	4-22	-	-
I.D.K. Salisbury	314.1	65	936	30	31.20	6-19	-	2
A.J. Tudor	127.3	17	526	16	32.87	6-101	-	1
B.C. Hollioake	169.2	34	594	17	34.94	4-54	-	-
J.E. Benjamin	211.0	39	759	13	58.38	3-52	-	-

Qualification: 100 overs, 10 wickets

LIMITED-OVERS BATTING AVERAGES 1997										
	M	I	NO	Runs	HS	Ave	100	50	c	st
A.J. Stewart	18	18	4	641	90*	45.79	-	6	19	2
G.P. Thorpe	16	16	2	552	100*	39.43	1	3	12	-
M.P. Bicknell	24	12	8	157	57*	39.25	-	1	4	-
A.D. Brown	24	24	1	877	203	38.13	2	4	6	-
C.C. Lewis	21	17	7	302	68*	30.20	-	1	12	-
A.J. Hollioake	22	20	0	546	80	27.30	-	4	5	-
B.C. Hollioake	21	19	1	472	98	26.22	-	3	3	-
M.A. Butcher	18	17	2	386	81	25.73	-	1	11	-
J.D. Ratcliffe	18	14	1	345	82	26.53	-	3	6	-
N. Shahid	15	14	5	219	52	24.33	-	1	2	-
I.J. Ward	10	9	3	81	31	13.50	-	-	1	-
I.D.K. Salisbury	20	11	5	79	23*	13.17	-	-	9	-
Qualification: 6 innings										

LIMITED-OVERS BOWLING AVERAGES 1997								
	O	M	Runs	W	Ave	BB	4wi	RPO
C.C. Lewis	156.3	15	611	31	19.71	4-21	1	3.90
M.P. Bicknell	181.0	15	758	36	21.06	4-28	2	4.19
Saqlain Mushtaq	92.2	4	423	18	23.50	3-30	-	4.58
A.J. Hollioake	111.2	3	650	27	24.07	5-38	1	5.84
I.D.K. Salisbury	143.5	2	670	23	29.13	4-53	1	4.66
J.E. Benjamin	127.0	3	549	17	32.29	4-19	1	4.32
B.C. Hollioake	144.2	3	785	20	39.25	3-47	-	5.44
Qualification: 40 overs, 10 wickets								

5 1998: Shattered Dreams

Although there had been very little movement in terms of playing personnel during the close season - Saqlain Mushtaq had been confirmed as Surrey's overseas registration, while Micky Bell, the 31-year-old left-arm swing bowler from Warwickshire, was the only new signing of any significance - changes had been required on the management and coaching side following the departures of Dave Gilbert and Tony Pigott to Sussex. Gilbert had become General Manager, while Pigott had taken on the role of Chief Executive. Keith Medlycott, whose second eleven side had won their 50-overs-per-side knockout trophy, had been appointed as the new Cricket Manager, while Alan Butcher had returned to the club that he had served so well as a player to take charge of the second team. It was terrific to see two popular former Surrey men installed in these two key roles.

On the debit side, Darren Bicknell was likely to miss the whole season after undergoing a serious operation on his injured back, though Surrey had sufficient confidence in their squad batsmen - Nadeem Shahid, Jason Ratcliffe and Ian Ward - to resist the temptation to go out and sign a replacement. Chris Lewis's shoes were obviously going to be far more difficult to fill, though it was hoped that the England all-rounder's departure would ensure that Ben Hollioake's development was not impeded.

Hollioake senior had meanwhile enjoyed a mixed winter following his appointment as England's ODI captain in September 1997. After leading a side that included three of his Surrey colleagues - Stewart, Thorpe and Brown - to victory in the Akai Singer Champions Trophy (Sharjah Cup) tournament, he had skippered a very similar squad to a 4-1 defeat in the ODI series in the West Indies. This followed a 3-1 setback in the Test series that had led to the resignation of Michael Atherton.

On the domestic front, it had been decided that a two-division structure should be put in place to increase competitiveness and reduce the number of meaningless end-of-season matches. The split was to be introduced first in the one-day league, with the counties finishing in the top nine places in the 1998 Sunday League to form Division One of the new National League in 1999 and the other teams to make up Division Two. A rather strange decision involved the Benson & Hedges Cup, which was to be cut from the fixture list after 1999 in order to reduce the amount of cricket that was being played. For its final season in 1999 it was to be rechristened the Benson & Hedges Super Cup, with only the top eight counties in the 1998 County Championship being invited to participate. It seemed odd to reward four-day success with entry to a one-day competition.

Although there were, for once, no last-minute dramas concerning the club's overseas registration, Saqlain Mushtaq was to miss the start of the season with an injured spinning finger, while Alec Stewart was to be rested from some of the early matches after a demanding winter schedule in the West Indies that had extended until 8th April.

The English season began with a decidedly soggy 'Sunday sandwich' against Northamptonshire at The Oval. After the first two days of the Championship match had yielded just thirty overs of action - during which Surrey made 88-1 after being put in - the Sunday League contest fell victim to a torrential downpour after thirty-four overs with the visitors having reached 162-5, thanks to Mal Loye's seventy-nine.

When the third day of the four-day fixture went the same way as the first had done, with not a single ball bowled, the contest looked dead in the water that stood in puddles around the Oval outfield. With attempts to revive the game on the final day having come to naught because the captains couldn't agree on a target for Northamptonshire to chase, Surrey took the chance to enjoy some batting practice. Taking advantage of some variable bowling, they gathered in a full hand of batting points by racing to 351-5, courtesy of fifties from Jason Ratcliffe, Nadeem Shahid and Graham Thorpe, and a violent century from Ali Brown that spanned just seventy-two balls and included six sixes and ten fours. Incredibly, he had scored just a single from his first fifteen deliveries.

With the batting points in the bag, Adam Hollioake declared and let his bowlers loose in an attempt to gain one or two for bowling, though this plan was scuppered by a declaration from the visiting skipper, Kevin Curran, as soon as Ben Hollioake (2-6) had removed Alec Swann to take his side within one wicket of a point. Since Northamptonshire had only forty-four runs on the scoreboard at the time, they were forced to follow on, 307 runs in arrears, by the Surrey captain as the match drew to a farcical conclusion. In the time that remained Hollioake (1-17) managed to dismiss the unfortunate Swann for the second time in twenty minutes before Richard Montgomerie and Graeme Swann played out the remaining overs, finishing on 46-1.

Two days later, the bookies' pre-season favourites, Warwickshire, captained by Brian Lara, were the visitors to The Oval for another Championship encounter. Almost inevitably, day one was rain affected, though Surrey enjoyed the better of the play that was available by claiming four wickets - including Dominic Ostler for a third successive Championship duck and the key scalps of Lara (38) and Nick Knight - while the Bears scored 102 runs.

A total reversal of fortunes looked likely on the second morning as Trevor Penney (46) and Dougie Brown (60) took their fifth-wicket stand to ninety-four, though it eventually transpired that 176-4 was to be the visitors' best position of the day and indeed the match. Ian Salisbury's excellent spell of 4-7, allied to the fall of Brown to Butcher (3-39), sent Warwickshire into an irretrievable tailspin that saw the last six wickets adding just thirty-one runs, before Butcher and Jason Ratcliffe rattled up an unbeaten opening stand of 162 by the close of play.

Although neither Surrey opener lasted long on day three after rain had delayed the start until 1.30pm - Butcher went for seventy-two and Ratcliffe fell just seven short of a century against his former county - the Bears' comeback was short-lived as Nadeem Shahid (90) and Graham Thorpe (114) batted brightly to add 190 for the third wicket. Wickets then tumbled to Neil Smith (5-128) as the home side tried to set up a declaration before stumps but their hopes of putting Warwickshire in again were foiled by further rain with the score on 405-6.

It was now a rare occurrence in county cricket but, for the second successive week, the Sunday League fixture interrupted the four-day match. This turned out to be rather fortunate, however, as the very wet conditions that saw the one-day game reduced to a farcical ten-overs-a-side contest would have wrecked the Championship match. After being put in by Brian Lara, the Lions batted rather unintelligently while scoring 81-5 in their allotted overs, and were then given a lesson in placement and running between the wickets by Neil Smith (48) and Nick Knight (25 not out), who saw Warwickshire through to a comfortable eight-wicket victory with five balls to spare.

With Adam Hollioake having, predictably, declared at Saturday's overnight score, Warwickshire were now left to bat out the final day of the Championship match to earn a draw. Although their prospects of achieving this looked good, given that the pitch was pretty placid, they got off to a poor start when Joey Benjamin and Martin Bicknell quickly removed the hapless Ostler (9) and Keith Piper (4), who was opening in place of the injured Knight. Determined resistance from Lara (57) and David Hemp (37) then followed, but once they were parted after adding seventy-nine for the third wicket Warwickshire again collapsed dramatically to lose the game by an innings and 49 runs before tea. While Bicknell, with 5-27, was the chief architect of the slump from 100-2 to 149 all out, Salisbury was again impressive in taking 2-30 to complete amazing match figures of 32.3-19-37-6, and Butcher claimed the key wicket of Lara - caught behind down the legside by Jonathan Batty - for the second time in the game.

(Empics/Surrey CCC)

(Empics/Surrey CCC)

AZHAR MAHMOOD

(Empics/Surrey CCC)

JONATHAN BATTY

JOEY BENJAMIN

(Empics/Surrey CCC)

MARTIN BICKNELL

(Empics/Surrey CCC)

DARREN BICKNELL

(Empics/Surrey CCC)

ALI BROWN

(Empics/Surrey CCC)

MARK BUTCHER

(Empics/Surrey CCC)

(Empics/Surrey CCC)

RIKKI CLARKE

The Benson & Hedges Cup group matches were next on the agenda, with the five fixtures being sensibly grouped together in the space of eleven days without any interruptions from games in the other competitions.

Surrey started their campaign in defence of the trophy with a match against Hampshire at Southampton and amassed a very useful total of 267-8, thanks largely to a 35-ball knock of forty-three from Ali Brown at the top of the innings and a fourth-wicket stand of ninety-five between Mark Butcher (67) and Graham Thorpe (48). Hampshire's bowling was very mixed, with the excellent efforts of Peter Hartley (3-32) and the 20-year-old all-rounder Dimitri Mascarenhas (4-28) being neutralised by the sixty-plus spells of the other three bowlers.

In reply, the hosts threatened briefly when they reached 116-2 through the efforts of Giles White (47) and Robin Smith (45) before Ian Salisbury (3-32) and Martin Bicknell (4-38) triggered a fatal collapse to 177-9. Although forty-two runs were added for the last wicket Hampshire were already out of the hunt and they eventually succumbed by forty-eight runs.

A bizarre case of déjà vu then followed as Surrey faced Gloucestershire on 30th April for the third successive season. Fortunately for the defending champions, Rob Cunliffe, who had scored a century in both of the previous contests, fell for a mere fifty-eight this time, though Gloucestershire still racked up a decent total of 266-7, with Jack Russell contributing eighty-three from number three in the order.

On a fine Oval pitch, Ali Brown (74) and Alec Stewart (39) rapidly reduced Surrey's requirement by compiling an opening partnership of eighty-eight from twelve overs, allowing Graham Thorpe (85), Mark Butcher (40 not out) and Adam Hollioake (23 not out) to see the side home by seven wickets in the forty-eighth over.

With two good victories in the bag, Surrey next welcomed British Universities to The Oval. The home side were delighted to include the fit-again Saqlain Mushtaq in their team for the first time, while the students' eleven again contained a large number of future county regulars (including Ben Hutton batting at number ten!). With the exception of Mark Chilton, who claimed 4-28, Hutton (2-43) turned out to be the pick of the Universities' attack, in fact, as the cup holders posted a slightly disappointing 263 all out that included half-centuries for Adam Hollioake (55) and the in-form Thorpe (58). Surrey's total always looked likely to be good enough against this opposition, however, and so it proved, with Ben Hollioake (3-23) taking the principal bowling honours as the visitors were dismissed for 158.

A potentially pivotal game against Kent at Canterbury was next on the fixture list. With both sides knowing that the victors would almost certainly seal their progress to the quarter-finals, Surrey asked their hosts to bat and, for the fourth consecutive match, the side batting first notched a total in the 260s. Kent's 260-9 was built around fifty-plus contributions from Trevor Ward (51), Carl Hooper (69) and Mark Ealham (56), while Ian Salisbury (2-36) and Joey Benjamin (1-37) were, by some distance, the visitors' best bowlers.

Although Surrey could only manage one individual half-century in reply - Graham Thorpe's masterful unbeaten eighty-five - near-misses from Ali Brown (46) and Alec Stewart (40), who again gave the innings a seven-runs-per-over start during their 93-run partnership, and Adam Hollioake (44), enabled them to reach their target with four wickets and eighteen balls in hand.

With qualification confirmed, Surrey rested both Graham Thorpe and Saqlain Mushtaq for the final group match against Somerset at The Oval, and gave Micky Bell his first-team debut. These moves looked fully vindicated as the home county piled up 296-6 from their fifty overs, with an outstanding partnership of 185 for the second wicket between Alec Stewart (108) and Ben Hollioake (91 from 98 balls) providing the bulk of the total. Hollioake's knock, which was especially encouraging after his slow start to the season, included a brutal assault on Mushtaq Ahmed (3-0-35-0), who was deposited over the midwicket boundary on three occasions during one particular over.

If Surrey felt their total had made victory a formality, they were soon made to think again as Dermot Reeve (60) and Michael Burns (95) put the visitors ahead of the clock while adding 158 for the first wicket. The tide slowly began to turn, though, when Reeve holed out at midwicket off Adam Hollioake (2-44) and Ian Salisbury (2-51) bowled both Burns and Marcus Trescothick before the total had passed two-hundred. With runs and wickets coming in almost equal measure during the tense closing overs, Martin Bicknell (3-51) and Ben Hollioake (3-62) managed to keep cool heads while Mushtaq Ahmed (26) and his fellow tailenders lost theirs, allowing Surrey to sneak in by nine runs with seven balls of the visitors' innings unused.

Having earned a home quarter-final tie against Lancashire by topping their Benson & Hedges Cup qualifying group, Surrey returned to Sunday League action with a trip to Headingley to take on Yorkshire.

In typical seamer-friendly conditions, Yorkshire struggled to 162-9 against the impressive Joey Benjamin (3-16), Martin Bicknell (2-26) and Saqlain Mushtaq, who bowled with great skill to concede just nineteen runs from his eight overs in alien conditions. With the Tykes' pacemen all in good form, their total looked undeniably handy, though, and it wasn't long before Surrey's strong batting line-up was being humbled. After an uncomfortable start, Alec Stewart fell lbw to Chris Silverwood (2-23) with the score on twenty-three, then an angry Darren Gough ran riot after an appeal for a catch at the wicket off Graham Thorpe was turned down. In gathering gloom, the England fast bowler steamed in to claim 5-25, reducing Surrey to a miserable 45-7 before rain eventually brought a merciful end to the unequal struggle with the total advanced to sixty-seven after 21.3 overs. Yorkshire ran out winners by fifty-one runs under the Duckworth-Lewis system and Surrey's Sunday League campaign was off to a dreadful start, with just two points having been gleaned from their three rain-affected matches.

A trip north was now followed by a journey south as the team made their second visit of the season to Southampton for Championship and Sunday League fixtures against Hampshire.

The four-day game saw Surrey handing the 20-year-old Alex Tudor his first start of the campaign and, in order to accommodate him - plus Alec Stewart and Saqlain Mushtaq, who also missed the last Championship match - Jason Ratcliffe and Nadeem Shahid, who had both scored nineties against Warwickshire, had to be omitted. One could only feel sorry for 'Ratters' and 'Nad' as Surrey's selection underlined the strength of their squad.

That potency was further amplified as Surrey dominated the match from start to finish after winning the toss. Alec Stewart (59) and Mark Butcher, who went on to compile a splendid 106, set their side off on the right track with an opening stand of 118, allowing Ali Brown to enter the fray at 247-3 and blast a 96-ball century that put Surrey in complete command. Although Nixon McLean ended the first day with three wickets to his name, the visitors were very well placed at 434-5, with Brown undefeated on 111 and Jon Batty, most encouragingly, unbeaten on fifty-one.

Adam Hollioake's team then extended their total to 591 on day two, with Brown eventually dismissed for 155 (from 147 balls) and Batty for sixty-three, before Alex Tudor (48) and Martin Bicknell (38) added to Hampshire's agony with a ninth-wicket stand of ninety-one.

Requiring 442 to avoid the follow on, Hampshire - already missing John Stephenson, who was confined to bed by a virus - recovered from the early loss of Jason Laney to reach 54-1 before the spinners began to weave their spell and rapidly reduced their hosts to 67-4. Although a partnership of fifty-two by Robin Smith and Dimitri Mascarenhas hinted at a revival, Surrey were not to be denied as Tudor (4-32) and Saqlain (3-62) swept away the lower order, leaving Mascarenhas stranded on sixty out of an inadequate total of 189. The visitors' very good day then became even better when White and Laney fell to Bicknell and Tudor respectively before close of play as Hampshire followed on.

With the weather set fair and the home side's morale already at rock bottom, it was no surprise that Surrey duly completed a comprehensive victory by an innings and 184 runs the following afternoon. Although there were pockets of resistance along the way - most notably from Adrian Aymes and Shaun Udal, who added sixty-two for the eighth wicket - the visitors' strong and varied attack, led by Bicknell (3-43) and Tudor (3-53), ensured that the contest was wrapped up with a day to spare, taking Surrey to the top of the nascent Championship table in the process.

Unfortunately, this second consecutive County Championship victory was followed by a third successive Sunday League defeat twenty-four hours later, as Hampshire produced a much-improved performance, while Surrey failed to hit the heights of the previous three days. The hosts' 239-8 centred around a second-wicket partnership of 124 between Giles White (58) and Robin Smith (62) as the Lions' bowlers turned in off-colour displays, while the visitors' response fizzled out completely after Ali Brown and Mark Butcher had scored forty from the first eight overs. Nadeem Shahid (48) was the only man to pass twenty-five as the wily Shaun Udal (5-43) gathered in a rich harvest of wickets from reckless charges and outfield catches that sent Surrey spinning to a 75-run defeat.

With fortunes in the two league competitions contrasting dramatically, Keith Medlycott took his team down to Taunton to play a Somerset side that had made a poor start to the season. Since Adam Hollioake, Alec Stewart, Graham Thorpe and Ali Brown were all included in England's Texaco Trophy squad to take on South Africa, and Saqlain was again nursing a damaged spinning finger, it was a much weakened Surrey team, captained for the first time by Mark Butcher, that got away to a flying start after inviting Somerset to bat on a damp, green wicket. With none of their top seven batsmen reaching double figures, the cidermen slumped to 65-7 before some decent hitting from the tailenders and a top-scoring thirty-five extras, including twenty-eight no-balls, allowed them to total 176. Martin Bicknell (4-14) was Surrey's star-turn with the ball, though Ben Hollioake (3-55) and Joey Benjamin (2-69) also played their part.

Unsurprisingly, in view of the conditions and their inexperienced batting line-up - including Ian Ward at number three and James Knott, playing as a specialist batsman, at number six - Surrey found the going no easier when they replied and by the close of the first day they were struggling at 156-7.

Thanks to the efforts of Ian Salisbury (51, his first half-century for Surrey), Jon Batty (39) and Joey Benjamin, the visitors managed to prolong their innings on the second morning, reaching 241 to earn a 65-run lead. By the time lunch arrived, Somerset were in serious strife at 21-2, and when Benjamin claimed his third scalp shortly after the resumption a Surrey victory looked quite likely, since the hosts were still trailing by thirty-eight runs. A fourth wicket then fell to Alex Tudor with the arrears only just cleared, before a match-turning partnership developed between Piran Holloway and Rob Turner, both of whom appeared to be untroubled by all the bowlers bar Salisbury on a pitch that had now dried and flattened out. This pair took the score to 253-4 by the end of day two, with Holloway on 110, Turner on seventy-four and the match back in the melting pot.

On the third morning the excellent Salisbury appeared to tilt the balance in favour of his team by removing both overnight batsmen - Holloway for 123 and Turner for 88 - after their stand had added 214 to the Somerset total. The Surrey seamers found it impossible to make any headway at the other end, though, which enabled Burns (40), Rose (76) and Caddick (37) to advance the score from 297-6 to 435-7 and put their team in control of the match. Although Salisbury eventually worked his way through the tail to finish with hard-earned figures of 5-98 from a marathon forty-seven overs, the hosts' final tally of 475 left Surrey to score a daunting 411 to win a match that had seemingly slipped from their grasp. Although Butcher and Ratcliffe knocked eighty-five off the target before the latter fell to Rose for thirty-three shortly before the close of play, the odds still favoured the home side as stumps were drawn.

Within minutes of the start of an overcast final day, the hosts had become red-hot favourites as their 18-year-old debutant left-arm swing bowler, Matthew Bulbeck, removed both Ian Ward and

Nadeem Shahid without a run added to the overnight total of ninety-two. Although Ben Hollioake (28) helped his skipper steady the ship for a while, Somerset's five seamers made full use of the favourable overhead conditions to hustle through the middle-order and leave the innings in tatters at 182-7. Amidst this carnage, Mark Butcher held firm to complete a most worthy century during a ninth-wicket partnership of forty-one with Martin Bicknell (23), thus becoming the first Surrey captain to carry his bat - for 109 out of 245 - as his side sunk to a 165-run defeat just before tea. The impressive Bulbeck completed a fine match by following his first innings' 3-52 with 3-48, while Andy Caddick (3-91) was the other principal destroyer as Somerset's first Championship victory of the season provided Surrey with their first setback in the premier domestic competition. Keith Medlycott's men maintained their top spot in the table, however, since other results fell kindly for them.

LEADING POSITIONS:- Surrey P4, Pts 60; Sussex P4, Pts 60; Derbys P4, Pts 54

A disappointing Taunton trip then ended with a second defeat that left Surrey bottom of the Sunday League table and almost certainly out of the running for the title before the end of May. Put in on another green pitch, the champions of 1996 were routed by Somerset's seamers for just 127, with forty-two of those runs coming from a ninth-wicket stand of forty-two between Ian Ward (45 not out) and Ian Salisbury (33). Although the hosts lost their first two wickets for twenty-two when they replied, they were eventually led to a convincing seven-wicket win with ten overs to spare by Mark Lathwell, who was unbeaten on sixty-four as Somerset claimed the four points that had always looked destined to be theirs once they had won the toss.

Although Adam Hollioake and Ali Brown - the latter fresh from a match-winning fifty-nine the previous day - had returned for the Sunday League game after England's 2-1 Texaco Trophy series defeat at the hands of South Africa, the loss of four batsmen for the County Championship game had proved to be too much of a handicap. Losing that number of players to England was always going to seriously weaken the side but the fact that all four were front-line batsmen made things far worse.

With a ten-day break between the ODI series and the first Test match, all of these absentees were able to take their place in a full-strength Surrey side for the Benson & Hedges Cup quarter-final against Lancashire at The Oval two days later.

After rain had delayed the start of play until 3.30pm Lancashire were put in by Adam Hollioake and made all the early running, thanks to Michael Atherton (93) and John Crawley (44), who shared a second-wicket partnership of 122 to put their side in sight of a big total at 148-1 after thirty-two overs. Surrey fought back dramatically, however, as Saqlain Mushtaq's dismissal of Crawley allowed Martin Bicknell (2-25) and Ian Salisbury (2-34) to engineer a slippage to 168-6 that restored balance to the contest. Saqlain (4-46) then returned to seal the hosts' fightback by claiming a last-over hat-trick, courtesy of catches at long-on, long-off and midwicket, leaving Lancashire all out for 203 and bringing a semi-final berth into view for his side.

After scoring 35-0 from eight overs by the end of the first day allocated to the match, Surrey returned to complete a fairly comfortable victory the next day. Although the home county squandered an 81-run opening partnership by Ali Brown (41) and Alec Stewart (31) to stand on the brink of collapse at 113-4, Mark Butcher (36) and Adam Hollioake (39 not out) were able to steady Surrey nerves with a match-clinching partnership of seventy for the fifth wicket. Ben Hollioake then joined his brother to see his team through to their thirteenth consecutive Benson & Hedges Cup victory, this one by five wickets with twenty-six balls to spare. The semi-final draw that followed this triumph suggested that thirteen could prove to be unlucky for Surrey, since it presented them with a trip to Grace Road to take on a confident Leicestershire side.

A return to four-day cricket now saw unbeaten Kent making the short trip to The Oval where, to everyone's surprise, Surrey had decided to play on the pitch that had already been used for both the Texaco Trophy ODI and the Benson & Hedges Cup quarter-final. This meant that it had already seen almost two-hundred overs of action as the captains tossed up. Adam Hollioake was, therefore, delighted when Steve Marsh called incorrectly and, predictably enough, the home skipper elected to take first use of a surface that provided generous turn before lunch. Neither Alec Stewart (86) nor Mark Butcher (51) seemed unduly perturbed, however, as they took Surrey to 136-0 at the interval. Although both openers departed soon afterwards, Graham Thorpe and Adam Hollioake built on their efforts with a 51-run stand for the third wicket before Carl Hooper ripped through the middle order with a four-wicket burst that sent the hosts sliding from 193-2 to 212-6. Order was then restored by Jon Batty and Ian Salisbury, with the latter still in occupation at the close of play, which came at 314-9.

Although Salisbury, who ended with a Surrey-best unbeaten fifty-six, and Martin Bicknell were only able to extend the total to 342 on the second morning as Hooper claimed the last wicket to finish with a career-best 7-93, an above-par score soon increased in value as Bicknell and Alex Tudor rattled out Fulton, Key and Hooper before lunch with just twenty-one on the board.

The Surrey spin twins, who had each been awarded their county cap the previous day, then took over in style during the afternoon, running through the rest of the batting with the assistance of Graham Thorpe, who held a total of six catches - one short of equalling the world record for an innings - as Kent were shot out for just 86. Allan Wells top-scored with twenty-four as Salisbury (3-13) and Saqlain (3-18) ran riot against batsmen who were simply incapable of dealing with high-class spinners on a turning surface.

With victory seemingly already in the bag for Surrey, Kent followed on 256 runs in arrears and immediately lost both of their openers for a duck to the new ball. Thereafter it became almost a straight fight between Carl Hooper and the spinners. Although Trevor Ward, Wells, and Matthew Fleming offered limited support, Hooper was the only man able to dominate as he played a quite superb innings of ninety-four that was characterised by brilliant footwork and strokeplay. When he departed late in the day to a catch behind the wicket off Saqlain he received a generous ovation from the fair-minded Oval crowd, while Adam Hollioake requested the extra half-hour in an attempt to complete a two-day triumph. This move yielded just one of the three wickets that were required, though it didn't take long for Saqlain (4-100) and Salisbury (3-75) to complete Surrey's victory by an innings and thirty runs the next morning.

The county's decision to play on a used pitch - which was said to have come about because the wicket that had originally been produced got damp in the lead-up to the game - was roundly condemned by Kent and some members of the media. This was rather rich coming from the county that had produced an under-prepared pitch at Canterbury the previous September, and also failed to acknowledge that the all-important bounce of the surface had been consistent and true throughout the match. It was simply a case of two excellent spin bowlers outclassing batsmen - bar the outstanding Hooper - who had failed to adapt to the prevailing conditions.

With Sussex failing to win ther match at Worcester, this victory took Surrey fourteen points clear at the top of the Championship table.
LEADING POSITIONS:- Surrey P5, Pts 83; Sussex P5, Pts 69; Durham P5, Pts 62

By beating Kent with almost two days to spare, Surrey had earned themselves some extra breathing space before their 'weakened' side - minus Graham Thorpe, the recalled Mark Butcher, and Alec Stewart, the new captain, all of whom were playing in the first Test against South Africa - took on Worcestershire at The Oval.

After Adam Hollioake had won the toss and elected to bat on a controversy-free brand new pitch, his stand-in top three did him proud as the hosts racked up 502-7 declared over the course of the first two days. On a rain-affected opening day, Jason Ratcliffe, who made exactly a hundred, and Ian Ward, who compiled a career-best sixty-four, batted superbly to launch the innings with a

164-run partnership, while Nadeem Shahid, in the company of a belligerent Ali Brown (72), led the way on day two with a sparkling innings of 124. Since the pitch was already offering slow turn for the spinners, Worcestershire did well to reach stumps at 104-2, with the in-form Graeme Hick - unbeaten on forty and fresh from registering his hundredth first-class century - looking perfectly capable of notching a fourth consecutive County Championship ton.

The third morning of the game saw Surrey making good progress as they raced through the visitors' middle-order batting, though Hick was not amongst the Worcestershire casualties during the slide to 155-6. Finally finding a supportive partner in Stuart Lampitt (43), Hick moved slowly but surely to his 101st first-class century - six of them having come against Surrey - before being dismissed for 119 by Martin Bicknell with the new ball. Although Lampitt then departed shortly afterwards to Alex Tudor with the score on 284, Richard Illingworth (45 not out) galvanised his tail-end team-mates into further dogged resistance that saw the visitors past the follow-on mark of 352 and on to 366-9 at the close of play

Even though Bicknell (3-61) quickly disposed of Alamgir Sheriyar with just one run added to the total the next morning, the game looked destined to end in a draw, not least because Surrey's potential fourth-innings match-winners, Saqlain Mushtaq (4-116) and Ian Salisbury (1-100), had delivered an incredible 110 overs between them during Worcestershire's 147-over first knock.

Adam Hollioake and his team clearly had other ideas, though, as they rattled up 130-4 in twenty-six overs up to lunch, with Ward (58) and the skipper himself (47 not out) to the fore. Much to everyone's surprise it was then announced that Surrey had declared and were challenging Worcestershire to score 266 from a minimum of 67 overs, which seemed a very reasonable target given Hick's current form.

With his side quickly losing Vikram Solanki to Tudor for the second time in the match, the visitors' key man was soon at the crease, though he and Abdul Hafeez made light of this early blow by rattling up fifty runs in eleven overs. Nervous Surrey fans were soon feeling more comfortable, however, when a delighted and animated Saqlain pinned Hick lbw, plumb in front of his stumps, for twenty-two, greatly increasing the home side's prospects of victory at a stroke. The Pakistani spin wizard was really relishing his task as he despatched Hafeez and Haynes shortly afterwards and, just as Hick dominated the visitors' first innings, Tom Moody began to take charge of the second. Adopting an aggressive approach against a weary-looking Salisbury, the giant Australian kept his side in with a chance of victory, while Saqlain continued to bemuse and remove the batsmen at the other end. With the score on 160-7, the Surrey leg-spinner took his revenge, however, having Moody caught behind off a googly for a fine sixty-two and leaving Worcestershire with no option but to play for the draw. Hard though they tried, Illingworth and Newport were unable to save their side, with the former becoming Saqlain's seventh victim when he unwisely padded up to an off-break and the latter being taken by Shahid at silly point off Salisbury (2-81) with less than fifteen minutes left for play. The Surrey celebrations, both on and off the pitch, made it clear that everyone regarded this as a superb victory, and the chief architect of the 79-run triumph, Saqlain Mushtaq, proudly waved his recently awarded cap to the crowd as they acknowledged his magnificent performance in returning career-best figures of 7-41. Much credit was also due to Adam Hollioake for a bold declaration that showed great faith in his bowlers. As he later said "Sometimes you have to risk losing a game in order to win it, and too many people aren't prepared to do that."

This win enabled Surrey to extend their lead at the top of the table to seventeen points, even though Sussex and Durham had maintained their surprisingly good early season form by beating Kent and Middlesex respectively.

LEADING POSITIONS:- Surrey P6, Pts 106; Sussex P6, Pts 89; Durham P6, Pts 85

With things going nicely in the Championship, attention now turned to the Benson & Hedges Cup semi-final at Grace Road, Leicester.

Having put their opponents in to bat on a greenish pitch on a breezy day, Surrey suffered from a mixture of bad luck and bad cricket as Leicestershire scored an impressive 311-4 from their fifty overs. The hosts' innings was constructed around a 172-run stand for the second wicket between Ben Smith (89) and Darren Maddy, who compiled a fine unbeaten 120 despite being 'dismissed' by two of the seven no-balls that the visiting bowlers delivered - he was caught on fifty-three and then bowled on 104. While 'avoidable misfortune' would be an apt way of describing these moments from the Surrey point of view, it was pure bad luck that had seen Ian Salisbury tear a groin muscle in the process of delivering his first ball of the match. With the leg-spinner unable to play any further part in the game, the team's run of thirteen wins in the competition looked as if it could, indeed, prove to be unlucky.

Surrey's reply was then quickly undermined by their old boy, Chris Lewis, who removed all three current Test men - Stewart, Thorpe and Butcher - to leave his erstwhile colleagues in dire straits at 72-4. When Ben Hollioake then went for sixty-three at 113-5 - caught by that man Lewis off James Ormond - the visitors looked down and out, but Adam Hollioake (85) overcame a poor start to enjoy stands of eighty with the excellent Jason Ratcliffe (41) and eighty-one with Martin Bicknell (38 not out) to keep the dream of retaining the golden trophy alive. Inevitably, however, the outstanding Lewis (4-40) was to have the last word, returning to produce an unplayable yorker for Hollioake that effectively decided the contest, enabling the Foxes to complete a 20-run triumph.

Forced into a return to Championship action just two days later by the crowded fixture list, Surrey needed to bounce back quickly at Chelmsford against an Essex side who had started the Sunday League season well but were struggling badly in four-day cricket.

It was therefore unfortunate that rain ruined the match, with only the second day unaffected by the elements. During the first half of a game played on a green pitch, Surrey took advantage of an attack in which only Mark Ilott (4-64) consistently located a good line and length, totalling 373 in just 87.5 overs before putting Essex in real trouble at 120-6. Ali Brown (79) and Adam Hollioake (59) had revived the visitors after they had struggled to 66-4 early on day one, while Jon Batty (52) and Saqlain Mushtaq, with a Surrey-best undefeated forty-five from 40 balls, had provided a real sting in the tail with a last-wicket stand of sixty-three. Ben Hollioake (3-21) had then put the hosts under the cosh by claiming the prime scalps of Hussain, Stuart Law and Irani.

Unfortunately for the visitors, the second half of the contest was decimated by rain - only fourteen overs were bowled on day three, which saw Martin Bicknell (3-68) claim two wickets to reduce Essex to 151-8, while fewer than forty further overs were possible on the last day, when Surrey dismissed their hosts for 203 and had them fighting for their lives at 75-4 (Bicknell 3-26) after enforcing the follow on. The failure of the bonus points system to reflect the play was underlined as the visitors took eleven points from the match to their hosts' eight. Surrey's haul had enabled them to extend their lead in the table, however, since rain around the country - which was suffering another of the wettest Junes on record - had resulted in most of the other games also being drawn.

LEADING POSITIONS:- Surrey P7, Pts 117; Durham P7, Pts 93; Sussex P6, Pts 89

The Sunday League clash between the two sides had been slotted in between days three and four of the Championship match, and Surrey had suffered further 40-over humiliation in a farcical rain-ruined contest.

When the weather first intervened, Essex were 136-3 after twenty-seven overs with the excellent bowling efforts of Joey Benjamin (8-0-22-0), Saqlain Mushtaq (5-0-12-0) and Alex Tudor (4-0-22-2) having been negated by expensive spells from the other bowlers.

After a lengthy delay, the Lions were then set a Duckworth-Lewis target of 137 to win in seventeen overs, which wasn't unreasonable given that Essex had been deprived of their last thirteen overs, during which they would have been likely to acclerate their rate of scoring. All was going well for the visitors when their chosen opening pair of Alec Stewart and Graham Thorpe - deputising for the injured Ali Brown - reached 32-0 after five overs but, perhaps irked by Essex skipper Nasser Hussain's time-wasting tactics, Thorpe threw his wicket away with a reckless stroke against Darren Cousins (3-23) and initiated a horrendous collapse to 41-5. With ten overs having to be completed for a result to be declared, and Surrey way behind the Duckworth-Lewis par score, Essex began racing around between overs, while each new batsman took an eternity to get to the middle. Farce reigned, and when another downpour necessitated a further suspension in play the visitors looked to have escaped defeat since only eight overs of their innings had been bowled. Unfortunately for the Lions, the rain soon eased and the umpires elected to restart the game in persistent drizzle, allowing the home side to complete a controversial 26-run victory as Surrey finished on 69-7 from eleven overs.

This win took Essex to the top of the Sunday League table and left Adam Hollioake's team rooted to the bottom with just two points to their credit after six matches, only two of which had been played as 40-overs-per-side contests because of poor weather. It was obvious that all hope of winning the title had gone and it would now require a good run of results to gain a place in the top half of the table and secure Division One status for next season.

After a disappointingly damp time in the usually dry east, the team now headed north to Manchester, a city notorious for its wet weather.

The Sunday League game against Lancashire was played on the Wednesday night preceding the Championship match since it was to be Old Trafford's first-ever competitive floodlit fixture. With fireworks, music, a party and a compere, Lancashire were clearly going for the razzmatazz in a big way, though there wasn't much to get excited about once the game got under way on a miserably damp afternoon. Electing to bat, the Lions of Surrey were soon struck by the Lightning of Lancashire as Peter Martin and Ian Austin left their visitors reeling at 27-3. Adam Hollioake, with seventy, and Ian Ward (55), with his maiden Sunday League half-century, then reconstructed the innings with what was, incredibly, Surrey's first fifty partnership of the season in the 40-over competition, before rain drove the players from the field with the scoreboard reading 182-6 after thirty-nine overs.

Eventually, after a further rain interruption one over into Lancashire's reply, the Duckworth-Lewis system set the home side a target of 132 from twenty-two overs, which looked to be a tricky task. At 85-6, with three batsmen having fallen to Joey Benjamin (3-30) and three to run outs, victory appeared to be beyond the reach of the Lightning, but Austin and Gary Yates then combined to produce an unbroken 50-run stand that swept them home with three balls to spare and took the red rose county to the top of the Sunday League table above Essex... and left Surrey marooned in eighteenth place.

The recent depressing weather continued unabated as the two sides switched to County Championship mode - the first day was washed out completely, while just 105 overs were bowled on the next two days, during which time Surrey were put in and then put out for 146 before Lancashire replied with 151-7. Given the overcast bowler-friendly conditions that prevailed, low scores were not unexpected, and the seamers enjoyed themselves immensely, with Wasim Akram (4-42) and Peter Martin (3-35) starring for the home side and Alex Tudor (5-43) impressing for the visitors.

Although the final day began with Lancashire declaring at their overnight total and attempting to win the game by bowling out the Championship leaders for a second time, it soon became clear that Surrey were not going to crumble again. Mike Watkinson therefore changed tack, introducing 'joke' bowlers to open up the match and allow a contrived finish. The willing concession of 130 runs in thirty minutes after lunch allowed Ian Ward (81 not out) and Nadeem Shahid (126 not out) to take their side to a declaration point of 254-1, leaving the red rose county to chase 250 to win in fifty-three overs.

While both sides were way below full strength for this game - Lancashire's absentees were Atherton, Fairbrother, Austin and Hegg, while Surrey were without Butcher, Stewart, Thorpe, Salisbury and Saqlain - the fact that the visitors were fielding a pretty inexperienced attack suggested that the home side might have got the better of the deal... though most people had thought that when Adam Hollioake had declared against Worcestershire.

This time, however, things didn't work out well for Surrey, as Nathan Wood (80 not out) and John Crawley (78) made light of the early departure of Paddy McKeown by adding 136 for the second wicket. Then, when the latter fell to Rupesh Amin with ninety-nine runs still needed from the last sixteen overs, Andrew Flintoff - on a pair after being dismissed by his good friend, Alex Tudor, in the first innings - entered the fray to hit his first ball for four and take sixteen from an Amin over. Suddenly, Lancashire were red-hot favourites to win and, with fifty required from the final thirteen overs, the contest was decided during an amazing Tudor over. Opening his shoulders to great effect and aiming in the arc between long-on and square leg, Flintoff smashed Surrey's young paceman for thirty-four runs in an over that cost thirty-eight in total since it contained two no-balls. Although Tudor was unlucky when the third ball of the over flew down to fine leg off an inside edge, every other shot in Flintoff's sequence of 6, 4, 4, 4, 6, 6, 0 seemed to come off the middle of the bat, and the bowler had to be grateful for the final 'dot ball' that saved him from breaking the world record for the number of runs off the bat in one over. Having reached his fifty from just twenty deliveries in the course of Tudor's over and ensured that his side would win the match, Flintoff went on to reach sixty-one from a mere 24 balls before being well caught on the boundary off Bicknell shortly before Lancashire closed out the game by six wickets with 8.4 overs in hand.

Surrey therefore left Old Trafford with just three points to show for their efforts, though they still held a twenty-point lead in the Championship race.

COUNTY CHAMPIONSHIP - TOP OF THE TABLE AT 21ST JUNE					
	P	W	D	L	PTS
Surrey	8	4	2	2	120
Durham	8	3	2	3	100
Yorkshire	7	3	2	2	95

A rather less demanding match followed as Surrey took on Buckinghamshire at The Oval in the first round of the Nat West Trophy. Although Adam Hollioake's men were perhaps guilty of not making the most of a 161-run opening partnership between Alec Stewart (97) and Jason Ratcliffe (71) as they piled up 315-9, their minor county visitors were never in the hunt as Alex Tudor (4-39) and Nadeem Shahid (3-30) played the major roles in dismissing them for 183.

While Surrey had avoided slipping up on their potential Nat West Trophy banana skin, Worcestershire, their opponents in the Sunday League four days later, had been the victims of a shock result, going down by four runs to Scotland in Edinburgh. Tom Moody's side were therefore keen to make amends by winning at The Oval, though this didn't look likely when they were bowled out for 180 after electing to bat. Significantly, extras top-scored with thirty-seven, thanks principally to the fifteen wides that resulted in the Lions failing to bowl their overs in time and, consequently, being docked an over from their reply.

With Surrey's batsmen struggling to find any real fluency until Jon Batty (35) and Martin Bicknell (30 not out) added fifty-three for the seventh wicket, fears that the deduction of the fortieth over might turn out to be crucial were realised when the Lions' last pair fell two short of the six runs they required to win the match from the thirty-ninth over. It now looked highly likely that Surrey would be playing Division Two one-day cricket in 1999 since they were already sixteen points short of ninth place with eight of their seventeen matches played.

The team's next County Championship assignment took them to Swansea to face the reigning champions, Glamorgan, who trailed their visitors by thirty-seven points and already had a real fight on their hands if they were to retain their crown. Since the game clashed with the third Test match of a series in which England trailed 1-0, both sides were below full strength. Surrey were lacking Alec Stewart, Graham Thorpe and Ben Hollioake - who had been selected in the squad despite his mediocre Championship form but didn't make the final eleven - while Glamorgan were, perhaps significantly, without Robert Croft at a St Helens ground that usually favoured the spinners. Knowing this, the visitors included Ian Salisbury in their team, even though he was still troubled by his groin injury. Mark Butcher - who, it transpired, had broken a thumb in the field at the end of the four-day game against Essex - was still out of action, forcing Surrey to select James Knott as a specialist batsman.

Despite losing the toss, which seemed to put them at a considerable disadvantage, the visitors started well, largely thanks to Adam Hollioake, who took three wickets to reduce Glamorgan to 61-4 after Alex Tudor had disappointed during his opening four-over spell. While Hollioake revelled in his unfamiliar role of third seamer, his opposite number, Matthew Maynard, held his team's innings together in the similarly alien role of opening batsman, making sixty-five before falling to the excellent Martin Bicknell (3-53). With Salisbury kept out of the attack, it was Hollioake who came back to finish off the innings and return career-best figures of 5-62 in a Glamorgan total of 197. This appeared to be a reasonable score on a pitch that had assisted both the seam bowlers and the off-breaks of Saqlain Mushtaq (2-38), and by the close of play Surrey were ruing the fact that they had donated fifty-one extras to the hosts' total. After losing Jason Ratcliffe to the first ball of their reply, the Championship leaders had struggled to 113-6, despite a very good fifty from the fast-maturing Ian Ward.

On the second day, Jon Batty, who constructed a steady thirty before falling to Darren Thomas (3-47), and Saqlain, who thrashed his way to twenty-five before being bowled by Owen Parkin (3-50), enabled Surrey to gain a very slender two-run first-innings lead. It was, however, very disappointing that Saqlain should depart to an ugly slog with his side one run short of a batting point.

The Pakistani spin king had plenty of time to redeem himself during Glamorgan's second knock, however, with the game now effectively reduced to a one-innings affair. Although Bicknell, as usual, removed Steve James - who had played in the second Test but been immediately discarded after scores of 10 and 0 - Surrey found further breakthroughs hard to come by as Maynard (71) and Adrian Dale dug in doggedly. It was only once Salisbury entered the attack in the twenty-eighth over to bowl in tandem with Saqlain that the visitors began to take a grip on the game. With the leg-spinner claiming four wickets in an excellent spell, the Welsh county slipped from 108-1 to 144-6, before Thomas and Shaw stopped the rot with an unbroken stand of twenty-six that left the game magnificently poised at the end of day two.

That balance was then maintained throughout a third morning's play that saw Salisbury adding three further scalps to his collection, allowing him to complete outstanding Surrey-best figures of 7-65 as Glamorgan were dismissed for 212. This left the visitors to score 211 for victory and by lunch they had lost Ratcliffe to Dean Cosker in reducing the target to 178.

When the left-arm spinner struck again after the break to dispose of Nadeem Shahid, and Thomas removed Hollioake for a duck, Surrey were struggling at 52-3, but Ward and Ali Brown turned out to be the perfect partnership at this time of crisis. While the former again batted with impressive patience and composure, the latter recovered from a nervy start to dominate Cosker and force an increasingly desperate Maynard to ask Thomas, Steve Watkin and Tony Cottey to experiment with their occasional off-cutters and off-breaks in the absence of Robert Croft. The champions were fighting a lost cause, though, and by the time Cottey trapped Brown lbw for an excellent 133-ball 100, including five sixes and six fours, Surrey were just six runs from victory. Ward was unbeaten on seventy-nine as the league leaders coasted home by six wickets with more than a day to spare and twenty points in the bag.

This win kept Surrey at the top of the tree, though Leicestershire had shot up to second place after drawing with Sussex and thrashing Durham.

COUNTY CHAMPIONSHIP - TOP OF THE TABLE AT 4TH JULY					
	P	W	D	L	PTS
Surrey	9	5	2	2	140
Leicestershire	9	4	5	0	122
Sussex	9	3	4	2	111

The Sunday League game between Glamorgan and Surrey started as a real basement battle - the two sides had just eight points and one win between them - and ended, after just sixty-six overs of action, with relegation a virtual certainty for the Lions after the hosts had secured a crushing 107-run victory. Glamorgan's total of 184 was built around Adrian Dale's patient sixty-five as Ben Hollioake (3-30) and the spinners enjoyed bowling on another pitch that tested the skill of the batsmen, while Surrey capitulated with depressing ease to 77 all out. After Owen Parkin (3-24) had accounted for the top order, Darren Thomas's combination of pace and reverse swing proved utterly irresistible as he cleaned up with 7-16, the best figures ever recorded by a Glamorgan bowler in limited-overs cricket, and the third-best in the history of the Sunday League.

Attention now turned back to the Nat West Trophy, where Surrey faced a second round clash against Gloucestershire at Bristol. With Mark Butcher still out of action and Graham Thorpe sidelined by a long-term back injury that had flared up again during the drawn third Test, Surrey struggled badly against Mike Smith (4-46) in the early stages of the game, sliding to a perilous 20-4 before being rescued by a wonderful partnership of 156 between the two England captains, Alec Stewart (89) and Adam Hollioake (88). Unfortunately for the visitors, some excellent Gloucestershire catching and ground fielding then brought about the second collapse of the innings, from 176-4 to 215 all out, which put the contest back in the balance.

Surrey were soon back in charge, however, as superb bowling at the start of the hosts' reply by Martin Bicknell (3-24), Joey Benjamin and Ben Hollioake left Gloucestershire in a deep hole at 45-5. Despite the best efforts of Mark Alleyne (39), and a strangely selfish innings by Jack Russell (49 not out), the home team were unable to get back into the match, as Saqlain (2-24) and Salisbury (2-28) teased out the lower order to wrap up a 52-run triumph for their side.

Although their form in the longer one-day competitions had been impressive, Surrey were still unable to reproduce it in the Sunday League as their performance in the next fixture demonstrated. The game against Leicestershire at The Oval was played on a Monday afternoon because of the Foxes' participation in the Benson & Hedges Cup final and resulted in another embarrassing defeat. Bouncing back well from their humiliating 192-run defeat by Essex at Lord's, the visitors knocked up 252-9 in thirty-eight overs, thanks to Phil Simmons (114), Ben Smith (87) and some utterly wretched Surrey fielding that would have shamed a decent club side. With the honourable exception of Ian Ward (68), none of the batsmen reached thirty as the toothless Lions fared little better with the bat and flopped to a ninth successive defeat in the 40-overs competition, this time by forty-four runs.

Fortunately, this debacle had been witnessed by just a handful of spectators, but there was a larger crowd at Guildford as Surrey returned to Championship action two days later.

Although visitors Middlesex were joint leaders of the 40-over competition they were making little impression in the four-day game, having won just two of their first nine matches. Their fortunes looked likely to improve, however, as Surrey slipped to 7-3 after electing to bat, with Mark Butcher, Alec Stewart and Adam Hollioake having all gone for ducks to the new-ball combination of Angus Fraser and Chris Batt, a tall 21-year-old left-arm seamer in his first season with the county. A stand of eighty-seven for the fourth wicket between Ali Brown (51) and Ian Ward (35), who had been selected ahead of Jason Ratcliffe and Nadeem Shahid as a result of his excellent recent form, then steadied the ship before Brown was caught off Phil Tufnell just before lunch.

A post-prandial collapse, again at the hands of Fraser (4-34) and Batt (5-51), then saw Surrey shot out for 150, with only Ian Salisbury (31) offering any resistance. It was worrying for the Championship leaders that they had now gone three matches without securing a batting point, following their dismissals for 146 at Old Trafford and 199 at Swansea.

With the ball continuing to swing, Middlesex soon hit problems of their own, however, as Mike Gatting became the day's third current or former England captain to fall for a duck when he was bowled by Martin Bicknell. Once Mark Ramprakash and Justin Langer had departed after constructing a solid second-wicket partnership of twenty-five, the visitors replicated Surrey's earlier collapses, nosediving to 47-5 and then, eventually, 115 all out when Tufnell hit the last ball of the day to cover point. Keith Brown, with thirty, had played a lone hand as his team-mates had succumbed to Bicknell (3-25), Alex Tudor (4-47) and Saqlain Mushtaq (2-15) and handed the league leaders a thirty-five run advantage on a day of twenty wickets.

On day two, with the Guildford C.C. pitch having been absolved of any blame for the opening day's batting traumas, Surrey set about building a winning position in their second innings. Although they lost Butcher to Batt for ten, the hosts batted far more convincingly the second time around, with Adam Hollioake (59) and Ali Brown (79) providing the middle-order ballast that put Surrey in control at 335-8 when stumps were drawn.

Salisbury's new Surrey-best of sixty-one and Tudor's impressive forty-one then extended the home side's advantage to 455 on the third morning during a 63-run ninth-wicket stand that snuffed out Middlesex's hopes of pulling the game out of the fire. With Gatting again bowled by Bicknell for nought - this time first ball - to complete an embarrassing pair, and the key men, Ramprakash and Langer, each failing to get past twenty, the writing was soon on the wall for the hapless visitors. From the depths of 48-4, David Nash and Keith Brown launched a recovery of sorts, advancing the total to eighty-eight before Adam Hollioake unleashed his spinners to complete the task of winning the match. Predictably enough, a flimsy lower order had no answer to the wiles of Salisbury (4-43) and Saqlain (2-52) as Surrey claimed victory by 280 runs, despite the efforts of Brown, who was left stranded on fifty-nine. The Middlesex wicketkeeper thus completed a clean sweep for the two Browns in the match, since they had provided the top score in each of the four innings!

Having failed to gain any batting points, Surrey found their lead at the top of the table cut by four points, as Leicestershire had pulled off the greatest run chase in County Championship history against Northamptonshire at Leicester. Left to score 204 from just twenty overs, the Foxes had got home by four wickets with five balls to spare, thanks largely to Vince Wells's fifty-eight from 32 balls and Chris Lewis's unbeaten 33-ball knock of seventy-one. With Lancashire having beaten both Worcestershire and the rain at Lytham, and Gloucestershire having dealt efficiently with Sussex at Cheltenham, the chasing pack remained very much on Surrey's tail.

COUNTY CHAMPIONSHIP - TOP OF THE TABLE AT 18TH JULY				
	P	W	D	L	PTS
Surrey	10	6	2	2	160
Leicestershire	10	5	5	0	146
Lancashire	9	5	3	1	131
Gloucestershire	9	5	1	3	128
Kent	10	4	4	2	120

Since Sunday League 'relegation' was now unavoidable, Surrey rested a number of key players for the Sunday League match against their high-flying London-based rivals, with Micky Bell, Gareth Batty and James Knott all getting first-team opportunities as a result. In front of a packed crowd, the afternoon started with the presentation of first eleven caps to two loyal squad men, Jason Ratcliffe and Nadeem Shahid, while Jonathan Batty received his second-eleven cap after impressing on a consistent basis since taking over from Knott as Alec Stewart's regular stand-in behind the stumps.

The England selectors had, meanwhile, included Ian Salisbury and Mark Butcher in their squad for the fourth Test, though they had omitted Ben Hollioake. On a bad day for the Hollioakes it had also been announced that the captaincy of the one-day international side was to pass from Adam to Alec Stewart, the England Test captain. Apparently, it was now felt that the 'split' captaincy didn't work and that it was better for the same man to lead both the Test and ODI sides.

There was plenty of news to digest, therefore, as Surrey elected to bat and raced to 169-1, with Ian Ward making a career-best ninety-one and Nadeem Shahid celebrating the award of his cap with a fine knock of fifty-eight. Some witless batting and running between the wickets by the Lions in the final ten overs allowed Middlesex back into the match, however, and a final total of 223-9 looked short of par for the Woodbridge Road ground.

When the visitors replied, some decent early bowling, particularly by Joey Benjamin, reduced the league leaders to 57-3 before Justin Langer (60) joined forces with David Nash (36) to lead another revival that put the visitors back on top again at 151-4. As the game continued to ebb and flow, the Australian left-hander then fell to a fine catch by Ali Brown at third man off Mark Butcher and, amidst a welter of runs and wickets, Keith Dutch (40) emerged as a potential hero for Middlesex with a sensible knock that put them on the brink of victory at 217-8. Needing seven from the final over bowled by Ben Hollioake, Dutch hit a boundary before losing the strike with a single from the third ball, thereby entrusting the task of scoring two runs from three balls to his tail-end partners. This task proved beyond both Jamie Hewitt, who was run out from the next ball, and Angus Fraser, who failed to get any bat on either of Hollioake's last two deliveries, much to the delight of an excited and partisan home crowd. Surrey had thus secured their first Sunday League win of the 1998 season - albeit by just one run - at the eleventh attempt, despite the fact that Alec Stewart, Martin Bicknell, Ian Salisbury, Saqlain Mushtaq and Alex Tudor had all been left on the sidelines.

The county's next Championship fixture took them to Cheltenham, where they faced fourth-placed Gloucestershire - including the deadly new-ball combination of Mike Smith and Courtney Walsh - without the services of Alec Stewart, Mark Butcher, Ian Salisbury (on England duty) and Graham Thorpe, who looked likely to miss the rest of the season.

After their visitors had elected to bat on a fast, bouncy wicket under heavy cloud cover, Gloucestershire proceeded to take the first-morning honours as Surrey lost five wickets for 138, with Smith claiming three scalps and Walsh the other two. Adam Hollioake had stood firm for much of the session after coming in at 44-2 and proceeded to play quite beautifully after the break, scoring freely all around the wicket and sharing a 115-run stand for the sixth wicket with the dogged James Knott (35) before the son of the former England wicketkeeper was undone by the medium pace of Tim Hancock. The Surrey skipper completed his first century for almost a year shortly afterwards, having faced 142 balls and hit eighteen fours and a six, before rain arrived to wipe out the rest of the day's play with the score at 265-6.

A refreshed Smith (6-66) and Walsh (3-57) then knocked over the last four wickets - including Hollioake for a magnificent 112 - the next morning for the addition of just thirty-two runs, leaving Keith Medlycott's men just three runs short of a third batting point at 297 all out.

Although Rob Cunliffe and Tim Hancock followed up their colleagues' fine bowling effort by compiling the first half-century opening partnership against Surrey in the 1998 Championship, the visitors soon hit back through Saqlain Mushtaq, who claimed two victims in reducing the hosts to 90-3. Gloucestershire rallied once again, however, through Dominic Hewson (52) and Matt Windows, who advanced the score to 145-3 before an astonishing collapse put the Championship leaders in control of the match. After Windows had cracked under pressure from Martin Bicknell, the total crept up to 166 before the hosts lost their last six wickets for the addition of just one run in the space of twenty-seven deliveries, finishing 167 all out. Russell, Lewis and Walsh all recorded ducks as Bicknell finished with 5-34 and Saqlain returned 4-84.

With a welcome but surprising first-innings lead of 130 to build on, Surrey expected a hostile response from the home side and were not disappointed as Walsh claimed two of the five wickets that fell before the close of play. At 111-5, the visitors led by 241, but still had work to do, since all of their top five batsmen were back in the hutch.

The third morning then saw the second amazing decline of the match as Walsh (6-47) ripped through Surrey's lower order, claiming four of the last five wickets that tumbled for the addition of a paltry twenty-four runs in just forty-six balls. Suddenly, the game was completely open, with Gloucestershire needing 266 to win.

Much to the visitors' disappointment, Cunliffe and Hancock again gave their side an encouraging start of forty-four before Saqlain, wheeling away at one end while Hollioake rotated his seamers at the other, struck two blows in the space of three balls. The balance of power then swung back and forth, with Surrey on top at 100-4 - when Cunliffe, having been dropped three times, was yorked by Ben Hollioake for fifty-three - but the hosts back in control at 161-4. Mark Alleyne and Matt Church then fell to Bicknell (3-81), giving Surrey a clear sight of victory, before Martyn Ball joined Matt Windows to forge a seventh-wicket partnership that was ultimately to prove decisive. Seventy-nine runs flowed from just sixteen overs and Gloucestershire were coasting home until Windows was caught off Saqlain (3-94) for sixty and Lewis went lbw to Tudor. Surrey's final chance to snatch the match then came and went as Nadeem Shahid dropped Ball (48 not out) off Tudor at deep backward square leg with the home side still twelve runs short of the winning post. Unfazed by this lucky escape, the ninth-wicket pair took their team through to a two-wicket triumph that was rightly celebrated by a large home crowd at the very attractive college ground. Surrey's players meanwhile headed for the dressing room knowing that they had thrown away a great opportunity to open up a lead of some thirty-six points at the top of the Championship table through some poor batting and a number of missed catches.

COUNTY CHAMPIONSHIP - TOP OF THE TABLE AT 25TH JULY					
	P	W	D	L	PTS
Surrey	11	6	2	3	166
Gloucestershire	10	6	1	3	148
Leicestershire	10	5	5	0	146
Lancashire	10	5	4	1	141

After an unscheduled day's break everyone was back at the college ground for the Sunday League match between the two counties. Understandably, Surrey again chose to omit their key bowlers from their 40-overs side and it showed as Gloucestershire piled up an impressive 261-8. Although Joey Benjamin was typically steady and Gareth Batty bowled his off-breaks intelligently to return figures of 1-32, the other bowlers suffered some rough treatment at the hands of Bobby Dawson (68) and Matt Windows (59).

Having had an over deducted from their allocation because of a slow over-rate, Surrey were soon in dire straits at 26-4 when they replied, with Lewis (3-45) and Hancock (2-30) having disposed of Ward, Brown, Shahid and Ben Hollioake. It looked to be a hopeless situation but Jason Ratcliffe (80, including four sixes) and James Knott first managed to stop the rot and then went on to add 157 in twenty-three overs, thereby breathing life back into the contest. The Lions' roar was only silenced, in fact, when Courtney Walsh (2-25) returned to the attack to bowl Knott for a splendid ninety-eight and spark a final disintegration from 231-5 to 239 all out.

Surrey's disappointing week in Cheltenham was then followed by a depressing defeat at The Oval against Derbyshire in the Nat West Trophy quarter-final. After opting to bat, the highly-fancied home side never came to terms with a hard-working visiting attack and only managed to reach a final total of 217-7 when Martin Bicknell (48 not out) and Ian Salisbury (34 not out) flayed fifty runs from the final five overs of Surrey's 60-over innings.

An examination of Derbyshire's batting line-up, which appeared to have a fragile middle order and a lengthy tail, suggested that all was not lost, though Surrey clearly needed to capture some early wickets. None were forthcoming, however, as Michael Slater (82) and Kim Barnett (60) took full advantage of some poor bowling and woeful fielding to construct a 162-run opening partnership that allowed the visitors to cruise home to a well-deserved victory with five wickets and as many overs in hand. Having lost three successive matches in three different competitions inside a week, Surrey's season was in danger of falling apart and the County Championship now represented their only chance of glory.

Luckily, a home game against Sussex, whose campaign had gone into serious decline after a promising start, offered a good opportunity to get back on the winning trail. The visitors had the best of the early exchanges after winning the toss and deciding, predictably enough, to take first use of a second-hand pitch - the one that had been used for the Nat West Trophy quarter-final. With Surrey seemingly suffering a hangover from that match, the visiting openers, Wasim Khan and Toby Peirce, scored eighty-three from the first twenty-one overs, during which time Alex Tudor had left the field with an injury after delivering just three overs. Rain then caused an 85-minute break in play, which worked wonders for the home side.

Having almost certainly received a dressing-down from an irate Adam Hollioake, who had been heard berating his players during the first period of play, Surrey were suddenly a different side when play resumed. After Martin Bicknell (2-35) started the rot by removing Khan for forty-one and Mark Newell for a duck, Saqlain Mushtaq mesmerised the rest of the batsmen with an incredible spell of 7-17 in sixty-six balls. Aided by Ben Hollioake, who disposed of the obdurate Peirce (54), the Pakistan magician transformed a score of 93-0 into 125 all out and ended with career-best figures of 7-30.

With Saqlain having achieved his success through skilful variations rather than any dramatic turn, Surrey provided further evidence that the pitch was perfectly acceptable by reaching 112-2 by the close of the first day and then pressing on to 364 all out - a lead of 239 - on day two. Although Justin Bates enjoyed some personal victories with his off-breaks to finish with 5-100, Alec Stewart (96) and Ali Brown (94) had long since ensured that the Championship leaders would be celebrating their seventh Championship win of the campaign before we reached the final day of the match. This looked increasingly certain when Sussex slumped to 59-4 before stumps were drawn, with Bicknell having single-handedly dismissed poor Newell for a pair and Saqlain having bagged the valuable scalp of Michael Bevan for the second time in the match.

Day three then saw Chris Adams fighting a lone hand as his team sank to defeat shortly after lunch by an innings and 69 runs. The Sussex skipper was desperately unlucky to be left high and dry on ninety-nine out of a total of 170 when Ian Salisbury (2-22) dismissed Mark Robinson to complete the good work done earlier in the innings by Bicknell (4-45) and Saqlain (4-74), who each reached fifty first-class wickets for the season during this innings. As Surrey reflected on their victory, their visitors were left to contemplate the sobering fact that only Khan, Peirce (twice) and Adams had managed to record a double-figure score in the course of the match.

With twenty-four points added to their season's tally, Surrey moved forty points clear at the top of the table, thanks largely to the fixture computer - it had scheduled the Lancashire versus Leicestershire match for a very wet four days in Manchester and given Gloucestershire a week off.

COUNTY CHAMPIONSHIP - TOP OF THE TABLE AT 3RD AUGUST					
	P	W	D	L	PTS
Surrey	12	7	2	3	190
Leicestershire	11	5	6	0	150
Gloucestershire	10	6	1	3	148
Yorkshire	11	4	5	2	148
Lancashire	11	5	5	1	147

Two floodlit Sunday League matches at The Oval - played on a Monday and a Wednesday - now brought everyone back down to earth with a bump. The lights were scarcely needed for the first game as the Sussex Sharks passed the Surrey Lions' pathetic 40-over total of 143-8 with eleven overs to spare, thanks to an unbroken partnership of 115 for the third wicket between Chris Adams (64 not out) and Michael Bevan (39 not out). Then, two days later, Derbyshire came, saw and conquered again as the Lions sank to their twelfth Sunday League defeat of the season, this time by twenty-eight runs. A 9,000-strong crowd was at least able to enjoy the floodlit spectacle this time as Surrey extended the game into the final over on a balmy early August night. They had, however, been hopelessly out of contention for most of their innings after slipping from 96-1 to 139-7 when chasing 246 to win. Michael Slater (58) and Phillip DeFreitas (56) had been the principal contributors to the Derbyshire innings, while Nadeem Shahid (58) and the two Battys, Jon (40) and Gareth (37), provided the best entertainment in the Lions' losing cause.

Having already recorded two limited-overs wins at The Oval, Derbyshire were now aiming for a Championship victory in London SE11 when the four-day game got under way the next day. There was a sensational start to the day, too, when the Surrey team was announced. With Alec Stewart, Mark Butcher and Ian Salisbury playing in the final Test of the series against South Africa at Headingley, and Graham Thorpe having undergone a back operation to finish his season, the club's resources were further stretched by the news that Alex Tudor had a stress fracture of the foot, and Jason Ratcliffe had been suspended for disciplinary reasons. As a result, the 44-year-old Alan Butcher was drafted into the team six years after his final first-class appearance for Glamorgan and twelve years after he had last played for the Surrey first eleven.

On a green-tinged pitch that had been prepared at quite short notice when the original choice of wicket had been deemed to be too dry, the home county eventually prospered after Ian Ward and Nadeem Shahid had fallen to the left-arm spin of Ian Blackwell, and Jon Batty - surprisingly elevated to the top of the order - had been dismissed by Phillip DeFreitas. Striking the ball as cleanly as ever after a shaky start, Ali Brown, with assistance from the Hollioakes, led his side from 57-3 to 198-6, at which point Alan Butcher strode to the wicket to great applause and struck his first ball through the covers for four. Although Butch senior's knock ended when he fell lbw to Kevin Dean (3-34) for twenty-two, he saw Brown through to an excellent century and then, shortly afterwards, received the news that his son had scored his maiden Test century up at

Headingley as England tried to build on their series-levelling victory at Trent Bridge. Meanwhile, at The Oval, Brown was finally caught off Blackwell (5-115) for 132 with the total on 287, but Surrey still managed to secure a third batting point and reach a final total of 333 thanks to thirties from Martin Bicknell and Saqlain Mushtaq. Derbyshire then lost Michael Slater and Michael May as they closed the day on 46-2, trailing by 287 runs.

Day two saw Surrey taking control of the match, as the visitors slipped from a high point of 62-2 to 139 all out, with Ben Hollioake bowling at a lively pace to return career-best figures of 4-36, and the other six wickets being shared between the equally impressive Bicknell (3-48) and Saqlain (3-42). Although the Championship leaders had secured a 194-run advantage, Adam Hollioake elected not to enforce the follow on, since the pitch was already taking spin and would clearly offer more to Saqlain and Rupesh Amin later in the game. This decision still appeared to be the right one, even though Surrey struggled in their second knock, reaching 148-7 by stumps, with no batsman passing twenty-seven and Alan Butcher making a dozen in what was, presumably, his last innings in first-class cricket.

The third morning's play then sealed Derbyshire's fate as James Knott's determined unbeaten forty-one and Bicknell's feisty eighty-one wiped out any lingering hopes the visitors might have had of pulling off a sensational victory and allowed the Surrey captain to declare at 238-9.

Chasing a theoretical 433 to win, the opening pair of Slater and May put together a partnership of ninety-three before the spinners started to take charge. After May (43) and Weston had fallen to Saqlain, Kim Barnett thrashed an Amin long hop to cover with the total at 160, and the innings crumbled away rapidly, with a succession of batsmen seemingly unable to decide whether to attack or resist passively. No other batsman reached double figures and the game was all but over when Slater perished to a fine overhead catch by Saqlain off his own bowling when one short of what would have been a high-class century. The Surrey off-spinner wrapped up a 226-run victory for his side shortly afterwards by trapping Dean lbw, thereby recording new career-best figures (8-65) for the third time in the season.

With Lancashire having beaten Gloucestershire, and Leicestershire having wiped the floor with Somerset - thanks to a nine-wicket haul from James Ormond - Surrey's advantage at the top of the table had grown by just a single point.

COUNTY CHAMPIONSHIP - TOP OF THE TABLE AT 9TH AUGUST					
	P	W	D	L	PTS
Surrey	13	8	2	3	213
Leicestershire	12	6	6	0	172
Lancashire	12	6	5	1	170
Gloucestershire	11	6	1	4	151

Ten days were to elapse between the demolition of Derbyshire and Surrey's next fixture against a struggling Nottinghamshire side at Trent Bridge. In that time England clinched a 2-1 Test series win over South Africa, thanks in part to a first-innings century from Mark Butcher; Alec Stewart, Adam Hollioake and Ali Brown were selected for the Emirates Triangular Tournament against South Africa and Sri Lanka; and wins for Lancashire and Gloucestershire in the Championship kept them very much in contention for the title.

The loss of four batsmen, plus Alex Tudor, who was likely to be out for the rest of the season, again stretched Surrey's resources in Nottingham, where Mark Butcher led the side and James Knott came into the team as a specialist batsman at number six. Having won the toss and invited their hosts to bat on a green wicket clearly designed to nullify the threat of Saqlain and Salisbury, Surrey's three seamers, Martin Bicknell (2-64), Joey Benjamin (3-59) and Ben Hollioake (3-45) caused all sorts of problems for the batsmen as Nottinghamshire slumped to 65-5 and then 112-7.

They eventually recovered to post 213, thanks to a gutsy unbeaten sixty-six from Chris Read, a highly promising wicketkeeper who had just turned twenty, but the visitors looked to be in the ascendancy at the close of the first day, having scored eighty-four for the loss of Ian Ward and Jason Ratcliffe.

The next morning, Mark Butcher (77) and Ben Hollioake (34) extended their third-wicket stand to ninety-three to establish a fine position for the Championship leaders at 130-2 before their departures, plus the loss of Knott for a duck, left the game back in the balance at 160-5. Nadeem Shahid's sixty-four, in an 85-run partnership with Jon Batty, then re-established Surrey's advantage until the brilliant run out of the visitors' wicketkeeper by Paul Strang set off a collapse that saw Andy Oram (4-37) tidy up the tail in a most efficient manner, leaving the visitors all out for an ultimately disappointing total of 270.

The loss of two batting points was soon forgotten, though, as Bicknell (3-51) and Hollioake set about dismantling Nottinghamshire's second innings in the remaining twenty-eight overs of the day. Grabbing three wickets apiece, they seemingly decided the contest in Surrey's favour by dumping their hosts in a deep hole at 79-7.

With Nottinghamshire unable to extend their advantage beyond sixty-eight before Ben Hollioake - completing career-best figures of 4-28 - and Joey Benjamin (2-21) polished off the innings, Surrey managed to wrap up a seven-wicket victory shortly after lunch on day three. Although the green Trent Bridge pitch had indeed kept the spinners out of the game, with Saqlain delivering just fourteen overs and Ian Salisbury remaining unemployed, it had certainly done the hosts no favours. The quality and preparation of pitches around the country clearly needed to be improved, since this was the sixth consecutive Championship match involving Surrey that had ended inside three days.

The position at the top of the table had scarcely changed during this round of matches since all the other title contenders had matched Surrey by winning their games.

COUNTY CHAMPIONSHIP - TOP OF THE TABLE AT 23RD AUGUST					
	P	W	D	L	PTS
Surrey	14	9	2	3	235
Lancashire	14	8	5	1	212
Leicestershire	13	7	6	0	196
Gloucestershire	13	8	1	4	195
Yorkshire	13	5	5	3	178

The team was then spared further meaningless Sunday League action when the jinxed Surrey versus Nottinghamshire fixture was abandoned for the third successive season. The 'loss' of two points was significant for the Lions, however, since it secured the wooden spoon for the 1996 champions.

Another week of inactivity followed for Surrey before the start of their next Championship match - against Yorkshire at Headingley - and in that time Leicestershire annihilated Nottinghamshire to move into second place in the table with 220 points. While Lancashire, like Surrey, had a week off, Gloucestershire picked up just seven points as they lost to Somerset, and Yorkshire squeezed home by one wicket against Essex at Scarborough. Once these points were added in to the table, it appeared that Gloucestershire, in fourth position on 202 points, and Yorkshire, just behind them on 201, were out of contention for the title as they had too much ground to make up on the top three sides.

With everyone bar the injured Thorpe and Tudor available, Surrey must have been feeling confident that they could produce a better display at Headingley than they had done in the Sunday League game earlier in the season. It also seemed highly significant that Yorkshire would be without their star overseas batsman, Darren Lehmann, who had left to join an Australian training camp, as well as the injured Darren Gough, though, on the credit side of the balance sheet, Craig White was fit to return to action after three months out with back problems.

Since Yorkshire were much the stronger of the two sides in the seam bowling department everyone was expecting to see a green, and slightly 'sporty', surface once the match got under way and they weren't to be disappointed. After a first-day washout had left players and spectators frustrated, the removal of the covers on the second morning revealed a strip that was barely distinguishable from the rest of the square, though Surrey could hardly complain, having played a couple of games on used, spinner-friendly tracks at The Oval. The visitors then won what seemed to be a vital toss but failed to take advantage of their good fortune as Yorkshire reached 150-2, largely through the determined efforts of Craig White, who opened the innings and made fifty-five, and David Byas, who scored fifty-two. Although they collapsed, late in the day, from 214-4 to 247-9 in the face of some steady bowling from Mark Butcher (4-41) and the Hollioakes, who each claimed two scalps, Yorkshire already looked to have a decent total on the board. Byas then declared as soon as his side had secured a second batting point at 250-9 and left the Surrey openers to face six overs, four of which they survived before bad light ended play at 17-0.

Day three always looked as if it could prove pivotal to the contest, and it went well for the visitors, initially, as Mark Butcher and Ian Ward extended their opening partnership to eighty. The innings went into swift decline, however, once the first-change seamers - Gavin Hamilton, a bowling all-rounder who was enjoying a good run of form, and Matthew Hoggard, a lively 21-year-old outswing bowler - got into their stride. Making full use of the available movement in the air and off the seam, as well as occasional variable bounce, these two ripped through the Surrey batting with remarkable ease, transforming the contest with four wickets before lunch - taken at 98-4 - and another six afterwards to leave the visitors all out for 147, 103 runs in arrears and without a batting point to their name. Hamilton's outstanding bowling earned him career-best figures of 7-50, while Hoggard was scarcely any less impressive in returning 3-18 as Surrey's ten wickets fell for just sixty-seven runs in twenty-eight overs. By the end of the day, Yorkshire had extended their lead by 151 runs for the loss of four wickets, with White playing much more aggressively than he had done in the first innings to reach eighty-two.

On the final morning the England all-rounder went on to complete an excellent century before Byas declared at 196-4, setting his visitors an unlikely target of 300 to win in a minimum of eighty-eight overs. The loss of Butcher, adjudged lbw to Chris Silverwood before a run had been scored, and Ward, to a catch in the gully off the same bowler with the total on eleven, quickly confirmed that a draw was the best Surrey could now aim for. At 47-2, with Shahid and Stewart having restored some stability to the innings, this looked possible, but once Hamilton and Hoggard were paired again the visitors lost four wickets for sixteen runs and appeared to be facing a heavy defeat. Although he was fighting a losing battle, Ben Hollioake (60) proceeded to reel off a stream of glorious boundaries in registering his highest Championship score of the season before being bowled by an unplayable gem of a delivery from Hamilton (4-22). With Silverwood quickly hustling out the tail to finish with 5-30, Surrey were dismissed for 135 by 3.20pm and Hamilton rightly led his team from the field to a standing ovation, having bowled beautifully throughout the game, albeit in favourable conditions, to earn career-best match figures of 11-72.

Since Leicestershire had registered their fourth successive Championship victory by overcoming Warwickshire at Edgbaston, Surrey's sixteen-week leadership of the table had been brought to an end. Wins for Lancashire and Gloucestershire, on top of Yorkshire's well deserved 164-run success at Headingley, had left Keith Medlycott's team in danger of being swamped at the last, while the final match of the season, at home to the Foxes, was increasingly looking like a potential title decider.

COUNTY CHAMPIONSHIP - TOP OF THE TABLE AT 4TH SEPTEMBER					
	P	W	D	L	PTS
Leicestershire	15	9	6	0	244
Surrey	15	9	2	4	239
Lancashire	15	9	5	1	236
Gloucestershire	15	9	1	5	223
Yorkshire	15	7	5	3	223

Frustratingly, Surrey had to return to The Oval to fulfil a Sunday League fixture before heading north again to play Durham at Chester-le-Street in their penultimate Championship match. It proved to be a pretty featureless contest, too, though it did provide the Lions with their second win of the summer. After being put in to bat, the Lions mustered 183-8 - with Jon Batty providing the top score of 38 not out from number seven in the order - then Kent fell foul of Micky Bell (3-36) and Adam Hollioake (4-18) as they ended up forty-one runs short of their hosts' total.

With the inconvenient Sunday League game out of the way, Surrey made their way to the very attractive Riverside ground hoping that the September weather in the north-east would be kind to them. They had been boosted by the news that Saqlain Mushtaq would be available for the final match against Leicestershire - earlier reports had suggested that he would be required by Pakistan for the Sahara Cup games against India in Toronto - and were able to field a full-strength side with the exception of Thorpe and Tudor.

Fortunately, only eleven overs were lost to rain on an opening day that saw Surrey win the toss and post a total of 323, thanks principally to two eighty-plus partnerships, the first between Ali Brown (51) and Ben Hollioake (34) and the second between Adam Hollioake (67) and Martin Bicknell (39 not out).

Having reached 32-0 by the close of day one, Durham had only progressed as far as 72-1 by the end of a second day that was wrecked by rain. This turned out to be a very bad twenty-four hours for Keith Medlycott's team, since Leicestershire were already looking certain to record a maximum-points win over bottom-of-the-table Essex. It was now essential for Surrey to find a way of winning their match.

That began to look increasingly unlikely, however, as day three at The Riverside was again badly truncated by rain. Play was suspended six overs after lunch, with John Morris having completed an impressively fluent century while guiding Durham to 231-3, and abandoned at 4.30pm, leaving Leicestershire holding all the aces in the title race. The Foxes had recorded a crushing victory over Essex, as expected, and were twenty-five points ahead of Surrey. A three-point draw would now be no use to Adam Hollioake's men, so they had to pray for good weather and some collusion with Durham's David Boon on the final day of the match if they were to retain a realistic chance of claiming that elusive Championship crown.

Although the previous evening's weather forecast had been dreadful, and a hefty shower had hit Chester-le-Street in mid morning, play got under way just an hour late, at 11.30am, on day four. It was soon evident that the two captains had indeed put their heads together while waiting for the action to start, since Jon Batty was immediately handed the ball and gifted Durham the twenty-two runs they required to gain the point that secured their best-ever County Championship placing of fifteenth. The hosts - in the form of Jon Lewis and David Boon - then generously donated 142 runs to the Surrey cause in 15.4 overs, before the sides arrived at the agreed target of 213 in a minimum of sixty-one overs. This looked to be weighted hugely in the home side's favour, but Adam Hollioake had been in no position to drive a hard bargain, knowing that his team desperately needed to win the match.

It was only when Martin Bicknell and Joey Benjamin started to bowl with a new ball that the full effects of the pitch having been covered for the best part of two days became obvious. With added assistance from overcast skies, they found plenty of encouragement off the pitch and through the air and, consequently, after a twenty-run opening stand between Lewis and Morris, began to tear into the Durham batting line-up. Supported by fine fielding, including a brilliant catch by Alec Stewart at second slip, Benjamin proved to be particularly lethal in capturing five wickets as the hosts crashed dramatically to 58-8 at tea.

Although time was now on Surrey's side, banks of slate grey clouds were rolling in towards the ground and threatening their victory prospects. After a tea break that felt considerably longer than twenty minutes, Benjamin quickly claimed a sixth victim with the score unchanged, but the last-wicket pair of John Wood and Steve Harmison proved hard to shift as drizzle began to fall. Eight overs of calculated hitting from the former and dogged defence from the latter caused much anxiety in the visitors' ranks before Ben Hollioake's belated entry into the attack, with the drizzle turning to rain, did the trick for the Championship chasers. His eleventh delivery turned out to be a fine yorker that shattered Wood's stumps, sealing a totally unexpected 121-run triumph with a theoretical twenty-three overs to spare, but potentially many fewer because of the rain and poor light. Surrey celebrations knew no bounds as the veteran Benjamin was applauded from the field with fantastic figures of 6-35 to his credit and his side still alive and kicking in the Championship race.

With the top five sides all winning, there was no real change in the standings, though Yorkshire and Gloucestershire were now out of the running. The 1998 County Champions would be either Leicestershire, Surrey or Lancashire.

COUNTY CHAMPIONSHIP - TOP OF THE TABLE AT 14TH SEPTEMBER					
	P	W	D	L	PTS
Leicestershire	16	10	6	0	268
Surrey	16	10	2	4	259
Lancashire	16	10	5	1	257
Yorkshire	16	8	5	3	247
Gloucestershire	16	10	1	5	244

Before departing for London to prepare for the big showdown with the Foxes at The Oval, Surrey ended their Sunday League season in style with a 101-run triumph over their seventeeth-placed hosts. After the Lions had built an impressive total of 237-6 around knocks of fifty-eight from Alec Stewart and eighty-five not out from Mark Butcher, Durham got away to a shocking start against Joey Benjamin (2-22) and Ben Hollioake and were never in the hunt thereafter. David Boon battled hard for his forty-seven before falling to Ian Salisbury, who then polished off the tail to return figures of 3-15.

SUNDAY LEAGUE TABLE 1998							
		P	Pts	W	L	T	A	NRR
1	Lancashire	17	54	12	2	0	3	12.18
2	Warwickshire	17	42	9	5	0	3	4.23
3	Essex	17	42	9	5	1	2	1.27
4	Leicestershire	17	40	9	6	0	2	15.13
5	Kent	17	38	8	6	0	3	1.19
6	Gloucestershire	17	36	7	6	0	4	-1.65
7	Worcestershire	17	36	7	6	1	3	-4.60
8	Hampshire	17	34	8	8	0	1	0.95
9	Yorkshire	17	34	8	8	0	1	-2.47

10	Glamorgan	17	32	7	8	0	2	-0.25
11	Nottinghamshire	17	32	7	8	1	1	-0.67
12	Middlesex	17	32	7	8	0	2	-4.90
13	Northamptonshire	17	32	6	7	1	3	2.80
14	Somerset	17	30	6	8	1	2	-0.10
15	Derbyshire	17	30	6	8	0	3	-5.10
16	Sussex	17	28	6	9	0	2	-1.84
17	Durham	17	24	4	9	1	3	-7.89
18	Surrey	17	16	3	12	0	2	-8.17

During the game at The Riverside, the club had received bad news - Saqlain Mushtaq was, after all, required by Pakistan in Toronto and would therefore miss what was to be the 'winner takes all' Championship decider. From Surrey's point of view it was good that Lancashire were still capable of snatching the title by winning their final match, since it meant that Leicestershire couldn't opt to play for a draw at The Oval.

Come the morning of the match, the home county's team included Graham Thorpe, who had made a surprisingly quick recovery from his back operation; Rupesh Amin, as the replacement for Saqlain; and Alec Stewart as wicketkeeper, taking the gloves from poor Jon Batty, who had been one of only two ever-presents in the Championship side until this match. Leicestershire - who could boast five ever-presents and three men who had missed just one game - were able to field their eleven of choice and then drew first blood by winning the toss and electing to bat.

The opening session of the game saw Surrey holding sway, with the seamers removing Maddy, Wells, Sutcliffe and Simmons for 125 runs, but thereafter it was a different matter as Ben Smith and Aftab Habib, who had come together with the total at 102, began to dominate. During the afternoon the hosts were further handicapped by the retirement of Martin Bicknell, who had suffered a knee injury after delivering thirteen overs, and this left the attack with a very threadbare look. With no Bicknell, Tudor and Saqlain - three-quarters of the first-choice bowling line-up - and Ian Salisbury not at his best after three disappointing and confidence-sapping Test match performances, Surrey seemed powerless to stop the Foxes' fifth-wicket pair, both of whom completed excellent centuries before the close of play. At 349-4, the visitors were in full control of the match and Surrey's Championship dreams were already fading away.

Although Smith and Habib were only able to extend their record-breaking stand by five runs, to 252, on the second morning before Ben Hollioake (3-106) had Habib (114) caught behind, any prospects of this triggering a significant collapse were soon scotched by a determined Paul Nixon. In the company of the very impressive Smith, the Leicestershire wicketkeeper built another significant partnership to finally grind Surrey's hopes into the dust. After the former was finally dismissed for a career-best 204 with the total on 480, the latter, supported by an aggressive Chris Lewis (54 not out), made his way steadily to a century that heralded a declaration at 585-6.

With twenty-one overs left to bat, and 436 runs needed to avoid the follow-on, the home county's tired players soon became easy prey for fresh and fired-up Foxes' bowlers. The extent of the devastation wreaked by the visitors was, however, quite incredible - Mark Butcher, Graham Thorpe and Nadeem Shahid all departed for ducks and Surrey didn't register their first run until the seventh over. The hosts' nightmare then continued when Ali Brown fell lbw to David Millns with the total on eight, and it was a blessed relief when bad light ended play for the day twelve overs early. At 13-4, with Millns and Alan Mullally having taken two wickets apiece, Surrey were looking down and out.

Although Alec Stewart and Adam Hollioake managed to advance the score to seventy-nine before being parted on the third morning, another dismal collapse to 85-8 followed, during which Leicestershire deservedly clinched their second Championship title in three years. With

Lancashire having missed out on all four batting points in their match, the Foxes knew that an 11-point draw would be good enough for them to claim the crown and, since they clearly couldn't lose this match, the capture of their third bowling point, which came when Vince Wells won an lbw verdict against Ian Salisbury, represented the moment of triumph. James Whitaker, the injured Leicestershire skipper who had missed most of the season, hobbled delightedly out to the middle with champagne and joined in his team-mates' celebrations before allowing them to continue their march to victory in the match. After dismissing Surrey for 146, despite a defiant unbeaten forty-six from Ben Hollioake, the new champions unsurprisingly enforced the follow on and were soon running through the dispirited home team's batting line-up again. There were only three periods of resistance - when Butcher and Ben Hollioake produced an opening stand of forty-seven; while Adam Hollioake (53) and Bicknell were adding seventy-one for the eighth wicket; and when the last pair of Hollioake and Rupesh Amin appeared to be dragging the contest into an unwanted fourth day. Eventually, in very poor light, Amin surrendered himself to a stumping off Matthew Brimson (3-62) with the total on 228, handing victory to the visitors by an innings and 211 runs. This was Surrey's heaviest defeat of the twentieth century and their worst ever humiliation in a home match. Leicestershire, meanwhile, had ended their Championship season with a sensational run of eight wins in nine games, with seven of those victories yielding maximum points, and it was typical of them that the twenty Surrey wickets in the decisive fixture had been shared around between six different bowlers. They were worthy champions and celebrated their triumph gleefully on the committee balcony at The Oval while the supporters and players of Surrey drifted away, wondering where it had all gone wrong.

	COUNTY CHAMPIONSHIP TABLE 1998						
		P	Pts	W	D	L	Bat	Bwl
1	Leicestershire	17	292	11	6	0	47	51
2	Lancashire	17	277	11	5	1	30	56
3	Yorkshire	17	269	9	5	3	47	63
4	Gloucestershire	17	267	11	1	5	23	65
5	Surrey	17	261	10	2	5	38	57
6	Hampshire	17	202	6	6	5	27	61
7	Sussex	17	201	6	4	7	30	63
8	Warwickshire	17	200	6	3	8	35	60
9	Somerset	17	192	6	4	7	30	54
10	Derbyshire	17	191	6	4	7	28	55
11	Kent	17	178	5	7	5	18	59
12	Glamorgan	17	176	4	7	6	36	55
=	Worcestershire	17	176	4	7	6	32	59
14	Durham	17	158	3	5	9	30	65
15	Northamptonshire *	17	146	4	8	5	31	52
16	Nottinghamshire	17	140	3	4	10	20	60
17	Middlesex	17	130	2	6	9	28	52
18	Essex	17	118	2	4	11	16	58
* 25pts deducted for producing a substandard pitch								

One match had, ultimately, decided the way that Surrey's season was viewed. Had they beaten Leicestershire to claim their first Championship title since 1971, it would have been lauded as a great campaign. Having lost the match and finished fifth, however, it ended up being regarded as a disappointing summer, with dismal performances in the Sunday League and Nat West Trophy balancing out a good, but ultimately unsuccessful, Championship campaign and a rather unfortunate defeat in the Benson & Hedges Cup semi-final. Surrey could have few complaints about finishing fifth in the four-day competition, since they had lost to all of the four counties who finished above them in the final table, with the defeat at Cheltenham felt by many to have been the turning point in the season. Had Adam Hollioake's team secured the victory over Gloucestershire that had looked to be there for the taking then they might well have proved unstoppable. In the final analysis, the seam bowling and batting hadn't been good enough, especially away from home, where four of the five Championship defeats had been sustained. To neutralise the Saqlain-Salisbury spin combination, most counties had produced a green, or slightly damp, surface that had shown up Surrey's lack of regular and effective back-up to the admirable Martin Bicknell. Although the youthful Ben Hollioake and Alex Tudor had, generally speaking, made encouraging progress, the 37-year-old Joey Benjamin - Durham deeds excepted - had looked to be in decline, while Micky Bell had been a real disappointment, never really doing enough in the second eleven to earn a first-team place. On the batting front, the absence of Darren Bicknell had been felt, while international calls had made life difficult, causing constant changes in personnel and the players' positions in the order. Ian Ward had made the most of his increased opportunities, however, and looked capable of claiming a regular place in the side in 1999.

As far as the limited-overs competitions were concerned, the fall from top to bottom in the Sunday League in just two seasons was remarkable, though probably explained by the fact that the team's efforts had been concentrated almost totally on the Championship once the 40-overs campaign had got off to such a disastrous start. Having said that, some of the performances were wholly unacceptable and deserved condemnation. The loss of two fine limited-overs all-rounders - Brendon Julian and Chris Lewis - in the space of two years had clearly been a major blow to Surrey in that form of the game, and it also hadn't helped the team's cause that Ali Brown, who had been excellent in four-day cricket, surprisingly struggled in the Sunday League, scoring just 209 runs from fourteen innings... which was just six more than he'd made in that one epic knock against Hampshire the previous season!

1998 SEASON SUMMARY

COMPETITION	P	W	D/A	L	POSITION/PROGRESS
County Championship	17	10	2	5	5th
Sunday League	17	3	2	12	18th - Relegated
Nat West Trophy	3	2	0	1	Quarter-final
Benson & Hedges Cup	7	6	0	1	Semi-final
TOTAL	44	21	4	19	No Trophy

1998 RESULTS SUMMARY

17/4	NORTHAMPTONSHIRE	OVAL	CC	Match Drawn
19/4	NORTHAMPTONSHIRE	OVAL	SL	Match Abandoned
23/4	WARWICKSHIRE	OVAL	CC	WON by an inns & 49 runs
26/4	WARWICKSHIRE	OVAL	SL	LOST by 8 wickets
28/4	Hampshire	Southampton	BHC	WON by 48 runs
30/4	GLOUCESTERSHIRE	OVAL	BHC	WON by 7 wickets
4/5	BRITISH UNIVERSITIES	OVAL	BHC	WON by 105 runs
6/5	Kent	Canterbury	BHC	WON by 4 wickets
8/5	SOMERSET	OVAL	BHC	WON by 9 runs
10/5	Yorkshire	Headingley	SL	LOST by 51 runs (D/L)
13/5	Hampshire	Southampton	CC	WON by an inns & 184 runs
17/5	Hampshire	Southampton	SL	LOST by 75 runs
21/5	Somerset	Taunton	CC	LOST by 165 runs

25/5	Somerset	Taunton	SL	LOST by 7 wickets
27/5	LANCASHIRE	OVAL	BHCqf	WON by 5 wickets
29/5	KENT	OVAL	CC	WON by an inns & 30 runs
3/6	WORCESTERSHIRE	OVAL	CC	WON by 79 runs
9/6	Leicestershire	Leicester	BHCsf	LOST by 20 runs
11/6	Essex	Chelmsford	CC	Match Drawn
14/6	Essex	Chelmsford	SL	LOST by 26 runs (D/L)
17/6	Lancashire	Old Trafford	SL	LOST by 4 wickets (D/L)
18/6	Lancashire	Old Trafford	CC	LOST by 6 wickets
24/6	BUCKINGHAMSHIRE	OVAL	NWT	WON by 132 runs
28/6	WORCESTERSHIRE	OVAL	SL	LOST by 1 run
1/7	Glamorgan	Swansea	CC	WON by 6 wickets
5/7	Glamorgan	Swansea	SL	LOST by 107 runs
8/7	Gloucestershire	Bristol	NWT	WON by 52 runs
13/7	LEICESTERSHIRE	OVAL	SL	LOST by 44 runs (D/L)
15/7	MIDDLESEX	GUILDFORD	CC	WON by 280 runs
19/7	MIDDLESEX	GUILDFORD	SL	WON by 1 run
22/7	Gloucestershire	Cheltenham	CC	LOST by 2 wickets
26/7	Gloucestershire	Cheltenham	SL	LOST by 22 runs
28/7	DERBYSHIRE	OVAL	NWTqf	LOST by 5 wickets
30/7	SUSSEX	OVAL	CC	WON by an inns & 69 runs
3/8	SUSSEX	OVAL	SL	LOST by 8 wickets
5/8	DERBYSHIRE	OVAL	SL	LOST by 28 runs
6/8	DERBYSHIRE	OVAL	CC	WON by 226 runs
19/8	Nottinghamshire	Trent Bridge	CC	WON by 7 wickets
23/8	Nottinghamshire	Trent Bridge	SL	Match Abandoned
1/9	Yorkshire	Headingley	CC	LOST by 164 runs
6/9	KENT	OVAL	SL	WON by 41 runs
9/9	Durham	Riverside	CC	WON by 121 runs
13/9	Durham	Riverside	SL	WON by 101 runs
17/9	LEICESTERSHIRE	OVAL	CC	LOST by an inns & 211 runs

COUNTY CHAMPIONSHIP BATTING AVERAGES 1998

	M	I	NO	Runs	HS	Ave	100	50	c	st
A.D. Brown	15	22	1	1036	155	49.33	4	6	20	-
A.J. Stewart	8	12	1	464	96	42.18	-	4	15	-
M.A. Butcher	12	18	1	661	109*	38.88	2	4	10	-
N. Shahid	12	22	3	683	126*	35.94	1	3	13	-
A.J. Hollioake	15	22	2	684	112	34.20	1	4	15	-
J.D. Ratcliffe	9	15	1	449	100	32.07	1	2	2	-
I.J. Ward	10	19	2	529	81*	31.11	-	5	9	-
I.D.K. Salisbury	12	13	2	285	61	25.90	-	3	6	-
B.C. Hollioake	16	24	3	455	60	21.66	-	2	7	-
M.P. Bicknell	17	21	1	433	81	21.65	-	1	5	-
J.N. Batty	16	19	2	351	63	20.64	-	2	39	6
Saqlain Mushtaq	12	15	5	176	45*	17.60	-	-	7	-
J.A. Knott	5	9	3	103	41*	17.16	-	-	1	-
A.J. Tudor	10	13	3	167	48	16.70	-	-	3	-
J.E. Benjamin	8	9	3	57	18*	9.50	-	-	1	-
Qualification: 8 innings										

COUNTY CHAMPIONSHIP BOWLING AVERAGES 1998

	O	M	Runs	W	Ave	BB	10wm	5wi
Saqlain Mushtaq	475.0	136	1119	63	17.76	8-65	3	3
M.P. Bicknell	494.1	141	1340	65	20.61	5-27	-	2
I.D.K. Salisbury	337.0	99	766	36	21.27	7-65	-	2
B.C. Hollioake	248.4	49	792	34	23.29	4-28	-	-
A.J. Tudor	184.2	34	737	29	25.41	5-43	-	1
M.A. Butcher	94.4	22	287	11	26.09	4-41	-	-
J.E. Benjamin	189.1	42	626	22	28.45	6-35	-	1

Qualification: 100 overs, 10 wickets

LIMITED-OVERS BATTING AVERAGES 1998

	M	I	NO	Runs	HS	Ave	100	50	c	st
M.P. Bicknell	20	15	11	198	48*	49.50	-	-	4	-
A.J. Stewart	16	16	0	584	108	36.50	1	3	15	8
G.P. Thorpe	12	11	1	345	85*	34.50	-	3	2	-
I.J. Ward	15	15	1	395	91	28.21	-	3	3	-
J.N. Batty	12	11	5	167	40	27.83	-	-	9	5
A.J. Hollioake	26	25	2	623	88	27.09	-	4	12	-
M.A. Butcher	17	16	3	301	85*	23.15	-	2	8	-
B.C. Hollioake	22	20	1	406	91	21.37	-	2	7	-
A.D. Brown	25	24	0	494	74	20.58	-	1	7	-
I.D.K. Salisbury	19	12	4	146	34*	18.25	-	-	6	-
N. Shahid	19	17	2	271	58	18.07	-	2	4	-
J.D. Ratcliffe	24	21	0	357	80	17.00	-	2	8	-
J.E. Benjamin	25	12	9	22	5*	7.33	-	-	3	-
Saqlain Mushtaq	12	7	1	37	11	6.17	-	-	3	-

Qualification: 6 innings

LIMITED-OVERS BOWLING AVERAGES 1998

	O	M	Runs	W	Ave	BB	4wi	RPO
B.C. Hollioake	140.3	6	758	32	23.69	3-23	-	5.39
I.D.K. Salisbury	125.0	7	586	23	25.48	3-15	-	4.69
Saqlain Mushtaq	98.5	5	397	15	26.47	4-46	1	4.02
A.J. Hollioake	149.3	2	796	30	26.53	4-18	2	5.32
M.P. Bicknell	156.5	9	646	23	28.09	4-38	1	4.12
J.E. Benjamin	186.0	21	747	22	33.95	3-16	-	4.02

Qualification: 40 overs, 10 wickets

6 1999: The Dream Fulfilled

Another quiet close season saw just one major addition to the playing staff, with Gary Butcher leaving Glamorgan to join his elder brother and his father at The Oval. With Darren Bicknell's return from injury sure to add strength to the batting, it was hoped that a squad that was one year older and wiser after the desperately disappointing climax to the 1998 season might be able to go one step further this time around. Adam Hollioake had serious doubts about whether this would be possible, however, for the very good reason that England was hosting the World Cup for the first time since 1983. This meant that all of Surrey's England ODI players, plus Saqlain Mushtaq, were likely to miss the first third of the season, depending on how far the host nation and Pakistan progressed in the competition. Since the Test players would then be absent again during the four matches against New Zealand that followed the World Cup, Hollioake had stated that he didn't expect the current Surrey squad to be seen at their strongest until the 2000 and 2001 seasons. His logic was sound, but everyone at the club was hoping he would be proved wrong.

The biggest change to the domestic game for 1999 was the introduction of the two-division 45-overs-a-side National Cricket League, which replaced the Sunday League. The original intention for matches to be played over the 50-overs-a-side duration used for ODIs had been scrapped, with a compromise length between that and the old 40-overs-a-side of the Sunday League adopted instead. In addition to the introduction of three-up, three-down promotion and relegation - which seemed to be one team too many for divisions of just nine teams - every county had to adopt a nickname for use in the competition, just as Surrey had done with their Lions moniker back in 1997.

In the County Championship, the points system had been amended in an attempt to stop sides producing 'result' wickets. Green and 'sporty' pitches were, quite rightly, felt to be hindering the development of young players, who were never likely to come across such surfaces in international matches if their career progressed that far. Win points were therefore reduced from sixteen to twelve, with draw points increasing from three to four, so that the value of two high-scoring draws now outweighed the value of a low-scoring victory plus a low-scoring defeat, rather than the other way round. It was hoped that this would discourage those counties who had previously prepared 'result' pitches on the premise that a win and a defeat yielded a better return than two draws. The Championship was to follow the one-day league by splitting into two divisions from 2000, with the top nine sides in the 1999 Championship to form the inaugural first division and the bottom nine to make up the second division. This, in itself, promised a more competitive summer in the four-day competition in 1999.

Finally, as the new season drew nearer, Surrey confirmed that Mark Butcher would captain the side while Adam Hollioake was absent with England's World Cup squad for the first part of the season.

The earliest ever start to a County Championship season saw Surrey hosting Gloucestershire at The Oval from the 13th to 16th April, and, though it was very cold, the weather didn't cause too much disruption. Although Gary Butcher was making his debut, the home team had to do without the services of Adam Hollioake, Alec Stewart and Graham Thorpe, who were all representing England in Sharjah, while the visitors were able to field a full-strength side that included their new signings, Kim Barnett, Jeremy Snape and the Australian all-rounder, Ian Harvey.

On a rain-truncated first day, Surrey's openers, Mark Butcher and Ian Ward, got the team's campaign away to a great start with an unbroken partnership of 124, though neither man lasted long the following morning when Harvey and Mike Smith engineered a collapse. After Butcher went for sixty-eight and Ward for seventy-eight, the home county dipped to 179-5, and needed a reviving stand of sixty-nine by Ben Hollioake (49) and Jon Batty (37) to reassert their authority.

Smith (4-93) then returned to start another slide to 283-9 before Martin Bicknell - surprisingly batting at number eleven - scored an undefeated forty-nine while dominating a last-wicket stand of fifty-nine with Ian Salisbury that enabled Surrey to total 342.

Having captured the wickets of Barnett and Dominic Hewson before the close of day two, the hosts continued to chip away at the Gloucestershire batting the next day, with Bicknell (3-56) and Salisbury putting their visitors in danger of following on at 160-8. Although a brief but violent innings of thirty from Harvey - batting at number ten because of a stiff back - ensured that this possibility was averted, Surrey still managed to secure a first-innings lead of 129 when Smith became the final victim in Salisbury's return of 5-44. Led by a very positive Mark Butcher, who looked in great form as he raced to ninety-eight, the home side then extended their advantage by 159 runs for the loss of five wickets - four of them to the persistent Smith - before stumps were drawn.

After losing Butcher (101) to Smith (5-42) as soon as he had reached his century on the final morning, positive batting from Batty and Gary Butcher allowed their captain to declare with seventy-three runs having been added to the overnight score in just ten overs. This left Gloucestershire to chase a highly unlikely 359 runs to win from a minimum of eighty-four overs, and they were soon in trouble when the openers departed with just seven runs on the board and Salisbury removed Hewson on the stroke of lunch. Thereafter wickets became increasingly hard to come by on a good pitch as the batsmen dug in, with Bicknell's 700th first-class wicket - Mark Alleyne, caught by Batty - being one of only two to fall during the afternoon session.

Matt Windows, unbeaten on fifty-three at tea, then found a perfect ally in Jack Russell to further thwart Surrey's attempts to force victory, and had moved on to ninety-eight when rain at 5pm brought an early closure to a game that the hosts were looking increasingly unlikely to win.

The team now had to travel up to Chester-le-Street for their first National Cricket League Division Two match on April 18th. Cold weather was to be expected in the north-east at that time of the year, so it was not a great shock when hailstones and snow stopped play at one point during the visitors' innings and reduced the match to a 26-overs-per-side affair. Surrey's 175-5 featured a rapid forty-five from Ben Hollioake, plus handy twenties from Ali Brown, Ian Ward and Nadeem Shahid, before the Durham Dynamos, chasing a Duckworth-Lewis revised target of 188, were put on course for victory by David Boon (55) and Jimmy Daley (41). With six wickets in hand and just nineteen runs required from the final three overs the hosts looked almost certain to win, but a clatter of wickets, resulting from suicidal batting and running between the wickets, led to a disastrous collapse from 170-4 to 186 all out and a rather fortunate Surrey victory by two runs.

With the National League campaign away to a winning start for the bookmakers' pre-season favourites, the next stop was New Road, Worcester, for the second County Championship fixture. As had been the case at The Riverside, Surrey were permitted to field their England players in order to give them some practice ahead of the World Cup, so there were several changes to the line-up that had taken on Gloucestershire. Jason Ratcliffe, Nadeem Shahid and Gary Butcher made way for Stewart, Thorpe and Adam Hollioake, though Mark Butcher retained the captaincy in order to maintain continuity.

Unfortunately, no one was to get much practice during four rain-soaked days that saw action only for a limited amount of time on day three. Put in to bat on an unsurprisingly damp pitch, Surrey batted aggressively in an attempt to gather in some batting bonus points, but only mustered one as they were bowled out for 223. Ben Hollioake took the batting honours for the visitors with a hard-hit fifty-five, while 19-year-old Chris Liptrot, who took 5-51 on his home debut, and Stuart Lampitt (4-47) were the bowlers who made the best use of the conditions. Worcestershire then scored 15-1 - with Philip Weston caught behind off Alex Tudor for a duck - before the game was consigned to its watery grave.

Returning to National League action at The Oval against the Northamptonshire Steelbacks, a below-par Surrey side posted just 207-9 from their forty-five overs after electing to bat. Although Tony Penberthy's return of 4-48, which included two wickets at each end of the innings, was significant in taming the Lions, the biggest problem was the inability of a string of batsmen to make a big score after getting a start.

Having lost their skipper, Matt Hayden, early on, Mal Loye put the visitors in the driving seat with a confident knock of fifty-five that enabled them to withstand a mid-innings crisis that saw them stumble to 126-5. With the match back in the balance, Penberthy (47 not out) again turned out to be a rock for the Steelbacks, allowing Graeme Swann the freedom to blast an unbeaten thirty from just nineteen balls to ensure victory by four wickets with ten balls to spare.

Thanks to a quirk of the fixture scheduling, Surrey had an early opportunity to avenge this defeat when they visited Northampton for the County Championship match three days later. With both sides at full strength - bar Alec Stewart, who was absent following a family bereavement - Surrey got away to a flying start after the hosts had elected to bat. Confounded by bounce and movement off what had looked to be a good pitch, the Northamptonshire batsmen struggled to cope with some fine seam bowling from Martin Bicknell, Alex Tudor and Mark Butcher, slumping to 91-7 shortly after lunch. Rob Bailey, who had opened the innings and taken eleven overs to get off the mark, was still battling away, however, and managed to form a vital alliance with Paul Taylor that endured for two-and-a-half hours and took the total on to 208. At this point, with the pitch having eased considerably, Bailey fell lbw to Bicknell (4-48) for seventy-five, leaving Taylor to eke out another forty runs with the tail before being last man out for seventy-one.

Having matched seventy-two of the hosts' 248 runs by the close of day one, for the loss of Ian Ward and the retirement of Nadeem Shahid, who had been struck a nasty blow on the wrist by Devon Malcolm, Surrey progressed nicely to 182-4 at lunch on the second day. This was thanks largely to a determined knock of fifty-two from their stand-in skipper, and a free-flowing undefeated forty-five by Adam Hollioake, who had timed the ball beautifully from the start of his innings. Well supported by brother Ben, Hollioake then manoeuvred his side into a strong position at 232-4 before Dave Follett (3-64) and Malcolm (3-82) claimed two wickets apiece to peg the visitors back to 283-9 and force Shahid, with his left wrist in plaster, to make a brave return to the middle. Although the Surrey man's injury had been confirmed as a broken wrist, he had decided to come out and bat one-handed in an attempt to help his team gain an extra batting point and his club captain secure the five runs he needed to complete his century. Unfortunately, neither goal was achieved as Hollioake was run out for ninety-six in trying to steal a bye to wicketkeeper David Ripley with the total on 286, leaving Surrey with a worthwhile, but ultimately disappointing, lead of thirty-eight runs. By the close of the day, Northamptonshire were ninety runs to the good, though they had lost Matt Hayden, who drove his first ball straight to mid-off, and Mal Loye, who made an attractive forty-seven before falling to a brilliant catch by Ben Hollioake in the gully.

A fascinating contest swung one way and then the other throughout day three. It started with Tudor claiming two early wickets during a fine, pacy spell, before David Sales and Tony Penberthy looked to have put the hosts back in the ascendancy with a 111-run stand that took the score up to 245-4 at lunch. Then, after the break, Tudor's second two-wicket burst of the day, which included the scalp of Sales for sixty-nine, tilted the balance back towards Surrey, only for the gutsy Penberthy to find an equally determined partner in Ripley. This combination added fifty-six seemingly vital runs as the impressive Tudor (5-64), who had looked to be the only truly penetrative bowler on a pitch that had flattened out considerably, finally ran out of steam. The visitors were fortunate, therefore, that Bicknell, armed with the new ball, came to the rescue in their hour of need, bowling Penberthy for a well-constructed eighty-eight and swiftly dealing with the tail to finish with figures of 4-78.

With Northamptonshire having subsided from 316-6 to 338 all out, Surrey were left to chase 301 to win in four sessions, and the first of these clearly belonged to the visitors as they reached 112-1 by stumps. After Butcher had fallen to Malcolm with the total on thirty, Ian Ward (35 not out) and Graham Thorpe (52 not out) put together a fine stand of eighty-two that gave their side a better than even chance of registering a first Championship victory of the season on the final day.

The pre-lunch session on day four proved decisive as the Ward-Thorpe stand extended to 147 before Ward was bowled by Graeme Swann for sixty-three. Unfazed by his partner's departure, Thorpe went on to complete a marvellous 162-ball hundred before lunch, by which time Ali Brown had helped him take Surrey to within seventy-one runs of their target. With Northamptonshire's spirit now broken, it was no surprise that victory was achieved without any further loss of wickets within an hour of the restart. Thorpe (138 not out) and Brown (66 not out) had every reason to feel satisfied as they left the field to a fine ovation from the visiting supporters, having secured Surrey's first Championship win at Wantage Road since 1982.

Following a day off to savour their success at Northampton, the players were back in National League action, and there was a surprise in store for them... after three consecutive abandonments in the short-course form of the game between 1996 and 1998, the Nottinghamshire Outlaws and the Surrey Lions finally made it out onto the park!

With his England men having departed for the duration of the World Cup, Mark Butcher won the toss at Trent Bridge, invited the home side to bat and then saw them overcome some fine bowling from Ian Salisbury and Ben Hollioake (3-47) to reach 237-8. This was a much better score than had been envisaged when Alex Wharf (38 not out) and Mark Bowen (22 not out) had come together at 179-8 and it proved to be too good for the Lions. Having looked comfortable in making their way to 69-1 through Ali Brown and Hollioake, Surrey were reduced to 81-6 by a four-wicket blast by Bowen (4-46) that appeared to have decided the contest. Ian Ward, with an excellent eighty from number six in the order, had certainly not given up hope, though, and shared in stands of sixty-seven with Gary Butcher (33) and seventy with Alex Tudor (28) before the latter's needless run out allowed the Outlaws to seal an 11-run triumph.

After a couple of World Cup warm-up matches that saw less-than-enthusiastic Surrey line-ups hammered by both New Zealand (108 runs) and the West Indies (88 runs), the team faced the more serious business of a County Championship encounter with Essex at The Oval. The hosts were forced to make a number of changes to the line-up that had triumphed at Northampton, owing to the absence of their England men and the injury to Nadeem Shahid. These included the return of Darren Bicknell, who was making his first Championship appearance since September 1997, and the inclusion of a second spinner in Rupesh Amin.

On a rain-affected opening day, Essex's Paul Prichard was very much to the fore, compiling an impressive 103 as his side posted 216-5 against some rather lacklustre Surrey bowling after winning the toss. There were no complaints about the bowling of Ian Salisbury (3-49) and Mark Butcher (3-18) on day two, however, as they swept through the visitors' lower order to leave Essex all out for 262 and put their side in the driving seat... or so it seemed. Under overcast skies, the Essex seamers created havoc, reducing the home side to 116-7 after Mark Butcher (39) had battled gamely at the top of the order, and it was only thanks to the efforts of Alex Tudor (33) and Martin Bicknell (27 not out) that Surrey were able to reach 195 before being bowled out just before the close of play.

The hosts then continued their fightback on day three, as Bicknell and Tudor removed Prichard, Robinson and Flanagan to put their visitors in a spot of bother at 43-3, and Ben Hollioake followed up by claiming the scalps of Irani and Grayson shortly before the score reached three figures. Stuart Law had looked in menacing form while completing a 57-ball half-century, however, so it was understandable that Surrey were mightily relieved when their captain brought himself into the attack and had the Queenslander caught behind for sixty-four with the total standing at 136. Hopes that a flimsy lower order might fold quickly were dashed, though, as wicketkeeper Barry Hyam (51) survived three dropped catches to register a maiden first-class fifty while supervising a period of resistance that pushed the Essex lead up to 261 with three wickets standing. With the game seemingly slipping away from Surrey at this point, it was just as well that Tudor (4-42) made a timely return to the attack to mop up the tail and leave the visitors all out for 204.

Requiring 272 - the highest score of the match - to claim victory, the home team were given a flying start by Butcher and Ward, who put on sixty-six before Peter Such and Paul Grayson took advantage of the wearing surface to capture three wickets and leave the game nicely poised when time was called at 110-3.

On the final morning the loss of the overnight batsmen - Jason Ratcliffe and nightwatchman Ian Salisbury - for the addition of just two runs, immediately put Surrey on the back foot and made Essex red-hot favourites to win. Ali Brown maintained a positive approach, however, seeing off the seamers in the course of completing a 58-ball fifty and dominating a sixth-wicket stand of eighty-seven with Ben Hollioake that regained the initiative for the home side. After his partner had been given out caught behind, Brown received further valuable support from Jon Batty as he advanced to a magnificent 148-ball century and piloted his team to a first County Championship triumph over Essex since 1991.

This win had added significance, since it moved Surrey to the top of the table almost exactly a year to the day since they had taken the lead in the 1998 Championship.
LEADING POSITIONS:- Surrey P4, Pts 50; Hants P3, Pts 49; Middx P4, Pts 49.

Although everything was going well in the four-day game, Surrey needed to get their National League campaign back on track quickly if they were to achieve their stated pre-season goal of gaining immediate promotion to the top echelon of the one-day league. Taunton - never a happy hunting ground for the county in the limited-overs game - was therefore not the best of venues for the Lions' next match, and memories of past disasters at the County Ground were soon recurring as the visitors slumped to a dismal 3-3 within ten balls of being put in to bat. From this hopeless position, they did pretty well to scrape together 184-9 against Somerset's seven seamers, but this never looked to be a challenging total despite the capture of two early wickets. Peter Bowler (70) and Rob Turner (63), both regular run-scorers against Surrey, sealed the visitors' fate with a 115-run third-wicket partnership that enabled the Sabres to cruise home with six wickets and thirty-nine balls in hand.

In a repeat of the situation when they played Northamptonshire, the fixture list granted Surrey an immediate opportunity to take revenge in a Championship match, as Somerset were the next visitors to The Oval. Having missed the round of matches that followed their win over Essex, the county's reign at the top of the table had been a short one and they found themselves in fifth place to Somerset's fourth as the visitors won the toss and opted to bat. After trouncing Leicestershire in their previous game, the cidermen must have been full of confidence, but this was soon undermined by Martin Bicknell (4-72), who picked up the wickets of Cox, Holloway and Trescothick by the time the total had reached thirty. On a good pitch, the batsmen continually found ways to get themselves out against keen Surrey bowling and fielding, with only Rob Turner (67) showing the required discipline as Ian Salisbury (3-35) and Ben Hollioake (2-26) mopped up the tail to leave Somerset one run short of a batting point. The visitors' total of 199 was then left looking wholly inadequate as their hosts progressed comfortably to ninety-four for the loss of Mark Butcher by the close.

Day two saw Surrey piling on the runs, with Ian Ward (76) and Jason Ratcliffe (86) enjoying big partnerships with Darren Bicknell, who laid the foundations on which his team could build a huge first-innings lead by scoring a chanceless 114 on only his second Championship appearance after his return from back surgery. Having scored steadily up until tea, the home side increased their run rate during the final session of the day, thanks largely to cameo knocks from Ali Brown (42) and Ben Hollioake (36) that enabled Surrey to close on 425-8.

The overnight pair of Salisbury and Bicknell then exceeded expectations by extending their partnership from thirty-four to 122 on the third morning before the latter ran himself out for sixty-nine with the total on 513. Salisbury took this as a cue to expand his repertoire of strokes and, almost before he knew it, he had surpassed his previous best score and was on the verge of a maiden first-class century. Receiving ideal passive support from last man Rupesh Amin, the Surrey leg-spinner eventually ran a delivery from Jason Kerr to third man for the single that took him to a treasured ton from 117 balls and brought an instant declaration at 558-9.

Although they held a massive 359-run advantage, the home team were soon reminded that there was plenty of hard work ahead of them on a slow turning pitch as Jamie Cox (54) and Marcus Trescothick (76) put on 132 for the first wicket. Amin accounted for them both during an excellent spell, however, and with Salisbury following up by bamboozling Holloway, the close of play arrived at 192-3, with Surrey still looking capable of securing a well deserved victory on the final day.

After the loss of Michael Burns to Ben Hollioake (2-58) for twenty-seven early the next morning, further determined defiance from Keith Parsons and Rob Turner saw Somerset through to lunch at 274-4, with their hopes of snatching a draw rising. Martin Bicknell's rapid removal of Parsons for seventy-seven after the break gave the home side a lift, however, before another frustrating stand developed for the sixth wicket. This partnership emulated its two predecessors by exceeding fifty before Amin prised out Turner (68) with a delivery that lifted and turned sharply to revive Surrey's fading hopes. Although the spinners had done much of the work during the day, Mark Butcher now made an inspired move by recalling Hollioake to the attack, and the young all-rounder quickly justified this decision by yorking Adrian Pierson for nought with the visitors still trailing by twenty runs. The appearance at number nine of Peter Bowler, who had been confined to bed by illness and a bad back, confirmed that Somerset weren't about to throw in the towel, so the capture of an eighth wicket - that of Jason Kerr, caught behind off Amin for thirty-five - with tea looming was most welcome for the hosts. At the break, the visitors were leading by five runs with two wickets standing.

Regular bowling changes after the interval failed to unsettle the ninth-wicket pair of Bowler and Caddick, however, and with banks of dark grey cloud moving in from the north-west Surrey had another potential foe capable of denying them victory. The last sixteen overs of the match had just begun when Salisbury eventually made the breakthrough for his side, having Caddick taken at silly point after nearly an hour-and-a-half of determined resistance, with Somerset leading by thirty-six runs. Further frustration then followed as Matt Bulbeck, a very capable lower-order batsman, helped Bowler run down the remaining overs with the skies continuing to darken and the game looking increasingly likely to end in stalemate. Finally, with the cidermen forty-five runs to the good and just eight overs to be bowled - two of which would be lost for the change of innings - the crunch over arrived and Salisbury knew that he simply had to find a way of capturing the final wicket. Bowler played out the first three deliveries before taking a single from the fourth, leaving Bulbeck to survive the last two balls. The first of these turned harmlessly down the legside but the second was a gem of a googly from round the wicket that spun past the left-hander's defensive bat to hit the top of off stump, sparking celebrations that were only muted by the increasingly threatening skies and the knowledge that the task of scoring forty-seven runs from five overs was a tall order.

It was now up to the batsmen to ensure that the fine efforts of Amin (54-30-87-4) and Salisbury (49-15-95-3) weren't wasted, but by the time Messrs Butcher and Brown emerged from the pavilion regular flashes of lightning were already visible in the distance. With all five bulbs on the 'bad light indicator' aglow on the scoreboard, Surrey quickly lost their skipper to a run out in Caddick's two-run opening over, before Hollioake and Brown each picked up a legside six during a second over, from Kerr, that also included the run out of Hollioake and ended with the score at 18-2. In virtual darkness, with thunder crashing and lightning flashing all around the ground, Jason Ratcliffe then produced an incredible stroke, driving Caddick into the pavilion for six during a third over that yielded eleven runs, and followed up with an edged drive for four in Kerr's next over to leave Surrey needing twelve runs from nine deliveries. With the rain somehow holding off, Ratcliffe picked up a brace of twos with off-side drives from the last three balls of the over, reducing the target to eight runs from Caddick's final over. After a leg-bye had been scampered from the first delivery, Ratcliffe increased his crucial contribution to the run chase to twenty-two runs from thirteen balls by crashing the England paceman's next delivery to the extra-cover boundary, before Caddick took revenge with a superb leg stump yorker that proved unplayable in the Stygian gloom. Since an almighty downpour was looking imminent, Ian Ward rushed out to the crease with Surrey now needing three runs from three balls and Brown - his eyes already attuned to the darkness - desperate to get on strike. Despite being warned twice by Caddick for backing up too far, he still managed to steal a bye to the wicketkeeper from Ward's first ball and then sent his team-mates and the Oval crowd into raptures of delight by whipping the next delivery to the midwicket boundary to seal an incredible seven-wicket victory at the end of a dramatic final day. Within minutes, as the celebrations continued, the heavens opened and a twenty-minute torrential downpour left the outfield flooded. Maybe this was to be Surrey's year?

Victory took the county back up to second place in the table, just behind Hampshire, who had followed a win over Middlesex at Lord's in the previous round of matches with a 261-run mauling on a Trent Bridge green-top that had enabled Nottinghamshire to move up to third.
LEADING POSITIONS:- Surrey P5, Pts 69; Hants P5, Pts 74; Notts P5, Pts 65.

Although England had crashed out of the World Cup after the opening phase of the competition earlier in the week, Surrey decided not to select Messrs Stewart, Thorpe and Hollioake for their next National League game against the Derbyshire Scorpions at The Oval. With the injury-hit visitors forced to field their 39-year-old coach, Colin Wells, plus a couple of unknown seam bowlers, Anthony Woolley and Michael Deane, it appeared that the Lions should be capable of registering their second National League victory without their disappointed England men. The Scorpions fought tooth and nail, however, producing a battling performance in the field that punished a dismal batting effort by the Lions on a tricky pitch and left the hosts all out for a miserable 153. Although Martin Bicknell and Alex Tudor (2-26) did their best to bring their side back into contention by reducing Derbyshire to 48-3, a fourth-wicket stand of seventy-four between Stephen Titchard (44 not out) and Robin Weston (36) proved decisive and left Surrey languishing in eighth place in the table.

A trip to Tunbridge Wells in the County Championship was next on the team's agenda. With their England World Cup players now ruled out by a reception at Buckingham Palace that clashed with the first day of the match, Surrey made one change to the eleven that had beaten Somerset, replacing the unfortunate Rupesh Amin with Joey Benjamin in conditions that looked certain to favour seam bowling. This view was soon confirmed on a showery opening day that ended with Surrey 92-2 after being put in on a difficult pitch that offered exaggerated bounce at one end.

With a lush, slow outfield adding to their problems, the batsmen continued to have a real battle on their hands on day two, though Darren Bicknell clearly relished the challenge as he defied the bowlers for four-and-a-half hours while making a vital fifty-seven from 190 balls. Ben Hollioake

(30) offered excellent support during a fifth-wicket stand of sixty-two but, once these two were dismissed, Surrey needed an eighth-wicket partnership of fifty-eight between Ian Salisbury (38 not out) and Martin Bicknell (27) in order to reach a very creditable total of 271. The nature of the pitch was demonstrated by the fact that the visitors had scored their runs at an uncharacteristically slow rate of just 2.74 an over, while Kent's seamers would have been disappointed that spinner Min Patel (3-59) returned the best figures of the innings.

Alex Tudor and Martin Bicknell certainly intended to enjoy themselves on this surface and they did so in style as they reduced Kent to a sorry 47-7 by the close of play. After Surrey's opening bowlers had captured two wickets apiece by tea, which was taken at 14-4, rain during the final session allowed just nineteen overs of action. The hosts still managed to lose another three batsmen in this time, however, with Tudor dismissing Matt Walker; Bicknell disposing of the dangerous Andrew Symonds; and Ben Hollioake getting in on the act by trapping Matthew Fleming lbw. Surrey were already looking set for another victory, provided that the unsettled weather was kind to them.

That triumph was almost sealed on day three, in fact, as Tudor (5-30) and Bicknell (4-32) wrapped up the home side's first innings for seventy-one to secure a 200-run lead, which on this surface was worth many more runs than that.

Although Kent put up sterner resistance second time around, largely as a result of losing just one wicket during the opening bursts from their first-innings destroyers, the damage had already been done. Surprisingly, the hosts' nemesis in their second knock turned out to be Jason Ratcliffe, whose height enabled him to achieve awesome bounce with his medium-pace deliveries. By picking up the wickets of Key, Walker and Symonds at a personal cost of twenty-eight runs he registered a new career-best performance and opened the door for Bicknell (3-23) and Hollioake to reduce their opponents to 142-8 and put Surrey on the brink of a three-day victory. Although Kent managed to survive the extra half-hour for the loss of Patel to Tudor (2-39), it only took four overs on the final morning for the visitors to sew up their expected emphatic victory by an innings and twenty-eight runs and move back to the top of the Championship table.

LEADING POSITIONS:-   Surrey P6, Pts 87;   Hants P6, Pts 85;   Notts P6, Pts 71; Yorks P6, Pts 71

Surrey's next fixture looked likely to be the toughest of the season - a trip to Grace Road to face Leicestershire, the County Champions, who had made a good start to the campaign and were currently sitting in fifth place in the table, seventeen points adrift of the leaders. Unbeaten at home in the Championship for four years, the Foxes looked sure to be title contenders again, especially as they were seldom affected by international calls and were capable of fielding a settled side.

Just to underline this point, Leicestershire selected the same side that had massacred Surrey at The Oval the previous September, with the exception of the inclusion of Australian paceman Michael Kasprowicz, who had replaced Phil Simmons as their overseas player. Surrey were meanwhile boosted by the return of Graham Thorpe and Adam Hollioake, though Alec Stewart was absent with an injured finger. Surprisingly, Mark Butcher retained the captaincy despite Hollioake's return, and promptly lost a seventh consecutive Championship toss, which resulted in the hosts taking first use of a good-looking pitch.

Up until lunch, taken at 115-4, the play followed a remarkably similar pattern to the sides' previous meeting, but thereafter it took a very different course. After reaching 267-5 through Aftab Habib (60), Chris Lewis (56) and Paul Nixon (33), the Foxes collapsed dramatically to 267-9 and then 272 all out as Alex Tudor followed up a highly effective pre-lunch spell of 3-12 with an even more devastating burst of 4-1 in twelve deliveries. Even though he wasn't always at his best, the big paceman finished with career-best figures of 7-77. Left with sixteen overs to bat at the end of the day, Mark Butcher then tore into the bowling, building on Tudor's efforts by racing to forty-nine as the visitors closed the day on 76-0.

Incredibly, Butcher was still at the crease at the end of the following day, too, having advanced his score to 253 out of a total of 469-7. With their stand-in skipper playing so well it was no surprise that Surrey dominated day two from start to finish, though no other batsman managed to score more than twenty-five after Ian Ward's dismissal for fifty-seven ended an opening partnership of 189. The visitors didn't need any other major contributions, however, as Butcher toyed with a strong attack during a superb exhibition of batsmanship. Messrs Mullally, Kasprowicz, Lewis, Millns, Brimson and Maddy had no answer to brilliant strokeplay that took the England left-hander to three figures from 147 balls, and then past his previous career-best score of 167 on to a maiden double-century that came from his 307th delivery.

Although he fell lbw to Alan Mullally (5-106) after adding just six runs to his score on the third morning, Butcher's 259 went into the record books as the highest score by a Surrey batsman against Leicestershire, and the best tally by an Englishman or a left-hander at Grace Road... as well as putting his side in a great position to end the hosts' unbeaten run on their home ground.

After they were finally bowled out for 501, Surrey were unable to capture a wicket before lunch, though they struck three times shortly afterwards as the hosts dipped from 74-0 to 86-3 against the combination of Tudor and Ian Salisbury. The visitors' leg-spinner continued to trouble the home side during the rest of the afternoon as he bowled unchanged from the pavilion end, but Habib and Nixon batted with great skill to build a partnership that endured beyond tea. Although Nixon (47) was eventually trapped lbw by Salisbury (3-71) in the final hour of the day, no further breakthroughs were forthcoming and Leicestershire made it to the close on 239-4, leading by ten runs, with Habib unbeaten on seventy.

With everything seemingly stacked in Surrey's favour - a new ball due; Vince Wells unlikely to bat after sustaining a nasty eye injury during fielding practice on the second morning; a fragile Leicestershire tail to come - it was particularly galling that rain should wipe out the whole of the final day's play, spoiling what had been a fascinating, hard-fought contest and, probably, denying the Championship leaders a victory that would have been very sweet indeed. Although Surrey's lead at the head of the table had grown by seven points, it could have been so much better had the Leicester weather not come to the champions' rescue.

COUNTY CHAMPIONSHIP - TOP OF THE TABLE AT 12TH JUNE					
	P	W	D	L	PTS
Surrey	7	4	3	0	99
Hampshire	7	3	2	2	90
Yorkshire	7	4	1	2	87
Middlesex	8	3	4	1	87
Warwickshire	7	3	3	1	85

Desperately needing to kick-start their National League campaign, Surrey now made their second visit of the season to Northampton, though this time they were to leave pointless. Despite fielding one of the longest and strongest batting line-ups imaginable they proved incapable of surpassing the Steelbacks' score of 235-8, which was built around knocks of fifty-four and forty-four by David Sales and Russell Warren respectively. Rocked back onto the ropes at 34-3 by Devon Malcolm (3-35) and Paul Taylor, the Lions never fully recovered despite the best efforts of Graham Thorpe (70) and Ben Hollioake (45), and fell six runs short of victory with the highly unlikely last-wicket pairing of Darren and Martin Bicknell at the crease. Having lost five successive games in the 45-overs-a-side league, promotion was already looking to be something of a pipe dream.

A welcome return to four-day cricket then saw Surrey taking on a Lancashire side that was languishing in sixteenth place in the table but looked certain to make rapid advances now that Muttiah Muralitharan had joined them following the World Cup. The controversial, but highly skilled, Sri Lankan off-spinner was fresh from claiming 14-117 against Warwickshire at Southport in his second Championship appearance, having been denied a chance to bowl on his debut at Bristol by almost non-stop rain. Unbelievably, Lancashire had lost the Southport match by nineteen runs, but everyone knew that they would soon be winning games with Murali in their ranks. Although spectators were denied the sight of a spin showdown between the Sri Lankan and Saqlain Mushtaq because Pakistan were still in the World Cup, the game looked likely to be highly competitive as Alec Stewart and Rupesh Amin came into the Surrey side to replace Martin Bicknell, who had suffered a freak 'electrical disturbance' to his heart during the NCL game at Northampton, and the injured Adam Hollioake. Mark Butcher, continuing as captain for an eighth game, again lost the toss and Lancashire chose, predictably, to bat.

Any thoughts that Surrey might struggle in the field without Bicknell and Saqlain were quickly dispelled as Lancashire were dismissed for 194 shortly after tea. The top score of the innings was John Crawley's thirty-six, while no partnership exceeded thirty-seven as Alex Tudor stepped into Bicknell's shoes by claiming 4-60 and Amin did a decent Saqlain impersonation with 2-35 in support of Ian Salisbury's 3-28. With Butcher (40) again looking in great form before falling to Andy Flintoff, and Ian Ward batting sensibly until being defeated by Muralitharan shortly before the close, Surrey certainly held the advantage in the match as they reached stumps at 98-2.

After the early loss of nightwatchman Ian Salisbury to Muralitharan on the second morning, the experienced England combination of Alec Stewart and Graham Thorpe played the Sri Lankan with great skill and gradually guided their side into a strong position. Although Thorpe eventually departed to a slip catch with the total on 186, giving Murali a third wicket in the innings, Surrey managed to press on to 220-4 before Brown appeared to lose patience against the off-spinner as lunch loomed and had his stumps rearranged.

A post-lunch collapse, which began when Stewart, having made an excellent ninety-five, became the third man to be bowled by Muralitharan, saw the hosts slide to 298 all out, two runs short of a third batting point but 104 runs ahead of their opponents' score. The Sri Lankan spin king finished with 6-87 from 41.5 beguiling overs, while Gary Keedy (3-87) worked his way through the tail despite the studied defiance of Darren Bicknell, who made a patient thirty-seven from the unfamiliar position of number seven in the order.

Lancashire then set out to wipe off their arrears through Mike Atherton (52) and Mark Chilton (37), and had almost achieved their objective when Mark Butcher brought himself into the attack and claimed three vital wickets as the day drew to a close. With the Surrey skipper removing both openers and John Crawley at a personal cost of two runs in the space of fourteen deliveries, the visitors slipped from 95-0 to 98-3, allowing their hosts to clamber back into the driving seat as stumps were drawn with just two runs added to the total.

When Alex Tudor then struck three blows of his own the next morning to reduce Lancashire to 120-6, Surrey looked set for a comfortable victory, but Warren Hegg was not about to give up without a fight. Having added thirty-seven for the seventh wicket with Graham Lloyd before the England coach's son became a fourth victim for Butcher, Hegg formed a very valuable alliance with Peter Martin that pushed the total up to 220. At this stage of the proceedings, the home side were feeling a little concerned, so they were most grateful to Rupesh Amin (2-43) when he lured Martin into a foolish charge down the pitch and then followed up by claiming Muralitharan lbw later in the same over. With just Keedy now for company, Hegg adopted a more positive approach, picking up a number of boundaries off Tudor until the tall paceman had his revenge with the new ball, luring the Lancashire captain into a miscued hook with his score on ninety-four and the total 260. Mark Butcher's final return of 4-30 was a career-best, while Tudor's dismissal of Hegg gave him 4-81 and left the Championship leaders requiring 157 to win with just over four sessions of the match remaining.

Although there was no pressure from the clock, Surrey's openers got them away to a flying start and the game was looking all but over at 78-0 in the nineteenth over, with Butcher going well on forty. Muralitharan and Keedy made their presence felt at this point, however, forcing a sudden reappraisal of the situation by claiming two wickets apiece in the space of thirty-one balls to reduce the home side to 85-4. When Ward then fell to Muralitharan for forty-three at 101-5, alarm bells were ringing and the game was wide open once again, with the spinners wheeling away and applying pressure with fielders around the bat. Although Surrey were temporarily put back on track by the sixth-wicket pair of Darren Bicknell and Ben Hollioake, who took the total up to 121 without too many problems, disaster struck from the penultimate ball of the day when the latter was taken at slip off Murali to restore equilibrium to the contest.

The final morning of the match, which started with the home team needing just thirty-six runs to win and the visitors requiring four wickets, served up a few nerve-wracking moments before Bicknell (24 not out) and Jon Batty (23 not out) eventually eased Surrey home without further loss after twenty-four tense and tight overs. One had to feel sorry for Muralitharan, who took 4-67 in the second innings to complete a second successive ten-wicket match for his adopted county yet ended up on the losing side again.

Having emerged triumphant from a fascinating contest, Surrey moved thirteen points clear at the top of the Championship table.

COUNTY CHAMPIONSHIP - TOP OF THE TABLE AT 18TH JUNE					
	P	W	D	L	PTS
Surrey	8	5	3	0	117
Warwickshire	8	4	3	1	104
Hampshire	8	3	3	2	101

Surrey's miserable run in the National Cricket League came to an end in dramatic style when the Glamorgan Dragons visited The Oval on 19th June. This game, in common with the week's other scheduled NCL matches, had been brought forward by a day to avoid clashing with Sunday's World Cup final, and the change suited the Lions nicely as they completed a 143-run win.

Having elected to bat and then lost Alec Stewart and Graham Thorpe early on, Mark Butcher (42) and Adam Hollioake (40) established the base for a decent total at 108-2. Once they were parted, however, a succession of run outs triggered a collapse to 187 all out that seemingly left the hosts facing yet another defeat in the competition.

This view warranted instant reassessment when Martin Bicknell's first-ball dismissal of Matthew Maynard set Surrey off on the right foot, and the Lions never looked back thereafter as the Dragons were slain for a mere forty-four runs in seventeen sensational overs. Ian Bishop, a 21-year old swing bowler formerly on Somerset's books, claimed 3-13 on his first-team debut as a replacement for the injured Alex Tudor, while Bicknell took the major honours by taking 7-30, the best figures ever recorded by a Surrey bowler in limited-overs cricket. Although the ball moved around quite dramatically for the two seamers, it seemed incredible that only Alun Evans (17) had been able to make it to double figures as the Lions duo became only the second pair of bowlers to dismiss a side unassisted in a domestic limited-overs game, matching the achievement of Keith Boyce and John Lever against Middlesex in 1972.

Having been a member of the Pakistan side that had been hammered by Australia in the World Cup final at Lord's, Saqlain Mushtaq found himself facing Scotland in the Nat West Trophy at the tiny but attractive Grange Cricket Club ground in Edinburgh three days later. Needless to say, he found the Scottish batsmen rather easier to deal with than the Australians, claiming 4-17 as Surrey bowled their hosts out for 147. After Ali Brown departed for a third-ball duck, the visitors cruised home to a simple seven-wicket victory, thanks to Alec Stewart's sixty-four and Graham Thorpe's unbeaten thirty-nine.

With their passage into the next round of the premier knockout cup secured, Keith Medlycott's men then headed off to Bristol to participate in a third different one-day competition in the space of eight days. Their opponents in the Benson & Hedges Super Cup were Gloucestershire, who put Surrey in to bat upon winning the toss and then took full advantage of overcast skies. After the dismissals of Brown and Stewart to Jon Lewis and Ian Harvey (4-42) for thirty-eight, only Graham Thorpe - who was dropped twice on fourteen - got to grips with the conditions, scoring eighty-four of the visitors' rather disappointing total of 220-9. A second-wicket stand of 104 between Kim Barnett (65) and Matt Windows (39) then provided the ideal platform for a Gloucestershire victory after Alex Tudor (2-41) had disposed of Tim Hancock with thirty-five on the board. Once they had seen off the outstanding Saqlain (10-3-19-1), the hosts sauntered home by seven wickets with two overs in hand and Jack Russell undefeated on fifty.

With this cluster of one-day games out of the way, attention turned back to the County Championship, with bottom-of-the-table Durham making the trip down to The Oval to face a Surrey team that showed no fewer than five changes from the eleven that had beaten Lancashire. Out went the four men who had been selected to play for England in the first Test against New Zealand - Mark Butcher, Graham Thorpe, Alex Tudor and Alec Stewart, who had lost the captaincy to Nasser Hussain - and in came the fit-again Adam Hollioake and Martin Bicknell, plus Jason Ratcliffe and Gary Butcher. Additionally, Saqlain Mushtaq replaced the unfortunate Rupesh Amin, who had again bowled well to return match figures of 4-78 against the red rose county.

With Adam Hollioake back in charge of the team, Surrey won their first toss of the season and batted for the whole of the first day to make 335 all out, which included half-centuries from Ian Ward (51), Ben Hollioake (50) and Ian Salisbury (53), as well as five other contributions in the 24-44 range. The 20-year-old Steve Harmison had generated genuine pace and disconcerting bounce from a lively Oval track to return figures of 5-76, while Surrey had been rescued from a rocky 215-7 by a 71-run partnership for the eighth-wicket between Salisbury and Jon Batty.

After a somewhat unsatisfactory opening day that had seen them bat in a rather cavalier fashion, the Championship leaders took a firm grip on the game during the final session of a rain-ravaged second day. All the good work done by John Morris (78) and Jon Lewis (36) in manoeuvring their side into a decent position at 129-1 shortly after tea was undone as Durham subsided to 182-7 against the spin of Salisbury (4-57) and Saqlain.

Neil Killeen, with twenty-nine, was then the only man to offer much resistance as Saqlain (5-72) claimed the last three wickets to tidy up the tail the next morning for the addition of just thirty-five runs.

With a handy lead of 118 to build on, Surrey proceeded to race along at four-an-over during a third-wicket stand of 143 between Jason Ratcliffe (91) and Ben Hollioake (71) that dominated the afternoon session and allowed Adam Hollioake to declare at 247-6 with twenty-two overs left for play. Needing 366 to win, Durham lost Michael Gough and Jimmy Daley to Martin Bicknell and Saqlain respectively before time was called at 32-2, leaving Surrey eight wickets from victory with ninety-six overs to come on day four.

It soon became obvious that the hosts wouldn't need anything like that number of overs to secure victory as they enjoyed another good session the following morning. The game was virtually in the bag, in fact, once the experienced middle-order pair of Morris (22) and David Boon (25) had become two of Saqlain's five pre-lunch victims that left the visitors' innings on the rocks at 129-7. Just sixty-seven balls were then needed after the resumption for Surrey to complete a resounding 226-run victory, with Saqlain removing Graeme Bridge and Simon Brown to complete figures of 7-38 before Salisbury delivered the final blow by having Lewis caught behind for forty-six, thereby preventing him from carrying his bat.

Although Hampshire won their match against Glamorgan to move back into second place, Warwickshire's defeat at Maidstone allowed Surrey to extend their lead in the Championship to sixteen points.

COUNTY CHAMPIONSHIP - TOP OF THE TABLE AT 3RD JULY					
	P	W	D	L	PTS
Surrey	9	6	3	0	136
Hampshire	9	4	3	2	120
Warwickshire	9	4	3	2	108
Leicestershire	9	3	5	1	108

Back in the National League, Surrey next visited Derby for a game against their fellow strugglers, the Derbyshire Scorpions. To everyone's surprise, Alex Tudor - whose unbeaten ninety-nine as nightwatchman had helped England to victory over New Zealand in the first Test the previous day - was included in the Lions' line-up and received a warm ovation from supporters of both sides when he appeared for the pre-match warm-ups. Extra special home applause was reserved for Kevin Dean, however, as he knocked over Surrey's top four batsmen to put the visitors in trouble at 62-4 and return figures of 4-35. The Lions made a great recovery, though, as Ali Brown, supported by Adam Hollioake's forty-five during a 114-run fifth-wicket stand in eighteen overs, powered his way to 105 from just 91 balls and enabled his team to post a total of 238-9. Martin Bicknell (3-27) then almost 'did a Dean' by claiming the first three Scorpions' wickets and starting a fatal slide to 64-5. With no one in their side capable of matching Brown's heroics, the hosts were never in contention as they made their way fairly aimlessly to 174 all out against eight different bowlers, seven of whom took a wicket.

A Nat West Trophy fourth round clash with Worcestershire at New Road followed hot on the heels of Surrey's third NCL victory of the season and produced another win to take Keith Medlycott's men into the quarter-finals. After electing to bat, the home side lost wickets at regular intervals and were consequently never able to break loose against some disciplined Surrey bowling led by Saqlain Mushtaq (3-30), Martin Bicknell (2-32) and Ben Hollioake. Although Graeme Hick's 90-ball knock of sixty-six underpinned the innings, and David Leatherdale contributed thirty-seven, Worcestershire's 204-9 looked a little below par, even on a pitch that had aided the bowlers. When the visitors slipped to 9-2 and then 42-3, the hosts were back in business, however, and it took a brilliant stand of 142 between Graham Thorpe (91 not out) and Mark Butcher (54) to put Surrey back on track and, ultimately, secure a comfortable five-wicket triumph with nineteen balls to spare.

Despite the fact that another round of Championship matches had been played since Surrey's victory over Durham, the leading positions had scarcely changed, which meant that Guildford would be staging a top-of-the table clash between leaders Surrey and second-placed Hampshire, who had been performing above expectations.

They continued their good form, too, on the first morning of the match, as a full-strength home side ran into all sorts of problems after Adam Hollioake had won the toss and elected to bat. Assisted by some very poor shot selection from the Surrey batsmen, Nixon McLean (4-63) and Peter Hartley (4-66) cut swathes through the batting line-up, dismissing half the side for just forty-five runs in a mere nine overs before further reducing their hosts to 74-7. Although the Surrey captain did his best to revive his side during partnerships of forty-three with Alex Tudor and forty with Martin Bicknell, he was eventually left high and dry on sixty-three when Shaun Udal (2-2) came into the attack to terminate the innings with the total on 171.

Memories of how Middlesex had collapsed to 115 all out after Surrey's dismissal for 150 in the previous season's match at Guildford then came flooding back as Bicknell pinned Jason Laney lbw for nought with the first ball of Hampshire's reply. Although Will Kendall also fell to Bicknell with the score advanced only as far as thirty-eight, the home team then found their path to a comeback blocked by the promising Derek Kenway and the veteran Robin Smith. Play was well into the final session, with seventy-eight runs added to the total, before the latter became Bicknell's third victim after making forty, then another frustrating stand developed between Kenway and Matthew Keech. At 160-3 it appeared that the visitors were going to hold all the aces at the end of the day, but the late introduction of Saqlain Mushtaq and Ian Salisbury provided manna from heaven for the beleaguered Championship leaders. With Salisbury accounting for Keech and John Stephenson, and Saqlain chipping in with the wicket of Adrian Aymes, Hampshire's advantage was eroded somewhat as they finished the day level with their hosts on 171-6.

After Bicknell (4-75) removed Kenway for an impressive sixty-three early the next morning, the visitors assumed control through the efforts of their tail-end batsmen. Dimitri Mascarenhas, Shaun Udal - before he was forced to retire hurt after being hit on the elbow by a Tudor delivery - and Peter Hartley were all merely support acts, however, as Nixon McLean topped the bill by smashing the Surrey bowlers all around the park. The lithe West Indian cracked two sixes and ten fours in a 52-ball career-best innings of seventy that enabled Hampshire to turn the near-parity of 175-7 into a significant first-innings lead of 151 before Ben Hollioake (2-31) brought the innings to a close at 322.

Although they had quite a mountain to climb if they were to get back into the match, the hosts made a good start through Butcher and Ward, though the latter had a lucky escape early on when a hopelessly miscued pull resulted in the ball landing safely in space behind the striker's stumps. With McLean unexpectedly removed from the attack after just five overs, and surprisingly defensive fields in place, the Surrey opening pair compiled a partnership of 107 in reasonable comfort before Ward fell to the occasional off-spin of Laney, who had been pressed into service in the absence of Udal. Butcher and Graham Thorpe then added another 118 to the total as the Championship leaders continued to fight back strongly against a Hampshire side whose self-belief seemed to be draining away rapidly. Although Butcher was eventually unseated by Hartley after making a splendid ninety-four, Salisbury kept Thorpe (60 not out) company through to the close at 239-2, with Surrey now eighty-eight runs to the good.

At the start of day three the balance of power swung back towards the visitors as Hartley removed Salisbury and Ben Hollioake in his opening spell, before Thorpe found valuable support forthcoming from Ali Brown. The England left-hander went on to complete a fine century from 183 balls shortly after losing Brown (40) to Udal, whose elbow was, fortunately, bruised rather than broken, and then dominated the afternoon session as the home side snatched the initiative away from their opponents. By the time Thorpe was run out for a magnificent 164, the total had advanced to 451-9, and when the last wicket fell, heralding the arrival of the tea interval after the addition of another thirty-one runs, Surrey appeared to be on course for an important victory. That looked even more likely by the close of play as both Laney and Kendall fell lbw to Bicknell for the second time in the match, then Saqlain snapped up Kenway and Keech to leave the south coast county struggling at 98-4 in pursuit of 332 to win.

Hampshire's slender hopes rested squarely on the shoulders of Robin Smith as the final day began, but he was powerless to do anything as nightwatchman Hartley perished to Bicknell (3-50) after being dropped three times and Aymes fell to Saqlain with almost two-hundred runs still required. When Stephenson was bowled by a quicker ball from the Surrey off-spinner after making a quick twenty-six, the writing was certainly on the wall, and the end came swiftly thereafter as Smith (46), McLean and Mascarenhas fell in the space of four balls from Saqlain, who finished with 6-44, and Salisbury. The Championship leaders had therefore completed an amazing comeback, turning a 151-run first-innings deficit into a victory by 156 runs. This enabled them to extend their lead in the title race to twenty-four points, despite Leicestershire's thrashing of Sussex that had taken them into second place. After what had happened the previous year everyone was very much aware of the threat that the Foxes could pose in the last third of the season.

COUNTY CHAMPIONSHIP - TOP OF THE TABLE AT 17TH JULY				
	P	W	D	L	PTS
Surrey	10	7	3	0	152
Leicestershire	10	4	5	1	128
Hampshire	10	4	3	3	127

Surrey knew that victory was essential if they were to retain any hope of promotion in the NCL when they took on the unbeaten Somerset Sabres the next day. After winning the toss and reaching 82-1 through the efforts of Mark Butcher (44) and Alec Stewart (33), the loss of four wickets for thirty-one runs to Steffan Jones (3-65) and the outstanding Paul Jarvis (4-28) put the visitors firmly in charge. Although Ben Hollioake (48) and Ian Ward (34) fought back well with a partnership of eighty for the sixth wicket, the Lions' final total of 225-9 looked to be around thirty runs short of par in the prevailing conditions.

The Sabres were rattled, however, by the loss of Jamie Cox for a duck, and a decline to 75-4 at the hands of an impressive Ben Hollioake (3-31), before they were put back on course by a fifth-wicket stand of seventy-one between Piran Holloway and Keith Parsons. Despite losing further partners with the total at 157, 163 and 201, the left-handed Holloway stayed calm and turned out to be the match-winner as he completed a fine century with three overs to go. He then had the luxury of watching Andy Caddick seal a two-wicket victory in the next over by heaving Ian Salisbury over the short legside boundary for successive sixes. Although Surrey's promotion prospects had disappeared along with the ball, that was no bad thing in many people's eyes since it enabled them to concentrate their efforts for the remainder of the season on winning the County Championship title.

Perhaps the most uplifting moment of an ultimately disappointing Sunday at Guildford had come with the tea-time presentation of county caps to Alex Tudor and Ben Hollioake. The fact that both men had been capped by England before their county underlined that the Surrey cap was, quite rightly, not given away lightly and had to be earned over a period of time.

Sixth-placed Warwickshire were Surrey's next opponents in the County Championship, and they looked sure to provide stiff opposition, since a victory would bring them into the title race. Neither side was even close to full strength, however, with Surrey lacking Butcher, Stewart and Thorpe (with England), plus Alex Tudor, who had been forced out of the Test by a knee injury, while the Bears were deprived of the services of the injured Neil Smith, Tim Munton and Trevor Penney. On a more positive note, they were boosted by the return of Allan Donald, who had been sidelined with an ankle injury since the World Cup.

Undeterred by a rather green-looking pitch, Surrey elected to bat upon winning the toss and came through a potentially difficult first session in a fine position at 118-1, as a clearly out-of-sorts Donald and Graeme Welch turned in below-par displays. Although the visitors were then pegged back to 159-3 within an hour of the restart when Jason Ratcliffe went for thirty-seven and Ian Ward (82) fell immediately after posting a new career-best score, Surrey were soon on top again as Ali Brown and the Hollioakes batted positively either side of tea during stands of seventy-four and 102. While Ben (34) and Adam (43) fell short of their half-centuries, Brown completed a superb hundred from just 116 balls before becoming the third of four victims in the day for Ed Giddins - clearly the pick of the bowlers - after reaching 108. Although the Championship leaders slipped from 335-4 to 340-6 after their centurion's departure, Gary Butcher and Jon Batty put them back on track with an unbroken stand of forty-nine that took the score to 389-6 at the close.

The second day didn't start well for Warwickshire, with Donald being forced off the field by a recurrence of his ankle injury after delivering just three balls, and the seventh-wicket pair going on to add another forty-two runs before Batty was dismissed for thirty-eight with the total on 431. Unfazed by the loss of his partner, Butcher continued to bat attractively, making seventy and guiding the visitors to 483 before he was last out to the persevering and deserving Giddins, who finished with figures of 6-90.

Since there had been clear signs that the pitch might offer some turn during the Surrey innings, the appearance of Saqlain and Salisbury was eagerly awaited by the visiting supporters - if not by the Bears' batsmen - as the hosts started out on their attempt to score 334 to avoid the follow on. Although Surrey's seam bowling, Martin Bicknell excepted, was far from impressive, Warwickshire were 62-3 before the spinners had even warmed up, with Mark Wagh running himself out, David Hemp caught behind off Adam Hollioake, and Anurag Singh going lbw to Bicknell for a duck. The hosts' captain, Nick Knight, who had feasted on some poor fare from the Hollioakes in reaching a 74-ball fifty, kept his side in the game during the partnership of sixty with Dominic Ostler that followed, before the spinners were eventually unleashed shortly before tea. As expected, both men immediately found plenty of turn and occasional awkward bounce, and it wasn't long before Ostler was brilliantly taken by Ben Hollioake at slip off Saqlain.

The final session of the day then turned out to be one long struggle for the batsmen once Knight was bowled by a perfect googly from Salisbury within six runs of what would have been an excellent century. From a safe position of 186-4 just prior to their skipper's demise, Warwickshire tumbled to a perilous 223-9 by the close, as the Surrey leg-spinner disposed of Dougie Brown (42), Graeme Welch and Allan Donald, while Saqlain chipped in with the scalp of Keith Piper.

Almost inevitably, the early capture of Ed Giddins's wicket by the excellent Salisbury (5-49) led to the hosts being invited to follow on 256 runs in the red on the third morning... and by lunchtime the game was over as a contest. Although Warwickshire managed to reach 55-1 after the loss of Knight to Bicknell for thirteen, they then lost three wickets in four balls, and four in thirteen, to the spinners as they plummeted to a desperate 58-5. Brown and Welch then steadied the ship for a while either side of the interval, but once they fell to consecutive deliveries - Welch bowled on the drive by a Salisbury googly, and Brown playing on to Saqlain - with the total advanced to 105, the end came quickly. By mid-afternoon, the Bears had been dismissed for 133, and the architects of their defeat by an innings and 123 runs, Saqlain (5-32) and Salisbury (4-46), were happily leading their team from the field with another twenty points in the bag and Surrey in sight of that elusive County Championship crown.

With Leicestershire being held to a draw by Worcestershire, and Hampshire defeated by a fast-improving Lancashire side in this round of matches, Surrey moved thirty-four points clear of the pack.

LEADING POSITIONS:- Surrey P11, Pts 172; Leics P11, Pts 138; Hants P11, Pts 129.

The only redeeming feature of Surrey's next NCL match was that it was played at the beautiful Ynysangharad Park in Pontypridd. After the Lions had named an eleven lacking Butcher, Stewart, Thorpe (on Test duty), Tudor (injured), Saqlain and Bicknell (rested), the Glamorgan Dragons won the toss and posted an imposing county-record total of 294-4. This score was based on a Glamorgan-best third-wicket partnership of 204 between Jacques Kallis - who scored a sublime unbeaten 155 from 141 balls on his debut for the Welsh county - and Matthew Maynard (79), and left Surrey with a mountain to climb. Three early wickets for Owen Parkin (3-41) merely added to the visitors' problems and it was left to Darren Bicknell (62) to salvage some pride for the Lions before Robert Croft (3-51) took advantage of wildly swinging bats to put the finishing touches to a 71-run victory for the Dragons.

With a full-strength team, bar Tudor, at their disposal for the Nat West Trophy quarter-final at Northampton that followed, Surrey turned in a much better performance and cruised past Northamptonshire with ease. For reasons best known to themselves, the hosts produced a pitch that offered generous turn for the spinners, enabling Saqlain Mushtaq (4-28) and Ian Salisbury (3-29) to run riot after the Swann brothers had feasted on the seam bowling of Bicknell and Benjamin to reach 90-1 after just thirteen overs. The last nine wickets fell for a paltry sixty-two runs as the home batsmen were caught in the spinners' web, leaving Surrey to score just 153 to win. Although the visitors slipped to 80-3 at one stage, in the face of some home spin from Graeme Swann (2-40), the fourth-wicket pair of Graham Thorpe (42 not out) and Ali Brown (39 not out) combined to revive memories of their match-winning partnership in the Championship encounter earlier in the season as they hurried their side to the winning post with more than fourteen overs in hand.

With dreams of the double still very much alive, Surrey next hosted a Glamorgan side whose 1997 feat of winning a first Championship title for twenty-eight years they hoped to emulate within the next three or four weeks.

While the pretenders to Leicestershire's throne fielded the same side that won at Edgbaston, since Butcher, Stewart and Thorpe were playing in the third Test against New Zealand, the Welsh county were forced into a late change when Steve Watkin withdrew with a neck injury and was replaced by the rookie fast bowler, Simon Jones, aged 20. Jacques Kallis, who had batted so beautifully at Ynysangharad Park in the NCL fixture, was making only his second Championship appearance for Glamorgan, but didn't trouble the Surrey bowlers on this occasion after Matthew Maynard had won the toss and opted to bat.

With the ball swinging around in humid conditions and the pitch looking to be one of the bounciest on the square, Martin Bicknell and Ben Hollioake proved to be a real handful as the visitors subsided to 79-7 at lunch. After a nightmare start that had seen the prolific Steve James fall once again to his nemesis, and Kallis dismissed by Hollioake for a duck, Glamorgan had been subjected to some outstanding new-ball bowling, with the first change only coming a few overs before the interval when Bicknell finally decided that he needed a breather after a spell of 15-6-24-3. Hollioake (5-51) kept going after the interval, however, to register his maiden five-wicket haul by dismissing Michael Powell, while Saqlain Mushtaq polished off the tail with 2-14 to leave the visitors all out for 101 in 40.5 overs.

Surrey now knew that if they could put a decent total on the board they would be set up for a win that would take them another step closer to the Championship title. Although the going was still tough for the batsmen, neither Simon Jones nor Darren Thomas had the control to emulate their Surrey counterparts and, consequently, the home side managed to cruise past their opponents' score with just three wickets down. While Ian Ward (41) was steadiness personified until he fell to Dean Cosker with 129 on the board, Ali Brown - benefiting from dropped catches when he was on ten and thirty-four - raced to a 64-ball fifty to keep his side very much on top. Although he lost two more partners, Ben Hollioake and Gary Butcher, before time was called at 184-6, Brown remained in occupation on sixty and represented a clear threat to the visitors' prospects of hauling themsleves back into the match on day two.

After suffering a double blow early the next morning when Simon Jones first forced Jon Batty out of the action with a short delivery that penetrated the grille of the Surrey wicketkeepers' helmet, and then dismissed Ian Salisbury for a first-ball duck, the hosts were quickly put back on course by Brown and his new partner, Martin Bicknell. With the Jones-Thomas combination again proving expensive, runs flowed freely, allowing Brown to complete a superb hundred from his 115th delivery, and the eighth-wicket partnership to grow rapidly in value to ninety-nine. At this point, Brown was caught at long-on off Robert Croft for 124 with the scoreboard reading 291-8 and the home county in a very powerful position despite the fact that Batty was at the local hospital having an x-ray that confirmed his injury as a fractured cheekbone. Although Bicknell and Saqlain now represented Surrey's last pair, they still managed to secure a third batting point for their side before Bicknell was out for fifty-seven shortly after lunch with the total on 309.

Trailing by 208 runs, Glamorgan then collapsed sensationally for a second time, leaving the match all but over by tea. Once Bicknell (3-18) and Hollioake had wiped out the top four batsmen - including Adrian Dale to a catch by Brown, who was standing in for Batty behind the stumps - the spinners got in on the act with three victims of their own to leave the visitors tottering on 76-7 at the break.

The Welshmen then surrendered their last three wickets in the space of a single over from Saqlain (5-18) shortly after the restart, with Brown claiming a stumping and a very fine catch in the process, handing Surrey victory by an innings and 124 runs with almost seven sessions of play to spare.

With Leicestershire's game against Warwickshire at Grace Road being badly affected by rain and ending in stalemate, Adam Hollioake's men were boasting a 41-point lead in the Championship by the time this round of matches was completed.

COUNTY CHAMPIONSHIP - TOP OF THE TABLE AT 7TH AUGUST					
	P	W	D	L	PTS
Surrey	12	9	3	0	191
Leicestershire	12	4	7	1	150
Kent	12	5	5	2	144

Although the Surrey Lions and the Nottinghamshire Outlaws had finally managed to get onto the field and complete a Sunday/National League match back in May, normal service was resumed on Sunday 8th August as the return NCL game between the two sides was again abandoned without a ball being bowled. This was the fourth time in five scheduled contests that rain had completely washed out this seemingly jinxed fixture.

How Surrey must have wished that the floodlit National League game against second-placed Sussex Sharks at Hove had gone the same way four days later. The side that was expected to take the field against Somerset at Taunton in the Nat West Trophy semi-final in two days time produced an abysmal batting display, with only Alec Stewart (37) and Graham Thorpe (31) passing thirty in a feeble total of 144 from 41.3 overs. With the exception of Adam Hollioake and Saqlain Mushtaq, the bowling performance that followed was hardly any better, as Chris Adams (51) led his side to victory by seven wickets with eleven overs to spare.

Unfortunately for Surrey, their performance on the day of the semi-final turned out to be as poor as the dress rehearsal against Sussex had been, with only three players making any mark at all as dreams of a double were turned to dust by an impressive Somerset side.

With the visitors opting to include Jason Ratcliffe in their side ahead of Joey Benjamin, their line-up looked to be short of a specialist seamer, and they were made to pay a heavy price after Adam Hollioake had invited his hosts to bat. Jamie Cox led the way with a splendid 114, and his partnerships of 135 for the first wicket with Peter Bowler (48) and ninety-two for the second wicket with Piran Holloway (45) enabled his team to reach a high point of 227-1 from which they were always going to control the game. Had it not been for an outstanding spell of 10-0-32-4 from Saqlain Mushtaq, Somerset would probably have posted a much higher total than their final 315-8, which included a shocking nineteen wides and ten no-balls.

In reply, Mark Butcher and Ian Ward provided a bright start with a stand of forty-one, but that was almost as good as it got for the leaders of the County Championship. Although Graham Thorpe tried to glue the innings together with a well-played sixty-two, and Ali Brown made thirty-nine before falling to a brilliant return catch by Paul Jarvis, no one else was able to make a contribution as Keith Parsons (4-43) rubber-stamped his side's emphatic 120-run victory.

Surrey needed to put this disappointment behind them quickly as they faced mid-table Sussex at Hove four days later in their next Championship fixture. Having been dropped by England for the fourth and final Test - after standing in as captain for the injured Nasser Hussain in the third - Mark Butcher returned to the Surrey side, though Ben Hollioake was ruled out by a calf injury and replaced by Joey Benjamin. Much to everyone's surprise, given the nature of the injury he sustained against Glamorgan, Jon Batty had been given clearance to play, provided that he wore a helmet when keeping wicket.

After an opening day washout, Adam Hollioake won the toss and Surrey took first use of a well-grassed pitch that was clearly designed to favour seam rather than spin. Although the wisdom of their skipper's decision was being questioned when the visitors crashed to 55-6 in the face of a four-wicket burst from James Kirtley (4-61), Surrey recovered much of the lost ground either side of lunch through a superb 121-run partnership between the captain himself and Martin Bicknell. When both men departed in quick succession - Hollioake for 61, Bicknell for 67 - the Championship leaders were pegged back to 181-8, but the lower order did at least ensure that their side picked up a batting point by pushing the total up to 224, at which point Robin Martin-Jenkins (4-50) had last man Joey Benjamin caught from a skied drive. Sussex then built on their fielding effort, with Richard Montgomerie and Toby Peirce posting a 58-run opening partnership before Saqlain Mushtaq struck twice in quick succession with his "wrong 'un", trapping Montgomerie lbw and then bowling the left-handed Michael DiVenuto. With Chris Adams keeping Peirce company until stumps were drawn at 99-2, the home side were justifiably able to claim the first-day honours.

The game changed dramatically on day two, however, as Surrey took complete control and left themselves well placed to register a sixth successive Championship victory. This amazing turnaround was triggered by an incredible Sussex collapse that saw the hosts subside to 115 all out in just eleven overs. After Peirce had completed his half-century from the first ball of the day and helped his skipper move the score on to 103-2, Martin Bicknell put the skids under the hosts by removing Adams, Peirce - the bowler's fiftieth first-class victim of the summer - and Umer Rashid in the space of two overs, before Saqlain took over as destroyer-in-chief. Having already had Tony Cottey taken at leg slip in the midst of Bicknell's successes, the Pakistani spin king stunned Sussex with a sensational hat-trick that left the hosts reeling at 109-9. After Nick Wilton had become Saqlain's first victim, caught at slip for a first-ball duck, James Kirtley and Jason Lewry were clean bowled by the off-spinner's next two deliveries to provide him with his second three-in-three of the summer, following his previous effort for Pakistan against Zimbabwe in the World Cup. Although Mark Robinson hung on gamely for four overs with a bewildered Robin Martin-Jenkins, who had been watching helplessly from the non-striker's end, the home team's number eleven batsman became another Saqlain scalp with his side 109 runs short of Surrey's 224. Having picked up 5-6 in six overs to complete an overall return of 7-19, the talented off-spinner led a happy visiting team back to their dressing room with the match having been turned on its head. Bicknell, meanwhile, finished with 3-46, including 3-9 from five overs during a sensational first hour of the day.

Although they lost both openers in extending their lead by fifty-nine runs before lunch, Surrey made good progress during the afternoon as Darren Bicknell played his natural game from number three in the order while Ali Brown scored fifty-nine at better than a run a ball at the other end. As the visitors pressed on towards a declaration, the tall left-hander completed a well-paced 158-ball century after tea and celebrated in an untypically emotional fashion before falling to James Kirtley (3-96) for 115. The closure came from Adam Hollioake shortly afterwards, with his team's score standing at 315-7 and Jon Batty unbeaten on forty-five from 46 balls.

Requiring an unlikely 425 to win, a shell-shocked Sussex lost Peirce and Montgomerie to Benjamin and Bicknell respectively in knocking fifty-six runs off that target, before Adams and DiVenuto took them safely through to the close at 94-2.

When the hosts lost their Tasmanian left-hander to Bicknell (2-46) in the second over of the final day, an early finish looked likely, but Adams and Cottey succeeded in delaying the inevitable with an 84-run fourth-wicket partnership that endured until lunch was within sight. Once Salisbury had deceived Cottey with a googly to end the stand, the Surrey spinners bounced back well from a surprisingly poor start to remove both Adams, for a fine seventy-two, and Martin-Jenkins before the interval arrived at 193-6.

Although the tail couldn't fail to offer greater resistance second time around, they were still unable to delay their visitors for long as Salisbury (4-45) and Saqlain (3-78) efficiently finished off the Sussex innings for the addition of twenty-four runs in fifteen overs, sealing Surrey's victory by 207 runs. With four games to go, Keith Medlycott's team now needed just thirty-one points to win the title.

LEADING POSITIONS:- Surrey P13, Pts 208; Leics P13, Pts 159; Kent P13, Pts 154.

Three days later the team were in Derby to take on eighth-placed Derbyshire in the first of those four matches, knowing that victory could see them crowned County Champions, if results elsewhere fell their way. Leicestershire's shrewd Cricket Manager, Jack Birkenshaw, had already conceded that the leaders were unstoppable but, after the doomed finale to the 1998 season, no one was taking anything for granted until the title was mathematically safe.

Surrey's line-up included Alec Stewart and Graham Thorpe, who had been part of England's team that had lost the Test series 2-1 with defeat at The Oval, and Ian Bishop, who was making his Championship debut in place of the out-of-form Joey Benjamin. Mark Butcher missed out with food poisoning and was replaced at the eleventh hour by Darren Bicknell.

On a rain-curtailed first day, the champions-elect were put in to bat by their hosts and progressed nicely until they lost the elder Bicknell to Paul Aldred with the score on forty-eight. Although Jason Ratcliffe was soon forced to retire hurt when he was hit on the helmet by a bouncer from the same bowler, Surrey dominated thereafter through Ian Ward and Graham Thorpe, who built an impressive partnership, during which Ward surpassed the career-best eighty-two he had posted a month earlier at Edgbaston. A chance to finally nail his maiden first-class century was put on hold by a shower that brought about an early tea with his score on ninety-eight, but he wasn't to be denied for long as he reached the mark with a top-edged hook for four over wicketkeeper Karl Krikken a few overs after the restart. Although he was dismissed for 103 immediately after completing his 196-ball ton, Ward had put Surrey in a position of strength that enabled them to shrug off the added loss of Ratcliffe, to the first ball he faced upon his return, and Thorpe for a well controlled eighty-nine just after he had taken his side to a second batting point at 250. Alec Stewart also fell before bad light ended play for the day, but at 285-5 the visitors were already very well placed to push for victory.

A second day of just forty-three balls, thirty runs, and one wicket - Adam Hollioake caught behind off Dominic Cork - seemed to reduce their chances of securing a win, though they soon made up for lost time when play resumed on day three. After notching the thirty-five runs they required to earn their final batting point, Surrey declared immediately and set out on the tough task of securing twenty wickets in less than two days on what was a fairly flat pitch. Even though

Derbyshire's batsmen were short of runs and confidence, their openers started well, taking the score to thirty-five and safely negotiating Ian Bishop's opening spell, only for the debutant's replacement, Jason Ratcliffe, to trap Adrian Rollins lbw in his first over and have Stephen Titchard caught at second slip in his second. Steve Stubbings (42) and Robin Weston then advanced the total to sixty-four shortly after lunch before Martin Bicknell and Saqlain Mushtaq joined forces in the attack to share four wickets and reduce the home team to 74-6, with Weston going for eleven, Cassar for one, Pyemont for a first-ball duck and Krikken also without scoring. A brief recovery to 95-6 was then ended when the dogged Titchard became a third victim for Bicknell (3-52) early in a shower-interrupted final session and, though Cork and Phillip DeFreitas (38 not out) added a defiant forty-seven runs for the eighth wicket, Bishop (2-45) returned to the fray in partnership with Saqlain (3-36) to claim the Derbyshire captain as his maiden first-class wicket and trigger a terminal collapse to 154 all out. Adam Hollioake's decision to enforce the follow-on was entirely predictable and produced the wicket of Stubbings, lbw to Bicknell for the second time in the day, before time was called with the home side struggling to save the game on 28-1, still 168 runs in arrears.

As the last day began, results elsewhere had already ensured that Surrey could no longer clinch the title at the County Ground, though no one was too worried about that as the players attempted to claim the win points from the current game. That began to look unlikely as Rollins and Titchard increased the value of their second-wicket stand to eighty-five, though the loss of the latter to Saqlain on the stroke of lunch gave renewed hope to the visitors.

The Surrey off-spinner and Bicknell (4-46) then sliced through the middle order like a knife through butter upon the resumption, with poor James Pyemont recording a king pair on his Derbyshire debut as the hosts dipped to a dismal 114-6. Knowing that his team was now in real danger of defeat, captain Cork counter-attacked bravely, reaching fifty from just 58 balls and adding forty for the last wicket with the injured Ian Blackwell before being stumped off Saqlain (5-59) for fifty-three with the scores level shortly after tea. Although Darren Bicknell fell lbw to Cork's first ball, Surrey secured the match-winning single nine balls later to move within eight points of becoming County Champions. The only slight worry for the champions-in-waiting was a leg injury that had resulted in Martin Bicknell leaving the field at the fall of Derbyshire's eighth wicket.

COUNTY CHAMPIONSHIP - TOP OF THE TABLE AT 27TH AUGUST				
	P	W	D	L	PTS
Surrey	14	11	3	0	228
Leicestershire	14	5	8	1	176
Kent	14	6	6	2	170

Frustratingly, Surrey had a couple of inconsequential NCL matches to fit in before they could close out the Championship title and they certainly couldn't afford any more injuries, especially to the bowlers. Worse still, these games were to be played in the three days before the potentially decisive Championship match against Nottinghamshire, which started on Wednesday 1st September. It was no surprise, therefore, that a number of key personnel were rested for the Sunday fixture with Durham and the Tuesday game against Middlesex.

In the first of these matches, Durham again threw away a great chance of recording a first-ever victory over Surrey, just as they had done back in April. At the end of the Lions' innings of 221-7, which leant heavily on Graham Thorpe's eighty-four and a hefty thirty extras, the visitors were docked an over from their reply because of their slow over-rate. This then became highly significant when the Dynamos lost their way late in their innings against Ian Bishop (4-34) and Adam Hollioake, having looked set for victory at 196-4 following a 102-run stand between Jon

Lewis (44) and Martin Speight (60). Despite the best efforts of tailenders Melvyn Betts and John Wood, Durham fell two runs short of their hosts' total and were left kicking themselves again.

An even closer game followed at Lord's on the eve of the big Championship match, when the Lions eventually shared the spoils with their London-based rivals after a helter-skelter pursuit of the Crusaders' 252-5, which was built around Owais Shah's 112 and Paul Weekes's eighty. Surrey's reply was akin to a rollercoaster ride as aggressive knocks from the top five batsmen - including fifty-seven from Jason Ratcliffe and forty-one from Adam Hollioake - kept the visitors in contention throughout. A late dip from 201-3 to 235-9 when Angus Fraser (4-35) returned to the attack, suggested that the train had come off the track, however, and it took a fine effort by Ian Bishop (15 not out) and Carl Greenidge to hit and scramble twelve runs off the final over from Richard Johnson to secure Surrey's first tie in Sunday/National League cricket since 1988.

The big match against Nottinghamshire arrived with the county's seam bowling resources stretched to breaking point. With Alex Tudor and Ben Hollioake already ruled out, and Martin Bicknell now joining them on the sidelines with the calf injury he picked up in the closing stages of the Championship win at Derby, the new ball was to be in the hands of Ian Bishop, and the Ulsterman Mark Patterson, who boasted a combined total of one County Championship appearance between them! Other than Patterson for Bicknell junior, the only other change saw Mark Butcher returning from his bout of food poisoning to replace Bicknell senior. It was most unfortunate that, after years of service to the county, both Bicknell brothers would be sitting on the sidelines if Surrey did indeed clinch their first Championship since 1971 in this match.

This looked likely to be the case by lunch on the opening day, as Nottinghamshire's woeful season showed no sign of improvement after Jason Gallian won the toss and decided to bat on a very dry-looking pitch. If Mark Patterson had any nerves on his debut they were soon settled when he trapped Guy Welton lbw with his eighth delivery, and it wasn't long before the other 'rookie', Ian Bishop, got in on the act by having the visiting skipper caught behind with the total on twenty-two. Great catches by Jason Ratcliffe - a one-handed leaping effort at square leg - and Alec Stewart then brought further joy for Patterson (3-25) and misery for Nottinghamshire, who were now struggling badly at 39-4. Usman Afzaal and Chris Read then steadied the ship slightly, adding thirty-six for the fifth wicket before the introduction of spin led to a rapid decline from 75-4 to 89-7 at lunch and 115 all out an hour afterwards. Once Afzaal was sixth out for forty-seven when he miscued a pull off Saqlain (3-15), there was no stopping the off-spinner and his partner-in-crime, Ian Salisbury (3-29), who claimed Paul Franks as his fiftieth first-class victim of the season to become the third member of the club that Bicknell had started at Hove and Saqlain had joined during the second innings at Derby.

With four bowling points in the bag, Surrey set out on their quest to score 350 and secure the four batting points that would bring Championship glory to the team. Although the prospects of this happening looked bright, initially, as Mark Butcher and Ian Ward took the total up to thirty-nine, a fine spell by Mark Bowen (3-30) earned him the wickets of Ward, Ratcliffe and Thorpe in the run-up to tea, which was taken at 61-3. When Butcher then fell to Vasbert Drakes soon after the resumption to leave Surrey struggling at 77-4, a total of 350 looked a long way off, and, in hazy conditions that now favoured the seamers, Ali Brown and Alec Stewart needed all their skills to ensure that Nottinghamshire didn't gain the upper hand in the match. Counter-attacking boldly yet sensibly, this pair took the champions-elect into the lead and up to 155-4 before Paul Franks was brought on for a second spell that instantly yielded the scalps of Brown (34), very well caught at second slip by Archer, and Stewart (49), who fell to an even better catch at first slip by Gallian. Since news had come through that Leicestershire had dropped a batting point at Grace Road, Surrey's requirement had dropped to three points, or three-hundred runs, though their hopes of achieving that total appeared to be snuffed out when Vasbert Drakes struck two killer blows, removing Salisbury and Adam Hollioake in quick succession to leave the hosts wobbling on 199-8 at the close. The game would now have to be won if Adam Hollioake's men were to seal their success here at The Oval.

After the ECB pitch inspectors had found nothing wrong with the bouncy surface on which eighteen wickets had fallen during the first day, Surrey started day two in dreadful style, losing their two remaining wickets in eleven balls without adding a run to their score. With Saqlain having been bowled by Drakes (4-53) from the sixth ball of the morning, Mark Patterson looked to steal a point-clinching single to the very same man at mid-on in the next over and failed to make his ground as an accurate throw hit the stumps at the non-striker's end.

With the Nottinghamshire openers, Welton and Afzaal, surviving the opening spells from Patterson and Bishop, and wiping twenty-nine runs from the arrears of eighty-four in the process, the morning session looked like it could turn out to be a high point in a season of mediocrity for the visitors. Surrey were awoken from their early slumbers by the introduction of Jason Ratcliffe and Saqlain Mushtaq, however, with the former having Welton nicely taken behind the wicket by Stewart, and the latter removing Gallian for a duck, courtesy of a juggling slip catch by Thorpe, to reduce Nottinghamshire to 31-2. Although Paul Johnson survived some anxious moments once Salisbury joined Saqlain in the attack, both he and Afzaal reeled off some surprisingly confident strokes as their partnership endured until lunch, by which time the visiting team had moved into a 15-run lead.

The third-wicket stand then began to look dangerous for the champions-in-waiting after lunch, passing the hundred mark at better than four runs an over as Afzaal got the better of Saqlain, even though there were a few edges mixed in with the powerful off-side drives and cuts. Thankfully for Surrey, their off-spinner eventually penetrated an ugly heave to leg by Johnson (41) with the total on 140, and soon removed Archer to regain the initiative for the home side. Afzaal then found another worthwhile ally in Chris Read, however, and further frustration followed for the home county until Hollioake pulled off another masterstroke by recalling Ratcliffe to the attack. The part-time medium-pacer snared Read lbw almost immediately, ending a 35-run partnership and pushing the door to victory open again with Nottinghamshire effectively 107-5 at this point. Undeterred by his colleague's departure, Afzaal pushed on to become only the second man to take a Championship century off the Surrey attack in the course of the season to date - Paul Prichard having achieved the feat back in May - reaching the mark from 163 balls and earning a generous ovation for his efforts. It was all to be downhill for the visitors from this point, though, as the dismissals of Wharf, Drakes and Afzaal (104) in consecutive overs left them in deep trouble at 207-8.

With everyone in the ground beginning to wonder if Surrey could finish the game inside two days, Franks and Bowen resisted stoutly up to and beyond tea. Spectators were arriving at The Oval by the minute in the hope that they could witness a piece of cricketing history, but time looked to be running out until Salisbury pinned Bowen lbw with a googly to end a frustrating 12-over partnership of twenty-two. With just one wicket to fall, Nottinghamshire were 145 runs ahead with twenty-nine overs - including the eight that constituted the extra half-hour - left in the second day's play. If Surrey were to have any hope of closing out the game, and the Championship, that night the last wicket was needed quickly and without the addition of too many more runs. It was fortunate for everyone, therefore, that Salisbury managed to snare last man Richard Stemp in identical fashion to Bowen in his next over with just a swept boundary by Franks off Saqlain having added to the task facing Surrey. As Saqlain (4-100) and Salisbury - whose final wicket in a return of 4-66 had been the six-hundredth of his first-class career - led their side from the field yet again after another display of superb spin bowling, the home dressing room faced a dilemma... to chase or not to chase a very stiff target of 150 in a maximum of twenty-seven overs to clinch the title in front of a good-sized crowd, who were creating a terrific atmosphere in the ground.

With the home crowd wondering how their team would approach this task, the appearance of the regular openers, Butcher and Ward, suggested that Surrey were going to concentrate first and foremost on winning the match, which was reasonable enough after a 28-year run without a Championship title. The spectators' expectations were raised, however, by a rollicking start from Butcher, who picked up boundaries off both the middle and the edge of his bat in speeding to twenty-two in six overs. Although Ward was only on seven, having faced very little of the bowling, a glut of extras had enabled the total to reach forty-two by this time, which put Surrey ahead of the run rate required to seal the title that evening. A couple of quiet overs then put the chase back in doubt before a pair of batting gloves was taken out to the middle, clearly with a message from the captain. For seven overs, as the total advanced at a steady pace to seventy-nine from fifteen overs, the crowd were left wondering about the timing of their celebrations - tonight or tomorrow? - then twenty-three runs flowed from the next two overs to erase any doubts. Butcher simultaneously completed a fine 55-ball fifty and raised the Surrey hundred with a boundary from the final ball of the seventeenth over, before the day's allocation of overs ran out with the home side forty runs away from popping the champagne corks. Rather than risk a lynching, the umpires agreed to the extra half-hour, and the decision was immediately vindicated when a flurry of five fours from overs twenty and twenty-one sent the score rocketing to 136-0. Given the hopelessness of their situation, captain Gallian now decided, understandably, to wave the white flag, inviting Afzaal to deliver the following over, which ended up costing thirteen runs and left Surrey two short of an incredible victory. After three nervy deliveries, Ward - having completed a 62-ball fifty in the previous over - eventually drove a Drakes off-break to the pavilion boundary, ending twenty-eight years of hurt by securing the county's sixteenth outright County Championship title. With arms raised in triumph all around the ground and out in the middle, the exhausted Ward and Butcher embraced before hurrying back to the dressing room to celebrate with their equally joyous team-mates.

Shortly afterwards, once everything had settled down, the Surrey heroes made their way up to the committee room balcony where Adam Hollioake - who was just eight days old when the 1971 Championship had been won - received the much-coveted trophy, accompanied by a huge roar from the fans gathered in front of him and down below on the hallowed turf. A perfect day then ended with the team wandering down onto the outfield to shake hands with the fans and show off the Holy Grail of cricket before everyone departed to enjoy their own celebrations. After the disappointment of the previous year's debacle against Leicestershire, this triumph was very sweet indeed.

LEADING POSITIONS:- Surrey P15, Pts 244; Leics P15, Pts 183; Yorks P15, Pts 182

With everyone still on cloud nine following the clinching of the Championship, the Surrey Lions completed their disappointing NCL season with two games under floodlights at The Oval, the first against the title-chasing Sussex Sharks and the second a London derby versus the Middlesex Crusaders.

In the Monday night match, Sussex showed why they were already assured of promotion, fighting back impressively with the ball, and then easing home to victory under the lights to go top of the second division table. James Kirtley (4-48) and Chris Adams were responsible for pegging the Lions back after forties from Mark Butcher, Stewart and Thorpe had put them in sight of a much bigger total than their final 217, before a sparky seventy-eight from Michael DiVenuto and a steady eighty from Richard Montgomerie enabled the Sharks to cruise in by nine wickets with two overs in hand.

The following night's game then saw the Lions ending the season with one of their best all-round performances of the NCL campaign as they trounced Middlesex by sixty-nine runs. Stewart (76) and Thorpe (70) were again very much to the fore as Surrey knocked up 243-5, the sort of total they should have posted the previous night, before a fine fielding display produced four run outs that prevented the Crusaders from building the necessary momentum to challenge the Lions' total. Significantly, the highest partnership of the Middlesex innings was just thirty-nine as they were bowled out for 174 in 41.2 overs and, as a result, saw their south London rivals leapfrog them to finish sixth in the Division Two table.

NATIONAL LEAGUE DIVISION TWO TABLE 1999								
		P	Pts	W	L	T	A	NRR
1	Sussex	16	54	13	2	0	1	11.95
2	Somerset	16	52	13	3	0	0	8.29
3	Northamptonshire	16	40	9	5	0	2	-0.49
4	Glamorgan	16	34	8	7	1	0	-1.34
5	Nottinghamshire	16	28	6	8	0	2	0.41
6	Surrey	16	24	5	9	1	1	0.83
7	Middlesex	16	22	5	10	1	0	-1.70
8	Derbyshire	16	20	4	10	1	1	-7.99
9	Durham	16	14	3	12	0	1	-10.30

With the title already sewn up, Surrey's Championship clash with Middlesex at Lord's had lost its edge before a ball had even been bowled. Despite being without the injured Alex Tudor and Ben Hollioake, plus Saqlain Mushtaq, who was required by Pakistan in Toronto, the newly-crowned champions dominated the first three days of the match before being denied a ninth successive County Championship victory on the final day by a typically assured and classy innings from Mark Ramprakash.

After winning the toss and electing to bat, Surrey amassed a total of 585 during the first four-and-a-half sessions of the contest, with records falling all over the place, especially during a fifth-wicket stand of 288 between Ali Brown (265) and Adam Hollioake (116). Brown's maiden first-class double-century came up in 294 balls and offered outstanding entertainment to everyone except the suffering Middlesex bowlers, of whom Phil Tufnell (3-90) and Angus Fraser (3-111) were the pick.

Surrey then did extremely well to dismiss their hosts for 284 on a very good pitch - largely through the efforts of Martin Bicknell (3-47) and Ian Salisbury (3-74) - after a fine knock of ninety-eight from the promising 22-year-old opener Andrew Strauss had enabled the home team to reach 115-1 without too many problems.

With the bowlers tired at the end of a long hard campaign, and the attack further depleted by the first-innings withdrawal of Ian Bishop with a calf strain, it was predictable that Middlesex would make a better fist of their second innings after following on. Receiving good support from Ben Hutton (50), Richard Kettleborough (69) and David Nash (56 not out), Ramprakash (209 not out) batted through more than 130 overs to become the first player to register three double-centuries against Surrey and secure the draw at 499-5.

LEADING POSITIONS:- Surrey P16, Pts 256; Lancs P16, Pts 199; Leics P16, Pts 189.

The final match of the summer pitted Surrey against old rivals, Yorkshire, the only team to have won more Championship titles than the men from The Oval. To celebrate the home county's successful season, drinks in the Members' bar in the pavilion were on sale at 1971 prices, meaning that a pint of beer or lager cost just 20p, while a bottle of wine could be purchased for a bargain £1.20.

There was plenty of time for everyone to visit the bar, too, because rain decimated the first half of the match, wiping out all of the first day and allowing just twenty-one overs to be bowled on day two, during which Yorkshire struggled to 50-5 against Martin Bicknell, who had been named as Surrey's Player Of The Year, and Carl Greenidge - son of West Indian legend, Gordon - who was making his Championship debut. With so much time having been lost, it already seemed certain that the match would be drawn, allowing Surrey to complete their first ever unbeaten season in the County Championship since it was officially constituted in 1890.

The game moved on so quickly on day three, however, that a positive result suddenly looked possible. After Yorkshire had recovered from the depths of 72-9 to reach 115, with Greenidge returning 5-60 and Bicknell 4-38, Surrey were dismissed in just thirty-three overs for 128. Ian Ward (27) and Ali Brown (18) were the only men able to offer any support to Graham Thorpe, who made a battling unbeaten fifty-eight as the new champions were sent into freefall from a high point of 101-4 by Chris Silverwood (5-28) and Anthony McGrath (3-18). The Tykes fared little better second time around, though, ending the day on 92-6 with a lead of just seventy-nine runs and facing defeat after Bicknell had added another three wickets to his season's tally.

With the contest having been completely dominated by the ball thus far, it was a major shock to everyone that Richard Blakey (71) and nightwatchman Ian Fisher, with a career-best fifty-one, survived the whole of the morning session on the final day. By dint of careful application, they added eighty-four runs for the seventh wicket and allowed David Byas the luxury of a mid-afternoon declaration at 213-9 that challenged his hosts to score 201 for victory in a minimum of forty-three overs. The loss of three wickets for twenty-two rapidly ensured that discretion would be the better part of valour, however, and Surrey were very happy to accept the umpires' offer of bad light at 57-4 with twenty-one overs remaining for play.

By drawing their final game, the club went undefeated through a season for the first time since 1864 - an amazing feat - and their final margin of victory in the 1999 Championship was a staggering fifty-six points, the largest since Essex topped the table by seventy-seven points back in 1979. Under the points system that had been in place in 1998 - where sixteen points were awarded for a win, rather than twelve - Surrey would have beaten their nearest rivals by an astounding seventy-two points.

COUNTY CHAMPIONSHIP TABLE 1999							
		P	Pts	W	D	L	Bat	Bwl
1	Surrey	17	264	12	5	0	36	64
2	Lancashire	17	208	8	5	4	37	55
3	Leicestershire	17	200	5	9	3	43	61
4	Somerset	17	194	6	7	4	38	56
5	Kent	17	194	6	7	4	34	60
6	Yorkshire	17	193	8	3	6	21	64
7	Hampshire	17	191	5	7	5	45	58
8	Durham	17	188	6	4	7	34	66
9	Derbyshire	17	187	7	2	8	34	61
10	Warwickshire	17	187	6	6	5	35	56
11	Sussex	17	185	6	6	5	29	60
12	Essex	17	181	5	5	7	38	63
13	Northamptonshire	17	171	4	6	7	35	64
14	Glamorgan	17	163	5	5	7	26	57
15	Worcestershire	17	159	4	7	6	18	65
16	Middlesex	17	157	4	8	5	24	53
17	Nottinghamshire	17	140	4	2	11	27	57
18	Gloucestershire	17	136	2	6	9	26	62

Surrey's domination of the County Championship in 1999 was quite incredible, especially when it was taken into account that they had suffered more than any other county in the country from player absences through injuries and international calls. The end-of-season statistics were simply awesome, with Keith Medlycott's men having outshone their opponents in just about every way imagineable - they scored their runs, and took their wickets, at a faster rate than anyone else; they conceded fewer runs per over, and per innings, than their rivals; and they had captured a phenomenal 304 opposition wickets in their seventeen matches - with rain having robbed them of the chance to capture twenty-five of the other thirty-six.

The four main bowlers - Martin Bicknell, Saqlain Mushtaq, Ian Salisbury and Alex Tudor - had claimed 228 wickets between them, yet the club had been able to field this first-choice attack in only one match, against Hampshire at Guildford. Bicknell had been outstanding, not only with the ball but also with the bat, and was a worthy winner of the Player Of The Season award again; Saqlain had simply overwhelmed opposition batsmen with his skill and variations, taking his wickets at a rate than was unheard of in the modern game; his spin-twin, Salisbury, had bowled as well as at any time in his life and, with Saqlain, formed the club's best spin partnership since Lock and Laker; while Tudor brought pace and bounce to the attack, complementing Bicknell's guile and swing perfectly.

This awesome and ideally balanced attack still needed the batsmen to put runs on the board for them, however, so it was fortunate that the club was also powerful in that area, with a good mix of accumulators and strokemakers in their squad. Although the bulk of the runs had come from Ali Brown, Mark Butcher and Ian Ward - the latter having matured into a highly dependable opener and become a regular member of the team - there were plenty of others who were able to make a valuable contribution if the team was struggling, including all the bowlers. In fact, it had been the case all season that someone had stepped up to the plate whenever a performance had been needed, as was demonstrated in the Nottinghamshire game, where Mark Patterson had played an important role on the first morning of his Championship debut. Additionally, the club possessed a talented and fast-improving wicketkeeper in Jon Batty, and excellent leaders both on and off the field. In Keith Medlycott, Surrey had a young and ambitious Cricket Manager who appeared to be highly skilled in the art of man-management, while the captaincy of both Adam Hollioake and his stand-in, Mark Butcher, was always positive and aggressive. The excellent start to the Championship season, when the club's international players were on World Cup duty, had been pivotal to the capture of the title, and also proved that the team was able to win games even when they were without the magical Saqlain Mushtaq. Those who claimed that this Surrey side was something of a one-man team were very wide of the mark indeed.

Predictably enough, given the effort required to win the Championship, the team's displays in the one-day game had often been less than inspiring. Work still needed to be done in that area - where the batting had again been a major problem - with a return to the first division of the NCL a priority for 2000. It was entirely understandable that the capture of the Championship title should have taken precedence, but there was no reason why Surrey's squad of talented players shouldn't be successful in the limited-overs form of the game as well.

Perhaps the most worrying thing for the other seventeen counties was the fact that the current Surrey team included a great many players who were still short of, or only just reaching, their peak. They looked hungry for further success, too, and it seemed certain that further trophies would follow. They would have to do without Darren Bicknell in 2000, though, since the 32-year-old left-handed opener - perhaps mindful of the younger Ian Ward's improvement - had decided to seek pastures new and looked likely to sign for Nottinghamshire. Additionally, Joey Benjamin, 38, whose effectiveness had been greatly reduced by the loss of a crucial yard of pace, was sadly, but predictably, not offered a new contract after eight seasons of largely excellent service. The other players who were not retained at the end of the season were James Knott, who wasn't quite up to the required standard with either bat or gloves, and Micky Bell, who had failed to live up to expectations after his move from Warwickshire.

1999 SEASON SUMMARY

COMPETITION	P	W	D/T/A	L	POSITION/PROGRESS
County Championship	17	12	5	0	1st
National League Div 2	16	5	2	9	6th
Nat West Trophy	4	3	0	1	Semi-final
Benson & Hedges Cup	1	0	0	1	Quarter-final
TOTAL	38	20	7	11	1 Trophy

1999 RESULTS SUMMARY

13/4	GLOUCESTERSHIRE	OVAL	CC	Match Drawn
18/4	Durham	Riverside	NL2	WON by 2 runs (D/L)
20/4	Worcestershire	Worcester	CC	Match Drawn
25/4	NORTHAMPTONSHIRE	OVAL	NL2	LOST by 4 wickets
28/4	Northamptonshire	Northampton	CC	WON by 8 wickets
3/5	Nottinghamshire	Trent Bridge	NL2	LOST by 11 runs
14/5	ESSEX	OVAL	CC	WON by 4 wickets
23/5	Somerset	Taunton	NL2	LOST by 6 wickets
26/5	SOMERSET	OVAL	CC	WON by 7 wickets
31/5	DERBYSHIRE	OVAL	NL2	LOST by 6 wickets
2/6	Kent	Tunbridge Wells	CC	WON by an inns & 28 runs
9/6	Leicestershire	Leicester	CC	Match Drawn
13/6	Northamptonshire	Northampton	NL2	LOST by 5 runs
15/6	LANCASHIRE	OVAL	CC	WON by 4 wickets
19/6	GLAMORGAN	OVAL	NL2	WON by 143 runs
23/6	Scotland	Grange CC	NWT	WON by 7 wickets
27/6	Gloucestershire	Bristol	BHSCqf	LOST by 7 wickets
30/6	DURHAM	OVAL	CC	WON by 226 runs
4/7	Derbyshire	Derby	NL2	WON by 64 runs
7/7	Worcestershire	Worcester	NWT	WON by 5 wickets
14/7	HAMPSHIRE	GUILDFORD	CC	WON by 156 runs
18/7	SOMERSET	GUILDFORD	NL2	LOST by 2 wickets
21/7	Warwickshire	Edgbaston	CC	WON by an inns & 123 runs
25/7	Glamorgan	Pontypridd	NL2	LOST by 71 runs
28/7	Northamptonshire	Northampton	NWTqf	WON by 7 wickets
4/8	GLAMORGAN	OVAL	CC	WON by an inns & 124 runs
8/8	NOTTINGHAMSHIRE	OVAL	NL2	Match Abandoned
12/8	Sussex	Hove	NL2	LOST by 7 wickets
14/8	Somerset	Taunton	NWTsf	LOST by 120 runs
18/8	Sussex	Hove	CC	WON by 207 runs
24/8	Derbyshire	Derby	CC	WON by 9 wickets
29/8	DURHAM	OVAL	NL2	WON by 2 runs
31/8	Middlesex	Lord's	NL2	Match Tied
1/9	NOTTINGHAMSHIRE	OVAL	CC	WON by 10 wickets
6/9	SUSSEX	OVAL	NL2	LOST by 9 wickets
7/9	MIDDLESEX	OVAL	NL2	WON by 69 runs
9/9	Middlesex	Lord's	CC	Match Drawn
15/9	YORKSHIRE	OVAL	CC	Match Drawn

COUNTY CHAMPIONSHIP BATTING AVERAGES 1999

	M	I	NO	Runs	HS	Ave	100	50	c	st
A.D. Brown	17	26	4	1127	265	51.22	4	2	31	1
G.P. Thorpe	9	13	2	561	164	51.00	2	2	13	-
M.A. Butcher	13	22	1	991	259	47.19	2	4	12	-
I.J. Ward	17	28	3	954	103	38.16	1	8	6	-
A.J. Hollioake	12	16	2	486	116	34.71	1	3	6	-
D.J. Bicknell	10	15	1	478	115	34.14	2	1	2	-
M.P. Bicknell	15	17	4	432	69	33.23	-	3	5	-
A.J. Stewart	7	10	1	262	95	29.11	-	1	10	2
B.C. Hollioake	12	18	0	468	71	26.00	-	3	12	-
J.N. Batty	14	18	5	294	45*	22.61	-	-	43	7
J.D. Ratcliffe	12	18	1	380	91	22.35	-	2	5	-
I.D.K. Salisbury	17	19	2	353	100*	20.76	1	1	5	-
Saqlain Mushtaq	7	8	5	46	25*	15.33	-	-	1	-
A.J. Tudor	9	11	2	91	33	10.11	-	-	3	-

Qualification: 8 innings

COUNTY CHAMPIONSHIP BOWLING AVERAGES 1999

	O	M	Runs	W	Ave	BB	10wm	5wi
Saqlain Mushtaq	290.5	90	660	58	11.37	7-19	2	7
M.P. Bicknell	545.4	156	1346	71	18.95	4-32	-	-
A.J. Tudor	281.3	66	836	39	21.43	7-77	-	3
I.D.K. Salisbury	558.2	145	1315	60	21.91	5-44	-	2
M.A. Butcher	168.0	47	400	16	25.00	4-30	-	-
B.C. Hollioake	234.5	47	754	20	37.70	5-51	1	-

Qualification: 100 overs, 10 wickets

LIMITED-OVERS BATTING AVERAGES 1999

	M	I	NO	Runs	HS	Ave	100	50	c	st
G.P. Thorpe	13	13	3	682	91*	68.20	-	6	6	-
A.J. Stewart	13	13	0	371	76	28.53	-	2	9	4
M.A. Butcher	17	17	1	423	54	26.43	-	1	4	-
A.D. Brown	20	20	1	488	105	25.68	1	-	9	-
I.J. Ward	20	19	3	395	80	24.69	-	1	3	-
B.C. Hollioake	16	15	0	314	48	20.93	-	-	6	-
J.D. Ratcliffe	10	10	1	169	59	18.77	-	1	2	-
A.J. Hollioake	17	15	0	263	45	17.53	-	-	2	-
A.J. Tudor	8	7	1	55	28	9.16	-	-	-	-
J.N. Batty	11	9	1	72	19	9.00	-	-	13	1
M.P. Bicknell	14	11	5	46	16	7.66	-	-	-	-
I.D.K. Salisbury	15	11	0	75	19	6.82	-	-	2	-

Qualification: 7 innings

LIMITED-OVERS BOWLING AVERAGES 1999								
	O	M	Runs	W	Ave	BB	4wi	RPO
Saqlain Mushtaq	72.0	10	206	20	10.30	4-17	3	2.86
I.E. Bishop	64.1	7	243	11	22.09	4-34	1	3.78
A.J. Tudor	61.2	5	297	11	27.00	2-26	-	4.84
M.P. Bicknell	114.0	14	490	18	27.22	7-30	1	4.29
A.J. Hollioake	67.2	3	397	14	28.36	3-47	-	5.89
B.C. Hollioake	94.0	6	440	14	31.42	3-31	-	4.68
Qualification: 40 overs, 10 wickets								

For a detailed account of the 1999 season, including exclusive interviews with the players, read **'The Dream Fulfilled - Surrey's 1999 County Championship Triumph'** (details given on page 350)

7 2000: Doubling Up With Delight

Since they had made no major signings during the winter, Surrey were to start the defence of their County Championship title with much the same squad that had performed so well in 1999. Although Darren Bicknell had completed his move to Nottinghamshire, his loss was likely to be covered by the increased availability of Mark Butcher and/or Graham Thorpe. While Butcher faced the possibility of being dropped from the England set-up after a disappointing winter in South Africa that saw him score just 166 runs at an average of 20.75 in the five Tests, Thorpe's situation was entirely dependent on how the selectors viewed his decision to opt out of the tour for family reasons. It was quite possible that it would count against him when it came to the selection of teams for the two-match series against Zimbabwe, though a return for the five West Indies Tests looked highly likely, since he was still regarded by many as the best batsman in the country. Both men had, in any case, been omitted from the group of twelve players who were to be contracted to the ECB for the six months that covered the summer series. Alec Stewart was the only Surrey man to be awarded one of these new central contracts, which gave the ECB complete control over the players' appearances in county cricket. The Honorary Club Captain was therefore likely to be absent for most of the summer, while Saqlain Mushtaq wouldn't be available to the county until the end of May, since he was playing for Pakistan in the West Indies. On a more positive note, Saqlain had been given permission to miss his country's brief tour to Sri Lanka in June.

As everyone prepared for the first season of two-division County Championship cricket, a further change had been made to the points system. Since the adjustment to the number of points awarded for wins and draws hadn't achieved a sufficiently significant reduction in the production of 'result' wickets, the allocation of bonus points had been tweaked. Only three bowling points were now available - at three, six and nine wickets - while the maximum number of batting points had been increased from four to five, to be awarded when reaching 200, 250, 300, 350 and 400 runs in the first 130 (rather than 120) overs of the first innings.

The season opened with what was probably the wettest Benson & Hedges Cup qualifying campaign on record. Surrey's first two matches - away to Essex and at home to Kent - were complete washouts, before the players were finally able to get on the field at Hove. Having been put in to bat by Adam Hollioake, Sussex struggled to a dismal total of 97 that featured an opening stand of thirty and a last-wicket partnership of twenty-five! Needless to say, there was nothing much in between as the Surrey seamers, led by Jason Ratcliffe with a career-best 3-15, dominated. The visitors' reply was then played out in drizzle until a heavy downpour ended the contest with Surrey, at 61-1 from twenty overs, having done enough to secure a 35-run Duckworth-Lewis victory.

A win that looked most valuable in a south group where the majority of the games had been abandoned then became even more precious when the match against Middlesex also fell foul of awful weather, despite a late switch of venue from a waterlogged Lord's to a sodden Southgate.

With so few games having been played, Surrey knew that if their final fixture against Hampshire at The Oval was abandoned they would go through to the quarter-finals, having been on the field of play for precisely sixty-four of a scheduled five-hundred overs. This looked likely to be the case, in fact, as the outfield was still very wet indeed on the day of the game, but the umpires, under pressure from a Hampshire side who needed a victory if they were to qualify, eventually decided to play a ten-overs-a-side match starting at 5pm.

Put in by Adam Hollioake, the visitors recovered well from a disastrous start of 14-3, thanks to Derek Kenway, who scored forty-seven from 29 balls to enable his team to post a reasonable total of 87-7. With a strong batting line-up at their disposal, this score looked well within Surrey's compass, especially once they had raced to 60-3 after six overs. Two outstanding overs from Shane Warne - during which he took 2-6 and also had Mark Butcher missed behind the wicket - turned the tables in Hampshire's favour, however, allowing Alan Mullally to secure a two-run victory for his side with an excellent final over. After initial fears that this defeat had dumped Surrey out of the competition, it emerged that their superior net run rate had allowed them to advance as one of the two best third-placed sides from the three groups, and the draw then presented them with a quarter-final tie against Yorkshire at Headingley.

With a most unsatisfactory Benson & Hedges qualifying competition out of the way, Surrey's defence of the County Championship got under way three days later at Taunton. The game had actually been due to start a day earlier but the County Ground was so wet that the first day's play was abandoned at lunchtime without a ball bowled.

When the contest did finally begin at 3pm on the second scheduled day, the champions got off to a poor start, being inserted in bowler-friendly conditions and bowled out before the close for 185. A stand of seventy-four for the fifth wicket between Ali Brown (47) and Adam Holliaoke (59) was all that stood between Surrey and humiliation as Steffan Jones (5-41) and Andy Caddick (3-71) made the most of the opportunity to bowl first.

The rain then returned on day three, allowing just five overs - one of which was a double wicket maiden by Martin Bicknell - and leaving the contest dead in the water when the final day got under way in bright sunshine at 11.30am. Since conditions were now much better for batting, it was no great surprise that Somerset dominated, scoring 302-8 declared, with Marcus Trescothick (85) and Michael Burns (81) making a good start to the season. For Surrey, Ian Salisbury (3-56), Martin Bicknell (2-48) and Ian Bishop, who took 1-24 in twelve tidy overs, all looked in fine fettle.

Moving on to Cardiff for their opening National Cricket League fixture, the Surrey Lions decided to bat first after winning the toss and posted 185-9 from their forty-five overs on a difficult slow pitch that stifled expansive strokeplay and rewarded good placement of the ball and running between the wickets. A second-wicket stand of ninety-one between Mark Butcher (47) and Graham Thorpe (61) formed the core of the visitors' total, with no other batsman able to pass sixteen against the Dragons' tight bowling and fielding led by Owen Parkin (3-39) and Robert Croft (2-28).

When Glamorgan replied Martin Bicknell quickly disposed of the pinch-hitters, Croft and Alex Wharf, for thirteen before Michael Powell (30) and Matthew Maynard (46) put their side back on course with a 59-run partnership for the third wicket. This turned out to be the biggest stand of the innings by some distance, however, as the Lions managed to snap up a wicket every time the hosts threatened to take control. With Ian Salisbury (2-32) capturing two middle-order scalps, including the dangerous Maynard, and Adam Hollioake doing his usual sound job at the sharp end of the innings, the Dragons were never able to get ahead of the clock and eventually fell ten runs short of Surrey's total with five balls remaining.

Having made an encouraging start in their attempt to gain promotion to the first division of the NCL, a positively evil piece of fixture scheduling sent Surrey straight up to Chester-le-Street for their second County Championship match. With the County Champions still boasting a one hundred percent record against Durham since the north-east county gained first-class status in 1992, this looked to be an early opportunity to get points on the board, provided that the weather was kinder at county cricket's most northerly outpost than it had been down in the south-west.

The first day of the match was blessed with surprisingly pleasant weather and produced some good cricket from two sides who were both without injured players - Alec Stewart was missing from the Surrey line-up, while John Wood and Michael Gough were out of action for the hosts, with the latter being replaced by 17-year-old Nicky Peng, a Durham Academy batsman who didn't even feature in the new Playfair Cricket Annual.

After putting his hosts in to bat, Adam Hollioake was delighted to see his seamers reduce Durham to 48-4, at which point the young debutant entered the fray with not too much batting talent left in the pavilion. It was immediately noticeable that Peng was very composed for one so young as he helped Paul Collingwood push the total on to 119 either side of lunch before the more experienced man fell to Alex Tudor for an impressive sixty-six.

Having unfurled some lovely strokes during the afternoon, Peng enjoyed a few moments of good fortune - including successive edged fours that took him to a well-played 104-ball half-century - in the midst of a testing spell from the excellent Bicknell (3-52) that brought the Surrey swing king the wicket of Martin Speight with the total at 143. The visitors seemed to have a slight advantage at this point, since Peng now had only the tail to support him, but the youngster responded positively by expanding his repertoire of strokes to dominate stands of thirty-two for the seventh wicket with Neil Killeen and forty-three for the ninth wicket with Steve Harmison. When Ben Hollioake (4-41) finally trapped Harmison lbw to make the score 219-9, Peng was on eighty-nine, with just Simon Brown for company and the tension around the ground tangible. A glorious straight-driven boundary off Hollioake eventually took him within two runs of his century before a fatal flash outside the off stump shortly afterwards gave the bowler revenge and left the 17-year-old with the consolation of having recorded the highest score by a Durham player on his Championship debut. The crowd rightly rose to applaud Peng's brilliant 145-ball effort as he left the field with Durham 234 all out, and it was good to see Adam Hollioake adding his own congratulations with a few words and a pat on the back.

With the hosts' total looking about par for the course in conditions that still favoured the seamers, Surrey got away to a sticky start against Brown and Betts, scoring just three runs from the first ten overs. Although run-scoring became a little easier once these two were replaced by Killeen and Harmison, the visitors lost two wickets before the close - Ian Ward to a brilliantly executed run out at the non-striker's end by Simon Katich from second slip as the batsmen tried to steal a single from Ward's let-off at third slip, and Graham Thorpe to a catch at the wicket off Harmison after struggling to eighteen. Having taken thirteen overs to open his account, Mark Butcher was still in occupation on ten after twenty-eight very testing overs from the Durham seamers.

As soon as Butcher's vigil ended, with his score on fifteen, after seven overs of the second day, Surrey collapsed in sensational style from 57-2 to 81-9, with Killeen (3-19) and Brown (3-29) using seam and swing, allied to a touch of variable bounce, to rip through the visitors' line-up. During this period of play, the hosts produced some of the best cricket seen against the reigning champions for some considerable time, with very fine bowling being supported by brilliant catches from wicketkeeper Speight - changing direction to snap up Ben Hollioake's inside edge - and from Collingwood - sprinting in from the boundary before diving full length to punish the Surrey skipper's miscued hook. Although the prospect of having to follow on was averted by a last-wicket stand of twenty-three by Salisbury and Bishop, Surrey were eventually all out in 55.5 overs for just 104, the lowest score recorded by any county against Durham.

The visitors clearly needed an outstanding second-innings bowling performance if they were to get back into the match, and soon rocked their hosts back on their heels at 14-4 as Bicknell and Tudor each claimed two wickets. Surrey lacked their opponents' depth in seam bowling, however, and found it hard to maintain their momentum as Katich dug in doggedly with help from Peng, who again batted attractively while making twenty-three, and then Speight, who fell to Tudor (3-45) shortly after tea for thirty-six. With dark clouds overhead making it pretty gloomy out in the middle, Bicknell managed to snap up a seventh wicket for his side by bowling Killeen for a duck before bad light finally prevailed and brought play to a close with Durham on 121-7, leading by 251 runs.

Since the task ahead of them was already looking pretty tough, Surrey definitely didn't need the 50-run partnership between Katich and Betts that gave the home county a great start to day three. Although Bicknell eventually claimed Betts lbw for twenty-three to secure his first five-wicket haul in the Championship since July 1998 - incredible but true! - the game already appeared to have slipped away from the champions. Ben Hollioake's belated two-wicket contribution, including the scalp of Katich, who was last out for a highly accomplished sixty-five, left Durham 316 runs ahead of their more illustrious opponents and clear favourites to claim their first-ever victory over the men from The Oval.

Although Butcher and Ward saw their side through to lunch at 39-0, the second innings turned out to be an even more embarrassing procession than the first had been once play resumed. Batting was made to look nigh on impossible by further top-class seam bowling that transformed a score of 41-0 into 66-9 and then 85 all out. Having beaten their own record for the lowest score against Durham, the county champions had been deservedly humbled by the crushing margin of 231 runs, with the north-east county's four seamers having all performed brilliantly throughout. As Messrs Brown (3-8), Killeen (3-14), Harmison (2-19) and Betts (2-36) savoured their triumph in front of an almost disbelieving gathering of members and supporters from both sides, Surrey were already appreciating that it would be harder to retain their Championship crown than it had been to win it.

Having had a day off to lick their wounds, Surrey reappeared in the guise of the Lions to take their revenge in the NCL match with the Durham Dynamos.

After being put in to bat, the visitors built on the foundations laid by Mark Butcher (27) and Alec Stewart (41) to rattle up a decent score of 230-7, with most of the late impetus being provided by Ben Hollioake (42 from 50 balls) and Jason Ratcliffe (25 from 24 balls) at the expense of Steve Harmison (9-0-66-1). Many of the runs conceded by the lanky speed merchant came from wides, which accounted for just over half of the top-scoring fifty-one extras that boosted Surrey's total.

Sadly for the Dynamos, their reply was anything but dynamic as Martin Bicknell and Alex Tudor (2-26) stifled and then dismissed the top order, leaving the rest of the batsmen with too much ground to make up. As the required run rate spiralled ever higher, Adam Hollioake outwitted and eradicated the middle and lower order, returning career-best figures of 5-29 and sending Durham into a nosedive from 99-3 to 164 all out that left the Lions victorious by sixty-six runs.

A rather tougher task faced Surrey as they next travelled to Headingley for the Benson & Hedges Cup quarter-final against a Yorkshire side that had made a promising start to the season.

After the visitors had named a team that included Carl Greenidge in place of Ian Salisbury, since the pitch looked tailor-made for seamers, David Byas won the toss and, predictably enough, asked Surrey to bat. Matthew Hoggard (4-39) then justified his skipper's decision by removing Messrs Butcher, Brown, Thorpe and Adam Hollioake with just thirty-nine runs on the board, though Byas could have earned a fifth wicket for his bowler had he not missed a difficult chance offered to second slip by Alec Stewart early in the innings. Thereafter, Stewart made sure that Yorkshire paid for reprieving him by anchoring the Surrey batting effort, while Ben Hollioake (44) played a highly significant role in a reviving stand of ninety-six for the sixth wicket. With Jason Ratcliffe giving the total a late boost by scoring fifteen runs from eleven balls, and Stewart accelerating to finish unbeaten on ninety-seven, the final total of 198-6 looked perfectly acceptable.

It began to resemble an above-par score, however, when the trusted firm of Bicknell and Tudor (2-39) reduced the Tykes to 15-3, thanks in part to a couple of excellent gully catches by Ben Hollioake. The balance of power then swung back towards the hosts as Matthew Wood (59) and Darren Lehmann (50) constructed a fine partnership of 109, before the burly Australian was erroneously adjudged caught behind down the legside off Adam Hollioake (2-30) with his team needing seventy-five to win at under five runs per over. This decision turned out to be crucial, since it allowed Surrey to engineer a collapse through a fine catch by Stewart and three direct-hit run outs as Yorkshire began to panic. The hosts' disintegration from 166-5 to 183-9 left them needing to score sixteen from two overs and, following a fine penultimate over from Adam Hollioake, twelve runs from the last six balls of the match. With all the main bowlers' overs now used up, Jason Ratcliffe was handed the ball in a totally unfamiliar situation and, luckily for Surrey, kept a cool head, bowling Ryan Sidebottom with the fifth delivery to secure a seven-run win and a semi-final against Glamorgan in Cardiff.

With things going well in the limited-overs competitions, Surrey were looking forward to their first home Championship game of the season after the two very disappointing trips to Taunton and Chester-le-Street.

The hosts and their visitors, Kent, were confined to their dressing rooms by rain on the first day, however, and when the match got under way twenty-four hours later Surrey could only muster 278-6 from 107 overs after being put in by Matthew Fleming. In awkward batting conditions, against steady bowling, only Ali Brown (60) managed to reach fifty, though it was one of the slowest of his career, taking 121 balls.

An unsatisfactory day for just about everyone was then followed by a third day that was almost as uninspiring. After Surrey had pressed on at four runs an over to 417 all out, largely through the efforts of Martin Bicknell (73) and Ian Salisbury (50), who shared a 113-run eighth-wicket partnership, Kent, with no hope of winning the game, plodded to 92-2 from thirty-four overs by tea. Rain and bad light then brought a mercifully early close eleven overs after the resumption, with just twenty-three added to the total and the game seemingly going nowhere.

How wrong can you be?! Much to everyone's surprise, the match was revived by the captains on the final morning, with Kent declaring at their overnight total, and Mark Butcher whacking four balls from Rob Key for seventeen runs before a Surrey closure left the visitors to chase 320 from a minimum of ninety-three overs.

The feeling that this represented a decent deal from the hosts' point of view was then confirmed when Bicknell and Tudor rattled out Smith, Key, Wells and Hockley with just forty-five on the board, though the man they really needed to see the back of was Rahul Dravid, who had made an unbeaten forty-four in Kent's first knock.

After harbouring realistic hopes of victory at lunch, when the visitors were 63-4, Surrey found the middle session hard going, as they failed to take a wicket until just before tea when Dravid fell to Bicknell for a polished seventy-one.

Although both sides briefly threatened to claim the spoils of victory after the resumption - first Kent, when Ealham (83) and Nixon (50 not out) took the score up to 199-5, then Surrey, when their visitors' eighth wicket fell with forty-six deliveries remaining - neither side could really claim to have done enough to earn victory as Kent finished on 255-8.

Strangely enough, Surrey's next match turned out to be the return Championship fixture against Kent at Canterbury, since the scheduled NCL London derby against Middlesex Crusaders at The Oval on Sunday 21st May was abandoned well before the starting time of 1pm because the outfield was waterlogged following very heavy rain in the capital.

Conditions were, unfortunately, no better at the St Lawrence ground, since one of the wettest springs on record had left water tables so high that grounds around the country - particularly in the south - were unable to absorb any more of the rain that fell intermittently. With just forty-seven overs possible on day one, fifty-six on day two and a mere fifteen on the last day, the Surrey innings of 348-8, anchored by Ian Ward's excellent career-best 158 not out, was spread out over the whole four days of the match. Players, umpires, spectators and ground staff were all left thoroughly frustrated as Surrey took seven points from the match to Kent's six.

A rain-drenched Sophia Gardens in Cardiff provided the venue for the team's next match, which was the Benson & Hedges Cup semi-final against Glamorgan. After electing to bat when play eventually got under way at 4pm on the first of the two days allocated to the match, the Welsh county scored 99-2 from 24.1 overs before bad light and further rain brought about an early close.

The third-wicket partnership between Michael Powell and Matthew Maynard that had its roots on day one at 27-2, took the total up to 160 the following day before the former was bowled by Alex Tudor (2-46) for sixty-seven. Glamorgan's promising position was then further strengthened by a 66-run stand by Maynard and Adrian Dale until the loss of their captain for a marvellous 109 triggered a decline to 251 all out, which included three run outs and three wickets for Adam Hollioake (3-36).

The visitors' chances of succeeding in their difficult run chase soon received a double blow when Brown and Tudor - surprisingly promoted to number three - fell to consecutive balls from Owen Parkin with the score on eleven, and Surrey never really got to grips with their task thereafter as the middle order was swept away by Alex Wharf (3-37) and Robert Croft (3-42). Although Alec Stewart (85) had survived the slide to 125-7, and put up a brave fight with support from Jason Ratcliffe (24) and Martin Bicknell (25), Surrey never seriously threatened a Duckworth-Lewis revised target of 245 in forty-six overs after two short rain breaks. Despite taking some heavy punishment, Parkin picked up the last two wickets to finish with 4-60 and see his side through to their first Lord's final since 1977.

After the continuing wet weather had claimed yet another match - the home NCL fixture against the Essex Eagles - the Lions were back on the park again for a floodlit NCL contest with the Hampshire Hawks at The Oval.

Unfortunately, a sizeable crowd didn't get to see very much action under the lights as the Lions gobbled up the Hawks in double-quick time, bowling them out for just ninety-four in 30.2 overs and then cruising home by seven wickets in just 21.1 overs. Martin Bicknell (3-18) and Alex Tudor, with career-best limited-overs figures of 4-26, were the architects of the victory, reducing Hampshire to 6-3, 15-4 and then 42-6, as the ever-positive Adam Hollioake supported them with attacking fields that, at times, included four slips. Although Shane Warne proved that he had recovered from the experience of recording a pair in each of his first two County Championship matches by top-scoring with thirty-four, he wasn't immune from Surrey's excellence as Ian Salisbury pulled off an outstanding catch in the covers to end the Hawks' innings. Ian Ward then scored forty-four of the ninety-five runs that the Lions needed to maintain their unbeaten record.

LEADING POSITIONS:- Warwicks P4, Pts 16; Notts P5, Pts 16; Surrey P5, Pts 16.

After a poor start to the campaign that had seen them win just two and lose eight of their matches in the three main competitions, the last thing Hampshire needed was to face a Surrey side bolstered by the return of Saqlain Mushtaq for a County Championship fixture at The Oval.

Having lost the toss and found themselves in the field, the visitors stuck to their task well throughout the opening day of the match, restricting Surrey to 268-8 from 100 overs. Although Graham Thorpe (58) had been the only top-order batsman to register a half-century as the hosts declined from 124-2 to 215-8 against the 21-year-old paceman Simon Francis (4-95) and the veteran John Stephenson, he was eventually joined in that particular club by both Martin Bicknell (59) and Alex Tudor (64 not out), as Surrey's bowlers again showed their ability with the bat in extending the total to 333 on the second morning. Tudor, in particular, produced some thrilling strokes during a last-wicket stand of fifty-five with Saqlain Mushtaq.

Bicknell then starred in his principal role, putting the home side on top by removing Jason Laney, Will Kendall and Robin Smith before lunch, only for Hampshire to win the afternoon session by a distance, as Giles White, supported by Adrian Aymes, led his side from the depths of

33-3 to 143-4 with a steady knock against Surrey's first-choice attack. Fortunately for the champions, Alex Tudor (3-52) and Saqlain Mushtaq then combined to great effect after the break and turned the tables on their visitors in style once White had been dislodged by the Pakistani off-spinner for a very well constructed ninety-six. The Hampshire opener's exit with the total on 151 triggered a collapse to 207-8 at the close, greatly increasing Surrey's chances of winning the match, especially as the pitch was already offering turn to the spinners.

The south coast county's last two wickets added just three runs to the total on the third morning as Bicknell (4-52) and Saqlain (3-65) rapidly accounted for Mascarenhas and Francis respectively, leaving the reigning champions with a very useful first-innings lead of 123. Adding to this proved to be something of a problem, though, as Mullally struck three times in an excellent opening spell to peg Surrey back to 44-4. A recovery to 90-4 either side of lunch by Adam Hollioake (41) and Jason Ratcliffe eventually came to an end when Warne induced the home captain to play on, and thereafter the Aussie legend held sway. Bowling round the wicket into the rough outside the right-handers' leg stump he confounded both Batty and Ratcliffe to put his opponents under pressure at 109-7. A note of controversy then crept into the match when umpire John Holder suddenly called a wide - which counted as two runs in the Championship between 1997 and 2002 - against Warne for negative legside bowling. This was a baffling decision, considering that the leg-spinner had already captured three scalps with the tactic he was employing. Although the bowler was understandably aggrieved, he simply raised his game still further and, belatedly joined in the attack by Mullally (4-31), picked up two further wickets to finish with 5-31 as Surrey's slide ended with their dismissal for a total of 142.

Hampshire were now back in the match, needing 266 to win, though they immediately ran into trouble as Laney fell to Tudor for a duck, thereby recording a pair and extending a miserable sequence of scores against Surrey. The home team then struck again with the score advanced to forty when White was stumped off Ian Salisbury after advancing down the wicket and being beaten by a leg-break, but the game was still wide open at the close, with Hampshire having made 58-2 from thirty-four tense and tight overs.

As the final day got under way, results from the Division One games that had started a day ahead of this match had ensured that the losers of this contest would sink to the bottom of the table, while the winners would go fourth. This knowledge gave the contest an added edge and seemed to affect Hampshire as Surrey's bowlers sprang out of the traps to send them plunging towards almost certain defeat at 87-6. Although Bicknell contributed an excellent spell of seven overs that brought him the prized wicket of Robin Smith, it was Tudor's quick one-two to remove Kenway and Aymes that twisted the knife and allowed Saqlain to remove Stephenson in double-quick time. From this seemingly hopeless position, Warne launched a counter-attack that briefly unsettled Surrey until Tudor struck again by having Kendall taken at slip shortly before lunch with the score on 125.

After the break, the Australian leg-spinner continued to bat positively, but once he was caught and bowled by Saqlain after completing a 65-ball half-century with the visitors still 105 runs short of victory the game appeared to be over. When Mullally then followed him back to the pavilion twelve runs later after becoming another victim of Saqlain (3-89), Surrey's win appeared to have been rubber-stamped, since Dimitri Mascarenhas was carrying an injury and last man Simon Francis boasted, if that was the right word, a career-best score of eleven.

Francis immediately looked a more capable batsman than Mullally, however, and though he enjoyed a few strokes of luck early in his innings, settled in to play a sensible second fiddle to Mascarenhas, who kept the scoreboard moving by thumping the occasional ball to the boundary. A series of milestones came and went - Francis's career-best; the fifty partnership; Mascarenhas's half-century; a new record partnership for Hampshire's last wicket against Surrey - as the batsmen edged their team closer to a highly unlikely victory, before the hosts were able to take a new ball with the delayed tea interval just two overs away and the visitors ten runs short of their objective. An edged four by Francis off Bicknell in the final over of the session then left the reigning County Champions just five runs away from plunging to the bottom of the Championship table.

When play resumed, two tense overs and two singles to Mascarenhas followed before the decisive over from Tudor arrived. Having missed out on a short, wide delivery first-up, and then mistimed a drive to mid-on from the second ball, Mascarenhas attempted to pull the next delivery, only to mistime the stroke horribly and dolly a simple catch back to the bowler. An elated Tudor promptly ran off to the Vauxhall end, pursed by his team-mates, and threw himself to the turf, football style, before being submerged by his colleagues. One had to feel sorry for Mascarenhas (59) and Francis (30 not out) as they left the field, followed shortly afterwards by a jubilant Tudor (5-57) and his happy colleagues. Surrey had secured a vitally important victory by two runs... and everyone's mind flashed back to the moment when John Holder had called Shane Warne for that legside wide.

LEADING POSITIONS:- Leics P6, Pts 57; Yorks P4, Pts 56; Lancs P5, Pts 55; Surrey P5, Pts 42

Derbyshire, who were without a win in eight games in the two league competitions, were Surrey's next opponents in both the Championship and the NCL, with the County Ground, Derby being the venue.

The four-day game was shrouded in controversy from the start, as a damp pitch greeted Surrey when they turned up on the first morning. Although the hosts offered numerous excuses for this, the simple fact of the matter was that this contravened Championship regulations.

In spite of the prevailing conditions, Surrey made two baffling decisions - firstly, to play both spinners instead of calling up a specialist third seamer, and then to bat first after winning the toss. Derbyshire immediately pounced upon what seemed to be a serious error of judgement as Tim Munton removed the out-of-touch Mark Butcher and Graham Thorpe in the space of three balls with the total on nine, and followed up by claiming the scalp of Alec Stewart twenty-two runs later. Ali Brown then fell to Paul Aldred with the total advanced to fifty-one before Ian Ward (41) and Adam Hollioake led a recovery that hinted at better things after lunch.

Alas, this proved to be a false hope as Munton - with three Championship wickets at 94.66 apiece before this game - returned to claim four more victims and send Surrey crashing from 93-4 to 138 all out. Although the former Warwickshire seamer had bowled well to return figures of 7-34, it would be fair to say that he'd probably not bowled on many pitches as 'sporty' as this one.

Needing to hit back quickly, the visitors managed to removed half the Derbyshire side for sixty-five either side of tea, with Bicknell and Tudor inevitably sharing the wickets, but the lack of a proper third seamer showed up thereafter as the hosts staged an impressive recovery. Mathew Dowman, who had opened the innings and survived the carnage, led the way with a determined sixty-nine, and received useful assistance from Karl Krikken and the combative Dominic Cork (44 not out) in lifting the score to 181-6 before Surrey fought back late in the day. After Tudor (5-64) dislodged Dowman and Aldred with successive deliveries, Jason Ratcliffe accounted for Trevor Smith in the next over before bad light brought play to a close at 7.30pm with the scoreboard reading 181-9. Since nineteen wickets had fallen in the day, it was no surprise to see Mike Denness, a member of the ECB's Pitches Liaison Committee, examining the surface shortly after the players had left the field.

Once Bicknell (4-75) had brought the Derbyshire innings to a swift conclusion on the second morning by having Munton caught behind with the hosts leading by fifty-three, Surrey again struggled at the start of their second knock, slumping to 28-3. With Munton having increased his match tally to nine wickets by disposing of Ward and Thorpe, and Cork having removed Butcher, the County Champions were in desperate trouble until Alec Stewart and Ali Brown rode to the rescue with all guns blazing. Adding eighty runs in quick time, the fourth-wicket pair brought their side back into the contest with a stream of glorious strokes until Cork (3-62) plucked an amazing return catch out of thin air to end Stewart's innings on forty-two just before lunch.

Although Brown and Adam Hollioake managed to sustain the fightback for a while after the resumption, advancing the score to 160 with more bold strokeplay, Matthew Cassar (3-46) eventually produced a deadly spell of 3-6 in nineteen deliveries to put his side back on course for victory. After dismissing Brown for an excellent seventy-two, he quickly followed up with the wickets of Hollioake and Ratcliffe to break Surrey's resistance and leave them gasping for breath at 183-9. Despite a brave effort from Salisbury and Saqlain, who added thirty-five for the last wicket, Derbyshire were left to chase 166 to win with seven sessions of play remaining.

The events of the post-tea period then appeared to seal Surrey's fate as the home side made a very positive recovery after the early departures of Stubbings and Dowman. Michael DiVenuto tore into Tudor with gusto, racing to a 47-ball half-century that enabled his side to shrug off Saqlain's dismissal of Cassar with the total on sixty-five and contemplate a two-day victory. Although the visitors regained a degree of control through their off-spinner and the returning Bicknell in the latter stages of the day, close of play arrived with DiVenuto and Rob Bailey having guided their team to within forty-seven runs of a first Championship win over Surrey since 1993.

Derbyshire duly completed a comfortable seven-wicket triumph the following morning, with DiVenuto finishing on ninety-two and Bailey on forty, though their joy was tempered by the announcement that they were to be deducted eight points for producing an unsatisfactory pitch. Having taken just three points from the match, Surrey had far greater problems, however, and clearly had to work out what had gone wrong. Putting the matter of pitches to one side, they would not have expected to lose to either Durham or Derbyshire, and would now need to perform very well for the rest of the season if they were to retain their Championship title. Having slipped down to fifth place in the table, they trailed Yorkshire, the current leaders, by twenty-eight points and had also played an extra game.

LEADING POSITIONS:- Yorks P5, Pts 73; Lancs P6, Pts 72; Leics P6, Pts 57; Somerset P5, Pts 54; Surrey P6, Pts 45

Surrey needed to show resilience after this latest setback - just as they had done at The Riverside - and they had an early chance to do this as they took on the Derbyshire Scorpions in the NCL two days later.

Despite a fine opening spell from Ian Bishop, who was standing in for the injured Martin Bicknell, the home side made all the early running after being invited to bat, reaching 131-2 from twenty-six overs, largely through the efforts of DiVenuto (31) and Cassar (56). The Lions roared back into contention, though, as fine stints from Saqlain (3-36) and Ratcliffe stifled the middle order and prompted a serious decline to 197-9.

Surrey's reply was launched in fine style by Ian Ward (53) and, once he departed with his side over halfway towards their target, Ali Brown, batting at number five, provided further momentum with a quick-fire thirty-four. Although Dominic Cork (3-31) picked up three quick wickets late in the game, the Lions always looked likely to maintain their unbeaten record in the NCL, especially while Graham Thorpe (45 not out) was at the crease.

LEADING POSITIONS:- Notts P6, Pts 20; Surrey P6, Pts 20; Warwicks P4, Pts 16

Although Surrey's position in the County Championship didn't look too promising, it was very much to their advantage that six of their remaining ten matches were at home, where they could prepare pitches that didn't offer undue assistance to seam bowling, which remained their weak suit in terms of strength in depth. Unlike at Derby, where Ian Salisbury hadn't bowled a ball in anger and Saqlain Mushtaq had been restricted to sixteen overs, the spinners could play a full part in the game, and they were doubtless itching for a serious bowl as fourth-placed Somerset came to The Oval.

With Jon Batty replacing Alec Stewart, who was playing in the first Test against the West Indies, and Jason Ratcliffe dropped in favour of Nadeem Shahid, the Surrey side showed two changes from the line-up that had lost to Derbyshire. Somerset, meanwhile, were short of seam bowlers, since Andy Caddick was with England, and Graham Rose and Matt Bulbeck were injured.

Adam Hollioake was therefore delighted to win the toss, give his side first use of a fine pitch, and then sit back and watch his top-order batsmen rack up the runs. Although Ian Ward missed out on the opportunity to post a good score against a rather thin-looking attack after being 'strangled' down the legside by Steffan Jones's fifth ball of the match, the previously out-of-form Mark Butcher and Graham Thorpe thrived. With both men probably feeling that they had a point to make to the England selectors, a stand of 190, to which Butcher contributed eighty-two, would have done them no harm. Although his team-mate had fallen short of the mark, Thorpe went on to register his first County Championship century since his epic 164 against Hampshire at Guildford the previous summer, while Shahid made an attractive seventy-seven on his return to the four-day side after an absence of fourteen months.

Having reached stumps on day one at 338-5, Surrey continued to torment the Somerset bowlers the next day, with Jon Batty completing a maiden first-class century, thanks to the support of his lower-order colleagues. There were echoes of the previous season's encounter between these two teams at The Oval, as Batty emulated Ian Salisbury's feat; Surrey scored well over five-hundred; and the first-time centurion needed considerable assistance from his last-wicket partner to reach three figures. While Rupesh Amin had seen Salisbury through to the mark in 1999, it was Saqlain Mushtaq on this occasion who had offered solid support to ensure that his team-mate was able to advance from seventy-nine to a hundred.

Facing a mammoth Surrey score of 548, Somerset started well, with Jamie Cox and Marcus Trescothick posting an opening stand of seventy-three, but once the spinners were paired and found their rhythm the picture changed dramatically. After Cox was pinned lbw by Saqlain for thirty-four, Trescothick (45) and Peter Bowler departed to successive balls from Salisbury; Piran Holloway was snapped up by Batty off the leg-spinner after scoring just one run in seventy minutes; and then Saqlain followed his spin twin's example by removing Keith Parsons and the debutant all-rounder Peter Trego with consecutive deliveries. A score of 95-1 had become 98-6 and the visitors were happy to make it through to the end of the day without incurring any further losses, at 111-6.

The Somerset tail then folded pretty quickly the following morning, with Saqlain snapping up three of the last four wickets to finish with 6-47, while Salisbury returned 4-31 in a final total of 145. Having been 73-0 just before Cox's demise, this represented a truly spectacular disintegration - albeit against two superb spin bowlers at the peak of their powers - and Somerset were forced to follow on a massive 403 runs in arrears.

With five-and-a-half sessions left for play, the visitors' cause looked absolutely hopeless, though the spirited resistance they had offered before losing so dramatically in London SE11 just over a year ago would have been in their minds as they set out on this most daunting of tasks. The loss of Trescothick for thirteen to a slip catch off Alex Tudor before the spinners had even thought about loosening up was clearly a bad blow, though Cox and Holloway provided a modicum of hope by surviving until lunch and pushing the total up to fifty-six in the process.

While seam had been Surrey's weapon of choice for all but a few overs before the break, it was spin that confronted the batsmen upon the resumption. Although different players tried different approaches, nothing seemed to work for very long as Salisbury dominated, picking up wickets at regular intervals and returning career-best figures of 8-60 as the visitors were dismissed an hour into the final session for 190. Although Bowler (37) had resisted grittily, and Ian Blackwell (32 not out) had played positively with the match all but over, no one had been able to come to terms with the leg-spinner's magnificent variations of spin and flight.

Surrey's three-day victory, by an innings and 213 runs, moved them up to fourth in the table and kept them in touch with their three most likely rivals for the Championship title.
LEADING POSITIONS:- Yorks P6, Pts 88;   Leics P7, Pts 75;   Lancs P6, Pts 72; Surrey P7, Pts 65

Having earned themselves an extra day off for rest and recuperation, Surrey were then able to enjoy a short break by the sea in Exmouth as they met Devon in the third round of the Nat West Trophy.

After Adam Hollioake won the toss and asked the minor county to bat, Martin Bicknell (3-19) produced an excellent opening spell that reduced them to 44-3, before Matthew Wood (43) and David Lye (56) put together a spirited stand of a hundred for the fourth wicket. They were never really able to break free against the spin of Saqlain (2-36) and Salisbury, however, and it was obvious that Devon's final score of 194-6 was unlikely to trouble the professionals. Although Mark Butcher departed early in the Surrey reply, Ali Brown (59), Alec Stewart (70 not out) and Graham Thorpe (46 not out) provided some fine entertainment for a good-sized holiday crowd as they swept their side home by eight wickets with six overs in hand.

A rather more serious test now faced Surrey as they headed straight up to Edgbaston for a floodlit NCL clash with the Warwickshire Bears. With both sides boasting unbeaten records, something had to give, and it was the home side that cracked under the lights as the Lions turned in an outstanding performance.

After the hosts chose to bat, Nick Knight (82) was the only man to pass twenty-five as Surrey's five bowlers, supported by almost flawless fielding, turned in excellent spells of nine overs. Bicknell (2-29) and Tudor were on the mark at the start; Saqlain (2-24) and Ratcliffe kept a tight grip during the middle of the innings as the Bears lost their way completely; then Ben Hollioake (2-28) proved to be a tough opponent towards the end of an innings that yielded a below-par score of 162-7. The Lions then produced an equally impressive and confident performance with the bat, cruising home by seven wickets with twenty-nine balls to spare, even though two very poor lbw decisions went against them. Ali Brown, with forty-five, and Alec Stewart, with an unbeaten seventy-two, were Surrey's star-turns as they made light of a slightly awkward pitch to take their team four points clear at the top of the table.
LEADING POSITIONS:- Surrey P7, Pts 24;   Notts P6, Pts 20;   Warwicks P5, Pts 16

Surrey's next fixture was the return NCL match at Southampton against the Hampshire Hawks, which was being played on the Tuesday afternoon preceding the Championship game between the two sides. With the Hawks struggling at the bottom of the table, having won just one and lost five of their matches to date, this seemed like a good time to be playing them.

When Ali Brown fell to the seventh ball of the match from Dimitri Mascarenhas (3-21) and Alan Mullally (2-20) followed up with a fine spell that reduced the Lions to 44-4 on a seemingly blameless pitch in beautiful weather, this view clearly needed to be reassessed. Hopes of halting the slide were then dashed by three unfortunate middle-order dismissals and, though Ben Hollioake (37) supervised the addition of forty-one runs for the last two wickets, Shane Warne (2-32) and Shaun Udal (2-18) maintained Hampshire's tight grip as Surrey were bowled out for 116 with an almost criminal seven overs of their allocation unused.

With their unbeaten record in real danger, the Lions roared back impressively as Martin Bicknell (3-14) dismissed both Giles White and Mascarenhas in his opening over and, ably assisted by the excellent Alex Tudor, put the Hawks in serious trouble at 18-4. John Stephenson and Jason Laney then dug in sensibly to see off the opening bowlers, leaving Adam Hollioake to decide who he should pair with Saqlain Mushtaq, his obvious choice as third bowler. Although his bold decision to opt for Ian Salisbury over one of his seamers looked flawed initially as his leg-spinner took time to settle and the fifth-wicket pair took the total up to fifty-seven, it eventually paid dividends as Salisbury (2-38) trapped Stephenson lbw with a googly to trigger a fatal collapse by the hapless Hawks. The outstanding Saqlain (3-12) completely mesmerised the lower order as the final six wickets tumbled for just sixteen runs, leaving Hampshire all out for 73 and Surrey triumphant by a quite remarkable forty-three runs.

LEADING POSITIONS:- Notts P8, Pts 28; Surrey P8, Pts 28; Glamorgan P7, Pts 18

With Hampshire's apparent inferiority complex when playing Surrey having been underlined again in the NCL game, the two counties went into the Championship encounter with the visitors already holding a strong psychological advantage.

The hosts fared reasonably well, however, on an opening day of twists and turns after Surrey had won the toss and elected to bat. Although the visitors enjoyed periods of dominance while making 331, they were frequently pegged back by Alan Mullally, who bowled well throughout the innings to take 6-75. With Shane Warne (2-90) proving surprisingly ineffective and receiving some rough treatment during a 119-run stand for the fourth wicket between Ali Brown (71) and Adam Hollioake (47), Mullally's contribution was vital to the hosts' cause, though he met his match in Martin Bicknell (56 not out), who sustained Surrey late in the day, following a slump from 216-3 to 231-6.

The balance of power then shifted dramatically towards the County Champions on day two as Saqlain Mushtaq and company again exposed Hampshire's batting insecurities. After Bicknell (2-25) had removed the openers with just seventeen runs on the board, Adam Hollioake's pairing of Saqlain (6-51) and Salisbury (2-40) sent the hosts crashing from a healthy position of 84-2 shortly before lunch to a sickly 167 all out by tea. Although his side had earned a lead of 164, the Surrey captain decided against enforcing the follow-on, leaving the home batsmen to contemplate the difficulties of facing his spinners on a third or fourth day surface. By the close of play the visitors had extended their advantage by 134 runs for the loss of Ward, Thorpe, and Saqlain to Warne and Udal, with Saqlain's approach to the job of nightwatchman having been particularly interesting. Although he fulfilled the main requirement of the role by surviving until the penultimate ball of the day, his five-over stay in the middle had included a slog-sweep for six off Udal and a couple of drives back over the bowler's head!

Having reached sixty the previous evening, Mark Butcher progressed to a fine 210-ball century the next morning, thereby disproving the theory that he had a serious weakness against spin bowling. Although Warne (5-90) picked up a few late wickets as Surrey moved towards a lunchtime declaration at 228-6, Butcher was not included in his bag of victims, remaining undefeated on 116 as Adam Hollioake's closure set Hampshire the task of scoring 393 to win.

At the conclusion of the first of the five sessions remaining in the match, the writing was already on the wall for the south coast county, with half their side dismissed for 120 on a pitch that was offering an increasing degree of turn. Following up his ninety-six in the match at The Oval, Giles White again looked an accomplished player, twice lifting Saqlain for six while compiling an impressive seventy-three before being bowled by Salisbury to leave Hampshire battling to avert a three-day defeat at 173-7. Although Udal eventually fell to Saqlain after a defiant stand of forty-three with the steadfast Adie Aymes, and Mullally went to the same bowler with eight balls of the extra half-hour remaining, the hosts managed to take the game into the final day at 265-9.

Only fourteen balls were required for Saqlain to win an lbw decision against Aymes (50) and wrap up a 120-run victory the next morning. By a strange statistical quirk, both Salisbury and

Saqlain ended with figures of 4-84 as Surrey closed the gap on the roses counties at the head of the Championship table.

LEADING POSITIONS:- Yorks P7, Pts 91; Lancs P7, Pts 89; Surrey P8, Pts 83

A swift return to limited-overs competition saw Surrey hosting Sussex at The Oval in a fourth-round Nat West Trophy tie. With awful weather allowing just two overs' play on the scheduled day of the game, the match was played out almost entirely on the reserve day, and saw Surrey ease to a seven-wicket victory after stifling the visitors' batting with some excellent bowling.

After being asked to bat, Sussex had looked reasonably well placed at 143-2 after thirty-seven overs, but once Michael Bevan (60) and Richard Montgomerie (53) were separated after a stand of 104, the visitors mustered just forty-nine runs for the loss of seven wickets from the final thirteen overs of their innings. Although Adam Hollioake (3-23) was the chief beneficiary of this collapse, the architects were Martin Bicknell (1-26), Saqlain Mushtaq (1-30) and Ian Salisbury (1-30), all of whom had delivered tight ten-over spells. The early departure of Ali Brown to Robin Martin-Jenkins (2-28) proved to be a mere blip as Mark Butcher earned his side an attractive home quarter-final tie against Lancashire with an unbeaten eighty-seven.

Since Surrey were due to face Leicestershire in a Championship match that started at Oakham School in Rutland the very next day, the players had to make a swift dash up the motorway as soon as Sussex had been vanquished. This was hardly ideal preparation for the first of four vital matches that would go a considerable way to deciding whether or not Surrey would be able to retain their Championship crown. Looking at the four-day fixtures in isolation, the game at Oakham was to be followed by three consecutive home matches against Yorkshire, Leicestershire and Lancashire, the sides that looked sure to be Surrey's main rivals for the title. If Keith Medlycott's men could put a good run of results together over the course of the next few weeks then the damage done by the defeats at Chester-le-Street and Derby could be rectified.

The ground at Oakham School, which was being used for a first-class fixture for the first time since 1938, was an absolute delight, with a beautifully manicured outfield and an almost white pitch that looked full of runs. Since this match clashed with the start of England's triangular ODI series against the West Indies and Zimbabwe, Surrey went into the game without Alec Stewart and Graham Thorpe, who had been recalled to the national side after his period in exile. Leicestershire, meanwhile, were at full strength and had adjusted well to the loss of key players such as Paul Nixon, Alan Mullally and David Millns in the close season.

Having won the toss on a grey and cloudy morning, Surrey elected to bat and were soon in deep trouble at 27-3, with the 22-year-old paceman James Ormond having taken advantage of a good fast pitch to remove Mark Butcher, Ian Ward and Adam Hollioake during a fine opening spell. To the relief of the visiting supporters, their team responded well to this crisis through the efforts of Ali Brown - who completed a sparkling half-century from seventy-four balls - and Nadeem Shahid, who between them took the total up to 112 by lunch.

Although the latter fell to Phillip DeFreitas soon after the resumption, and Ben Hollioake followed soon afterwards with the total on 125, Brown continued on his own sweet way, completing a stunning first Championship century of the season from 139 balls, shortly before losing two further partners. The dismissals of Jon Batty (181-6) and Martin Bicknell (190-7) left Surrey in danger of posting a seriously substandard total, but the batting ability of their bowlers once again proved invaluable as Alex Tudor dropped anchor while Brown continued to wreak havoc. Reaching 150 from the 203rd delivery of his innings and then progressing with even greater speed to a sensational double-century fifty-four balls later, the middle-order maestro supervised the addition of 141 runs for the eighth wicket before Tudor (22) was caught off Vince Wells shortly before stumps were drawn at 334-8.

If Leicestershire had hoped to close out the Surrey innings quickly on day two they were to be disappointed. Although Ian Salisbury was removed by DeFreitas (3-115) with just thirty runs added to the overnight total, Saqlain Mushtaq was still in occupation with Ali Brown by the time lunch arrived almost two hours later. By this time, Brown had passed his 250 (from 331 balls) and moved on to a career-best 269; Saqlain had posted a new Surrey-best score and was just four runs short of his half-century; and the last-wicket stand was worth ninety in a total of 454-9. The fielders were already looking pretty dispirited at this stage, but they had further suffering to endure after the break as Ormond (3-92) grassed a dolly caught-and-bowled chance from Brown on 270 shortly after Saqlain had completed an excellent 87-ball fifty. Although Wells and the ineffective Anil Kumble managed to slow the run-rate slightly, Surrey continued to make steady progress to 505, with Brown five runs short of his triple-century, before the Foxes' skipper finally found a good delivery to defeat Saqlain (66) and terminate the last-wicket partnership at 141. The Surrey off-spinner looked crestfallen at having left his partner high and dry on 295 - the highest score ever recorded in Rutland - but his Surrey-best contribution to a stand that, in common with the 141-run eighth-wicket partnership, was a record for Surrey versus Leicestershire matches, had been magnificent.

The crowd's generous applause for Brown's superb innings was still fresh in the memory when the home side's openers emerged from the pavilion to start a reply that was, incredibly, almost over by tea. With Bicknell (3-41) and Tudor (3-34) picking up three wickets apiece, and Ben Smith running himself out in attempting a sharp single, the Foxes flopped to 51-7, still 305 runs short of avoiding the follow-on, and suddenly on course for a crushing defeat.

Although Neil Burns (30) and Phil DeFreitas (38) rallied their team briefly with a 55-run stand after the break, Adam Hollioake's decision to turn to spin eventually paid dividends as Saqlain had the latter taken at silly point, and Salisbury induced Kumble to play on, during a slow final session that ended with Leicestershire in dire straits at 134-9.

After Saqlain (2-25) finally wrapped up the Foxes' first innings for 143 the following morning, the hosts immediately hit trouble again when they followed on 362 runs behind, losing Darren Maddy to a catch by Batty off Bicknell from the first ball of their second knock. With Sutcliffe, Wells and Habib also back in the hutch by lunch, taken at 42-4, Leicestershire were looking set for a three-day defeat until rain struck, keeping the players off the field for more than two hours. Since the skies were still grey, and the weather forecast for the final day was very poor, there was suddenly a degree of concern in the Surrey ranks.

When play did finally resume at 4pm, Ben Smith's early departure to Bicknell (3-44) was followed by the hosts' most protracted resistance of the match, as Darren Stevens, supported by Chris Lewis and DeFreitas, reeled off some very pleasant strokes while compiling Leicestershire's first individual half-century of the contest from just sixty-one balls. Having reached sixty-eight, however, he was bowled by Saqlain as he padded up to a sharply turning off-break, leaving the hosts in peril again at 149-7. Although DeFreitas and Burns managed to defy the spinners for a while thereafter, the Pakistani spin king eventually struck another blow for his side by having Burns caught behind as drizzle began to turn to rain. With it looking increasingly likely that the visitors would need to act fast if they were to wrap up the game with a day to spare, Saqlain (5-35) worked the oracle, dismissing both Kumble and Ormond - to somewhat contentious umpiring decisions, it must be said - in the space of three deliveries in quite heavy rainfall. Surrey had won, just in the nick of time, by an innings and 178 runs.

As Keith Medlycott's men celebrated a magnificent first away victory against Leicestershire since 1993 the rain began to lash down... and it was still falling, in prolonged showery bursts, until late the next afternoon. Had Saqlain not finished the game when he did then the match would certainly have been drawn, since there would have been no chance of play on the final day. Maybe the tide was turning in Surrey's favour, since Yorkshire and Lancashire were both easily held to a draw, by Durham and Derbyshire respectively, in their matches, allowing Adam Hollioake's team to take over at the top of the league.

COUNTY CHAMPIONSHIP - TOP OF THE TABLE AT 10TH JULY					
	P	W	D	L	PTS
Surrey	9	4	3	2	103
Yorkshire	8	4	3	1	98
Lancashire	8	4	4	0	96

It was a throwback to the olden days as Yorkshire came to The Oval for a top of the table clash in the County Championship on 12th July. Neither side was at full strength for the game, but with each county having two players away with England - Stewart and Thorpe for Surrey, Gough and White for Yorkshire - and a seam bowler out injured - Surrey's Tudor and Yorkshire's Hamilton - there was a nice balance to the list of absentees.

A very tight first day saw Yorkshire secure a definite advantage as Surrey failed to make full use of winning the toss on a typical Oval pitch that was expected to give increasing assistance to the spinners. With no batsman able to fully establish himself against the three-pronged pace attack of Chris Silverwood, Matthew Hoggard and Ryan Sidebottom, the hosts enjoyed only two brief periods of supremacy, when Ian Ward and Nadeem Shahid were adding sixty-one for the second wicket, and then while Martin Bicknell and Ian Salisbury were sharing a partnership of seventy-three after their side had slipped to 148-7. Yorkshire were otherwise on top, thanks to some fine swing bowling from Sidebottom (5-40) and Hoggard (4-70) that kept Surrey to a below-par total of 226, which included a top score of forty-eight from Adam Hollioake.

After rain had delayed the start of play on day two until 1.30pm, Yorkshire made good progress from their overnight position of 33-1 - David Byas having fallen to Salisbury's final ball of the opening day - despite the loss of Richard Blakey with the score at sixty-four. Once Michael Vaughan was joined by Darren Lehmann the spinners were put under the cosh, with the Australian taking a particular liking to a below-par Salisbury and forcing him out of the attack with a series of boundaries on his way to a scintillating 45-ball half-century. With their total seemingly shrinking by the minute, it was just as well for Surrey that Bicknell's return to the attack soon produced his 800th first-class wicket. The prize scalp of Lehmann (55), who miscued a pull to mid-on, was well timed, too, since it allowed the hosts to regroup during the tea interval that arrived shortly afterwards at 175-3.

With the Championship's leading run-scorer now out of the way, Adam Hollioake reverted to an all-spin attack, with excellent results for the home county. Once Vaughan had fallen lbw for eighty to Saqlain's quicker ball with the total on 189, the Yorkshire innings folded rapidly as seven wickets fell for fifty-three runs, restricting the visitors' first-innings lead to just sixteen. Although the smiles were back on Surrey faces as the perpetrators of the Tykes' decline to 242 all out, Saqlain (6-63) and Salisbury (3-105), led their side from the field, they were soon wiped off as Butcher fell lbw to Silverwood during the two overs that the home team had to face before the close of play.

Knowing that they couldn't afford to lose a cluster of wickets to Yorkshire's fired-up pacemen at the start of the third day, Surrey batted with extreme caution during the morning session, wearing down Messrs Silverwood, Hoggard and Sidebottom as they reached 62-2 from thirty overs at lunch, with the only casualty having been nightwatchman Salisbury, who had hung around for seventeen of those overs.

The match turned in Yorkshire's favour after the restart, however, as Ward (39) and Adam Hollioake fell to the off-spin of James Middlebrook and the gentle medium pace of Gary Fellows respectively with Surrey leading by just sixty-nine runs. With the new batsman, Ali Brown, seemingly immune to the pressure of the situation and making a confident start against this pair of bowlers, Byas made the logical decision to switch back to his pacemen, though it failed to produce the results he desired. Looking tired from their exertions in the match to date, they were unable to peg back the scoring rate as the fifth-wicket partnership raced past fifty and Shahid completed an excellent half-century from 104 balls. This left the Yorkshire captain with no alternative but to revert to his back-up bowlers and, as a result, the balance of power shifted rapidly towards the Championship leaders. With Brown racing to a 52-ball fifty and the value of his alliance with Shahid expanding to three figures in just nineteen overs, Surrey were holding the whip hand as tea arrived at 197-4.

Although Shahid fell lbw to Middlebrook (4-119) not long after the restart, his fine knock of eighty had proved most valuable in changing the course of the match. Since the hosts were leading by 213 at the time of his departure, they could afford to shrug off the loss of Ben Hollioake and Jon Batty in rapid succession shortly after Brown had completed a marvellous century from his 106th delivery. By the close of play, Surrey had advanced to 320-7, with Brown (130 not out) and Bicknell (25 not out) having added to the Tykes' misery with an unbroken stand of fifty-five, during which Lehmann was penalised four times for negative legside bowling. This demonstrated just how far and how quickly the game had slipped away from Yorkshire.

Having elected to continue batting on the final morning of the match, Adam Hollioake's declaration came after four overs, at 345-8, when Bicknell fell to Silverwood for forty, leaving Brown unbeaten on 140. This set the visitors a target of 330 to win in a minimum of ninety overs, though it soon became obvious that a draw was now the best they could hope for. Despite the fact that he was carrying a knee injury, Martin Bicknell took the new ball and removed both openers during an outstanding first spell of 8-4-17-2 that prefaced the introduction of Saqlain and Salisbury just before lunch.

Having been 55-2 at the break, the visitors then fell apart spectacularly during the afternoon session. After Anthony McGrath had departed to a bat-pad catch off Saqlain with the score unchanged, the key wicket of Lehmann came eleven overs later - with just ten singles added to the total - when the clearly frustrated left-hander finally cracked, advancing on Salisbury and mistiming a drive to wide mid-on where Brown took a good low catch. With their talisman gone for seventeen, Yorkshire then dipped dramatically to 68-6 as the former England leg-spinner took wickets in each of his next two overs to complete a deadly spell of 3-1 in twelve balls. This prompted a change of approach from the visitors, with the remainder of their batsmen attempting to get after the Surrey spin twins, but with very limited success. Although Fellows, Middlebrook and Silverwood all managed to pick off a couple of boundaries, Saqlain was quick to hit back each time, taking two wickets in four balls on two separate occasions to finish the innings off at 126 with a devastating spell of 4-9 in fourteen deliveries. With Surrey's first Championship victory over Yorkshire since 1995 sealed by a margin of 203 runs with more than a session to spare, Saqlain (5-41 in the innings and 11-104 in the match) and Salisbury (3-36) led their team back to the dressing room to the applause of a home crowd who were starting to think in terms of back-to-back Championships for their team.

With Lancashire having drawn at Taunton, Keith Medlycott's men now led the way by sixteen points, though both of their roses rivals had a game in hand.

COUNTY CHAMPIONSHIP - TOP OF THE TABLE AT 15TH JULY				
	P	W	D	L	PTS
Surrey	10	5	3	2	119
Lancashire	9	4	5	0	103
Yorkshire	9	4	3	2	102

Having won nine successive games in the three major competitions since their defeat at Derby, Surrey were now really flying, and they managed to take their victorious streak into double figures the next day when the Glamorgan Dragons were comprehensively beaten by sixty-seven runs in the NCL at The Oval.

The match didn't start well for the Lions, as Alex Wharf (2-37) removed both Mark Butcher and Nadeem Shahid with just nine runs in the bank but, thereafter, the hosts gradually took control, first through a 63-run alliance between Ian Ward and Ali Brown, and then by means of a fourth-wicket partnership of 181 between Ward and Adam Hollioake. The Surrey captain dominated both the stand and the Glamorgan bowlers in scorching to 111 from just ninety-eight deliveries, with the second fifty of his century coming from a mere thirty-eight balls. Ward, meanwhile, played a sensible supporting role, finishing unbeaten on ninety when the innings closed at 268-5.

With an excellent opening spell by Martin Bicknell (7-0-16-0) preventing the Dragons from getting away to the flying start that they needed, Surrey were able to retain pole position throughout Glamorgan's reply. Having also struggled to make any headway against Saqlain Mushtaq, the visitors' fate was finally sealed when Ben Hollioake (4-42) dismissed Steve James (36) and Michael Powell (31) in quick succession after they had taken their side to 113-2 from twenty-five overs. With the required run rate already up to eight an over, and two new batsmen at the crease, the decline that followed - to 201 all out - was almost inevitable.

Having maintained their unbeaten record, Surrey moved four points ahead of the Outlaws again and, perhaps more significantly, twelve points ahead of Glamorgan in fourth place.

NCL DIVISION TWO - TOP OF THE TABLE AT 16TH JULY					
	P	W	L	T	A	PTS
Surrey	9	7	0	0	2	32
Nottinghamshire	8	7	1	0	0	28
Warwickshire	8	5	2	1	0	22

The third of Surrey's four key Championship clashes brought Leicestershire to Woodbridge Road, Guildford, still smarting, no doubt, from their humiliation at Oakham School just two weeks previously. Having just beaten Durham at Grace Road they were still very much in contention for the title, twenty-five points behind Surrey in fourth place but with a game in hand, as Vince Wells won the toss and decided to bat in ideal conditions.

Despite the fact that everything looked nicely set up for the batsmen, Martin Bicknell still managed two strikes with the new ball, claiming the wicket of Darren Maddy, caught behind, for the third time in three Championship innings with the score on sixteen and then following up by accepting a simple return catch offered by Darren Stevens ten runs later. With Carl Greenidge - deputising for the injured Alex Tudor - unable to break through at the other end, Iain Sutcliffe and Ben Smith stabilised the innings up until lunch.

The return of Bicknell after the break provided Surrey with a third wicket, when Sutcliffe (37) edged to second slip with the total on ninety-five, though successes were hard to come by for the home side during the rest of the afternoon. With Saqlain Mushtaq getting no joy from the pitch, and Ian Salisbury being allowed to rest an injured shoulder, Smith shared two further fifty-plus stands, first with Aftab Habib and then with his captain, before completing a fine century from 182 balls shortly before tea. Although he had been dropped at square leg by Greenidge off Ben Hollioake when on eighteen, nothing could detract from a magnificent effort that had put his side in a good position at 213-5 as the interval arrived.

Fortunately for the hosts, the final session of the day had a dream start as the indefatigable Bicknell had Smith (102) caught at slip from the fourth delivery, with the batsman having failed to add to his score. The Foxes' middle-order man left the field to a fine round of applause, having become the first man to score a Championship century against Surrey in 2000.

Bicknell's haul of five wickets then became six with the total advanced to 226 when Neil Burns edged to his opposite number, leaving the home team in the box seat for the first time since Leicestershire had been reduced to 26-2 early in the morning. Phillip DeFreitas and Dominic Williamson, aided by a glut of extras, put their side back on top, though, by adding eighty-six for the eighth wicket until equilibrium was restored late in the day when they departed to consecutive deliveries - Williamson to a disputed catch by Batty off Adam Hollioake after making a career-best forty-seven, and DeFreitas (27) to a catch at point from an angry slash at the next ball bowled by Saqlain.

When play resumed the next morning, Martin Bicknell completed well-deserved figures of 7-72 - his best return since 1991 - by having Anil Kumble caught behind with the total on 318, before Surrey's reply got away to a dreadful start when Mark Butcher was erroneously given out caught down the legside off James Ormond from the third ball of the innings. Nadeem Shahid (47) then played very attractively in partnership with Ian Ward before falling to Kumble on the stroke of lunch, just as the home side had been threatening to take command, while the loss of Adam Hollioake early in the middle session of the day maintained the balance of the game at 123-3. Although Ward continued to hold his end up, reaching fifty from the 129th ball of his innings, Surrey suffered another setback when Ali Brown was forced to retire from the fray after taking a nasty blow on the wrist from Ormond, who was confirming the good impression he had made at Oakham School. On top of his other qualities, the strapping paceman demonstrated great versatility later in the afternoon after Ward and the out-of-form Ben Hollioake had taken the score to a very promising 198-3. With his options dwindling, Wells asked Ormond to deliver some off-breaks, and with his fifth delivery the Leicestershire opening bowler had the younger Hollioake caught at short leg off bat and pad. Jon Batty then went to Kumble with just eleven runs added to the total, putting the game back in the melting pot, before the welcome reappearance of Brown enabled the hosts to reassert their authority either side of tea by moving to within fifty-two runs of the Foxes' score with five wickets in hand. With Ward having just completed his second Championship century of the season from 206 balls after almost five hours of impressive concentration, Surrey looked sure to earn a first-innings lead until Brown (34) fell to Ormond in the next over. Unfortunately for the home county, this wicket was the first of four that tumbled in five overs as 266-5 became 273-9, with the lower order that had performed so well in the first game at Oakham crumbling away in the face of hostile bowling from Ormond, who suddenly had six wickets to his name. Although the 22-year-old paceman failed to add to his haul, since Kumble (3-68) finished off the Surrey innings by claiming Greenidge lbw with the total on 288, he still finished with the impressive figures of 6-87 as the Foxes' players left the field with a small, but largely unexpected, first-innings lead of thirty to build on in the remaining fourteen overs of the day.

Any sense of contentment that the visitors felt after regaining the initiative late in the Surrey innings was to be wiped away before stumps were drawn. Their second knock started badly when Maddy once again fell to Bicknell - bowled by an absolute peach of a delivery that plucked out his off stump with the innings just six balls old - and the left-handed Sutcliffe lost his middle stump as he drove at the fourth ball of the Surrey swing king's second over. From 7-2, Darren Stevens and Ben Smith stabilised the innings for seven overs, taking the total up to thirty-one in the process, before a devastating decline set in to drive the home crowd wild. Almost inevitably, it was the Guildford C.C. old boy, Bicknell, who was responsible for a sensational Leicestershire slide from 31-2 to 33-5, as he had Stevens caught at second slip; trapped nightwatchman Burns lbw four balls later; and then induced an edge from Habib that was again picked up at second slip. With Bicknell boasting figures of 5-24 in the innings - and 12-96 in the match - to date, it was little wonder that the fans were at fever pitch, and the sudden realisation that the game was now at Surrey's mercy was underlined when Greenidge won an lbw verdict against Smith as he played no stroke to the second ball of the day's final over. This belated reward for Greenidge, who had been plugging away accurately from the railway end, left the Foxes very much on the run with their innings in tatters at 33-6 as stumps were drawn.

Day three started with a volley of strokes from the Leicestershire seventh-wicket pair of Vince Wells and Phillip DeFreitas that saw seven fours and an incredible square-driven six by Wells off Bicknell flowing from the first seven overs. With forty-seven runs having been added to the overnight total in this time, Bicknell then got back amongst the wickets, having DeFreitas brilliantly picked up by Mark Butcher diving low to his left at second slip and then following up two balls later by inducing an outside edge from Wells that flew to Ali Brown at first slip. At 81-8 the game looked to be all over for the visitors, since the pitch was still playing well, and the only remaining question was how many wickets Bicknell would end up with. Four overs later we knew the answer. After Kumble had been caught at square cover from the third ball of the Surrey seamer's thirteenth over, Ormond had his off stump knocked back two balls later to leave Leicestershire all out for eighty-seven and the brilliant Bicknell with a whole host of feats and records to his name as he left the field to a rapturous ovation from spectators and players alike - he had become the first man in the country to reach fifty first-class wickets for the season when dismissing Kumble; his final innings figures were 9-47 and his match figures 16-119, with the former being his best in the Championship and the latter, not surprisingly, the best of his career; and his match figures were the best recorded in England since Jim Laker's 19-90 in the Old Trafford Test of 1956.

At this moment in time, however, the most important thing for Surrey was that Bicknell's astonishing performance had set the team up for a vital Championship victory that would maintain their position at the head of the table. Needing just 118 runs to eclipse the County Champions of 1996 and 1998, Butcher and Ward knocked fifty-three off the target in nineteen overs before lunch and then completed their side's sixth consecutive Championship win at Woodbridge Road in a further twenty overs after the break.

With both Lancashire and Yorkshire recording 20-point victories in their matches, Surrey's lead in the title race had actually been cut, though it appeared that defeat at Guildford had probably put Leicestershire out of contention.

COUNTY CHAMPIONSHIP - TOP OF THE TABLE AT 22ND JULY				
	P	W	D	L	PTS
Surrey	11	6	3	2	136
Lancashire	10	5	5	0	123
Yorkshire	10	5	3	2	122

Having had their lead in one league trimmed by three points, Surrey now had a chance to extend their advantage in NCL Division Two by four as the Nottinghamshire Outlaws came to Guildford for a big first-versus-second showdown.

As things worked out, the contest more closely resembled a top-versus-bottom clash as the Lions dished out a 127-run mauling, dominating their opponents almost from start to finish. The only time that the visitors were on top was when David Lucas removed Mark Butcher for six in the third over, since that wicket brought Graham Thorpe to the crease to share a 139-run second-wicket partnership with Ian Ward (51). Thorpe scored at a run a ball throughout his innings, reaching a superb century from the 99th delivery he faced and going on to score an unbeaten 126 from 127 balls as Surrey - aided by late blasts from Brown (37 from 24 balls) and Adam Hollioake (21 from 19) - powered their way to 273-3.

Facing this daunting total, Nottinghamshire started well with a 57-run opening partnership that included the first Bicknell versus Bicknell confrontation since Darren's move north. This battle within a battle ended with honours even when the elder Bicknell was run out for fourteen, but the game as a whole was always flowing Surrey's way, especially once Saqlain Mushtaq (3-25) and Jason Ratcliffe (3-39) joined forces to strangle the life out of the middle-order batting. After losing seven wickets for fifty-four runs to this pairing in subsiding to 111-7, the tail was swept aside by the Hollioakes as the Outlaws crashed to 146 all out after 35.2 overs.

NCL DIVISION TWO - TOP OF THE TABLE AT 23RD JULY						
	P	W	L	T	A	PTS
Surrey	10	8	0	0	2	36
Nottinghamshire	9	7	2	0	0	28
Middlesex	10	5	3	1	1	24

Two very important matches against Lancashire now followed, with the Nat West Trophy quarter-final draw having presented the red rose county with a tie at The Oval just a week before they were due to visit London SE11 in the County Championship. With both sides chasing the Championship-Nat West double, the matches seemed likely to be hard-fought close-run affairs. Well, that was the theory anyway.

The Nat West match turned out to be a major disappointment for Surrey as they failed to perform to their usual high standard and suffered an eight-wicket thrashing that brought their sequence of twelve consecutive competitive victories shuddering to a halt.

Although they reached 80-0 from the first twenty overs through Ian Ward (28) and Alec Stewart (49), only Graham Thorpe (55) and Ian Salisbury (21 not out from 21 balls) made any impression with the bat thereafter as Lancashire's three spinners - Chris Schofield (4-41), Gary Yates (2-40) and Gary Keedy (1-40) - took control on a pitch that provided them with plenty of assistance. It was a case of Surrey being hoisted by their own petard as a series of inappropriate strokes led to a slump from 99-1 to 182-7 and a disappointing 50-over total of 210-7.

Alex Tudor's third-ball uprooting of Michael Atherton's off-stump that proved to be the zenith of the home side's display in the field as Andrew Flintoff strode in to take full advantage of Martin Bicknell's absence with a back strain. Rushing to a 40-ball half-century that included three consecutive fours off Carl Greenidge and two successive sixes off Jason Ratcliffe, he put Lancashire in complete command at 71-1 from twelve overs. Although he was a little more circumspect against the spinners, the England all-rounder soon put Lancashire's victory beyond doubt and went on to complete a wonderful hundred from just eighty-eight deliveries during a 190-run partnership with Saurav Ganguly, who fell to Tudor (2-48) for fifty-one shortly before Flintoff closed out the match. There were fourteen overs remaining when the big all-rounder made the winning hit and left the field to a well deserved ovation with 135 runs, nineteen fours and four sixes to his name.

With Surrey now left to concentrate their efforts on the two leagues, they had a week off, during which the roses counties went head-to-head in a vital Championship encounter at Headingley. After Yorkshire had the better of the first three days, a fourth-day washout was excellent news for Surrey, leaving the white rose county with eleven points and the red rose county with nine. All three title contenders had now played eleven games and the position at the top of the Championship couldn't have been much tighter, since Surrey had 136 points to Yorkshire's 133 and Lancashire's 132. This just added to the importance of the clash against unbeaten Lancashire at The Oval two days later.

With England's third Test against the West Indies at Old Trafford claiming the services of Messrs Thorpe, Stewart and Atherton - the latter two earning their 100th cap - neither side was at full strength, though the home team were boosted by the return of Alex Tudor from his side strain. When John Crawley called incorrectly at the toss, it was inevitable that Surrey would bat, and on a first day shorn of thirty-six overs by rain that halted play just before tea, the hosts made 191-6, which was thanks almost entirely to the middle-order trio of Ali Brown and the Hollioake brothers, since Michael Smethurst had reduced the Championship leaders to 12-3 during an opening burst of 9-5-7-3. Adam Hollioake's eighty was the key to the recovery, with Brown (54) playing the major role in helping him to add ninety-six for the fourth wicket, and brother Ben (24) playing second fiddle during a stand of fifty-six for the fifth wicket.

After further rain on day two had allowed just eleven overs' play before tea, the impressive Smethurst (6-63) pegged Surrey back to 237-8 before a vital partnership of fifty-seven for the ninth wicket between Ian Salisbury and Alex Tudor, enabled Surrey to post a total of 310. With just two days left for play a draw was looking the most likely result.

The events of the third morning prompted a reappraisal of that view, however, as Tudor produced a devastating opening spell of 4-28 to plunge the visitors into desperate trouble at 33-5. His nicely controlled burst brought him the scalps of stand-in opener Glen Chapple, Neil Fairbrother, Graham Lloyd, and Saurav Ganguly, who trod on his stumps while playing back to his first delivery. When Saqlain Mushtaq followed up by having the dangerous Andrew Flintoff (36) caught at short leg just before lunch with the total on eighty-five it was clear that the red rose was wilting.

Surrey had an additional capped player on the field after the interval, since Ian Ward had been awarded his first-eleven cap during the break. He wasn't the only player from the home team to have something to celebrate, though, as Tudor returned to the attack opposite Saqlain (2-28) to return career-best figures of 7-48 by wiping out the Lancashire tail. After Joe Scuderi had been caught behind off the off-spinner, the tall paceman had Chris Schofield miscuing an ugly pull to mid-off; Gary Keedy picked up at third slip; and a desperate Warren Hegg bowled as he heaved to leg. Having been dismissed for just 120 in 39.1 overs, the visitors conceded a 190-run deficit, though they were not forced to follow on as Adam Hollioake elected to bat his opponents out of the match. This tactic looked to be the right one, too, as Surrey progressed smoothly to 117-1 at tea, and then accelerated to a declaration at 227-4 from 51.5 overs during the final session. Mark Butcher (95) and Nadeem Shahid (62) had led the way with attractive, well-paced knocks before Ali Brown and Adam Hollioake had indulged in a big-hitting competition at the expense of Schofield, between them striking three mighty sixes into the upper reaches of the pavilion. Although Surrey failed to pick up a wicket in the last eight overs of the day as Lancashire scored nineteen of the theoretical 418 runs they required for victory, they still had a realistic chance of notching another important win on the final day of the match.

With Alec Stewart having scored a century in his hundredth Test on the occasion of the Queen Mother's hundredth birthday the previous day, Surrey began the hunt for ten Lancastrian wickets in good heart the next morning, and they were soon making inroads into the visitors' batting line-up again. After Tudor (2-42) had taken his match tally to nine by luring Chapple and Flintoff into poor strokes to short deliveries, Adam Hollioake brought Saqlain into the attack and gained almost immediate reward with a catch at silly point to remove Crawley with the total on forty-five. Although Ganguly and Fairbrother offered determined resistance during a 44-run stand for the fourth wicket, the introduction of Salisbury shortly before lunch brought the wicket of the Indian Test batsman, who played a delivery onto his stumps after making twenty-seven.

When Graham Lloyd then fell to Saqlain (3-45) immediately after the break, Surrey appeared to be likely winners, though they had to remain patient during a partnership of thirty-eight between Fairbrother (47) and Scuderi before Salisbury stormed through the rest of the batting. Taking four of the last five wickets - including Hegg, brilliantly caught by a diving Butcher at backward square-leg from a full-blooded sweep at a full-toss - to return figures of 5-46, the leg-spinner engineered a final collapse from 132-5 to 145 all out, allowing Surrey to claim a 272-run victory and eighteen points to Lancashire's three.

While the reigning champions had been destroying their nearest rivals in just two-and-a-half days of actual playing time, Yorkshire were securing a 10-point draw at Taunton, despite putting in a pretty poor performance. Lancashire's first Championship defeat of the campaign left them nineteen points adrift of Surrey, while their white rose rivals trailed by eleven.

COUNTY CHAMPIONSHIP - TOP OF THE TABLE AT 5TH AUGUST				
	P	W	D	L	PTS
Surrey	12	7	3	2	154
Yorkshire	12	5	5	2	143
Lancashire	12	5	6	1	135

Buoyed by their sixth successive comprehensive victory in the Championship, Surrey now returned to NCL action with a trip to Lord's to put their unbeaten record on the line against the Middlesex Crusaders, who were lying just outside the promotion places in fourth spot. The Lions' second division supremacy was never threatened in the slightest, however, as they dominated a rather uninspiring contest. After electing to bat, Middlesex were kept on the leash by excellent Surrey bowling throughout the innings, with Mark Ramprakash (53) making the only substantial score, and Simon Cook (28 not out from 28 balls) the only man to really get after the bowlers in a total of 167-8.

Although the visitors spluttered along unimpressively at the start of their reply, and then lost both openers with the total on thirty-two, Ali Brown and Adam Hollioake (47) provided much needed impetus at better than a run a ball while Nadeem Shahid (50 not out) kept his hand on the tiller to steer Surrey home to a comfortable five-wicket victory with thirty-five balls to spare.

Following this derby triumph, the Lions led the table by twelve points and were close to securing promotion, since Glamorgan, the team now in fourth place, trailed them by sixteen points.

LEADING POSITIONS:- Surrey P11, Pts 40; Notts P10, Pts 28; Warwicks P10, Pts 26

Three days later, Surrey had a chance to move even closer to sealing their place in Division One for 2001 as they played their first ever first-team match at Whitgift School in South Croydon. The school ground provided a lovely setting for a county cricket match as the Warwickshire Bears, lying third in the league, became the latest team to attempt to score an NCL victory over the rampant Lions.

Although the pitch was something of an unknown quantity, despite the fact that it had been used for second eleven cricket, Surrey opted to bat upon winning the toss and were sustained largely by the outstanding Graham Thorpe, who completed a fine half-century from just 49 balls and went on to score sixty-two from fifty-seven deliveries. Although his departure at 180-6 led to a late collapse to 211-9 at the hands of Allan Donald (3-40), he seemed to have put his side in with a very good chance of victory on a slightly tricky surface.

This was soon confirmed as the Bears slipped to a dire position of 24-4, from which they never recovered. Trevor Penney (35) and Ashley Giles (28) were the only men to offer much resistance as the visitors crumbled to 108 all out in just thirty overs to give the Lions victory by 103 runs. Whitgift's successful debut looked likely to secure its immediate future as an outground venue for the county side.

Surrey now stood on the very threshold of promotion after registering their tenth win in twelve NCL matches. Additionally, two more wins would probably be sufficient to seal the title, since Nottinghamshire were sixteen points behind with just six matches to play.

LEADING POSITIONS:- Surrey P12, Pts 44; Notts P10, Pts 28; Warwicks P11, Pts 26

After a week's break to fulfil some NCL fixtures, the top three sides returned to battle in the Championship race. Surrey's run-in was most interesting, since they were to host relegation threatened Derbyshire and Durham, while also facing trips to Scarborough and Old Trafford to face their title rivals. If the home games could be won then draws in the two away matches would probably suffice to keep the coveted trophy at The Oval.

The first of these four matches brought Derbyshire to London for a contest that was sure to be played on a much drier surface than had been the case in Derby. Knowing exactly what to expect, the visitors included two young spinners in an eleven that was lacking both Dominic Cork, who was playing in the fourth Test against the West Indies, and Karl Krikken, who was nursing a broken thumb. Surrey, meanwhile, were making do, as ever, without England's Alec Stewart and Graham Thorpe, and had finally decided that the out-of-form Ben Hollioake should give way to Gary Butcher, who had been scoring runs and taking wickets in the second eleven.

When Tim Munton, Derbyshire's stand-in skipper, won the toss he made the obvious decision to take first use of a good dry surface, but then saw his team struggle to 69-3 at lunch, with Stubbings, DiVenuto and Bailey having fallen to Surrey's three main seamers.

Things then went from bad to worse for the visitors during the afternoon, as Bicknell's dismissal of Mathew Dowman (85-4) and Luke Sutton (106-5) led to a rapid decline to 118 all out. After Saqlain had taken his fiftieth first-class wicket of the season by pinning Matt Cassar lbw, the final slide to submission turned out to be swifter than anyone could possibly have imagined. Having had Paul Aldred caught by his brother at second slip - courtesy of Bicknell's parry from third - with the sixth ball of a new spell, Gary Butcher went on to claim Munton via a catch at third slip by Bicknell with the first ball of his next over and then complete a hat-trick by having the left-handed Kevin Dean caught by the same man in the same position. Needless to say, this was the cue for Surrey celebrations, with the bowler receiving a standing ovation from the crowd as he was mobbed by his ecstatic team-mates. A sensational return to the first team then became a history-making performance when Lian Wharton was trapped lbw by the next delivery, giving Butcher four wickets in four balls and Surrey-best figures of 5-18. As he led his team from the field it was revealed that this was only the thirty-second time that four-in-four had been achieved in first-class cricket - the most recent occurrence prior to this one having been in 1996 - and that the last person to perform the feat in the County Championship was Surrey's very own Pat Pocock, against Sussex at Eastbourne way back in 1972.

Adam Hollioake's team had now given themselves a great chance to move twenty points closer to retaining their Championship crown, and they weren't about to waste it. By 6pm, they had overtaken Derbyshire's dismal total, with Mark Butcher and Ian Ward having completed half-centuries, and though both men fell before time was called at 161-2, the former for seventy-eight and the latter for fifty-seven, they had played their part in ramming home the advantage earned earlier in the day by the younger Butcher and Martin Bicknell (3-36).

With their promotion to NCL Division One having been confirmed by Middlesex's victory over Warwickshire under the lights at Edgbaston the previous evening, day two started well for Surrey as they recovered from the early loss of Nadeem Shahid to move rapidly into a powerful position at 219-3 through nightwatchman Ian Salisbury and Adam Hollioake (42 from 34 balls). Once Kevin Dean, the left-arm seamer, entered the fray and began to swing the ball prodigiously it became a different game, however, and the hosts slumped almost as dramatically as their opponents had done. Putting a poor performance on day one behind him to turn figures of 0-35 into 6-51, he ripped through the rest of the batting in no time at all, with Surrey's last seven wickets tumbling for just forty-one runs. Incredibly, the last five had gone for a mere five runs to a mixture of unplayable deliveries and loose strokes, leaving the Championship chasers with just two of their five batting points and a lead of 142 rather than the 250-plus that had looked likely.

Although the loss of bonus points was of some concern, the match was now so far advanced that Surrey were well placed to force a victory... though they probably didn't expect to have the win sewn up before tea. All seemed to be going pretty well for the visitors as openers Steve Stubbings and Luke Sutton saw off the seamers in reducing their team's deficit to seventy-four runs, but the introduction of the spinners soon changed the picture in most sensational style. With Salisbury's fifth and sixth deliveries earning him the wickets of Stubbings (41) and DiVenuto (0) to identical bat-pad catches by Shahid at short leg, the slump was under way, and Saqlain needed no second invitation to sweep the Derbyshire middle order aside in double-quick time. After removing Bailey (0) with the last ball of his fourth over, he wiped out Sutton (23), Cassar (0), and Lacey (0) with balls two, four and six of his next over as the hapless visitors crumbled from 68-0 to 70-6. Having taken 4-0 in seven balls, Saqlain then had to wait a while for his next victim as Salisbury nipped in with the wicket of Aldred, who was stumped by a distance for four to make the score 75-7. With the game long since over as a contest, and Derbyshire's professional pride destroyed, the Surrey off-spinner tidied up the tail with another deadly burst, this time of 3-0 in eleven balls, to leave the visitors all out for 97 and defeated by an innings and 45 runs inside five sessions. It seemed barely possible, but Tim Munton's team had actually lost all ten wickets for the addition of just twenty-nine runs, with high-class spin bowling having proved to be far too good for some club-standard batting.

As Saqlain followed the now familiar routine of leading his side from the pitch with a wave of his Surrey cap to the members in the pavilion, he had the incredible figures of 9.3-5-11-7 to his name, while Salisbury finished with 3-25.

In the other matches affecting the top of the table, Yorkshire were held to a draw by Leicestershire at a very damp Grace Road, while Lancashire beat Kent in a low-scoring match at Old Trafford. The net effect was for Surrey to increase their lead over their roses rivals to eighteen points.

COUNTY CHAMPIONSHIP - TOP OF THE TABLE AT 19TH AUGUST				
	P	W	D	L	PTS
Surrey	13	8	3	2	171
Yorkshire	13	5	6	2	153
Lancashire	13	6	6	1	151

With just the Division Two title to play for now in the NCL, Surrey took another step towards that goal by inflicting a six-wicket defeat on the Derbyshire Scorpions at The Oval. While Surrey had gone from strength to strength since their disappointing reversal at the County Ground in June, Derbyshire had gone into freefall and had just one NCL victory and that Championship win at Surrey's expense to their credit from a truly dreadful season. Their lack of confidence showed, too, as they mustered a disappointing 175-9 from their forty-five overs, with only Michael DiVenuto (30) and Rob Bailey (43) making any real impression against tight Surrey bowling led by the spinners, Salisbury (3-32) and Saqlain (2-34).

Although the Lions looked to be in danger of another shock loss to Derbyshire when they slumped to 83-4 after twenty-four overs, Adam Hollioake (48 not out) and Jason Ratcliffe (42 not out) put together a sensible stand of ninety-three to shepherd their team to an eleventh NCL victory of the campaign with an over to spare.

NCL DIVISION TWO - TOP OF THE TABLE AT 20TH AUGUST					
	P	W	L	T	A	PTS
Surrey	13	11	0	0	2	48
Nottinghamshire	12	8	3	0	1	34
Warwickshire	13	7	5	1	0	30
Middlesex	13	6	4	1	2	30

An opportunity to clinch the NCL Division Two title came three days later when Surrey played the Essex Eagles in a day-night game at Castle Park, Colchester. Unfortunately, they were to fluff their lines on the big occasion as the hosts inflicted a first defeat of the season on a full-strength Lions' side that fell twenty-three runs short of Essex's total on a pitch that became more difficult to bat on as the game progressed.

Having won an important toss, the Eagles soared to 128-0 after twenty-five overs before Surrey started to take a grip on the game thanks to some excellent bowling from Ian Salisbury (4-32) and Adam Hollioake (4-38). Once the opening stand of 161 between Stuart Law, who made a classy ninety-two, and Nasser Hussain (57) was broken, Essex collapsed to 206-8 against the resourceful Lions' skipper and his inspired leg-spinner, who recovered well from conceding eleven runs in his first over. Surrey then struggled for the greater part of their reply, with no one able to make a big score after getting a start, and the only partnership of note coming from Adam Hollioake (36) and Ian Ward (25), who added fifty-four for the fifth wicket to briefly raise hopes of victory. Once these two departed in fatally quick succession, panicky batting from the lower order led to a rapid and decisive decline to 183 all out.

LEADING POSITIONS:- Surrey P14, Pts 48; Notts P12, Pts 34; Warwicks P13, Pts 30

While Surrey had a week's break before their next Championship game - the big clash with Yorkshire at Scarborough - Lancashire's fixture with Leicestershire at Grace Road offered the men from Old Trafford a chance to draw level with Surrey at the head of the table if they could secure a maximum-points win. Despite having the better of the game, they were unable to convert a 202-run first-innings lead into the victory they required, largely because Phil DeFreitas had a fine game with the bat, scoring ninety-seven in the first knock and an unbeaten 123 in the second. Consequently, Surrey led the way by eight points as they prepared to head north.

LEADING POSITIONS:- Surrey P13, Pts 171; Lancs P14, Pts 163; Yorks P13, Pts 153

By the time they arrived in Scarborough, Keith Medlycott's team had secured the NCL Division Two title, thanks to the Middlesex Crusaders' victory over the Nottinghamshire Outlaws at Richmond C.C. It was rather ironic that Surrey's London-based rivals had sealed matters for them at the ground of a club that was based within the Surrey borders despite playing in the Middlesex League, but everyone was delighted to have another trophy in the cabinet in any case.

LEADING POSITIONS:- Surrey P14, Pts 48; Notts P13, Pts 34; Middlesex P14, Pts 34

There were numerous reasons why Yorkshire were likely to leave some grass on the pitch at North Marine Road - they were strong in the seam bowling department; they needed to win the match in order to close the gap on their visitors; and they wished to negate the deadly spin twins, Saqlain and Salisbury, since their batsmen invariably struggled against high-class spinners. No one had quite expected the pitch to be virtually indistinguishable from the outfield, however, and there were fears that this crucial showpiece match could be spoiled by an unreliable surface as a big crowd built up in the ground and Mike Denness, one of the ECB's Pitch Liaison Officers, prowled around out in the middle.

Surrey had suffered a significant blow before play started, with Martin Bicknell ruled out by a back injury, adding to the absence of Stewart and Thorpe with England for the final Test at The Oval. Yorkshire were in a similar position, though, since they were lacking the injured Ryan Sidebottom in addition to their own Test men, Gough, White and Vaughan. While the hosts replaced Sidebottom with Greg Lambert, a 20-year-old debutant paceman, Surrey recalled Ben Hollioake to take the new ball.

Having lost the toss, the visitors were, predictably, asked to bat and managed to reach lunch at a highly satisfactory 106-2, thanks to a mixture of good batting from Ian Ward and Nadeem

Shahid and some poorly directed bowling in conditions that had, as expected, offered a good deal of lateral movement and occasional eccentric bounce.

Although Matthew Hoggard (3-100) produced a much better spell after lunch to unseat both Ward, for an excellent fifty-nine, and Adam Hollioake (37), it was Gavin Hamilton (2-53) and the medium-paced Fellows (2-27) who bowled the most consistently testing line and length as Surrey gradually subsided from 147-2 to 197-7 in the course of the afternoon.

The Championship leaders were put back on course by the lower order during a productive final session, however, as Silverwood and Hoggard bowled too short to Jon Batty (47), Ian Salisbury (47 not out) and Alex Tudor (23 not out), leaving David Byas, the Yorkshire captain, tearing his hair out with frustration long before stumps were drawn at 330-8. As a crowd estimated at 6,000 filtered out of the ground, it was clear that Surrey had taken another significant stride towards becoming the first county since Warwickshire (1994 and 1995) to retain a County Championship title.

Controversy reigned before a ball had been bowled on day two, since the pitch appeared markedly less green, with rumours suggesting that a significant amount of grass had been taken off the surface that morning. This was a clear case of the goalposts having been moved ahead of Yorkshire's innings and further soured relations between the two sides.

With the hosts looking likely to be punished by the Pitches Liaison Officer, their visitors stayed focused on the game in hand, adding twenty-six runs to their overnight total before being bowled out, with four batting points to their credit, for 356. Salisbury (57 not out from 111 balls) had played extremely well to record the second half-century of a Surrey innings that represented a great team effort, with seven scores in the 24-59 range.

The excellence of the visiting team's batting was then underlined in sensational style when Alex Tudor trapped Simon Widdup lbw with the first ball of Yorkshire's reply and had Anthony McGrath caught behind with the second. Although he failed to pull off an incredible hat-trick, praise was due to another crowd in the region of 4,500 for offering up warm applause at the end of an amazing opening over that had seriously damaged the Tykes' fading title challenge. Their hopes then dimmed further when Ben Hollioake bowled Vic Craven with a superlative yorker in the next over to make the score 4-3, and the white rose county's prospects would have been snuffed out completely at 4-4 in Tudor's second over had the bowler not overstepped the crease when Darren Lehmann edged to Jon Batty. After all this early drama the hosts gradually hauled themselves back from the brink in the second half of the morning session, though they did lose another wicket when Byas was taken at short leg off Ben Hollioake with the total advanced to seventy-three.

With the prolific Lehmann leading a comeback after the break, it appeared that Yorkshire might yet be able to give the Championship leaders a game until Fellows snicked Tudor to Batty with the total at 112 and, following a short break for rain, a furious Lehmann (66) was run out when Hamilton belatedly changed his mind about taking a single to Ward in the covers. Since Surrey were now cock-a-hoop and the home side were in the pits of despair, it was no surprise that the tail folded quickly thereafter, with 123-5 becoming 158 all out when Saqlain Mushtaq (2-0) claimed two wickets in seven balls following Tudor's departure from the field with an attack of cramp.

With Tudor's immediate participation uncertain, and Ben Hollioake having already bowled nineteen overs in the day, Adam Hollioake decided that his side would bat again, rather than enforce the follow on. Surrey then made their way to fifty-three for the loss of Ward and Shahid before bad light brought an early close at 6.10pm with no fewer than twenty-two of the day's scheduled overs remaining to be bowled.

It was bad news all round on the third morning of the match. While Yorkshire had been deducted eight points for preparing a pitch deemed to be 'poor' by the ECB Pitches Panel, obliterating their slender title hopes at a stroke, heavy overnight rain had seeped under the desperately inadequate covering of the bowlers' run-up at the pavilion end of the ground, causing the start of play to be delayed. This was immensely frustrating for the spectators and the Surrey team alike. With the home side making it abundantly clear that they were no longer interested in playing, everyone was left to hang around in bright sunshine until the umpires decreed that play should start at 3.30pm, by which time dark clouds were looming in the distance. After just eleven overs, during which Mark Butcher advanced his score to forty-nine, Adam Hollioake fell to Silverwood, and the score moved on to 89-3, the heavens opened, putting an end to the day's action and almost certainly condemning the game to a draw.

Further overnight rain then kept the players off the field until 4pm on the final day, leaving just thirty-two overs for play. Although Surrey declared immediately at their overnight score, Yorkshire's openers were able to reach 68-0 from twenty-five overs in relative comfort before the inevitable draw was declared and hostilities ceased.

With Lancashire not involved in this round of matches, Surrey's eleven points had enabled them to extend their advantage to nineteen, while Yorkshire's net return of minus one point from 'the war of Scarborough' saw them sink back to fourth place on 152 points. Although they felt hard done by to be deducted eight points, they had been incredibly lucky to escape without penalty earlier in the season when a rogue pitch at Headingley for the match against Kent had seen thirty-four wickets fall while 423 runs were scored.

COUNTY CHAMPIONSHIP - TOP OF THE TABLE AT 4TH SEPTEMBER					
	P	W	D	L	PTS
Surrey	14	8	4	2	182
Lancashire	14	6	7	1	163
Leicestershire	14	4	8	3	159

With the NCL title already secured and an important Championship match against Durham coming up, Surrey now faced a game against the Nottinghamshire Outlaws at Trent Bridge that they could have done without. Predictably enough, they rested all their front-line bowlers, fielded a pretty young side - including two first-team debutants in Tim Murtagh and Phil Sampson - and lost what turned out to be a pretty dire match.

In magnificent batting conditions, Nottinghamshire racked up an imposing 288-4 after receiving a county record-breaking 196-run start from openers Darren Bicknell (115) and Jason Gallian (84), with young Murtagh's impressive first spell and Ali Brown's career-best 3-39 the only positive features for the Lions' fans. Accurate new-ball spells from Paul Reiffel and A.J. Harris then killed the game off early in Surrey's reply, leaving Nadeem Shahid's 108-ball innings of 109 as the only source of entertainment while the visitors pottered along aimlessly before falling sixty-three runs short of the Outlaws' total on 225-3.
LEADING POSITIONS:- Surrey P15, Pts 48; Notts P14, Pts 38; Warwicks P14, Pts 34

Surrey's nineteen-point advantage in the Championship had almost assured them of the title, provided that they could beat a Durham side that were all but mathematically relegated. With just one other win to their credit - at home to Derbyshire - since their stunning and well deserved victory over Keith Medlycott's men at The Riverside in May, the dispirited visitors were unlikely to find a pitch to suit their seamers in London SE11. That alone made Surrey strong favourites to either clinch the title, or come very close to it, before they had to travel to Old Trafford for their final game on 13th September.

Although the international season had ended, Surrey were not allowed to field Alec Stewart or Graham Thorpe, so their team showed one change from the Scarborough game, with Martin

Bicknell fit to return in place of Ben Hollioake. Durham's line-up differed from their victorious Riverside eleven in three key areas - Nick Speak had been deposed as captain and replaced by Jon Lewis, Andy Pratt had taken over from Martin Speight behind the stumps, and, most disappointingly, Nicky Peng had been dropped after enduring a woeful run of form since his brilliant debut innings. Just to add to the struggling visitors' woes, Lewis lost the toss, allowing his hosts to bat first.

After the opening session of play had been restricted to just 5.5 overs by a couple of rain breaks, Mark Butcher and Ian Ward gorged themselves on some variable Durham bowling for the rest of the day, with Butcher completing a 215-ball century just one delivery before Ward reached the same personal landmark from 232 balls in the penultimate over from Nicky Phillips. With the scoreboard reading 243-0 at the close, Surrey were not only in an immensely powerful position but also virtually guaranteed the full hand of batting points that would make Lancashire's job of catching them so much more difficult.

The Butcher-Ward alliance extended well into the second morning of the match, first breaking the record for the highest Surrey partnership against Durham at 246, and then setting a new mark for any wicket by any county against the men from The Riverside at 323. Since the visitors had spurned a couple of chances to break the stand, and endured moments of misfortune along the way, the hosts couldn't really complain when their opening pair were finally split up, after adding 359 runs, by an awful lbw decision that went against Ward on 144. Lunch came soon afterwards at 381-1, and thereafter the champions-elect looked to strike out for a declaration, with Butcher reaching 191, the highest score by a Surrey batsman against Durham, before being bowled by the deserving Harmison (2-105), who also picked up the wicket of Adam Hollioake before the closure came at 453-4. With unsettled weather forecast for the rest of the match, this was a good positive move that gave the home team seven-and-a-half sessions in which to take twenty wickets.

After one-and-a-half of those sessions, Surrey had six wickets in the bank, with one coming before tea - Lewis bowled by Bicknell as he shouldered arms - and five arriving after the break when the spinners took charge. Once Saqlain Mushtaq had dismissed Michael Gough for twenty-eight with the total on sixty-six, Ian Salisbury, supported by excellent catches from Tudor and Ward, ripped out the middle order, with his most important scalp coming just before the close. Simon Katich, the 25-year-old Australian left-hander had played the spinners quite beautifully in completing a 75-ball fifty and moving on to seventy-seven when he charged recklessly at the leg-spinner, missed a wild hit to leg and was stumped. With Katich gone and the close of play score 165-6, a Durham follow-on looked pretty inevitable.

Frustration reigned on day three as wet weather kept the players in the pavilion until 3pm, leaving just forty-three overs to be bowled in the day and ruling out any prospect of a three-day victory for Surrey. With the light quite poor under grey skies, Adam Hollioake had no option but to use his spinners, even though the wet ball made life difficult for them to operate with, and a touch of anxiety started to creep in as the overnight pair of Pratt and Phillips survived thirteen overs leading up to tea.

Since they couldn't afford to leave themselves with too much to do on a last day that was predicted to be rain-affected, Surrey badly needed to pick up wickets after the restart. It came as something of a relief, therefore, when Salisbury eventually removed Pratt (36) courtesy of a stumping by Jon Batty with the total advanced to 205, though it took another ten overs in increasingly poor light for the home side to strike again when the same bowler won an lbw verdict against Neil Killeen with a faster googly delivered from round the wicket. Fortunately for Surrey, the last two wickets fell relatively quickly, with Saqlain (2-91) finally unseating Phillips (29), and Salisbury completing figures of 7-105 by dismissing Harmison with the total on 241.

Forced to follow on 212 runs in arrears, Durham's openers were immediately faced by the spinners with the new ball since the light was still barely playable, but with the score 10-0 after 5.4 overs the umpires decided that it was too dark even for the slow men to be operating and called a halt to the day's proceedings.

With Lancashire's match having started two days after Surrey's, and the red rose county having enjoyed a fine first day by dismissing Somerset for 132 and replying with 142-3, the onus was now on the Championship leaders to beat Durham if they were to avoid the possibility of a very tricky test up at Old Trafford the following week.

Alex Tudor ensured that his side got away to a fantastic start on a grey final morning of the game by removing Lewis, lbw, and Katich, to a superb diving catch in front of first slip by Batty, with his third and fourth deliveries. Unfortunately, by the time Martin Bicknell had completed the second over of the day, the light was so poor that Adam Hollioake had to revert to spin, though this move quickly yielded another wicket in a rather fortunate manner as Salisbury deflected Michael Gough's drive onto the non-striker's stumps with poor Paul Collingwood backing up out of his crease. The skies then brightened a little, allowing Tudor (3-41) to return to the attack in place of Saqlain, and his partnership with Salisbury soon brought wickets with consecutive deliveries, as Gough drove the paceman to extra cover and Jimmy Daley was bowled by the leg-spinner's googly. From the depths of 43-5, Martin Speight and Andrew Pratt saw their side through to lunch and beyond, though the latter had more than his fair share of anxious and edgy moments en route, particularly against Bicknell. Finally, though, in the tenth over of a fine post-lunch spell, Surrey's senior seamer had his man caught at fifth slip with the score at 120, bringing sighs of relief from the team's players and supporters alike and clearing the path to victory. With the spinners back in tandem, Saqlain had Phillips taken at the wicket, then Salisbury came up with a double-wicket maiden, reaching fifty first-class wickets for the season in the process, by dismissing Speight for a well-played forty-eight and Harmison for a duck to leave Durham on the brink of defeat at 133-9. Victory - and to all intents and purposes - the Championship was then clinched four overs later when Killeen gloved a sweep at Salisbury (4-49) to Batty with the total on 144. Since Lancashire appeared to be on course for a maximum-points win in Manchester, the title wasn't mathematically secured, but the players formed a celebratory huddle out on the square while the small crowd offered their congratulatory applause. Even though the Surrey team - led by Ian Salisbury, with match figures of 11-154 - were accorded a standing ovation upon their return to their dressing room, this was all very low-key after the dramatic clinching of the 1999 Championship. By opening bottles of champagne and making their way down onto the outfield to shake hands with their supporters, the players indicated that they believed the title had been retained but, since it was still just remotely possible for Lancashire to score a 20-0 points victory at Old Trafford the following week, the trophy couldn't be presented, despite the fact that it was at The Oval, along with the ECB's Tim Lamb.

As expected, Lancashire completed a three-day twenty-point win over Somerset the following day, leaving Surrey needing a single point at Old Trafford to confirm their status as the County Champions of 2000.

COUNTY CHAMPIONSHIP - TOP OF THE TABLE AT 10TH SEPTEMBER					
	P	W	D	L	PTS
Surrey	15	9	4	2	202
Lancashire	15	7	7	1	183
Yorkshire	15	6	7	2	172

Fielding the same inexperienced side that had lost at Trent Bridge in their previous NCL match, Surrey ended their successful Division Two campaign with defeat at the hands of the Durham Dynamos the next day. After Carl Greenidge (2-49) had captured two early wickets, Jimmy Daley (105) and Paul Collingwood (86) emulated the feat of Nottinghamshire's Bicknell and Gallian by posting a record-breaking Sunday/National League stand for their county, adding 177 for the third wicket in a total of 251-5. This turned out to be fifty-nine runs too many for the Lions as they crumbled to 192 all out at the hands of Nicky Phillips (4-30) and Ian Hunter (3-23) after Ali Brown (51 from 38 balls) and Ian Ward (41 from 43 balls) had given them a perfect platform with an opening stand of eighty-seven in twelve overs. Having registered their first Championship win over Surrey back in May, Durham now had a limited-overs victory to their credit too.

LEADING POSITIONS:- Surrey P16, Pts 48; Notts P15, Pts 42; Warwicks P15, Pts 38

With just three wickets or two-hundred runs required to rubber-stamp their second successive Championship title, Surrey headed off to Old Trafford in fine spirits. Sadly, the ECB had felt it necessary to warn Adam Hollioake against declaring with his side eight wickets down if they were in danger of failing to score two-hundred - thereby sealing the title by denying Lancashire a bowling point. The Surrey skipper had assured them that he would play fair, though the ECB really did seem to be making something out of nothing, since the chances of Lancashire scoring 400-2, bowling their opponents out for under two-hundred and winning the match were minuscule in the extreme.

At the toss, which was won by Warren Hegg, who was standing in for appendicitis victim John Crawley, Surrey named the same team that had beaten Durham in the Championship fixture, while Lancashire were allowed to include Michael Atherton but not Andy Flintoff.

Although Atherton soon went lbw to Martin Bicknell after the home side had decided to bat, Surrey were kept waiting for the all-important point as Mark Chilton and Saurav Ganguly rode their luck during a stand of eighty-nine that saw both men dropped and Ganguly bowled by a Saqlain Mushtaq no-ball. With lunch in sight, and the total one shy of three figures, Chilton's good fortune finally ran out when he was run out for thirty by a direct-hit throw from cover by a delighted Alex Tudor, leaving the Indian international and Neil Fairbrother to bat through to the interval and further delay the moment when Surrey's title was confirmed.

As it happened, they didn't have to wait too long after the resumption, though the desperately unlucky Tudor saw Fairbrother missed twice in the slips before Ganguly flashed outside the off stump and found his edge excellently taken by Adam Hollioake diving to his left from third slip. With the title having been officially signed, sealed and delivered at 1.36pm precisely, the twelfth man, Ben Hollioake, rushed out on to the field to join a celebratory huddle on the square and Surrey were able to relax after their nervy morning display.

The visitors then looked keen to finish the season in style as Tudor immediately yorked Graham Lloyd, and Saqlain (4-81) swept through the middle order to leave the red rose county in terrible strife at 154-7, but Warren Hegg showed great character to score an excellent unbeaten ninety-three and, with assistance from Gary Keedy (a career-best 34) and Mike Smethurst, push the total up to 324. This turned out to be the highest score made against Surrey during the season, though no one was too bothered about that - or the loss of Mark Butcher and Nadeem Shahid for twenty-eight before stumps - as the triumphant visitors were presented with the Championship trophy on the top tier of the pavilion in gathering gloom. Although photographers were there to capture the moment, and the usual champagne-spraying took place, there were very few people present to witness celebrations that were extremely muted compared to those of the previous season. Not that it really mattered... the bottom line was that Surrey were County Champions again.

With both sides understandably less than fully motivated, for very different reasons, the newly confirmed champions posted a reply of 297-9 on a second day that featured a delayed start because of rain, and interruptions towards the close of play by bright sunshine that left the batsmen dazzled by reflected light. In between times, Surrey were always second-best as they lost wickets at regular intervals after a stunning morning cameo by Adam Hollioake (49 from 39 balls) had been terminated by Smethurst. Chris Schofield (4-94) was largely responsible for bringing about a decline to 193-8 before Gary Butcher's steadying sixty-six and an unbroken last-wicket stand of fifty-four restored balance to the match.

A complete washout on the third day promptly finished the game as a contest, leaving us with a final day that was dominated by facts, stats and farce. In extending their partnership to 116, and Surrey's first innings to 359, both Saqlain (54) and Bicknell (79 not out) registered half-centuries, with Bicknell's runs taking him to a total of exactly five-hundred in the 2000 Championship. Lancashire's second innings of 304-9, which was dominated by occasional bowlers, then yielded a career-best score of sixty-six by Smethurst; career-best bowling figures of 5-86 for Mark Butcher bowling off-breaks; and maiden first-class wickets for Jon Batty and Ali Brown, who, after nine years and more than a hundred overs of trying, finally claimed his first scalp by trapping Neil Fairbrother lbw for ninety.

Having earned one more batting point than their opponents, Surrey finished the season twenty points clear of Lancashire, which was quite an achievement considering that they had trailed the red rose county by twenty-seven points after their sixth match, at Derby in June, had ended in defeat.

COUNTY CHAMPIONSHIP DIVISION ONE TABLE 2000							
		P	Pts	W	D	L	Bat	Bwl
1	Surrey	16	213	9	5	2	44	41
2	Lancashire	16	193	7	8	1	35	42
3	Yorkshire *	16	188	7	7	2	36	48
4	Leicestershire	16	165	4	9	3	42	39
5	Somerset	16	145	2	10	4	41	40
6	Kent	16	140	4	8	4	18	42
7	Hampshire *	16	112	3	4	9	20	48
8	Durham	16	112	2	5	9	27	41
9	Derbyshire *	16	111	2	8	6	19	44

* 8 points deducted for substandard pitch

With the Nottinghamshire Outlaws and the Warwickshire Bears each claiming a victory during the season's final round of NCL matches, Surrey finished just two points clear of Nottinghamshire in the final Division Two standings, though that certainly wasn't an accurate reflection of their domination of the division.

NATIONAL LEAGUE DIVISION TWO TABLE 2000							
		P	Pts	W	L	T	A	NRR
1	Surrey	16	48	11	3	0	2	11.93
2	Nottinghamshire	16	46	11	4	0	1	-2.18
3	Warwickshire	16	42	10	5	1	0	7.10
4	Middlesex	16	38	8	5	1	2	-0.26
5	Essex	16	32	7	7	0	2	0.36
6	Glamorgan	16	32	7	7	2	0	-2.19
7	Durham	16	20	5	11	0	0	0.32
8	Hampshire	16	20	5	11	0	0	-5.78
9	Derbyshire	16	10	2	13	0	1	-9.00

Although the team had again proved themselves to be the best in the country by a distance, Surrey's 2000 County Championship triumph had been very different from their 1999 success. While they had led the way for most of the previous campaign, the setbacks at Chester-le-Street and Derby had left them needing to come from behind in 2000, and the manner in which they had done that was quite incredible. The run of seven successive victories - all by overwhelming margins, with four of them coming against their main rivals - showed a side at the peak of its powers, with every major player producing a stunning performance at some point during that sequence. Another major difference had been the fact that the 1999 Championship had been the last all-play-all competition, whereas this one had come in the first year of the two-tier system, with every other side being played both home and away, which clearly made it a tougher league to win. Significantly, Surrey had come through the six matches against their principal opponents - Lancashire, Leicestershire and Yorkshire - with a record of four wins and two draws.

In addition to spawning a more competitive brand of cricket, 2000 had seen an improvement in the overall quality of pitches, with a couple of obvious exceptions. Surrey's tracks at The Oval had been rated the best in the country for four-day cricket, with their award-winning groundsman, Paul Brind, being instructed to prepare the best possible surface for every match, while Bill Clutterbuck's Guildford wicket was also highly commended. The days of Surrey using an occasional second-hand pitch for a Championship fixture were a thing of the past. Away from home, the tracks at Southampton, Canterbury, Taunton, Old Trafford and Oakham had all rated in the good to excellent bracket, while there had been sympathy for Durham's groundsman at The Riverside - his square was still taking time to settle down, and the whole ground had been soaked by rain ahead of Surrey's visit. It was therefore just the wickets at Derby and Scarborough - normally a fine batting surface - that had been disappointing. While it was easy to understand why some counties wanted to give a helping hand to their seamers against Surrey, since that kind of pitch was always likely to expose the champions' Achilles heel, it was perfectly reasonable for the ECB to crack down on counties who prepared tracks that were not conducive to good four-day cricket and the development of high-quality young cricketers. The message to those clubs seemed to be "prepare a 'result' pitch at your peril - it could cost you points".

As far as one-day cricket was concerned, it was pleasing to see the team gaining promotion to the first division of the NCL, where Surrey surely belonged, though the cup defeats at the hands of Glamorgan and Lancashire had represented the low points of an otherwise excellent campaign. The National League performances had been consistently impressive until the title had been sewn up - at which point younger players had, quite rightly, been given some opportunities - though it was noticeable that Division Two cricket was of a poor standard at times. With counties of the calibre of Lancashire, Yorkshire, Kent, Leicestershire and Gloucestershire all participating in the upper echelon, the second division definitely had a second-class feel to it and Division One was sure to present much more of a challenge in 2001. To sum up 2000, one would have to say that it had been immensely successful, since Surrey had completed their first ever double-winning summer, even if the NCL Division Two title didn't count as a 'major'.

As far as individual performances were concerned, the 'big four' of Bicknell (66 wickets), Tudor (47), Saqlain (66), and Salisbury (52) had again proved to be the most dominant group of bowlers in county cricket bar none, capturing a combined tally of 231 scalps compared to the 228 that they had managed in 1999. Their consistent excellence was amply illustrated by the fact that only one batsman - Ben Smith at Guildford - had managed to score a Championship century against Surrey. Ben Hollioake, with eleven, was the only other man to take more than ten wickets, and the 117.5 overs he delivered exceeded the next heaviest workload by a Surrey bowler in the Championship by seventy-five. All of the main four bowlers also contributed vital runs down the order, with Martin Bicknell earning the distinction of being the only player in the country to complete the double of five-hundred runs and fifty wickets in the Championship. This enabled him to be viewed as a genuine all-rounder in the county game, and made him a justified winner of Surrey's Player Of The Season awards again, yet it somehow failed to convince the England selectors that he was worthy of another chance at Test level. Although it was disappointing for the players concerned, it was good news for the county that he and the prolific Ali Brown continued to be ignored. Brown led the way in the batting averages with 935 runs at 51.94 per completed innings, while the openers, Mark Butcher and Ian Ward, had both scored almost nine-hundred runs at over forty. The fact that no one reached the magical thousand runs mark could probably be explained by lack of opportunity, since Surrey had often only batted once in a match, with the openers' twenty-five visits to the crease being the most managed by anyone.

Looking ahead to 2001, Surrey decided to retain all their existing players, though some strengthening in the seam bowling department looked necessary. Although Bicknell and Tudor had remained largely free of injury throughout 2000, there was no guarantee that this would be the case in future seasons, and there was always a chance that Tudor - if not Bicknell - could receive a recall to England colours if he kept on performing well. With the club's young support seamers having been starved of first-team opportunities, and probably not ready to make the step up on a full-time basis anyway, the signing of an experienced paceman looked like it would be a good move. Everyone was also hoping that Ben Hollioake would be able to kick on again in 2001 after enduring a miserable 2000 campaign, during which form and fortune appeared to desert him completely.

2000 SEASON SUMMARY

COMPETITION	P	W	D/A	L	POSITION/PROGRESS
County Championship	16	9	5	2	1st
National League Div 2	16	11	2	3	1st - Promoted
Nat West Trophy	3	2	0	1	Quarter-final
Benson & Hedges Cup	7	2	3	2	Semi-final
TOTAL	42	24	10	8	2 Trophies (1 Major)

2000 RESULTS SUMMARY

15/4	Essex	Chelmsford	BHC	Match Abandoned
16/4	KENT	OVAL	BHC	Match Abandoned
18/4	Sussex	Hove	BHC	WON by 35 runs (D/L)
21/4	Middlesex	Southgate	BHC	Match Abandoned
24/4	HAMPSHIRE	OVAL	BHC	LOST by 2 runs
26/4	Somerset	Taunton	CC1	Match Drawn
30/4	Glamorgan	Cardiff	NL2	WON by 10 runs
2/5	Durham	Riverside	CC1	LOST by 231 runs
6/5	Durham	Riverside	NL2	WON by 66 runs
9/5	Yorkshire	Headingley	BHCqf	WON by 7 runs
11/5	KENT	OVAL	CC1	Match Drawn
21/5	MIDDLESEX	OVAL	NL2	Match Abandoned
23/5	Kent	Canterbury	CC1	Match Drawn
27/5	Glamorgan	Cardiff	BHCsf	LOST by 32 runs (D/L)
29/5	ESSEX	OVAL	NL2	Match Abandoned
30/5	HAMPSHIRE	OVAL	NL2	WON by 7 wickets
1/6	HAMPSHIRE	OVAL	CC1	WON by 2 runs
7/6	Derbyshire	Derby	CC1	LOST by 7 wickets
11/6	Derbyshire	Derby	NL2	WON by 3 wickets
14/6	SOMERSET	OVAL	CC1	WON by an inns & 213 runs

Date	Opponent	Venue	Comp	Result
21/6	Devon	Exmouth	NWT	WON by 8 wickets
23/6	Warwickshire	Edgbaston	NL2	WON by 7 wickets
27/6	Hampshire	Southampton	NL2	WON by 43 runs
29/6	Hampshire	Southampton	CC1	WON by 120 runs
5/7	SUSSEX	OVAL	NWT	WON by 7 wickets
7/7	Leicestershire	Oakham School	CC1	WON by an inns & 178 runs
12/7	YORKSHIRE	OVAL	CC1	WON by 203 runs
16/7	GLAMORGAN	OVAL	NL2	WON by 67 runs
19/7	LEICESTERSHIRE	GUILDFORD	CC1	WON by 10 wickets
23/7	NOTTINGHAMSHIRE	GUILDFORD	NL2	WON by 127 runs
26/7	LANCASHIRE	OVAL	NWTqf	LOST by 8 wickets
2/8	LANCASHIRE	OVAL	CC1	WON by 272 runs
6/8	Middlesex	Lord's	NL2	WON by 5 wickets
9/8	WARWICKSHIRE	WHITGIFT SCHOOL	NL2	WON by 103 runs
16/8	DERBYSHIRE	OVAL	CC1	WON by an inns & 45 runs
20/8	DERBYSHIRE	OVAL	NL2	WON by 6 wickets
23/8	Essex	Colchester	NL2	LOST by 23 runs
30/8	Yorkshire	Scarborough	CC1	Match Drawn
3/9	Nottinghamshire	Trent Bridge	NL2	LOST by 63 runs
6/9	DURHAM	OVAL	CC1	WON by an inns & 68 runs
10/9	DURHAM	OVAL	NL2	LOST by 59 runs
13/9	Lancashire	Old Trafford	CC1	Match Drawn

COUNTY CHAMPIONSHIP BATTING AVERAGES 2000										
	M	I	NO	Runs	HS	Ave	100	50	c	st
A.D. Brown	16	23	5	935	295*	51.94	2	4	16	-
M.A. Butcher	16	25	4	891	191	42.42	2	3	13	-
I.J. Ward	16	25	3	894	158*	40.63	3	3	4	-
N. Shahid	9	12	0	434	80	36.16	-	3	13	-
M.P. Bicknell	15	18	2	500	79*	31.25	-	4	5	-
A.J. Hollioake	16	23	0	689	80	29.95	-	3	27	-
A.J. Tudor	14	16	6	283	64*	28.30	-	1	5	-
I.D.K. Salisbury	16	19	6	313	57*	24.07	-	2	6	-
G.P. Thorpe	8	12	0	280	115	23.33	1	1	6	-
J.N. Batty	13	16	2	276	100*	19.71	1	-	29	7
Saqlain Mushtaq	12	14	2	217	66	18.08	-	2	8	-
B.C. Hollioake	10	14	1	142	29	10.92	-	-	8	-

Qualification: 8 innings

COUNTY CHAMPIONSHIP BOWLING AVERAGES 2000								
	O	M	Runs	W	Ave	BB	10wm	5wi
Saqlain Mushtaq	451.2	127	1016	66	15.39	7-11	2	6
M.P. Bicknell	413.2	115	1052	60	17.53	9-47	1	3
I.D.K. Salisbury	380.3	101	984	52	18.92	8-60	2	3
A.J. Tudor	304.3	71	1071	47	22.78	7-48	-	3
B.C. Hollioake	117.5	25	407	11	37.00	4-41	-	-

Qualification: 100 overs, 10 wickets

LIMITED-OVERS BATTING AVERAGES 2000										
	M	I	NO	Runs	HS	Ave	100	50	c	st
A.J. Stewart	12	12	4	513	97*	64.12	-	4	8	1
G.P. Thorpe	14	13	4	482	126*	53.55	1	3	8	-
N. Shahid	7	7	2	239	109*	47.80	1	1	6	-
I.J. Ward	21	17	1	497	90*	31.06	-	3	4	-
A.J. Hollioake	21	18	5	403	111	31.00	1	-	8	-
J.D. Ratcliffe	20	13	6	165	42*	23.57	-	-	5	-
M.A. Butcher	16	16	3	296	87*	22.76	-	1	5	-
A.D. Brown	21	21	0	427	59	20.33	-	2	11	-
B.C. Hollioake	13	9	0	142	44	15.77	-	-	6	-
I.D.K. Salisbury	11	6	3	44	21*	14.66	-	-	7	-
A.J. Tudor	16	8	3	32	10*	6.40	-	-	3	-

Qualification: 6 innings

LIMITED-OVERS BOWLING AVERAGES 2000								
	O	M	Runs	W	Ave	BB	4wi	RPO
A.J. Hollioake	90.4	2	411	32	12.84	5-29	3	4.53
M.P. Bicknell	139.0	21	373	23	16.21	3-14	-	2.68
Saqlain Mushtaq	104.0	11	356	21	16.95	3-12	-	3.42
A.J. Tudor	118.0	16	490	25	19.60	4-26	1	4.15
I.D.K. Salisbury	74.4	3	276	12	23.00	4-32	1	3.69
B.C. Hollioake	73.5	0	335	13	25.76	4-42	1	4.53
J.D. Ratcliffe	123.5	7	494	17	29.05	3-15	-	3.98

Qualification: 40 overs, 10 wickets

For a detailed account of the 2000 season, including exclusive interviews with the players, read **'Doubling Up With Delight - Surrey's Twin Triumphs 2000'** (details given on page 350)

8 2001: A Mixed Return

At the end of the 2000 season, with Surrey having won back-to-back Championships and kept the same group of players together, it was hard to see any of the other counties stopping them in 2001. When an already powerful squad was then augmented by two key signings during the close season, the prospects of becoming the first county for thirty-three years to win three consecutive titles grew brighter still. Ed Giddins, the former Sussex and Warwickshire seamer who had played three Tests for England the previous summer before seemingly fading out of contention, joined the club in the autumn after allegedly falling out with Bob Woolmer, the Bears' coach, and looked to be the ideal experienced seamer that Surrey needed to bolster their attack. This useful acquisition was then followed by an even better one in the New Year when Mark Ramprakash finally cut his ties with Middlesex after much wrangling and crossed the Thames to join the County Champions. Disillusioned by the way the club he had served for fourteen seasons was being run, and keen to play first division cricket in order to try to regain his England place, he was one of three men to leave the north London-based county, the others being Richard Johnson and Keith Dutch. Since the departure of these players had been preceded by the dismissals of Mike Gatting (Director Of Coaching) and Ian Gould (Coach) in August 2000, it was clear that all was not well on the other side of the river. Once Ramprakash had secured his release, Surrey were always the favourites to land his signature, for a number of reasons - they were successful and likely to maintain a place in the first division; the team was London-based; the pitches at The Oval were the best in the country; and many of Surrey's players were known to him, and were said to be amongst his closest friends in the game. It was hard to see any reason why he would want to play his cricket anywhere else, so the announcement of his move to The Oval came as no surprise at all. With the addition of Ramprakash and Giddins to the staff, Surrey now had a quite incredible thirteen internationals on their books. Another Middlesex player, Ben Scott, a highly-rated 19-year-old wicketkeeper, had also joined the County Champions as cover for Jon Batty, since Alec Stewart's England commitments meant that he was unlikely to be around very often.

Although Stewart and Graham Thorpe were the only two Surrey players centrally-contracted to England, it was quite likely that others might receive international recognition during the summer, including Ian Ward, who had been a huge success on the England 'A' tour to the West Indies. As part of an experiment by the West Indies Cricket Board, the 'A' squad had been invited to participate in the domestic first-class competition, the Busta Cup, and Ward had made three centuries - against Trinidad & Tobago, Guyana and Barbados - while scoring 769 runs at an average of 64.08 to finish second in the first-class batting averages behind Carl Hooper.

After two years of dramatic change, including the introduction of the two-division system in both four-day and one-day cricket, the English domestic competitions were, for once, left relatively untouched during the close season. The principal change for 2001 concerned over-rate penalties. With the old system of fines having failed to make any significant impact, the ECB had introduced new schemes that involved the deduction of points in four-day cricket and the imposition of penalty runs in the one-day competitions. All teams were required to bowl at a rate of sixteen overs per hour and, at the end of each Championship match, a side would be deducted 0.25 of a point for every over they fell below par. So, for example, if they bowled for ten hours in the match and managed to deliver just 158 overs they would be two overs below par (10 x 16 - 158) and would therefore be docked 0.50 of a point. Allowances were, of course, to be made for the capture of wickets and unavoidable hold-ups... just to complicate matters. In the limited-overs competitions, sides would be given a cut-off time by which they had to deliver the appropriate number of overs for the innings concerned, and any overs that hadn't been started by the time the cut-off point was reached were to result in a six-run penalty, to be agreed and signalled by the umpires. So a shortfall of one over would add six runs to the opposition's total, two would be penalised by twelve runs etc etc. It would be interesting to see how often the umpires would be brave enough to enforce these penalties.

The season began with a most disappointing Championship match against Kent at The Oval. Although rain washed out the final day's play, the game was already a certain draw by then, with the two sides having cancelled one another out over the course of the first three rain-affected days. After winning the toss, Kent piled up an imposing total of 456-8 declared on a flat dry pitch, with openers Dave Fulton (111) and Rob Key (101) putting on 198 for the first wicket, and Matt Walker sustaining the rest of the innings with 105. Once the home side had got over the shock of losing Mark Butcher to Martin Saggers for a duck before stumps on day two, they found batting to be just as easy, as Mark Ramprakash became the first player to score a century on his debut for the county since Adam Hollioake performed the feat against Derbyshire at Ilkeston in 1993. In addition to Ramprakash's excellent 231-ball knock of 146, there were half-centuries from Ian Ward (70), Ali Brown (72) and Jon Batty (59) as the reigning champions were bowled out for 473 by the end of the third day, with Min Patel (4-117) and Mark Ealham (3-80) producing the only bowling figures of note in the whole match.

After this damp squib of an opening fixture, Surrey were in for an even more disappointing time in Manchester, the venue for their Championship game with Lancashire two days later. Following on from the wettest winter on record, April rain at Old Trafford had left the outfield so waterlogged that everyone was left hanging around aimlessly for three long days. It would have been four, but for the fact that the umpires made the sensible decision to abandon the final day's play at breakfast time, fully appreciating that there was no hope of the sodden outfield drying out, and leaving each side with just four draw points. A survey of the record books revealed this to be Surrey's first total washout of a first-class match since 1981, when a three-day game against Hampshire at The Oval had suffered the same fate.

The Benson & Hedges Cup qualifying campaign then got away to an equally watery start as the game against Middlesex at The Oval saw just thirty-five overs of play - during which Surrey made 146-2, thanks largely to Ian Ward's unbeaten seventy-one - before the following day's encounter with Sussex was abandoned without a ball bowled.

With Hampshire's debut match at their Rose Bowl ground in West End, on the outskirts of Southampton - a Benson & Hedges fixture against Essex - having been abandoned, Surrey turned out to be the south coast county's first opponents at the new venue. On a slow low pitch that made batting very difficult, the visitors mustered a respectable 194-7, with seven men making scores of between fifteen and thirty-three, and Neil Johnson claiming 3-41 for the hosts. Hampshire then found life no easier as their innings closely mirrored Surrey's, with seven batsmen reaching double figures but no one getting past thirty, and Ben Hollioake (3-29) being the three-wicket man as the hosts fell twenty-four runs short of making a winning start at their new home.

Essex then visited The Oval the next day and posted 222-8 from their fifty overs after winning the toss. The visitors' innings followed a remarkably similar course to their NCL innings at Colchester the previous August, as Nasser Hussain (63) and Stuart Law (55) set Essex up for a big total at 114-1, only for Ian Salisbury (1-34) and Adam Hollioake (4-36) to come up with fine spells of bowling that brought their team back into the game. Thankfully for Surrey, their performance with the bat was far better than at Castle Park, with an excellent 151-run partnership for the second wicket between Mark Ramprakash (97 not out) and Alec Stewart (59) enabling them to cruise home by six wickets with three overs in hand.

The final group match took Surrey to Canterbury, with Adam Hollioake's men needing a victory to be sure of qualifying for the quarter-finals. When Kent won the toss, elected to bat, and reached 115-1, courtesy of a 102-run second-wicket stand between Rob Key (45) and James Hockley (55), they looked on course for an imposing total, but Ian Salisbury brought the visitors back into contention with a fine spell of 2-45 that helped peg the score back to 176-6. Paul Nixon (65 not out) and James Golding (26) swung the balance back in favour of Kent in the latter stages of the innings, however, despite the best efforts of Adam Hollioake (3-49), leaving Surrey to chase 266 for victory. This target looked beyond the visitors when they sank to 92-4, with Ward, Ramprakash, Thorpe and Brown all back in the pavilion, though Alec Stewart was still there and, with support from his captain, looked to be turning things around until Golding brought him to book for ninety-two. Although the news that Essex had beaten Middlesex at Chelmsford guaranteed Surrey second place in the group - and qualification - they still pulled out all the stops to try to win the game from 154-6, though the brave efforts of Ben Hollioake (50 not out), Alex Tudor (28) and Martin Bicknell (24) were foiled at the last. Hollioake had taken his side to within two runs of victory by smiting the last ball of the penultimate over for six, but this left Ed Giddins exposed at the start of the final over and it only took Golding (3-47) one ball to claim him lbw and secure a one-run victory for Kent.

With the Benson & Hedges Cup games out of the way and Surrey facing a trip to Hove in the quarter-finals, the County Champions travelled to Northampton for the third match in defence of their title. After four fairly futile days on a very flat track, the batsmen left with greatly enhanced averages, while the bowlers came away with aches and pains as reward for their hard labour.

Unsurprisingly electing to bat first upon winning the toss, Northamptonshire made steady progress to 476 over the first day-and-a-half of the game, with two partnerships forming the bedrock of their innings - 173 for the second wicket between Mike Hussey (75) and Jeff Cook (80), then 161 for the fifth wicket by Alec Swann (96) and Tony Penberthy (75). Surrey's three main bowlers - Ian Salisbury (4-130), Martin Bicknell (3-129) and Alex Tudor (2-89) - all toiled for thirty-plus overs before settling back to watch Graham Thorpe (148) and Ali Brown (122) give the hosts a taste of their own medicine after Penberthy (4-66) had claimed Mark Butcher and Mark Ramprakash with successive balls when the total was fifty-one. With half-centuries from Ian Ward (79), Adam Hollioake (50) and Martin Bicknell (56) coming either side of the 193-run stand between Thorpe and Brown, Surrey were eventually dismissed for 607 on the final morning, giving them a lead of 131. This was nowhere near enough on such an easy-paced wicket, as the hosts proved by batting out the rest of the day to score 304-1, with Mal Loye (167 not out) making his first Championship century for two years and occasional bowlers being employed well before the end of a truly tedious day.

Returning to The Oval for the start of their first campaign in NCL Division One, Surrey then found Nottinghamshire's top-order batsmen to be in similar form to Northamptonshire's, with Greg Blewett (69), Darren Bicknell (50) and Usman Afzaal (49) setting them up for a big total at 216-3, before Adam Hollioake (3-56) dragged them back to a final score of 233-8. This still proved to be too many for the Lions, however, as their top five failed to deliver sufficient runs at a fast enough pace when faced by tight bowling from Greg Smith (3-32), Gareth Clough (2-33) and Richard Stemp (1-36). Ben Hollioake tried to rescue the situation with an excellent unbeaten seventy from 66 balls, but the task of scoring sixty-three from the final five overs proved to be beyond his powers as Surrey finished on 216-9.

Poor weather was still prevalent at this stage of the season, and it returned with a vengeance to wipe out the first two days of Surrey's next Championship fixture, at home to Leicestershire. Although this looked likely to condemn the game to a draw, the hosts made an impressive start after Leicestershire elected to bat, with a four-wicket burst from Martin Bicknell (4-61) bringing about a collapse from 70-2 to 88-6 after Ed Giddins had removed the openers cheaply during his first spell. The visitors made an impressive recovery, however, with Jon Dakin (69) sharing successive stands of fifty-nine and ninety-two with Neil Burns (45) and Carl Crowe (42) respectively before Giddins returned to spark a terminal decline from 239-7 to 246 all out and finish with Surrey-best figures of 5-48.

With Alec Stewart, Graham Thorpe and Ian Ward - earning his first cap - engaged in the opening Test of the summer against Pakistan at Lord's, Surrey's reshuffled batting order, featuring Nadeem Shahid as an opener, hit problems on the final day. After looking to be on course for a couple of batting points at 108-2, the hosts dipped disappointingly to 158-9 against a combination of James Ormond (4-55) and off-spinner Crowe (a career-best 4-47), before Salisbury's top-scoring unbeaten thirty-six took his side up to a more respectable total of 190. In the remaining time, the visitors struggled to 94-5 in the bowler-friendly conditions, with Bicknell returning 3-25 and Tim Murtagh claiming Daniel Marsh - son of the legendary Australian wicketkeeper, Rodney - as his maiden first-class victim for Surrey on his Championship debut. With poor weather affecting matches all around the country, and very few positive results having been registered as a consequence, just sixteen points separated the top and bottom teams in the nascent league table.

The Lions and the Foxes went head-to-head in the NCL the next day, with the two sides producing an entertaining game that ended in a four-wicket win for the visitors. After electing to bat, Surrey lost Messrs Mark Butcher, Ramprakash and Shahid to Scott Boswell (3-32) with only forty runs on the board, before Ali Brown took control in the company of the Hollioakes. After Adam had helped him stabilise the innings, Brown (111 not out from 129 balls) shared an unbroken stand of 127 with Ben (64 not out from 63 balls) during the final twenty overs to see the Lions through to a total of 230-4.

The points looked like they could be coming Surrey's way when Alex Tudor (2-35) claimed two early wickets, but the game turned in the Foxes' favour during a 77-run fifth-wicket partnership at a run a ball between Daniel Marsh (97 not out from 102 balls) and Darren Maddy (46 from 47 balls). As Marsh steered his side home with just three balls to spare, life in the first division was already looking rather more difficult than the Lions had expected.

A trip down to Hove for the Benson & Hedges Cup quarter-final against Sussex was next on Surrey's agenda. The visitors, who had a full-strength team at their disposal, elected to bat when Adam Hollioake won the toss and, after losing Alec Stewart for a duck, they were set up for a decent total by Ali Brown and Mark Ramprakash, who added 125 runs for the second wicket in twenty-four overs. Brown went on to complete his second century in four days, finishing unbeaten on 108 in a total of 239-7, and then kept his fingers crossed that he wouldn't end up on the losing side again. That looked possible while Richard Montgomerie (83) and Chris Adams (37) were adding exactly a hundred for the third wicket, but a tricky target of 102 from the final fifteen overs proved to be way too difficult once Alex Tudor (2-37) had bowled both Adams and Will House in quick succession on his return to the attack. When Ben Hollioake (3-13) removed Montgomerie shortly afterwards the hosts subsided meekly to 186 all out, leaving Surrey victorious by fifty-three runs.

Boosted by the news that they had been given a home draw against Nottinghamshire in the Benson & Hedges Cup semi-finals, Surrey returned to Championship action as near neighbours Essex made the trip to The Oval. Having named a full-strength side bar the injured Adam Hollioake, Surrey's honorary captain, Alec Stewart, won the toss and found his side in a degree of trouble at 206-6 by mid-afternoon, with all the good work done by Mark Butcher (52) and Ian Ward (43) during an opening stand of seventy-six having been undone by Ricky Anderson and Mark Ilott, who had shared five of the wickets. The stand-in skipper and Alex Tudor made light of the situation, however, and both stood on the brink of a century at the end of day one, by which time they had advanced the total to a very healthy 393 and smashed the county's partnership record for the seventh wicket against Essex.

By the time this pair were parted the next morning, with Stewart (106) having fallen to Anderson (4-154) after completing his first Championship century since September 1997, the stand had exactly doubled the score to 412 and Tudor had reached an excellent maiden first-class century. When the Surrey paceman was finally dismissed by Mark Ilott (3-127) for 116, Martin

Bicknell (38) and Ian Salisbury (26) twisted the knife to push the final total up to 498 and leave Essex needing 349 to avoid the follow on. Had it not been for a superb knock by the prolific Stuart Law, who reached stumps unbeaten on 132 out of 265-7, they might well have been batting again before the close of play.

Surrey then strengthened their position on the third morning when Bicknell (4-65) and Salisbury (3-46) polished off the innings at three-hundred - Law having made 153 before falling to the leg-spinner - thereby securing a 198-run advantage. With Stewart eschewing the option of enforcing the follow on, the hosts knocked up 206-5 at four-an-over with Mark Butcher (72) and Mark Ramprakash (52) to the fore, before declaring and leaving the visitors to chase 405 in four sessions.

Having survived the first of those sessions with all wickets intact at the end of day three, Essex continued their defiance the next day after Bicknell (2-27) had come up with two early strikes. With Surrey not helping themselves by spilling a number of catches, Paul Grayson's 329-ball innings of 115 formed the cornerstone of a fine rearguard action by the visitors that also yielded half-centuries for Law and Ronnie Irani and earned them a surprisingly easy draw at 312-4.

Without a league win to their credit from five Championship and two NCL matches, Surrey were hoping to break their duck as they travelled to Northampton for a National League game against the Northamptonshire Steelbacks. With Stewart, Thorpe, Ward, Salisbury and Tudor all missing from their line-up, this looked a tall order but a decent bowling performance, led by the excellent Ed Giddins (2-22), restricted the home side to 213-6, which included a knock of eighty from Mike Hussey.

Mark Butcher then got the Lions' reply off to a great start with a 63-ball knock of fifty-five, but once he had departed with the total on ninety the visitors subsided to 155-6 in the face of some typically tight bowling from Tony Penberthy (3-43). Although a Surrey requirement of fifty-nine runs from eight overs seemed to make the Steelbacks favourites at this point, Mark Ramprakash (85 not out from 100 balls) now had a perfect ally in Jon Batty (21 not out), and this pair upped the tempo to steer their side home with two overs to spare.

Although this win had improved the county's early standing in the NCL, things were not looking so promising in the Championship, where a week's break had led to a slide to sixth place in the table. It was important, therefore, that the first NCL win was followed by a first Championship victory. Surrey's next match - at home to Somerset - offered them hope, as the cidermen had been soundly beaten on their last couple of trips to The Oval.

While Alex Tudor was still ruled out by the side strain that had led to him missing the win at Northampton, Ian Salisbury returned to the team despite a lingering problem with a finger on his bowling hand. With England involved in the Nat West Series after a 1-1 draw in the Test series with Pakistan, Ian Ward was back in the Surrey fold, though Alec Stewart, Graham Thorpe, Ali Brown and Ben Hollioake had all been selected in the ODI squad, along with Somerset's Marcus Trescothick and Andy Caddick.

The game didn't start too promisingly for the home side as Adam Hollioake, who had returned from injury at Northampton, lost the toss, allowing Somerset to bat first. The men from the west country then laboured to 260-6, with a 140-run fourth-wicket partnership between Peter Bowler (73) and Mark Lathwell, who fell to Rupesh Amin (3-80) in the penultimate over for ninety-nine, causing Surrey considerable frustration.

Despite the best efforts of Martin Bicknell (4-62), who took three wickets the next morning, Somerset managed to extend their total to 377, thanks largely to Richard Johnson, who was last out for fifty-one. Finally free to inject some urgency into the game, the hosts then rattled up 322-3 by the close, with Mark Ramprakash compiling an unbeaten 116 in good time, and Mark Butcher (76) and Nadeem Shahid (65) playing significant roles in ensuring that the run rate exceeded four

(PA/Empics)

(Empics/Surrey CCC)

ADAM HOLLIOAKE

(Empics/Surrey CCC)

(Empics/Surrey CCC)

BEN HOLLIOAKE

(Peter Frost)

(Empics/Surrey CCC)

CHRIS LEWIS

(Empics/Surrey CCC)

JAMES ORMOND

JASON RATCLIFFE

(Empics/Surrey CCC)

MARK RAMPRAKASH

(Empics/Surrey CCC)

SAQLAIN MUSHTAQ

(Empics/Surrey CCC)

IAN SALISBURY

an over. A good day for Surrey had been especially memorable for Jon Batty, who had been awarded his county cap after five years of fine service to the club.

Ramprakash and Adam Hollioake continued to push on when play resumed on day three, but having established a powerful position to total 500-plus for the third successive home Championship fixture against Somerset, an almighty collapse set in. Hollioake's departure to Steffan Jones (3-82) for forty-eight at 365-4, followed by Ramprakash's demise at the hands of the same bowler for a superb 143 at 386-6, completely unhinged the hosts, allowing Johnson (3-66) and Keith Dutch (4-96) to demolish the tail and complete Surrey's capitulation to 403 all out. The reigning County Champions had, however, re-established control by stumps as Ian Salisbury built on successes at the top of the order by Bicknell and Ed Giddins to work his way through the middle order and leave Somerset struggling on 190-8.

Although it took Surrey eighteen overs to capture the last two wickets on the final morning, for the addition of forty-four runs, Salisbury (5-95) was able to lead his team from the field confident in the knowledge that he had set up an important win for his team. With the home county needing 209 to win at under three runs an over, Mark Butcher and Ian Ward added forty-one for the first wicket before Ramprakash came in to play a most commanding innings of ninety from 99 balls that sealed Surrey's victory. Although he became a third victim for Dutch (3-55) at 182-4 when he was caught at long-on, his knock had ensured an easy passage by six wickets with more than twenty-five overs to spare.

Although their 20-point win had allowed Surrey to make a dramatic leap up to second place in the table, Yorkshire were already twenty-four points ahead of the field, having won four of their first six games.

LEADING POSITIONS:- Yorks P6, Pts 89; Surrey P6, Pts 65; Lancs P6, Pts 63

Sadly, the following day's NCL match between the two counties was reduced by rain to a ten-overs-a-side farce... though Somerset probably didn't mind too much in the end as they ran out convincing winners by eight wickets, having used up just thirty-nine of the sixty deliveries to which they were entitled. Bowling straight and full, the Sabres' five seamers - led by Ian Jones (3-14), a last-minute replacement for Richard Johnson, who had been taken ill - restricted their hosts to an extremely inadequate 68-5 before Ian Blackwell hammered an unbeaten thirty-three from just eighteen balls to secure the four points.

Three weeks on from Surrey's disappointing home draw with Essex, the two counties locked horns again at Valentine's Park, Ilford, though it was Ronnie Irani's side who dominated most of the match on this occasion.

The visitors got away to an appalling start after electing to bat, losing early wickets to some wanton strokes and finding themselves in deep trouble at 47-4 before they were pulled around by Adam Hollioake and Gary Butcher. This pair added ninety-nine for the fifth wicket and had evened up the contest when Butcher's departure to Ashley Cowan (3-64) for thirty-six set off the second disastrous collapse of the innings. From 146-4, Surrey subsided to 198 all out as Ronnie Irani picked up four cheap wickets, including that of his opposite number for seventy-seven, to finish with figures of 5-58.

Showing commendable spirit, the visitors then hit back impressively to reduce Essex to 145-7 by the close, with four different bowlers getting in on the act and the hosts' innings having followed a similar pattern to that of their opponents. After his side had been reduced to 42-4, Irani, who was undefeated on fifty-five at stumps, had found an able collaborator in 19-year-old debutant Richard Clinton - son of former Surrey player and coach, Grahame - who had played well to make thirty-six during an 86-run partnership that revived the Essex effort.

On the second morning, the County Champions seemed to lose their way completely, as Irani dominated stands of forty-two for the eighth wicket and eighty-seven for the ninth wicket to complete a fine century before being last out for 119 with the total advanced to a previously unthinkable 296. By the end of a rain-shortened day, Surrey were really up against it at 93-3, still trailing by five, and with much resting on Mark Ramprakash, who was unbeaten on forty-nine.

Unfortunately for the visitors, Ramprakash was harshly adjudged lbw to Ilott for sixty-one early the next day, and it took another good partnership between Adam Hollioake (52) and Gary Butcher (56) to keep Surrey afloat and take the score up to 195-4. The return of Ricky Anderson looked to have proved decisive, however, as his four-wicket burst reduced the visitors to 278-9, before the last-wicket pair of Ian Salisbury and Ed Giddins managed to hang around for fourteen overs while adding twenty-eight runs. Although this partnership appeared to be merely delaying the inevitable at the time, it actually turned out to be of far greater significance than anyone could have imagined. By the time Anderson (5-79) managed to dislodge Salisbury (37) the home team's outside chance of a three-day victory had gone, though a final day triumph looked odds-on as Clinton and Stuart Law took their side to 65-2 at the close after Bicknell had struck twice with the score on thirty-five.

As lunch approached on day four - with Essex still only two wickets down and just fifty-six runs short of victory - so did banks of rainclouds that proceeded to deposit their contents all over Valentine's Park for most of the rest of the day. While Clinton (66 not out) and Law (58 not out) kicked their heels in the pavilion, the outfield became completely saturated, forcing the umpires to declare that no more play would be possible and enabling Surrey to escape with a draw that extended their twelve-month unbeaten run in the Championship.

Despite having won just one of their seven matches, Keith Medlycott's team retained second place in the table, though Yorkshire's draw with Somerset had enabled the Tykes to extend their lead to twenty-seven points

LEADING POSITIONS:- Yorks P7, Pts 99; Surrey P7, Pts 72; Somerset P7, Pts 68; Kent P7, Pts 68

After a seven-day break, Surrey returned to action with an NCL fixture against the unbeaten Kent Spitfires at The Oval, and were delighted to welcome back Saqlain Mushtaq, whose Test and Nat West Series commitments with Pakistan were at an end. The off-spinner's presence wasn't much help on this occasion, however, as a line-up lacking Stewart (rested by the ECB), Thorpe and Ramprakash (both injured) mustered just 154 runs in 44.2 overs. After Martin Saggers (3-21) and Ben Trott (2-19) had reduced the Lions to 23-4, the Hollioakes - Ben with 46, Adam with 36 - had combined to add eighty-five for the fifth wicket before another collapse at the hands of Mark Ealham (2-41) and Matt Walker (3-21) had left the hosts to defend a total that looked wholly inadequate.

Alex Tudor (4-36) and Martin Bicknell (2-16) appeared to have saved the day when the Spitfires nosedived to 70-6, but they had reckoned without debutant Geraint Jones making thirty-nine and sharing a crucial partnership of fifty-four for the seventh wicket with Matthew Fleming (26 not out). Once Jones had departed, the Kent captain saw his team home by two wickets with help from Saggers (15 not out), and Surrey were left to rue the sixteen wides that they had conceded in a low-scoring game. Having now lost four of their five games, the Lions were only being kept off the bottom of the table by the point-less Northamptonshire Steelbacks.

Fortunately, the performance against Kent was soon forgotten as the team put up an altogether better performance the following day to thrash Nottinghamshire by 174 runs in the Benson & Hedges Cup semi-final at The Oval. It really was one of the most one-sided limited-overs matches imaginable, reminiscent of the 1997 semi-final win over Leicestershire, with Surrey on top from start to finish after winning the toss and electing to bat.

Having received a racing start from Mark Butcher (84 from 86 balls) and Ian Ward (58 from 50), who shared a 112-run opening partnership in seventeen overs, the middle-order batsmen all scored at a phenomenal rate to keep Nottinghamshire's suffering bowlers under pressure. Nadeem Shahid's 21-ball cameo knock of thirty-two was followed by a run a ball sixty-seven from Alec Stewart and then explosive late innings from Ali Brown (49 from 37 balls) and Ben Hollioake (39 not out from 23) that took the total past three-hundred in the forty-second over and on to a final 361-8. This was a record high total against a first-class county in the Benson & Hedges Cup and the highest score recorded in a domestic fifty-overs match.

Facing such a mammoth total, the visitors soon sank to 47-4, with Martin Bicknell (2-43) removing his brother for fifteen en route. Usman Afzaal (37) and the 21-year-old Kevin Pietersen (78 not out from 67 balls) brought a little bit of respectability to the Nottinghamshire effort with a stand of sixty-eight for the fifth wicket but they were always fighting a hopeless cause and it was only a last-wicket partnership of forty-four that enabled the visitors to total 187 and avoid the ignominy of suffering the heaviest defeat by a first-class county in the Benson & Hedges Cup.

With Surrey having so completely outplayed their opponents to reach their first Lord's final since they lifted the Benson & Hedges Cup in 1997, it was hard to understand why Nottinghamshire were currently lying third in the NCL and Surrey were languishing in eighth.

Two days later, the team played in a third different limited-overs competition in the space of four days, taking on the Surrey Cricket Board XI at Guildford in the third round of the Cheltenham & Gloucester (formerly Nat West) Trophy. Unsurprisingly, the Board's collection of the best players from the club sides in the county were no match for the professionals of Surrey, scoring just 158 and then seeing Mark Butcher (73 not out) and Ian Ward (70 not out) knock off the runs in just 27.1 overs.

Having sat out a round of Championship matches since their lucky escape at Valentine's Park, Surrey had slipped to fifth in the table, so their next match, against second-placed Lancashire at The Oval, had taken on greater importance. In a game that was to see Saqlain Mushtaq and Muttiah Muralitharan going head-to-head, Adam Hollioake won an important toss and elected to bat, though his batsmen failed to take advantage, with only Mark Ramprakash (59) and Martin Bicknell (50) making more than twenty-eight as Surrey spluttered to 248 all out by the end of the opening day. Glen Chapple (2-45) and Peter Martin (2-56) did most of the early damage, allowing Murali (5-81) to cast his spells over the rest of the batting until he met stern resistance from Bicknell and Ian Salisbury (23) during a ninth-wicket stand of sixty-two.

Lancashire's reply then occupied day two, with most of their runs coming from the top of the batting order, as Jamie Haynes (57) and John Crawley (43) gave them a 110-run start before Saqlain worked his way through the rest of the batting. Andy Flintoff, with forty from number three in the order, and Warren Hegg, with a fine unbeaten seventy-four, were the only men to prosper thereafter as Surrey's overseas spinner outdid his red rose counterpart by claiming 6-89 in a Lancashire total of 276.

A very tight contest, played with the intensity of a Test match, then saw Surrey bat all the way through the third day to make 285-8, with Mark Butcher (86) and Adam Hollioake (73) enabling their side to reach a high point of 182-2 before Muralitharan (55-23-72-3) and company slowly evened up the contest again, leaving a fascinating last day in prospect.

Unfortunately, the game then fizzled out unexpectedly as Lancashire declined to make any attempt at victory once Adam Hollioake had declared at midday, setting the visitors a target of 293 from a minimum of seventy-seven overs. Even the hard-hitting Flintoff (34 from 119 balls) got his head down defiantly as John Crawley (84 not out from 219 balls) shepherded his team to a disappointing stalemate at 170-2 from seventy-one overs.

Although the eight points gained from this draw had enabled Surrey to advance to third place in the table, their inability to bowl sides out was becoming something of a worry, and there was much work to be done if Yorkshire, the runaway leaders, were to be caught.

LEADING POSITIONS:- Yorks P8, Pts 119; Lancs P8, Pts 91; Surrey P8, Pts 80

The next destination for Keith Medlycott's draw specialists was Grace Road, Leicester, where they had to face the fourth-placed Foxes without Alec Stewart, Ian Ward, Mark Butcher, Graham Thorpe and Mark Ramprakash. The first three were all playing in the first Ashes Test of the summer, while the latter two would have joined them had they not been injured. Surrey's line-up consequently showed three changes, with both Nadeem Shahid and Gary Butcher earning recalls, and Michael Carberry, the 20-year-old left-handed opener, making his first-class debut.

At the end of an incredible first day's play, it looked certain that the game would yield a positive result one way or the other, since Leicestershire were 79-0 in their **second** innings. Although the pitch appeared to hold no great terrors, twenty wickets fell in eighty-one overs after Vince Wells, the home captain, had won the toss and elected to bat.

Surrey set the ball rolling by dismissing their hosts for 165 in forty-three overs, with Trevor Ward (46) providing the only top-order resistance as his side slipped to 88-7, and Neil Burns (45) and Phillip DeFreitas (22) managing only a limited repair job with an eighth-wicket stand of forty-seven. Just three bowlers had been used during this demolition job - Martin Bicknell (4-54), Saqlain Mushtaq (4-60) and Alex Tudor (2-45).

The visitors were not so pleased with themselves by the end of the afternoon, however, as they were bundled out for just 102 in thirty-eight overs by the 38-year-old Devon Malcolm, who claimed his County Championship best figures of 8-63 by using a combination of pace and swing to take advantage of some inept batting. While Carberry, with a top-scoring twenty-three, had acquitted himself well in his debut innings, few of his team-mates had matched his application and concentration as the hosts had secured a 63-run lead, which Ward and Sutcliffe extended to 142 by the close.

Leicestershire then batted for most of the second day under a scorching sun, compiling 472-8 at a rate in excess of four an over before declaring and setting their visitors the small matter of 536 to win with a little more than two days of the match to run. The Foxes' second innings was built around Ben Smith's superbly constructed 179 and also featured good aggressive knocks from Daniel Marsh (82) and Neil Burns (66), while Surrey - hampered by the absence of broken toe victim, Ian Salisbury - owed a debt of gratitude to Saqlain, who had delivered forty-seven consecutive overs while returning 5-172.

Having ended day two on 28-1 - Shahid having been an early victim for Malcolm - Surrey battled gamely through a grim and grey third day that was shorn of twenty-seven overs by rain and bad light, though defeat still looked on the cards at 281-6. This was in spite of battling efforts from, first, Adam (64) and Ben Hollioake (59), who added 103 for the fourth wicket, and then Gary Butcher (26 not out) and Alex Tudor (45 not out), who batted through the last twenty-five overs of the day.

Day four turned out to be every bit as cloudy and unsettled as day three, though the first serious rainfall came just a couple of minutes too late to save Gary Butcher, who was bowled by Marsh for thirty-eight after sharing in a defiant stand of 128 that had taken the score up to 318-7. After eleven overs had been lost to the rain, Surrey continued to fight on, and they looked likely to get through to lunch without incurring another loss until Alex Tudor's marvellously determined knock of eighty-six from 148 balls came to an end when his off stump was removed by DeFreitas armed with the new ball. Although this appeared to be a fatal blow to the visitors' already slim chances of saving the game, another shower during the interval delayed the restart until 2.10pm. With nobody sure whether Salisbury would be able to bat because of his broken toe - and, if he did, how effectively - Jon Batty and Martin Bicknell were facing a seemingly lost cause, and the end appeared to be nigh when the Surrey wicketkeeper was unlucky to be bowled, via his thigh pad, by Malcolm with thirty-nine overs still remaining for play. The prospect of further rain was the only thing that kept hopes alive as Salisbury hobbled out to the crease with a runner, though the last-wicket pair were still together at 3.30pm, with the score on 424-9 and Bicknell having completed a fine 59-ball half-century, when another heavy downpour sent the players scurrying off for an early tea.

Unfortunately for Surrey, only eight overs had been lost by the time play resumed at 4.20pm with twenty-five overs and three balls remaining to be bowled. Almost immediately, Devon Malcolm switched to round the wicket in an attempt to soften up the batsmen, though Bicknell and Salisbury were sufficiently well set to deal with this as they took the score past 450 and then completed a hundred partnership. By now, James Ormond was back in the attack and he caused a couple of late scares as the game moved into the final four overs - first, Bicknell's leading edge towards point landed safely between two fielders, then, in the penultimate over of the match, the same batsman had to dig out a superb yorker and survive a concerted appeal for a catch in the slips when a rearing delivery struck him above the wrist. With every Surrey supporter in a small crowd praying that their team wouldn't be denied at the death, Salisbury carefully blocked out the last six balls of the contest from Marsh to complete one of the greatest rearguard actions in the history of the club. Bicknell, who finished three runs short of his career-best score on eighty-five from 133 balls, and Salisbury, who ended unbeaten on thirty from 127 balls, had held firm for an incredible thirty-nine overs and one ball while adding 109 for the last wicket and most certainly deserved the heroes' welcome they received from the delighted Surrey fans, and their team-mates, upon their return to the pavilion with a total of 478-9 shining out from the electronic scoreboard. This was the highest fourth-innings score ever recorded by the county and the third-highest by any county in the Championship since 1900. With six batsmen having survived for over a hundred deliveries in the visitors' second innings, the four points that had been snatched from the jaws of defeat rewarded a fine team effort... though everyone was still left wondering how a game that had seen twenty wickets fall on day one had managed to endure until the final delivery of the last day. This had been a truly amazing match.

Although Surrey's totally unexpected draw was well worth celebrating, results elsewhere meant that the team slipped back to fifth in the table, below Yorkshire, Lancashire, Somerset and Kent.

The gritty, fighting display in the Championship game was then followed by a dismal 128-run surrender in the following day's NCL match with the unbeaten table-topping Foxes. Although the Surrey team was further depleted by the absence of Messrs Bicknell, Salisbury and Tudor, there were few, if any, high points as the Lions replied to Leicestershire's 240 with a feeble innings of 112 that included just one boundary. Gareth Batty's bowling stint of 2-32, followed by a top-scoring innings of thirty, made him Surrey's most impressive player on the day, while the chief architects of the Foxes' triumph were Darren Stevens (63) and Darren Maddy, who scored forty-four from 33 balls and then wrapped up the Lions' innings with three wickets in four deliveries to return figures of 3-1.

With Surrey now equal last in the NCL, and forced to contemplate the possibility of instant relegation back to Division Two, confidence must have been at a low ebb as they made the trip to Headingley to take on a buoyant Yorkshire side in the fourth round of the C&G Trophy.

A match that featured numerous stoppages for rain, forcing it to be completed on the reserve day, saw Surrey compiling a useful 243 after they had been put in to bat, with much being owed to Ian Ward (81) and Mark Ramprakash (51), whose 92-run second-wicket partnership gave the innings a sound base. Martin Bicknell (3-34) then won lbw verdicts against Byas (12), Wood (24) and the dangerous Lehmann (0) as Yorkshire struggled to 84-4, though the hosts had fought their way back into the match at 131-4 from twenty-nine overs when play was suspended at 8pm on the first day.

The terrific battle that had been anticipated the next morning never materialised, however, as Gary Fellows (80 not out) and Craig White (73 not out) knocked off the required 113 runs in just 19.1 overs with surprisingly few alarms.

This defeat was hardly ideal preparation for Surrey ahead of the Benson & Hedges Cup final against Gloucestershire, though it had to be remembered that the 1997 triumph over Kent at Lord's had been preceded by a wretched performance against Nottinghamshire in the Nat West Trophy.

While Keith Medlycott's team were clearly not in the best of form as the big day arrived, having won just three of their seventeen matches outside of the Benson & Hedges Cup, Gloucestershire appeared to be losing the air of invincibility that had helped them to win five one-day trophies in the previous two seasons - including four wins in four knockout cup finals at Lord's. Although they had cruised through their matches in the Benson & Hedges competition, they had won only three of their eight NCL games and had just been dumped out of the C&G Trophy by Durham. It therefore seemed that confidence might be in short supply all round, leaving the side who could best raise their game on the day to claim the spoils of victory.

With Ian Salisbury's broken toe ruling him out of the match, Surrey's team selection was pretty straightforward, with their line-up consisting of eleven internationals, while Gloucestershire had been without Mike Smith - victim of a deep-seated groin problem - virtually all season, and had recently lost Jon Lewis to a serious back injury.

After rain had delayed the start by half an hour, Surrey won the toss, decided to bat, and lost Mark Butcher lbw to Ian Harvey with just seven on the board, before Ian Ward and Mark Ramprakash steadied the ship with a second-wicket stand of sixty-four. Having played quite beautifully to reach thirty-nine, Ramprakash surprised everyone by holing out to deep midwicket off Mark Alleyne, prompting a steady decline to 97-4 as the Gloucestershire skipper added Alec Stewart and Ali Brown to his bag of victims. When Ward then departed at 118, having compiled an excellent fifty-four, the cup holders were very much on top, leaving the Hollioake brothers to carry out much-needed repair work. With Ben clearly relishing the Lord's atmosphere, as usual, and playing the leading role, equilibrium was gradually restored to the contest during a stand of eighty-four. This ended when Adam fell lbw to Martyn Ball, shortly after his brother had completed a marvellous 54-ball half-century with a six over midwicket off Mark Hardinges, and the total had advanced by just two runs to 204 when Alex Tudor became another leg-before victim for the Gloucestershire off-spinner, putting Surrey in some danger again. An important 38-run stand between Martin Bicknell and Hollioake ensured that a respectable total would be posted, however, before the latter's mature knock of seventy-three from 76 balls was ended by James Averis in the forty-ninth over of the innings. Just two runs were added thereafter as the cunning Harvey bowled Bicknell and Ed Giddins with successive deliveries to leave Surrey all out for 244 from 49.5 overs.

Although the London-based county looked to have a decent score on the board, it was important that they didn't let Gloucestershire get away to a flying start. Bicknell and Tudor produced opening spells that were, therefore, nigh on perfect, with the latter completely bottling up Kim Barnett during five excellent overs that cost just seven runs before he gave way to Giddins. The former Warwickshire paceman promptly reaped the rewards of his team-mate's labours as a frustrated Barnett was bowled by the new bowler's third delivery, having scored just seven runs from thirty balls. With Gloucestershire's other opener, Jack Russell, playing an anchoring role at one end, and the run-rate stuck at three an over, the reigning Benson & Hedges champions needed to make progress at the other end, and in trying to do this lost further wickets. After Dominic Hewson had fallen to Saqlain Mushtaq with the total on sixty-eight, Giddins struck two major blows for his side by removing the extremely dangerous Harvey lbw at 71 and then hitting Matt Windows's off stump eighteen runs later. With Surrey now clearly on top, the hugely experienced Russell and Alleyne worked hard to haul their team back into contention during a stand of forty-two for the fifth wicket at almost a run a ball, with the former England wicketkeeper reaching fifty from eighty-four balls along the way. The game was virtually decided, however, when these two fell in quick succession - Russell caught behind off the returning Tudor at 131, and Alleyne caught-and-bowled by Saqlain at 133 - with the west country side still more than a hundred runs short of victory. Jeremy Snape and Chris Taylor tried their best to revive their rapidly expiring team, but once Taylor had become a third victim for the Surrey off-spinner, Tudor earned further reward for his fine bowling by polishing off the tail with help from Bicknell, tying up a comfortable 47-run triumph with twenty-five balls of Gloucestershire's innings unused. Having brought their opponents' run of wins in cup finals at Lord's to an end, the Surrey squad celebrated the third Benson & Hedges Cup victory in the club's history with a lap of honour after receiving the trophy. The men from The Oval had now won six trophies in six years - five of them 'majors' - which was a magnificent achievement... and the run looked sure to continue.

BENSON & HEDGES CUP FINAL 2001
GLOUCESTERSHIRE v SURREY at Lord's

Saturday 14th July — Surrey won by 47 runs
Surrey won the toss and elected to bat — Umpires:- John Hampshire & Ken Palmer

SURREY

Fall Of Wkt	Batsman	How	Out	Score	Balls	4s	6s
1-7	M.A. Butcher	lbw	b Harvey	0	7	-	-
5-118	I.J. Ward	c Russell	b Hardinges	54	59	5	-
2-71	M.R. Ramprakash	c Taylor	b Alleyne	39	33	7	-
3-89	A.J. Stewart +	c Snape	b Alleyne	8	18	-	-
4-97	A.D. Brown	c Harvey	b Alleyne	3	10	-	-
6-202	A.J. Hollioake *	lbw	b Ball	39	65	-	-
8-242	B.C. Hollioake	c Alleyne	b Averis	73	76	4	2
7-204	A.J. Tudor	lbw	b Ball	1	7	-	-
9-244	M.P. Bicknell		b Harvey	19	21	-	1
	Saqlain Mushtaq	Not	Out	1	2	-	-
10-244	E.S.H. Giddins		b Harvey	0	1	-	-
	Extras	(4lb, 3w)		7			
	TOTAL	**(49.5 overs)**		**244**			

Bowler	O	M	R	W	NB	Wd
Harvey	9.5	2	43	3	-	2
Averis	10	1	65	1	-	1
Alleyne	10	1	51	3	-	-
Ball	10	0	39	2	-	-
Hardinges	7	0	31	1	-	-
Barnett	3	0	11	0	-	-

GLOUCESTERSHIRE

Fall Of Wkt	Batsman	How	Out	Score	Balls	4s	6s
5-131	R.C. Russell +	c Stewart	b Tudor	62	96	7	-
1-35	K.J. Barnett		b Giddins	7	30	-	-
2-68	D.R. Hewson	c Bicknell	b Saqlain	11	12	1	-
3-71	I.J. Harvey	lbw	b Giddins	1	5	-	-
4-89	M.G.N. Windows		b Giddins	10	15	2	-
6-133	M.W. Alleyne *	c &	b Saqlain	26	32	1	1
8-190	J.N. Snape	c Stewart	b Tudor	22	35	-	-
7-161	C.G. Taylor		b Saqlain	12	16	2	-
9-194	M.A. Hardinges	c Stewart	b Bicknell	12	21	-	-
	M.C.J. Ball	Not	Out	3	7	-	-
10-197	J.M.M. Averis		b Tudor	1	6	-	-
	Extras	(16lb, 14w)		30			
	TOTAL	**(45.5 overs)**		**197**			

Bowler	O	M	R	W	NB	Wd
Bicknell	10	1	38	1	-	2
Tudor	9.5	3	28	3	-	1
Giddins	8	1	31	3	-	-
Saqlain	8	0	37	3	-	5
B.C. Hollioake	10	0	47	0	-	1

Gold Award Winner - Ben Hollioake

Having had just three days to savour their success, Surrey travelled into the heart of the county for the annual Guildford festival, with Northamptonshire the visitors for both Championship and NCL matches.

In common with Essex and Glamorgan, the two other sides who had been promoted from Division Two at the end of 2000, Northamptonshire were currently resident in the relegation zone, and therefore seemed likely to be up for a scrap in the hope of dragging their hosts into the dogfight. They were boosted by the fact that Surrey were making history by providing the whole of the England middle-order for the second Ashes Test, leaving Adam Hollioake and Keith Medlycott to put together a side without the services of Messrs Mark Butcher, Thorpe, Ramprakash, Stewart and Ward - who were filling the numbers three to seven slots at Lord's - for the second successive Championship fixture. There were a couple of changes to the team that had played at Grace Road, as Surrey elected to field an extra bowler, Ed Giddins, in place of Gary Butcher, and move Jon Batty up to open the innings with Michael Carberry, which allowed Nadeem Shahid to drop to number three. Ian Salisbury, meanwhile, returned to the side, having made a quick recovery from the broken toe he had sustained at Leicester, though the early indications were that he might not play a big part in the game, due to a bouncy and slightly uneven pitch that gave encouragement to the seamers after Northamptonshire had elected to bat. Having reached lunch in a comfortable position at 106-3, the visitors fell apart in amazing fashion after the break as Alex Tudor transformed morning figures of 7-0-44-0 into 13-3-54-5, thanks to a stunning burst of 5-3 in thirty-one balls that sent Northamptonshire into freefall from 115-3 to 120 all out. Although he hadn't reaped the same rewards as Tudor, Giddins had already justified his inclusion in the team by exploiting the pitch to the full in returning an outstanding analysis of 17-9-18-3.

Apart from a spell just after tea, when they slipped from 78-0 to 97-3 as Michael Strong (3-104) took three wickets in twenty-three balls, Surrey controlled the rest of the day. After the makeshift opening pair - Carberry with forty-six and Batty with thirty-nine - had provided a good start, Adam Hollioake (47) and Ali Brown (55 not out) added eighty-one for the fourth wicket in fourteen overs to enable their side to reach 209-5 before stumps were drawn.

Although Brown had been diagnosed with a broken thumb - the legacy of a missed slip catch during the visitors' innings - it scarcely showed as he completed an excellent 131-ball century the next day before falling to his off-spinning namesake, Jason Brown (4-91), for 103. With Tudor having already contributed a rapid thirty-five, and Salisbury making an unbeaten forty-two either side of lunch, Surrey were able to total 368 and claim a 248-run lead that looked sure to prove decisive against a side that was lacking in confidence.

Despite the loss of Adrian Rollins to Martin Bicknell before tea, the visitors seemed to be fighting back nicely as Michael Hussey (40) and Mal Loye took the score up to 80-1, but a late blast by Surrey's senior seamer blew away the Northamptonshire middle order and all but sealed the reigning champions' victory. Minds were cast back to Bicknell's end-of-day demolition of Leicestershire twelve months previously as he shot out Loye, Warren, Hussey and Penberthy - the cream of the visitors' batting - in the space of twenty-four deliveries to leave them in a hopeless position of 99-5 at the close.

When Bicknell removed Toby Bailey and David Ripley in his first five overs the next morning, there were thoughts of him going one better than his 9-47 in 2000, but Giddins then claimed the scalp of Graeme Swann (41) to reduce the Championship strugglers to 151-8 and bring a pre-lunch victory into view. Knowing that his job was done, Bicknell retired to the outfield with excellent figures of 7-60, allowing Ben Hollioake and Alex Tudor to polish off the tail with the total on 193 and leave Surrey victorious by an innings and fifty-five runs.

Even though this was only Surrey's second Championship win of the season, they were back up to equal fourth place in the table, with everyone but leaders Yorkshire in their sights.
LEADING POSITIONS:- Yorks P9, Pts 129; Somerset P10, Pts 115; Kent P10, Pts 107; Leics P10, Pts 106; Surrey P10, Pts 106

The Northamptonshire Steelbacks and the Surrey Lions had just one NCL victory apiece as they went head-to-head two days later but, by the end of a very disappointing afternoon, Adam Hollioake's team had been cast adrift at the bottom of the table. Since their batting resources were stretched to the absolute limit by the added absence of the injured Ali Brown and Ben Hollioake, it was no real surprise that the hosts could only muster a score of 195 in front of the Guildford public, with the captain's innings of sixty-six receiving little support from his inexperienced colleagues. There was, however, no excuse for the dreadful bowling that followed, since Ian Salisbury was the only absentee from the full-strength line-up. Martin Bicknell's superb spell of 8-1-16-2 stood out like a beacon amongst the dross as the Steelbacks easily chased down a Duckworth-Lewis revised target of 176 in thirty-seven overs after a shower had swept across the ground. Such was the dominance of Michael Hussey (96 not out) and Mal Loye (70 not out) that Northamptonshire sailed home by eight wickets with almost seven overs to spare.
BOTTOM OF THE TABLE:- Somerset P9, Pts 12; Yorks P7, Pts 8; Northants P8, Pts 8; Surrey P7, Pts 4

Another NCL defeat the following Sunday, this time at the hands of the Warwickshire Bears at Edgbaston, was even more dispiriting, as it was 'achieved' with four of the county's England men back in the Lions' line-up. Graham Thorpe was the exception, since his right hand had been broken by a Brett Lee delivery during the Test match.

After being put in on a rather unreliable surface, Surrey were dismissed for 136 in 42.2 overs, with Ben Hollioake almost single-handedly saving his side from total embarrassment by scoring a fine unbeaten fifty-two. Although he received belated assistance from Saqlain Mushtaq (20) during a 49-run eighth-wicket partnership, the damage had already been done by Dougie Brown (3-14) and Vasbert Drakes (3-35).

There seemed to be just a glimmer of hope for the Lions when Ed Giddins (2-30) reduced the Bears to 55-4 on his return to Edgbaston, but Dougie Brown (63) added heroics with the bat to his excellence with the ball during a partnership of seventy-three with Trevor Penney (35) that enabled Warwickshire to romp home by three wickets with forty-five balls in hand. Following this latest setback, things were looking increasingly desperate for Surrey at the foot of the table.
BOTTOM OF THE TABLE:- Somerset P9, Pts 12; Yorks P8, Pts 12; Northants P8, Pts 8; Surrey P8, Pts 4

Having missed a round of Championship matches, Surrey had fallen to sixth place in the table and now trailed Yorkshire, who were their next opponents, by forty-three points. A win was essential if they were to retain any hope of retaining their title, yet they also had to keep looking back over their shoulder at results in the relegation zone.

Headingley had not been a happy hunting ground for Surrey at the best of times, but on this occasion their assignment looked particularly tough, since Yorkshire were a confident table-topping outfit, while the men from The Oval were again stripped of five players, since Alex Tudor had earned a recall to the England side. Had Graham Thorpe been fit then Surrey might well have provided more than half the national team for the third Test. Although Darren Gough and Craig White were absent for Yorkshire, balancing the scales slightly, the visitors needed all the luck they could get as Adam Holllioake won the toss and elected to bat. While no batsman dominated, Surrey did manage to reach 105-2 before Ryan Sidebottom and the Tykes' new pace ace, Steve Kirby (4-90), ripped through the middle order to put their visitors in real trouble at 127-6.

The lower order came to the rescue, however, with Ian Salisbury's fifty-four, plus thirties from Martin Bicknell and Saqlain Mushtaq, boosting the final total to an acceptable 278. Ed Giddins then removed the Yorkshire openers, Matthew Wood and Chris Taylor, before time was called, leaving honours even at 61-2.

Day two very much belonged to Surrey, once Darren Lehmann (52) was sixth out with the total on 171 shortly before lunch. Giddins (4-50) had bowled well to keep his side in the game during the morning session, but it was Bicknell (3-67) and Saqlain (3-23) who routed the tail for a further thirty-three runs after the break to give the reigning County Champions a first-innings lead of seventy-four over the pretenders to their throne. By close of play they had batted purposefully to reach 171-4, with Michael Carberry again impressing while making forty-six and Ali Brown still in occupation on forty-two.

Although Brown didn't last long on the third morning, becoming a fourth victim in the innings for the young off-spinner Richard Dawson - who was due to celebrate his twenty-first birthday on the final day of the game - Ben Hollioake took over the leading role before a heavy shower interrupted the visitors' progress at 219-5. With forty-two overs lost, Surrey reassessed their tactics and attempted to push on briskly once play resumed, though this was only partially successful as they added sixty-two runs for the loss of their last five wickets in seventeen overs. During this frenetic little spell of play, Ben Hollioake reached sixty-eight before falling to Gavin Hamilton (3-68), while Dawson returned career-best figures of 6-98.

Requiring 356 to win from a minimum of 120 overs, the Championship leaders reached fifty for the loss of Chris Taylor before stumps, which left the game nicely poised going in to the final day. It would be an especially important day for Surrey, since victory would put them back in the Championship race, whereas a draw would leave them with far too much to do to close the gap on the white rose county.

It was very unfortunate, therefore, that rain should arrive after six overs the next morning, with Bicknell having trapped Anthony McGrath lbw for fourteen and had Lehmann missed at leg slip before he had scored. Although the umpires managed to save some time by taking an early lunch, twenty-one overs were lost and the stuffing seemed to have been knocked out of the visitors when play resumed at 1.30pm. In sixty-one further overs they failed to capture another wicket, while Wood (85 not out) and Lehmann (106 not out) added 190 runs to the total, leaving Yorkshire on 244-2 when everyone shook hands on a draw that suited the home side down to the ground and left Surrey's hopes of a Championship hat-trick in tatters.

The Yorkshire Phoenix then topped off Surrey's typically disappointing trip to Leeds by beating the Lions in the following day's NCL contest, running up 230-7 in their forty-five overs before dismissing their visitors for 163. The Surrey line-up had again shown plenty of changes, with Ian Ward and Mark Ramprakash having been drafted into the side following a three-day defeat for England at Trent Bridge that had enabled the Australians to register a 3-0 winning lead in the series. With Adam Hollioake unfit, Martin Bicknell had captained the side and been far and away his side's best bowler with 3-20 as Yorkshire had built on a fine start given to them by Gavin Hamilton (57) and Matthew Wood (47). In reply, Surrey had little to offer apart from Ramprakash's fifty-eight at the top of the order and an unbeaten thirty-eight by Saqlain Mushtaq when the game was already over as a contest, thanks to Chris Elstub's career-best 4-25. Since Surrey were now twelve points from safety, their position was starting to look nigh on hopeless.

BOTTOM OF THE TABLE:- Yorks P9, Pts 16; Somerset P9, Pts 12; Northants P9, Pts 8; Surrey P9, Pts 4

With the Benson & Hedges Cup triumph looking increasingly like a golden lining to the very grey cloud that represented the season as a whole, Surrey returned to The Oval for a County

Championship fixture against Glamorgan, who currently shared eighth place in the table with Northamptonshire.

Since Surrey were fielding a side that was at full strength bar their injured skipper, they appeared to have a good chance of recording their third victory of the season to silence those who felt the champions of 1999 and 2000 could yet get sucked into the relegation dogfight. When the stand-in captain, Martin Bicknell, won the toss and elected to bat first everything seemed to be going to plan, though Mark Butcher appeared to be the only man to relish a lively pitch as the hosts slumped to 70-4. The England left-hander was utterly dominant as he completed a magnificent 142-ball century out of 204-6 and went on to reach 145 not out before running out of partners with the total on 281. Even Glamorgan's star performers with the ball, Darren Thomas (3-69) and Andrew Davies (3-76), had been unable to contain Butcher as he became the first Surrey batsman to carry his bat since he himself had performed the feat at Taunton in 1998.

It was always likely that the home seamers would also enjoy bowling on a pitch with good carry and bounce, and Bicknell certainly had fun as he removed the visiting openers before the close of play and then picked up three more wickets to reduce the Welsh county to 83-6 early on day three after the second day of the match had been completely washed out by rain. Surrey were held up thereafter by a partnership of ninety-four for the seventh wicket between Mark Wallace and Darren Thomas that endured into the middle session of the day, before the latter was bowled by Tudor for fifty-seven. With the resistance broken, Saqlain Mushtaq (2-21) helped Bicknell (6-69) lop off the tail to leave Wallace unbeaten on sixty-three in a total of 223.

Although a lead of fifty-eight runs wasn't as many as the hosts would have hoped for earlier in the day, it still looked pretty handy as they embarked on their second innings. This didn't start well, however, as Butcher and Ramprakash fell to Simon Jones before tea - taken at 29-2 - and things then went from bad to worse during the final session of the day. With Davies picking off Tudor and Stewart - the latter to a breathtaking diving catch in front of first slip by Wallace - after Watkin had disposed of Ben Hollioake and Ali Brown, Surrey were suddenly in danger of defeat at 95-7. It was therefore just as well for the home side that the old firm of Bicknell and Salisbury were able to staunch the flow of wickets by adding thirty-four runs to the score before stumps.

Hopes that Surrey's dependable tail might add another fifty-plus runs to the total on the final morning were quickly dashed by Watkin (4-28) and Jones (3-36), who tidied up the innings for the addition of just twelve, leaving the relegation-threatened visitors to score exactly two-hundred for victory.

After Jimmy Maher failed to survive Bicknell's opening spell for the second time in the match, and Matthew Maynard fell to Ed Giddins for fourteen with the score on fifty-two, Glamorgan gradually took control of the game, and were over halfway to their target before Ian Thomas (59) finally fell to Saqlain after enjoying something of a charmed life. Mike Powell (51) and Adrian Dale then appeared to have sewn up a Welsh win with a 62-run stand for the fourth wicket before Bicknell returned to the attack and, with the assistance of two great diving catches by Stewart, claimed four wickets in seven balls to send the home crowd into raptures and leave the match in the melting pot at 167-7 as tea arrived.

Sadly for Surrey, they were unable to maintain their momentum after an interval that had probably come at just the right time for their visitors. Although Bicknell (5-48, and 11-117 in the match) and Saqlain managed to find the edges of both batsmen's bats, nothing went to hand, and the eighth-wicket pair of Wallace and Davies duly sealed victory for their team, simultaneously improving their chances of avoiding the drop back to Division Two and leaving the reigning champions contemplating a scenario that had seemed out of the question at the start of the summer. Having been extremely fortunate not to lose at Ilford and Leicester, Surrey's superb run in Championship cricket had finally come to an end, and they were now just 11.5 points above the drop zone, with half a point having been deducted at the end of the match when it was revealed that the hosts had fallen two overs short of par on their over-rate. For the record, this was Surrey's first defeat in twenty-two Championship matches stretching back to June 2000, and their first in a home Championship fixture since September 1998.

COUNTY CHAMPIONSHIP - BOTTOM OF THE TABLE AT 11TH AUGUST				
	P	W	D	L	PTS
Surrey	12	2	9	1	119.50
Glamorgan	12	2	7	3	108.00
Northamptonshire	12	1	7	4	101.00
Essex	12	1	5	6	82.00

It might not have been a great consolation prize, but Surrey did at least manage a second NCL victory of the season the following day when the Gloucestershire Gladiators were vanquished by two wickets with two balls to spare in a match reduced to 41-overs-per-side by pre-match rain. The visitors' total of 176 owed just about everything to a fifth-wicket stand of 109 between Matt Windows (70) and Jeremy Snape (49), as a young Lions' attack, including Carl Greenidge (2-39), Gareth Batty (2-5) and Ben Hollioake (3-24), produced a spirited effort, and Jon Batty picked up five victims behind the stumps. The Hollioakes - Adam with fifty-six and Ben with forty-two - then broke the back of Surrey's task by taking the score from 78-3 to 154-3, before a late clatter of wickets to Snape (3-30) made the finish rather closer than it should have been.
BOTTOM OF THE TABLE:- Yorkshire P9, Pts 16; Somerset P9, Pts 12; Northants P10, Pts 10; Surrey P10, Pts 8

A trip to Canterbury for a day-night game against second-placed Kent two days later didn't offer too much hope of continued NCL success, especially once the Spitfires had won the toss and elected to bat in daylight. Having slumped to 34-3 against Martin Bicknell (3-35) in the early stages of their innings, the home side were rescued by Andrew Symonds, who rattled off seventy-four from 68 balls to put them in a promising position at 151-4. Once he departed, however, the Spitfires were spun out for 207 in forty-two overs by Gareth Batty (4-36) and Saqlain Mushtaq (2-36), giving the Lions a fair shot at victory. With Ali Brown (27 from 25 balls) and Adam Hollioake (43 from 50 balls) having supplied impetus and Ian Ward (51) anchoring the innings, they looked well placed at 147-3 after thirty-two overs, but madness took hold once the Surrey opener had fallen to a direct-hit run out by Matthew Fleming. After Symonds had picked up two quick wickets, the Kent captain proceeded to hit the stumps on three further occasions in the space of four balls as the lower order panicked in quite unbelievable fashion, and the Lions capitulated to 164 all out. While the Spitfires moved within two points of the Leicestershire Foxes at the head of the table, Surrey now looked doomed to the drop, especially as Yorkshire and Somerset had each picked up a vital victory.
BOTTOM OF THE TABLE:- Yorkshire P10, Pts 20; Somerset P10, Pts 16; Northants P10, Pts 10; Surrey P11, Pts 8

One relegation in a season would be disastrous enough, let alone two, so Surrey were hoping for better things from the Championship encounter with Kent that started two days later. With Ian Ward returning to the side, having been dropped by England after five Tests in which his top score was thirty-nine, Surrey were lacking four England men - Stewart, Butcher, Ramprakash and Tudor - plus the injured Thorpe, when Adam Hollioake won the toss and chose to bat. Although this appeared to be the correct decision, his team slumped to 95-6 before lunch, Martin Saggers (4-58) having taken out the top order with a spell of three wickets in two overs, and a minor recovery to 83-4 having been scotched with the interval looming.

Fortunately for Surrey, Martin Bicknell applied himself diligently after the break, sharing stands of sixty-four with Jon Batty (40) and seventy-four with Ian Salisbury (34) to help pull his side round before being adjudged lbw to Andrew Symonds (3-35) when twenty-two runs short of an elusive maiden first-class century. Although the visitors' final total of 258 was a lot better than it might have been, it wasn't looking too clever when Dave Fulton and Rob Key took Kent to 43-0 at stumps.

It was looking even less impressive the next day when the hosts shrugged off the early loss of Fulton to Bicknell to reach 153-1 half-an-hour after lunch. In their hour of need it was almost inevitable that Surrey's inspiration should be their senior seam bowler, who removed Rob Key (79), Symonds (0), and Ed Smith (37) in the space of seven deliveries to peg Kent back to 154-4. With the initial breach made, Saqlain Mushtaq (2-60) and Salisbury extended the decline to 199-7, before Paul Nixon (66 not out) and Min Patel (38) took their side into the lead with a most valuable partnership of eighty-four. As the day drew to a close, Ben Hollioake (2-39) and Salisbury (2-58) closed out the Kent innings efficiently by capturing the last three wickets for eighteen runs to leave the hosts all out for 301.

Trailing by forty-three runs on first innings, Surrey made an absolutely disastrous start to day three and by mid-morning they looked set for an embarrassing defeat at 44-6. The top-order batting had failed yet again as Saggers (3-37) and Ben Trott (3-48) had picked up three wickets apiece, leaving the visitors just one run in front with four wickets left and five-and-a-half sessions remaining for play. Surrey seemed certain to suffer a second consecutive Championship defeat, which would leave them perilously close to the relegation zone. Batty and Bicknell managed to take their team through to lunch without further loss, however, and were then able to put their feet up until 3pm, thanks to rain that began falling just before play was due to resume.

Once the action got under way again, Bicknell quickly completed his second fifty of the match, though his pleasure was soon tempered by the loss of Batty and Salisbury inside the next four overs. The Surrey stalwart remained unfazed by these dismissals, though, and with Saqlain offering solid support at the other end, moved on to a career-best score of ninety at tea, having picked up a couple of twos with snicks either side of slip off Patel in the final over of the session.

Even though light rain was falling, play restarted on time after the break, but Bicknell probably didn't mind getting wet as he eventually dabbed a Symonds off-break to third man for the three runs that completed a long-awaited maiden first-class century from 139 balls and earned him a well-deserved ovation from everyone in the ground.

By 5.20pm, with the rainfall becoming increasingly heavy, and Bicknell unbeaten on 110 in a total of 193-8, the umpires decided that enough was enough and took the players off the field for what turned out to be the last time in the match. Heavy rain overnight and from about 10am on the final morning left areas of the field too wet for play, much to the frustration of the Kent team and their supporters. Surrey had been lucky again, though they certainly owed the four draw points here to the magnificent Bicknell as much as the weather. Although the England selectors continued to ignore him, he was now the county's leading run-scorer in the Championship (660) as well as the nation's leading wicket-taker (60).

Having gained twelve points from a draw with Essex, Glamorgan had closed the gap between themselves and Surrey to just 8.5 points.

COUNTY CHAMPIONSHIP - BOTTOM OF THE TABLE AT 20TH AUGUST					
	P	W	D	L	PTS
Surrey	13	2	10	1	128.50
Glamorgan	13	2	8	3	120.00
Northamptonshire	13	1	8	4	111.00
Essex	13	1	6	6	91.00

Taunton was not a good place for Surrey to be going in search of an NCL victory to keep alive their extremely slender hopes of avoiding relegation back to Division Two, especially with five senior players missing through either injury or Test duty. Despite this, the Lions recovered well from the early departures of Ian Ward and Gareth Batty to Steffan Jones, reaching 182-2, thanks to an excellent partnership of 155 in twenty-four overs between Ali Brown (98 from 89 balls) and Adam Hollioake (70 from 77 balls). Unfortunately for the visitors, the loss of these two batsmen in quick succession gave Ian Blackwell (3-16) the chance to bring his side back into the match and the innings rather fizzled out at 236-8.

Blackwell and Peter Bowler then got the Sabres away to a flying start by plundering forty-four runs from the first six overs, and they rarely looked back thereafter. While Bowler (86) maintained a steady tempo at one end, Michael Burns (53 from 47 balls) ensured that his side never fell below the required run-rate as Surrey's bowlers, Ed Giddins (3-31) excepted, failed to exert sufficient control under the floodlights. There were four overs remaining when Somerset strolled home by four wickets to all but confirm Surrey's demotion.

BOTTOM OF THE TABLE:- Yorkshire P11, Pts 20; Somerset P12, Pts 20; Northants P11, Pts 10; Surrey P12, Pts 8

The two sides then locked horns in the Championship, with Somerset sitting in second place in the table, though they were forty points behind champions-elect Yorkshire. Since both teams required a win - Surrey to ensure they didn't drop into the relegation zone and Somerset to retain the slimmest of chances of becoming champions - a typically good batting track at Taunton didn't really suit either side... nor did the drizzle that wiped out the first morning's play.

Once the game did get under way, a visiting side that included Gareth Batty, making his Championship debut, fought back well to hold the advantage at the end of the opening day. Somerset had been very much in control at 142-1 after electing to bat, but the sudden loss of Jamie Cox (76) and Michael Burns (38) had sparked a collapse to 159-5 at the hands of Martin Bicknell (3-84) and Saqlain Mushtaq. By capturing Rob Turner's wicket with the last ball of the day, Ed Giddins had kept the hosts on the back foot at 207-6.

Ian Blackwell dominated the rest of his team's innings the next day, scoring an impressive 120 and supervising the addition of 107 runs for the last wicket with Jamie Grove in extending the total to 373, despite the best efforts of Saqlain (6-107). Surrey's hopes of challenging their hosts' total were then undermined by the regular loss of wickets throughout the afternoon, and Somerset definitely held the whip hand by the close of play, since the visitors were still 149 runs in arrears with just four wickets standing.

With Richard Johnson (5-62) and Steffan Jones (3-98) sharing the remaining wickets for the addition of fifty-four runs the following morning, the visitors suddenly found themselves in a spot of bother. Their disappointing total of 278 included just one half-century - Ben Hollioake's fifty-six - while Turner claimed six catches to help secure a handy 95-run lead for the home side. Although news had meanwhile come through that Yorkshire had beaten Glamorgan at Scarborough to clinch their first Championship title since 1968, Somerset proved they were still keen to secure second-place prize money by pushing on to 265-5 at stumps, with Burns (70) having led the charge.

Jamie Cox's fourth-morning declaration at 311-6, which came when Blackwell (67) was caught off Saqlain (3-114), challenged Surrey to score an unlikely 407 in eighty-three overs. The loss of three wickets for ninety appeared to rule out any chance of a bold attempt at victory, though fine knocks from Adam Hollioake (83), Ali Brown (64) and Ben Hollioake (56) did briefly raise hopes of an exciting finale. Ultimately, however, the flat pitch and an over-cautious declaration resulted in a fairly predictable stalemate at 294-6, though Rob Turner at least had something to celebrate -

by claiming another three catches in the innings he had equalled the Somerset wicketkeeping record of nine in a match.

Although Glamorgan's defeat at Scarborough had been good news for the visitors, Northamptonshire had claimed a last-session victory over Leicestershire at Northampton to move within 7.5 points of Surrey.

COUNTY CHAMPIONSHIP - BOTTOM OF THE TABLE AT 26TH AUGUST				
	P	W	D	L	PTS
Surrey	14	2	11	1	137.50
Northamptonshire	14	2	8	4	130.00
Glamorgan	14	2	8	4	123.00
Essex	14	1	7	6	98.00

Results in other matches since their last NCL outing had already confirmed Surrey's National League relegation by the time they took on the Warwickshire Bears at Whitgift School for a second successive season. Perhaps inevitably, with the pressure now off, the Lions roared to a 123-run victory in a match that almost exactly mirrored the previous season's contest. As in 2000, Surrey's total was built around one major innings, which on this occasion was Ali Brown's stunning 116 from 108 balls that took the hosts from the depths of 15-3 to a final score of 231. While the home county had totalled twenty runs more than they had managed twelve months previously, Warwickshire made no progress at all, replicating their dismal score of 108 all out, though achieving it in 29.5 overs, as opposed to thirty overs in 2000. After reaching 44-0 through the efforts of Nick Knight (34) and Mark Wagh, the Bears lost all ten wickets for the addition of sixty-four runs as Ben Hollioake (3-10) and Tim Murtagh (a career-best 4-31) ran amok.
BOTTOM OF THE TABLE:- Yorks P14, Pts 24; Glos P13, Pts 22; Surrey P13, Pts 12; Northants P13, Pts 10

The Lions then registered back-to-back NCL victories for the first time in over a year by beating relegation-threatened Yorkshire Phoenix by seven wickets in a day-night match at The Oval. Not for the first time, Saqlain Mushtaq (3-44) was Surrey's most successful bowler against Yorkshire as the visitors compiled 214-8, with six batsmen reaching twenty-two but no one bar Darren Lehmann (47) exceeding twenty-eight. After rain had led to the Lions being set a Duckworth-Lewis revised target of 186 from thirty-four overs, Gareth Batty put his fellow Yorkshiremen to the sword, scoring an undefeated eighty-three from 78 balls to see his team home with four balls to spare.
BOTTOM OF THE TABLE:- Glos P14, Pts 26; Yorks P15, Pts 24; Surrey P14, Pts 16; Northants P14, Pts 14

After a nine-day break from Championship action, Surrey took on the new - and worthy - County Champions in the first of the two matches that would decide their fate in the premier domestic competition.

While Surrey were back to full strength, bar the injured Tudor and Thorpe, Yorkshire elected to rest Darren Lehmann, Richard Blakey and Ryan Sidebottom, possibly with an eye on their forthcoming NCL relegation tussle with the Gloucestershire Gladiators. The visitors' line-up was still fairly close to that which had led the way in the Championship for almost the whole season, and they fully expected to give their hosts a good run for their money when David Byas won the toss and elected to bat on a first day shortened by rain to eighty-five overs. Yorkshire were made to work very hard for their runs all day long and had mustered just 179-5 by the time stumps were drawn, with Martin Bicknell (3-43) having claimed three of the wickets and Anthony McGrath still in occupation on sixty-nine.

Although McGrath managed to progress to a fine century the next morning, he received precious little support from lower-order batsmen who were hopelessly bamboozled by the skills of Ian Salisbury (4-49) and Saqlain Mushtaq (2-70). The former England 'A' batsman was undefeated on 116 when Yorkshire were finally bowled out for 235 after 114.4 overs, and by the close of play the recently deposed County Champions were already leading by fifty-six runs with five wickets in hand. Having been given a great start by Mark Butcher (90) and Ian Ward (63), who posted 164 runs for the first wicket against some rather wayward bowling, the hosts lost their way against off-spinner Andy Gray, dipping to 222-5 before being put back on course by Mark Ramprakash (53 not out) and Ben Hollioake (43 not out).

The Ramprakash-Hollioake alliance then moved the home county into a position of great strength on the third day, with Ramprakash (131) registering his third Championship century of the summer, and Hollioake (118) finally recording a maiden first-class ton for Surrey, during a stand that extended to 215 before Gray (4-128) claimed the former Middlesex batsman as his fourth victim. The hosts' lead had reached 281 by the time Adam Hollioake called a halt at 516-9 after just 130.4 overs of batting, giving his side forty-two overs in which to make inroads into the County Champions' second innings. Although Chris Taylor and Matthew Wood were back in the pavilion by the time the score had reached sixty-five, stern resistance followed from Michael Vaughan (55 not out) and McGrath (52 not out), who added an unbroken 106 runs for the third wicket, leaving Surrey with plenty of work to do on the final day if they were to secure a much needed victory.

The capture of a vital twelve win points actually turned out to be much easier than expected the next morning as Bicknell (3-83) and Saqlain quickly rattled through the Yorkshire batting once the former had disposed of McGrath for seventy-three (195-3) and the latter had unseated Vaughan for sixty-one (207-4). Only Simon Guy, who remained undefeated on twelve, reached double figures thereafter as Surrey's two main bowlers remained in harness until victory was clinched by an innings and forty-six runs four balls after lunch. Saqlain, in particular, was simply irresistible as he returned season's-best figures of 7-58 to ease his county's relegation fears.

The picture was now much clearer at the bottom of the table. Glamorgan's defeat at the hands of Leicestershire had seen them demoted alongside Essex, while Northamptonshire's draw with Kent left Surrey needing a maximum of four points to retain their cherished Division One status.

COUNTY CHAMPIONSHIP - BOTTOM OF THE TABLE AT 10TH SEPTEMBER				
	P	W	D	L	PTS
Surrey	15	3	11	1	157.50
Lancashire	15	4	6	5	146.00
Northamptonshire	15	2	9	4	141.00
Glamorgan	15	2	8	5	126.00
Essex	15	1	7	7	101.00

With the season now drawing to a close, Surrey continued their good late form in the NCL with an impressive five-wicket win in a high-scoring encounter with the Nottinghamshire Outlaws at Trent Bridge. After inviting their hosts to bat, the Lions' very limited attack was blasted for 277-7, with John Morris (102 from 103 balls), Usman Afzaal (50 from 59 balls) and Kevin Pietersen (61 not out from just 34 balls) all enjoying themselves immensely.

Although Scott Newman, making his first-team debut along with Rikki Clarke, registered a second-ball duck, Surrey were put firmly on the road to victory by Ali Brown, who made a 65-ball hundred, and Gareth Batty (63 from 71 balls), who shared a second-wicket stand of 189. A.J. Harris (4-42) then caused panic by grabbing three quick wickets, including Clarke for a duck, and when the same bowler also removed Brown for a sensational 97-ball 130 with the total on 228 the game looked wide open again. Adam Hollioake (43 not out) and Nadeem Shahid kept cool heads, however, to lead the Lions to victory with two overs to spare.

The final Championship match of the season arrived with Surrey confident about securing the four points they needed to ensure their survival in the first division, though it was quite incredible that the team was in this position, having been firm favourites to win the title at the start of the season.

By the end of an opening day that was truncated by rain, Surrey were just a single point away from confirming their Division One status for 2002, having bowled Glamorgan out for 258 in 74.4 overs to earn the maximum three bowling points. After the home side had elected to bat, they lost three wickets with their score on thirty - Steve James, almost inevitably, to Martin Bicknell; Jimmy Maher and Ian Thomas to Ben Hollioake - before recovering to 143-4 through Michael Powell (56) and their 20-year-old debutant, Jonathan Hughes. Ed Giddins (4-71) then came up with a four-wicket burst that rocked the Welsh county back to 170-8, only for Robert Croft to make amends for the three-ball pair he had recorded in the match at The Oval in August by scoring an unbeaten seventy to steer his side out of immediate danger.

On a rain-wrecked second day, Surrey progressed comfortably to 140-1, with Ian Ward making sixty-three, and his fellow left-handers, Michael Carberry (44 not out) and Mark Butcher (30 not out), the men charged with securing the all-important fourth bonus point the next day.

Having achieved this with ease, by taking the score to 224 before Carberry fell for a career-best eighty-four, the game was, thereafter, suffocated by weight of runs on a very flat Sophia Gardens track. With Adam Hollioake refusing to open the game up and force his tired players to partake of one final competitive effort in the field, despite the fact that victory could have secured third place in the table, Surrey batted on to score 701-9 declared from 191.3 overs. This was the fifth-highest score ever recorded by the county, and their highest ever total against Glamorgan, but it meant little else as Mark Butcher (230), with the second double-century of his career, Adam Hollioake (97) and Ali Brown (115) filled their boots against a pretty toothless attack. The Surrey captain's decision to bat on earned condemnation from the Glamorgan chairman, and it was only because Alec Stewart was struggling with an elbow injury that a declaration was eventually forthcoming late on the final afternoon.

With fourteen overs to bat, the Welsh county scored 69-1 as Hughes impressed with a quick-fire forty-nine before falling lbw to Ben Hollioake.

	COUNTY CHAMPIONSHIP DIVISION ONE TABLE 2001							
		P	Pts	W	D	L	Bat	Bwl	Ded'n
1	Yorkshire	16	219.00	9	4	3	50	45	0.00
2	Somerset	16	203.00	6	8	2	55	44	0.00
3	Kent	16	175.00	4	9	3	48	44	1.00
4	Surrey	16	169.50	3	12	1	43	43	0.50
5	Leicestershire	16	165.00	5	5	6	38	47	0.00
6	Lancashire	16	153.00	4	7	5	38	39	0.00
7	Northamptonshire	16	148.00	2	9	5	52	36	0.00
8	Glamorgan	16	133.00	2	9	5	36	37	0.00
9	Essex	16	116.00	2	7	7	28	36	0.00

Surrey's National League season at least ended on a high note with a fourth successive victory that spelt bad news for Gloucestershire, since it condemned the Gladiators to relegation alongside the Lions and the Steelbacks, and allowed Yorkshire to retain their Division One status.

On a typically awkward low-and-slow Bristol pitch, Gareth Batty, with fifty-four from 61 balls, was the only man to find any fluency against tight Gloucestershire bowling during the visitors'

45-over innings of 157-8. The Gladiators found the going even tougher, however, slipping to 31-4 as the impressive Tim Murtagh produced a killer spell of 3-0 in six balls, and they never recovered, with Batty (2-20) removing Matt Windows (37) and Mark Alleyne, before Adam Hollioake (4-19) polished off the tail to secure a 36-run victory for his team.

NATIONAL LEAGUE DIVISION ONE TABLE 2001							
		P	Pts	W	L	T	A	NRR
1	Kent	16	50	11	2	1	2	4.26
2	Leicestershire	16	46	11	4	0	1	7.82
3	Warwickshire	16	38	8	5	0	3	1.58
4	Somerset	16	32	7	7	1	1	-4.60
5	Nottinghamshire	16	30	7	8	0	1	-8.04
6	Yorkshire	16	28	7	9	0	0	9.66
7	Gloucestershire	16	26	6	9	0	1	1.48
8	Surrey	16	24	6	10	0	0	-5.05
9	Northamptonshire	16	14	3	12	0	1	-9.02

A season that had started with hopes of a third successive Championship title had ended up being hugely disappointing, despite the capture of the Benson & Hedges Cup... and it could have been a lot worse. Although the team had finished fourth in the Championship, losing just one match, they had been extremely fortunate to escape with draws from the rain-affected games at Ilford, Leicester and Canterbury. Surrey didn't only have poor weather to thank for saving them from a closer brush with the relegation zone. The biggest factor in their survival was Martin Bicknell, whose incredibly consistent displays with bat and ball made his selection as the club's Player Of the Year a formality. Without his 748 runs at 46.75, and seventy-two wickets at 21.36, the County Champions of 1999 and 2000 would surely have been playing Division Two Championship cricket in 2002, since so many of his colleagues struggled to reproduce the form and figures of the previous two seasons. With the bat, Ali Brown and Ian Ward both had disappointing campaigns, their confidence seemingly affected by unsuccessful runs with the ODI and Test teams respectively, while Alex Tudor and Ian Salisbury rarely produced the results that were expected of them with the ball. The same could be said for Ed Giddins, who had disappointed in all but a handful of National League games and the Benson & Hedges Cup, while even Saqlain Mushtaq found the going tougher, having appeared rather jaded at times after several years of non-stop cricket. Although it was partly explained by a clear improvement in the quality of pitches around the country, the inability to bowl sides out in the fourth innings of a match had certainly become a worry, with Essex, Lancashire and Yorkshire all finding it easy to save games that Surrey might well have won when their attack was at its peak in 1999 or 2000. The club's decline was, of course, hotly debated in many circles, with any number of theories being put forward. Personally, I felt the biggest problem was the loss of no fewer than nine players to international cricket at various stages of the season - Stewart, Thorpe, Butcher, Ramprakash, Ward and Tudor had all played in Tests; Ali Brown and Ben Hollioake had been selected for the Nat West Series of ODIs; while Saqlain Mushtaq had been away with Pakistan. As a result, the side was constantly changing, with no chance of any continuity developing, and the batting order, in particular, was frequently disrupted by the loss of three, four and sometimes five batsmen. In the circumstances it was little wonder that players struggled to perform consistently, especially those who were coming back from matches against a very strong Australian side with their self-belief having taken a battering.

Given that a settled line-up is considered to be even more important in the one-day game than it is in the four-day format, it was perhaps not surprising that the club struggled in the National League. It also appeared to be significant that the team's form improved towards the end of the season when fresh, young blood was introduced to the side, with players such as Gareth Batty and Tim Murtagh producing performances of promise, just as Michael Carberry had done in the Championship line-up.

It was certainly no coincidence that the competition in which Surrey were successful - the Benson & Hedges Cup - was the one in which they were able to field a reasonably settled side. After squeezing into the quarter-finals, they had replicated their 1997 feat of winning the trophy despite losing to Kent in the qualifying stages, and were worthy winners of the trophy after beating Sussex, Nottinghamshire and Gloucestershire with ease.

At the end of the season there were four departures, with Ian Bishop and Mark Patterson both released, and Gareth Batty (Worcestershire) and Carl Greenidge (Northamptonshire) finding themselves new counties in order to develop their careers. Surrey had been desperately keen to hang on to Batty but the promise of regular first-team cricket and a three-year contract at New Road was always likely to prove too much for his current employers to compete with. Since there were three seamers leaving The Oval, it was a fair bet to assume that at least one would be coming in, with James Ormond of Leicestershire known to be well respected in Surrey circles after some outstanding performances against the team in recent times.

One other change at the end of the year saw the Chairman Of Cricket, Vic Dodds, standing down after six years, during which he had made an important contribution to the club's revival.

2001 SEASON SUMMARY

COMPETITION	P	W	D/A	L	POSITION/PROGRESS
County Championship	16	3	12	1	4th
National League Div 1	16	6	0	10	8th - Relegated
C&G Trophy	2	1	0	1	4th Round
Benson & Hedges Cup	8	5	2	1	Winners
TOTAL	42	15	14	13	1 Trophy

2001 RESULTS SUMMARY

Date	Opponent	Venue	Comp	Result
20/4	KENT	OVAL	CC1	Match Drawn
25/4	Lancashire	Old Trafford	CC1	Match Abandoned
1/5	MIDDLESEX	OVAL	BHC	Match Abandoned
2/5	SUSSEX	OVAL	BHC	Match Abandoned
4/5	Hampshire	Rose Bowl	BHC	WON by 23 runs
5/5	ESSEX	OVAL	BHC	WON by 6 wickets
7/5	Kent	Canterbury	BHC	LOST by 1 run
9/5	Northamptonshire	Northampton	CC1	Match Drawn
13/5	NOTTINGHAMSHIRE	OVAL	NL1	LOST by 17 runs
16/5	LEICESTERSHIRE	OVAL	CC1	Match Drawn
20/5	LEICESTERSHIRE	OVAL	NL1	LOST by 4 wickets
23/5	Sussex	Hove	BHCqf	WON by 53 runs
25/5	ESSEX	OVAL	CC1	Match Drawn
3/6	Northamptonshire	Northampton	NL1	WON by 4 wickets
6/6	SOMERSET	OVAL	CC1	WON by 6 wickets
10/6	SOMERSET	OVAL	NL1	LOST by 8 wickets
13/6	Essex	Ilford	CC1	Match Drawn
24/6	KENT	OVAL	NL1	LOST by 2 wickets
25/6	NOTTINGHAMSHIRE	OVAL	BHCsf	WON by 174 runs

27/6	Surrey Cricket Board	Guildford	CGT	WON by 10 wickets
29/6	LANCASHIRE	OVAL	CC1	Match Drawn
4/7	Leicestershire	Leicester	CC1	Match Drawn
8/7	Leicestershire	Leicester	NL1	LOST by 128 runs
11/7	Yorkshire	Headingley	CGT	LOST by 6 wickets
14/7	GLOUCESTERSHIRE	LORD'S	BHCf	WON by 47 runs
18/7	NORTHAMPTONSHIRE	GUILDFORD	CC1	WON by an inns & 55 runs
22/7	NORTHAMPTONSHIRE	GUILDFORD	NL1	LOST by 8 wickets (D/L)
29/7	Warwickshire	Edgbaston	NL1	LOST by 3 wickets
1/8	Yorkshire	Headingley	CC1	Match Drawn
5/8	Yorkshire	Headingley	NL1	LOST by 67 runs
8/8	GLAMORGAN	OVAL	CC1	LOST by 3 wickets
12/8	GLOUCESTERSHIRE	OVAL	NL1	WON by 2 wickets
14/8	Kent	Canterbury	NL1	LOST by 43 runs
16/8	Kent	Canterbury	CC1	Match Drawn
21/8	Somerset	Taunton	NL1	LOST by 4 wickets
23/8	Somerset	Taunton	CC1	Match Drawn
30/8	WARWICKSHIRE	WHITGIFT SCHOOL	NL1	WON by 123 runs
3/9	YORKSHIRE	OVAL	NL1	WON by 7 wickets (D/L)
5/9	YORKSHIRE	OVAL	CC1	WON by an inns & 46 runs
9/9	Nottinghamshire	Trent Bridge	NL1	WON by 5 wickets
12/9	Glamorgan	Cardiff	CC1	Match Drawn
16/9	GLOUCESTERSHIRE	Bristol	NL1	WON by 36 runs

COUNTY CHAMPIONSHIP BATTING AVERAGES 2001

	M	I	NO	Runs	HS	Ave	100	50	c	st
M.A. Butcher	10	15	1	844	230	60.28	2	5	11	-
M.R. Ramprakash	9	14	0	776	146	55.42	3	4	4	-
M.P. Bicknell	15	22	6	748	110*	46.75	1	4	5	-
A.J. Tudor	7	11	1	399	116	39.90	1	1	2	-
A.J. Hollioake	13	20	1	758	97	39.89	-	7	15	-
A.D. Brown	13	20	0	630	122	31.50	3	2	3	-
I.J. Ward	11	18	0	561	79	31.16	-	4	5	-
M.A. Carberry	6	10	0	311	84	31.00	-	1	6	-
B.C. Hollioake	12	19	0	586	118	30.84	1	4	18	-
I.D.K. Salisbury	15	21	4	440	54	25.88	-	1	9	-
G.P. Butcher	4	8	1	175	56	25.00	-	1	2	-
N. Shahid	7	12	0	208	65	17.33	-	1	8	-
J.N. Batty	10	16	1	239	59	15.93	-	1	26	2
Saqlain Mushtaq	9	14	5	131	38	14.55	-	-	1	-
E.S.H. Giddins	12	14	8	36	9*	6.00	-	-	2	-

Qualification: 8 innings

COUNTY CHAMPIONSHIP BOWLING AVERAGES 2001

	O	M	Runs	W	Ave	BB	10wm	5wi
M.P. Bicknell	541.5	132	1538	72	21.36	7-60	1	3
Saqlain Mushtaq	411.2	109	952	43	22.13	7-58	-	4
E.S.H. Giddins	352.5	83	1102	30	36.73	5-48	-	1
A.J. Tudor	206.2	46	732	19	38.52	5-54	-	1
I.D.K. Salisbury	396.2	72	1151	27	42.63	5-95	-	1

Qualification: 100 overs, 10 wickets

LIMITED-OVERS BATTING AVERAGES 2001

	M	I	NO	Runs	HS	Ave	100	50	c	st
M.R. Ramprakash	13	13	2	529	97*	48.09	-	5	3	-
B.C. Hollioake	20	17	5	563	73	46.92	-	5	3	-
A.D. Brown	22	20	2	787	130	43.72	4	1	9	-
G.J. Batty	12	11	2	317	83*	35.22	-	3	3	-
I.J. Ward	18	18	2	548	81	34.25	-	6	3	-
A.J. Stewart	8	8	0	264	92	33.00	-	3	9	-
M.A. Butcher	14	14	2	370	84	30.83	-	4	-	-
A.J. Hollioake	24	21	2	482	70	25.37	-	3	8	-
N. Shahid	14	13	1	175	43	14.58	-	-	2	-
G.P. Butcher	8	7	2	62	17	12.40	-	-	1	-
M.P. Bicknell	20	13	2	136	24	12.36	-	-	5	-
A.J. Tudor	12	8	0	96	28	12.00	-	-	3	-
Saqlain Mushtaq	14	12	4	94	38*	11.75	-	-	4	-
J.N. Batty	17	11	2	86	21*	9.56	-	-	20	2
T.J. Murtagh	8	6	4	14	4*	7.00	-	-	1	-
E.S.H. Giddins	24	10	3	6	3	0.85	-	-	8	-

Qualification: 6 innings

LIMITED-OVERS BOWLING AVERAGES 2001

	O	M	Runs	W	Ave	BB	4wi	RPO
A.J. Hollioake	100.0	5	498	26	19.15	4-19	2	4.98
B.C. Hollioake	115.2	9	551	28	19.67	3-10	-	4.77
A.J. Tudor	100.5	15	427	20	21.35	4-36	1	4.23
G.J. Batty	54.3	4	256	11	23.27	4-36	1	4.69
M.P. Bicknell	161.0	19	568	24	23.66	3-20	-	3.52
T.J. Murtagh	62.5	5	308	11	28.00	4-31	1	4.90
E.S.H. Giddins	183.5	19	805	25	32.20	3-31	-	4.37
Saqlain Mushtaq	95.5	4	465	11	42.27	3-37	-	4.85

Qualification: 40 overs, 10 wickets

9 2002: From Tragedy To Triumph

Surrey's 2001-2002 close season was relatively quiet and uneventful until 23rd March 2002. Up until that point, the principal news had involved the expected signing of James Ormond from Leicestershire, and Alec Stewart's decision to miss England's winter visits to Zimbabwe, India and New Zealand in order to have operations on his elbows. Then everything changed with the truly awful news that Ben Hollioake had been killed in a car crash in Perth, Western Australia at the age of twenty-four. Everyone in the cricket world, but particularly at The Oval, was stunned and shocked by this terrible tragedy, the second of its type to strike Surrey in just over five years, following the untimely death of Graham Kersey on New Year's Day 1997. As on that occasion, it was one of the most likeable and loved members of the squad who had been lost with so much of his life and career ahead of him.

Players and officials of the club flew out to Australia for the funeral mass in Perth, where Adam paid a tearful and emotionally-charged tribute to his brother, during which he announced that he and his seven-months pregnant wife, Sherryn, planned to name their baby daughter Bennaya, after Ben and his girlfriend Janaya, who had been seriously injured in the accident. The club made it clear to Adam that he should put his family first at this tragic time and that he should take as much time away from the game as he needed, whether it was one month, three months or the whole season if necessary. Paul Sheldon, the Surrey Chief Executive, had meanwhile announced that the club would dedicate the 2002 season, and any trophies that were won, to the memory of Ben. With the new season just four weeks away it was hard to know what effect the tragedy would have on a team that had already been installed by the bookmakers as favourites to regain the County Championship title. Cricket was almost certainly a very long way from the players' minds at this moment in time, as indeed it was for the supporters and officials, and anyone who knew or loved Ben.

County cricket then suffered a second tragic loss just nine days later when Sussex's Umer Rashid, aged twenty-six, drowned with his younger brother at a notoriously dangerous beauty spot in Grenada, while on the club's pre-season tour, where they were taking part in a triangular tournament with Northamptonshire and Yorkshire. These two incidents cast a shadow over the English domestic game as everyone prepared for the new season.

Surrey were left to make some important decisions in the wake of their tragic loss. Since they would be unlikely to see much of the centrally-contracted Mark Butcher and Graham Thorpe, and had to prepare themselves for the worst-case scenario of Adam Hollioake missing the whole season, they elected to reverse a decision not to employ a replacement overseas player to cover the early season absence of Saqlain Mushtaq, who was playing in Pakistan's home series against New Zealand. As a result, Azhar Mahmood, the 26-year-old Pakistani all-rounder, was to be engaged for the first five weeks of the season. Azhar, who was a good friend of Saqlain, and was well known to most of the Surrey players, having had injuries treated at The Oval in the past, was a high-class all-rounder who could provide the cover that the club needed at this time. Additionally, it was announced that Mark Butcher would captain the side until the international season began in the middle of May, and that Graham Thorpe was to be rested from the early matches on the orders of the ECB.

By a twist of fate, Surrey's opening fixture pitted them against Sussex, giving added poignancy to the two-minute silence that preceded the start of play. It must have been very hard for these two sets of players to concentrate fully on a game of cricket after all that they had been through in recent weeks but, to their credit, they did so.

Having won the toss, it was no surprise that Surrey chose to bat on a wonderful Oval track that produced some magnificent batting, especially on day one. After James Kirtley had removed both openers with just thirty-three runs on the board, Mark Ramprakash and Alec Stewart put their side firmly back on track with a stand of 143 that was eventually ended when Sussex's new signing from Yorkshire, Paul Hutchison, had Ramprakash caught behind down the legside for a nicely constructed fifty-six. Having seen Ali Brown, on twenty, missed by Matt Prior behind the wicket, the left-arm seamer then had the considerable consolation of claiming Stewart's scalp with the total on 229, when the unfortunate batsman edged a drive to Prior on ninety-nine. The rest of the day belonged to Brown and Nadeem Shahid as they reeled off a succession of marvellous strokes in taking the total to 461-4 by close of play. Both men completed a memorable century - Brown's, from 110 balls, was his first against Sussex in the County Championship, while Shahid's 109-ball hundred was his first in Championship cricket since June 1998 - and each of them was understandably emotional upon reaching the milestone. There could have been no finer tribute to their late team-mate, and it seemed entirely appropriate that both players ended the day unbeaten on 132, since they had batted with equal brilliance.

Surrey then took a firm grip on the game on day two, extending their first innings to 575-8 declared - with Brown's innings ending on 177 and Shahid's on a career-best 150 - before working their way through the Sussex batting to leave them struggling at 308-9 when stumps were drawn. Alex Tudor (4-84) had made the early breakthroughs, reducing the visitors to a perilous 111-4 in mid-afternoon, while Azhar Mahmood (3-59) and James Ormond, with 2-52 on his debut, had snuffed out a middle-order fightback led by the determined Michael Yardy (93).

Once Ian Salisbury had ended Sussex's first innings with the second ball of the third day, Surrey enforced the follow on and saw Tudor pin Richard Montgomerie lbw with his second delivery, before a partnership of 110 developed between Murray Goodwin (34) and a very positive Chris Adams. Although Salisbury managed to terminate this stand just before lunch by having the former Zimbabwe batsmen taken at silly point, Adams found another fine ally in Tony Cottey and sailed on to complete the third fine century of the match, from 112 deliveries. With this pair having advanced the score to 198 - sixty-nine runs shy of making Surrey bat again - Adams played on to Tudor for 114, opening the door for the hosts to storm through and knock out the middle order in quick time. With Azhar claiming two victims, and Ormond and Salisbury one apiece, Sussex declined to 262-7 just before tea, leaving the home side well placed to push for victory in the final session. Although Cottey went on to register a brave 140-ball century and shared successive partnerships of fifty-five with, first, Kirtley and then Jason Lewry, his departure to a catch at the wicket off Salisbury (3-93) for 114 ensured that Surrey's season would start on a winning note. With Martin Bicknell taking the new ball and quickly ending the innings at 379 by having Hutchison taken at fourth slip, the hosts were left to score 113 to win, twenty-three of which were knocked off, without loss, before time was called.

Mark Butcher (68 not out) and Ian Ward (43 not out) duly saw their side home to a ten-wicket victory the next morning, with the only slight disappointment coming in the form of a post-match 0.25-point deduction for failing to achieve the required over-rate during the game.

Buoyed by their first opening-match victory in the County Championship since 1995, Surrey travelled up to Headingley to take on the reigning County Champions, Yorkshire. Whereas this fixture would normally have been approached with some trepidation, on this occasion there were reasons for guarded optimism. While the visitors fielded an unchanged side, the home team were denied the services of Michael Vaughan and Matthew Hoggard (rested by the ECB), as well as the injured Darren Gough, Craig White and Anthony McGrath. Additionally, Surrey appeared to be going into a game at Headingley with a more impressive battery of seamers than their hosts for the first time in living memory. It seemed that Yorkshire also felt this might be the case, since the pitch they had prepared was merely tinged with green, though this didn't stop Mark Butcher from inserting his opponents when he won the toss.

Messrs Bicknell, Tudor, Ormond and Azhar then justified their skipper's faith in them by producing a near-perfect display of seam and swing bowling that left Yorkshire all out for 140 in 75.5 overs by tea. Although Alex Tudor (4-31) and Azhar Mahmood (3-33) returned the best figures, it was Martin Bicknell (2-39) who enjoyed the most memorable moment of the day when Darren Lehmann clipped a delivery straight to Mark Ramprakash at square leg to become the Surrey stalwart's nine-hundredth first-class victim. By a strange statistical quirk, the Australian left-hander had provided Bicknell with his eight-hundredth wicket at The Oval in 2000.

By the time stumps were drawn, twenty-eight overs later, the visitors were within twenty-five runs of their hosts' total, on 115-0, with Mark Butcher having scored fifty-three, and Ian Ward on fifty-one, after exploiting some wild and woefully misdirected bowling at the start of the innings from Steve Kirby and Chris Silverwood. Day one had been Surrey's by a country mile.

The second day turned out to be no better for the County Champions. Once Butcher (83) and Ward (70) had fallen in quick succession after posting 161 for the first wicket, Mark Ramprakash and Alec Stewart twisted the knife with a 137-run third-wicket partnership, before the former 'walked' for a catch down the legside - just as he had done against Sussex in the opening match - after making sixty-five. Stewart then suffered bad luck of a different kind with the total advanced to 381-4, as he sliced a drive at Gary Fellows to Matthew Wood at backward point with his score on ninety-six. After tea, positive knocks from Nadeem Shahid (45) and Azhar Mahmood (64 not out) ensured that Surrey passed the magical five-hundred mark, before the persevering Kirby (5-129) and Fellows (3-90) ended Yorkshire's suffering at 510.

Although the agony in the field was over, there was still more misery to be piled on the hosts before the day was out. Despite the fact that there was only time to bowl two overs, Surrey managed to claimed two wickets without conceding a run, as Wood was caught behind off Bicknell's fourth ball, thereby bagging a 'pair', and Scott Richardson was bowled by Tudor's evil second delivery that shot almost straight along the deck. Yorkshire were already in need of a miracle if they were to save the game.

Heavy overnight rain, which was followed by morning drizzle, meant a late start at 1.25pm the next day, though it merely delayed the inevitable as Yorkshire were already almost down and out inside the first two hours of play. Having been reduced to a miserable 32-5 by Bicknell (3-43) and Tudor, the hosts had made a very minor recovery to 96-7 by the time another shower arrived to send the players off for an early tea at 3.20pm. Luckily for Surrey, play was able to resume at 4pm and, though the 21-year-old Chris Taylor dug in at one end, while Richard Blakey (31) and Chris Silverwood (38) put bat to ball at the other, Yorkshire were all out for 202 by 5.45pm. Ormond (2-40) and Azhar, who bowled quite beautifully to claim 3-18, finished off the lower order efficiently, leaving Taylor undefeated on a career-best fifty-two from 126 balls as the visitors ended a 29-year run without a Championship victory at Headingley in style, by a margin of an innings and 168 runs. This win also brought to a close Surrey's sequence of ten consecutive draws away from home in the premier domestic competition, with the last positive result having been the victory at Oakham School in July 2000.

Having made such a brilliant start in the Championship, it was a great disappointment when Surrey's Benson & Hedges Cup qualifying campaign began with an eight-wicket thrashing at the hands of Middlesex at Lord's. After being put in to bat in damp, seamer-friendly conditions, only Mark Butcher, with fifty-one, was able to make any impression against Angus Fraser (1-22), Chad Keegan (3-24) and Ashley Noffke (4-34) as Surrey were bowled out for 123 in just thirty-eight overs. Despite having a fine hand of five seamers at their disposal, the visitors were unable to find a way back into the match as the pitch eased slightly, with Owais Shah scoring a fine unbeaten fifty to see Middlesex home to a very comfortable victory with almost twenty overs to spare.

Hampshire then visited The Oval for the next game in the group and posted a decent total of 243, thanks to positive early knocks by Neil Johnson (46 from 35 balls) and Derek Kenway (40 from 45 balls), plus a more measured sixty-four from Robin Smith that enabled the visitors to survive a collapse to 140-6 at the hands of Azhar Mahmood (2-29) and Ian Salisbury (2-48). After reaching 106-2 through the efforts of Alec Stewart (52) and Mark Ramprakash (39), Surrey then lost their way in mid innings against Shaun Udal (4-36) and Will Kendall, and were in serious danger of defeat at 157-6 after forty overs. Azhar then brought his side back into the game by scoring exactly fifty from thirty-two balls, but once the Pakistani all-rounder had been run out, Alex Tudor (28 not out) just failed to see Surrey home. Needing two from the final delivery to secure victory for his team on the basis of them having lost fewer wickets, the big paceman couldn't beat the mid-on fielder with his drive and was only able to manage a single, leaving the visitors victorious by one run.

Having lost their first two matches, there was now real pressure on the reigning Benson & Hedges champions to beat Essex at Chelmsford in their next fixture. Thanks to Mark Butcher's 60-ball knock of sixty-two, the visitors were well placed at 107-1 after twenty-one overs, but thereafter Mark Ramprakash (70 not out) was left to play a lone hand as Surrey were bowled out for 223, with Essex skipper Ronnie Irani very much to the fore by claiming 4-38. Although Martin Bicknell (3-24) gave his side an early lift by reducing the hosts to 8-2 during an excellent opening spell, Andy Flower bedded in at one end during successive stands of sixty-nine with Graham Napier (41) and forty-six with Irani (30), and then blossomed during a decisive partnership of sixty-two with Aftab Habib (27). It was unfortunate for the Zimbabwean left-hander that his brilliantly paced innings should be terminated two runs short of a well deserved century, but he had done enough by then to enable Essex to cruise home by four wickets with almost five overs to spare.

Surrey were now most unlikely to qualify for the quarter-finals, though they showed that they hadn't given up hope of sneaking through as one of the best third-placed teams by beating Kent at The Oval two days later. The hosts' challenging total of 257-9 owed a good deal to Ali Brown's explosive seventy-three from 58 balls and Graham Thorpe's measured innings of sixty-one from 76 balls that ensured his team-mate's early blast was not wasted. Although Rob Key (59) sustained Kent during a shaky start, and Dave Fulton and Matt Walker contributed forties from the middle order, Surrey's seamers, led by Alex Tudor (3-28) and Benson & Hedges Cup debutant Phil Sampson (3-42), always appeared to have the situation under control and duly led their team to a comfortable 44-run victory.

The final group game took Surrey down to Hove, where their ultra-slim qualification hopes were finally extinguished by a Sussex side that had already secured their place in the last eight. In a match reduced to 46-overs-a-side, the visitors looked set for a huge total when Ali Brown (97 from 89 balls) and Ian Ward (46) were going great guns at 145-2, but they began to misfire once Ward - captaining the side in the absence of the injured Butcher - was bowled by Will House. Mark Davis (2-47) and James Kirtley (2-36) promptly hauled the hosts back into the game by ripping out the middle order, before Billy Taylor (4-23) claimed a hat-trick, dismissing James Ormond, Phil Sampson and Ed Giddins to wind the innings up eight balls early for 220.

The balance of power then swung back and forth during a Sussex reply that relied heavily on Richard Montgomerie's sixty-six and seemed to be going off the rails when his dismissal led to a slump from 133-3 to 163-6. Although Azhar Mahmood pulled out all the stops for his side to finish with 4-34, useful cameos down the order managed to bring the scores level at 220-8 with one ball to be bowled, enabling Sussex to win by virtue of having lost fewer wickets, despite the last-ball dismissal of Kirtley. There was great disappointment in the Surrey camp at the failure to progress in the competition, since it was said to be the trophy that the players most wanted to win for Ben Hollioake, the Gold Award-winning hero of both the 1997 and 2001 finals.

Returning to Championship action, Surrey welcomed Lancashire to The Oval for a contest between the only two sides to have won their first two matches, and with all England players permitted to participate it looked set to be quite a match.

For Surrey, Graham Thorpe's return led to the omission of the desperately unlucky Nadeem Shahid, who had scored 150 and forty-five in his first two Championship innings of the season, while Lancashire were delighted to include Andrew Flintoff in what appeared to be their strongest available eleven.

After the visitors won the toss and elected to take first use of what looked to be another superb Oval wicket, a rather ordinary morning session that ended with honours even at 108-3 was followed by a quite remarkable post-prandial period that saw 212 runs scored for the loss of seven wickets in thirty-eight overs. Flintoff was, inevitably, at the eye of the storm, scorching from four to 137 in this period, with his century coming from just seventy-five balls, including two sixes and seventeen fours. With Ian Salisbury and, to a lesser extent, Martin Bicknell, the only men able to contain the England all-rounder, the batsmen at the other end simply had to keep Flintoff company in order for the red rose county to amass a huge score. Surrey managed to keep chipping away with wickets, however, and were probably relieved that the total had risen no further than 320 when Salisbury (3-30) claimed Flintoff as his final victim to end the innings. After the big man had been lured down the track and beaten by what turned out to be a googly, Alec Stewart was able to complete a routine stumping, leaving Flintoff to receive a standing ovation from the crowd on his way back to the pavilion, having hit three sixes and twenty fours from the 106 deliveries that he faced.

The events of the day's final session then sent Lancashire's players and supporters home with big smiles on their faces. After Glen Chapple had picked up a trio of fine scalps - Butcher, Ramprakash and Thorpe - Ian Ward was run out for forty-eight after a mix-up with Ali Brown, before Flintoff (2-32) and the 18-year-old Kyle Hogg nipped in with three more wickets to reduce Surrey to a sickly 92-7. Although Salisbury and Tudor had increased the total to 106 by stumps, it was clear that the home county had a lot of work to do if they were to avoid the follow on.

That became more unlikely the next morning when Salisbury was bowled as he shouldered arms to a quite incredible break-back delivery from Chapple with the total on 129, though Tudor offered hope with some fine early strokes and, in partnership with Martin Bicknell, took the total beyond 150. Unfortunately for Surrey, they were still seven runs short of saving the follow-on when Bicknell fell to Gary Keedy's second delivery, though this turned out to be something of a blessing in disguise. Encouraged by his left-arm spinner's success, Warren Hegg retained him in the attack for too long, allowing Tudor to complete an excellent 79-ball half-century with a slog-sweep for six, and the last-wicket pair to add fifty-two precious runs before the deserving Chapple (5-65) trapped Tudor lbw for sixty-one. With James Ormond unbeaten on thirty-five, Surrey had at least narrowed the deficit to 104 runs by reaching 216.

Lancashire's lead had grown to 228 by the time bad light halted play shortly after tea, though Surrey - or to be more precise, Azhar Mahmood - had captured five wickets by then. Only Mark Chilton (35) got past thirty as the Pakistani all-rounder, well supported by the equally impressive but unlucky Ormond, moved the ball both ways in the air and off the pitch to claim the aforementioned Chilton lbw, have Swann, Byas and Lloyd caught behind by Stewart, and remove Flintoff's middle stump with an outstanding late inswinging yorker.

Surrey then continued their comeback the next morning when Azhar won a rather debatable lbw verdict against Stuart Law (39) to make Lancashire 154-6, and then picked up two further victims courtesy of catches by Stewart, with the second of these being an absolute corker low down in front of first slip to get rid of the left-handed Hogg with the total advanced to 180. The Surrey wicketkeeper - who seemed sure to regain his England place, since his winter stand-in, James Foster, was injured - now had ten victims to his name in the match, while Azhar had all eight wickets in the innings. Dreams of an 'all ten' were swiftly scotched, however, when Ormond pinned John Wood lbw in the very next over and, after a frustrating little partnership of nineteen for the last wicket, yorked Hegg (43) to terminate the innings at 200 and leave the hosts a victory target of 305. With the outstanding figures of 25-5-61-8 to his name, Azhar Mahmood quite rightly led his team from the field and received a hearty ovation from home supporters, who had clearly enjoyed having him at the club as a locum for Saqlain Mushtaq.

Although time wasn't going to be a factor, with five sessions of play remaining, the hosts' target looked to be quite a tall order for the fourth innings of the match, and the feeling that Lancashire were favourites was maintained for most of the rest of the day as a wicket fell every time Surrey looked to be levelling up the contest - Butcher fell at 42, Ward at 78, Thorpe at 104 and Brown at 139. By tea, Mark Ramprakash had become the second Surrey batsman to register a fifty in the match, having reached the landmark in eighty-four balls, and had Stewart for company, with the home side over halfway to their goal at 159-4. The final session of the day looked like it could be pivotal to the outcome of the game.

Although bad light curtailed play within fourteen overs of the restart, Surrey had very much the better of things, scoring forty-one runs without losing another wicket. With Ramprakash on seventy-one and Stewart on twenty-five, the home side now looked to have a slight edge going into the final day.

The overnight pair had increased the value of their partnership to 109, taking Surrey to within fifty-seven runs of victory, before Lancashire finally made the breakthrough they so badly craved when Stewart (46) fell to a catch at short extra cover by David Byas off Mark Chilton, who had been called into the attack almost as a last resort. The visitors' hopes of a comeback were soon dampened, however, as Azhar made a confident start to his innings, and Ramprakash completed an excellent century - the fifty-sixth of his first-class career - from 197 balls. Although Wood managed to unseat Azhar with the total advanced to 281, and Alex Tudor fell lbw to Keedy at 290 after a bizarre three-ball innings of eight, Ramprakash finally sealed a three-wicket victory in style by driving Keedy into the Bedser Stand for six to finish unbeaten on 119, having given a superlative demonstration of how to chase down a big target.

With Surrey having won their first three Championship matches of the summer for the first time since 1958, it was no surprise to see them leading the nascent league table.
LEADING POSITIONS:- Surrey P3, Pts 55.75; Leics P3, Pts 45; Lancs P3, Pts 40

Surrey then added to their success in the Championship fixture by emerging victorious in the following day's NCL Division Two match between the two counties, which turned out to be one of the shortest on record. The Lions had the game done and dusted by 4.18pm, thanks to excellent new-ball spells from Martin Bicknell (5-26) and Ed Giddins (2-8) that sent the Lightning crashing from a high point of 31-1 to 41-7. After a brief flurry of strokes from Warren Hegg (17) - whose innings was ended by a brilliant catch off his own bowling by Phil Sampson (2-18) - the visitors slumped to 68 all out, which equalled their lowest score in the Sunday/National League. Surrey raced home in 11.5 overs for the loss of four wickets to get their promotion campaign off to the best possible start.

After a week's break, during which Leicestershire and Lancashire were both held to draws in the Championship, allowing Surrey to remain on top of the pile, Keith Medlycott took his team down to Bristol for an NCL encounter with the Gloucestershire Gladiators. It turned out to be quite a bizarre game, too, as the balance of power swung violently one way and then the other. Having been put in to bat, Surrey were given a stunning start by Ali Brown (54 from 41 balls) and Ian Ward (27), who posted an 86-run opening partnership inside fourteen overs, even though conditions were favouring the bowlers. Once these two had fallen to consecutive deliveries, however, batting began to look almost impossible, with Jon Lewis (4-22) and

Mark Hardinges (2-46) responsible for a dramatic collapse to 103-7. Fortunately for the Lions, Jon Batty batted with great sense to make an unbeaten twenty-eight and push the total up to 163-9, having received assistance from an unlikely source in Ed Giddins, who posted a career-best undefeated thirteen during a last-wicket stand of thirty-two.

Boosted by his batting, Giddins (3-31) then joined forces with Martin Bicknell (3-24) to leave the Gladiators in desperate trouble at 64-5. Martyn Ball clearly relished the battle, however, as he dragged his side back into contention with help from, first, Chris Taylor and then James Averis. When the excellent Saqlain (1-20) then had Averis caught by Giddins to peg Gloucestershire back to 115-8 the points appeared to be heading for The Oval, only for Jon Lewis (27 not out) to show unexpected talent with the bat. Having survived the loss of Ball for forty-five at 146-9, and a difficult chance to Ian Ward at slip with two runs required, the Gladiators' seamer saw his side through to a thrilling one-wicket victory with nine balls to spare.

Surrey's next County Championship match saw them locking horns with Somerset, the only other unbeaten side in Division One. The cidermen had a dreadful recent record at The Oval in four-day cricket, having lost in each of the previous three seasons, so the hosts were favoured to win, even though the visitors were able to field Marcus Trescothick and Andy Caddick. On the debit side, Richard Johnson missed out with a knee injury. Surrey, meanwhile, welcomed back Saqlain Mushtaq in place of Azhar Mahmood, who had been an excellent stand-in, and looked to be at full strength.

After rain had delayed the start by forty-five minutes, Mark Butcher won the toss, elected to bat and then saw his side struggle all day in seamer-friendly conditions. While Ian Ward scored sixty-two to hold the top half of the innings together, Alex Tudor and the Surrey spin twins all made twenties in the lower order to enable their side to post a total of 220. With showers breaking the home side's innings into segments of twenty-two, twenty-three and twenty-four overs, Somerset were able to use their three main seamers - Caddick (5-66), Matt Bulbeck (4-60), and Steffan Jones - for all but four overs, which was greatly to their advantage.

Somerset didn't find the going any easier when they replied on day two, and at 115-5 shortly after lunch, with Alex Tudor (3-64) having claimed the wickets of Trescothick, Cox and Burns, the game was nicely balanced. Ian Blackwell soon changed that, though, coming through a few anxious moments early in his innings to power his way to a 44-ball fifty while adding 106 for the sixth wicket with Rob Turner (36). Since they were facing the prospect of conceding a sizeable first-innings deficit at this point, Surrey were extremely grateful for Bicknell's burst of three wickets in nine balls that followed, pegging the visitors back to 225-8. When Blackwell then fell lbw to Ian Salisbury for an impressive ninety-eight, with Somerset's lead just seventeen, the hosts' comeback was almost complete. Although Bicknell was unable to improve on his 4-72, Saqlain Mushtaq (2-31) nipped in with his second wicket to finish off the innings at 253 and leave Surrey with twenty-seven overs to bat before the close of play. During this time they made 87-3, with Butcher and Ramprakash having been dismissed before the arrears were cleared, and Thorpe having fallen to Blackwell late in the day to leave Somerset on top.

With the third day's play having been completely washed out, Somerset looked the more likely winners as the final day got under way, and the early capture of nightwatchman Salisbury's wicket seemed to confirm that. Although Ian Ward (67) and Ali Brown (46) then reduced the threat of defeat with an 83-run stand for the fifth wicket, Keith Dutch revived his side's hopes by bringing both men to book as lunch approached. A sturdy and sensible partnership of eighty-seven between Alec Stewart (53) and Alex Tudor (44) ensured stalemate during the afternoon, however, and a game that had been spellbinding for two-and-a-half days fizzled out with Surrey finally dismissed for 332 and Somerset batting out time on 45-1.

LEADING POSITIONS:- Surrey P4, Pts 63.75; Leics P5, Pts 62; Hants P5, Pts 55; Lancs P4, Pts 51

As the team prepared to head off to Edinburgh for a C&G Trophy match against Scotland, everyone was delighted to hear that Adam Hollioake's wife, Sherryn, had given birth to baby Bennaya. Better still, Adam would be returning to England within a couple of weeks to continue his cricket career, scotching rumours that suggested he had decided to retire from the game. It was fantastic to discover that a man who still had so much to offer would be returning to action before too long.

Up in a very wet Edinburgh, no play was possible on the designated day for the Scotland versus Surrey fixture, so everyone returned to the pleasant little Grange Cricket Club ground on the reserve day. Fortunately, the teams managed to play enough cricket for a Duckworth-Lewis result to be declared, with Surrey emerging victorious by fifty-five runs. Surrey's 246-2 was built around Mark Ramprakash's unbeaten 101 and Nadeem Shahid's undefeated sixty-five, after poor Ali Brown had recorded a first-ball duck to go with the third-ball duck he had registered on this ground in 1999. Scotland were never remotely in contention when they replied, stuttering along to 63-4 from 24.1 overs before further rain caused play to be abandoned.

With the game having dragged on deep into the reserve day, Surrey had missed their flight to Manchester for the return Championship match against Lancashire, so a fleet of hire cars had to be hastily booked to transport the players down the motorway to Old Trafford. It wasn't the ideal preparation for what was sure to be another tough game.

Thankfully, Ian Ward - captaining Surrey for the first time in a Championship match - won the toss and decided that his side should bat. With Butcher, Stewart, Thorpe and Tudor all playing in the second Test against Sri Lanka, the visitors' team showed four changes from that which had taken on Somerset, with Nadeem Shahid, Michael Carberry, Jon Batty and Rikki Clarke - making his Championship debut - all drafted into the side.

Although Carberry didn't last too long as Surrey made a very slow and sticky start on a lively looking pitch, Ian Ward and Mark Ramprakash managed to put together an excellent partnership of 133 either side of lunch to give their side a fantastic platform for a big total. Unfortunately, the loss of two wickets in three balls - Ramprakash, brilliantly run out for seventy-one when attempting a second run to Kyle Hogg at deep midwicket, and Shahid lbw to Gary Keedy - set them back on their heels at a crucial time, and before they knew it they were 177-5. After Ward (61) had become a maiden first-class victim for James Anderson, a 19-year-old debutant fast bowler, and Ali Brown had been bowled by Keedy for twenty-eight, Clarke and Batty carried out some valuable repair work, taking their side through to tea without further loss and then extending their sixth-wicket stand to 102 after the break. Although Clarke (41) became Anderson's second victim after showing great promise in an innings that included some glorious drives down the ground, and Martin Bicknell was bowled by Keedy (5-122) in the last over of the day, Surrey were comfortably placed on 292-7 at stumps, with Batty still in occupation, having reached fifty from 147 balls shortly before Bicknell's dismissal.

The second day belonged very much to Surrey. In the morning, Batty (104) completed a most valuable 211-ball century, with largely passive support from Ian Salisbury and Saqlain Mushtaq, as the visitors took their total on to 382, then Lancashire struggled with the bat, reaching 163-7 from sixty-four overs by the close of play. Having made a solid start through Alec Swann and Mark Chilton, the former was run out in similar fashion to Ramprakash on the first day, with Clarke's brilliant stop and throw from deep midwicket earning Surrey their opening breakthrough with the total on thirty-three. Chilton was then dismissed by Ormond in the next over, when Batty pulled off a stupendous catch down the legside via the batsman's glove, and the vital wicket of Stuart Law came shortly before tea in similar style, with the Surrey keeper picking up a brilliant catch off Bicknell from a genuine leg glance.

Saqlain Mushtaq then teased and tormented the Lancashire batsmen during a final session that yielded just sixty-nine runs for the loss of four wickets in thirty-three overs. While Ormond accounted for Graham Lloyd, the Pakistani off-spinner dislodged Neil Fairbrother, Warren Hegg and Kyle Hogg, leaving Glen Chapple, unbeaten on thirty-five, to attempt to save his side from following on the next day.

Although Saqlain (4-43) and Salisbury (2-16) quickly dealt with the tail in the morning, dismissing Lancashire for 194 after Chapple (51) had completed an impressive 100-ball half-century, Surrey decided against enforcing the follow on despite having a lead of 188 runs. That seemed reasonable enough, provided that the weather stayed fine... but the forecast suggested that there could well be some rain around before the end of the match. Surrey then ground out fifty-three runs from twenty pre-lunch overs, effectively putting the red rose county out of the match, before showing a little more urgency during the afternoon, despite the loss of Carberry and Ramprakash to successive deliveries from the distinctly pacy Anderson (2-22). Ward (106) led the way, completing his first century for Surrey since September 2000 from his 167th ball just before tea, though he fell shortly afterwards as the visitors accelerated towards a closure at 246-6. This left Lancashire a theoretical target of 435 from 116 overs, but the first twenty of these overs were immediately wiped out by rain that started falling soon after the declaration had been made and ensured that no more play would be possible on day three.

Unfortunately for Surrey, further rain then ruined the final day, with just nine overs bowled before tea and seventeen afterwards. In this time the hosts scored 112-3 as Ward posted ultra-attacking fields for Bicknell and Ormond, but there was no escaping the fact that the decision not to enforce the follow-on had backfired on the visitors and allowed Lancashire to escape with an undeserved draw.

This result cost Surrey the leadership of the table, with Leicestershire going top after beating the County Champions, Yorkshire, at Grace Road. The 2001 champions had now lost four of their first five matches and were already looking unlikely to retain their title.

LEADING POSITIONS:- Leics P6, Pts 80;   Surrey P5, Pts 73.75;   Hants P6, Pts 64; Lancs P5, Pts 57

Having raced from London to Edinburgh, and then from Edinburgh to Manchester, Surrey now had to travel down to Northampton overnight for the National League match that had been scheduled for the Bank Holiday Tuesday marking the Queen's Golden Jubilee. It was perhaps no surprise, therefore, that they made a slow start after Northamptonshire had decided to bat. Although they had been well contained in the early stages by Ed Giddins, the Steelbacks' opening pair still managed to post 127 in twenty-seven overs before Giddins returned to the attack for a second spell to remove Mike Hussey (69) and David Sales with successive deliveries. With Ian Salisbury (2-35) and Saqlain Mushtaq proving difficult to get away, and Martin Bicknell dismissing Mal Loye for eighty-six, the hosts needed Tony Penberthy's late run-a-ball innings of thirty-eight to reach a total of 229-6.

Ali Brown (55 in 36 balls) and Ian Ward (25 in 23 balls) then launched the Lions' reply in sensational style by putting fifty on the board inside four overs, with the former Surrey seamer, Carl Greenidge, coming under particularly heavy fire. Although Ward departed with the score on sixty-eight, and Brown went when it was eighty-four in the eleventh over, sensible batting was all that the visitors needed now, since the required run-rate was down to four an over. Ricky Anderson (3-30), and Jason Brown managed to pull their side back into the game, however, by pegging the Lions back to 117-4, before a steady partnership of sixty-three between Mark Ramprakash and Rikki Clarke seemed to have sealed the Steelbacks' fate. The game took another twist, though, when Darren Cousins held a wonderful, leaping overhead catch off Anderson at mid-off to remove Ramprakash (44) with Surrey needing fifty runs from eleven overs.

Neither Bicknell nor Tudor lasted long, and when Greenidge was bravely reintroduced into the attack he removed Clarke (52) - who had compiled an excellent maiden limited-overs fifty from 67 balls - and Saqlain with his first two deliveries, and then bowled Salisbury in the final over to secure a five-run win for the Steelbacks and return figures of 3-49. Surrey now had one win from three NCL matches, but it could so easily have been three out of three had they held their nerve here and at Bristol.

After a week's break, Surrey faced fifth-placed Kent at The Oval in their next Championship match. With their four England men again engaged in battle with Sri Lanka, the home team showed just one change in personnel from Old Trafford, with Michael Carberry being replaced by Ed Giddins, and Jon Batty consequently moving up the order to open the batting. With conditions damp and overcast when play eventually got under way at 1.40pm after heavy overnight rain, it was no surprise that Ian Ward elected to insert the opposition when he won the toss. His seamers then wasted little time in rewarding his decision by dismissing Kent for 153 in just 43 overs, with the only serious resistance coming from Paul Nixon (54) and Mark Ealham, who added fifty-two for the sixth wicket. Martin Bicknell, aided by brilliant catches from Batty behind the stumps and Salisbury in the gully, completed a full set of five-wicket hauls against all the other counties as he finished with 6-42, while James Ormond was almost as impressive in claiming 3-56.

Surrey then found life almost as difficult against Amjad Khan and Matthew Fleming (4-68), who claimed five wickets between them before time was called at 111-5, with Ali Brown on forty-nine, having made batting look ludicrously simple.

Day two's play then started an hour-and-a-half late because the Kent players had been caught in an almighty traffic jam in central London, caused by a burst water main in Buckingham Palace Road. They might have wished that they hadn't got to the ground at all, however, as Brown reproduced his scintillating form of the previous evening, dismantling their attack with consummate ease to reach a breathtaking century from exactly a hundred balls, eighteen of which he had struck to the boundary. Dominating a series of handy stands with the Surrey bowlers - eighty-six with Bicknell; sixty-five with Salisbury; fifty-six with Saqlain; and forty-six with Ormond - Brown rattled on past his 150 from 161 balls and moved his team into an increasingly commanding position. By the time he was last out to Min Patel, caught at long-off for a brilliant 188 from 208 balls that included twenty-nine fours and a six, the total was 361 and Surrey were leading by 208 runs.

With an awkward twenty-six overs to bat before the close, Kent were hit by an early blow when Ormond trapped Key lbw for four, though the batsman appeared to be unlucky, having almost certainly got an inside edge onto his pad. Dave Fulton and Ed Smith didn't let this unfortunate setback affect their concentration, however, as they battled through twenty overs before bad light terminated play almost four overs early with the scoreboard reading 79-1.

The third morning of the contest then proved decisive, with the early departure of Fulton for forty-eight getting Kent's day off to an awful start. No blame could be attached to the batsman, though, since he had fallen to Salisbury's second blinding gully catch of the match. While Khan had been caught high away to the fielder's left in the first innings, Fulton's nicely middled cut off Ed Giddins was intercepted low and right-handed as Salisbury dived full-length towards point - it was a sensational effort. When Giddins then trapped Smith lbw shortly afterwards to make the score 99-3 it established a pattern that repeated through the rest of the morning session, with wickets falling in pairs. Matt Walker and Andrew Symonds took the score to 130-3 before the former fell to Bicknell and the latter stupidly ran himself out, then Mark Ealham and Matthew Fleming departed in rapid succession to Saqlain Mushtaq, leaving the visitors in desperate trouble at 162-7. There appeared to be no hope for Kent now, even though Patel managed to plunder five boundaries off the Surrey off-spinner in the final overs before lunch, which was taken at 200-7.

Although Patel (37) was dismissed by Giddins (3-80) immediately after the break, the crowd's entertainment was extended further into the afternoon by another counter-attacking innings, as Amjad Khan crashed his way to a career-best unbeaten forty-two from forty-seven balls. Paul Nixon, who was undone by Bicknell's fine catch off his own bowling, and Martin Saggers, who edged Ormond to third slip, were unable to see the Danish paceman through to a fifty, however, as the innings came to an end at 268.

Facing the simple task of making sixty-one to win, Surrey strolled home in 22.3 overs for the loss of their skipper for fifteen to go back to the top of the table, following a defeat for Leicestershire at Edgbaston.

LEADING POSITIONS:- Surrey P6, Pts 92.75; Leics P7, Pts 86; Hants P7, Pts 73

COUNTY CHAMPIONSHIP - TOP OF THE TABLE AT 15TH JUNE				
	P	W	D	L	PTS
Surrey	6	4	2	0	92.75
Leicestershire	7	3	2	2	86.00
Hampshire	7	1	5	1	73.00

Sunday 16th June saw Adam Hollioake's return to action, as he skippered the team in the NCL match against the Hampshire Hawks at The Rose Bowl. Although he had arrived in England before the Kent game, he had elected to play in a second eleven fixture at Canterbury in order to get some match practice. It was wonderful to see him back in Surrey colours, and the crowd at Hampshire's new ground offered up a series of warm and sympathetic ovations for him throughout the afternoon, which did them much credit.

With the ball generally dominating the bat, just as it had in the Benson & Hedges Cup qualifier at the start of the summer, the hosts recovered to post 178-8 from their forty-five overs after a dreadfully slow start had seen them crawl to 29-2 from the first fourteen overs delivered by the excellent Martin Bicknell (2-15) and Ed Giddins (2-34). John Crawley (34) top-scored for the Hawks before being caught behind off the third ball delivered by Hollioake, who went on to return 3-45. The Lions' reply then leant heavily on Ian Ward's anchoring innings of fifty-one from ninety balls, though it looked like being in a losing cause when his departure to Chris Tremlett (3-25) at 121-5 was followed by Hollioake's exit, for fifteen, seven runs later. The combined efforts of Jon Batty (15), Martin Bicknell (19 not out) and Ian Salisbury (15 not out) managed to get the target down to five runs from the last over, however, before Salisbury heaved Lawrence Prittipaul's first ball high over deep midwicket for a match-winning six. With two wins to go with their two defeats, Surrey now occupied sixth spot in the table, though they were just six points adrift of leaders Gloucestershire.

The team's next fixture was a home C&G Trophy fourth-round tie against Glamorgan... and it turned out to be quite a game. After Adam Hollioake had, quite predictably, elected to bat first after winning the toss on a beautiful morning, Surrey got away to a fairly sedate start of 35-0 after seven overs before the contest, and Brown in particular, exploded into life. A sudden rush of boundaries off Andrew Davies and Darren Thomas saw the total soar into three figures in the fourteenth over, before Brown raced past his previous best Nat West/C&G Trophy score of seventy-two and on to a fantastic 80-ball century that included four sixes and ten fours. With Ian Ward flying along in his partner's slipstream to reach his personal fifty from 61 balls, Surrey's two-hundred arrived in the twenty-seventh over, after the Glamorgan spinners, Dean Cosker and Robert Croft, had received the same rough treatment that had been meted out to the seamers. The Brown-Ward partnership then became the highest for any wicket in limited-overs matches for Surrey when twenty-two runs flowed from the next over by Thomas, who ended his second spell of the innings with the horrendous figures of 5-0-70-0. By now, it was quite obvious to the fairly small crowd that they were witnessing something very special, and the pace showed no sign of slackening as Brown completed his 150 from his 104th delivery and Ward registered a new career-best limited-overs score of ninety-seven. At this point, with the stand worth 286 in thirty-five overs, the Welshmen finally claimed their first wicket, when Croft somehow got a ball through Ward's defences with the batsman just short of what would have been an excellent century. The left-handed opener's innings had occupied just ninety-five balls and had helped to set Surrey up for a huge total.

Following Ward's departure, Brown dominated to an even greater extent, completing his second limited-overs double-century from a mere 134 balls, ten of which had disappeared for six and twenty of which had been despatched for four. The total was now up to 350, with eight overs still to be bowled, and in the following over Brown set a new mark for the highest individual score made in a limited-overs match in the UK when he moved on to 209. Although he didn't know it, the world-best individual score of 222 by Graeme Pollock was now within reach, and it wasn't long after Adam Hollioake arrived at the crease, at 376-3, that this record also tumbled to Brown. Having already left a trail of shattered records in his wake, the Surrey master-blaster then took twenty-two from Davies's eighth over - the forty-eighth of the innings -to breeze past 250 from 153 deliveries and leave the Glamorgan seamer nursing figures of 8-0-88-0. These were inexpensive, however, compared to the 8-0-101-2 that Thomas had against his name as he started the penultimate over of the innings with Surrey already boasting the highest total made in a limited-overs match anywhere in the world. Although his final over cost him a 'bargain' seven runs, Thomas still ended with the most expensive figures ever recorded in the one-day form of the game, 9-0-108-3, while Brown had reached an incredible 268. The first ball of the final over, delivered by Michael Kasprowicz, turned out to be the last of the Surrey batsman's phenomenal knock, as a yorker defeated his attempted flick to fine leg and rattled his timbers. Having faced just 160 deliveries and scored twelve sixes and thirty fours, Brown received a handsome ovation from everyone in the ground, including a number of the Glamorgan players who sportingly made a special effort to offer their congratulations. As the Surrey innings finally came to a close at 438-5, everyone began to fully appreciate that they had just witnessed one of the most incredible sporting feats of all time, since Brown had smashed Pollock's 28-year-old record by an unbelievable forty-six runs and led his side to a total of a magnitude that had never been recorded before in a limited-overs match at this level of the game.

Since no team had ever made anything like four-hundred when batting second in a limited-overs match, Glamorgan appeared to have no chance of winning the game as they began their fifty overs, though they got away to a great start, with Robert Croft hitting Martin Bicknell's first five deliveries to the boundary. When seventeen runs then came from the second over, bowled by Ed Giddins, the visitors had almost seen to the odd thirty-nine of the 439 they needed to win... and they kept on coming at the Surrey seamers. After Giddins had been removed from the attack with figures of 2-0-28-0, James Ormond found his first over disappearing for fifteen, making the score 76-0 after just six overs, with Croft having completed a stunning fifty, comprising a six and eleven fours, from a mere twenty-two balls. Everyone kept expecting the Welsh dragon's fire to burn itself out, but it didn't happen, even after Hollioake had run out Ian Thomas with the total on 113 at the start of the eleventh over. Croft was still blazing away with great success and reached a marvellous century from his fifty-sixth delivery in the fourteenth over with the run-rate still almost ten an over, receiving a fine ovation from the crowd for a very brave and entertaining innings. The applause was then repeated five overs later - though it was tinged with relief as far as the home fans were concerned - when the Glamorgan skipper skied a delivery from his opposite number into the covers after making 119 from 69 balls, three of which he had hit for six and eighteen of which had brought him four runs. At 163-2 after eighteen overs, the visitors were still a long way from their target, however, and Giddins's dismissal of the dangerous Matthew

Maynard for twenty-one in the twenty-fourth over, with the total advanced to 197, allowed Surrey to breathe more easily. Although he wasn't recognised as an especially powerful or fast-scoring batsman, Adrian Dale played an important innings at this stage, picking off a number of boundaries while David Hemp progressed to a fifty that was, by the standards of the game, relatively sedate, since it had taken sixty balls. Having reached this mark, however, Hemp stepped on the accelerator, taking successive sixes off Saqlain in a 17-run over that left the visitors needing 144 runs from fifteen overs. With his side very much in need of a breakthrough, Adam Hollioake now returned to the attack and picked up two wickets - Dale (49) to a catch at cover, and Mike Powell to a catch at deep mid-on for a second-ball duck. Despite the loss of two partners with the total on 295, Hemp was becoming a real menace to the hosts, and took rapid revenge on Hollioake when the Surrey captain reappeared in the attack three overs later, after a switch of ends - sixteen runs came from the over as the former Warwickshire left-hander moved on to ninety-nine. He duly completed the third fine century of the match, from eighty-five balls, in the following over from Saqlain before being brought to book for 102, including three sixes and ten fours, by the returning Bicknell. With the visitors now 341-6 after forty-one overs, it seemed that this could be the beginning of the end, especially once Mark Wallace became the second victim for the expensive Bicknell (10-0-84-2) two overs later. This was not the case, however, as Darren Thomas assumed the leading role in a partnership with Kasprowicz that kept Surrey under real pressure. Having raced to a 30-ball half-century in the forty-sixth over, and taken his team past four-hundred in the forty-seventh, Thomas watched his Australian partner hammer twelve runs from over number forty-eight, bowled by Hollioake, leaving the visitors to score twenty-four from the last two overs. Unfortunately for Glamorgan, Kasprowicz was then run out at the non-striker's end by a great throw from long-on by the Surrey captain from the third ball of the penultimate over with just two runs added to the total, which left them with a mountain to climb. Confirmation that the chance of an unbelievable victory was slipping from their grasp came when Giddins restricted the batsmen to just three singles from the second half of an excellent over, meaning that the plucky Welshmen had to score nineteen from Hollioake's final over. The game finally looked to be all over for the visitors when the first two deliveries yielded just one run and the wicket of Davies, caught at wide mid-on, but, with the batsmen having crossed, the big-hitting Thomas (71 not out) was at least back at the striker's end. By pulling the next ball over backward square leg for six, the left-handed all-rounder gave his side renewed hope, but that vanished, after a legside wide, when he lost the strike with a single from ball four. Needing ten runs from two deliveries, Dean Cosker swung wildly and had his off stump removed by a perfect yorker to leave Surrey triumphant by just nine runs at the end of a sensational day's cricket. Hollioake (5-77) had, as ever, kept a cool head to capture five wickets, with his performance, in the final analysis, having been almost as important as Brown's 268 in securing victory.

As the spectators rose as one to show their appreciation for a most entertaining day's cricket and Glamorgan's amazingly gutsy performance, which had made this a truly great match, the statisticians were left to count up all the personal bests, national, competition, and world records that had been broken. It was a match that no one who was at The Oval that day would ever forget.

For an over-by-over account of this match and Ali Brown's incredible innings, including interviews with the players and full statistical analysis, read **'268 - The Blow-By-Blow Account Of Ali's Amazing Onslaught'** *(details given on page 350)*

Everyone had just about got their breath back four days later when the Sussex Sharks came to The Oval for an NCL match. Although the game was played on the same pitch that had been used for the historic C&G Trophy contest, and the overhead conditions were similar, spectators saw little more than a third of the number of runs that had been scored on the Wednesday as the Sharks were routed for 150 and Surrey cruised home by six wickets with more than six overs to spare. The more bowler-friendly white ball used in the National League was thought to be the principal reason for the very significant decrease in the run-count, though Ed Giddins certainly used it extremely well, recording career-best limited-overs figures of 5-20 as he reduced his former county to a sorry 40-5. Although they made a minor recovery through Robin Martin-Jenkins (50 from 76 balls) and Kevin Innes, who doubled the score after coming together at 53-6, their total seemed unlikely to test the hosts on the '268' pitch. After struggling to 46-3 from the first nineteen overs of their reply, the Lions gradually picked up the pace, and a major assault on Mark Robinson by Adam Hollioake (42 not out from 34 balls) and Nadeem Shahid (50 not out) as the game moved into the final ten overs sealed victory for the home side. The only blot on the landscape as far as Surrey were concerned was a serious injury to Martin Bicknell, who fell heavily in his follow-through during his sixth over of the match and was later diagnosed with a broken right wrist that was likely to keep him out of action for some time. On a happier note, Mark Ramprakash had been presented with his Surrey cap during the tea interval.

Having sat out the midweek round of Championship matches, but retained top spot because neither of their closest rivals were playing, Surrey had to make a special trip to Manchester to play Lancashire Lightning the next Sunday. With the men from Old Trafford seemingly a fading force in one-day cricket - having secured just one win from their first six NCL matches - the Lions looked to have a good opportunity to improve their position in the table, after moving up to third following their victory over Sussex. Unfortunately, the only winner on the day was the Manchester weather. Although the game started on time, rain arrived to cause an abandonment after Ali Brown had blasted fifty-six from forty-two balls, and Mark Ramprakash (39 not out) and Rikki Clarke (28) had then taken the score on to an impressive 152-3 from thirty-one overs.
LEADING POSITIONS:- Derbys P5, Pts 14; Glos P6, Pts 14; Surrey P6, Pts 14; Essex P4, Pts 12

Since Surrey's next fixture, a Championship match against Somerset at Taunton, clashed with the Nat West ODI series, the visitors were forced to make do without Stewart, Thorpe and Tudor, while the hosts were deprived of the services of Marcus Trescothick. Additionally, both sides were hit by injuries to key players, with Somerset lacking Cox, Caddick and Johnson, and Surrey shorn of Mark Butcher and Bicknell. With so many key men missing, particularly those who would have operated with the new ball, it was hard to know what to expect from the game. As it turned out, the absence of the bowlers far outweighed the loss of the batsmen on a typically good batting track, and runs flowed from the start to the finish of a game that always seemed likely to end in a draw.

With heavy rain having fallen almost non-stop for eight hours the previous evening, it was a major surprise that play got under way on time, but no surprise that Michael Burns asked Surrey to bat once he'd won the toss. The early loss of wickets at Taunton had often spelt disaster for Surrey in the past, but not on this occasion. After Jon Batty had fallen lbw to the tenth ball of the day from Steffan Jones, and Ian Ward had snicked Simon Francis to first slip with the total on thirty-two, Mark Ramprakash and Nadeem Shahid (51) added 130 for the third wicket either side of the lunch break before the latter went lbw to Ian Blackwell shortly after completing a battling 78-ball fifty. Although Ali Brown quickly came and went for ten, Ramprakash progressed smoothly to a classy century from 170 balls as Adam Hollioake got his bearings in his first Championship innings since his return. It didn't take the Surrey skipper long to do this, and by tea he had already completed his fifty at close to a run a ball, with Ramprakash on 129.

The final session then saw Surrey amass 172 runs from thirty-two overs, with Hollioake making eighty-seven from eighty-three balls before becoming a third victim for the persevering Francis (3-104), and Clarke notching a fine maiden Championship half-century in 75 balls.

All the while Ramprakash continued to play sublime strokes all around the wicket, ending the day undefeated on 199 in a total of 448-5, with Clarke at the other end on sixty.

With the pitch having eased rapidly during the first day's play, Michael Burns's decision to insert Surrey had ended up looking rather foolish, though the visiting batsmen certainly weren't complaining. Ramprakash had enjoyed himself immensely and needed just four balls of the second morning to reach his double-century from 301 balls. Clarke was the man who dominated the early stages of the day, however, rushing through to an excellent maiden first-class century from the 123rd delivery of his innings and celebrating his achievement joyously with his batting partner. Ramprakash had been strangely becalmed thus far and, having added just nineteen runs to his overnight score in sixteen overs, got a bottom edge onto his stumps in attempting to hook Jones and departed to well-deserved applause for a magnificent 218. With the scoreboard already reading 527-6, the new batsman, Ian Salisbury, had licence to thrill and proceeded to do exactly that, crashing the ball all around the park in making an unbeaten forty-six from just thirty balls before the visitors declared at 608-6, with Clarke undefeated on 153 from 180 balls.

It was now Somerset's turn to enjoy Phil Frost's fine batting track and they made a great start through Piran Holloway and Matthew Wood, who posted a stand of 202 for the first wicket, with Wood playing really well to complete a century shortly after tea from just 139 balls. Although Ormond eventually removed both men - Wood for 106 and Holloway for seventy-seven - during a wholehearted spell from the old pavilion end, none of the other bowlers were able to make much impression until Ed Giddins claimed Peter Bowler lbw with the total advanced to 261. By the time stumps were drawn at 304-3 yet another batsman, Michael Burns, had a fifty to his name and Somerset were firmly on course to save the follow on and kill the game off as a contest.

After another fine burst by Ormond, during which he saw two catches go down, Somerset gradually reasserted themselves on the third morning, with the overnight pair extending their partnership to 117 before both fell lbw to Rikki Clarke - Parsons for forty-seven and then Burns for ninety-nine. Even though they had dipped slightly to 401-5, the hosts still looked certain to avoid the follow on, though they were given a minor scare shortly before reaching the magical 459 when Ormond (3-137) and Clarke (3-104) each picked up a third scalp. Rob Turner ensured that there were no slip-ups, however, and with help from the tail pushed the home team on to a final total of 554. With an insignificant lead of fifty-four to build on, Ian Ward (31 not out) and Jon Batty (63 not out) took Surrey through to the close at 96-0 from thirty-three overs and it appeared that we were in for a very dull final day.

With the pitch continuing to be a batsman's dream, the overnight pair extended their partnership to 153 the next morning before Ward was unseated by Bulbeck for seventy-five, though this didn't staunch the run-flow as Batty progressed serenely to his third first-class century from the 168th ball of his innings and Mark Ramprakash compiled a feisty fifty. Having made fifty-three from just forty-three balls, the latter fell to Blackwell with lunch imminent, then Salisbury, promoted to number four, went to Parsons from the final ball of a session that ended with Surrey on 261-3 and Batty unbeaten on 122.

The feeling that Adam Hollioake was planning a declaration was then underlined by a positive approach after the interval that saw Rikki Clarke blast a quick-fire twenty-one and the visitors' wicketkeeper advance rapidly to a maiden 150, from exactly 200 balls, before holing out in the deep off Parsons (3-91) for 151 to trigger a closure at 324-5. Challenged to chase 379 in fifty-seven overs, Somerset used the twenty-three overs remaining in the afternoon session to reach 103-1, leaving stalemate as the most likely outcome of the match.

Matt Wood and Michael Burns (68) kept their side in with an outside chance of victory after tea, however, taking the total on to 216 before the latter was caught in the deep by Clarke off Saqlain, allowing the big-hitting Ian Blackwell to enter the fray with 163 runs required from sixteen overs. Having hit his fourth ball for six, the powerfully-built left-hander then joined the crowd in saluting Wood for completing his second century of the match from 127 balls, thereby becoming the first man to perform the 'twin tons' feat against Surrey since Neil Taylor of Kent in 1990. Fortunately for the visitors, Blackwell (22 from 14 balls) was outwitted by Saqlain and stumped before he could do too much damage, though Wood suddenly struck Salisbury for 4-6-4 to keep his side in with a chance of pulling off a special win, despite the fact that the target was still a fearsome 112 from eleven overs. When the 21-year-old Devonian - who had played for the minor county in their match with Surrey at Exmouth in 2000 - fell in almost identical fashion to Blackwell three overs later for a career-best 131, Somerset's hopes gradually faded, with boundaries hard to come by against Hollioake and Saqlain (4-111) bowling with most of the fielders posted on the boundary. Eventually, with 286-3 having become 324-7, the home side called off the chase and the game was played out as a draw. Hollioake's declaration had at least produced an entertaining final day to a contest that had yielded 1,815 runs, beating the British match aggregate record by seven runs.

With poor weather having dogged the other matches being played in this round of fixtures, Surrey's twelve-point draw enabled them to extend their lead at the head of the table.
LEADING POSITIONS:- Surrey P7, Pts 104.75; Leics P8, Pts 94; Hants P8, Pts 80; Kent P7, Pts 79.50

Having had an overnight dash back from Taunton, Surrey faced the Middlesex Crusaders in a National League match at a rather damp Southgate the next day.

After the visitors had won the toss and put their hosts in to bat, a brief shower early in the Crusaders' innings reduced the match to 42-overs-a-side. Tim Murtagh (3-38) promptly took advantage of the initial movement available to the seamers by taking out the top order of Strauss, Alleyne and Koenig for thirty-four runs, before Owais Shah and Ed Joyce (31) stabilised the innings with a stand of fifty-five for the fourth wicket. With their middle order never able to break completely free from the shackles imposed by the combination of Saqlain Mushtaq and Jason Ratcliffe - playing his first match since September 2000 following a career-threatening knee injury - the Crusaders could only total 194-8 despite the best efforts of Shah, who made seventy-four from 92 balls. After a Duckworth-Lewis recalculation left Surrey to chase 194, rather than 195, to win, Ali Brown made an early exit to Ian Jones, and Ian Ward went to Simon Cook with the total on seventy-six, before Mark Ramprakash (87 not out) and Rikki Clarke (62 not out from 59 balls) shared an unbroken partnership of 121 to see their side home with ten balls and eight wickets in hand.
LEADING POSITIONS:- Glos P7, Pts 18; Surrey P7, Pts 18; Hants P5, Pts 14; Northants P5, Pts 14

An improving Warwickshire outfit were Surrey's next opponents in the Championship, with the teams meeting in the premier domestic competition for the first time since the introduction of two divisions. The Bears were just starting to find their feet following promotion from the second division, and looked capable of giving the Championship leaders a decent game as they arrived at The Oval with a line-up that included Shaun Pollock but lacked Nick Knight and Ashley Giles, who were both participating in the Nat West Series.

After naming the same side that had played at Taunton, Adam Hollioake elected to bat on winning the toss, and at the end of a day that was cut to fifty overs by frequent showers his team had made 191-5. The score could have been a lot better for the home team after Ian Ward and Jon Batty had posted fifty-seven for the first wicket, but also a lot worse, since this stand was immediately followed by the loss of four men for two runs in twenty-three deliveries. Although Dougie Brown, who had taken three of these wickets, gave Adam Hollioake a few early scares, the Surrey captain battled back well to dominate proceedings in the final session and complete a

61-ball half-century before having his off stump plucked out by Melvyn Betts with his score on fifty-six. Mark Ramprakash was still there on fifty-seven at stumps, having arrived at a polished fifty from 108 balls.

Surrey then made exceptional progress on the second morning, with Ramprakash in magnificent form as he punished some very wayward bowling to complete a fine 174-ball century during a stand of 175 with Rikki Clarke (79). Clarke had also looked in great touch before falling to the combative Brown shortly before lunch, which was taken at 339-6.

The hosts then built on an already powerful position during the afternoon as Ramprakash progressed smoothly to 150 from 270 balls before losing two more partners - Salisbury and Saqlain - in quick succession with the total just past four-hundred. Although James Ormond provided him with useful support for a while before becoming a sixth victim for Brown, Ramprakash needed a sterling batting effort from Ed Giddins in order to secure the last twenty-one runs that he required to achieve the very rare feat of registering a double-century in two consecutive matches. Having reached the mark from 305 deliveries, with his virtually flawless innings having included thirty-one fours and a six, it was announced that the former Middlesex man had become the first player to perform the feat in the County Championship since Aravinda De Silva in 1995, and the first England-qualified batsman to turn the trick since Graeme Hick in 1986. With his job done, Giddins soon skied a return catch to the hard-working Brown (7-110), leaving Ramprakash to savour a fantastic ovation as he returned to the pavilion with an unbeaten 210 to his name in a total of 475.

By the end of the day this score was looking even more impressive, since Warwickshire had slipped to 120-5, with Ormond having accounted for the openers, Powell and Wagh, and Saqlain Mushtaq having removed the middle-order trio of Bell, Ostler and Troughton after the Bears had fought back to reach 79-2.

Although showers caused a couple of stoppages the next morning, the Bears made good progress in the twenty-one overs that were bowled, advancing their score by 108 runs for the loss of Brown, who had been bowled by Ormond with the total on 162. While Pollock had been no slouch in moving on to forty-nine, it was Neil Smith who had boosted the scoring rate so effectively, taking fours off six successive deliveries from Ormond, spread over two overs, in rushing to a 45-ball half-century.

Fortunately for Surrey, Ormond (5-116) pinned Pollock lbw as soon as the South African had reached fifty from 78 balls after the restart, and then had Keith Piper taken at slip to leave Warwickshire struggling again at 261-8. Although Smith had enjoyed some success against Saqlain, plundering sixteen runs from one particular over, the Pakistani off-spinner eventually took revenge when he had his tormentor taken at short leg for a belligerent seventy-four from just seventy balls at 281, allowing Giddins to bring the curtain down on the innings twelve runs later by having Betts caught behind.

Since his opponents trailed by 182 runs with only four-and-a-half sessions remaining for play, Adam Hollioake decided to enforce the follow on, and then saw Powell and Wagh (43) erase eighty-five runs from the deficit before Ian Salisbury trapped the latter lbw shortly after tea. With the spinners wheeling away unchanged for the rest of the day, the Warwickshire skipper, Powell, did very well to reach stumps undefeated on sixty-six out of a total of 165, though he lost two further partners along the way - Bell lbw to an undetected Salisbury googly to make the score 113-2, and Ostler, much to his disgust, adjudged caught at short leg off Saqlain at 132.

With Warwickshire still trailing by seventeen runs at the start of the final day, Surrey remained favourites to win the match, though they were forced to endure a miserable opening session as Michael Powell and Jim Troughton extended their fourth-wicket partnership to 113, before Giddins finally trapped Powell lbw for a very plucky ninety-five with lunch imminent.

Further frustration followed for the hosts after the break, with Troughton and Shaun Pollock taking Warwickshire's lead into three figures and both looking comfortable until James Ormond produced another breakthrough for his side, luring the South African into a pull that resulted in a top edged skier that Ali Brown took nicely over his shoulder running back from slip. The strapping former Leicestershire paceman then followed up by claiming two further wickets in his next three overs, having Dougie Brown caught at second slip and then extracting Neil Smith's middle stump with a superb yorker, at which point the Bears led by 127 runs with three wickets standing and forty-six overs left for play. Another eighteen runs were added to the total before Ormond struck for a fourth time, capturing the key scalp of Troughton for an excellent ninety-four, courtesy of a good overhead catch by Saqlain on the third man boundary from the Warwickshire left-hander's sliced drive. With Surrey's target becoming more testing as the runs required increased and the available overs decreased, it was just as well that their big fast bowler was still on a roll and completed a five-wicket haul, and his first ever ten-wicket match, by spearing a deadly yorker through Melvyn Betts's defences to send the off stump cartwheeling and reduce the visitors to 337-9. Although Ormond (5-62) was unable to extend his devastating spell of 4-15 in twenty-seven deliveries, Saqlain ended the innings shortly afterwards with the total on 350, leaving his side to chase 169 for victory from thirty-four overs after tea.

A required run-rate of five an over seemed unlikely to worry the Championship leaders too much, as long as they could get away to a good start... but they didn't. Shaun Pollock's opening over brought him the wickets of Jon Batty and Mark Ramprakash - who followed his double-century with a duck when he got a thin edge to a magnificent delivery - to sow a few seeds of doubt in Surrey minds. When Ian Ward was then brilliantly taken behind the wicket by Piper off Carter (2-37) in the fourth over with just twenty-one on the board, and Nadeem Shahid nicked the same bowler to Pollock at slip to make the score 32-4, the match was right back in the balance. Ali Brown and Adam Hollioake were not to be fazed by this tricky situation, however, and responded in the way they knew best, taking the attack to the bowlers during a stand of seventy-one in twelve overs that appeared to put their side firmly back on track for their fifth Championship victory of the season. The match turned again, though, on the run out of Brown (33) - with sixty-six runs needed from fourteen overs - since it gave the Bears a vital fillip and inspired them to storm back with a vengeance. Once Dougie Brown (2-26) had trapped Rikki Clarke lbw with the total on 111, and the returning Pollock had snapped up Ian Salisbury fourteen runs later, much depended on the Surrey captain, who had just completed a storming 52-ball half-century, containing the unusual mix of four sixes and one four. Having played out the first five deliveries of Brown's next over it appeared that he might even have decided to settle for the draw, before a sixth-ball bouncer tempted him into a hook which he top-edged high on the legside for Carter to catch with great aplomb after hurtling in from the boundary. At 126-8, Surrey now had no option but to try and play out the remaining seven overs, but the task proved beyond them. After Pollock had claimed Saqlain Mushtaq lbw with twenty-seven balls to go, Neil Smith rewarded his captain's decision to throw him the ball for the penultimate over by winning a rather dubious leg-before verdict against James Ormond with his first delivery. The Warwickshire players were understandably ecstatic to have completed such a dramatic comeback and to have secured their first County Championship victory at The Oval since 1975, while Surrey were left to reflect on a disappointing second-innings batting display that had ultimately cost them the match.

Fortunately for Keith Medlycott's team, this result didn't affect their position at the head of the table, since the other three games in this round of matches were all drawn.
LEADING POSITIONS:- Surrey P8, Pts 112.75; Leics P9, Pts 104; Hants P9, Pts 90; Kent P8, Pts 89.50

Before Surrey headed off to Hove for a C&G Trophy quarter-final against Sussex, the club's players, officials and supporters had a date at Southwark Cathedral for a 'Service Of Thanksgiving For The Life Of Ben Hollioake'. Attended by over eight-hundred people, including more than 140 professional cricketers from just about every county side in the country, it was an understandably emotional event, featuring readings by Alec Stewart and Paul Sheldon, before Mark Butcher gave a courageous rendition of a song entitled "You're Never Gone", which he had composed in memory of his late friend and team-mate. A moving tribute by a clearly distressed Adam Hollioake was then followed by an address from the former Prime Minister and Club President, John Major, before everyone filed out of the cathedral into glorious sunshine. The service had been a fitting tribute to Ben, and it must have left the Surrey players even more determined to win the Championship title for the much-loved team-mate they had lost.

Just two days later Adam Hollioake produced an incredible performance at Hove to see his side safely into the semi-finals of the C&G Trophy by fourteen runs. After he had won the toss and elected to bat, the Surrey skipper watched his side recover from a slightly shaky position of 48-2, thanks to a 141-run third-wicket partnership between Mark Ramprakash and Rikki Clarke (55), before striding out at number five to play a quite sensational innings. Although 35.3 overs had already been used up, Hollioake managed to power his way to an unbeaten 117 from just fifty-nine balls, smiting eleven fours and five sixes along the way as he supervised the addition of 148 runs from the last eighty-seven balls of an innings that ended on 337-3. Ramprakash (107 not out) sensibly fed his skipper as much of the strike as he could while completing a quite superb century of his own - albeit in a totally different style - from just ninety-eight deliveries. Despite giving his team-mate a 76-run start, Hollioake reached his 52-ball ton just two overs later, leaving Sussex to 'do a Glamorgan' if they were to get close to their winning target. The south coast side certainly made a brave attempt to score the required 338, with Richard Montgomerie (88 from 93 balls) reaching fifty from only forty-four deliveries before becoming rather becalmed by Saqlain Mushtaq and Rikki Clarke and eventually falling to Jason Ratcliffe with the total on 174. Murray Goodwin then did his best to keep his team in contention by racing to a 43-ball fifty that developed into a magnificent 78-ball century, but Surrey always had just enough runs in hand as the hosts tried to chase down targets of forty-four from the last four overs, thirty-five from three, and twenty-six from two. Saqlain's five-run penultimate over finally sealed their fate, leaving the unfortunate Goodwin unbeaten on 110 from eighty-six balls as the innings closed on 323-8.

Understandably keen to get back to winning ways in the Championship after their shock defeat at the hands of Warwickshire, Keith Medlycott's men travelled to Canterbury to take on Kent, with team selection presenting the Manager and his captain with something of a dilemma. Although the ECB had ruled Alec Stewart out of the game, and asked that Alex Tudor should also be rested, since he was suffering from shin splints, they wanted both Mark Butcher and Graham Thorpe to play ahead of the first Test against India. Butcher had been promised a game, in order to test the knee that had undergone surgery after the series against Sri Lanka, while Thorpe - who was going through a turbulent period in his private life - had missed the last four matches of the Nat West Series with a calf strain and had then made the surprising decision to retire from one-day international cricket with immediate effect. Although they had, generally speaking, always done their best to assist England in the past, Surrey were not able to help them on this occasion, since Ward, Ramprakash, Hollioake and Brown were essential selections, along with Butcher, while Rikki Clarke had to fill the final place in the top six to balance the attack as third seamer. Thorpe therefore had to be left on the sidelines, which didn't go down well with the England hierarchy.

After Adam Hollioake had called incorrectly at the toss, Kent got away to a flying start through Dave Fulton and Rob Key, as Surrey's early bowling and catching let them down badly, though Saqlain Mushtaq provided succour just before lunch by removing both openers - Fulton for sixty-two, Key for fifty-seven - after their stand had reached 121.

Andrew Symonds then dominated the middle session with a tremendous 94-ball century that was largely responsible for the hosts piling on 199 runs in thirty-eight overs for the loss of three further wickets. At 285-3, the picture had been looking truly bleak for Surrey, but Ian Salisbury's dismissal of James Hockley for forty-six, ending a 130-run partnership for the fourth wicket, and Paul Nixon for eight, had enabled them to regain a toehold on the game as tea approached.

The visitors then continued their comeback after the break, with Saqlain bowling Symonds after the big Australian had added just six runs to his tea score of 112, and the spin twins then sharing the remaining four wickets equally after Mark Ealham and James Golding had added an increasingly confident forty-two runs for the seventh wicket. With Salisbury claiming Ealham and Min Patel to finish with 4-59, and Saqlain removing Amjad Khan and Martin Saggers in the space of four balls to complete a return of 5-122, Kent suddenly subsided from 371-6 to 374 all out, restoring a degree of balance to the contest. The loss of Ian Ward to Khan before the close confirmed the impression that it had, without any question, been Kent's day.

The second morning of the match then saw the hosts take complete control of the contest as Surrey suffered a shocking early collapse from their overnight position of 20-1 to 34-4, with Saggers picking off nightwatchman Salisbury and Mark Ramprakash in slightly fortunate style - played on, and caught down the legside, respectively - before Khan produced an unplayable lifter for Rikki Clarke. The visitors then sank further into the mire when Mark Butcher edged Khan to slip (59-5), and Ali Brown had his stumps rearranged by Saggers's excellent yorker (77-6), leaving the Championship leaders 148 runs short of avoiding the follow on with just four wickets to fall. Shrugging off these setbacks, Adam Hollioake adopted a positive approach, and was already on the brink of a rapid half-century when he lost another partner, Jon Batty, at 126-7. The Surrey captain - clearly struggling with a leg injury of some kind - again came up with an aggressive response, hooking Ealham for six in the next over to reach his personal landmark from fifty-four balls faced, and then taking two more 'maximums' from the first over bowled by Patel shortly before lunch arrived at 157-7.

With Saqlain Mushtaq and James Ormond falling for the addition of just twenty-seven runs after the restart, the visitors were looking almost certain to follow on as Ed Giddins made his way out to the middle. Knowing that he would be unlikely to receive anything more than passive support from his number eleven, Hollioake simply stepped up the ferocity of his attack, taking twenty-two runs from a Saggers over to complete a sensational 95-ball century - his first in the Championship since September 1999 - and then a couple more boundaries from Khan (4-91) in the next over to put his side within two runs of saving the follow-on. The Danish paceman then attempted to keep Hollioake off strike for the next over by delivering a bouncer, but the ball passed so high over the batsman's head that umpire Trevor Jesty was forced to call it a no-ball, thereby enabling Surrey to achieve their objective. This was just as well, since Giddins was cleaned up by Saggers (5-66) in the following over, leaving Hollioake to take the crowd's applause as he returned to the dressing room undefeated on 122 from 103 balls, seven of which he had hit for six, and fourteen of which had gone for four.

Although the visitors had avoided the follow-on, they still trailed by a daunting 149 runs as they took to the field, minus their injured captain, to try to find a way back into the game. When Giddins removed Fulton, and Ormond dismissed Smith, with just thirty-three runs on the board, there appeared to be a glimmer of hope, but Key and Symonds quickly re-established Kent's superiority with a partnership of ninety-seven that was only broken on the stroke of tea when the Australian was taken at short leg off Saqlain shortly after completing a fine 52-ball half-century.

Having gone to tea at a very comfortable 135-3, the hosts found themselves rather less well placed at 145-6 six overs after the restart as Salisbury and Saqlain struck three times to leave Kent grateful for the contribution of Key, who had completed a valuable fifty from ninety-six balls during this mini-collapse. Fortunately for the home side, they had stabilised the innings again at

174-6 by the time rain arrived to bring the day's action to an early conclusion with Surrey already facing a fourth-innings target of 323.

With the skies overcast as the third morning's play got under way, the visitors' stand-in skipper, Mark Butcher, opted to pair James Ormond and Ed Giddins, and this looked to be a good decision as the former soon removed Key for sixty-eight and the latter dislodged Golding with the total on 203. The ninth-wicket pair of Min Patel and Amjad Khan survived the seamers' wholehearted bursts, however, forcing Butcher to turn back to his spinners, with Kent's lead already looking good enough to win them the match. Although these bowling changes failed to disturb a positive Patel (43 not out), Salisbury and Saqlain (4-60) eventually won lbw verdicts against Khan and Saggers respectively to end the innings on 260, which meant that Keith Medlycott's team would need to score a highly unlikely 410 to win.

With Min Patel leading Kent in place of Dave Fulton, who had a finger injury, Surrey set out shortly before lunch on their attempt to surpass the club's record fourth-innings winning total of 354-9 (versus Gloucestershire at Gloucester in 1994) and were delighted when their openers raised fifty for the first wicket. Martin Saggers then struck two crucial blows shortly afterwards, with Mark Butcher edging to second slip, and Mark Ramprakash getting a faint touch to wicketkeeper Nixon. Fortunately for Surrey, these losses prefaced a fine riposte from Ian Ward and Rikki Clarke, as the third-wicket pair took the Championship leaders safely through to tea at 158-2, with the former completing a half-century from 80 balls, and the latter, looking in especially fine fettle, having got to the same mark at exactly a run a ball.

Faint hopes of a sensational Surrey victory then appeared to be dashed completely after the break, as Clarke (66), Ali Brown and Jon Batty all fell to Symonds operating as an off-spinner, while the first-innings hero, Adam Hollioake, snicked Saggers to Nixon, leaving the visitors in danger of a three-day defeat at 191-6. Ward continued to battle away, though, and had reached ninety-nine when Mark Ealham, returning to the attack in place of Saggers, bowled Ian Salisbury to leave Surrey staring down the barrel at 208-7. Although it appeared that his effort would be in vain, the former England left-hander duly completed an outstanding century from 208 balls, some thirty-two deliveries after he had moved on to ninety-nine, and appeared to have steered his side through to the close at 223-7 until Patel badgered the umpires into allowing his side the extra half-hour in the hope of finishing the game a day early. Having not taken a wicket for nine overs, the request - and the umpires' response - appeared questionable, though it didn't benefit Kent in any case as the eighth-wicket pair added a further forty-one runs to the total in the eight overs that were bowled. These runs included a six over extra cover by the typically unorthodox Saqlain Mushtaq off Saggers (3-85) in the penultimate over.

The Championship leaders were 264-7 as the final day began, with Ward on 115 and Saqlain on thirty-one, and everyone in the crowd was aware that their entertainment might not last very long, especially as Kent had a new ball due in ten overs' time. Neither side ventured very much up until that point, with Surrey adding just nineteen runs against a combination of Ealham, Patel and Symonds bowling his off-breaks. Saggers and Khan were then thrust into the action, and the latter almost claimed Saqlain's scalp with his first delivery when the batsman skied the ball behind the bowler, but survived when the nearest fielders failed to take responsibility for getting under the ball, leaving Patel to make a belated and unsuccessful attempt from his position at mid-on. The batsman promptly celebrated his reprieve by blasting Khan over long-on for six later in the over and then picking off three fours in the following two overs to complete a brave half-century from eighty-eight balls. Having played the major role in helping Ward to add 105 for the eighth-wicket, and brought Surrey's target down below a hundred, he then fell for sixty when he chipped a ball from Khan to mid-on, making Kent hot favourites to sew up victory before lunch, even though James Ormond made a confident start to his innings. This was not how it worked out, though, as the ninth-wicket pair saw off the new-ball bowlers and then eased their way to a fifty partnership against the spinners, leaving their side just forty-one runs away from a most unlikely victory at the break, with Ward having just reached 150 from his 336th ball.

Surprisingly, Patel opted to pair Ealham and Golding upon the resumption, despite their lack of success with the ball in the match to date. Ormond wasn't objecting, however, as he reeled off a couple of high-class strokes to create a new ninth-wicket partnership record for Surrey versus Kent and take his team within twenty-five runs of their target. With just Giddins to come, everyone knew that one wicket could soon become the two that the hosts required for victory, but the Championship leaders' prospects were suddenly improved when thirteen runs came from an over by Patel, who had replaced Golding in the attack. Saggers was now widely expected to make a belated return to the action, but he was again overlooked, this time in favour of Khan, when Patel made the obvious decision to take himself out of the firing line, with Ward having reached a new career-best score and the total having passed four-hundred. After a series of singles had been gathered in, amidst increasing tension, Ormond drove a Khan half-volley over extra cover for a boundary to level the scores before very nearly playing the last ball of the same over down onto his stumps. Thankfully, Ward kept his team-mates and supporters waiting for only another three deliveries before punching a ball from Ealham down the ground for the match-clinching single that sparked off celebrations on the visiting team's dressing room balcony and amongst the small group of away supporters who had optimistically stayed on in Canterbury. It was 2.35pm and the Championship leaders had clinched one of the greatest wins in their club's history by two wickets, having compiled Surrey's highest fourth-innings score to win a match and taken a giant step towards securing another Championship title. As the two heroes of the hour left the field with the visitors fully enjoying their first win in the premier domestic competition at the St Lawrence ground since 1989, Ward had 168 runs to his name, having played surely the greatest innings of his life, and Ormond a Surrey-best forty-three. Since the seventh wicket had fallen at 208, Surrey had added a phenomenal 202 runs for the loss of just one wicket, thanks to Ward's 367-ball epic and two marvellous efforts from his lower-order partners.

Had Kent won the match they would have been just 8.25 points behind Surrey and challenging for the title, but instead they found themselves trailing the leaders by 32.25 points. At this stage of the season, no one looked capable of denying Keith Medlycott's men a third Championship title in four years.

COUNTY CHAMPIONSHIP - TOP OF THE TABLE AT 22ND JULY				
	P	W	D	L	PTS
Surrey	9	5	3	1	128.75
Leicestershire	9	3	4	2	104.00
Sussex	10	2	6	2	104.00

It seemed incredible, but the reigning County Champions, Yorkshire, were bottom of the table, twenty-four points adrift of safety, as they came to Guildford for a fixture that was vitally important for both sides. Neither team was remotely close to full strength for the game, since England's opening Test against India had claimed the services of Surrey's Stewart, Thorpe and Butcher, as well as Yorkshire's Vaughan, White and Hoggard. The Tykes were also missing the injured Steve Kirby, who was replaced by David Wigley, a 20-year-old debutant paceman, though they had the consolation of winning the toss, which resulted in Yorkshire taking first use of what looked to be a good track. Darren Lehmann, the visiting skipper, probably wasn't aware that batting had been hazardous on the first day at Guildford in recent years, though the hapless Matthew Wood immediately appreciated this fact when Ed Giddins's second ball of the match took the shoulder of his bat and looped to Ian Salisbury in the gully, leaving the batsman to contemplate his third successive Championship duck of the season against Surrey. Although Vic

Craven and Anthony McGrath then added fifty-three for the second wicket, the Championship leaders hit back strongly to reduce Yorkshire to 127-6 by lunch, thanks to two further wickets from Giddins (3-48) and a couple for James Ormond, including the valuable scalp of Lehmann, courtesy of a breathtaking catch by Rikki Clarke diving full length away to his left from third slip.

Clarke, who had removed Gary Fellows before the break, then added Richard Dawson and Chris Silverwood to his bag of victims to finish with a career-best 3-41 as he and Saqlain Mushtaq polished off the visitors' innings at 172 within a dozen overs of the restart. Having earned themselves a great opportunity to heap further misery upon their struggling visitors, Surrey soon lost Ian Ward and Mark Ramprakash to consecutive deliveries from Silverwood before taking charge either side of tea through, first, Nadeem Shahid (45) and then Ali Brown (50), while Jon Batty sensibly anchored the innings. By stumps, the hosts were nicely placed at 207-5, with Batty still there on seventy-eight.

After the early loss of Adam Hollioake to Ryan Sidebottom the next morning, the home side went on to extend their advantage to 210 by adding 175 runs in just thirty-eight overs before being bowled out just after lunch. Yorkshire had threatened a comeback when the unfortunate Batty fell to the persevering Sidebottom (3-57) for ninety-nine to make the score 250-7, but Clarke's excellent fifty-six from 57 balls on his home club ground quickly took the game away from the visitors, allowing Saqlain (44) and the hard-hitting Ormond (39 from 22 balls) to enjoy themselves at the expense of the long-suffering bowlers. Yorkshire's second innings was then given an 83-run start by Wood (43) and Craven (56) before Giddins and Ormond, with help on each occasion from Batty, claimed three wickets for thirty-four runs to put the County Champions under severe pressure early in the final session. They hit back well in the last twenty-eight overs of the day, however, with Michael Lumb (68 balls) and Darren Lehmann (82 balls) each completing a half-century to take their side into a 44-run lead at 254-3.

Although the visiting captain was able to add only six runs to his overnight fifty-five before being adjudged lbw to Ed Giddins early the next morning, Lumb progressed from sixty-eight to a fine 157-ball century during a 68-run partnership with Gary Fellows. Unfortunately from Yorkshire's point of view, neither man was able to make it through to lunch, as Adam Hollioake removed Fellows for thirty-three with the total on 337, and Ian Salisbury ended Lumb's career-best 124 in the penultimate over of the session with twenty-nine further runs added to the score.

The Surrey skipper clearly expected Yorkshire's lower order to fold to spin - as it had done many times before - after the break, but Richard Blakey (50) and Richard Dawson managed to successfully rebuff the best efforts of Saqlain and Salisbury while taking the score past four-hundred, and it was the seamers who finally brought the tail to book. After Ormond dislodged Dawson with the total at 413, the new ball was taken and helped to secure the last three wickets for thirty-three runs, with Giddins (4-113) adding one to his haul for the innings, and Clarke two. Needing 236 to chalk up their sixth Championship victory of the season - and Yorkshire's sixth defeat - Surrey were given a safe 52-run start by Ward and Batty before a slight decline set in shortly before the close, with the latter being joined back in the pavilion by Ramprakash and Shahid. At 110-3, with Ward unbeaten on sixty-seven, the hosts still looked the more likely winners on the final day.

After making a positive start the next morning, with nightwatchman Ian Salisbury very much to the fore, Surrey found their task much easier than expected, as the visitors' heads dropped with surprising rapidity. Salisbury reached an excellent 66-ball fifty in the same over that Ward completed an outstanding century from his 190th delivery, and a comfortable six-wicket victory was sealed just a few overs after the nightwatchman had fallen to Lehmann for fifty-nine. As their left-handed opener returned to the pavilion with an unbeaten 124 against his name, having completed a thousand first-class runs for the season en route, Surrey had moved 33.25 points clear at the top of the table.

COUNTY CHAMPIONSHIP - TOP OF THE TABLE AT 27TH JULY				
	P	W	D	L	PTS
Surrey	10	6	3	1	147.75
Kent	10	4	3	3	114.50
Sussex	11	2	6	3	111.00

With everything going to plan in the Championship, Surrey now faced a run of one-day matches that offered the chance to consolidate their position in the NCL and make progress in the C&G Trophy.

The first of these games was a National League clash with the Essex Eagles at Guildford, which gave Surrey a chance to round off the festival week with a second victory. Ronnie Irani's questionable decision to insert his hosts on a blisteringly hot afternoon was punished to the tune of 310-7, as Ian Ward (62 from 57 balls) and Mark Ramprakash (74 from 76 balls) provided a great base for a late assault that saw the Lions plunder ninety-two runs from the final eight overs of the innings. Assisted by aggressive knocks from Nadeem Shahid, with thirty-four runs from twenty-seven deliveries, and Ian Salisbury, who scored nineteen from eight, Jason Ratcliffe crashed the ball all around the park in making an unbeaten fifty-three from a mere thirty-one balls, leaving the visitors with a daunting target.

After Tim Murtagh (2-41) had undermined Essex's early efforts by reducing them to 95-4 from eighteen overs, Andy Flower (50 from 49 balls) and Mark Pettini (51 from 46) brought the Eagles back into contention with a fifth-wicket stand of ninety-nine, only for Ratcliffe (4-44) and Salisbury (3-44) to cause as much mayhem with the ball as they had with the bat. Once Pettini's leg stump had been uprooted by Ratcliffe, the innings disintegrated from 194-4 to 237 all out, leaving Surrey with four more points towards their promotion bid.
LEADING POSITIONS:- Glos P10, Pts 30; Surrey P8, Pts 22; Northants P7, Pts 18

Surrey's hopes of ending their miserable run of failures in the Nat West/C&G Trophy were then well and truly crushed by Yorkshire at the end of four farcical days in Leeds. A spell of awful weather in the lead-up to the match left the Headingley outfield under water on the scheduled day of the game, and with each of the two reserve days also being blighted by rain it appeared that the contest would have to be decided by a bowl-out. After much discussion between the two counties and the ECB - including the suggestion, rejected by Yorkshire, that the tie could be played on a neutral ground further south, where the weather was fine - it was decided that an extra reserve day should be allocated on Sunday 4th August, two days after the second official reserve day. Although this presented a slight problem, since each county had a National League fixture on the Saturday, everyone was understandably prepared to do anything to avoid having a semi-final decided by a bowl-out. Surrey felt it would be crazy to send their team down to Croydon to play Northamptonshire at Whitgift School and then rush everyone back to Headingley that evening for the rescheduled C&G Trophy contest, so they cobbled together a side to fulfil the NCL game (see the report that follows), while Yorkshire, whose match was at home, used the designated semi-final pitch for their National League fixture with Nottinghamshire. Since they were not keen to play Surrey on a 'used' surface that had taken some spin, the host county proceeded to cut a fresh pitch for the delayed semi-final the next morning, much to the annoyance of both the visitors and the umpires. Since it hadn't been properly covered during the wet weather, this new track started out very damp and it was therefore inevitable that Adam Hollioake would lose the toss and find his side being asked to bat. Although they were fielding a strong side, Surrey never got into the game at all, losing in embarrassing fashion by ten wickets with almost eighteen overs to spare. With the bat, only Mark Ramprakash, who made a masterful sixty-three, progressed past twenty-one as Craig White (4-35), Matthew Hoggard (2-21) and company restricted their opponents to 173-8, while the visitors' bowling was even less impressive. Although there were far too many 'four balls' on offer, White still batted splendidly in the company of Matthew Wood (57 not out) to complete an utterly comprehensive victory with the same stroke that took him to a sensational personal hundred from just seventy-eight deliveries.

With the Surrey 'reserve' team having, not unexpectedly, lost to the Northamptonshire Steelbacks the previous day, the defeat at Headingley was even harder to swallow. The Lions' eleven that played at Whitgift School is worth recording, since it was an amazing collection of first-team players, second-eleven regulars and a 'blast from the past'. The line-up was:- David Ward, Scott Newman, Michael Carberry, Jon Batty (wicketkeeper), James Benning, Ian Salisbury (captain), Gary Butcher, Ben Scott, Phil Sampson, Danny Miller and Rupesh Amin, with three men making their Surrey first-team debut - Benning, Scott and Miller - and David Ward, who was now the master in charge of cricket at the school, making a fleeting return to the side six years after his last appearance. It was most unfortunate for Jason Ratcliffe that his troublesome knee prevented him from playing, and it turned out that his five-star performance against the Essex Eagles at Guildford had been his swan song in first-class cricket.

The match saw the Lions' 'cubs' competing well in the field, even though the Steelbacks rattled up 277-5 in a rain-reduced allocation of forty overs, with Mal Loye (101 not out from 111 balls) batting through the innings while David Sales (67 from 50) and Matt Cassar (54 from 38) provided the fireworks. Following a heavy shower, Surrey's Duckworth-Lewis revised target was a daunting 265 from twenty-nine overs, which would have been tough enough with a full-strength eleven at their disposal. Although victory always looked out of the question, David Ward provided the crowd with some terrific entertainment as he turned back the clock with a sensational knock of seventy-eight from fifty-two balls that included fourteen fours and a six. It was almost inevitable that his departure at 125-2 in the seventeenth over would set off a substantial collapse, though the extent of it was rather disappointing. The Northamptonshire trio of Jeff Cook (3-8), Graeme Swann (3-16) and Jason Brown (3-30) knew far too much for Surrey's largely inexperienced line-up as wickets tumbled by the over, leaving the hosts all out for 162 and the Steelbacks to claim second place in the league table.

LEADING POSITIONS:- Glos P11, Pts 34; Northants P8, Pts 22; Surrey P9, Pts 22

The Lions' slim hopes of catching NCL Division Two leaders, Gloucestershire, then received a body blow three days later when the second game of the Whitgift festival resulted in Middlesex's first victory over Surrey in Sunday/National League cricket for thirteen years. The home team's performance was poor enough to cast doubts over their ability to maintain a promotion place, since the Crusaders had few problems in amassing 274-8 before dismissing the Lions for 209 in just 38.1 overs. Owais Shah, well supported by Andrew Strauss (74), was the star of the show for Middlesex, scoring an excellent 110 from ninety-three balls as the admirable Tim Murtagh (1-26) received very little support from his fellow Surrey bowlers. Similarly, the hosts' reply contained only one contribution of note, a stunning ninety-four from sixty-three balls by Ali Brown that delighted the crowd and kept the home team very much in contention until his dismissal in the eighteenth over reduced them to 135-5. Thereafter, the off-spin of Paul Weekes (3-32) and Jamie Dalrymple (2-29) proved too good for everyone, allowing the men from Lord's to end their embarrassing run against their London-based rivals in the short-course competition.

LEADING POSITIONS:- Glos P12, Pts 36; Northants P9, Pts 26; Surrey P10, Pts 22

Having lost three one-day games in the space of four days, the team badly needed to revive their faltering NCL promotion challenge as they took on the Sussex Sharks under the floodlights at Hove the following evening. After the hosts won the toss and elected to bat, Ed Giddins (4-39) soon reduced their chances of posting a big score by removing Montgomerie, Goodwin, Cottey and Prior during an excellent opening spell of seven overs, and the Lions maintained control thereafter - despite Chris Adams's battling sixty - until Kevin Innes (50 not out) and Mark Davis (27 not out) battered forty-nine runs from the last six overs of the innings. Their unbroken stand of eighty-four for the eighth wicket enabled the Sharks to post a respectable total of 194-7, though this appeared to gain in value as James Kirtley (2-25) and Robin Martin-Jenkins reduced the visitors to 25-3. Surrey gradually reasserted their superiority, however, as Mark Ramprakash (60) and Nadeem Shahid (74 not out) compiled a match-winning 131-run partnership for the fourth wicket, allowing Adam Hollioake to fire off a volley of fine strokes that sealed a much needed six-wicket victory with thirty-four balls to spare. This important win enabled the Lions to move six points clear of fourth-placed Middlesex.

LEADING POSITIONS:- Glos P12, Pts 36; Northants P9, Pts 26; Surrey P11, Pts 26; Middx P11, Pts 20

Surrey's bowling resources were seriously depleted as they arrived in Hove for their Championship match against Sussex. With Bicknell (wrist) and Ormond (hand) out injured, Saqlain away in Morocco with Pakistan, and Salisbury allowed to miss the game because his wife was about to give birth, Keith Medlycott was relieved to have Alex Tudor back in the ranks after the big paceman had been released from England's squad for the second Test. Given their problems in the bowling department it was understandable that Surrey had signed the former Pakistan leg-spinner, Mushtaq Ahmed, as a short-term overseas replacement for Saqlain. On a less happy note, Graham Thorpe had decided to take an indefinite break from all cricket in order to attempt to sort out his domestic problems.

Although the match started on time, the pitch was still damp after receiving a thorough dousing during a floodlit NCL match earlier in the week, so it was no surprise to see Surrey inserted when Chris Adams won the toss. Almost inevitably, the batsmen found life difficult against Sussex's four seamers, with wickets falling at regular 20-30 run intervals up to 157-5 before Kevin Innes (4-41) wiped out the lower order with surprising ease, the last five wickets tumbling for thirty-six to leave Ali Brown as top-scorer with forty-nine. The Championship leaders hit back well during the post-tea session, however, inspired by wickets in the second and third overs of the hosts' reply - Richard Montgomerie was brilliantly taken by Shahid at short leg off Giddins, while Murray Goodwin was bowled by a Tudor break-back. From the depths of 4-2, Sussex were partially revived by contributions of twenty-plus by their four middle-order batsmen until Tudor and Murtagh swung the game dramatically in Surrey's favour late in the day by capturing three wickets with the score at 112, leaving Mark Davis and Kevin Innes to bat through to stumps at 139-7.

The visitors' hopes of earning a first-innings lead were dashed the following morning, as Innes (41 not out) continued to enjoy a good match by supervising the addition of another sixty-four runs for the last three wickets, two of which fell to Tudor, giving him excellent figures of 5-66. Surrey's second innings was then launched in impressive style by Ian Ward and Jon Batty (46), who posted an opening partnership of 121 before the latter was very well caught at silly point off Davis. Unfortunately, it all went wrong for the London-based county during the final session, with the Sussex off-spinner turning out to be the unexpected destroyer. From an excellent position of 140-1 at tea, Surrey crumpled to 190-6, with Ward the first to go, caught behind off Davis for a well-played seventy-six, and the middle-order quartet of Shahid, Brown, Hollioake and Clarke all being bowled for single-figure scores. While Shahid was unlucky to receive an unplayable shooter from Kirtley, the others were guilty of inappropriate strokes to well-flighted turning deliveries from Davis, though the bowler deserved full marks for being brave enough to give the ball plenty of air. Although Ramprakash (64) and Tudor (28) then repaired some of the damage by adding fifty for the seventh wicket, both departed before the close of play to put the game back in the balance at 261-8. Having added Tudor to his bag of victims when the big fast bowler missed a slog-sweep and was bowled, Davis (6-97) left the field to a fine ovation with six wickets to his credit.

Although the off-spinner was unable to add to his haul the next morning, it only took thirty-two balls for James Kirtley (3-59) to bring the innings to a conclusion, though Mushtaq Ahmed (47 from 31 balls) had pushed the total on to 296 in that time. At this point, with Sussex needing 287 to win and ninety-six overs remaining in the day, the match looked likely to be completed with a day to spare, but increasingly heavy rain prevented any play after lunch, by which time the hosts had scored 85-2, with Giddins having removed Montgomerie for ten and Murtagh having disposed of Cottey for twenty-two.

The morning session of the final day saw some excellent Surrey bowling from Giddins, Tudor and Mushtaq on a pitch that had become rather untrustworthy, yet they only picked up the wicket of Matt Prior - bowled by Tudor for twenty after leading a charmed life - before lunch. Murray Goodwin, who had appeared fortunate to survive a confident appeal for a catch at the wicket, was still there on sixty-seven, having reached a gutsy fifty from 108 balls, but the total had only advanced by sixty runs in thirty-four overs.

Having weathered the pre-lunch storm successfully, Goodwin and Chris Adams took control after the break, with the Sussex skipper advancing his score to sixty-two before he fell to Tudor with fifty-three runs required for victory. It looked to be a case of too little too late for the Championship leaders, though the underemployed Tim Murtagh gave the hosts something to think about by trapping Goodwin (100) lbw in the over after the former Zimbabwe batsman had completed a wonderful century from the 223rd delivery of his innings. With the score now 238-5, the visitors stepped up their efforts to turn the match around, but they were only able to capture one more wicket - when the highly impressive Murtagh (3-47) pinned Tim Ambrose lbw with the total advanced to 265 - before Robin Martin-Jenkins and Kevin Innes saw their side home to a first Championship victory over Surrey for eight years, and their first against their London-based rivals at Hove since 1990.

Surrey's first Championship defeat away from home since June 2000 - equating to an incredible run of twenty-six months and sixteen matches unbeaten - allowed Kent to close the gap at the top of the table to 19.25 points. The Championship leaders' win at Canterbury three weeks ago suddenly looked even more important.

COUNTY CHAMPIONSHIP - TOP OF THE TABLE AT 11TH AUGUST				
	P	W	D	L	PTS
Surrey	11	6	3	2	150.75
Kent	11	5	3	3	131.50
Sussex	12	3	6	3	127.00

As they headed up to Leicester for their next match, it was clear that Surrey still had work to do if they were to become the 2002 County Champions. Their team showed a number of changes from Hove, with Martin Bicknell finally able to return after his wrist injury and James Ormond also fit to take his place in the line-up. Ed Giddins and Tim Murtagh dropped out of the side as a result, while another change saw Nadeem Shahid giving way to Mark Butcher, since the ECB wanted the England batsman to have some more match practice.

After Adam Hollioake had won the toss and elected to bat, it wasn't too long before Butcher - batting at number three - was out in the middle with a minor crisis on his hands, the visitors having subsided from 61-0 to 74-3 against Matthew Whiley and Darren Maddy. Since the pitch and overhead conditions were conducive to batting, Surrey's subsequent recovery wasn't a great surprise, with Ali Brown blazing his way to a 47-ball fifty after being badly dropped by Devon

Malcolm off his own bowling when on four, and Butcher having reached the milestone a little earlier from eighty-three deliveries. Having completed 10,000 first-class runs for Surrey while compiling his half-century, Brown went on to blast a couple of mighty sixes off Mohammad Kaif, the Indian international batsman, on the way to a quite brilliant 91-ball century before falling to Maddy shortly before tea for 104, with the partnership having added 211 and taken the score on to 285-4.

Surrey then pressed on purposefully after the break, adding 161 runs from thirty-two overs, with Butcher moving through to a most disciplined century from 156 balls before becoming another Maddy victim after reaching 116, and Adam Hollioake scorching his way to a hugely entertaining eighty - including thirteen fours and a six - from just seventy-four deliveries. After the visiting captain had been dismissed by the extremely occasional off-spinner, Trevor Ward, courtesy of a catch behind the wicket with the total on 419, Rikki Clarke took over the lead role, completing a composed half-century from seventy-eight balls to take the close of play score to 454-6.

Although Alex Tudor and Mushtaq Ahmed became early victims for Phillip DeFreitas on the second morning of the match, Clarke - badly hampered by a back injury sustained playing football the previous evening - found a sound ally in Martin Bicknell, and the ninth-wicket pair added fifty-two runs to take the total beyond five-hundred. The young Surrey all-rounder fell five runs short of a century, however, when Darren Maddy (5-104) returned to the attack to have him caught behind, and the innings then came to a close on 540 when Ormond had his stumps rearranged by the same bowler.

The Leicestershire openers then took advantage of the excellent pitch to score sixty-five largely untroubled runs before Tudor claimed the wicket of Ward during a fine eleven-over stint either side of lunch. Surrey then failed to make any further breakthroughs before tea as Sutcliffe and Maddy repelled excellent spells from Ormond and Mushtaq in the heat of the afternoon to reach the interval at 142-1, with Maddy having just completed a fine fifty from eighty-five balls.

Having defied the Surrey attack for 155 balls while scoring forty-eight, Sutcliffe eventually departed with the total at 167 when he was adjudged to be caught behind off Mushtaq, who had therefore secured his first wicket for his new team after fifty-five largely impressive but luckless overs. With the spirited second-wicket partnership having been broken, the visitors proceeded to make further gains before the close, as Bicknell picked up the first wicket of his comeback by inducing Darren Stevens to play on (196-3), and the decision to reunite Ormond with Mushtaq yielded three hard-earned wickets for fifteen runs late in the day. Once the leg-spinner had trapped both Mohammad Kaif and Maddy (81) lbw with googlies, the former Fox sent Rob Cunliffe's off stump rocketing out of the ground with a superb yorker. Although Phil DeFreitas and Neil Burns then stopped the rot with an unbroken stand of twenty-five, the hosts were clearly in a spot of bother at 265-6 when time was called.

A flimsy looking Leicestershire tail of Jamie Grove, Matthew Whiley and Devon Malcolm surrendered rapidly the next morning once Mushtaq had removed DeFreitas's middle stump with an undetected googly at 271 in the second over. With Grove bowled by another googly, Whiley run out when he carelessly wandered out of his crease, and Malcolm gloving a short ball from Ormond (2-46) through to Batty, Burns was left stranded on twenty-nine as the innings folded for 290. Having taken 5-71, Mushtaq deservedly led the side from the field, and then reappeared with his team-mates ten minutes later, since the follow-on had, predictably enough, been enforced.

Trailing by 250 runs, Leicestershire were again indebted to Sutcliffe and Maddy for giving their innings a sound base after Ward had fallen lbw to Bicknell for sixteen with the total on twenty-six. With Maddy impressively fluent in completing a fifty from just fifty-four balls, and Sutcliffe showing more strokes than in the first knock to complete his half-century from his 123rd delivery, the score rushed past 150 and on to 182 before Surrey gained a much needed breakthrough. The Foxes' skipper had progressed to sixty-four when Brown intercepted his skimming drive off Bicknell at cover, and when Stevens again failed to impress by falling to a bat-pad catch off Mushtaq for fourteen, with the hosts still forty-seven runs in arrears, the visitors were starting to scent victory.

The speed with which Surrey's triumph arrived was rather surprising, however, as Leicestershire went into freefall after taking tea at 219-3. Ormond's first ball after the restart trapped Maddy plumb in front of his stumps for an excellent ninety-four, before a 31-run partnership between Kaif (43) and Burns proved to be the hosts' last stand of note. Once the Foxes' wicketkeeper had been well caught at silly point off Mushtaq (3-115), Tudor (4-54) returned to the attack to clean up Kaif and the tail with a four-wicket burst that left the home team all out for 289. Needing just forty-two to seal their victory with a day to spare, Surrey sprinted to the winning post in 6.1 overs, though they did lose Ward, Batty and Butcher to Whiley and Malcolm in the process.

With Warwickshire having thrashed Kent to move up to third in the table, Surrey now led the way by a massive 36.25 points, though the Bears had a game in hand and still had to play host to the leaders in a couple of weeks time.

COUNTY CHAMPIONSHIP - TOP OF THE TABLE AT 17TH AUGUST				
	P	W	D	L	PTS
Surrey	12	7	3	2	170.75
Kent	12	5	3	4	134.50
Warwickshire	11	5	4	2	133.00

A return to National League action against the Derbyshire Scorpions at The Oval then produced an extremely disappointing defeat that represented a genuine setback to Surrey's hopes of earning promotion back to the first division. After Adam Holioake had won the toss and elected to bat, Ian Ward took five successive fours off Kevin Dean as he and Ali Brown rattled up forty-three runs from the first four overs, before Derbyshire's other five seamers took control. Mark Ramprakash (78), who registered his fourth half-century in his last five NCL innings, was the only batsman to make any impact as the hosts slipped steadily to 190 all out. Despite losing DiVenuto and Bassano for thirty-eight, the Scorpions' reply got away to a brisk start that put them ahead of the clock and allowed them to ride out a slight stumble to 128-5 when Tim Murtagh (2-38) and Ian Salisbury began to exercise strict control in mid innings. Steve Selwood (50) and Jason Kerr (34 not out) shared a 61-run sixth-wicket stand to ensure that their side cruised home by four wickets with thirty-seven balls to spare and moved into contention for promotion.
LEADING POSITIONS:- Glos P13, Pts 40; Northants P11, Pts 30; Surrey P12, Pts 26; Derbys P11, Pts 22; Essex P10, Pts 20

Surrey now needed to produce a positive response when they took on eighth-placed Hampshire Hawks under the lights at The Oval three days later. After choosing to bat first they were boosted by an opening stand of seventy-six in thirteen overs by Ward (38) and Brown (49 from 40 balls), before the ultra-consistent Ramprakash (50) reached the half-century mark for the seventh time in his last eight limited-overs innings during an 82-run partnership with Scott Newman (37). Although both men then fell in the same over from Neil Johnson (3-42) they had established a platform at 187-4 that allowed Nadeem Shahid (32 from 21 balls) to play the lead role in the addition of seventy-five runs from the final nine overs, despite the best efforts of Dimitri Mascarenhas (4-45). Chasing a demanding 263 to win, the visitors made a spirited start through Johnson (44) and Jason Laney (25) before the combination of Mushtaq Ahmed and Adam Holioake proved deadly. While the little leg-spinner tied the batsmen down during a fine spell of

9-2-19-1, the Surrey skipper thwarted their attempts to accelerate by picking up 5-43 as the visitors sank to 192 all out in 41.3 overs.
LEADING POSITIONS:- Glos P13, Pts 40; Northants P11, Pts 30; Surrey P13, Pts 30; Lancs P13, Pts 24; Derbys P11, Pts 22; Essex P10, Pts 20

With two victories from their last four games looking likely to be enough to sew up the Championship title, Surrey hosted sixth-placed Hampshire in optimistic mood. The south coast county had struggled on a regular basis against the men from The Oval in recent years and were lacking three key players - John Crawley, who was playing for England in the third Test against India, and the injured seamers, Alan Mullally and Chris Tremlett. Surrey were meanwhile missing Stewart, Butcher and Tudor (England) and Clarke (injured), but welcomed back Salisbury, Shahid and Saqlain, and gave a first-class debut to 22-year-old opening batsman Scott Newman, who had been scoring heavily in club and second eleven cricket.

In view of the late finish to the previous evening's floodlit match, the sides had agreed to start the first day of the Championship fixture at midday, with the day's allocation of overs being reduced from 104 to eighty-eight. The sixteen 'lost' overs would then be added to the quota of overs for days two, three and four.

Although the opening day was shorter than normal there really was no excuse for Hampshire to take the whole of it to score 190 in 85.2 overs after winning the toss and electing to bat. Their tactic at the start of play seemed to be to bat for as long as possible and grind out the biggest score they could manage in the hope of earning a draw, but it backfired badly, since their passive approach allowed Adam Hollioake to set attacking fields, especially for the spinners. Nick Pothas, with fifty-eight from number six in the order, was the only man to play with any positive intent whatsoever, and he shared in the only worthwhile partnership, sixty-eight for the seventh wicket with Dimitri Mascarenhas, as Saqlain Mushtaq (5-59) and Ian Salisbury (3-44) enjoyed their return to the team.

Having handed the initiative to their hosts straight away, Hampshire were now really up against it, especially once Surrey reached lunch on day two at 132-0. After getting away to a magnificent start, the debutant Newman offered three catching chances off Shaun Udal either side of completing a fine half-century from eighty balls, before reaching the break on seventy-three, with Ian Ward at the other end on fifty-seven.

With runs flowing freely off the seamers after the resumption, the Surrey openers soon managed to level the scores in the match before disaster befell Newman. Having made his way to ninety-nine, he elected to pad up to a delivery from his fellow debutant, James Tomlinson, and fell lbw as the ball went straight on rather than swinging away. It was good thinking and bowling by the Hampshire left-arm seamer, and an unfortunate misjudgement by the batsman, but Newman could still be proud of his performance as he returned to the pavilion to a fine ovation with the scoreboard reading 198-1. Ward then followed shortly afterwards for eighty-seven, caught at slip off a sharply turning off-break from Udal, and Hampshire also claimed the scalps of Mark Ramprakash and Nadeem Shahid during the afternoon session, though Surrey were already holding all the aces when tea arrived at 295-4.

Having given the bowlers a taste of what might follow by smiting two sixes in scoring thirty-five before the break, Ali Brown completed a marvellous 43-ball fifty shortly afterwards, despite having lost his skipper to Tomlinson for nine at 316-5. The visitors were denied further breakthroughs thereafter as Brown found a good ally in Jon Batty and completed the thirty-first first-class century of his career, from just 104 balls, four overs before stumps. By the close, Surrey led by 220 runs, at 410-5, and their eighth Championship victory of the summer was looking assured unless bad weather came to Hampshire's rescue.

The Championship leaders showed no mercy the next morning as the sixth-wicket pair extended their partnership to 154 before Udal finally snared Brown, courtesy of a fine over-the-shoulder catch by Jason Laney, with the batsman's score on 135 and the total on 470. Martin Bicknell and Ian Salisbury then came and went for quick-fire twenties as Surrey pressed the accelerator, reaching 575-8 before Lawrence Prittipaul polished off the innings by dismissing Saqlain and Batty (89) in the space of nine deliveries. As the players left the field with Surrey all out for 576, leading by 386, it was hard to know who deserved more sympathy - Batty for falling eleven short of his century, or Udal, who returned figures of 4-213 after toiling through forty-seven overs with little support.

It was clear from the start of Hampshire's second innings that they were going to be more positive, but it was rather too late to save them from the desperate position they had put themselves in. Although the two openers contributed thirties, before Johnson was undone by Saqlain, and Laney was spun out by Ormond - mixing his off-breaks with his seamers - the visitors needed fifties and hundreds if they were to have even the slightest hope of avoiding a heavy defeat. Will Kendall and Robin Smith did at least manage to get their side through to tea without further loss at 134-2, but things went downhill rapidly thereafter as Saqlain hit a real purple patch. By claiming the wickets of Smith and John Francis with consecutive deliveries at 142 - both to catches by Shahid, with the second one a fine reflex effort away to his right - and then striking again twice in quick succession to remove Kendall and Prittipaul, the Pakistani spin king took his innings haul to five and his match haul to ten, reducing the visitors to 167-6. Surrey's hopes of completing a three-day victory were thwarted, however, as Mascarenhas, assisted by Pothas, Udal and Hamblin, played his natural game to complete a 69-ball half-century and see his side through to stumps at 303-8, despite Hollioake claiming the extra half-hour.

By the time the final day got under way, Surrey knew that their position at the top of the Championship had been strengthened, since neither Kent nor Warwickshire had been able to win their match. Victory was soon tied up by Salisbury (3-104), who picked up the last two wickets, including Mascarenhas, last out for ninety-four at 326 when Ormond managed to hang on to a sharp overhead catch in the covers. As Saqlain (6-121) led his side from the field, closely followed by his spin twin, Surrey had extended their lead in the Championship to an incredible 45.25 points.

COUNTY CHAMPIONSHIP - TOP OF THE TABLE AT 25TH AUGUST				
	P	W	D	L	PTS
Surrey	13	8	3	2	190.75
Kent	13	5	4	4	145.50
Warwickshire	12	5	5	2	143.00

As the team made their way up to Edgbaston for their next game they knew it was possible for them to clinch the title if they could beat the Warwickshire side that were now their only realistic challengers. With Surrey's England men resting between the third and fourth Tests against India, the only change in their line-up saw the fit-again Rikki Clarke replacing the very unfortunate Scott Newman.

When Michael Powell won the toss, he elected to bat in conditions that looked ideal for wielding the willow and scored thirty-six himself before becoming one of two victims for Saqlain during an opening session that came to a close with the hosts on 110-2.

After lunch, a third-wicket stand of fifty-nine between Nick Knight and Ian Bell was ended with the total on 146 when Jon Batty swooped low in front of the slips to pick up a sensational catch offered by Bell (34) off Martin Bicknell. The visitors were still unable to grasp the initiative while Knight was at the crease, but once he departed for seventy-four to another brilliant Batty catch - this time off the inside edge, with James Ormond the bowler - Surrey quickly removed Shaun Pollock and Dougie Brown to leave the hosts struggling a little at 196-6. Unfortunately for the Championship leaders, Jim Troughton was already into his stride and, with steady support from Tony Frost, took his side through to tea at 223-6, with Surrey's surge having been stalled.

The final session of the day was fairly evenly balanced as the Bears advanced to 300-9, with Troughton eventually falling for an impressive sixty-one, and Frost hanging around for a hundred balls while making thirty-five. Overall honours were just about even, too, but if Keith Medlycott's team could put together a good reply then victory, and the Championship, could yet be theirs by the end of the match.

Surrey didn't enjoy the best of starts on the second morning, however, as the last-wicket pair of Mo Sheikh and Melvyn Betts added another forty-five runs to the total before Betts was caught on the long leg boundary by Saqlain (4-94) off Ormond (4-108) for forty-seven. This partnership, which had added sixty-six runs in total, had shown how good the pitch was and gave the visitors hope of building a decent first-innings lead. Although they didn't start well, losing Batty to Betts with the total on thirty-two, they prospered thereafter, in the form of Ian Ward and Mark Ramprakash, who batted until tea, by which time the score was 208-1, with Ward on eighty-six and Ramprakash on ninety.

Although neither man made it through to stumps, Ward at least had the consolation of reaching three figures, from 198 balls, whereas Ramprakash became the fourth Surrey batsman to record a Championship ninety-nine during the season when he fell lbw to Dougie Brown with the partnership worth 204 runs. Having moved on to 114, Ward made his exit within fifteen runs of his erstwhile partner, with the total on 251, but there still looked to be plenty of runs in both the pitch and the Surrey batting line-up when time was called at 319-3, with Shahid on forty-three and Brown on twenty-five.

This certainly turned out to be the case on day three as the Championship leaders raced along during the morning session - the overnight pair took the total to 397 before Brown (57) was stumped off Ashley Giles, then Adam Hollioake joined forces with Shahid to add another seventy-seven runs to the score. During this partnership for the fifth wicket, Shahid arrived at an excellent century from 144 balls, and he went on to reach 116 before he was taken at slip off Giles with 474 runs on the board. By the time lunch arrived, Hollioake had completed a terrific 39-ball half-century though he had also lost Rikki Clarke for ten to the same Frost-Giles combination that had unseated Ali Brown.

After the break Surrey folded with surprising rapidity from 510-6 to 544 all out. Hollioake was left stranded on eighty-two from 77 balls, as Giles removed Bicknell to finish with 4-134, and Dougie Brown made short work of Salisbury, Saqlain and Ormond to end with the rather flattering figures of 4-124. Surrey therefore held a 199-run advantage with 148 overs left in the match as Warwickshire's second innings got under way at 3pm on the third day. By a strange quirk of fate, these figures and timings almost exactly mirrored those from the match at The Oval earlier in the season, with the only difference being that Surrey's lead on that occasion was 182. When the home team's openers saw their side through to tea at 83-0 from just twenty overs, with both Powell and Wagh on thirty-six, there was still scope for Warwickshire to emulate their Oval comeback.

The final session of the day was slow but absorbing, with Surrey taking the early honours by claiming three quick wickets through Saqlain and Ormond, before Troughton and the injured Knight, batting with a runner, shepherded their side along from 105-3 to 154-3 by the close. With the pitch still playing well, it was going to be a tall order for the champions-elect to win the match and clinch the title, but with the Bears showing little or no ambition to try and claim victory themselves it appeared that Surrey would be all but mathematically the champions by the end of the contest.

For the first ninety minutes of day four, the visitors were held at bay by the overnight pair, as Troughton completed his second impressive half-century of the match from 110 balls, but with Warwickshire's lead standing at fifteen the belatedly introduced Salisbury trapped the 23-year-old left-hander lbw for sixty-three. Although Knight looked like he might be hard to shift as he moved his overnight score of fourteen on to forty-one, Surrey made another breakthrough in the last over of the session when Shaun Pollock was held at short leg off Saqlain, leaving the Bears effectively 26-5 with sixty-five overs left to play after the break.

The visitors needed to continue their wicket-taking progress during the afternoon session but found Knight and the new batsman, Dougie Brown, to be in defiant mood as they took the total past 250 and ate up valuable overs. With the home side starting to feel a little more comfortable at 257-5, Saqlain (4-80) struck, however, as his "wrong 'un", or "doosra" as it had now been christened, took the outside edge of Brown's bat to give Batty a catch and earn the off-spinner his fiftieth first-class wicket of the season. Knight now seemed to hold the key to the match as he completed one of the slowest fifties of his career, from 194 balls, though he had a very determined new partner in Tony Frost. While the Bears' wicketkeeper remained steadfast on nought for fifty-two balls, Knight began to find gaps in the field with some pleasing strokes, taking the hosts closer and closer to safety. By the time rain brought an early tea at 3.30pm, the seventh-wicket pair had been together for twenty vital overs and added forty-four runs, with Frost having taken a two from his fifty-third ball and moved his score on to seven.

Although no playing time was lost, Surrey's hopes were fading fast, and a flurry of runs off Bicknell and Clarke when the new ball was taken merely added to the feeling that the visitors were not going to be able to claim the title in this match. Although Frost eventually fell when he gloved a catch to Batty while attempting to hook Clarke, having played an excellent defensive knock of thirteen from eighty-six balls, the game was all but dead by then, and the only remaining matter of interest was whether or not Knight could reach his century. Having played really well throughout a 260-ball innings spanning five-and-a-half hours, he finally reached that personal milestone and, with his team's safety assured, he could even afford a smile when he became Ian Ward's maiden County Championship victim, trapped lbw for a superb 133 by the part-time medium-pacer's fourth ball.

As the players left the field following Warwickshire's 5.20pm declaration at 404-9, Surrey were so near yet so far from a third County Championship title in four years.

COUNTY CHAMPIONSHIP - TOP OF THE TABLE AT 30TH AUGUST				
	P	W	D	L	PTS
Surrey	14	8	4	2	202.75
Warwickshire	13	5	6	2	152.00
Kent	13	5	4	4	145.50

With the NCL Division Two promotion race still wide open, Surrey now faced a key floodlit match at the County Ground, Derby, against the Derbyshire Scorpions. The Lions started well after their hosts had won the toss and chosen to bat, with Ed Giddins removing the openers for six, before 21-year-old all-rounder, Nathan Dumelow (52), and Dominic Cork (51) added 111 for the third wicket in nineteen overs to put the Scorpions on top. Excellent spells in mid-innings by Rikki Clarke and Ian Salisbury then dragged Surrey back into the game, allowing Adam Hollioake to make an amazing impact when he entered the attack after thirty-four overs. With the visiting captain capturing four wickets in quick succession, Derbyshire slumped from 162-3 to 190-9, and needed a last-wicket stand of twenty-three to haul them up to a final total of 213.

The Lions' fortunes fluctuated wildly when they replied, as they hit early problems at 17-2, recovered well to 123-3, and then collapsed to 172-7 against Mathew Dowman and Graeme

Welch. With just six overs to go at this point, the visitors' hopes seemed to be resting on Clarke, who was playing a fine knock despite struggling with a knee injury. Salisbury then made a vital contribution by taking three boundaries from the forty-third over bowled by Cork, leaving his side to score just five runs from twelve balls, only for Mohammad Ali (3-42) to remove the leg-spinner and Tim Murtagh in the space of three deliveries with the total on 210. After Giddins had appeared fortunate to survive a confident lbw shout from the first ball of the final over from Cork, a wide, followed by a single to the Surrey number eleven, enabled the impressive Clarke to seal a tense one-wicket victory with two balls to spare and leave the field to a hero's welcome from his team-mates with ninety-eight runs to his name.

With Essex on a good run and Northamptonshire starting to fade badly, it was still pretty tight at the top of the table.

LEADING POSITIONS:- Glos P14, Pts 40; Surrey P14, Pts 34; Essex P13, Pts 32; Northants P13, Pts 30; Derbys P13, Pts 26

On Saturday 7th September, before Surrey next took to the field, they were confirmed as the 2002 County Champions, since neither Kent nor Warwickshire were able to win their match while the leaders were sitting out the round of games that started on 4th September. It was a wonderful achievement by a group of players who had been confronted by a second tragedy in five years at the start of the season, and it was no surprise that the team's triumph was immediately dedicated to the memory of Ben Hollioake. Talking about the club's decision to dedicate the title to his brother, Adam Hollioake said, "For me, personally, that was never a factor - to me it doesn't bring Ben back. The other guys would be likely to treat it more that way, because they probably thought it was a way of paying their respects to him. I just found it a nice gesture from the club to say that." Continuing his tribute to his team-mates, he went on to say, "What they have done for the club, and for me and my family, has been more than a tale of winning the Championship. I feel honoured to know them, they are a special bunch. People within cricket talk about us as being a hated side, but if you get to know these people you could never say that."

COUNTY CHAMPIONSHIP - TOP OF THE TABLE AT 8TH SEPTEMBER				
	P	W	D	L	PTS
Surrey	14	8	4	2	202.75
Warwickshire	14	5	7	2	161.00
Kent	14	5	5	4	157.50

Within twenty-four hours of regaining the title of County Champions from Yorkshire, who were now almost certain to be relegated, Surrey were back in action in the NCL, facing the Essex Eagles in a crunch match at Chelmsford. After being put in to bat by their hosts, the Lions struggled throughout an innings that owed much to Adam Hollioake's violent twenty-seven from just sixteen balls, and a crucial 32-run ninth-wicket partnership between Saqlain Mushtaq (28) and Tim Murtagh (14 not out), that enabled a final total of 162 to be posted.

Although the visitors then set the Eagles back on their heels at 63-4, a fine stand of seventy-four between Ronnie Irani (41) and Paul Grayson (29) appeared to have decided the game in favour of the in-form hosts. The picture changed, however, when Irani missed a slog at Martin Bicknell (2-28) with his side needing just twenty-six runs from fifteen overs. Even though Grayson followed shortly afterwards with the total on 145, it was only once Essex had reached 155-6 with eleven overs remaining that Adam Hollioake (3-11) and Ed Giddins (3-43) really came into their own, lopping off the tail at a cost of just five runs in the space of twenty-four balls to leave Surrey victorious by two runs. As the Lions' players celebrated their amazing last-gasp comeback on the outfield, Northamptonshire were losing to Lancashire at Old Trafford, thereby

confirming Surrey's promotion, since the only two sides who could overtake the Lions - the Eagles and the Steelbacks - were due to meet the following week.
LEADING POSITIONS:- Glos P15, Pts 44; Surrey P15, Pts 38; Essex P14, Pts 32; Northants P14, Pts 30

With Surrey having secured the Championship title, and Hampshire already relegated, both clubs gave opportunities to a few of their younger players when the two sides met at The Rose Bowl. Having had a change of heart about sitting out the rest of the season, Graham Thorpe returned to action for the visitors in an attempt to prove his form and fitness ahead of the winter's Ashes tour, while Adam Hollioake missed the game in order to take part in a floodlit match that Sussex had organised in memory of Umer and Burhan Rashid.

Ian Ward therefore skippered the Surrey side for a fixture that had an 'end of term' feel to it and, surprisingly, featured plenty of runs. Most pitches at The Rose Bowl had been uneven in bounce and very much favoured the bowlers, but this track played extremely well as Surrey racked up 348-7 on the first day after Ward had elected to bat and justified his own decision by scoring a fine 112. Nadeem Shahid (82) and Ali Brown (59 not out) also enjoyed themselves, while Saqlain was the man responsible for taking the total up to 418 on the second morning, making fifty-five after Brown had added just a single to his overnight score. Hampshire then rattled up 327 from seventy-six overs by the close of play, with John Crawley (82) and John Francis (59) leading the way with the bat, and James Ormond (4-87) and Saqlain Mushtaq (3-68) doing most of the damage with the ball.

The match continued to progress at a furious pace on day three, with Ward again setting a fine example to his team, completing his second hundred of the match - thereby emulating Adam Hollioake at Taunton in 1996 - and his third in successive first-class innings, making him the first Surrey man to perform that feat since John Edrich in 1965. With Thorpe (143) also reaching three figures, and his third-wicket stand with Ward (156) realising 239 runs, the County Champions totalled 422-8 in the day, allowing their stand-in skipper to declare overnight and set the hosts a notional target of 514 to win on day four.

When Martin Bicknell (5-56) removed Laney, Adams and Crawley with just twenty-seven runs on the board, and then followed up to dismiss Will Kendall at 65-4, it appeared that the game would be finishing early. Neil Johnson (86) led a recovery either side of lunch, however, and the lower middle-order then took advantage of some tired Surrey bowling during the afternoon to scorch along at more than five an over and take the game into the final session at 294-7. The brave and bold efforts of Dimitri Mascarenhas (67 from 62 balls) and the unfortunate Nick Pothas, who fell to a slip catch by Brown off Salisbury (4-116) when on ninety-nine, counted for naught, though, as Surrey eventually dismissed their opponents for 390 to record a 123-run victory.
LEADING POSITIONS:- Surrey P15, Pts 222.75; Warwicks P15, Pts 181.00; Kent P15, Pts 176.50

Surrey's final Championship game of the season saw them playing host to Leicestershire. Although Adam Hollioake returned to captain the side, Martin Bicknell and Saqlain Mushtaq were both rested, allowing 22-year-old Phil Sampson to make his Championship debut.

After the home side had won the toss, Ian Ward and Scott Newman put together an opening stand of 227, with Ward compiling a fourth consecutive first-class century to become only the third Surrey batsman, after the great Tom Hayward (1906) and Sir Jack Hobbs (1920 and 1925), to achieve the feat. The opening pair then surpassed the previous record first-wicket stand for Surrey versus Leicestershire matches when their partnership reached 209, before Newman had a personal landmark to celebrate as he completed his maiden first-class century from 129 balls. Although Ward departed soon afterwards for 118, Newman and Jon Batty added 125 for the second wicket to heap further misery on their visitors as the bowlers began to wilt and the run rate increased. The Foxes did manage to remove both men before the close - Newman for an excellent 183 with the total on 352, and Batty for seventy-four in the final over before bad light stopped play eleven overs early - but a score of 397-3 underlined the feeling that Surrey were already in control of the game. The presentation of the County Championship trophy, followed by all the usual celebrations and photo opportunities, then rounded the day off very nicely indeed.

On the second morning, the home county progressed to 490-5 without too many problems before collapsing dramatically to 494 all out in the space of seventeen deliveries. During this decline, Javagal Srinath took a hat-trick that passed almost completely unnoticed - even by the bowler himself - as he followed his capture of the scalps of Salisbury and Ormond from the second and sixth balls of his twenty-sixth over by clean bowling Hollioake and Sampson with the first two deliveries of his twenty-seventh to bring the innings shuddering to a halt.

Requiring 345 to avoid the follow on, Leicestershire's reply leant heavily on three innings. After Iain Sutcliffe (72) had got his team away to a good start, the two Darrens, Maddy and Stevens (53), enabled them to reach the promising position of 277-3, only for Adam Hollioake (2-39) and his young seamers - Phil Sampson (3-52) and Tim Murtagh (3-62) - to scythe through the rest of the batting for the addition of just fifty runs. Maddy was left undefeated on 127, having batted with the assistance of a runner throughout his innings.

After deciding against enforcing the follow on, Surrey then batted for 105 overs to increase their advantage to an unlikely 625 before declaring with just fifty-two overs remaining for play on the final day. Although Ian Ward had failed in his quest for a fifth successive ton - falling to a controversial 'catch' after making twenty-two - Ali Brown, with 107, and Adam Hollioake, who registered his maiden double-century from 241 balls before falling for 208, had made merry while adding 282 for the fifth wicket, a record partnership for any wicket in Surrey versus Leicestershire matches.

Following Hollioake's belated declaration, the Foxes' task of batting out the game looked simple enough, but Murtagh and Sampson quickly reduced them to 11-4 as Sutcliffe's decision to promote his youngsters up the order backfired spectacularly. Neil Burns, with an aggressive sixty-eight from 61 balls, accompanied by the skipper himself, then looked to have steadied the ship at 99-4 until Hollioake clung on to a stinging return catch from the Leicestershire wicketkeeper and once again opened the door to victory. Murtagh, with a career-best 5-39, and Salisbury (2-28) proceeded to work their way through the rest of the batting as the light began to fade and eventually secured a crushing 483-run triumph by bowling their visitors out for 142 with a theoretical thirteen overs to spare. The margin of victory was the biggest in terms of runs in the club's history and enabled them to end the season 44.75 points ahead of the pack in the Championship. This was the most significant gap since Surrey themselves ended fifty-six points clear in 1999, and the second largest since 1979.

	COUNTY CHAMPIONSHIP DIVISION ONE TABLE 2002							
		P	Pts	W	D	L	Bat	Bwl	Ded'n
1	Surrey	16	242.75	10	4	2	59	48	0.25
2	Warwickshire	16	198.00	7	7	2	42	44	0.00
3	Kent	16	195.50	7	5	4	48	44	0.50
4	Lancashire	16	172.00	6	6	4	33	43	0.00
5	Leicestershire	16	171.00	5	6	5	42	46	1.00
6	Sussex	16	154.00	3	7	6	43	47	0.00
7	Hampshire *	16	131.00	2	9	5	35	44	0.00
8	Somerset	16	126.75	1	8	7	39	44	0.25
9	Yorkshire	16	124.75	2	6	8	35	45	3.25

* 8 points deducted for substandard pitch

With Gloucestershire confirmed as champions, and Surrey already promoted, it was no surprise that the final NCL match of the season between the two sides at The Oval was a rather low-key affair. After the Lions won the toss, they slipped to 58-4 against Mike Smith (5-30) before Graham Thorpe, with a magnificent 114 from 105 balls, led a spirited recovery to 263-8. The Division Two champions then made a fine start to their reply, as Craig Spearman (37) and Jack Russell (31) put on sixty-eight in thirteen overs, but their innings faded away thereafter to 184 all out in the face of fine bowling from Adam Hollioake (4-24) and Saqlain Mushtaq.

NATIONAL LEAGUE DIVISION TWO TABLE 2002							
		P	Pts	W	L	T	A	NRR
1	Gloucestershire	16	44	10	4	0	2	12.74
2	Surrey	16	42	10	5	0	1	6.53
3	Essex	16	40	10	6	0	0	3.93
4	Derbyshire	16	34	8	7	0	1	-0.98
5	Lancashire	16	32	7	7	0	2	-6.96
6	Northamptonshire	16	30	7	8	0	1	7.60
7	Hampshire	16	26	6	9	0	1	-2.81
8	Sussex	16	20	4	10	0	2	-7.43
9	Middlesex	16	20	4	10	0	2	-12.51

Surrey's achievements in 2002 would have been remarkable in any season, but they were particularly praiseworthy given the tragedy that hit everyone so hard in the lead up to the campaign. I'm sure that Ben would have been proud of his team-mates as they produced a series of stunning performances in his memory. As far as individuals were concerned, there were so many achievements to admire, including Ali Brown's 268 in the C&G Trophy; Ian Ward's record-equalling run of hundreds; Mark Ramprakash's back-to-back double-centuries; Adam Hollioake's incredible tons at Hove and Canterbury; Jon Batty's dramatic improvement with the bat; and Rikki Clarke's very impressive debut season. The fact that the most eye-catching feats came from the batsmen was not a great surprise, since pitches around the country continued to improve. Despite that, Surrey managed to dismiss the opposition twice in all ten of their Championship victories, which was a major feather in the cap of the bowlers, led by Saqlain Mushtaq and James Ormond, who both exceeded fifty wickets. Ormond's signing proved to be every bit as shrewd as had been expected, since Martin Bicknell and Alex Tudor played only sixteen matches between them because of injury in the case of the former, and a mixture of injuries and England calls for the latter. The bowling line-up was frequently unsettled, in fact, with the personnel who formed the attack often changing significantly from game-to-game. The two locum overseas players - Azhar Mahmood and Mushtaq Ahmed - had both done very well while standing in for Saqlain and had each produced a match-winning display, which in Azhar's case had potential significance, since counties were to be allowed to field two overseas players in every match in 2003. He had therefore made a good case for his return on a permanent basis. Whether the increase in overseas players was necessary was another matter, however, since the county game was increasingly becoming flooded with 'foreign' players who qualified as non-overseas registrations because they held a passport from a European Union country. While it was true that the quality of the domestic game was continuing to improve - Chris Adams said that the match against Surrey at Hove was the hardest, most intense cricket he'd played since he tasted Test cricket on England's 1999-2000 tour of South Africa - it was almost certainly more to do with having two divisions and better pitches than the influx of EU passport holders.

On the limited-overs front, it was pleasing that Surrey would be plying their trade in Division One of the NCL again in 2003, after finishing second in Division Two. Had the Lions won at Bristol in May, instead of going down by one wicket, they would have been able to celebrate a two-trophy season just as they had done in 2000. A glance at the statistics underlined that the NCL success had been very much a team effort, with no one bar Mark Ramprakash with the bat, and Ed Giddins with the ball, turning in a prolific season in a constantly changing side. Ramprakash had scored almost a thousand runs in the one-day games, which was a fantastic performance on top of his 1,073 Championship runs, while Giddins's limited-overs form made up for another disappointing season in Championship cricket. With James Ormond having established himself as a first-choice selection in the team, and Tim Murtagh showing increasing promise, it was no real surprise that the former Sussex, Warwickshire and England bowler was released at the end of the season and joined Hampshire. With opportunities few and far between for them at The Oval, Rupesh Amin (Leicestershire) and Michael Carberry (Kent) also decided to pursue their careers elsewhere, while Gary Butcher was released, and Jason Ratcliffe was to take on a role with the Professional Cricketers' Association following his enforced retirement from the game. Graham Thorpe, meanwhile, had another change of mind about the Ashes tour and pulled out of the squad, leaving his immediate future with England uncertain, as he clearly needed time to sort out his marital problems.

One other departure to record was that of the Surrey Chairman, Michael Soper, whose increased involvement with the ECB led to him stepping down towards the end of the year, after seven successful seasons at the helm. He was replaced by the Club Treasurer, David Stewart, who had also played a significant role in turning Surrey's fortunes around since the dark days of 1995.

2002 SEASON SUMMARY

COMPETITION	P	W	D/A	L	POSITION/PROGRESS
County Championship	16	10	4	2	1st
National League Div 2	16	10	1	5	2nd - Promoted
C&G Trophy	4	3	0	1	Semi-final
Benson & Hedges Cup	5	1	0	4	Group stage
TOTAL	41	24	5	12	1 Trophy

2002 RESULTS SUMMARY

19/4	SUSSEX	OVAL	CC1	WON by 10 wickets
24/4	Yorkshire	Headingley	CC1	WON by an inns & 168 runs
28/4	Middlesex	Lord's	BHC	LOST by 8 wickets
1/5	HAMPSHIRE	OVAL	BHC	LOST by 1 run
2/5	Essex	Chelmsford	BHC	LOST by 4 wickets
4/5	KENT	OVAL	BHC	WON by 44 runs
6/5	Sussex	Hove	BHC	LOST on more wkts lost
8/5	LANCASHIRE	OVAL	CC1	WON by 3 wickets
12/5	LANCASHIRE	OVAL	NL2	WON by 6 wickets
19/5	Gloucestershire	Bristol	NL2	LOST by 1 wicket
24/5	SOMERSET	OVAL	CC1	Match Drawn
29/5	Scotland	Grange CC	CGT	WON by 55 runs (D/L)
31/5	Lancashire	Old Trafford	CC1	Match Drawn
4/6	Northamptonshire	Northampton	NL2	LOST by 5 runs

219

12/6	KENT	OVAL	CC1	WON by 9 wickets
16/6	Hampshire	Rose Bowl	NL2	WON by 3 wickets
19/6	GLAMORGAN	OVAL	CGT	WON by 9 runs
23/6	SUSSEX	OVAL	NL2	WON by 6 wickets
30/6	Lancashire	Old Trafford	NL2	Match Abandoned
3/7	Somerset	Taunton	CC1	Match Drawn
7/7	Middlesex	Southgate	NL2	WON by 8 wickets (D/L)
10/7	WARWICKSHIRE	OVAL	CC1	LOST by 31 runs
17/7	Sussex	Hove	CGTqf	WON by 14 runs
19/7	Kent	Canterbury	CC1	WON by 2 wickets
24/7	YORKSHIRE	GUILDFORD	CC1	WON by 6 wickets
28/7	ESSEX	GUILDFORD	NL2	WON by 73 runs
3/8	NORTHAMPTONSHIRE	WHITGIFT SCHOOL	NL2	LOST by 102 runs (D/L)
4/8	Yorkshire	Headingley	CGTsf	LOST by 10 wickets
6/8	MIDDLESEX	WHITGIFT SCHOOL	NL2	LOST by 64 runs
7/8	Sussex	Hove	NL2	WON by 6 wickets
8/8	Sussex	Hove	CC1	LOST by 4 wickets
14/8	Leicestershire	Leicester	CC1	WON by 7 wickets
18/8	DERBYSHIRE	OVAL	NL2	LOST by 4 wickets
21/8	HAMPSHIRE	OVAL	NL2	WON by 70 runs
22/8	HAMPSHIRE	OVAL	CC1	WON by an inns & 60 runs
27/8	Warwickshire	Edgbaston	CC1	Match Drawn
2/9	Derbyshire	Derby	NL2	WON by 1 wicket
8/9	Essex	Chelmsford	NL2	WON by 2 runs
11/9	Hampshire	Rose Bowl	CC1	WON by 123 runs
18/9	LEICESTERSHIRE	OVAL	CC1	WON by 483 runs
22/9	GLOUCESTERSHIRE	OVAL	NL2	WON by 79 runs

COUNTY CHAMPIONSHIP BATTING AVERAGES 2002										
	M	I	NO	Runs	HS	Ave	100	50	c	st
A.J. Hollioake	9	13	2	738	208	67.09	2	5	10	-
I.J. Ward	16	29	3	1708	168*	65.69	7	7	9	-
M.R. Ramprakash	14	24	4	1073	218	53.65	3	6	6	-
A.D. Brown	16	26	2	1211	188	50.45	5	3	18	-
R. Clarke	9	14	1	580	153*	44.61	1	4	7	-
M.A. Butcher	6	11	1	385	116	38.50	1	2	3	-
J.N. Batty	12	22	2	740	151	37.00	2	3	41	5
N. Shahid	12	19	1	647	150	35.94	2	2	25	-
G.P. Thorpe	4	8	0	274	143	34.25	1	-	1	-
M.P. Bicknell	10	14	5	258	35*	26.66	-	-	6	-
Saqlain Mushtaq	10	13	2	278	60	25.27	-	2	4	-
A.J. Tudor	6	9	0	176	61	19.55	-	1	1	-
I.D.K. Salisbury	14	20	2	340	59	18.88	-	1	11	-
J. Ormond	15	17	4	208	43*	16.00	-	-	6	-

Qualification: 8 innings

COUNTY CHAMPIONSHIP BOWLING AVERAGES 2002								
	O	M	Runs	W	Ave	BB	10wm	5wi
Azhar Mahmood	109.2	27	345	20	17.25	8-61	-	1
A.J. Tudor	202.1	44	739	31	23.83	5-66	-	1
Saqlain Mushtaq	488.4	112	1359	53	25.64	6-121	1	3
M.P. Bicknell	326.0	78	1067	34	31.38	6-42	-	2
I.D.K. Salisbury	341.3	50	1192	37	32.21	4-59	-	-
J. Ormond	485.1	87	1780	51	34.90	5-62	1	2
E.S.H. Giddins	208.5	41	696	19	36.63	4-113	-	-

Qualification: 100 overs, 10 wickets

LIMITED-OVERS BATTING AVERAGES 2002										
	M	I	NO	Runs	HS	Ave	100	50	c	st
M.R. Ramprakash	23	23	6	952	107*	56.00	2	7	5	-
A.D. Brown	24	24	0	899	268	37.45	1	6	9	-
A.J. Hollioake	15	13	3	351	117*	35.10	1	-	9	-
R. Clarke	15	14	2	379	98*	31.58	-	4	8	-
N. Shahid	22	21	4	432	74*	25.41	-	3	6	-
I.J. Ward	24	24	0	596	97	24.83	-	4	6	-
J.N. Batty	15	9	2	122	30	17.42	-	-	20	2
I.D.K. Salisbury	13	10	3	118	21	16.85	-	-	6	-
A.J. Tudor	10	8	3	79	28*	15.80	-	-	2	-
A.J. Stewart	11	10	1	126	52	14.00	-	1	16	1
Saqlain Mushtaq	13	6	1	56	28	11.20	-	-	2	-
E.S.H. Giddins	22	10	7	31	13*	10.33	-	-	5	-
M.P. Bicknell	14	10	2	74	19*	9.25	-	-	2	-
T.J. Murtagh	9	6	2	32	14*	8.00	-	-	3	-

Qualification: 6 innings

LIMITED-OVERS BOWLING AVERAGES 2002								
	O	M	Runs	W	Ave	BB	4wi	RPO
A.J. Hollioake	80.1	2	446	30	14.86	5-43	4	5.56
M.P. Bicknell	112.1	18	444	22	20.18	5-26	1	3.95
Azhar Mahmood	44.4	1	181	8	22.62	4-34	1	4.05
E.S.H. Giddins	170.0	15	771	34	22.62	5-20	2	4.53
T.J. Murtagh	77.3	3	353	13	27.15	3-38	-	4.55
I.D.K. Salisbury	67.1	1	329	9	36.55	3-44	-	4.89
A.J. Tudor	77.5	3	388	9	43.11	5-28	1	4.98
J. Ormond	65.3	2	349	8	43.62	3-52	-	5.32
R. Clarke	75.3	3	421	9	46.77	2-27	-	5.57
Saqlain Mushtaq	98.0	4	422	8	52.75	1-14	-	4.30

Qualification: 40 overs, 8 wickets

For a detailed account of the 2002 season, including exclusive interviews with the players, read **'From Tragedy To Triumph - Surrey's Bittersweet Championship Success 2002'** (details given on page 350)

10   2003: Two In Blue

Everyone at The Oval felt very optimistic about the team's prospects as the 2003 season came into view. Although there had only been one major addition to the staff, with Azhar Mahmood having been signed as the county's second overseas player, the Surrey squad looked very strong indeed, and seemed unlikely to lose too many players to international calls. Following Graham Thorpe's decision to miss the Ashes tour, Alec Stewart and Mark Butcher were the only players centrally contracted to England, while Saqlain Mushtaq and Azhar Mahmood were the only other players likely to be called up for Tests or One-Day Internationals. Thorpe would clearly have to work hard and score plenty of runs if he was to convince Duncan Fletcher and Nasser Hussain that his problems were behind him, so there was every chance that Surrey would benefit from his presence in their side for most, or even all, of the summer. The bookmakers therefore rated Keith Medlycott's team as favourites to secure a fourth Championship crown in five years.

As far as the set-up of domestic cricket was concerned, things seemed to have settled down, with the only major change seeing the Benson & Hedges Cup replaced by a new competition, the Twenty20 Cup, which, as the name implied, was to feature matches of 20-overs-a-side duration, starting at 5.30pm in most cases. All counties were to play five games in three regional qualifying groups over the course of a two-week period, with the best four teams from those groups qualifying for a Finals Day - featuring the two semi-finals and the grand final - at Trent Bridge in mid-July. It was going to be interesting to see how the public took to the new format, since many people within the game had serious reservations about its appeal and the effect it might have on players' techniques, as well as the commitment of many counties to the competition. There was potential for it to be an almighty flop, with clubs fielding virtual second elevens and spectators having problems getting to grounds during the day's 'rush hour' period. Twenty20 cricket was going to be new and innovative... but would it work? All would be revealed in June.

The season started in more conventional style, with Surrey meeting Lancashire in a Championship match at The Oval. Doubtless attracted by some fine weather, high-class opposition, and the fact that it was Good Friday, a crowd estimated to be well in excess of 3,000 attended the first day's play. Surrey's team selection provided early interest, with Alec Stewart rested by the ECB, despite the fact that England's dismal World Cup campaign in South Africa had ended on March 2nd, and Mark Butcher controversially omitted from the Champions' line-up due to the fact that the club had a surfeit of fine batsmen, and wished to play Rikki Clarke as an all-rounder at number six. The bowling resources, on the other hand, were fully stretched, since Martin Bicknell, James Ormond and Phil Sampson were not fully fit, and Azhar Mahmood was concluding his wedding celebrations back home in Pakistan.

Fears that a seam attack led by Alex Tudor and Tim Murtagh, with back-up from Clarke and Adam Hollioake, might be a little lightweight were soon realised after Warren Hegg won the toss for Lancashire and elected to bat on what looked to be a typically fine Oval strip. All the early honours went to the visitors as their opening pair of Iain Sutcliffe and Alec Swann (57) compiled a 108-run partnership in twenty-eight overs before the latter was run out shortly before lunch. With Lancashire's two close season signings, Sutcliffe and Mal Loye, now together, the hosts continued to struggle, and a further sixty-one runs had been added to the total before Saqlain Mushtaq offered his team a degree of hope by trapping the former Leicestershire batsman lbw for seventy. Unfortunately for Surrey, this was to be their last success of the day as Loye and Stuart Law combined to flay the bowling all around the park during an unbroken stand of 222 that took the red rose county through to 391-2 by stumps. Although Law had struggled during the Australian domestic season, and offered a chance to Tudor, at backward point, off Salisbury when he was on twelve, he looked to be in fine form as he progressed smoothly to a 156-ball century and was joined on three figures by his partner towards the end of the day. Loye was understandably thrilled to have completed a 210-ball debut hundred for his new county, and he had moved on to 104, with Law on 129, when time was called with the visitors having exposed the limitations of Surrey's ring rusty attack.

After bad light and drizzle had allowed just ten overs' play on a grey second morning, the overnight pair increased the value of their alliance to 282 before Clarke removed both men - Loye for 126, then Law for 169 - in the same over, bringing Andrew Flintoff to the crease with the scoreboard already reading 460-4. Although the England all-rounder reeled off some fine strokes while scoring forty-two from 39 balls, Surrey gradually chipped away at the visitors' batting, with the admirable Salisbury (42-10-116-4) very much to the fore as Lancashire lost their last six wickets for seventy-six runs to finish with a total of 599. Much to Surrey's relief, bad light prevented them from starting their reply after tea, leaving Warren Hegg's men two days in which to dismiss their hosts twice.

After losing Batty to Anderson for thirteen at 35-1, the Champions recovered well during the third morning's play until Ian Ward (49) fell to the same bowler shortly before the interval with the total at 106. Things went badly wrong after lunch, however, as the pacy Anderson reduced his hosts to 140-5 in the space of six overs, thanks to a combination of fine bowling, poor batting and a dubious umpiring decision. With Ramprakash (50), Brown, and Thorpe having helped boost Anderson's figures to 5-50, and Surrey now in real trouble, Adam Hollioake and Rikki Clarke launched a fierce counter-attack, adding sixty-four for the sixth wicket at almost a run a ball. When Hollioake was brilliantly caught one-handed by a leaping Flintoff at first slip after scoring forty-three from 42 balls, the home side were unable to respond again and slipped to a very disappointing 280 all out at tea, with three of the last four batsmen having been caught off Chris Schofield (3-77). The final catch of the innings was taken by Anderson, who finished with 5-61 and was the man most responsible for Surrey being required to follow on for the first time since the last match of the 1998 season.

The reigning champions then lost two second-innings wickets in indifferent light - Batty for four and Ramprakash for thirteen - before conditions became too poor for play to continue, with Ward unbeaten on forty and the total on sixty-one.

Survival was clearly the name of the game for Surrey on the final day, and their hopes of saving the game were rising until Graham Thorpe fell to a miscued hook for the second time in the match, with his side still trailing by 195 runs and lunch just half an hour away. One disappointing dismissal was then followed almost immediately by another as Ali Brown attempted an almost impossible single to mid-off and was run out by a distance at the non-striker's end. Although Ward then had a lucky escape on seventy-three when he was bowled by a no-ball from Schofield, Surrey managed to reach the break in reasonable shape at 150-4.

Their hopes of defying the bowlers for another sixty-six overs received a shattering blow, however, when Adam Hollioake fell to the third ball of the afternoon from Kyle Hogg, with his side still 169 runs short of making Lancashire bat again. Much now depended on Clarke, who made a confident start to his innings with three early boundaries, and Ward, who successfully attacked Schofield to complete a marvellous 156-ball century, thereby extending his run of Championship hundreds to five from his last seven innings. With the pitch still playing very well, and both batsmen punishing any loose deliveries very effectively, a match-saving partnership developed as Ward completed his 150 from 211 balls and Clarke registered an 85-ball half-century just before tea, at which point Surrey's arrears had been reduced to thirty-four.

Although disaster struck soon after the restart when Ward was caught at cover off Anderson for a brilliant 158, Alex Tudor looked secure from the start of his innings and played a fine supporting role as Clarke continued to reel off a series of fine strokes. Lancashire were eventually able to take a new ball, but this made no difference as the 21-year-old all-rounder completed a wonderfully mature 139-ball century that snuffed out the visitors' victory hopes and allowed Surrey to escape with a draw. When the players finally shook hands at 379-6, Clarke was unbeaten on 127, while Tudor had batted for sixty-eight balls to score eleven.

After their disappointing start in the Championship, Surrey opened their NCL Division One season with a trip to Chelmsford to take on another of the promoted sides, the Essex Eagles. Put in by Ronnie Irani in conditions that gave early assistance to the bowlers, the Lions were reduced to a desperate 82-6 after twenty-one overs by the Essex seamers, led by Graham Napier (3-50). The innings was then transformed over the course of the next twenty-one overs by Adam Hollioake and Azhar Mahmood, who added 154 runs in sensational style to set a new seventh-wicket record for the Sunday/National League, beating the 132-run stand compiled by Keith Brown and Neil Williams for Middlesex against Somerset at Lord's in 1988. The strokeplay from both men during a stunning counter-attack was tremendous, with Hollioake completing his fifty from forty-six deliveries, and Azhar following him to the mark shortly afterwards in forty-five. When the Surrey skipper finally perished to Scott Brant at 236-7, he had scored a marvellous seventy-seven, including four sixes and six fours, from 66 balls, but Azhar remained until the penultimate ball of the innings, when he was bowled by Jon Dakin (3-51) two runs short of what would have been an outstanding century. The Pakistani all-rounder's ninety-eight from 73 balls, nine of which had brought him four runs and three of which had disappeared for six, had enabled his side to reach an imposing 268-8, giving the Lions a fine chance of starting their campaign with an important victory.

Although Essex's reply was given a flying start by the 6' 10" Will Jefferson (47 from 36 balls), the visitors began to restore some order to the proceedings after his departure to the impressive Tudor at 71-2. The home side then stayed up with the required run-rate for a while, despite a superb first spell of 7-0-16-2 from Saqlain Mushtaq, though they lost the wickets of Hussain, Flower and Grayson in achieving this, and stood at 146-5 after twenty-six overs. Irani's exit to Rikki Clarke's second delivery - ending a feisty knock of sixty-four from 60 balls at 178-6 - looked like it could prove decisive, but James Foster (41 from 37 balls) prospered for a while to keep his side in contention until Saqlain (3-27) and Tudor (3-57) returned to capture the vital scalps of Dakin and Foster respectively, leaving the tail with too much to do against Hollioake and Azhar. Since the Lions had historically struggled in the Sunday/National League when starting their campaign with a series of defeats - and succeeded when posting early-season wins - this 15-run victory appeared to be important.

Having looked rather under-prepared during their first Championship match, Surrey were hoping to produce an improved performance when Warwickshire visited The Oval a few days later. With Ian Salisbury having sustained a finger injury while batting against Lancashire, and the rest of the attack having looked rather impotent, it was no surprise to see James Ormond, Martin Bicknell and Azhar Mahmood coming into the side, though there were shocks for both Graham Thorpe and match-saving hero Rikki Clarke, who were omitted in order to accommodate Mark Butcher and the inclusion of the extra bowler. The replacement of Jon Batty with Alec Stewart was less of a surprise, but still unfortunate for Batty, since he had set a new Surrey record in the opening game, conceding no byes in Lancashire's massive total of 599.

With Michael Powell injured, Ashley Giles was skippering Warwickshire and it was entirely predictable that he should choose to bat upon winning the toss. Although Martin Bicknell and James Ormond found plenty of movement in the early stages of the morning, they had no luck against the determined Nick Knight and Tony Frost, who then took advantage of some surprisingly poor fare from Azhar Mahmood and Saqlain Mushtaq to post an opening stand of 153. Once Bicknell had returned to dislodge Frost for a fine seventy-eight and Knight for a patchy fifty-eight just after lunch, Surrey bounced back into contention, however, as Alex Tudor (3-92) sliced through the middle order with a fine spell that brought about a decline to 215-5.

Fortunately for Warwickshire, Mark Wagh kept calm despite the rapid loss of four partners, and became the third batsman to record a half-century, from 98 balls, shortly before losing Dougie Brown to a much-improved Saqlain on the stroke of tea with the total on 237 and the game nicely balanced.

Although Ormond produced a good burst after the break to secure his first two wickets of the season, the visitors managed to edge the final session of the day, as Wagh (91 not out) received fine support from Giles, Mo Sheikh and Neil Smith to move the score on to 342-8.

After heavy overnight rain had left the ground wet enough to wipe out the first twenty-four overs of day two, Surrey snapped up the wicket of Smith with just a single added to the overnight score, before they were forced to endure a frustrating last-wicket stand of seventy. Once Wagh had completed a magnificent 167-ball century, there was very little to commend the hosts' performance as the total grew to 413 in the space of just fifteen overs either side of lunch, until the Bears' number three finally fell to the deserving Ormond (3-83) for 136. Fortunately, Surrey's batsmen were able to redeem the shocking display in the field during the rest of the day's play, though it wasn't plain sailing as Ian Ward made an early exit, and three wickets fell for eight runs after Mark Butcher (64) and Mark Ramprakash (45) had put on 101 for the second wicket. From the decidedly dicey position of 121-4, the County Champions were propelled to a close of play score of 237-4 by a superb unbeaten knock of eighty-seven by Adam Hollioake, who completely dominated an unbroken stand of 116 with Alec Stewart. Reaching his half-century in 55 balls, after surviving a straightforward stumping chance off Giles on forty-nine, Hollioake put his team right back in the match with a series of bold and brilliant strokes.

With rain preventing any play on day three until 2pm, and then allowing just twenty-nine overs of action thereafter, the game looked to be heading for a certain draw as Surrey advanced their score to 349-7 with some good, positive batting. Although Stewart (50) was more aggressive than on the previous day, converting his overnight twenty-nine into a 99-ball half-century before being caught off Brown, he was still overshadowed by his captain, who completed a fantastic hundred from just 114 deliveries. When Brown also ended Hollioake's fun at 122, with the total advanced to 309, Azhar and Tudor continued to push on until the rain returned.

Tudor (55) then dominated the scoring the following morning, seeing his side through to a fourth batting point and a final total of 390 with a classy 66-ball fifty before Brown tidied up the tail to finish with 5-96. Leading by twenty-three on first innings, Warwickshire then fell foul of Tudor again as the big paceman claimed the wickets of Frost and Wagh before lunch, with fifty-one runs having been added to their advantage.

Two double-strikes during the afternoon then briefly raised hopes of an exciting conclusion to the match. After Bell fell to Saqlain, and Troughton was again undone by Tudor (3-56), with the score on seventy-two, Dominic Ostler and Brown were both taken by Hollioake at silly point in the space of three balls from Saqlain (3-29) with the total at 117 and the lead 140. Knight remained steadfast as ever, though, completing a valuable 112-ball fifty and, in the company of Giles (33), making the game safe after tea. Ramprakash and Brown - who claimed his second first-class wicket when he had Giles caught behind - then rattled through seventeen overs in quick time to ensure their team avoided an over-rate penalty, and when Stewart and Ward took a turn with the ball Knight took the opportunity to move within sight of a century late in the game. By 5.30pm he was only on ninety-three, but Stewart took pity and delivered a few rank deliveries in order for him to reach three figures from 222 balls and take the final score to 221-7.

For the NCL match between the two sides that followed the Championship encounter, Surrey fielded the same eleven that had won at Chelmsford, which suggested that, barring an injury to Jon Batty, Alec Stewart - who had been available for selection - might have played his last one-day match for the county. With the pitch looking to be another beauty, and Adam Hollioake having elected to bat, the Lions got away to a great start, posting their hundred after just 12.4

overs, thanks to explosive efforts from Ali Brown (28 in 21 balls) and Ian Ward (47 from 45). Mo Sheikh and Ashley Giles then calmed things down slightly in the middle of the innings, though Mark Ramprakash (63) and Graham Thorpe (58) had no need to do anything but work the ball around the field in any case, after being given such a fine platform to build upon. Once Ramprakash had departed at 185-4, further fireworks came from Rikki Clarke (26 from 17 balls) and Azhar Mahmood (19 from 12), allowing the Lions to total 281-8.

Warwickshire clearly needed a good start to their reply but didn't get one as they were rocked back on their heels by magnificent new-ball bowling from Azhar (2-34) and Martin Bicknell (2-30), who had claimed the wickets of Frost, Wagh and Bell by the time the Bears had thirty-six runs on the board. Alex Tudor then followed up by dismissing Jim Troughton for the third time in five days during a fine spell of 4-45 that left the visitors down and almost out at 127-7. Nick Knight had again survived the carnage, however, and completed a brave half-century from sixty-one balls, before blasting a rapid second fifty from just thirty deliveries to reach a brilliant century and give his side an outside chance of victory. Although his departure to a catch on the boundary by Ramprakash off Hollioake for 108 sealed the Bears' fate shortly afterwards, some impressive late-order hitting by Graham Wagg (31 from 11 balls) entertained the crowd and reduced the final margin of defeat to twenty-five runs.

Twenty-four hours later the Lions had a chance to make it three NCL wins from three starts when they visited New Road for a televised match against the Worcestershire Royals. Having recorded just two Sunday League victories away to Worcestershire in fourteen attempts over the years, it looked likely to be a tough assignment, especially as the previous day's hero, Alex Tudor, was ruled out with a knee injury. As a result, James Ormond was included in an otherwise unchanged Surrey line-up and ended up taking the first wicket of the innings after the Royals had won the toss and decided to bat. Although there were already eighty-five runs on the board by the time the strapping pace bowler pinned Vikram Solanki lbw for forty, the opening partnership had used up almost seventeen of their side's forty-five overs. With Surrey's bowling and fielding being both tight and tidy, the home team continued to make steady but unspectacular progress throughout their innings, with Graeme Hick being denied the strike as much as possible, and Kadeer Ali taking a long time to establish himself against the excellent Ormond and Saqlain Mushtaq. Although both batsmen completed half-centuries and accelerated towards the end of the innings, with Hick making eighty-one from 69 balls and Kadeer fifty-two from 75 deliveries, the hosts' final score of 244-5 looked no better than par for the course in good batting conditions.

This feeling was soon confirmed after Surrey had lost Ian Ward for four to the third ball of their reply, since Ali Brown and Mark Ramprakash quickly took charge with some stunning strokeplay. After Brown had completed a magical 43-ball fifty, the Lions' hundred came up in just 14.5 overs, and this was followed soon afterwards by Ramprakash's equally fine half-century from 47 balls. Although Gareth Batty and David Leatherdale then proved rather more accurate than Messrs Kabir Ali, Mason and Hayward had been, Surrey's 150 arrived in the twenty-second over and the game looked to be all over bar the shouting. It seemed to be nothing more than a minor inconvenience when Brown (81 from 67 balls) and Ramprakash (67 from 68) fell in quick succession to Batty, since their replacements, Graham Thorpe and Rikki Clarke put together a 49-run stand to take the score on to 209-3. The game turned quite dramatically, however, when Thorpe was run out for thirty-eight, since Kabir Ali (3-43) and Hayward (3-66) each followed up with a devastating burst that saw them remove five batsmen for thirty runs. The last of these dismissals, which left Surrey at 239-9 and spectators on the edge of their seats, was highly controversial as it was evident to most people in the ground, apart from umpire Lloyds, unfortunately, that Saqlain's outside edge had not been caught cleanly by wicketkeeper Rhodes. Luckily for all concerned, the umpire's error didn't turn out to be decisive, since Bicknell and

Ormond each struck an off-drive to the boundary to seal a very tense one-wicket victory for the visitors and maintain their one hundred percent NCL Division One record.

A trip to Stone to play Staffordshire in the C&G Trophy was next on Surrey's agenda. There was a good crowd at the attractive little Stone C.C. ground and they enjoyed an entertaining day's cricket on a very flat pitch, with Surrey emerging triumphant by just nine runs at the end of a game that wasn't quite as close as the final margin suggested.

After being put in to bat, the visitors' total of 273 was due almost entirely to Ian Ward's maiden limited-overs century, which came from just eighty balls and was reached in spectacular style with three successive sixes, and Rikki Clarke's forty-seven from 41 balls. Once Staffordshire's most likely match-winner, Kim Barnett, had gone for twelve, the feeling that Surrey weren't operating at full throttle was underlined by Adam Hollioake's decision to give Ward a full spell of ten overs, and to keep himself and Saqlain Mushtaq out of the attack until the final overs of the match. Dave Womble (49), Graeme Archer (65) and Paul Shaw (55 not out) did their very best to make Surrey pay for their apparent complacency, though targets of ninety-three runs from seven overs, sixty-four from four, and twenty-five from the final over were always likely to prove too testing for the valiant minor county side.

As the early season matches continued to come thick and fast, Keith Medlycott's team headed straight off to Trent Bridge for their third Championship fixture of the campaign, with their hosts surprisingly top of the nascent table, despite being without many of their best players. Surrey, meanwhile, named the same team that had drawn with Warwickshire and were not unhappy to lose the toss and end up in the field, since the pitch looked far from perfect.

It soon became clear that it was a poor surface, though it didn't seem to hold too many fears for Jason Gallian, the Nottinghamshire captain, as he came safely through the morning session on thirty-eight out of a total of ninety-two. Three of his colleagues had departed by this time, however, with Azhar Mahmood claiming two scalps and Mark Butcher, surprisingly brought on for one over before lunch, bowling Usman Afzaal with his second delivery.

Although Bilal Shafayat didn't last long after the break, becoming a third victim for Azhar (3-46) with just four runs added to the score, Gallian found a steadfast ally in Chris Read and went on to complete a gritty half-century from 131 balls. The fifth-wicket pair succeeded in taking the total up to 155, putting their side in a good position, before Surrey started their fightback when Read played on to James Ormond after making twenty-two. Although he was scoreless for twenty-four deliveries, Paul Franks then kept Gallian company while the score was advanced by another twenty-two runs, before Ormond - with a little help from Alex Tudor, who disposed of Steve Elworthy - reduced the home side to 185-9. With his team's feeble looking tail subsiding so swiftly, Gallian sensibly moved on to the offensive to reach an excellent century from 198 balls, and take the total up to 211, before Ormond completed figures of 5-42 by having last man Charlie Shreck taken at the wicket. As he left the field, the Nottinghamshire skipper received a warm round of applause from his home crowd, having carried his bat for 112 and, on a personal level at least, justified his decision to take first use of a pitch that had already shown signs of being inconsistent in bounce.

Surrey's reply then got away to a wretched start when Mark Butcher was adjudged to have feathered Elworthy's first ball of the innings through to Read, and Ward edged Greg Smith to first slip with the total on four. This terrific start by the Nottinghamshire opening bowlers looked to have put the hosts on top again, but Alec Stewart rapidly restored equilibrium to the contest by taking advantage of some truly unintelligent bowling to race to a 33-ball fifty. With Mark Ramprakash joining in the fun as the home seamers completely lost the plot, the Surrey hundred came up in the twentieth over, and the third-wicket pair had taken the score to 147-2 by the time Stewart fell two runs short of what would have been an excellent century, bottom-edging an attempted pull shot into his stumps. The England wicketkeeper's marvellous 70-ball knock contained seventeen fours and had put his side in pole position in the match until the late loss of Ramprakash (38) and Brown levelled things up slightly at 159-5.

On the second morning, the remaining batsmen followed Stewart's lead by adopting an extremely positive approach against some poor Nottinghamshire bowling. The inability of the bowlers to adhere to the basic principles of line and length on an untrustworthy surface was simply staggering, and everyone cashed in gleefully, as Adam Hollioake (35 from 25 balls) got his side away to a flier and then sat back to watch Azhar Mahmood take the visitors into the lead during a 49-run stand with a surprisingly subdued Saqlain Mushtaq. Once the off-spinner had gone for twenty-four at 251-7, Azhar completed a tremendous 42-ball half-century and took Surrey through the three-hundred barrier in only the fifty-fifth over of the innings during an eighth-wicket stand of eighty-two with Alex Tudor. The hosts' only other success of the morning came when Gallian - undoubtedly embarrassed by the fact that his seamers had conceded 162 runs in the day's first twenty-two overs - came on to deliver an accurate spell, during which he had Tudor caught behind for twenty-seven. Azhar was unbeaten on eighty-two at lunch and Surrey were 345-8.

After twenty overs had been lost, following a shower during the interval, Azhar took sixteen runs from Elworthy's first over of the afternoon session before falling to a fine running, diving catch by Read from a top-edged hook two overs later, thereby emulating Stewart in missing out on a century by just two runs. Although Martin Bicknell then crashed five boundaries in two overs, Surrey were dismissed just seven runs short of securing their final batting point when Ormond holed out to mid-on off Greg Smith (4-81), who had easily been the pick of a very poor bunch of bowlers. Trailing by 182 runs on first innings, Nottinghamshire's position deteriorated further when Martin Bicknell claimed brother Darren lbw with the fifth ball of the home team's second knock shortly before another shower brought an early tea at 6-1.

When play finally resumed at 4.25pm, the visitors continued to show their hosts how to bowl on a poor pitch, with Ormond (3-26) accounting for Welton, Afzaal and Shafayat to put the early Championship leaders in deep trouble at 35-4, before Gallian and Read once again came together to steady the Nottinghamshire ship. They had only taken the score as far as seventy-one, though, when Bicknell nipped in with the important wicket of Gallian - lbw for twenty-eight - and then erased any hope of the home side escaping defeat by having Read well taken by Azhar at third slip five runs later. Although Surrey were unable to complete a two-day victory, with Franks and Elworthy holding firm until the close at 94-6, everyone knew that the points were now in the bag for the reigning County Champions, weather permitting.

Although Elworthy (52) added fifty-two for the seventh wicket with Franks, and thirty-eight for the last wicket with Shreck, on his way to a 71-ball half-century, he wasn't able to make Surrey bat again the following morning. With Tudor's suspect knee keeping him off the field, and Ormond also struggling with a knee problem, Bicknell (5-83) and Azhar (2-59) had been left to polish off the innings for 176, completing a very comfortable victory by an innings and six runs and securing twenty-one points - four for batting, three for bowling and fourteen (up from twelve in 2002) for the win.

LEADING POSITIONS:- Warwicks P4, Pts 49.75; Surrey P3, Pts 39; Lancs P3, Pts 35

Boosted by their opening Championship victory, Surrey returned to The Oval for a match against Leicestershire, who included Virender Sehwag in their line-up for the first time and were able to select a full-strength team. Surrey, meanwhile, had to do without the injured Alex Tudor and James Ormond, replacing them with Rikki Clarke and Ian Salisbury, and leaving Graham Thorpe on the sidelines yet again.

When Phil DeFreitas won the toss for the visitors he decided to bat, only for his team to instantly throw away the advantage by collapsing to 92-7 by lunch. Although there was a lot resting on their shoulders, as their side's only two frontline seamers in this match, Martin Bicknell and Azhar Mahmood rose to the occasion brilliantly to reduce the visitors to 47-5, with Azhar gaining particular pleasure from removing Sehwag with the first ball he bowled to the Indian strokemaker during an opening spell of 4-30. Mark Butcher then picked up two 'golden arm' wickets as the Foxes continued to self-destruct, before DeFreitas and David Masters added twenty-two unbroken runs for the eighth wicket before the interval.

This pair more than doubled the score to 155, with the Leicestershire skipper reaching fifty from just 48 balls, before Azhar returned to oust Masters for thirty-three, thereby completing a five-wicket haul. With only Charlie Dagnall and Devon Malcolm left to bat, DeFreitas tried to adopt an even more aggressive approach thereafter, but he didn't succeed for long as Saqlain Mushtaq defeated his slog-sweep with his score on sixty-five at 167-9. To everyone's surprise, the last-wicket pair managed to take the visitors through to a batting point at two-hundred before Saqlain had Malcolm caught, leaving Dagnall unbeaten on a career-best twenty-three, and Azhar with final figures of 5-78.

Needing a very good bowling performance to atone for some poor batting, Leicestershire did manage to make one early breakthrough when DeFreitas removed Ian Ward with thirty-nine on the board, but they had to wait until the score had reached eighty before Mark Butcher perished to the belatedly introduced Malcolm. Thereafter it was all Surrey, as Mark Ramprakash (59 not out) and Alec Stewart (58 not out) saw their side through to stumps at 182-2.

Day two then saw the hosts piling on the runs, with the morning session being particularly painful for the Foxes. Although Stewart only added thirteen to his overnight tally before being caught in the gully off DeFreitas, Ramprakash progressed to a fine 208-ball century as he built a new partnership with Ali Brown that realised 141 runs either side of lunch. Having scored just thirteen runs in his first four Championship innings of the season, Brown was especially pleased to make it through to a half-century from 68 balls, though he was disappointed to fall to Jeremy Snape for seventy-three with the total on 345. Adam Hollioake then proceeded to blast an ideal forty-one from only 24 balls before he and Ramprakash (152) were dismissed by consecutive deliveries from Dagnall and DeFreitas, while Rikki Clarke found life difficult before becoming a fourth victim for the Foxes' captain to make the score 423-7. When Snape then claimed the visitors' eighth wicket at 461 by removing Azhar Mahmood, it looked like the Champions could be bowled out by tea, but the Surrey spin twins had other ideas. With Salisbury playing the lead role, and Saqlain supporting, they shared an unbroken partnership of ninety-nine that ended with a declaration as soon as Ian Salisbury had completed his second first-class century with a straight six off Snape from his 160th ball. Adam Hollioake's closure at 560-8 left his side with a massive 360-run advantage and seven overs to bowl before the end of the day. In that time, Leicestershire lost Ward and nightwatchman Masters to Bicknell, which left them praying for rain with two days left to play.

The forecast of unsettled weather duly proved to be correct, as just five overs were bowled on day three, during which the visitors advanced to 32-2, and the wet outfield then kept the players in the pavilion until 1.10pm on the final day.

With only seventy-two overs remaining in which to pick up eight wickets, Surrey found Sehwag to be in sparkling form, as he saw off Bicknell and Azhar with a series of fantastic strokes to reach a 52-ball fifty and force the home skipper to introduce Saqlain Mushtaq in place of Bicknell. This change quickly brought about the downfall of Sehwag - adjudged lbw, despite having advanced down the pitch to the off-spinner - for a magnificent eighty-one, and gave Surrey a glimmer of hope. Although Saqlain was looking very much on song, and was soon joined in the attack by his spin twin, the fourth-wicket pair of Darren Maddy and Brad Hodge looked reasonably comfortable while adding sixty-one runs to the total. The picture changed, however, when Maddy was bowled by the Pakistani in the twenty-ninth over of the day, since it prefaced a collapse to 172-6, with three wickets falling in eight balls - Maddy (40) and Nixon to Saqlain, and Stevens to Salisbury. With ominously grey clouds gathering over the ground and tea imminent, the off-spinner struck a crucial blow by having Hodge caught at short leg for a very well played forty-seven, keeping alive Surrey's hopes of beating the rain. The interval had arrived at a bad time, though, and only eight balls were possible after the resumption - with the last of these bringing the wicket of DeFreitas to a very fine reflex catch by Hollioake off Saqlain (5-46) - before the heavens opened and saved Leicestershire from what looked to be a certain defeat with thirty overs still to be bowled.

Since Warwickshire had not been playing in this round of matches, and the other two games were drawn, Surrey's twelve points took them top of the table.

LEADING POSITIONS:- Surrey P4, Pts 51; Warwicks P4, Pts 49.75; Lancs P4, Pts 46

The Kent Spitfires were welcomed to The Oval the following day, with Surrey hoping to extend their winning start in the NCL. In good batting conditions, Mark Ealham, Kent's stand-in captain, decided to put the Lions in to bat and was probably soon regretting it as Ian Ward, with thirty-one from 27 balls, and Ali Brown, whose breathtaking forty-four came from just 24 deliveries, piled up seventy-eight runs from the first eight overs. Although the tempo inevitably dropped after Peter Trego dismissed both Surrey openers in quick succession, Mark Ramprakash and Graham Thorpe kept the scoreboard ticking over nicely until another double strike, this time by the impressive James Tredwell (2-35), brought Kent the scalps of both Thorpe (36) and Rikki Clarke with the total on 165 after twenty-seven overs. After Adam Hollioake had been and gone for a quick-fire fifteen, Azhar Mahmood entered the fray to play a violent innings that sent the score soaring. Having taken six balls to get off the mark, the Pakistani all-rounder rushed to a 35-ball half-century shortly before Ramprakash completed a magnificent century from his 96th delivery, bringing up the Lions' three-hundred in the process. Azhar was eventually caught off Trego (4-66) in the last over of the innings after advancing his score to seventy from 41 balls with another rush of boundaries, while Ramprakash ended unbeaten on 107 from 99 deliveries as the hosts finished on 322-7, the highest total ever made in the history of Surrey versus Kent encounters in Sunday/National League cricket.

The Spitfires' task was daunting in the extreme, since they needed to break their hosts' League record score for a side batting second and winning - 317-6 against Nottinghamshire at The Oval in 1993, when games were 50-overs-a-side. With Martin Bicknell producing a tight opening spell, and Azhar removing Ealham with the total on fourteen, the visitors' assignment immediately became more difficult. Trego and Rob Key seemed to be putting their side back on track, however, by adding forty-eight for the second wicket, only for Tim Murtagh - replacing the injured Ormond in Surrey's side - to remove them in consecutive overs and peg Kent back to 71-3. With Ed Smith and Greg Blewett struggling to make much of an impact against Murtagh and the accurate Saqlain Mushtaq, the required run rate rose so dramatically that it was standing at 9.3 when the Australian was bowled by the Pakistani with the total at 137. The realisation that this was now a do-or-die situation prompted an instant response from Smith and his new partner, Matt Walker, as they meted out some very rough treatment to Murtagh and the Lions' skipper, raising a century partnership in just ten overs, with Walker contributing a 38-ball fifty in the process. Surrey's bowling and outcricket became increasingly ragged under pressure from the fifth-wicket pair and, as the Spitfires' target came down to thirty-one runs from the last four overs, they suddenly looked favourites to score an impressive victory. The game took a vital twist, however, when Azhar produced a wonderful reverse-swinging yorker with his penultimate delivery to remove Smith's off stump, and terminate a terrific 86-ball innings with the batsman one run short of what would have been a wonderful century. Although Kent were still well placed, needing twenty-three from three overs, Surrey fought hard through Hollioake and Clarke to retain their one

hundred percent record. With Walker kept off strike for all but six of those last eighteen balls, and Geraint Jones, Michael Carberry and James Tredwell unable to find a boundary, the Lions eventually got home by six runs in a nerve-jangling finish.
LEADING POSITIONS:- Surrey P4, Pts 16; Glam P3, Pts 12; Essex P4, Pts 12

Since Alec Stewart and Mark Butcher were playing for England in the first Test against Zimbabwe, Jon Batty and Graham Thorpe were recalled to Surrey's team for the next match, which was a Championship fixture against Essex at Chelmsford. Rikki Clarke, meanwhile, was unlucky to miss out again as James Ormond returned from injury to bolster the attack.

With the pitch looking quite green and grassy on an overcast morning, it was no surprise that Ronnie Irani should ask Surrey to bat after he had won the toss. The visitors then got away to a terrible start when Scott Brant pinned Ian Ward lbw with the second ball of the match, and Jon Batty followed his partner back to the pavilion soon afterwards when he edged Jon Dakin to James Foster. Graham Napier took over as destroyer-in-chief thereafter with a three-wicket burst that reduced the visitors to 51-5, before Graham Thorpe and Azhar Mahmood carried out some badly needed repair work to add 111 runs for the sixth wicket either side of lunch. The more aggressive Azhar was first to a half-century, from just 48 balls, though Thorpe's 100-ball effort was every bit as valuable, especially as he had, perhaps unsurprisingly, looked a little out of touch for much of his innings. Unfortunately for Surrey, the England left-hander (52) fell shortly after reaching his personal milestone, becoming a fourth victim for Napier (4-92), and his erstwhile partner departed six runs later when he played on to Brant, having scored a valuable seventy-seven. At 168-7, the visitors were back under the cosh, so they were grateful that their prolific lower-order was able to come to the rescue again, with Martin Bicknell and Ian Salisbury (30) putting together a stand of ninety that only ended shortly before tea when the leg-spinner was run out by Paul Grayson from cover. By this time, Bicknell had completed a fine fifty from seventy-one deliveries and Surrey were feeling much happier on 258-8.

Success continued to elude Essex during a final session cut short by bad light, as Bicknell found another sound ally in Saqlain Mushtaq, and the ninth-wicket pair pushed Surrey's score beyond three-hundred, with the former closing in on the second County Championship century of his career. Despite a couple of nervous moments in the nineties - first when a lofted drive off James Middlebrook just cleared the 6'4" Dakin at long-on to take him to ninety-nine, and then when Essex appealed for a bat-pad catch from the next ball - Bicknell reached the mark from his 148th delivery and fully deserved the ovation that followed. He had added seventeen to his tally, to take the score up to 337-8, when Ronnie Irani's decision to take the new ball prompted the umpires to offer the light to the batsmen, who duly accepted.

The visitors' innings lasted for another 9.3 overs on the second morning, during which time they added thirty-nine runs, with the ninth-wicket partnership extending beyond a hundred before Saqlain (30) was bowled by Brant (3-94), and Bicknell last out to Dakin for a brilliant 141 from 196 balls with the total on 376.

After the break between innings, which was extended by rain, the Surrey swing king was soon in the thick of the action again. Once James Ormond had claimed Darren Robinson lbw, Bicknell removed Grayson, Jefferson and Habib to leave the hosts struggling at 29-4 as lunch arrived. What a difference twenty-four hours - and Bicknell - had made.

Essex's position was stabilised for a while after the break by Andy Flower and Ronnie Irani, who saw off the opening bowlers with a stand of eighty-two for the fifth wicket before the home skipper was, once again, guilty of throwing his wicket away with a reckless stroke in a game against Surrey, badly miscuing a pull at Azhar Mahmood to cover. The Pakistani all-rounder then struck another important blow for his side with the score advanced to 132, when Flower (51) was taken in the gully not long after arriving at a determined half-century from 88 balls. This left the visitors in a powerful position, though they still had to work hard for their breakthroughs on an increasingly easy pitch as James Foster and Jon Dakin added forty-seven runs either side of tea. When Foster eventually became another victim for Bicknell (4-67), Essex were still forty-eight runs short of saving the follow-on, but their fears were erased with surprising ease by Dakin and the new batsman, James Middlebrook, both of whom struck some impressive boundaries. The former went on to complete a valuable fifty from his seventy-first ball, before Adam Hollioake's decision to pair Salisbury with Ormond (3-68) brought about a final Essex collapse, with the paceman snaring the eighth-wicket pair - Dakin for fifty-nine and Middlebrook for twenty-nine - and Napier being brilliantly caught, one-handed, by a tumbling Saqlain at wide mid-on off Salisbury. The last three wickets had fallen for nine runs in seventeen balls to leave the home side all out for 252, a deficit of 124.

After bad light had prevented Surrey from extending their advantage by more than seven runs on the second evening, Ian Ward and Jon Batty secured their side's position with a 102-run opening partnership on the third morning. Although Ward fell one short of fifty, with the visitors leading by 226, Batty went on to complete a 76-ball half-century, and had advanced to seventy-two by lunch, despite losing Mark Ramprakash and Graham Thorpe to Graham Napier.

Surrey then pressed on relentlessly after the interval, with Ali Brown butchering Napier in racing to an incredible 32-ball fifty before holing out off Middlebrook for sixty-four, and Batty completing his fifth first-class century from his 167th ball. Adam Hollioake, with a half-century from sixty-five deliveries, then helped his wicketkeeper take the score to 302-4 at tea, with the lead standing at 426.

Since Essex's success in their 2002 promotion-winning season was based almost entirely on chasing significant totals in the fourth innings of matches, it was clear that Surrey would not want to offer their hosts any hope at all with their declaration. They were denied the chance to make one before the close of the day, however, as poor light and drizzle left Hollioake with no option but to bat on until increasingly heavy rain ended play sixteen overs early, with Surrey on 381-7 and Batty having advanced to a career-best unbeaten 168.

The inevitable overnight declaration - setting Essex a purely hypothetical 506 to win - left the visitors with ninety-six overs in which to secure their second Championship victory of the season, and they got away to the right sort of start when Ormond claimed the three-hundredth first-class wicket of his career by trapping Jefferson lbw in the fourth over. The big paceman's tally then increased to 301 six overs later when Grayson was brilliantly caught one-handed by Batty diving away down the legside, and it stood at 302 by the time a fine twelve-over opening burst was complete - after Azhar had dismissed Flower with a brute of a delivery that took the batsman's glove on the way through to Batty, Ormond won an lbw verdict against an unhappy Robinson three balls later, thereby reducing the home side to 69-4. That was where the Championship leaders' run of success ended for a while, however, as Aftab Habib and James Foster put together a fine partnership of 119 that extended deep into the afternoon session. With Salisbury surprisingly kept out of the attack, and Surrey becoming increasingly desperate for another wicket, Habib completed a battling 85-ball fifty, before Ormond returned to the fray to pin Foster lbw for forty-two with tea just half-an-hour away. Having secured this vital breakthrough, the visitors then claimed two more in the next two overs, as Irani went to Saqlain and, most importantly, Habib (61) was finally unseated by an Ormond delivery that was not dissimilar to the one that Azhar had produced for Flower earlier in the day. Although Dakin and Middlebrook saw their side through to the interval at 225-7, an increasingly grey sky now seemed to present as much of a threat to Surrey's victory hopes as the batsmen.

It was therefore of some concern that light drizzle was in the air as play resumed, with the visiting side requiring three wickets in the thirty-nine overs that remained, weather permitting. Since the light was quite poor, Hollioake immediately gave the ball to Saqlain, who had Dakin taken at slip by Azhar with the second ball of the session, and brought Salisbury into the attack for the following over. Fears that the light, the rain or the batsmen might deny Surrey a well deserved success were then rapidly expunged as the leg-spinner dismissed Middlebrook and Brant with the first two balls of his third over to complete a 258-run triumph. Having played a major role in his county's first Championship victory at Chelmsford for a staggering fifty-three years, Ormond led a happy Surrey side from the field with figures of 5-82 to his name.

With Warwickshire having been held to a draw in a rain-affected game at Edgbaston, the leaders' advantage was now 12.25 points.

LEADING POSITIONS:- Surrey P5, Pts 72; Warwicks P5, Pts 59.75; Sussex P4, Pts 52

Although they stayed top of the table, Surrey lost their one hundred percent NCL record when their game at Bristol against the Gloucestershire Gladiators was washed out on Sunday 25th May. With heavy morning rain being followed by a torrential downpour in mid-afternoon there was never any chance of the game starting.

LEADING POSITIONS:- Surrey P5, Pts 18; Glam P4, Pts 16; Essex P4, Pts 12

The C&G Trophy draw had given Surrey a testing fourth-round tie at Taunton against Somerset, and the early sequence of events was familiar to visiting fans who had witnessed previous one-day encounters between the two sides at the County Ground - Somerset won the toss, put Surrey in to bat, and then claimed early wickets. On this occasion, however, the visitors didn't register an inadequate total and lose the match. This was due to a marvellous century from Graham Thorpe (102 not out from 103 balls), who masterminded his side's recovery from 34-2, and a maiden limited-overs fifty from Jon Batty (55 not out from 46 balls) that provided late impetus to take the total to 281-6.

Surrey's seamers, led by the outstanding Martin Bicknell (10-2-23-1), then picked up three wickets - including the important scalps of Cox and Trescothick - for fifty-one runs, before the middle-order trio of Burns (47), Parsons (83) and Blackwell (39) regained the advantage for Somerset at 222-4. The balance of power shifted again, though, when Saqlain Mushtaq (2-58) removed Parsons and Blackwell in quick succession, leaving Adam Hollioake (3-19) to clean up the tail and secure a 6-run victory in a tight finish.

Surrey's next Championship opponents were Sussex, who had been the most erratic side in the competition thus far, with two wins and two defeats resulting from their four matches. Having selected the same eleven that had triumphed at Chelmsford, Adam Hollioake won the toss, elected to bat and then watched his side slip to 22-2 as James Kirtley and Billy Taylor picked off an opening batsman apiece during excellent opening spells. Although Taylor's stint came to an unfortunate end when he pulled up with a leg injury, Sussex's bowlers still managed to restrict their hosts to 79-2 at lunch, with Mark Ramprakash having struggled to twelve and Graham Thorpe having looked in fine fettle while making forty.

With Thorpe completing his fifty from 83 balls soon after the restart, and Ramprakash suddenly finding his touch and timing, Sussex looked in for a hard afternoon until Mushtaq Ahmed had the right-hander caught at cover with the total on 132. The visitors' joy was short-lived, though, as the arrival of Ali Brown produced an immediate surge in the scoring rate that sent the total rocketing past the 150 mark and quickly on to two-hundred. Although Mushtaq caused a few problems every now and again, the seamers began to suffer as Brown sailed through to fifty from just 47 balls and Thorpe reached a sublime 156-ball century shortly before the fourth-wicket partnership became worth a hundred in a mere seventeen overs. The introduction of Michael Yardy's left-arm seamers managed to slow the scoring, however, and, with tea imminent, Kirtley offered his side further hope by having Brown (74) very well caught by Murray Goodwin at backward point to make the score 263-4.

With Brown replaced at the wicket by the equally destructive Hollioake, it was no surprise that the Championship leaders maintained their onslaught after the break - after the Surrey skipper had raced to a half-century in 49 balls, Thorpe reached 150 from 264 deliveries and the total passed 350 at almost four runs an over. Sussex enjoyed a mini-revival late in the day, though, as four wickets fell for thirty-five runs, with Thorpe going to Mushtaq for a brilliant 156 and Azhar falling to Kirtley for a duck, before Robin Martin-Jenkins struck twice with the new ball, taken with six overs remaining for play. After Bicknell had gone for eleven, and Hollioake for an entertaining seventy-seven from 78 balls, Salisbury and Saqlain batted through to stumps at 401-8.

Chris Adams's men were then frustrated for sixteen overs the following morning as the overnight pair batted positively to add seventy-nine runs to the total. Although Martin-Jenkins (3-86) and Mushtaq (3-159) each added a scalp to their collection to terminate the merry-making of Salisbury (45) and Saqlain (32), Sussex now faced the task of scoring 331 to avoid the follow-on.

The events of the hour's play leading up to lunch suggested that they might not make it, as Montgomerie, Yardy and Adams were sent packing by Ormond and Azhar with just twenty-four runs scored, leaving Goodwin and Ambrose to ensure that Surrey made no further inroads before the interval.

With Bicknell having suffered a similar fate to Taylor after bowling just three overs in the pre-lunch session, Adam Hollioake kept Ormond and Azhar going after the break, though they suddenly found life more difficult as Goodwin reeled off eight boundaries in seven overs to complete a fluent fifty from 58 deliveries. This sustained assault on the seamers prompted a bowling change that produced almost instant results for Surrey when Saqlain Mushtaq bowled the former Zimbabwe batsman for sixty with a big off-break, putting the visitors back in serious trouble at 98-4. Although the new batsman, Martin-Jenkins, initially looked uncertain against Salisbury, who had joined his spin twin in the attack, he survived to share a very valuable stand of ninety-one with Tim Ambrose and register a half-century in exactly the same number of balls as his colleague at the top of the order. The tall all-rounder's unhappy departure for sixty-one to an lbw decision in favour of the returning Azhar, then triggered a decline, as the loss of two wickets to the spinners either side of tea left Sussex struggling at 220-7. Mushtaq Ahmed responded to this situation by launching a counter-attack against Salisbury and Saqlain that prompted Hollioake to replace his leg-spinner with Ormond (4-81), which proved to be a wise move, since the strapping paceman removed both members of the eighth-wicket partnership in rapid succession - after Ambrose had been taken at gully for a very mature seventy-five, with the stand worth fifty-nine, Mushtaq fell lbw for forty-one scored at almost a run a ball with the total on 282. Despite the fact that the last-wicket pair of Kirtley and Taylor were able to add only twenty-five of the forty-nine runs required to save the follow on, Surrey elected to bat again anyway, reaching 22-0 by stumps.

With their side leading by 195 runs at the start of play, Surrey's openers made slow progress against Kirtley and Martin-Jenkins in the early stages before accelerating against Innes and Mushtaq to record individual fifties and a century opening partnership. Although Jon Batty (56) chopped a Mushtaq googly onto his stumps with the total on 137, Ian Ward had progressed to ninety-three by lunch, with the home side's lead standing at 338.

The left-handed opener duly completed his second Championship ton of the season after the break, and his perfectly paced 137-ball innings appeared to have put Surrey in a position to declare sometime around tea with a lead of 450-500. A series of showers that dogged the rest of the day completely scuppered Surrey's plans, however, forcing Adam Hollioake to close the innings at 233-3 (Ward 135) when a last 'window' of play arrived at 5.50pm. Needing 407 to win from a minimum of 109 overs, the Sussex openers ended up facing just twenty-three deliveries before bad light terminated proceedings for the day at 12-0.

On the final morning, the visitors recovered from the loss of Murray Goodwin to Azhar Mahmood for twenty-six to reach a comfortable 83-1 before Saqlain Mushtaq produced a brilliant three-wicket burst to reduce them to 85-4 and put the Championship leaders firmly on the road to victory. Their path was then blocked by two totally different innings, as Michael Yardy got his head down in defensive mode, while Robin Martin-Jenkins took the attack to the bowlers during the afternoon session. The Sussex all-rounder reached his fifty from 63 balls and had advanced to eighty-eight from a further thirty deliveries before an outstanding inswinging yorker from Azhar provided the home side with a much needed breakthrough. With forty-two overs left for play at this point, Surrey clearly wanted a sixth wicket before tea and, thanks to Matt Prior's miscued hook at Azhar, which was very well caught by Mark Ramprakash at deep backward square, they managed to get it with the total on 218.

When Kevin Innes was dismissed by Saqlain four overs after the restart, and James Kirtley fell to a fine catch by substitute Nadeem Shahid off Salisbury at 242-8 after defending defiantly for thirty-three balls, Sussex looked to be in grave danger of defeat. Yardy was still there, though, having just completed a 180-ball half-century, and he found Mushtaq Ahmed to be a very positive ninth-wicket partner. With the little leg-spinner leading the way, this duo put together a fifty stand that ate up thirteen valuable overs before Saqlain finally broke through, trapping his compatriot lbw with thirty-seven balls remaining in the match. Although the limping Billy Taylor, emerging at number eleven, looked potentially easy prey for Surrey, it turned out to be the limpet-like Yardy (69) who failed to last the distance, edging a fine delivery from Ormond into the safe hands of Azhar at second slip to seal the hosts' victory by 113 runs. The Sussex left-hander was disconsolate as he trudged off at the end of a 241-ball marathon of concentration, while the Surrey team were thrilled to have earned a well deserved win that enabled them to extend their lead at the top of the table to twenty-eight points.

COUNTY CHAMPIONSHIP - TOP OF THE TABLE AT 2ND JUNE					
	P	W	D	L	T	PTS
Surrey	6	3	3	0	0	94.00
Lancashire	5	1	4	0	0	66.00
Warwickshire	5	1	2	1	1	88.00

After a five-day break, the team's next fixture was an NCL clash with the third-placed Essex Eagles at The Oval. Despite the fact that Martin Bicknell had joined Alex Tudor on the injured list, Adam Hollioake opted to insert his visitors, and this move appeared to pay dividends as Phil Sampson and Azhar Mahmood disposed of the openers, Jefferson and Flower, by the time the score had reached thirty-five. With both James Foster and Mark Pettini failing to build on confident starts in the middle order when confronted by Saqlain Mushtaq and the outstanding James Ormond, Essex moved unconvincingly to 126-4 after twenty-eight overs before Darren Robinson and Paul Grayson started to impress. By adding sixty-seven runs in the next ten overs they put the Eagles in prime position to register a challenging score, but a sensational spell of bowling from the returning Azhar transformed the innings once Robinson (78) had lost his middle stump to a superlative yorker. The Lions' all-rounder was simply irresistible as he took five wickets for twelve runs in sixteen balls to finish with the excellent figures of 6-37 and complete an Essex slump from 193-4 to 220 all out.

Although Surrey's chase got away to a poor start when Scott Brant dismissed their openers for seventeen, the in-form Thorpe shared successive partnerships of seventy-two, forty and forty-eight with Ramprakash, Clarke and Hollioake to put his team in control at 177-4. Grayson then caused a few flutters by claiming two quick wickets when he entered the fray belatedly with his left-arm spin, but Thorpe (79 not out) and Saqlain (14 not out) ensured that there were no more alarms as they knocked off the final twenty-four runs to see the Lions home by three wickets with thirteen balls in hand.

With the Glamorgan Dragons also winning, the top two were looking strongly placed at this early stage of the season.

LEADING POSITIONS:- Surrey P6, Pts 22; Glam P5, Pts 20; Glos P6, Pts 14

Surrey had suffered some very disappointing Nat West/C&G Trophy defeats in recent years, but none were as bad as the trouncing they suffered at the County Ground, Derby in their quarter-final encounter on 11th June. On a pitch that looked a little 'sporty', Derbyshire did brilliantly to rack up a total of 271 after being put in by Adam Hollioake, with the home team's overseas batsmen, Michael DiVenuto (51) and Mohammad Kaif (81) taking full advantage of some indifferent bowling from all bar Azhar Mahmood (4-49) and the immaculate Saqlain Mushtaq (10-0-24-0). Surrey's reply then hit the rocks straight away as the excellent Dominic Cork (2-17) and Kevin Dean (2-26) reduced their visitors to 26-4. Although Graham Thorpe (37) and Hollioake briefly threatened a revival, Graeme Welch followed up the new-ball pairing's efforts with a fine spell of 4-26 to complete the rout of the visitors for a miserable 134 in just 33.4 overs. Having pulled off a couple of great catches in the course of a fine performance in the field, Derbyshire fully deserved their crushing 137-run triumph as they became the first team to beat Surrey in any competition since 18th August 2002, some twenty-two games ago. Surrey's conquerors on that occasion, in an NCL match at The Oval, had been... Derbyshire.

Attention now switched to the new Twenty20 Cup, with Surrey's campaign starting at The Oval against the Middlesex Crusaders. On a lovely mid-summer's evening, a crowd of around 10,000 packed into The Oval, immediately giving food for thought to those who had doubted whether the new competition would be a success. Having put their visitors in to bat, Surrey held the whip hand after ten overs, thanks to James Ormond's four-wicket salvo that left the Crusaders struggling at 90-6. When Ben Hutton then fell to Adam Hollioake at 103, Andrew Strauss (52) and Robin Weston (30) had to waste valuable overs steadying the innings before Ormond returned to dismiss Strauss with the total on 139 and complete amazing figures of 5-26. Azhar Mahmood then claimed the final two wickets to leave his side chasing 156 to win.

Although there were only four balls remaining when Mark Ramprakash drove the boundary that completed a four-wicket win, the hosts always looked to have the game under control, with Ward making thirty-one at the top of the order, and Messrs Benning, Hollioake and Thorpe all contributing twenties at much better than a run a ball. Having seen two sixes, forty-two fours, sixteen wickets and a last-over finish, most of the crowd would have gone home happy.

Surrey then recorded another good attendance for their second match, against the Essex Eagles at Imber Court, Esher, the following evening. After being invited to bat, the hosts were given a flying start by Ian Ward (30 from 19 balls), who was largely responsible for them notching forty-two runs from the first four overs, before the visitors fought back well to reduce Surrey to 80-4 at the mid-point of the innings. The Lions enjoyed an excellent second half, however, as Graham Thorpe (50 from 35 balls) and Azhar Mahmood, with an explosive 18-ball knock of forty-three, including three sixes and six fours, boosted the total to 182-9.

A bright knock of thirty from 18 balls by Andy Flower at the top of the order was pretty much all the Eagles had to offer in reply, as they never came to terms with the task facing them. Ronnie Irani and Mark Pettini also passed twenty-five, but not at anything like the required tempo, as Tim Murtagh (2-26) did a great job in the first half of the innings, allowing Azhar (4-20) and Adam Hollioake (2-18) to wrap up a very comfortable 44-run triumph.

Returning to Imber Court for their third home game in four days, Surrey then took a major step toward securing a Finals Day place by registering a straightforward victory over the Sussex Sharks. Handicapped by a slow start from their opening pair of Matt Prior and Bas

Zuiderent (35), Sussex never looked like making a big score, as only Chris Adams, with thirty-six from 22 balls, managed to get to grips with some very good bowling by Ian Salisbury (2-20), Phil Sampson (2-29) and Adam Hollioake (4-31). With the Sharks totalling a below-par 143-8, the hosts always seemed likely to triumph, even when Ward and Brown fell before the score had reached forty. Although Mushtaq Ahmed emulated his Lions counterpart by returning 2-20, Surrey produced a team effort with the bat, with no one exceeding James Benning's twenty-seven as they cruised home by four wickets with eleven balls to spare.

After a six-day gap, Surrey resumed their campaign against the Kent Spitfires at a well-populated St Lawrence Ground, Canterbury. With Kent having won two and lost one of their three games, this represented an important match at the top of the South Division table, and the unbeaten leaders looked in trouble when they reached the halfway point of their innings at 82-4 after being put in to bat. Although Andrew Symonds (4-1-17-1) proved very hard to get away, the other bowlers were easy prey in the final ten overs for both Mark Ramprakash (53 from 35 balls) and Azhar Mahmood (57 from 31), who smashed eight sixes between them in advancing the total to 186-8.

Kent's hopes of securing the required 187 runs immediately took a dive when the extremely dangerous Symonds fell to Tim Murtagh in only the second over. The Spitfires then subsided to 44-4 after six overs, before the combination of Ed Smith and Matt Walker that had almost won the NCL match at The Oval earlier in the season offered some hope with a partnership of forty-five. Once Walker had fallen to the excellent Ian Salisbury, the odds were stacked against Kent, however, and their last chance went when Smith was run out by Benning for fifty-six at 130-7 in the sixteenth over. Two fine end-of-innings overs by Murtagh saw him finish with figures of 3-37 as the hosts ended nineteen runs short of their victory target at 168-9 and the visitors celebrated their safe passage through to Finals Day.

Despite the fact that the fate of both sides had already been sealed when Surrey played Hampshire at The Rose Bowl in the final group match, a crowd of 6,500 filled the ground, showing how the public had taken to the new competition. The glorious weather that had blessed just about every match around the country was maintained right until the last as Surrey looked to complete a South Division 'grand slam' with a much changed bowler-heavy line-up. Having elected to bat, the Lions were given a 75-run platform by Scott Newman and Ali Brown (33 from 26 balls) in the first nine overs, but struggled thereafter on a tricky pitch. Apart from Newman, who anchored the innings with a run a ball fifty-nine, only Martin Bicknell reached double figures as Surrey ended up with a total of 140-9.

Bicknell then played a leading role with the ball, conceding just six runs in his first spell of three overs and claiming the wicket of James Hamblin as the Hawks got away to a safe but unspectacular start, reaching 51-1 after ten overs. Although Simon Katich (45 from 49 balls) and Derek Kenway (27 from 18) added forty-two for the fourth wicket to allow their side to reach 101-3 with four overs to go, no one was able to provide the necessary late acceleration against the wily Adam Hollioake, who claimed 5-21 in three overs as the Hawks slumped dramatically to 121 all out. Bicknell's final figures of 4-1-11-2 equalled the most economical in the competition to date as Surrey ended with a perfect five out of five record in the South Division.

FINAL TWENTY20 CUP (SOUTH DIVISION) TABLE				
	P	Pts	W	L
Surrey Lions	5	10	5	0
Sussex Sharks	5	6	3	2
Essex Eagles	5	4	2	3
Kent Spitfires	5	4	2	3
Middlesex Crusaders	5	4	2	3
Hampshire Hawks	5	2	1	4

With the Twenty20 Cup qualifying games completed, and the competition having received rave reviews in the media, Surrey faced their first Championship game for almost four weeks as they crossed the Thames to take on Middlesex at Lord's. This was the first meeting between the two London-based counties since the premier domestic competition split into two divisions, which promised to add a little extra spice to the contest.

Since the Nat West Series of ODIs was currently in full swing, Keith Medlycott's team was lacking the services of Rikki Clarke, who had just made his first few appearances for England, but included Mark Butcher and Alec Stewart. Butcher remained a member of the Test set-up only, while Stewart had, as expected, given way to Chris Read, even though he hadn't officially announced his retirement from ODIs. The other major change to the Surrey side since their last four-day match saw the fit-again Alex Tudor replace the injured Azhar Mahmood. After Andrew Strauss won the toss for Middlesex and elected to bat, Surrey had the better of the first half of the day, reducing their hosts to 148-5, thanks to some outstanding bowling by Martin Bicknell, who claimed four of the wickets during two fine ten-over spells on a good pitch. The second half belonged to Middlesex, though, as Ben Hutton received solid support from Abdul Razzaq, Paul Weekes and David Nash while compiling a valuable century from 179 balls, before being bowled for 101 by the criminally neglected Ian Salisbury's penultimate ball of the day.

From an overnight position of 311-7, Middlesex progressed as far as 370 all out on the second morning, with James Ormond (3-103) capturing the three remaining wickets and Bicknell returning final figures of 5-92. The Surrey batsmen then enjoyed themselves on the placid Lord's surface to run up 274-3 during the rest of the day, with Ian Ward's excellent 104 forming the backbone of the innings, and Mark Ramprakash still in residence on sixty-eight at stumps after registering one of the slowest half-centuries of his career from 143 balls.

Ramprakash then made history the following morning by becoming the first man to register a first-class century against all eighteen first-class counties when he reached three figures from his 236th delivery. Although the former Middlesex man departed soon afterwards for 110, nightwatchman Saqlain Mushtaq progressed to a Surrey-best sixty-nine, and Alec Stewart notched eighty-seven to guide his team through to a final total of 568, giving them a lead of 198. The visitors were unable to dislodge either of the Middlesex openers in the remaining nineteen overs of the day, however, leaving them with quite a task on their hands if they were to force a final-day victory.

Heavy overnight rain, followed by morning showers, then ensured that the game would end in stalemate, with play not getting under way until 1.30pm. Although Strauss and Koenig both completed personal half-centuries before another burst of rain wiped fifteen more overs from the day, neither man was able to reach three figures as the hosts finished on 218-2 - Strauss fell to Salisbury for ninety-five, while Koenig was dismissed by Adam Hollioake for eighty-nine.

Having played two and won two since their defeat at The Oval, a Mushtaq-inspired Sussex had moved up into second place in the Championship table, just six points adrift of Surrey.

COUNTY CHAMPIONSHIP - TOP OF THE TABLE AT 30TH JUNE				
	P	W	D	L	PTS
Surrey	7	3	4	0	106.00
Sussex	7	4	0	3	100.00
Lancashire	6	2	4	0	88.00

Crossing back to the southern side of the Thames, Surrey next took on Kent, who were struggling in the relegation zone after a sticky start to the season. The hosts' plan to select an unchanged side was scuppered by the late withdrawal of Adam Hollioake, whose father had been taken ill, which left Mark Butcher to captain the side, while Kent included their recent signing, Mohammad Sami, the Pakistani fast bowler, and gave a Championship debut to left-arm spinner Rob Ferley.

On a rain-hit opening day, Surrey won the toss, batted first and made 245-3, with Butcher leading from the front by scoring a sparkling unbeaten 117 that was full of superb strokes. Graham Thorpe also batted very well, scoring sixty-eight in a third-wicket stand of 138 before becoming a distinguished maiden Championship scalp for Ferley.

With another thirty-one overs lost to rain in the first half of the second day, Surrey elected to press the accelerator in order to make up for lost time, scoring 156 runs in 31.2 overs. Ben Trott (4-73) and Rob Ferley (4-76) both profited from their hosts' belligerent approach as they captured six of the seven wickets that fell for 108 runs after Butcher had been dismissed for 144 with the total on 293. Having only just managed to pocket their final batting point, thanks to a last-wicket stand of forty-two between Ian Salisbury and James Ormond, Surrey then set out to pick up bowling points and a victory, but found Ed Smith and Andrew Symonds blocking their path after David Fulton and Michael Carberry had been dismissed with forty runs on the board.

Kent's third-wicket pair extended their overnight partnership of sixty-one by another fifty runs on the third morning before Symonds became Martin Bicknell's second victim of the innings shortly after completing an 83-ball half-century. Smith, who had arrived at that mark earlier in the morning from 76 balls, then linked up with Matt Walker to strengthen Kent's position, taking advantage of some poor Surrey bowling to advance to a very fine century from the 138th delivery of his innings. Having reached lunch at 240-3, with the fourth-wicket pair having already added eighty-nine runs in good time, the visitors made an important announcement - Muttiah Muralitharan had been signed for the last two months of the season. This seemed to ease their relegation fears at a stroke and, buoyed by this news, the Kent batsmen pressed on with increasing haste, both before and after the departure of Smith for a marvellous 135 from 177 balls. With Geraint Jones giving him fine support at a rate of almost a run a ball, Walker took his side on to 352-5 and moved within seventeen runs of a century before Dave Fulton caught everyone on the hop by declaring forty-nine runs in arrears. It seemed that he felt Kent's best chance of securing a much needed victory was to chase runs on a fine Oval pitch in the fourth innings, and he had obviously come to some arrangement with his Surrey counterpart, who had left the field for a while during the latter stages of the Kent innings.

The remainder of the day was therefore dedicated to the home side increasing their lead, with the quality of the bowling gradually being relaxed during the forty-four overs that were bowled until stumps were drawn at 249-3. Butcher scored a fine ninety from 74 balls when the bowling was at its best, before Thorpe (46) and Brown (64 not out) feasted on some less impressive offerings from Carberry, Walker and Smith towards the end of the day.

After something of a pantomime at the start of the final day, which saw Surrey add just two runs from twenty balls, Mark Butcher's declaration came rather earlier than most people had expected, leaving Kent to score 301 from a minimum of ninety overs. This reflected the fact that Fulton had held the whip hand during the previous day's negotiations, since there had been no chance of Surrey winning the match at that particular time. They now had to try to take advantage of the second chance they had been given, and they certainly made a decent start when James Ormond claimed the scalps of Fulton for eleven and Smith for a sixth-ball duck with the total on twenty-one. After a recovery to 61-2, Saqlain then struck a further blow for the home side, taking his tally of first-class career wickets to seven-hundred by having Carberry well caught by Stewart behind the stumps.

Any regrets Fulton might have had about opening up the game then grew immediately after the restart when Symonds cut Tudor to the left of Salisbury at deep backward point, and saw the fielder cling on to the fast-travelling chance to reduce Kent to 67-4. There now appeared to be only one side that could win the match, since the bottom half of the visitors' batting line-up looked rather short on quality and experience. This was confirmed once Saqlain had removed Walker and Ealham before the total had risen to eighty, since the tail was exposed and then disposed of in quick time by the spinners bowling in tandem. Salisbury finished with 3-11 and Saqlain 4-27 as Kent subsided to 114 all out shortly after 3pm, with forty overs to spare. Fulton's bold gamble had failed in spectacular fashion, with Surrey having produced a brilliant display in the field to redeem their truly awful effort in the first innings and claim twenty points from the match. With Sussex not playing, and Lancashire failing to beat Essex at Chelmsford, this haul enabled Keith Medlycott's team to move twenty-six points clear at the head of the table.

COUNTY CHAMPIONSHIP - TOP OF THE TABLE AT 5TH JULY					
	P	W	D	L	PTS
Surrey	8	4	4	0	126.00
Sussex	7	4	0	3	100.00
Lancashire	7	2	5	0	96.00

There was good news off the field, too, with Adam Hollioake's father, John, recovering well from his illness, allowing the Surrey captain to make a swift return to the team for the next match. After a month's break from National League action, Surrey were looking to maintain their unbeaten record when bottom-of-the-table Yorkshire Phoenix came to The Oval. The hosts certainly got off to the best possible start when Matthew Wood, Yorkshire's stand-in captain, won the toss, elected to bat and then edged Martin Bicknell's first delivery to the right of slip, where Graham Thorpe pulled off a terrific diving catch. Although the Phoenix recovered from this instant setback to reach 139-3, thanks to Stephen Fleming, who completed a fine fifty from 58 balls during a third-wicket partnership of sixty-five with Michael Lumb, the introduction of Ian Salisbury (3-40) to join forces with an initially below-par Saqlain Mushtaq (2-39) changed the course of the innings. Four wickets tumbled for thirty-six runs as the spinners took a grip on the game for the Lions, then a minor recovery from 175-7 to 196-7 was abruptly ended by Adam Hollioake, who captured the last three wickets - including Fleming for a high-class ninety - in the space of five deliveries. A final total of 199, with nineteen balls of their innings unused, looked unlikely to be enough for Yorkshire to seriously test the league leaders.

Although Steve Kirby removed Ali Brown, courtesy of a fine catch by Richard Blakey behind the wicket in the second over, Surrey had no problems thereafter as Mark Butcher and Mark Ramprakash shared a 158-run partnership for the second wicket, during which Butcher registered his maiden limited-overs century from just 101 balls. After the England left-hander fell to off-spinner Andy Gray for an excellent 104, Ramprakash guided his side through to an easy seven-wicket win with almost seven overs to spare, finishing unbeaten on sixty.

With Glamorgan having played, and lost, an NCL game in the midst of their Twenty20 fixtures, and then been beaten by Kent at Maidstone while Surrey were hammering Yorkshire, the league leaders now held a six-point advantage.

NCL DIVISION ONE - TOP OF THE TABLE AT 6TH JULY					
	P	W	L	T	A	PTS
Surrey	7	6	0	0	1	26
Glamorgan	7	5	2	0	0	20
Gloucestershire	7	4	2	0	1	18

Adam Hollioake for Ali Brown, and Azhar Mahmood for Alex Tudor, were the only two changes from the previous Championship line-up when Surrey took on Warwickshire at Edgbaston. Having declared his eleven, Hollioake won the toss and elected to bat.

On a day when fortunes swung one way and then the other, the visitors had a poor morning, with the top four batsmen all getting a start but none of them going on past thirty, leaving Warwickshire the happier of the two sides with a lunch score of 115-4.

Surrey then took control after the break, though only after Warwickshire had spurned the opportunity to put their visitors in real trouble at 124-6 by missing chances offered by both Alec Stewart and Adam Hollioake. The hosts were made to pay a heavy price for their mistakes as the fifth-wicket pair put together a wonderful partnership of 150, with Hollioake leading the way by launching ferocious attacks on Waqar Younis and Graham Wagg that took him to an amazing 41-ball half-century. Stewart also played well in reaching a more sedate 82-ball fifty, shortly before a mid-afternoon drinks break turned out to be a watershed in the Surrey innings. After Dougie Brown had removed Hollioake for eighty-eight, scored at almost a run a ball, with the score at 253, Stewart and Azhar Mahmood added another thirty-five runs before the visitors lost four wickets in five balls without addition to the score to slump to 288-9. Azhar went first, caught behind off Wagg, before Neil Carter dismissed Stewart (74) and Ian Salisbury with the first two deliveries of the following over - both men also caught behind the wicket, giving Frost a wicketkeeper's hat-trick - and then had Saqlain Mushtaq taken at short leg two balls later. Having claimed a couple of scalps in the morning session, Carter (5-75) suddenly had five wickets to his name, and the innings had been totally transformed. There was then another twist in the Surrey tail as the last-wicket pair of Martin Bicknell (25 not out) and James Ormond (33) added sixty-seven priceless runs to earn their team another two batting points, at 300 and 350, before Brown removed the latter's off stump with the total at 355.

After tea, Warwickshire's reply was given a sound base by Michael Powell and Mark Wagh, who compiled an opening stand of sixty-two before Powell was brilliantly caught by a diving Azhar at slip off Salisbury. When time was called, seven overs later, the hosts had advanced to 85-1, with Surrey's old foe, Nick Knight, unbeaten on thirty-seven.

The second day's play saw the Bears riding a similar rollercoaster to their opponents, as they dipped to 120-5 from a high point of 114-1, thanks to some fine bowling from Azhar Mahmood, who claimed three wickets in eight balls, and Martin Bicknell. Dougie Brown and Tony Frost then restored equilibrium to the contest by adding seventy runs for the sixth wicket before lunch, only for Surrey to regain the initiative immediately after the break. Azhar (4-61) was once again the man to make the initial breakthrough, three balls into the day's middle session, when he had Frost caught at second slip, allowing Bicknell (3-62) and Ormond (2-57) to run through the tail after Brown (61) and Wagg had added twenty-nine for the seventh wicket. Losing their last four wickets for twenty-one runs in five overs was something of a disaster for Warwickshire, since it handed the Championship leaders a first-innings advantage of 110 runs, which looked to be significant on a pitch of occasional inconsistent bounce. Surrey didn't let the vagaries of the playing surface bother them, though, as Mark Butcher and Mark Ramprakash quickly overcame the early loss of Ian Ward to complete magnificent centuries before the close of play. The bowling was treated with disdain, and the run rate raced along at five an over, as Butcher's truly outstanding ton came from just 102 balls, while Ramprakash was also wonderfully fluent in reaching three figures from his 144th delivery. Although Neil Smith eventually had Butcher caught behind for 118 and then claimed the wicket of Thorpe, courtesy of a dollied return catch, Ramprakash (121 not out) was still there at the close, with Surrey on 282-3, leading by 392 runs.

With Warwickshire's fate surely already sealed, it was just a case of how long Adam Hollioake wanted to bat on for as day three began. He had clearly decided that some morning mayhem would suffice for his team as he and Azhar enjoyed their 'licence to thrill' once Alec Stewart had gone for forty-five at 319-4. Hollioake blasted thirty from 25 balls before falling lbw to Wagg, while his Pakistani team-mate contributed a thunderous unbeaten innings of fifty from just 26 balls to allow a declaration at 450-5 half-an-hour before lunch. Ramprakash, who had been no slouch himself in adding sixty-one to his overnight score during the morning's twenty-five overs, finished undefeated on 182, confirming Warwickshire as one of his favourite opponents in the process.

Chasing a purely hypothetical 561 in a minimum of 173 overs, the hosts lost their key man, Nick Knight, for eight, immediately after the interval, before battling back to lose just one more wicket in the rest of the session - Wagh well taken in front of first slip by Stewart off Hollioake for fifty-one with the total on 138.

Although Powell (91) had his middle stump removed by a near shooter from Ormond shortly after tea, Ian Bell and Jonathan Trott then batted most attractively to post a century partnership, during which Bell completed a half-century from 84 balls and Trott reached the same mark from 67 deliveries. At 289-3, the more optimistic Bears' fans might have been pondering the possibility of an outrageous victory for their side, but their dreams were shattered in the closing half-hour of the day as Hollioake pulled off two masterstrokes. Having brought himself into the attack and pinned Trott lbw for fifty-one with his first ball, he gave way to Saqlain after just one over and watched Bell hole out to Salisbury at wide mid-on from the off-spinner's second delivery. Warwickshire knew there was no way back for them as they closed on 304-5.

To give the home side credit, they didn't fold meekly the next day, with Dougie Brown recording his second fifty of the contest as the spinners wheeled away throughout the morning session, picking up Frost, Wagg and Carter without too much fuss, but being held up by Smith and Waqar. The last-wicket pair actually managed to extend the match beyond lunch, though only by seven deliveries before Brown fell to Saqlain (5-134) with his score on fifty-six and the total on 425. Surrey therefore emerged victorious by 135 runs, and maintained their 26-point advantage in the Championship, since Sussex had equalled the leaders' 21-point win in beating Essex by six wickets.

Although no one knew it at the time, this was Alec Stewart's final appearance for Surrey after twenty-three seasons at The Oval. It was a great shame that the county's fans were not able to give him an appropriate send-off in Surrey colours, but he had at least gone out on a high note with scores of seventy-four and forty-five, three catches and a victory.

COUNTY CHAMPIONSHIP - TOP OF THE TABLE AT 12TH JULY				
	P	W	D	L	PTS
Surrey	9	5	4	0	147.00
Sussex	8	5	0	3	121.00
Lancashire	7	2	5	0	96.00

The Bears were on a run of three straight NCL wins as they clashed with their unbeaten visitors in the following day's 45-overs-a-side contest. They certainly had the best of the early exchanges after Surrey had won the toss, with Waqar Younis (4-35) putting the Lions in trouble at 45-3 after twelve overs, and Neil Smith nipping in with the wicket of Ian Ward - batting out of position at number five - with the total advanced to eighty-seven. Although Mark Ramprakash and Adam Hollioake then added forty-seven for the fifth wicket, they were never able to entirely free themselves of the shackles imposed by the wily Smith and the young Kenyan leg-spinner, Collins Obuya, who eventually bowled the Surrey captain with a good quicker ball. Warwickshire then built on an already promising position by ridding themselves of Ramprakash for a steady fifty-seven and the dangerous Azhar Mahmood for seventeen at 166-7, leaving the Lions in danger of posting a decidedly below-par total. Two splendid late cameos ensured that they ended with a good score of 242-9, however, with Jon Batty making twenty-eight from 25 balls, and Ian Salisbury a magnificent thirty-three from 17 balls, including twenty-two runs - courtesy of a sequence of 6-4-6-6 - from the final over of the innings bowled by Obuya (3-65).

Although Azhar struck early in the Bears' reply to remove Neil Carter for eighteen, Nick Knight (74) and Jonathan Trott (51) then compiled a match-winning partnership of 131 in twenty-one overs, with Knight reaching fifty in 58 balls and Trott in sixty-two. Although Surrey briefly threatened a comeback by removing the second-wicket partners and Jim Troughton for the addition of just one run, their hopes were just as quickly snuffed out by Ian Bell and Michael Powell. Bell, who played beautifully from the start, reached fifty in just 42 balls, and finished on fifty-nine, while Powell was undefeated on twenty-six as the Bears strolled home by six wickets with almost three overs to spare. Although Martin Bicknell had endured a rare off day with the ball as Surrey had slipped to their first NCL defeat since they lost to Derbyshire on 18th August 2002, twelve games ago, he had the small consolation of having become the county's all-time leading wicket-taker in Sunday/National League cricket when dismissing Troughton. His tally of 235 wickets had taken him past the long-time record holder, Robin Jackman.

LEADING POSITIONS:- Surrey P8, Pts 26; Glam P8, Pts 24; Glos P7, Pts 18

Saturday 19th July was Twenty20 Cup Finals Day at Trent Bridge, and there was a near-capacity 15,000 crowd in the ground by the time the first semi-final between the Leicestershire Foxes and the Warwickshire Bears got under way. Once the Bears had triumphed, they sat back to watch the nation's one-day kings, Gloucestershire, take on the County Champions, Surrey, in what promised to be an absorbing match.

Since they wanted to play both their spinners on a dry pitch, Surrey were forced to leave Martin Bicknell out of their side in favour of James Ormond, while James Benning, who had played in the qualifying games during Rikki Clarke's absence in the Nat West Series, was a little unfortunate to have to give way to the county's latest England player.

Clarke struggled, in fact, after the Lions had elected to bat and lost Ali Brown for eighteen with the total at twenty-six in the fourth over. Unable to find his timing, the young all-rounder laboured for twenty-three balls in making fifteen, which left his side under pressure at 50-2 when he was stumped off Mark Hardinges in the ninth over. Surrey were greatly relieved that the outstanding Mike Smith (4-0-11-0) had completed his spell by this stage, though they still had four overs to come from the equally skilful Ian Harvey. While Ian Ward anchored the innings with a run-a-ball forty-nine, Adam Hollioake and Azhar Mahmood sparkled brightly but briefly at the other end, with the latter raising the Surrey hundred in the fourteenth over before becoming a third victim for Hardinges (3-37). When Graham Thorpe and Ward then fell in Harvey's first two overs - the fourteenth and sixteenth of the innings - it became clear that the Lions were not going to be able to post a huge total, and with Martyn Ball (2-26) proving even more difficult to score off at the other end during the 'death' overs, the champions of the South Division had to settle for a score of 147-9. It didn't look likely to be enough, though it was the highest total that the Gladiators had conceded in this competition when bowling first, none of the previous four teams having got past 134.

This offered a degree of hope, as did the first four overs of the Gloucestershire reply, during which James Ormond and Azhar swept away their opponents' three greatest threats with the bat - Craig Spearman, Jonty Rhodes and Ian Harvey. When Matt Windows then fell to Saqlain Mushtaq to make the score 36-4 in the eighth over, the Lions appeared to be almost home and hosed, though the Gladiators' two young all-rounders, Hardinges and Alex Gidman, had other ideas. These two added fifty-two in seven overs before Hollioake bowled Hardinges in the fifteenth over to keep his side on top, but the next over from Ian Salisbury cost nineteen runs, allowing Gidman to complete an impressive 41-ball half-century and leaving Gloucestershire needing thirty-eight runs from the last four overs. Surrey quickly reasserted their authority, however, as a brilliant seventeenth over of the innings by Hollioake, yielding just three runs, was followed by an Azhar yorker that shattered Gidman's stumps with the batsman on sixty-one. This left the Gladiators requiring twenty-eight runs from fourteen deliveries. Although Chris Taylor hit the first ball of the penultimate over for six, Hollioake followed up with five good deliveries, leaving Azhar with plenty of runs to play with as he started the final over. Needing an unlikely seventeen runs, Gloucestershire fell six short of victory at 142-6.

The inaugural Twenty20 Cup final therefore saw Warwickshire taking on Surrey just six days after the Bears had vanquished the Lions in the NCL at Edgbaston. The floodlit climax to a lengthy day's entertainment started at 7.15pm with Surrey in the field after Nick Knight had decided that his team would bat first, before the lights came into play. The Lions fielded an unchanged side - with Azhar Mahmood participating despite being inconvenienced by a thigh strain - and made a fantastic start that left them with one hand on the trophy inside seven overs. After Neil Carter and Nick Knight had taken six runs from James Ormond's opening over, and ten from the next delivered by Azhar, Surrey claimed five wickets in the next five overs to leave the Bears in a pit of despair at 33-5. The slide started when Carter dragged a ball from Ormond on to his stumps in the third over (16-1), and continued with Knight and Jim Troughton both falling in the big paceman's following over - the former emulated his fellow opener by playing on (20-2) and the latter was caught by Ali Brown at first slip (22-3). Azhar then got in on the act by producing a nasty lifter that flew from the shoulder of Ian Bell's bat to Rikki Clarke at backward point (32-4), before Ormond had Dougie Brown taken at the wicket from another fine delivery (33-5) to complete a magnificent spell of 4-0-11-4. The sixth-wicket pair of Trevor Penney and Tony Frost now faced a very difficult situation, and took different options. While Frost attempted to steady the ship, Penney took the aggressive route, making thirty-three from 22 balls before Adam Hollioake's inswinger defeated him with the total on sixty-three. Graham Wagg then went in similar fashion to leave the Bears almost down and out at 83-7, and it required a battling partnership of twenty-nine in four overs by Frost (31) and Collins Obuya (17) to take the total into three figures and give it a hint of respectability at 112-7. Unfortunately for Warwickshire, their innings then ended much as it had begun, with a clatter of wickets, as the eighth-wicket partners both holed out in the deep off Saqlain Mushtaq in the eighteenth over, and Neil Smith was run out from the first ball of the nineteenth, leaving eleven balls unused - a criminal number in a 20-over innings. With just three runs added for the last three wickets, Surrey needed to score just 116 to become the first winners of the Twenty20 Cup.

Any hopes Warwickshire might have harboured of being able to defend such a poor total were dashed in Neil Carter's opening over of the Lions' reply, when Ian Ward took boundaries from each of the last four balls, after the first delivery had flicked off his pads and scuttled away for four leg byes. Twenty runs had come off the over and the Bears were all but beaten. Although Waqar Younis started reasonably well, and Carter atoned for his first over with a four-run second, the Surrey openers still managed to raise the fifty in the sixth over, with victory now seemingly a formality for the London-based side. Dougie Brown's second over after replacing Carter - the seventh of the innings - then yielded a six to Ali Brown and two fours to Ward, before Waqar ended his spell with his worst over, costing eleven runs, as each batsman picked up a pulled boundary. With the score now 77-0 the Lions were roaring home, and they even managed to increase an already fantastic run-rate by taking eighteen off Collins Obuya when he replaced Brown, with the openers again matching one another stroke for stroke by notching a six apiece. An even more dramatic over, delivered by Graham Wagg, then saw the scores levelled - Ward completed a brilliant 26-ball fifty with an on-driven boundary before being caught at mid-on with the total on exactly a hundred, then a wide, two no-balls, and two fours to Brown completed a truly awful over. Brown's second boundary had taken him through to a superb half-century from

32 balls, and allowed Mark Ramprakash to crack the winning four off a white flag-waving Nick Knight with an astonishing 9.1 overs to spare. Although the Lions openers had played brilliantly, it was no surprise when James Ormond was named Man Of The Match, shortly before David Morgan, the Chairman of the ECB, presented the impressive new trophy to Adam Hollioake and then stood back to let the Surrey celebrations begin. With seven wins from seven games, no one could deny that the Lions were worthy winners of the inaugural Twenty20 Cup.

TWENTY-20 CUP FINAL 2003
SURREY LIONS v WARWICKSHIRE BEARS at Trent Bridge
Saturday 19th July — Surrey Lions won by nine wickets

Warwickshire Bears won the toss and elected to bat — Umpires:- Barry Dudleston & John Holder

WARWICKSHIRE BEARS

Fall Of Wkt	Batsman	How	Out	Score	Balls	4s	6s
1-16	N.M. Carter		b Ormond	8	12	0	1
2-20	N.V. Knight *		b Ormond	8	6	1	0
4-32	I.R. Bell	c Clarke	b Azhar	5	11	0	0
3-22	J.O. Troughton	c Brown	b Ormond	1	3	0	0
6-63	T.L. Penney		b Hollioake	33	21	2	2
5-33	D.R. Brown	c Batty	b Ormond	0	3	0	0
8-112	T. Frost +	c Ormond	b Saqlain	31	35	1	0
7-83	G.G. Wagg		b Hollioake	5	6	0	0
9-115	C.O. Obuya	c Ward	b Saqlain	17	11	1	1
10-115	N.M.K. Smith	run	out	1	2	0	0
	Waqar Younis	Not	Out	0	1	0	0
	Extras	(2w, 4nb)		6			
	TOTAL	(18.1 overs)		115			

Bowler	O	M	R	W	NB	Wd
Ormond	4	0	11	4	-	-
Azhar Mahmood	3	0	22	1	-	1
Saqlain Mushtaq	4	0	35	2	1	1
Clarke	4	0	20	0	1	-
Hollioake	3.1	0	27	2	-	-

SURREY LIONS

Fall Of Wkt	Batsman	How	Out	Score	Balls	4s	6s
1-100	I.J. Ward	c Waqar	b Wagg	50	28	8	1
	A.D. Brown	Not	Out	55	34	6	3
	M.R. Ramprakash	Not	Out	4	5	1	0
	R. Clarke	did not bat					
	A.J. Hollioake *	did not bat					
	Azhar Mahmood	did not bat					
	G.P. Thorpe	did not bat					
	J.N. Batty +	did not bat					
	I.D.K. Salisbury	did not bat					
	Saqlain Mushtaq	did not bat					
	J. Ormond	did not bat					
	Extras	(4lb, 2w, 4nb)		10			
	TOTAL	(10.5 overs)	(for 1 wkt)	119			

Bowler	O	M	R	W	NB	Wd
Carter	2	0	20	0	-	-
Waqar Younis	4	0	29	0	-	-
Brown	2	0	24	0	-	-
Obuya	1	0	18	0	-	-
Wagg	1	0	20	1	2	2
Knight	0.5	0	4	0	-	-

Man Of The Match - James Ormond

With one trophy safely tucked away in the cabinet, Surrey made their annual visit to 'Fortress Guildford' to take on Middlesex with a much-changed team. With Alec Stewart and Mark Butcher playing in the first Test against South Africa, and Adam Hollioake and Azhar Mahmood having picked up injuries at Trent Bridge, Jon Batty, Ali Brown, Rikki Clarke and Alex Tudor returned to the side, with Ian Ward taking over the captaincy.

When Andrew Strauss won the toss he asked his hosts to bat and, on a day shortened by a couple of brief showers, watched them run up 375-9, which represented a good recovery from low points of 20-2, 131-5 and 232-7. Graham Thorpe (51) had led the first stage of the recovery before falling to Simon Cook (3-77), while Rikki Clarke had made a very impressive eighty-five before he was eighth out to Ashley Noffke (3-91) with the total on 283. Ian Salisbury (40), Saqlain Mushtaq (40 not out) and James Ormond (32 not out) then boosted the total to unexpected heights during the final session.

On the second morning, Saqlain advanced to an unbeaten sixty-one, Ormond to a Surrey-best forty-seven and the hosts to a total of 411. Middlesex then responded positively, with Strauss and Sven Koenig (42) posting a 101-run opening stand before Tudor removed the latter just before the break.

The batsmen continued to dominate after the restart, bringing up their side's 150 in the thirty-fourth over and taking the score up to 163-1 before a quite extraordinary couple of overs appeared to transform the game. After Ormond trapped Strauss lbw for a fine eighty-seven with the first ball of his eleventh over, he followed up by capturing the scalps of Ben Hutton (very well caught down the legside by Batty), Ed Joyce (lbw) and Paul Weekes (bowled) with balls four, five and six, to set the crowd alight and reduce the visitors to 165-5. Ormond's hat-trick of left-handers was the first recorded instance in the County Championship, as was his capture of four left-handers in six deliveries. When Bicknell then removed Owais Shah in the next over, Surrey had taken five wickets in nine balls, and Middlesex, at 165-6, suddenly looked be struggling to save the follow-on. It was hugely disappointing for the hosts, therefore, that the innings took a rapid about-turn at this point, with David Nash and Abdul Razzaq (78) adding 155 for the seventh wicket - thanks partly to a few dropped catches of varying difficulty - either side of tea. By the close, Nash (69 not out) had taken the visitors to within sight of Surrey's score, at 346-8.

Since the contest was evenly balanced, it was a shame that rain wrecked the rest of the match, with day three wiped out completely - the first time a whole day had been lost to the weather at Guildford since 1985 - and only forty overs bowled on the final day, during which Middlesex were bowled out for 385 (Nash 96 not out, Bicknell 4-102, Ormond 4-106) and Surrey replied with 94-0.

Having won their game in hand while Surrey sat out the round of Championship matches prior to Twenty20 Finals Day, and then drawn with Nottinghamshire at Trent Bridge, Sussex were now just five points behind the leaders.

COUNTY CHAMPIONSHIP - TOP OF THE TABLE AT 28TH JULY				
	P	W	D	L	PTS
Surrey	10	5	5	0	159.00
Sussex	10	6	1	3	154.00
Lancashire	9	2	7	0	117.00

Surrey looked to have a good opportunity to get back to winning ways in the NCL when they took on the Worcestershire Royals on the Sunday of the Guildford Festival, since the visitors had lost their last four matches in the competition and languished in eighth place in the table. The Lions were hit by a couple of new injuries, however, with Graham Thorpe and Ian Ward forced to miss the game, though Adam Hollioake returned from a back complaint.

When the Surrey captain won the toss he elected to field, with the ground and pitch very damp after all the rain that had fallen in the previous forty-eight hours. His decision was clearly correct, and it was soon justified as Ormond (3-46) and the outstanding Bicknell (9-4-17-1) reduced the

Royals to 40-3 after ten overs. With the hosts' two most experienced bowlers having delivered sixteen of the first eighteen overs, a lot of responsibility was now left on the shoulders of the rest of the attack, and the canny Ben Smith recovered from a difficult start to exploit this. Receiving useful support from Andrew Hall (32) and Gareth Batty (23 not out from 20 balls), he completed a very mature fifty from 80 balls and then batted through the rest of the innings to finish unbeaten on a well-paced ninety-three out of a total of 219-6.

With Worcestershire having a strong hand of seamers, and the ball still moving around quite dramatically, 220 looked to be a testing target, and so it proved. Once Kabir Ali (4-30) had removed Brown and Ramprakash for four apiece during an excellent opening spell of 7-1-23-4, Surrey's inexperienced batting line-up was exposed, and it quickly crumbled away to leave the home side in desperate trouble at 55-5. Although captain Hollioake (33) did his best to refloat the sinking ship, Matt Mason then produced an impressive burst of 4-34 to sweep away the rest of the middle order, leaving Saqlain Mushtaq (27 not out) and his fellow tailenders to give the score a degree of respectability by adding forty-one for the last two wickets, taking it up to 140. This was the home county's lowest total in a one-day game at Guildford since 1982, and their 79-run defeat enabled Gloucestershire and Glamorgan to close ranks at the head of the league table.

NCL DIVISION ONE - TOP OF THE TABLE AT 27TH JULY							
	P	W	L	T	A	PTS	NRR
Gloucestershire	9	6	2	0	1	26	9.21
Surrey	9	6	2	0	1	26	1.09
Glamorgan	9	6	3	0	0	24	7.68

Surrey's season now reached a crucial stage with their next two matches being against their principal rivals in the two leagues - after a Championship match against Sussex at Hove, they were to face Gloucestershire under lights at The Oval in the NCL. The results of these games would go some way towards deciding if they would end the season with one, two or three trophies in the cabinet.

At Hove, Surrey were without Alec Stewart, Mark Butcher (England) and Alex Tudor (injured), but welcomed back Azhar Mahmood, while second-placed Sussex had both Kevin Innes and Jason Lewry unavailable through injury. When Chris Adams won the toss he elected to bat, and enjoyed the morning session as his openers racked up 148 runs from thirty-five overs. After a few early edges to third man by Richard Montgomerie off Martin Bicknell, the opening pair were quick to take advantage of some uncharacteristically indisciplined Surrey bowling. Murray Goodwin was first to a fine fifty from just 58 balls, while Montgomerie completed a more patchy effort from 84 deliveries, though neither man was able to go on and reach three figures. The Zimbabwean departed shortly after lunch for seventy-five, losing his off stump to a great delivery from James Ormond, while Montgomerie laboured long into the afternoon session before eventually being bowled by Ian Salisbury for ninety after the leg-spinner was belatedly introduced into the attack. By tea, the home side had reached 246-3, with the previously out-of-form Adams having batted increasingly well to complete an 85-ball half-century.

The Sussex captain then confirmed he was back to his best by reaching his first Championship century for fifteen months during the final session of the day. His tremendous 169-ball innings couldn't have come at a better time for his side and had certainly put the south coast county in the driving seat when stumps were drawn at 362-4. Surrey's only post-tea success had come when the criminally underbowled Salisbury had Tim Ambrose (43) taken at slip by Azhar Mahmood after the Anglo-Australian had added ninety-eight with his captain for the fourth-wicket.

On a rain-truncated second morning, Surrey made something of a comeback, with Adams (107) sportingly walking when Batty held a fine legside catch off Ormond (4-106) from the second ball of the day, and two more wickets falling to the same bowler in his next two overs. When Bicknell then removed Robin Martin-Jenkins for forty at 415-8, the visitors were looking highly likely to polish off the innings before lunch, but rain swept in to drive the players from the field just after noon.

Although Bicknell and Azhar soon lopped off the Sussex tail after play resumed at 1.45pm, with the hosts having added just sixty-seven runs to their overnight score for the loss of six wickets, the rest of the session belonged to the home side as they plunged their visitors into danger at 116-5. With the Sussex bowlers seemingly much more fired-up than their Surrey counterparts, and the conditions more conducive to bowling than they had been on the first day, only Mark Ramprakash batted with any degree of certainty as Sussex took charge.

Fortunately for the Championship leaders, Ramprakash eventually found a solid ally in Bicknell, after Azhar had fallen lbw to Mushtaq Ahmed with the total on 126, and the seventh-wicket pair managed to bat through to the close at 212-6, with Ramprakash on seventy-four and Bicknell on forty-two.

Surrey needed a further sixty-eight runs to avoid the follow-on as the third day began, and ended up achieving this quite easily, despite the loss of both Bicknell and Salisbury to Mushtaq (4-123) with only five runs added to the overnight score. Although there was a great deal of pressure on Ramprakash and his ninth-wicket partner, Saqlain, when they first came together, they survived a couple of scares to add eighty-four runs and keep their team out of immediate danger. Saqlain had certainly looked fortunate to survive a run out appeal with the total on 248, while Ramprakash should probably have been caught from the miscued hook shot that took him to a battling century, constructed with the utmost skill from 211 balls. Although the Surrey number three fell shortly afterwards, to James Kirtley's first delivery with the new ball, for 104, Saqlain (68) and Ormond (42 not out) then enjoyed themselves immensely during a last-wicket partnership that took their side's final total up to 355 before Martin-Jenkins (3-67) bowled Saqlain.

The visiting bowlers then tested Sussex's resolve with some much improved second-innings bowling that restricted the hosts to 67-2 from twenty-eight overs, before Goodwin and Adams accepted an offer to go off for bad light with thirty-seven overs remaining for play. Since their team was already leading by 143 runs, it seemed a slightly strange decision by the batsmen, but it was their prerogative to go off and wait for the light to improve. Unfortunately, the grey clouds over the County Ground refused to budge and no further play was possible.

Hopes of an interesting final day receded somewhat during the morning session, as Sussex added ninety-eight runs in thirty-four overs for the loss of Goodwin (29) and Adams (23). With Surrey unable to win the match by bowling the opposition out, everything now depended on whether the home side wanted to declare and set up a run chase later in the afternoon, which seemed a possibility, since Sussex's remaining fixtures looked more demanding than the matches facing the County Champions. Chris Adams clearly didn't see things that way, however, as he elected to bat on until the score was 302-5 and the game was a certain draw, much to the disappointment of many in the ground, including a large proportion of his own supporters. Towards the end of the Sussex innings, Surrey had revealed their frustration, with Saqlain and Salisbury sending down a couple of overs of seamers, and Hollioake delivering an over of leg-spin, though they really only had themselves to blame for the situation they found themselves in, having performed so poorly for the first day-and-a-half of the contest.

With Sussex taking twelve points from the match to Surrey's eleven, they had succeeded in trimming the leaders' advantage by a single point.

LEADING POSITIONS:- Surrey P11, Pts 170; Sussex P11, Pts 166; Lancs P10, Pts 139

While the status quo had been maintained in the Championship, Keith Medlycott's men had ground to make up in the NCL, since Gloucestershire had moved four points clear at the top -

thanks to a victory over the Yorkshire Phoenix - while Surrey had been completing their match at Hove. Luckily for all concerned, the floodlit top-of-the-table clash at The Oval was blessed with fine weather, though the two teams had disparate news to report at the toss. While the Lions were able to field something akin to a full-strength side, their visitors were without three key men, since Jonty Rhodes and Mike Smith were injured, and Ian Harvey was away with Australia.

Surrey were then further boosted by winning the toss, and no one was surprised when they elected to bat first. After Ian Ward had made a fairly early exit at 34-1, the second-wicket pair of Ali Brown and Mark Ramprakash piled into the Gladiators' bowling to raise the Surrey hundred in the fifteenth over, by which time Brown had completed a stunning 37-ball half-century. Although he then departed four overs later to a fine catch by Jon Lewis at long-off with the total on 130, Brown's 61-ball eighty-four had set the Lions up for a very big score. With Ramprakash moving along steadily at one end, and Graham Thorpe and Rikki Clarke able to be a little more expansive at the other while each scoring thirty-six, the pace of the innings rarely slackened and the total reached 250 in the forty-first over, shortly after the former Middlesex batsman had been dismissed for eighty-three from 102 balls. Azhar Mahmood then put the icing on the Surrey cake by scoring twenty-one from thirteen deliveries, leaving the Lions sitting pretty with a total of 297-6.

In front of a crowd in the region of 7,500, Gloucestershire made a flying start to their reply, with Craig Spearman and Philip Weston putting seventy on the board inside nine overs, before Bicknell broke through by having the latter well caught by Jon Batty standing up to the stumps. Unperturbed by this loss, Spearman went on to complete a sensational half-century from 33 balls, and when the Gladiators' hundred came up in the twelfth over it was clear that the Lions had a real battle on their hands. Fortunately for Surrey, with the total advanced to 114, Rikki Clarke produced a fine piece of fielding to throw down the non-striker's stumps from backward point, thereby removing Alex Gidman for fifteen, and then came up with an 'action replay' in the next over to dispose of Matt Windows with just three runs added to the score. Then, quite incredibly, Shoaib Malik became the visitors' third run-out victim in five overs shortly afterwards - with Thorpe the man to score a direct hit on the stumps this time - leaving Gloucestershire struggling a little at 125-4. The decisive moment of the innings came with the score on 156, however, when Spearman clipped a Clarke full-toss straight to James Benning, a substitute fielder, at deep backward square leg, ending a marvellous knock of eighty-five from 73 balls. With their main man gone, the Gladiators never looked likely to threaten Surrey's total again, losing two more wickets to run outs and two to Clarke (3-48) in subsiding to 231 all out. The Lions' 66-run triumph not only enabled them to draw level on points with Gloucestershire at the top of the table, it also reduced the gap that existed between the sides in terms of net run rate, which had the potential to be decisive at the end of the season if two teams had the same number of points and wins.

NCL DIVISION ONE - TOP OF THE TABLE AT 5TH AUGUST						
	P	W	L	T	A	PTS	NRR
Gloucestershire	11	7	3	0	1	30	7.31
Surrey	10	7	2	0	1	30	3.76
Glamorgan	11	6	5	0	0	24	0.39

Following a week's break, Surrey broke new ground by staging their first-ever Championship match at Whitgift School, South Croydon, against bottom-of-the-table Nottinghamshire. The visitors had proved to be every bit as unpredictable as many had felt they might be at the start of the summer, with their performances on grass not matching up to those they looked capable of achieving on paper! Their line-up for the Whitgift debut match looked far stronger than the eleven that had performed so poorly at Trent Bridge in May when they had sat fleetingly atop the table, with Stuart MacGill, Chris Cairns, Kevin Pietersen and Russell Warren all available this time round. Surrey, meanwhile, were lacking their England men plus the injured James Ormond as Adam Hollioake won the toss on a glorious morning and elected to bat.

No one was exactly sure what to expect from the playing surface as the game got under way, though the first impressions were very good and, by the end of day one, it was clear that the pitch inspectors wouldn't need to be called in... Surrey were 488-8! After losing Ian Ward and Jon Batty for seventeen apiece by the time the score reached forty-one, the third-wicket pairing of Mark Ramprakash and Graham Thorpe batted quite beautifully to add 241 in fifty-seven overs against some largely unimpressive bowling on a track that possessed more than enough pace and bounce to make for interesting and entertaining cricket. After completing relatively sedate half-centuries shortly after lunch, from 106 and 107 balls respectively, Thorpe and Ramprakash accelerated during the afternoon before the former was caught behind off Cairns for ninety-nine from 162 deliveries and the latter reached a flawless century from his 168th ball. Having taken tea at 310-3, the hosts then pressed on positively, with Ramprakash continuing to play with textbook excellence at one end, while Rikki Clarke, Ali Brown and Azhar Mahmood notched run-a-ball twenties and thirties to keep the suffering bowlers under pressure in the heat. Paul Franks, who removed Brown and Hollioake with consecutive deliveries, was the only man to enjoy much success, while the two overseas bowlers, Cairns and MacGill received some particularly rough treatment. With Ramprakash unbeaten on 191 at close of play, having given everyone a batting masterclass, Surrey could reflect on a fine first day that had left them holding all the aces.

After making a surprisingly edgy start to day two, Ramprakash eventually moved through to the ninth double-century of his career from 311 balls, earning a well-deserved ovation for his supreme efforts. Any hopes Nottinghamshire might have had about wrapping up the Surrey innings quickly were wrecked by Ian Salisbury and Saqlain Mushtaq, who not only supported their top-order colleague but also matched him stroke for stroke during successive record-breaking hundred-plus partnerships that extended the Surrey score to 693 and the visitors' misery until lunchtime. Salisbury (65 from 66 balls) helped Ramprakash add 129 for the ninth wicket before falling to the deserving Franks (3-91), then Saqlain (50 from 57 balls) notched his third successive Championship half-century during a last-wicket stand of 107 before being well caught down the legside off Greg Smith (3-110), who had probably been the best of Nottinghamshire's bad bunch. Although Ramprakash was left stranded on 279 after batting for 400 balls and hitting forty fours and four sixes, he'd at least had the satisfaction of recording a new career-best; setting a new mark for the highest individual score in Surrey versus Nottinghamshire matches; and sharing in two record-breaking stands for this fixture.

Needing the small matter of 544 to avoid the follow-on, the visitors were immediately plunged into desperate trouble by Martin Bicknell, who removed their top three batsmen - including brother Darren lbw - for twenty. Russell Warren and Kevin Pietersen then fought back briefly in their different styles, but the loss of the latter to Saqlain for seventy-nine with the total on 133 shortly after tea was a body blow to Nottinghamshire. Although Chris Cairns, captaining the side in Jason Gallian's absence, made twenty-six before becoming the first of two victims in two overs for the returning Bicknell, it was nowhere near enough as his side stumbled towards the inevitable follow-on. Despite having been reduced to 196-6 by Bicknell's excellent burst that had completed a five-wicket haul for the Surrey seamer, Warren and his new partner, Paul Franks, resisted stoutly for a while and looked like they might take their side safely through to the close. Disaster struck in the closing overs, however, as Hollioake's decision to replace Bicknell (5-42) and Azhar with Salisbury and Saqlain paid dividends - after 189 balls of grim defiance, Warren was trapped lbw for seventy-six by a Salisbury googly, then Franks was caught at slip off Saqlain from the last ball of the day, leaving the visitors in dire straits at 224-8.

Nottinghamshire's first innings was polished off with indecent haste on the third morning, with the Surrey spinners taking just thirty-four deliveries to share the remaining spoils. Having added just sixteen runs, to be all out for 240, the visitors trailed by a massive 453 runs, and by lunch they had virtually surrendered. After losing Guy Welton for a pair to the first ball of the second over bowled by Azhar, Bicknell nipped in with the wicket of Usman Afzaal, before the Pakistani removed the Nottinghamshire Bicknell for three and Warren for nine to leave the visiting team in real strife at 19-4. Both bowlers then continued to wreak havoc as Azhar (4-45) had Cairns very well caught at fourth slip by Hollioake with the score on thirty-five, and Bicknell lured the dangerous Pietersen into driving a catch to extra cover to make the score 45-6. Although Chris Read and Paul Franks then put together a stand of eighty-four that extended beyond lunch, with Read completing a game fifty from 74 balls shortly after Franks's departure to Hollioake, Surrey were already sure to clinch their sixth Championship victory of the season. Another impressive stand of 104 between Read and Smith (42) delayed the inevitable, though the end came quickly once the Nottinghamshire wicketkeeper was taken at slip off Salisbury for a brave ninety-three at 233-8. Saqlain quickly disposed of Smith and MacGill to seal victory by an innings and 211 runs, with the visitors having done marginally better second time around, recording a total of 242 as opposed to 240.

With the Surrey players and supporters celebrating an impressively efficient win, and the Whitgift authorities basking in the glow of a successful first foray into staging a four-day county match, it seemed that just about everyone bar the visiting team was happy.

Although this victory took Surrey twenty-six points clear of Sussex at the time it was completed, the south coast side managed to pull off an incredible last-gasp triumph over Lancashire two days later to move back within five points of the leaders and seemingly reduce the title race to a straight fight between the two home counties teams.

COUNTY CHAMPIONSHIP - TOP OF THE TABLE AT 17TH AUGUST					
	P	W	D	L	PTS
Surrey	12	6	6	0	192.00
Sussex	12	7	2	3	187.00
Lancashire	11	3	7	1	146.00

Having suffered three defeats in their last four NCL games, the Glamorgan Dragons arrived at Whitgift needing to beat the Surrey Lions if they were to stay in contention for the title.

After naming the same side that had beaten the Gloucestershire Gladiators, Adam Hollioake won the toss and elected to bat on what appeared to be another fine pitch, though his side struggled a little early on as Ali Brown fell to Andrew Davies, and Michael Kasprowicz bowled a tight opening spell. Although the scoring rate began to pick up once the big Australian was removed from the attack after delivering six overs, the Dragons still maintained a fair deal of control, with Dale removing Ian Ward (44) with the total on ninety-three, and the scoreboard showing 123-2 after twenty-seven overs. At this point, with Mark Ramprakash having just completed a fine half-century from 57 balls and Graham Thorpe having begun to establish himself at the crease, the Glamorgan spinners were despatched for forty-five runs from five overs. Surrey never looked back thereafter as Ramprakash stormed through to a marvellous 91-ball century before falling to the occasional seamers of Jimmy Maher for 101, and Thorpe accelerated to his personal fifty from 56 balls. Azhar Mahmood then contributed twelve runs from just five deliveries before Adam Hollioake entered the fray to blast an incredible forty-one from sixteen balls, four of which he hit for six and two for four, until he became a third victim for Maher (3-0-29-3). With Thorpe also locating the boundary on a number of occasions in the closing stages to finish unbeaten on seventy-seven from 72 balls, an astonishing 110 runs had been added from the final nine overs of an innings that ended on 298-5.

Needing to produce a run-chasing display not dissimilar to the one that took them so close to a historical victory in the famous C&G Trophy game of 2002, Glamorgan suffered two early setbacks, with Maher and Croft (31) both back in the pavilion by the end of the ninth over with the total on fifty. Mike Powell and Matt Maynard brought them right back into contention, however, with a stand of eighty-seven for the third wicket, during which the former completed an excellent fifty from just 37 balls. It was a real blow to the Dragons' hopes, therefore, when Powell was bowled by Saqlain for sixty-one in the twenty-first over, especially as it prefaced a very good seven-over period for the Lions, during which the off-spinner (1-36) and the recalled Ormond restricted the scoring and piled pressure on the batsmen. Maynard (41) eventually cracked, punching a catch back to Ormond (2-45) with the total on 159, and with the required run rate quickly rising to nine an over, Glamorgan were guilty of some panicky batting, especially against the Surrey captain when he belatedly brought himself into the attack for the thirty-fifth over. From 189-4 after thirty-three overs they collapsed to 240 all out in 39.4 overs, with Hollioake claiming 3-22 to seal his side's 58-run victory and take them to the top of the table.

NCL DIVISION ONE - TOP OF THE TABLE AT 17TH AUGUST						
	P	W	L	T	A	PTS	NRR
Surrey	11	8	2	0	1	34	5.58
Gloucestershire	11	7	3	0	1	30	7.31
Glamorgan	13	7	6	0	0	28	-0.83

As Surrey prepared to head up to Leicester for their next matches in the two leagues - which now both looked to be two-horse races - they were forced to leave Martin Bicknell behind, since he had received a shock call-up from the England selectors for the fourth Test against South Africa at Headingley. With the likes of Harmison, Hoggard, Jones and Johnson all out injured, it appeared that the Surrey veteran would finally play for his country again after ten years in the wilderness, and everyone was hoping he would show the selectors how wrong they had been to ignore his very valid claims for so long.

The National League game at Grace Road was a floodlit affair, so it preceded the Championship fixture and gave Surrey a chance to move eight points clear at the head of the table. With Ian Salisbury having been announced as Bicknell's replacement in the Lions' side, Phil DeFreitas won the toss for the sixth-placed Foxes, chose to bat, and then opened the innings himself with John Maunders. The latter departed quickly to James Ormond, who bowled his nine overs off the reel to claim 2-38, his second victim having been DeFreitas for thirty-nine with the total on seventy-three at the end of the seventeenth over. Although Darren Maddy and Brad Hodge then took the score into three figures in the twenty-first over and posted a 40-run stand that ended with the Australian's dismissal for forty-six, Surrey were on top for most of the remaining overs of the innings, thanks to the outstanding combination of Salisbury (1-37) and Hollioake (4-35). While Maddy progressed to a half-century from 69 balls and went on to make sixty-six from 87 deliveries, John Sadler (27 from 23 balls) was the only other batsman to make a significant impact as the innings fizzled out at 217-8.

With DeFreitas unable to take the field after being struck on the toe by a yorker during his innings, the Foxes were already up against it as Surrey began their reply, and though they started well, with Dagnall having Ali Brown badly missed at slip on one, it wasn't long before the Lions' openers took control. After the visitors' fifty had been raised in the eighth over, Brown roared on to a brilliant 37-ball half-century during a 23-run opening over from David Masters that included two sixes and two fours. When the former Kent seamer then conceded a further fourteen runs from his second over, taking the score to 106-0 after twelve, the game suddenly looked to be as good as over, and Surrey decided that they had a great opportunity to improve their net run rate.

Once Brown fell to Hodge for a sensational eighty-nine (65 balls, fourteen fours, two sixes) with the total on 131 after 15.3 overs, Azhar Mahmood (11 from 10 balls), Adam Hollioake (28 from 21) and Rikki Clarke (14 not out from 9) were promoted up the order to provide some fireworks. Ian Ward, meanwhile, reached fifty from just 47 deliveries, and ended unbeaten on seventy from 65 balls as the Lions raced to a seven-wicket victory in 28.2 overs, taking their net run rate ahead of Gloucestershire's. If they could maintain that supremacy then it would be worth an extra point come the end of the season.

NCL DIVISION ONE - TOP OF THE TABLE AT 20TH AUGUST						
	P	W	L	T	A	PTS	NRR
Surrey	12	9	2	0	1	38	8.45
Gloucestershire	11	7	3	0	1	30	7.31
Glamorgan	13	7	6	0	0	28	-0.83

With the Championship fixture starting on the same day as the Test Match, Surrey received an early boost with the news that Martin Bicknell had been selected at Headingley - creating a new record by returning to Test cricket after an absence of 114 matches - and had taken two early wickets.

His county side meanwhile elected to bat after deciding to omit the unlucky Ali Brown from their side in favour of an extra bowler in Tim Murtagh, and made steady progress to reach 88-0 at lunch on what looked to be a good pitch. Although the Leicestershire captain, Phil DeFreitas - clearly struggling with his injured toe - quickly went on the defensive after lunch, his side gradually worked their way back into the game at 178-3, with both Surrey openers making their exits shortly after reaching fifty and Mark Ramprakash (59) doing likewise after playing quite beautifully for seventy deliveries. The final session of the day saw Surrey taking charge, however, with Graham Thorpe (77 balls) and Rikki Clarke (55 balls) making it five out of five batsmen to record a fifty during a 169-run stand for the fourth wicket. Although the partnership ended in the penultimate over of the day when Thorpe (87) was adjudged to have been caught down the legside by wicketkeeper Paul Nixon off Jeremy Snape, Surrey were well placed on 349-4 at stumps, with Clarke unbeaten on ninety.

Despite the early loss of nightwatchman Saqlain Mushtaq for thirteen the next morning, Clarke progressed to a splendid century from 133 balls and, in partnership with his captain, took the total beyond four-hundred, despite some much improved Leicestershire bowling with the second new ball. Once Adam Hollioake played on to Vasbert Drakes (3-85) with the score on 420, Surrey's innings fell away to 501 all out, though, as they lost four wickets to the West Indian paceman and Snape (3-108), and Azhar Mahmood to the local A&E Department when the helmetless all-rounder top-edged a sweep into his nose. In the midst of this mini-collapse, Clarke's fine innings had ended at 139 from 199 balls.

Having started their reply shortly after lunch, the visitors found themselves in real trouble by tea, with half their side out for ninety-eight. After Ormond and Murtagh had removed the openers, Maunders and Maddy, Clarke's excellent match had continued with a three-wicket burst that took out the middle-order trio of Hodge, Sadler and Snape. It wasn't all good news for Surrey, however, since their skipper had left the field with what was said to be a viral infection, while Mark Ramprakash had been struck a fearful blow on the shoulder while fielding at short leg and looked to be in severe discomfort for the rest of the session.

With the rest of the day blighted by bad light, the Championship leaders were only able to make two further breakthroughs - when Murtagh (3-68) bowled both Damian Brandy and Phil DeFreitas for four apiece - leaving their hosts in even greater strife at 112-7 before Nixon and Drakes took them through to the early closure at 127-7. Since Sussex had already thrashed Essex by an innings and 120 runs at Colchester, Surrey knew that they had to go on and win this game in order to stay top of the table. At the halfway point in the match, that seemed quite likely, so long as the weather didn't interfere.

It appeared even more certain the following morning when Salisbury and Clarke, who returned career-best figures of 4-31, finished off the Foxes for 166, and forced them to follow on 335 runs in arrears.

With Adam Hollioake surprisingly back in action, but Mark Ramprakash (shoulder) and Azhar Mahmood (confirmed broken nose) confined to the dressing room by their injuries, the visitors made an important breakthrough before lunch when Maddy was caught behind off Clarke with the total on forty-nine, though the afternoon session turned out to be something of a nightmare for them. After a fairly quiet start, John Maunders stepped up a gear to complete a 134-ball fifty, while Brad Hodge rushed to the same mark in a mere fifty-two deliveries, raising the hundred partnership in the process. With Azhar's absence suddenly becoming a factor, the Victorian continued to find the boundary with astonishing regularity, converting his half-century into a hugely impressive hundred in the space of a further thirty-five deliveries, while Maunders registered a career-best score when he reached seventy-seven. By the time tea arrived, the score had advanced to 257-1, with the visitors having lost control during a session that saw Leicestershire add 201 runs and ended with Hodge on 118 and Maunders on ninety.

The appearance of Azhar after tea suggested that the visitors were concerned about the situation, though he was unable to make a breakthrough for his side during a brave spell that saw Maunders arrive at his maiden first-class century from the 219th delivery of his innings. The former Middlesex batsman's fine knock had pulled his side right back into the game, and he continued to defy the bowlers after Hodge departed to a catch by Batty off Salisbury for a magnificent career-best 157 from 169 balls that had included no fewer than twenty-nine fours. Although the last ten overs of the day from the spinners yielded a few scares for the batsmen and just eighteen runs, taking the total from 330 to 348, Leicestershire led by thirteen runs and had greatly improved their chances of securing a draw on the final day.

With a new ball in their hands and the skies overcast at the start of play, Surrey were optimistic about claiming some early wickets, but Maunders and John Sadler resisted stoutly and survived everything that the bowlers could throw at them throughout the morning session, during which the former completed his 150 from 355 balls and the latter reached a 129-ball fifty. Surrey's hopes of victory looked to be fading fast since the Foxes, on 454-2 at lunch, led by 119 runs.

Hopes that Phil DeFreitas might want to set up a run chase later in the day, since his eighth-placed side needed a win as badly as his opponents did - were then dashed during the afternoon as the home side continued to bat on. Although Maunders (171) fell to Salisbury shortly after the restart, it soon became obvious that the match was heading for a draw, and the visitors showed their disappointment by resorting to 'joke' bowling from Ian Ward and Graham Thorpe. Sadler took advantage of this to emulate his erstwhile partner by recording a very valuable maiden first-class hundred from 186 balls, the vast majority of which had been delivered by the front-line bowlers, and progressed to 145 before perishing to Thorpe. Although DeFreitas did eventually declare at 636-4, setting his visitors a notional 302 to win in eighty-five minutes plus sixteen overs, they unsurprisingly batted out the game at 117-2, thereby conceding the lead in the title race to Sussex.

COUNTY CHAMPIONSHIP - TOP OF THE TABLE AT 24TH AUGUST				
	P	W	D	L	PTS
Sussex	13	8	2	3	209.00
Surrey	13	6	7	0	204.00
Lancashire	12	3	8	1	156.00

A crass piece of fixture-scheduling now left both Surrey and their opponents, Lancashire, just one day's break before they clashed at Old Trafford in what appeared to be a vital match for both sides - Surrey needed to win in order to regain the leadership of the Championship from Sussex, while Lancashire had to triumph if they were to retain any hope of winning the title.

Although Azhar Mahmood and Adam Hollioake were passed fit to play in the match, Mark Ramprakash missed out because of his shoulder injury, and Martin Bicknell - who had picked up a hamstring strain while taking 2-50 and 2-75 in England's defeat at Headingley - was allowed to rest, in the hope that he would retain his place in the squad for the final match of the series at The Oval.

After Warren Hegg had revealed that Mal Loye was to miss the game because of back spasms, he lost the toss - to his obvious annoyance - and found his weary side condemned to a day in the field. It looked like it would be a long day, too, when Jon Batty and Graham Thorpe added 104 for the second wicket after the early exit of Ian Ward to Peter Martin, but they fought back well after lunch. Having removed Thorpe for fifty-seven, they captured the middle-order scalps of Clarke, Brown and Hollioake for just five runs as Surrey subsided to 148-5. Batty, who had played quite immaculately to reach a half-century from 97 balls just before the interval, then found an ideal ally in Azhar Mahmood, and this pair put together an excellent stand of 113 either side of tea to regain the initiative for the visitors. The Surrey wicketkeeper had already registered a superb 205-ball century when he lost Azhar (63) to Gary Keedy (3-62), though his side remained on top while Ian Salisbury and Saqlain Mushtaq played supporting roles at the other end during stands of thirty-seven and thirty-one. Unfortunately for the visitors, their hopes of subjecting their tired hosts to another lengthy period in the field the next morning were shattered in indifferent light at the end of the day when two wickets fell in three balls to John Wood with the total on 330.

With Martin dismissing Tim Murtagh early the next morning, Jon Batty was left stranded on 154, becoming the first Surrey player to carry his bat against Lancashire since Tom Hayward in 1907, and the first batsman from the county to do so at Old Trafford since Harry Jupp in 1870. It had been an absolutely terrific innings, spanning 283 balls, and had been almost entirely responsible for his team totalling 337.

By removing Iain Sutcliffe and Mark Chilton before lunch, the visitors looked to have gained a clear advantage, but a third-wicket stand of 109 between Stuart Law and Mark Currie - the 23-year-old debutant Cheshire batsman who was standing in for Mal Loye - put the hosts back on top during the first half of the afternoon. Ian Ward, who had taken over the captaincy from the ailing Adam Hollioake after lunch, managed to come up with a winning combination at this point, though, pairing Salisbury and Ormond to great effect. Once Law had gone for an excellent sixty-seven and the thrice-dropped Currie's good fortune had run out at fifty-six, the home side crumbled to 183-6, with each bowler bagging a pair of scalps. A minor recovery to 221-6 by Carl Hooper and Warren Hegg was then followed by another stumble to 262-9 against Azhar and Salisbury (3-70), leaving the red rose county in a spot of bother, since they were still trailing by seventy-five runs. Having been joined at the wicket by Gary Keedy, Hooper responded positively by completing a 71-ball half-century, and then proceeded to play a masterful innings that had the Surrey team tearing their hair out. Manipulating the strike with stolen singles and thumping the ball to the boundary in between times, the former West Indies captain left Keedy with very few balls to face, while also increasing the total at a rate of knots. There was a distinct feeling that the balance of power was shifting as Hooper raced to a tremendous ton from 124 balls and took his team into the lead before carving a delivery from Azhar (4-76) with the new ball to Salisbury at third man. While Hooper had made his way to a breathtaking 114 out of a total of 341, Keedy had contributed just one run from 36 balls to a vital last-wicket stand of seventy-nine. Since the light had closed in quite badly, Surrey were spared the need to bat before the close, but there was no doubt about which side would be the happier with the match position at the halfway stage of the contest.

Day three started with good news on the NCL front, since Gloucestershire's defeat at the hands of Kent the previous evening had left the Lions four points clear of the Gladiators with a game in hand. Things didn't go so well in the match Surrey were playing, however, as they slipped to 23-3 in bowler-friendly conditions after overnight rain and morning drizzle had delayed the start until 11.45am. They almost lost Ali Brown shortly afterwards, too, with umpire Barrie Leadbeater erroneously giving the batsman out caught behind off his helmet before realising his mistake and changing his mind, much to the relief of the Surrey players and supporters. Brown and Graham Thorpe then proceeded to restore some balance to the contest with a battling partnership of seventy before the visitors self-destructed at the hands of Gary Keedy (4-57). Once Thorpe (38) had edged Wood to Hegg, the left-arm spinner disposed of Azhar, Hollioake, Salisbury and Brown (61) at a cost of four runs in the space of twelve deadly deliveries, with three of the batsmen playing a significant part in their own demise. Although rain ended play for the day after Saqlain Mushtaq and James Ormond had taken the total from a grisly 122-8 to 137-8, Lancashire now looked highly likely to win tomorrow and put a huge dent in Surrey's title hopes.

There were no heroics form the tail on the final morning as Saqlain - caught off Martin, who finished with 3-20 - and Ormond - stupidly run out - lasted just seven balls. Needing a paltry 135 to win, Lancashire hustled home in 30.4 overs for the loss of two wickets, leaving Sussex as red-hot favourites to claim their first-ever Championship crown.

COUNTY CHAMPIONSHIP - TOP OF THE TABLE AT 29TH AUGUST					
	P	W	D	L	PTS
Surrey	14	6	7	1	210.00
Sussex	13	8	2	3	209.00
Lancashire	13	4	8	1	176.00

The team needed to put the disappointment of their first Championship defeat in over a year behind them quickly, since they had a very important NCL fixture at Headingley against the bottom team in the division, Yorkshire Phoenix, two days later.

With Mark Ramprakash still sidelined because of his injury, and Saqlain Mushtaq having been surprisingly called up at short notice to play for Pakistan in a Test against Bangladesh, the Lions' side showed two changes from their last National League outing, as Mark Butcher and Martin Bicknell were allowed a run-out ahead of the final Test at The Oval. Just to add to Surrey's problems in the Championship, Graham Thorpe had been recalled to the England squad in place of the injured Nasser Hussain, which meant he would miss the next game, against Kent at Canterbury.

Having lost the toss and been put in to bat by Anthony McGrath, the visitors made a very promising start, reaching 90-1 in the sixteenth over, before Ali Brown was bowled by the Yorkshire captain immediately after completing a very fine fifty from just 49 balls. This turned out to be the first of four wickets for McGrath (4-41) as Surrey slumped to 126-6, and from that point onwards their innings was sustained almost entirely by a combination of Rikki Clarke's mature unbeaten forty-six, and thirty-one extras, including twenty wides. With Jon Batty the only batsman in the bottom half of the order to reach double figures, the innings ended four balls early when the visitors were bowled out for 202.

The Lions' seamers hit back well, however, with Bicknell (1-21) removing the dangerous Stephen Fleming for twenty-seven, and James Ormond (2-28) picking up two wickets in rapid succession as the Phoenix struggled to 68-4. Michael Vaughan and Vic Craven joined forces to steady the ship, however, adding 120 runs for the fifth wicket and seemingly putting the relegation-threatened side on course for a priceless victory. With just fifteen runs needed from twenty balls, Clarke finally broke the partnership, running Craven out for forty-seven at the striker's end with a fine piece of footwork, though it appeared to be little more than a consolation wicket, especially when Vaughan clipped Azhar to square leg for four in the next over, reducing his side's target to just nine from fifteen deliveries. Then, with three further singles added to the total, the England captain attempted an unnecessary second run to Ward at deep midwicket and was beaten by the fielder's brilliant pick up and throw. Despite the loss of Vaughan for ninety at 198-6, there still seemed no way Yorkshire could fail to win, since there were eleven balls remaining to be bowled... but the panic that ensued in fading light was quite something to behold. Having failed to score from any of the next four balls, Richard Dawson was bowled by Clarke, then Richard Blakey had his stumps rearranged by Azhar three balls later with the total still stuck on 198. Although the hosts only needed one good stroke to level the scores at this stage, Steve Kirby proved incapable of getting a bat on the next ball and then managed just a single from the penultimate delivery when Hollioake failed to hang on to an awkward catching chance at backward point. With Darren Gough only able to find one run from the last ball, instead of the boundary Yorkshire needed, Surrey ran out most unlikely winners by two runs, thereby extending their lead over the Gladiators to eight points and pushing the Phoenix closer to Division Two.

NCL DIVISION ONE - TOP OF THE TABLE AT 31ST AUGUST							
	P	W	L	T	A	PTS	NRR
Surrey	13	10	2	0	1	42	7.71
Gloucestershire	13	8	4	0	1	34	5.35

With Gloucestershire having squeezed home to a two-run victory of their own against the Warwickshire Bears the day after Surrey's amazing victory at Headingley, the gap at the top of the table was back down to four points as the Lions took on the Kent Spitfires in a day-night game at Canterbury on Wednesday 3rd September. With the home side hovering just above the relegation zone, and Surrey's record in Sunday/National League games on Kentish soil showing just two wins from fifteen attempts, it promised to be a tough fixture. There was also the usual partisan Kent crowd to reckon with, plus the fact that Mark Butcher, Graham Thorpe and Martin Bicknell were now absent with England. Their replacements were Mark Ramprakash, Nadeem Shahid and Franklyn Rose, the former West Indian fast bowler who had been signed late in the day, as an overseas locum for Saqlain Mushtaq, to bolster the seam attack. Although his line-up was lacking Ed Smith, another player on duty with England, Dave Fulton quite predictably chose to bat after winning the toss.

With each of their overseas seamers picking up the scalp of an opening batsman to reduce Kent to 14-2, Surrey were out of the blocks quickly and dominated the first twelve overs, keeping the scoring rate below two runs per over. The picture then changed rapidly as Andrew Symonds cut loose, racing through to a brilliant 37-ball half-century during a partnership of fifty-seven for the fourth wicket with his skipper, after Matt Walker had gone for nineteen in the sixteenth over. Eight overs later, at 109-3, the Spitfires were looking set for a big total, but the game was rapidly transformed when Adam Hollioake snared both Fulton and Symonds in his opening over. Unfortunately for Kent, this turned out to be the start of a most amazing collapse that saw them slip to 142 all out in 31.4 overs, with the Lions' captain snapping up six wickets for seventeen runs in twenty-six deliveries to record career-best figures and put his side on course for victory.

On a pitch that had seemed better suited to bowlers than batsmen, Surrey's task didn't look entirely straightforward, and that was confirmed as the visitors lost wickets at regular intervals in making their way to 73-4 from twenty-one overs. Luckily for the Lions, a typically steady and determined Mark Ramprakash found the perfect foil in his captain, with Hollioake doing the majority of the scoring during a match-winning partnership of sixty that took the league leaders within touching distance of their target. Although Hollioake was caught off Amjad Khan for a nicely judged thirty-eight with the total on 133, Ramprakash was still there on forty-two when Azhar Mahmood sealed a five-wicket triumph with a boundary off the final delivery of the thirty-seventh over. Surrey were now within one victory of winning their second competition of the season.

NCL DIVISION ONE - TOP OF THE TABLE AT 3RD SEPTEMBER					
	P	W	L	T	A	PTS
Surrey	14	11	2	0	1	46
Gloucestershire	14	9	4	0	1	38

Hopes of making it a trophy treble had all but vanished following the results at Grace Road and Old Trafford, with Keith Medlycott's team now needing to win both of their remaining matches and hope that other results fell kindly for them. Their chances of pulling off the first of those victories were greatly reduced, however, by the injuries and Test calls that deprived them of the services of around half of their first-choice line-up for the next game, against Kent at Canterbury. Those hopes then receded further during a morning session that saw Dave Fulton (71) and Michael Carberry (92) piling up 158 runs without loss after the hosts had won the toss. Although Franklyn Rose, on his debut for Surrey in the Championship, and Tim Murtagh hauled Kent back to 191-3 after the break, the visitors' fate was sealed during the rest of the day, as Andrew Symonds notched a sparkling 123 from 121 balls and Mark Ealham weighed in with an unbeaten eighty by the time stumps were drawn at 435-5.

Murtagh (4-130) and Rose (3-101) then performed a decent damage-limitation exercise on the second morning to keep the home team's total down to 535 (Ealham 93), only for Surrey's top-order batting to be blown away before lunch by Amjad Khan and Martin Saggers, who passed fifty first-class wickets for the season in the process of claiming three scalps. After Jon Batty and Rikki Clarke had restored a modicum of respectability to proceedings by taking the score on from 30-4 to 64-4, a further collapse proved fatal, with the last six wickets tumbling for sixty-one to Saggers (4-40), Khan (3-50) and Muttiah Muralitharan (2-11).

Unsurprisingly forced to follow on, 410 runs in arrears, Surrey performed only marginally better second time around, finishing a truly awful day on 169-7, with Ian Ward (53) and Ali Brown (40) the only men to pass twenty and save their side from the ignominy of being bowled out twice in a day.

Although James Ormond (32 from 40 balls) and Franklyn Rose (36 from 26) batted brightly to entertain the small crowd on the third morning, the game was over well before lunch as Saggers (3-37) and Muralitharan (4-90) completed Kent's crushing victory by an innings and 155 runs. Surrey's title hopes had come to a traumatic end, therefore, after suffering their first back-to-back Championship defeats since September 1997, when their conquerors had also been Lancashire and Kent.

LEADING POSITIONS:- Sussex P14, Pts 231; Surrey P15, Pts 213; Lancs P14, Pts 197

Everything was not completely gloomy on the Surrey front, however, as Graham Thorpe - with a first-innings century - and Martin Bicknell - with six wickets - played significant roles in England's series-levelling win over South Africa at The Oval two days later. Alec Stewart, who scored thirty-eight in his last innings, had the satisfaction of ending his 133-Test career with a victory on his home turf.

Having had a week to get over the debacle at Canterbury and get one or two of their injured players fit, Surrey headed off to Cardiff for their penultimate NCL game, against the Glamorgan Dragons, knowing that victory would clinch the title for them.

Sophia Gardens was abuzz with gossip before the game even started, with Alec Stewart having announced his retirement from first-class cricket - having mused earlier in the season about playing one last season with his county side - and Ian Ward having revealed that he was leaving the club to pursue his career elsewhere. The parting of the ways was said to be amicable, yet Ward did not appear in Surrey's line-up and spent his afternoon in the television commentary box while Scott Newman took his place in the team. Although the England pair of Thorpe and Bicknell returned to the Lions' eleven, James Ormond and Azhar Mahmood both missed out through injury.

Having won the toss and elected to bat on a poor-looking wicket, Surrey struggled against the Dragons' seamers in the early stages and were in trouble at 61-4 when Rikki Clarke was bowled by Alex Wharf in the seventeenth over. Luckily for the league leaders, Mark Ramprakash and Adam Hollioake then reprised their efforts that had sealed victory against the Kent Spitfires at Canterbury, putting together a fine partnership, with the skipper playing the role of principal aggressor. Appreciating that run-scoring would be difficult throughout the game on a slow low pitch, the fifth-wicket pair hadn't attempted anything too adventurous in advancing the score to 111-4 after thirty-one overs, until Hollioake launched a calculated attack on Dean Cosker. During a potentially pivotal thirty-second over of the innings, the visiting captain struck two fours and two sixes to complete a very sensible 49-ball fifty and put his team on track for a competitive total. Although Hollioake then perished to Croft in the next over for fifty-one, Ramprakash stayed around long enough to supervise the addition of another twenty-two runs and reach his own half-century from 91 balls before becoming the first of four late victims for Adrian Dale (4-35). Brief but bright contributions from Jon Batty and Ian Salisbury in the latter stages of the innings ensured that the final total of 198-9 gave their side every chance of clinching the title.

After Jimmy Maher (21 from 17 balls) had got Glamorgan's reply got off to a positive start, the capture of two wickets with successive balls - Maher caught behind off Bicknell and Wharf run out - soon levelled things up for the Lions. A brilliant diving catch down the legside by Batty off Franklyn Rose to dismiss Ian Thomas with the score at fifty-one then strengthened Surrey's position before a dangerous-looking stand developed between Mike Powell and David Hemp. At 100-3 after 23 overs, the Dragons were undeniably on top, but the balance of power swung dramatically in favour of the Lions when Tim Murtagh (3-44) bowled Powell for forty and then found Hemp's outside edge to allow Batty to pull off another fantastic catch. With Mark Wallace becoming a fourth victim for the Surrey wicketkeeper shortly afterwards, thereby rewarding Clarke for an excellent first spell of seven overs, Glamorgan were in the mire at 114-6, and the introduction of Hollioake himself then further damaged their chances as he dismissed Dale in his third over with the total advanced to 130. The soon-to-be-deposed NCL Champions kept on battling, however, as stands of thirty-one for the eighth wicket and twenty-three for the ninth left them just fifteen short of victory with three overs remaining when the last pair of Cosker and David Harrison came together. Having scraped together five runs from the first of these overs from Hollioake (2-29), the responsibility of bowling the penultimate over fell to Clarke (2-19), and he rose to the occasion superbly by extracting Harrison's middle stump with a fine yorker to secure an eight-run victory and the NCL Division One title for the Surrey Lions.

Having won the Sunday/National League title for only the second time in the competition's history - emulating the feat of the 1996 side, who started Surrey's run of success on this very ground almost seven years ago to the day - the players were presented with the trophy and celebrated, in a surprisingly muted fashion, on the outfield.

NCL DIVISION ONE - TOP OF THE TABLE AT 14TH SEPTEMBER					
	P	W	L	T	A	PTS
Surrey	15	12	2	0	1	50
Gloucestershire	15	10	4	0	1	42

Although Surrey were still in with a chance of claiming second place, and the associated prize money, they opted to field a very young and inexperienced side in their last Championship match of the summer, at home to Essex. James Benning, Ben Scott and Neil Saker all made their Championship debuts, while Scott Newman and Phil Sampson made their first appearance of the season in the major domestic competition. Jon Batty played as a specialist opening batsman, in order to give Scott a chance with the gloves, while the team was led by Ian Salisbury, who won the toss and elected to bat.

Surrey's first-innings batting was rather gung-ho at times as they compiled a total of 318 in 81.3 overs. Nadeem Shahid played some fine strokes in a 54-ball innings of sixty-seven from number three in the order, but the only other knocks of any substance came from Jon Batty (87) and his wicketkeeping understudy, Ben Scott, who grafted his way to an unbeaten fifty-eight. Graham Napier, who topped and tailed the innings to finish with 3-58, and James Middlebrook, who filleted the middle order to return 4-93, were the principal wicket-takers for Essex.

The visitors then made a racing start to their reply on the first evening through the highly impressive 18-year-old left-hander, Alistair Cook, and Andy Flower, reaching 112-1 in twenty overs, with Cook's fifty coming from just 32 balls.

On the second day, Flower dominated with a double-century after Cook (84) had become Saker's maiden Championship victim. Mark Pettini, with seventy, was the other main contributor as the Zimbabwean left-hander reached his landmark just in time, before Essex were bowled out for 464.

Surrey's second innings was then wrecked by Mohammad Akram on the third day, with his opening spell of 11-6-17-4, during which he swung the ball at pace, being particularly impressive. At one point he'd boasted figures of 5.3-5-0-4 as the hosts had slipped to 26-4. Although Batty and Benning resisted stoutly with forty-seven apiece during a fifth-wicket stand of ninety-six, the excellent Akram (8-49) returned to pick up four more wickets, and would have had a chance of all ten had he not missed a difficult return chance offered by Salisbury. Napier eventually polished off the innings at 194, leaving his side to score forty-nine to win, which they managed for the loss of two wickets to Sampson.

COUNTY CHAMPIONSHIP DIVISION ONE TABLE 2003								
		P	Pts	W	D	L	T	Bat	Bwl	Ded'n
1	Sussex	16	257.00	10	2	4	0	62	47	0.00
2	Lancashire	16	223.00	6	8	2	0	64	43	0.00
3	Surrey	16	219.00	6	7	3	0	63	44	0.00
4	Kent	16	198.00	6	5	5	0	47	47	0.00
5	Warwickshire	16	171.50	4	6	5	1	50	37	2.50
6	Middlesex	16	169.00	3	10	3	0	46	41	0.00
7	Essex	16	156.00	3	7	5	1	34	45	0.00
8	Nottinghamshire	16	132.00	2	6	8	0	36	45	1.00
9	Leicestershire	16	125.50	1	9	6	0	36	40	0.50

Unfortunately, the NCL champions then ended their season with a truly dismal showing at The Oval against the Leicestershire Foxes, who needed to win in order to have any chance of maintaining their first division status. It was easy to tell which side had something to play for as the Lions' fairly young and inexperienced side ended up on the wrong end of a 168-run mauling, with Leicestershire amassing 283-9 before bowling their hosts out for just 115 in a mere twenty-two overs. Darren Maddy (69 from 62 balls), Brad Hodge (43 from 36) and John Sadler (35 from 27) gave their side a brilliant platform after John Maunders had fallen to the second ball of the match from Phil Sampson (3-68), before James Benning (4-43) and Ian Salisbury restored some order to proceedings. Vasbert Drakes then provided late acceleration with an unbeaten forty-three from 47 balls, leaving the Lions with a target that proved way too big for them. Ali Brown top-scored with twenty-seven from 28 balls, and Benning showed further promise with a 15-ball knock of twenty-five, but no one else made any impression at all as Phil DeFreitas (5-40) and Charlie Dagnall (3-21) completed a record-breaking rout - this was the biggest defeat, in terms of runs, that Surrey had suffered in thirty-five seasons of Sunday/National League cricket. At the end of the game, the squad was re-presented with the Twenty20 Cup and the NCL Division One trophy, though the celebrations were again distinctly low-key, and it was disappointing to see that a few players were missing from the celebrations. It seemed clear that all was not well.

NATIONAL LEAGUE DIVISION ONE TABLE 2003							
		P	Pts	W	L	T	A	NRR
1	Surrey	16	50	12	3	0	1	2.99
2	Gloucestershire	16	46	11	4	0	1	4.48
3	Essex	16	34	8	7	1	0	3.80
4	Warwickshire	16	32	8	8	0	0	-0.57
5	Glamorgan	16	32	8	8	0	0	-0.94
6	Kent	16	30	7	8	1	0	3.51
7	Leicestershire	16	28	7	9	0	0	-3.83
8	Yorkshire	16	20	5	11	0	0	-6.96
9	Worcestershire	16	16	4	12	0	0	-1.16

At the end of a season that had seen the side winning two of the three major limited-overs crowns and recording twenty-seven match victories to just seven defeats, you would have expected everyone at The Oval to be cock-a-hoop, but that wasn't the case. The loss of the Championship to Sussex - who were worthy first-time winners of the trophy - was clearly a major disappointment, while the poor run-in to the season had left many supporters talking about 'the end of an era'. A number of fans had spoken on the outfield at Sophia Gardens about how appropriate it was that the club's run of success should be ending where it began, which seemed to be a surprisingly gloomy viewpoint. As the weeks went by, though, it began to look as though they could be right, since the wind of change was positively howling through the club. On the eve of "Adam's Journey" - a 2,000-mile trek by foot, bicycle and boat that Adam Hollioake and a few friends were undertaking in aid of The Ben Hollioake Fund - the Surrey captain announced that he would be retiring from first-class cricket at the end of the 2004 season, saying:- *"After much soul searching I have decided that 2004 will be my final year. I have many things that I want to do with my family, charity work with The Ben Hollioake Fund and my business interests in Perth. I will continue to give everything I can to the club in the next twelve months, and in years to come."* This news was then followed by another Press Release a few days later announcing that Jon Batty would be taking over as captain for 2004, which came as a major surprise, since no one had thought of Batty as a future skipper, and he had a lot on his plate already if he was to carry on opening the batting as well as keeping wicket. Ian Ward had been felt to be the heir apparent to Hollioake, but his departure, which was still shrouded in mystery, had scuppered that plan and added to the feeling that a lot of things were going on behind the scenes. This was then confirmed on 27th November when Surrey informed the media that Keith Medlycott was leaving the club, which certainly came as something of a bolt from the blue, especially since he had enjoyed so much success and had a year to run on his contract. The Surrey Manager's statement in an official Press Release read as follows:- *"It has been a privilege to have managed the side since 1998 through a period of unrivalled success. To have been part of this era gives me enormous pleasure and pride. I now feel that, following Adam's decision to stand down as captain, the time is right for me to leave to pursue other opportunities and fresh challenges. Adam and myself formed a fantastic winning partnership and it's now time for me to look forward to the future. I believe I have taken Surrey as far as I can and that under a new manager and a new captain in Jonathan Batty, the club can continue to be successful."*

It wasn't only 'all change' on the playing side, either, since the club announced a new sponsorship deal in January 2004, with Brit Insurance Holdings plc taking over from the previous sponsors, AMP. The deal was to be worth £500,000 a year to Surrey, making it the largest of its kind in English cricket, and as part of the package the ground was to be renamed 'The Brit Oval'. Additionally, the Vauxhall end of the ground was to finally be redeveloped, with a major new stand to be built. Work was to start in February 2004 and would be completed by the end of May 2005.

Back on the playing front, Surrey were able to announce that they had secured the services of Steve Rixon, the highly successful New South Wales and former New Zealand coach. He was to take over the reins, on a two-year contract, in March 2004, once his current contract with NSW had expired.

2003 SEASON SUMMARY

COMPETITION	P	W	D/A	L	POSITION/PROGRESS
County Championship	16	6	7	3	3rd
National League Div 1	16	12	1	3	1st
C&G Trophy	3	2	0	1	Quarter-final
Twenty 20 Cup	7	7	0	0	Winners
TOTAL	42	27	8	7	2 Trophies

2003 RESULTS SUMMARY

18/4	LANCASHIRE	OVAL	CC1	Match Drawn
27/4	Essex	Chelmsford	NL1	WON by 15 runs
30/4	WARWICKSHIRE	OVAL	CC1	Match Drawn
4/5	WARWICKSHIRE	OVAL	NL1	WON by 25 runs
5/5	Worcestershire	Worcester	NL1	WON by 1 wicket
7/5	Staffordshire	Stone	CGT	WON by 9 runs
9/5	Nottinghamshire	Trent Bridge	CC1	WON by an inns & 6 runs
14/5	LEICESTERSHIRE	OVAL	CC1	Match Drawn
18/5	KENT	OVAL	NL1	WON by 6 runs
21/5	Essex	Chelmsford	CC1	WON by 258 runs
25/5	Gloucestershire	Bristol	NL1	Match Abandoned
28/5	Somerset	Taunton	CGT	WON by 6 runs
30/5	SUSSEX	OVAL	CC1	WON by 113 runs
8/6	ESSEX	OVAL	NL1	WON by 3 wickets
11/6	Derbyshire	Derby	CGTqf	LOST by 137 runs

Date	Opponent	Venue	Comp	Result
13/6	MIDDLESEX	OVAL	2020	WON by 4 wickets
14/6	ESSEX	IMBER COURT	2020	WON by 44 runs
16/6	SUSSEX	IMBER COURT	2020	WON by 4 wickets
23/6	Kent	Canterbury	2020	WON by 18 runs
24/6	Hampshire	Rose Bowl	2020	WON by 19 runs
27/6	Middlesex	Lord's	CC1	Match Drawn
2/7	KENT	OVAL	CC1	WON by 186 runs
6/7	YORKSHIRE	OVAL	NL1	WON by 7 wickets
9/7	Warwickshire	Edgbaston	CC1	WON by 135 runs
13/7	Warwickshire	Edgbaston	NL1	LOST by 6 wickets
19/7	GLOUCESTERSHIRE	TRENT BRIDGE	2020sf	WON by 5 runs
19/7	WARWICKSHIRE	TRENT BRIDGE	2020f	WON by 9 wickets
23/7	MIDDLESEX	GUILDFORD	CC1	Match Drawn
27/7	WORCESTERSHIRE	GUILDFORD	NL1	LOST by 79 runs
30/7	Sussex	Hove	CC1	Match Drawn
5/8	GLOUCESTERSHIRE	OVAL	NL1	WON by 66 runs
13/8	NOTTINGHAMSHIRE	WHITGIFT SCHOOL	CC1	WON by an inns & 211 runs
17/8	GLAMORGAN	WHITGIFT SCHOOL	NL1	WON by 58 runs
20/8	Leicestershire	Leicester	NL1	WON by 7 wickets
21/8	Leicestershire	Leicester	CC1	Match Drawn
26/8	Lancashire	Old Trafford	CC1	LOST by 8 wickets
31/8	Yorkshire	Headingley	NL1	WON by 2 runs
3/9	Kent	Canterbury	NL1	WON by 5 wickets
4/9	Kent	Canterbury	CC1	LOST by an inns & 155 runs
14/9	Glamorgan	Cardiff	NL1	WON by 8 runs
17/9	ESSEX	OVAL	CC1	LOST by 8 wickets
21/9	LEICESTERSHIRE	OVAL	NL1	LOST by 168 runs

COUNTY CHAMPIONSHIP BATTING AVERAGES 2003

	M	I	NO	Runs	HS	Ave	100	50	c	st
M.R. Ramprakash	14	22	4	1239	279*	68.83	5	2	7	-
M.A. Butcher	6	8	0	527	144	65.87	2	2	10	-
A.J. Stewart	6	8	1	451	98	64.42	-	5	20	-
G.P. Thorpe	11	18	2	880	156	55.00	1	7	8	-
J.N. Batty	10	19	4	794	168*	52.93	2	4	25	2
R. Clarke	9	14	2	513	139	42.75	2	1	11	-
Azhar Mahmood	10	13	2	441	98	40.09	-	4	17	-
M.P. Bicknell	11	11	3	318	141	39.75	1	-	1	-
I.J. Ward	15	24	1	856	158	37.21	3	2	8	-
I.D.K. Salisbury	14	18	4	455	101*	32.50	1	1	6	-
Saqlain Mushtaq	14	15	2	421	69	32.38	-	4	4	-
A.J. Hollioake	13	18	0	567	122	31.50	1	3	10	-
A.D. Brown	12	19	2	481	74	28.29	-	5	12	-
J. Ormond	12	14	5	198	47	22.00	-	-	2	-
T.J. Murtagh	5	8	4	61	21	15.25	-	-	-	-
Qualification: 8 innings										

COUNTY CHAMPIONSHIP BOWLING AVERAGES 2003							
	O	M	Runs	W	Ave	BB	10wm	5wi
M.P. Bicknell	326.4	83	1023	39	26.23	5-42	-	3
Azhar Mahmood	262.2	48	994	34	29.23	5-78	-	1
J. Ormond	366.1	65	1363	44	30.97	5-45	-	2
Saqlain Mushtaq	471.0	100	1364	41	33.26	5-46	-	3
I.D.K. Salisbury	371.1	60	1224	33	37.09	4-116	-	-
T.J. Murtagh	115.0	13	475	11	43.18	4-130	-	-
R. Clarke	130.1	13	607	12	50.58	4-21	-	-
A.J. Tudor	144.0	24	532	10	53.20	3-56	-	-

Qualification: 10 wickets

LIMITED-OVERS BATTING AVERAGES 2003										
	M	I	NO	Runs	HS	Ave	100	50	c	st
M.R. Ramprakash	16	15	3	750	107*	62.50	2	6	6	-
G.P. Thorpe	16	15	5	522	102*	52.20	1	3	9	-
I.J. Ward	13	13	1	371	108	30.91	1	1	1	-
A.D. Brown	18	18	0	496	89	27.55	-	4	10	-
Azhar Mahmood	15	14	2	313	98	26.08	-	2	4	-
A.J. Hollioake	18	18	0	463	77	25.72	-	2	5	-
M.P. Bicknell	13	6	4	47	14*	23.50	-	-	4	-
J.N. Batty	18	14	4	215	55*	21.50	-	1	22	4
R. Clarke	16	16	3	270	47	20.76	-	-	4	-
Saqlain Mushtaq	13	7	3	57	27*	14.25	-	-	1	-

Qualification: 6 innings

LIMITED-OVERS BOWLING AVERAGES 2003								
	O	M	Runs	W	Ave	BB	4wi	RPO
A.J. Hollioake	95.5	1	546	28	19.50	6-17	2	5.69
Azhar Mahmood	115.0	9	578	24	24.08	6-37	2	5.02
J. Ormond	114.0	9	549	18	30.50	3-46	-	4.81
R. Clarke	78.0	1	498	13	38.30	3-48	-	6.38
M.P. Bicknell	109.0	14	482	12	40.16	2-30	-	4.42
Saqlain Mushtaq	106.0	1	523	13	40.23	3-27	-	4.93

Qualification: 40 overs, 10 wickets

For a detailed account of the 2003 season, including exclusive interviews with the players, read **'Two In Blue - Surrey's Double-Winning 2003 Season'** (details given on page 350)

11 2004 And Beyond

After so much upheaval during the close season, the summer of 2004 was always likely to prove difficult for Surrey, though I don't think anyone had envisaged it being as tough as it turned out. With an inexperienced captain in place, and a new Manager arriving just a matter of weeks before the season began, it was unlikely that the team would get away to a flying start, but problems surfaced early on and the season just didn't get off the ground for weeks. In the Championship, Surrey were lucky to escape with a draw in the home match against Sussex; lost to Middlesex at Lord's; drew a rain-wrecked game with Northamptonshire; and then lost at Edgbaston, a sequence that immediately put the team under the microscope, especially as they had already lost three of their first four National League matches and suffered a very embarrassing defeat to Ireland in the second round of the C&G Trophy. The media soon latched on to Surrey's struggles as a story of a big club in decline and ran articles about it, asking all and sundry what they thought had gone wrong. Everyone had different theories, of course, but the most likely reasons included:- a short and poor pre-season build-up; Alex Tudor being struck down by injury with the season having barely started; Saqlain Mushtaq being forced to give way to his long-standing knee problems after less than a month of the campaign; a basic loss of confidence, as the side found itself in the alien position of being on a losing streak; and the plain and simple fact that Jon Batty was overburdened - with the squad short of an opening batsman to partner Scott Newman, following Ian Ward's departure, he had no choice but to add that role to his wicketkeeping and captaincy commitments.

With Steve Rixon finding that he had inherited a much bigger and more difficult job than he had expected, Surrey were soon struggling at the bottom of NCL Division One and towards the foot of the Championship table, though there were a few bright spots and fine individual achievements, even during these dark days - Scott Newman had started his first full season brilliantly and had instantly risen to the challenge of playing regular first-team cricket; Martin Bicknell claimed his 1000th first-class wicket during the game against Kent at the newly christened Brit Oval, while Jon Batty equalled world records by claiming ten victims - including eight in the first innings - and scoring a hundred in the same match that Bicknell reached his milestone. Only two victories - one in the NCL and one in the Championship - were recorded until the Twenty20 Cup qualifying competition started on July 2nd and yielded five wins to take the Lions through to Finals Day and spark a short-term recovery in the National League. Successive Championship defeats to Warwickshire at Guildford - Surrey's first four-day setback there since 1994 - and Northamptonshire at Wantage Road left the team in real danger of a relegation double, especially as Martin Bicknell and Ian Salisbury had been added to the injured list by this time. With Saqlain Mushtaq having already been ruled out for the rest of the season, and belated attempts to replace him with another overseas player having failed to produce any results, the club was grateful that left-arm spinner Nayan Doshi - son of former Indian Test spinner, Dilip - was making rapid progress after being plucked from club cricket earlier in the summer. This was particularly important once Salisbury joined his spin twin in being sidelined for the rest of the summer after the Northamptonshire defeat, which also turned out to be Adam Hollioake's final Championship appearance for the club - because of a knee problem, it was decided that the former skipper should concentrate his efforts on the one-day game. An absolutely crucial encounter with fellow relegation candidates, Worcestershire, at The Brit Oval then produced a compelling contest and a vital victory by sixty-eight runs, thanks largely to twin centuries from Mark Ramprakash and a lion-hearted second-innings bowling performance from James Ormond, who claimed 6-62. Another plus point from this match was the performance of Richard Clinton - son of the club's former opener and coach -

who had played very well to score seventy-three and twenty-seven, as well as holding a fine, and undoubtedly pivotal, catch to dismiss Graeme Hick in the visitors' first innings. After trying five different opening partners for Scott Newman - Batty, Butcher, Shahid, Hollioake and Clarke - Surrey finally looked to have found a solution to that particular problem. Although the team then lost to the Leicestershire Foxes in the Twenty20 Cup final, after a nail-biting one-run win over Lancashire in the semi-finals, and fell away again in the NCL to finish bottom, there was no stopping them now in the Championship as they recorded three wins from their last four games to secure a final placing of third in the table. During this impressive run-in, Azhar Mahmood was capped; Ali Brown completed a full-set of first-class centuries against the other counties by scoring a quite brilliant 154 at Old Trafford; Nayan Doshi returned match figures of 11-182 in that same match and followed up with 10-183 at Hove in the final game; while Jon Batty also enjoyed Surrey's superb win in Manchester by claiming eleven victims behind the timbers.

Having struck such a fine late run of form, Steve Rixon and his players were probably disappointed that the season ended when it did, though the main mid-season goal of retaining first division status in the Championship after such a bad start had at least been achieved. The club's Player Of The Season, Mark Ramprakash, was one of three men to pass 1,000 runs in the Championship, the others being Ali Brown and Scott Newman, as bat continued to increase its domination over ball in the English domestic game. Meanwhile, Jon Batty ended with 899 runs after enjoying a renaissance once he had moved down into the middle order. With the ball, Nayan Doshi had emerged at a crucial time for the club to capture thirty-three wickets at 26.51, while Azhar Mahmood and Martin Bicknell were the only other regular bowlers to average under thirty... just. James Ormond's statistics - forty-eight wickets at 37.50 - did not truly reflect how well he had bowled and how hard he had worked for the team. Although he had endured a very tough season as captain, Jon Batty had performed really well with both bat and gloves in all competitions and had conducted himself with great dignity in a difficult situation.

At the end of the season, it was decided that Mark Butcher should take over the captaincy in 2005 - with Mark Ramprakash to act as vice-captain when Butcher was away with England - while the club said goodbye to four senior players with a combined total of almost forty Surrey seasons between them. While Adam Hollioake and Nadeem Shahid both retired from the first-class game, Alex Tudor and Saqlain Mushtaq were not retained, largely due to their injury problems. Tudor eventually joined Essex, where it was to be hoped he would regain full fitness, while Saqlain was released on the basis that he was most unlikely to recover from operations on both knees in time to be fit to play in 2005. It was sad to see these players departing, but it underlined the fact that the club was at the end of an era and was in the process of rebuilding. While Nayan Doshi and Richard Clinton were rewarded for their efforts in the latter part of the season by being given two-year contracts, Surrey also made two new signings, with Mohammad Akram joining from Sussex, and Harbhajan Singh, the Indian off-spinner, being registered as the club's second overseas player alongside Azhar Mahmood.

Hopes were brighter for 2005 and beyond, with Steve Rixon looking to mould the team in his preferred style during an extended pre-season period and declaring that he had a long-term view of how he wanted the club and team to progress. With the impressive new OCS Stand to be opened at the end of May, it looked like rebuilding was very much the theme at The Brit Oval.

12 Team Statistics - Surrey Versus The Rest

As the following table shows, Gloucestershire and Lancashire were the only other counties to secure more than two trophies during Surrey's outstanding spell of success between 1996 and 2003. Neither of these teams managed to win the County Championship, however, while the second most successful Championship side of this particular era, Leicestershire, who took the title in 1996 and 1998, failed to win a limited-overs trophy. This leaves Glamorgan and Yorkshire as the only sides apart from Surrey to have captured both the Championship and a one-day crown during the period, which suggests that it has become more difficult to be simultaneously successful in both the four-day and the short-course versions of the game. This could be because some of the smaller counties target the one-day game, viewing success in limited-overs cricket as the pinnacle of their aspirations at the start of a new season. Back in 1996, Surrey probably saw the capture of a one-day title as a stepping stone to success in the four-day game, but other clubs view the shorter game as their only realistic chance of claiming some silverware, with Gloucestershire having been the prime example of this in recent times. It certainly seemed that their coach, John Bracewell, had accepted that winning the Championship was beyond his side's capabilities when he elected to replace Courtney Walsh, a match-winning fast bowler in four-day cricket, with Ian Harvey, a very talented all-rounder who became the linchpin of the team's one-day success without making many significant contributions in Championship cricket. This turned out to be an inspired move as Gloucestershire began to dominate the domestic limited-overs scene, and you certainly can't criticise a coach for taking this path to success if his resources are limited. The County Championship has always been the most important competition for Surrey, however, and it is the performance in that form of the game that matters most to the majority of members and the players. For a proud club that had failed to win a significant trophy since 1982, the Sunday League triumph of 1996 was of great significance, though, since it brought that barren run to an end.

ROLL OF HONOUR 1996-2003						
	TOTAL	Champ	SL/NL	NWT/C&G	B&H	20/20
Surrey	8	3	2	0	2	1
Gloucestershire	6	0	1	3	2	0
Lancashire	5	0	2	2	1	0
Leicestershire	2	2	0	0	0	0
Glamorgan	2	1	1	0	0	0
Yorkshire	2	1	0	1	0	0
Warwickshire	2	0	1	0	1	0
Essex	2	0	0	1	1	0
Sussex	1	1	0	0	0	0
Kent	1	0	1	0	0	0
Somerset	1	0	0	1	0	0

In an attempt to see how Surrey's overall performance compared to the overall performance of the other seventeen first-class counties between 1996 and 2003 I compiled tables for each of the four major competitions.

For the two league-based competitions I calculated each team's average position attained over the course of the eight seasons, accounting for the split into two divisions by awarding each year's tenth place to the side winning the second division, eleventh place to the county finishing second in that league and so on down to eighteenth place for the side propping up the Division Two table at the end of each summer. Although this system isn't perfect, a table based on the won-drawn-lost playing records of each team would clearly give a completely false picture, since a victory in the second division does not equate to a victory in the first division where the quality of the opposition is clearly superior. Using the 2004 County Championship to underline this point, Nottinghamshire, who topped Division Two by winning nine games, were obviously not a better side than Warwickshire, who were crowned county champions with five victories to their credit.

For the two knockout cup competitions I elected to go with a points system, awarding an increasing number of points to the counties the further they progressed in the tournament. Cup winners were therefore awarded six points; losing finalists four points; losing semi-finalists three points; and the losing quarter-finalists two points. Those falling at an earlier hurdle were awarded either one point or no points, depending on the competition.

Surrey's Overall Performance In The County Championship

It is no surprise to see Surrey topping the 1996-2003 County Championship table, as they had finished in the top five places in seven of those eight seasons. Kent and Leicestershire rightly shared second place, having been commendably consistent in maintaining first division status since the introduction of two divisions, while Lancashire, the only side to have been ever-present in the top echelon apart from these two and Surrey, clearly deserve fourth spot. Four times Championship runners-up since 1998 - twice to Surrey, once behind Sussex and once to Leicestershire - the Red Rose county actually come close to matching Surrey in terms of finishes since 1998. The final order of teams in this table seems to reflect performance very accurately, with the only major surprise perhaps being Nottinghamshire's equal-last position. Their recent record in the premier domestic competition is far worse than I'd imagined.

	AVERAGE FINAL POSITION IN THE COUNTY CHAMPIONSHIP 1996-2003									
		Ave Pos'n	1996 Pos'n	1997 Pos'n	1998 Pos'n	1999 Pos'n	2000 Pos'n	2001 Pos'n	2002 Pos'n	2003 Pos'n
1	Surrey	3.25	3	8=	5	1	1	4	1	3
2	Kent	4.75	4	2	11	5	6	3	3	4
=	Leicestershire	4.75	1	10	1	3	4	5	5	9
4	Lancashire	5.50	15	11	2	2	2	6	4	2
5	Yorkshire	5.88	6	6	3	6	3	1	9	13
6	Warwickshire	8.00	8	4=	8	10	15	12	2	5
7	Somerset	8.38	11	12	9	4	5	2	8	16
8	Essex	10.00	5	8=	18	12	11	9	10	7
9	Hampshire	10.25	14	14	6	7	7	10	7	17
10	Sussex	10.50	12	18	7	11	18	11	6	1
11	Glamorgan	10.63	10	1	12=	14	12	8	14	14
12	Worcestershire	11.13	7	3	12=	15	14	15	13	10
13	Middlesex	11.75	9	4=	17	16	17	14	11	6
14	Derbyshire	12.13	2	16	10	9	9	18	15	18
=	Gloucestershire	12.13	13	7	4	18	13	13	17	12
16	Northamptonshire	12.88	16	15	15	13	10	7	16	11
17	Durham	14.38	18	17	14	8	8	17	18	15
=	Nottinghamshire	14.38	17	13	16	17	16	16	12	8

Surrey's Overall Performance In The Sunday/National League

Given Surrey's extremely inconsistent performances in the Sunday/National League, their mid-table position - with an average league placing between eighth and ninth - is not unexpected. Warwickshire lead the way, having frequently been top-four finishers, while Kent and Leicestershire again feature in the top three of the table, largely as a result of their unbroken membership of the top division between 1996 and 2003.

Considering that both counties won the one-day league twice during the period under investigation, Lancashire and Surrey will reflect that overall positions of seventh and eighth in this table are not especially impressive. Their placings do, however, accurately reflect both (a) the inconsistency of the two teams in the 40- and 45-overs-a-side competition, and (b) the capricious nature of a league that was won by no fewer than six different sides in the eight years covered by this book.

	AVERAGE FINAL POSITION IN THE SUNDAY/NATIONAL LEAGUE 1996-2003									
		Ave Pos'n	1996 Pos'n	1997 Pos'n	1998 Pos'n	1999 Pos'n	2000 Pos'n	2001 Pos'n	2002 Pos'n	2003 Pos'n
1	Warwickshire	4.50	4	1	2	7	12	3	3	4
2	Kent	4.63	10	2	5	3	5	1	5	6
3	Leicestershire	5.63	12	4	4	6	4	2	6	7
4	Yorkshire	5.88	3	10	9	5	2	6	4	8
5	Worcestershire	6.88	8	8	7	2	7	12	2	9
6	Gloucestershire	7.13	16	11	6	4	1	7	10	2
7	Lancashire	7.63	9	3	1	1	8	15	14	10
8	Surrey	8.63	1	5	18	15	10	8	11	1
9	Somerset	8.88	5	6	14	11	6	4	7	18
10	Northamptonshire	9.75	6	9	13	12	3	9	15	11
=	Nottinghamshire	9.75	2	12	11	14	11	5	9	14
12	Glamorgan	10.00	13	13	10	13	15	10	1	5
13	Essex	10.13	17	7	3	9	14	16	12	3
14	Hampshire	13.00	15	15	8	8	17	13	16	12
15	Middlesex	14.00	7	16	12	16	13	17	18	13
16	Sussex	14.38	14	18	16	10	9	14	17	17
17	Derbyshire	15.13	11	14	15	17	18	18	13	15
=	Durham	15.13	18	17	17	18	16	11	8	16

Surrey's Overall Performance In The Nat West/C&G Trophy

The Nat West/C&G Trophy table proves something of a revelation, since few Surrey supporters would expect to see their team in sixth place. Although the club hasn't come remotely close to lifting the trophy in recent times, three appearances in the semi-finals and three in the quarter-finals are sufficient to give surprising respectability to the county's overall record.

Three-times winners Gloucestershire are pipped to the top spot by Lancashire, the winners in 1996 and 1998, because the men from Old Trafford have been more consistent over the course of the eight years in question... though these two counties are well clear of third-placed Somerset, the 2001 champions, and Yorkshire, who were victorious in 2002. This leaves Essex as the only winners of the trophy during the period 1996-2003 to finish below Surrey in the Overall Performance table.

OVERALL PERFORMANCE IN THE NAT WEST/C&G TROPHY 1996-2003									
		Pts	1996	1997	1998	1999	2000	2001	2002	2003
1	Lancashire	25	W	16	W	Q	S	S	16	S
2	Gloucestershire	24	16	16	16	W	W	16	Q	W
3	Somerset	20	Q	16	16	F	16	W	F	16
4	Yorkshire	19	S	Q	16	S	16	Q	W	16
5	Warwickshire	18	16	F	Q	16	F	S	16	Q
6	Surrey	17	S	16	Q	S	Q	16	S	Q
7	Essex	16	F	W	16	x	16	16	Q	16
8	Leicestershire	14	16	16	S	16	16	F	16	Q
9	Derbyshire	13	Q	Q	F	16	16	x	x	S
10	Glamorgan	11	x	S	16	Q	Q	16	16	16
=	Hampshire	11	Q	16	S	16	S	x	16	x
=	Kent	11	16	x	16	Q	16	Q	S	16
=	Sussex	11	Q	S	x	16	16	16	Q	16
=	Worcestershire	11	16	16	x	16	x	Q	Q	F
15	Middlesex	9	16	Q	Q	x	Q	X	x	Q
16	Northamptonshire	8	16	16	x	Q	Q	16	16	x
=	Nottinghamshire	8	x	Q	Q	16	x	16	16	16
18	Durham	7	16	x	16	x	Q	16	16	16

W=Winners (6pts); F=Finalists (4pts); S=Semi-finalists (3pts); Q=Quarter-finalists (2pts); 16=Reached last sixteen (1pt); x=Failed to reach last sixteen (0pts)

Surrey's Overall Performance In The Benson & Hedges Cup

Having won the trophy in 1997 and 2001, Surrey lead the way in the Benson & Hedges Cup table, edging out Gloucestershire, the winners in 1999 and 2000, by a single point. Yorkshire's consistency earns them third place, even though they failed to win this trophy during the last seven years of its existence, while the victors in 1996 (Lancashire), 2002 (Warwickshire) and 1998 (Essex) fill the next three positions in the list.

Although no one could dispute the supremacy of Surrey and Gloucestershire in the Benson & Hedges Cup, the figures for this competition are slightly distorted by the fact that fewer than half of the eighteen first-class counties participated in 1999, when the tournament was dubbed the Super Cup and entry was restricted to the sides who filled the top eight slots in the 1998 County Championship. It seemed strange to reward the teams who had played the best four-day cricket with exclusive entry to a one-day competition.

OVERALL PERFORMANCE IN THE BENSON & HEDGES CUP 1996-2002									
		Pts	1996	1997	1998	1999	2000	2001	2002
1	Surrey	23	Q	W	S	Q	S	W	z
2	Gloucestershire	22	Q	z	z	W	W	F	Q
3	Yorkshire	19	S	Q	S	F	Q	S	Q
4	Lancashire	18	W	z	Q	Q	S	z	S
=	Warwickshire	18	S	Q	z	S	z	Q	W
6	Essex	15	z	Q	W	x	z	z	F
7	Leicestershire	14	z	S	F	Q	z	z	Q
8	Sussex	12	z	z	z	S	Q	Q	Q
9	Kent	11	Q	F	Q	x	z	z	z
=	Northamptonshire	11	F	S	z	x	z	z	z
11	Glamorgan	10	Q	z	z	x	F	z	z

		Pts	1996	1997	1998	1999	2000	2001	2002
12	Durham	9	z	z	Q	x	Q	Q	z
=	Hampshire	9	z	z	z	Q	Q	z	z
14	Nottinghamshire	8	z	z	z	x	z	S	z
=	Somerset	8	z	Q	z	x	z	Q	z
=	Worcestershire	8	z	z	z	x	z	z	S
17	Middlesex	7	z	z	Q	x	z	z	z
18	Derbyshire	6	z	z	z	x	z	z	z

W=Winners (6pts); F=Finalists (4pts); S=Semi-finalists (3pts); Q=Quarter-finalists (2pts); z=Eliminated at zonal/group stage (1pt); x=Did not qualify for the competition (0pts). 1999 Super Cup only included teams who finished in the top eight of 1998 County Championship

Having assessed Surrey's overall records in the four major competitions, it is now time to delve a little deeper and examine their playing records against each of the other counties in these competitions.

Surrey's Playing Record In The County Championship

Having never finished below eighth place in the County Championship during their 1996-2003 glory years, it is inevitable that the analysis of Surrey's four-day results over that period of time throws up some impressive statistics.

Of 132 matches played, Surrey won no fewer than sixty-three and lost just twenty, with the remaining forty-nine being drawn. The home record during this time is especially remarkable, as the county won forty of sixty-six matches and suffered just eight defeats. Essex inflicted two of these losses, six other counties managed the feat just once, while ten found the most difficult challenge in county cricket beyond them. Although The Oval saw plenty of Surrey success, the Guildford Cricket Club ground at Woodbridge Road proved to be a real fortress for the county - all seven County Championship matches played there between 1996 and 2002 ended in victory for the home side before rain spoiled the 2003 match against Middlesex and brought about a stalemate.

Away from home, Surrey tended to struggle in the West Country, as the three counties on whose soil they failed to secure a victory were Gloucestershire, Somerset and Worcestershire. In Surrey's defence, they only played twice in Gloucestershire and Worcestershire during their glory years since both of these counties were languishing in the second division from 2000 to 2003. Additionally, the two matches at Worcester were completely decimated by rain, with a potential eight days of cricket producing just 183 overs of action. There was, however, no excuse for failing to taste success in five attempts at Taunton, where Surrey would have been expected to do better on the good pitches produced by the Somerset groundsman, Phil Frost. Apart from in 1998, when stand-in captain Mark Butcher failed to prevent his severely weakened side from going down by 165 runs, and in 2000, when rain completely ruined the match, the games tended to be high-scoring draws.

Looking more closely at results against individual counties, Hampshire emerge as the number one whipping boys for Surrey, having lost all eight encounters between the two sides, while five wins and a draw from six matches equates to a success rate of 91.67% for the south London-based county against Nottinghamshire. Durham's stunning, and totally unexpected, victory at the Riverside in 2000 represented their first ever triumph over the men from The Oval, but defeat in the other five contests between the two counties ensures that they rank as Surrey's third-favourite opponents of the period. At the other end of the scale, only one county failed to fall victim to Surrey in Championship matches between 1996 and 2003... Gloucestershire. Regarded for much of this era as one-day specialists, the West Country team actually won two and drew two of their four fixtures against the side whose record in the County Championship at that time was second to none. Gloucestershire are also the only side against whom Surrey's percentage success rate is below 50%, while Worcestershire (over the course of four matches) and Essex (eight games) emerge as the only teams to have an even 50-50 record against the County Champions of 1999, 2000 and 2002.

CHAMPIONSHIP RECORD v OTHER COUNTIES 1996-2003									
	HOME			AWAY			TOTAL		
County	W	D	L	W	D	L	W	D	L	% success
Derbyshire	2	1	0	1	1	1	3	2	1	66.67
Durham	3	0	0	2	0	1	5	0	1	83.33
Essex	1	1	2	1	3	0	2	4	2	50.00
Glamorgan	1	1	1	1	2	0	2	3	1	58.33
Gloucestershire	0	1	1	0	1	1	0	2	2	25.00
Hampshire	4	0	0	4	0	0	8	0	0	100.00
Kent	3	3	0	2	2	2	5	5	2	62.50
Lancashire	3	2	1	1	3	2	4	5	3	54.17
Leicestershire	3	2	1	2	4	0	5	6	1	66.67
Middlesex	2	1	0	1	2	0	3	3	0	75.00
Northamptonshire	2	1	0	1	2	0	3	3	0	75.00
Nottinghamshire	3	0	0	2	1	0	5	1	0	91.67
Somerset	3	2	0	0	4	1	3	6	1	60.00
Sussex	4	0	0	2	1	1	6	1	1	81.25
Warwickshire	2	1	1	2	1	1	4	2	2	62.50
Worcestershire	1	0	1	0	2	0	1	2	1	50.00
Yorkshire	3	2	0	1	2	2	4	4	2	60.00
TOTAL	40	18	8	23	31	12	63	49	20	66.29

NB - '% success' = [{(no. of wins x 2) + (no. of draws x 1)} x 100] / [no. of matches x 2]

Championship Defeats Season-By-Season

Surrey's record of losing just twenty County Championship matches in eight seasons is very impressive - and the last three of these defeats came right at the end of the club's golden era as things were beginning to pall. The games they lost are catalogued in chronological order in the following table, with each entry giving the date on which the game was lost, the opponents, the venue, and the margin of defeat.

It is interesting to note that between the defeats by Lancashire on 12th September 1997 and 29th August 2003, a period of almost six years, Surrey's eleven losses came at the hands of eleven different counties - Kent, Somerset, Lancashire, Gloucestershire, Yorkshire, Leicestershire, Durham, Derbyshire, Glamorgan, Warwickshire and Sussex. I suspect it is highly unlikely that any county side had ever before gone through a period of almost six seasons without losing twice to at least one other side in the competition.

This table also helps to highlight the three spells where Surrey went undefeated in the Championship for over a year - 13th April 1999 to 4th May 2000; 10th June 2000 to 11th August 2001; and 12th August 2002 to 29th August 2003. To enjoy three unbeaten runs of that length in the course of eight years is a quite remarkable achievement.

Another remarkable feature is the magnitude of the defeats. All but a handful would have to be described as 'heavy' defeats... proving that when Surrey lost during their glory years they still did it in style!

SURREY'S COUNTY CHAMPIONSHIP DEFEATS 1996-2003			
1996 (Two Defeats)			
10/6	Yorkshire	Middlesborough	221 runs
22/9	Worcestershire	The Oval	124 runs
1997 (Five)			
16/5	Gloucestershire	The Oval	9 wickets
7/6	Essex	The Oval	147 runs
5/7	Warwickshire	Edgbaston	5 wickets
12/9	Lancashire	The Oval	An innings and 55 runs
20/9	Kent	Canterbury	5 wickets
1998 (Five)			
24/5	Somerset	Taunton	165 runs
21/6	Lancashire	Old Trafford	6 wickets
24/7	Gloucestershire	Cheltenham	2 wickets
4/9	Yorkshire	Headingley	164 runs
19/9	Leicestershire	The Oval	An innings and 211 runs
1999 (Unbeaten Season)			
2000 (Two)			
4/5	Durham	Riverside	231 runs
9/6	Derbyshire	Derby	7 wickets
2001 (One)			
11/8	Glamorgan	The Oval	3 wickets
2002 (Two)			
13/7	Warwickshire	The Oval	31 runs
11/8	Sussex	Hove	4 wickets
2003 (Three)			
29/8	Lancashire	Old Trafford	8 wickets
6/9	Kent	Canterbury	An innings and 155 runs
19/9	Essex	The Oval	8 wickets

Surrey's Playing Record In Limited-Overs Cricket (excluding Twenty20 Cup)

Although Surrey's limited-overs record can't compare with their County Championship record - largely because of numerous unpredictable catastrophies in the Nat West/C&G Trophy and their wildly fluctuating fortunes in the Sunday/National League - the club's overall statistics for the period would stand up well against those of most other counties. An overall success rate of 61.05% and a record of 110 wins against seventy defeats is pretty impressive, especially when you consider that Surrey were, in effect, relegated twice during this time - in 1998, when the Sunday League was split into two divisions, and again in 2001.

The table of results reveals a few surprises upon examination. Who would have thought, for example, that Gloucestershire would be the team against whom Surrey had recorded the most wins and boasted the second-best success rate? Only Durham, in fact, have fared worse against Surrey in limited-overs cricket than the undisputed one-day kings of recent times. Hampshire, meanwhile, rank highly amongst the whipping boys again, though they did record three wins over the men from The Oval... just! One of their three triumphs came in the 2000 Benson & Hedges Cup game, which ended up as a ten-overs-per-side contest that was decided by just two runs, and another was by a single run in the same competition two years later.

Looking at the other side of the coin, while Gloucestershire were the only county to keep Surrey below the 50% success mark in Championship cricket, five sides managed it in the limited-overs form of the game. The identities of these teams are rather surprising, however, with Northamptonshire emerging as Surrey's principal bogey side, followed by Somerset, Nottinghamshire, Leicestershire and Yorkshire, none of whom could really be regarded as one-day giants between 1996 and 2003. In fact, their combined tally of limited-overs trophies during this period is two Nat West/C&G Trophies - one for Yorkshire and one for Somerset.

Although Surrey's home record is, as expected, significantly better than their away record, there is another shock in store, with Derbyshire showing up as the county to have recorded more one-day wins at The Oval than any other team. Their four victories from six matches came courtesy of Sunday/National League triumphs in 1998, 1999 and 2002, plus the wholly unexpected 1998 win in the Nat West Trophy quarter-final. Surrey do, however, manage to square the series of matches with the midlands county by virtue of an impressive record at the County Ground, Derby, their only defeat in recent times having come in the C&G Trophy quarter-final of 2003 - another shock result. As for Surrey's record at other away venues, Taunton again proves to have been an unhappy hunting ground, with one victory being dwarfed by five defeats, while successes at Headingley have also been few and far between.

	LIMITED-OVERS RECORD v OTHER TEAMS 1996-2003															
	HOME				AWAY				NEUTRAL				TOTAL			
	W	L	T	A	W	L	T	A	W	L	T	A	W	L	T	A	%age
Derbyshire	2	4	0	0	3	1	0	1	0	0	0	0	5	5	0	1	50.00
Durham	3	1	0	0	4	0	0	0	0	0	0	0	7	1	0	0	87.50
Essex	3	2	0	1	3	4	0	1	0	0	0	0	6	6	0	2	50.00
Glamorgan	5	0	0	0	3	3	0	0	0	0	0	0	8	3	0	0	72.73
Gloucs	6	0	0	0	4	3	0	1	1	0	0	0	11	3	0	1	78.57
Hampshire	4	2	0	0	6	1	0	0	0	0	0	0	10	3	0	0	76.92
Kent	4	2	0	1	2	3	0	0	1	0	0	0	7	5	0	1	58.33
Lancashire	3	1	0	0	1	1	0	1	0	0	0	0	4	2	0	1	66.67
Leics	2	3	0	0	2	2	0	0	0	0	0	0	4	5	0	0	44.44
Middlesex	3	1	0	2	2	1	1	2	0	0	0	0	5	2	1	4	68.75
Northants	1	3	0	1	2	3	0	0	0	0	0	0	3	6	0	1	33.33
Notts	2	2	0	2	1	2	0	2	0	0	0	0	3	4	0	4	42.86
Somerset	3	2	0	0	1	5	0	0	0	0	0	0	4	7	0	0	36.36
Sussex	3	3	0	1	6	2	0	0	0	0	0	0	9	5	0	1	64.29
Warwicks	4	1	0	0	2	3	0	0	0	0	0	0	6	4	0	0	60.00
Worcs	1	2	0	0	2	1	0	0	0	0	0	0	3	3	0	0	50.00
Yorkshire	3	1	0	0	2	5	0	0	0	0	0	0	5	6	0	0	45.45
First-class counties	52	30	0	8	46	40	1	8	2	0	0	0	100	70	1	16	58.77
Brit Univs	2	0	0	0	0	0	0	0	0	0	0	0	2	0	0	0	100.00
Bucks	1	0	0	0	0	0	0	0	0	0	0	0	1	0	0	0	100.00
Devon	0	0	0	0	1	0	0	0	0	0	0	0	1	0	0	0	100.00
Holland	1	0	0	0	0	0	0	0	0	0	0	0	1	0	0	0	100.00
Ireland	0	0	0	0	1	0	0	0	0	0	0	0	1	0	0	0	100.00
Scotland	0	0	0	0	2	0	0	0	0	0	0	0	2	0	0	0	100.00
Staffs	0	0	0	0	1	0	0	0	0	0	0	0	1	0	0	0	100.00
Surrey CB	0	0	0	0	1	0	0	0	0	0	0	0	1	0	0	0	100.00
TOTAL	56	30	0	8	52	40	1	8	2	0	0	0	110	70	1	16	61.05

NB - '% success' = [{(no. of wins x 2) + (no. of ties x 1)} x 100] / [no. of completed matches x 2]

Although Surrey featured in quite a lot of close matches in the limited-overs form of the game (see the tables that follow) it is rather surprising that they were involved in only two tied matches between 1996 and 2003. One of these - the Benson & Hedges Cup zonal game against Sussex at Hove in 2002 - was then decided, under the rules of the competition, in Sussex's favour since they had lost one fewer wicket, leaving just the National League contest against Middlesex at Lord's in 1999 as an officially recognised tie. Of the twenty-eight matches that were decided by fewer than ten runs or three wickets, eighteen (64%) ended in a win for Surrey, which is probably what you would expect, given that the team's one-day record was pretty good during that period. It is interesting to note, however, that both Surrey (twelve of their eighteen narrow victories) and their opponents (six out of ten) scraped home to victory more often when defending a total than when chasing one. This is not totally unexpected since Surrey possessed some fine end-of-innings bowlers - primarily Adam Hollioake, Azhar Mahmood, Ed Giddins and Saqlain Mushtaq - during their glory years, though the statistic also suggests that the side batting second in a one-day game is more likely to buckle under pressure as the contest reaches its conclusion.

Looking at the bigger picture, twenty-eight close finishes from a total of 181 completed matches is a disappointingly small number, revealing that only one game in six or seven results in a nail-biting finale for the players and spectators. If Twenty20 Cup matches were to be included in these statistics in years to come then I would expect this figure to improve, since the likelihood of a close match clearly increases as the number of overs played decreases.

NARROW SURREY VICTORIES IN LIMITED-OVERS MATCHES 1996-2003				
Margin	Opponents	Venue	Comp'n	Season
1 run	Middlesex	Guildford	SL	1998
2 runs	Durham	Riverside	NL	1999
2 runs	Durham	The Oval	NL	1999
2 runs	Essex	Chelmsford	NL	2002
2 runs	Yorkshire	Headingley	NL	2003
6 runs	Somerset	Taunton	CGT	2003
6 runs	Kent	The Oval	NL	2003
7 runs	Yorkshire	Headingley	BHC	2000
8 runs	Glamorgan	Cardiff	NL	2003
9 runs	Somerset	The Oval	BHC	1998
9 runs	Glamorgan	The Oval	CGT	2002
9 runs	Staffordshire	Stone	CGT	2003
1 wkt	Derbyshire	Derby	NL	2002
1 wkt	Worcestershire	Worcester	NL	2003
2 wkts	Warwickshire	The Oval	SL	1996
2 wkts	Northamptonshire	The Oval	SL	1996
2 wkts	Glamorgan	The Oval	SL	1997
2 wkts	Gloucestershire	The Oval	NL	2001
Qualification: Victory by fewer than 10 runs or three wickets				

NARROW SURREY DEFEATS IN LIMITED-OVERS MATCHES 1996-2003				
Margin	Opponents	Venue	Comp'n	Season
Tied*	Sussex	Hove	BHC	2002
1 run	Worcestershire	The Oval	SL	1998
1 run	Kent	Canterbury	BHC	2001
1 run	Hampshire	The Oval	BHC	2002
2 runs	Hampshire	The Oval	BHC	2000
5 runs	Northamptonshire	Northampton	NL	1999

Margin	Opponents	Venue	Comp'n	Season
5 runs	Northamptonshire	Northampton	NL	2002
1 wkt	Gloucestershire	Bristol	NL	2002
2 wkts	Somerset	Guildford	NL	1999
2 wkts	Kent	The Oval	NL	2001
* Sussex won by virtue of losing fewer wickets				
Qualification: Victory by fewer than 10 runs or two wickets				

Surrey played enough games in the Sunday/National League and the Benson & Hedges Cup between 1996 and 2003 for a breakdown of figures in those competitions to be worthwhile.

Surrey's Playing Record In The Sunday/National League

Although they were hugely erratic in the one-day league between 1996 and 2003, Surrey still boast a very respectable record of sixty-eight wins to fifty-one defeats. There were some truly awful performances at The Oval in that time, yet the home record is still impressive, with thirty-eight victories comfortably exceeding the twenty-two losses that were incurred. It is perhaps a little disappointing, however, that no fewer than six visiting counties - Derbyshire, Leicestershire, Northamptonshire, Somerset, Sussex and Worcestershire - boast a winning record on Surrey soil.

Away from home, thirty Surrey wins were almost exactly balanced by twenty-nine defeats, with only seven counties coming out on top overall in their clashes with the men from London SE11. The county of Somerset turns out to be the only one in which Surrey failed to win a Sunday/National League match during their glory years, and a dismal overall record of one win to six defeats marks the cidermen down as a real bogey side in this competition. Northamptonshire also had the Indian sign over Surrey, winning the series of matches by 6-2.

On the other hand, Surrey enjoyed a great deal of success against Durham and Hampshire (6-1), Glamorgan (7-2), Gloucestershire (6-2) and Middlesex (5-1).

SUNDAY/NATIONAL LEAGUE RECORD v OTHER COUNTIES 1996-2003												
	HOME				AWAY				TOTAL			
	W	L	T	A	W	L	T	A	W	L	T	A	% success
Derbyshire	2	3	0	0	3	0	0	1	5	3	0	1	62.50
Durham	2	1	0	0	4	0	0	0	6	1	0	0	85.71
Essex	2	1	0	1	2	3	0	0	4	4	0	1	50.00
Glamorgan	4	0	0	0	3	2	0	0	7	2	0	0	77.78
Gloucestershire	4	0	0	0	2	2	0	1	6	2	0	1	75.00
Hampshire	3	0	0	0	3	1	0	0	6	1	0	0	85.71
Kent	3	1	0	0	1	2	0	0	4	3	0	0	57.14
Lancashire	2	0	0	0	1	1	0	1	3	1	0	1	75.00
Leicestershire	1	3	0	0	2	1	0	0	3	4	0	0	42.86
Middlesex	3	1	0	1	2	0	1	1	5	1	1	2	78.57
Northamptonshire	1	3	0	1	1	3	0	0	2	6	0	1	25.00
Nottinghamshire	1	1	0	2	1	2	0	2	2	3	0	4	40.00
Somerset	1	2	0	0	0	4	0	0	1	6	0	0	14.29
Sussex	1	3	0	0	2	1	0	0	3	4	0	0	42.86
Warwickshire	4	1	0	0	1	3	0	0	5	4	0	0	55.56
Worcestershire	1	2	0	0	1	1	0	0	2	3	0	0	40.00
Yorkshire	3	0	0	0	1	3	0	0	4	3	0	0	57.14
TOTAL	38	22	0	5	30	29	1	6	68	51	1	11	57.08

NB - '% success' = [{(no. of wins x 2) + (no. of ties x 1)} x 100] / [no. of completed matches x 2]

Surrey's Playing Record In The Benson & Hedges Cup

The first thing to note is that Surrey didn't cross swords with Derbyshire, Durham, Northamptonshire, Warwickshire or Worcestershire in this competition. This was primarily because the qualifying groups were, generally speaking, organised geographically to save on travel costs and allow more regional derbies. Consequently, Surrey played the majority of their games against the other home counties, and the fact that trips to 'bogey grounds' like Taunton and Headingley were a rarity may explain why the club's away record is almost as good as their home record in this competition! Surprisingly, Hampshire are revealed as the only side to win twice at The Oval, though Surrey more than made up for this by winning all three encounters played at Southampton or The Rose Bowl.

BENSON & HEDGES CUP RECORD v OTHER TEAMS 1996-2002											
	HOME			AWAY			NEUTRAL			TOTAL	
	W	L	A	W	L	A	W	L	A	W	L	A	% success
Essex	1	0	0	1	1	1	0	0	0	2	1	1	66.67
Glamorgan	0	0	0	0	1	0	0	0	0	0	1	0	0.00
Gloucestershire	2	0	0	1	1	0	1	0	0	4	1	0	80.00
Hampshire	1	2	0	3	0	0	0	0	0	4	2	0	66.67
Kent	1	1	1	1	1	0	1	0	0	3	2	1	60.00
Lancashire	1	0	0	0	0	0	0	0	0	1	0	0	100.00
Leicestershire	1	0	0	0	1	0	0	0	0	1	1	0	50.00
Middlesex	0	0	1	0	1	1	0	0	0	0	1	2	0.00
Nottinghamshire	1	0	0	0	0	0	0	0	0	1	0	0	100.00
Somerset	1	0	0	0	0	0	0	0	0	1	0	0	100.00
Sussex	1	0	1	3	1	0	0	0	0	4	1	1	80.00
Yorkshire	0	1	0	1	0	0	0	0	0	1	1	0	50.00
All first-class counties	10	4	3	10	7	2	2	0	0	22	11	5	66.67
British Universities	2	0	0	0	0	0	0	0	0	2	0	0	100.00
Ireland	0	0	0	1	0	0	0	0	0	1	0	0	100.00
TOTAL	12	4	3	11	7	2	2	0	0	25	11	5	69.44

NB - '% success' = [(no. of wins x 2) x 100] / [no. of completed matches x 2]

13 Player Statistics

This section concentrates on the individual performances of Surrey players during the 1996-2003 glory years, looking first at the County Championship and then at limited-overs cricket.

Eight-Year Averages - County Championship Batting

Mark Ramprakash made a remarkable impact at The Oval in his first three seasons after crossing the Thames - his figures are so good, in fact, that Surrey supporters would probably suggest that he could have walked across the river! Graham Thorpe joins his former England team-mate in averaging over fifty for the club in Championship matches during the period covered by this book, while no fewer than eight players average over forty, which is widely considered to be the mark of excellence. I believe that the bottom portion of this list is the most telling, however, with only five men failing to average twenty, and just two obvious 'rabbits' - neither of whom played very often - in evidence. The length of Surrey's batting so often proved vital in the Championship, and this list shows that their four most regular bowlers of the period all managed to score over twenty runs per innings on average - Martin Bicknell comes in at 30.25, Alex Tudor at 23.76, Ian Salisbury at 22.33 and Saqlain Mushtaq at 22.16. It's no wonder it was often said that Surrey were never bowled out until the last wicket had fallen!

COUNTY CHAMPIONSHIP BATTING AVERAGES 1996-2003										
	M	I	NO	Runs	HS	Ave	100	50	ct	st
M.R. Ramprakash	37	60	8	3088	279*	59.38	11	12	17	-
G.P. Thorpe	57	89	9	4177	222	52.21	14	18	59	-
M.A. Butcher	93	153	12	6498	259	46.09	14	38	99	-
R. Clarke	18	28	3	1093	153*	43.72	3	5	18	-
A.J. Hollioake	107	159	13	6174	208	42.29	11	38	111	-
A.J. Stewart	51	76	6	2942	271*	42.03	3	18	109	5
I.J. Ward	88	147	12	5604	168*	41.51	14	30	47	-
A.D. Brown	117	179	17	6629	295*	40.92	21	27	125	1
Azhar Mahmood	13	17	3	537	98	38.36	-	5	20	-
B.P. Julian	16	23	2	759	119	36.14	2	3	9	-
D.J. Bicknell	36	61	4	2041	162	35.81	6	5	12	-
M.P. Bicknell	114	141	31	3327	141	30.25	2	15	37	-
N. Shahid	61	100	8	2726	150	29.63	5	13	68	-
C.C. Lewis	21	32	3	831	94	28.66	-	4	23	-
J.N. Batty	78	113	17	2748	168*	28.63	5	10	210	30
J.D. Ratcliffe	46	77	5	2019	135	28.04	2	11	17	-
G.P. Butcher	12	18	2	426	70	26.63	-	3	3	-
G.J. Kersey	15	20	4	402	68*	25.12	-	3	45	1
R.M. Pearson	15	15	9	143	37	23.83	-	-	4	-
A.J. Tudor	60	78	19	1402	116	23.76	1	4	15	-
B.C. Hollioake	65	98	4	2197	118	23.37	1	12	58	-
I.D.K. Salisbury	101	127	22	2345	101*	22.33	2	9	50	-
Saqlain Mushtaq	72	89	25	1418	69	22.16	-	8	26	-
J. Ormond	27	31	9	406	47	18.45	-	-	8	-
J.A. Knott	10	18	6	221	41*	18.42	-	-	9	1
J.E. Benjamin	34	40	15	359	38*	14.36	-	-	3	-
E.S.H. Giddins	18	21	12	59	9*	6.55	-	-	4	-
R.M. Amin	14	18	8	35	12	3.50	-	-	6	-
Qualification: 15 innings										

Eight-Year Averages - County Championship Bowling

Although his influence waned somewhat towards the end of Surrey's glory years, Saqlain Mushtaq's figures remain exceptional and prove what an important part he played in the club's Championship triumphs. The same, of course, can be said of Martin Bicknell, though his contribution was perhaps even greater because he missed so few games, offering reliability to his captain week-in week-out season after season. Alex Tudor and Ian Salisbury were the perfect foils to these two, proving how effective bowlers can be when they hunt in pairs... or, in the case of Surrey between 1999 and 2002, as a group of four!

Mark Butcher may be the surprise man in this list, appearing in fourth position, though it should be pointed out that the vast majority of his overs were delivered in the early years of the period under investigation when pitches tended to be rather more helpful to seam bowlers. If the pitches in this country continue to improve as they have done in recent years then bowling averages will continue to rise, with very few bowlers able to average under thirty over the course of a season. Economy rates below three runs per over could also become a thing of the past.

COUNTY CHAMPIONSHIP BOWLING AVERAGES 1996-2003									
	O	M	Runs	Wkts	Ave	BB	10wm	5wi	Econ
Saqlain Mushtaq	2843.0	749	7087	356	19.91	8-65	10	30	2.49
M.P. Bicknell	3601.1	945	10173	451	22.56	9-47	2	17	2.82
Azhar Mahmood	371.4	75	1339	54	24.80	8-61	-	2	3.60
M.A. Butcher	445.4	99	1328	53	25.06	5-86	-	1	2.98
A.J. Tudor	1450.2	302	5173	191	27.08	7-48	-	10	3.57
I.D.K. Salisbury	2699.0	592	7568	275	27.52	8-60	2	10	2.80
B.P. Julian	447.4	86	1762	61	28.88	6-37	-	3	3.94
C.C. Lewis	552.2	116	1859	60	30.98	5-25	-	2	3.37
T.J. Murtagh	200.1	29	779	25	31.16	5-39	-	1	3.89
B.C. Hollioake	969.0	188	3329	101	32.96	5-51	-	1	3.44
J. Ormond	851.2	152	3143	95	33.08	5-45	1	4	3.69
J.E. Benjamin	792.4	166	2680	75	35.73	6-35	-	1	3.38
E.S.H. Giddins	561.4	124	1798	49	36.69	5-48	-	1	3.20
R.M. Amin	417.3	121	1053	25	42.12	4-87	-	-	2.52
A.J. Hollioake	674.3	133	2303	53	43.45	5-62	-	1	3.41
R. Clarke	206.4	20	1005	22	45.68	4-21	-	-	4.86
R.M. Pearson	501.0	105	1599	33	48.45	5-142	-	1	3.19

Qualification: 20 wickets

County Championship Appearances

It is probably quite significant to Surrey's success in the County Championship that the top four men in this list are a batsman, a seam bowler, a spinner and their very influential captain. They were very few games, therefore, when the side was without at least one leading performer in each of those areas of the team. The fact that the England selectors decided that Brown, Bicknell, Adam Hollioake and Salisbury were not worthy of selection on very many occasions was very much to Surrey's advantage as it left them with the nucleus of a strong side at almost all times.

Looking more closely at the figures, Ali Brown's record of appearing in 117 games out of a maximum 131 (four seasons of seventeen matches, three of sixteen, and one of fifteen in 2001, when the match at Old Trafford was abandoned without teams being declared) is quite remarkable. The fact that he played in 89.3% of the Championship matches during the club's glory years is testimony to a fine fitness record and a consistency of performance that meant he was rarely dropped from the team. The same applies to Martin Bicknell, who suffered from a spate of injuries earlier in his career yet was hardly ever missing from the team sheet between 1996 and 2003, playing in 87.0% of the county's Championship fixtures - a fine record for an opening bowler. Although Ian Salisbury is some way behind Brown and Bicknell in terms of the number of matches played, it should be remembered that he didn't join Surrey until the 1997 season. He therefore runs Brown very close when the percentage of games played during his time at the club is calculated, since his 101 appearances from a maximum possible 114 games equates to an 88.6% appearance record.

As one would expect, Alec Stewart and Graham Thorpe, regular members of England's Test and one-day sides, fail to feature in this table, having played in fifty-one and fifty-seven Championship matches respectively during the period under investigation. It is testament to Surrey's strength in depth that they were able to cope so admirably with the frequent absences of these two highly influential players.

MOST COUNTY CHAMPIONSHIP APPEARANCES 1996-2003	
Player	Appearances
Alistair Brown	117
Martin Bicknell	114
Adam Hollioake	107
Ian Salisbury	101
Mark Butcher	93
Ian Ward	88
Jonathan Batty	78
Saqlain Mushtaq	72
Ben Hollioake	65
Nadeem Shahid	61

County Championship Runs

There are no real surprises in the table of leading run-makers, though Mark Ramprakash does fantastically well to make the top ten after playing for just three 'glory years' seasons, 2001-2003. After a slow start to his Surrey career with the bat, Jonathan Batty's form in 2002 and 2003 enables him to take ninth place, while the combination of Martin Bicknell's average and sixth position in the list of run-scorers underlines his right to be considered a true all-rounder at county level.

MOST COUNTY CHAMPIONSHIP RUNS 1996-2003		
Player	Runs	Average
Alistair Brown	6629	40.92
Mark Butcher	6498	46.09
Adam Hollioake	6174	42.29
Ian Ward	5604	41.51
Graham Thorpe	4177	52.21
Martin Bicknell	3327	30.25
Mark Ramprakash	3088	59.38
Alec Stewart	2942	42.03
Jonathan Batty	2748	28.63
Nadeem Shahid	2726	29.63

County Championship Centuries... And Near Misses

When it comes to Championship centuries no one can touch Ali Brown, who is well known for his ability to convert fifties into hundreds... and then hundreds into big hundreds. Although his impressive average of a century every 8.52 innings is trumped by both Mark Ramprakash and Graham Thorpe, who notched a ton every 5.45 and 6.36 innings respectively, it is only fair to point out that Brown has generally batted one or two positions below these two in the order, which has clearly put him at a slight disadvantage when it comes to completing centuries.

As well as boasting the second-best innings-per-century average, Thorpe turns out to be the only man to have scored a Championship hundred in each of the eight seasons covered by this book, which is a fantastic achievement given that he only played in a handful of matches in 1998, 2001 and 2002.

The biggest surprise when looking at this table is surely the lowly position of Alec Stewart, scorer of just three tons from seventy-six innings. It should be noted, however, that he was dismissed in the nineties on no fewer than six occasions between 1996 and 2003. Had he been able to convert these into centuries, his average in this table would have matched that of Brown. Mark Butcher, with five nineties, is the one man to come close to Stewart's tally of six, while the only two players on this list to avoid being dismissed in the notoriously nervous nineties are Ian Ward and Darren Bicknell.

Looking at the bigger picture, Surrey batsmen registered twenty-seven completed innings in the nineties during the period under consideration, while opposition batsmen notched thirty-two scores of that magnitude, with an unexpectedly high number of these - fourteen - being recorded in 2002 and 2003.

Another statistical quirk turns up when examining the grounds on which these nineties were scored. No fewer than sixteen of the twenty-seven racked up by Surrey players came at The Oval, while another four were made on the home soil of Guildford and Whitgift School. Even allowing for the fact that Surrey's pitches have tended to be more batsman-friendly than some of those away from home - allowing a greater number of batsmen to compile innings of ninety and beyond - one would have expected a more even balance between nineties recorded at home and nineties scored on opposition grounds. An analysis of the near misses by opposition batsmen reveals almost exact parity between home and away scores in the nineties, with thirteen of the thirty-two nineties being made at The Oval, one at Guildford and one at Whitgift.

Before moving on to Championship half-centuries, we should spare a thought for those batsmen who fell just a single short of the magical three figures. Five Surrey batsmen - Alec Stewart, Jon Batty, Scott Newman, Mark Ramprakash and Graham Thorpe - suffered this fate during the club's glory years, with the first four instances coming in 2002 and Thorpe's ninety-nine coming in 2003. Curiously, Stewart's 'one short' against Sussex at the start of the 2002 campaign was the first by a Surrey player in the Championship since Paul Atkins was dismissed on the brink of his century against Nottinghamshire in July 1992. After such a long gap, I suppose it was inevitable that three further ninety-nines should follow later in the 2002 season!

There were also five opposition batsmen who fell one short of three figures in Championship matches involving Surrey between 1996 and 2003, though these near misses were more evenly spread out over the course of the eight years - Trevor Penney (1997), Michael Slater (1998), Mark Lathwell (2001), Michael Burns and Nick Pothas (both 2002) were the men who were left to rue their misfortune.

MOST COUNTY CHAMPIONSHIP CENTURIES 1996-2003			
Player	100s	No. of inns	Inns/100 average
Alistair Brown	21	179	8.52
Mark Butcher	14	153	10.93
Graham Thorpe	14	89	6.36
Ian Ward	14	147	10.50
Adam Hollioake	11	159	14.45
Mark Ramprakash	11	60	5.45
Darren Bicknell	6	61	10.16
Jonathan Batty	5	113	22.60
Nadeem Shahid	5	100	20.00
Rikki Clarke	3	28	9.33
Alec Stewart	3	76	25.33

County Championship Half-Centuries

An examination of the number of innings of fifty-plus scored by Surrey batsmen between 1996 and 2003 reveals that Mark Butcher was the only man to amass a half-century of half-centuries. It also shows that there isn't a lot to choose between the regular top-six batsmen of the period, with each of them passing fifty roughly every third or fourth innings.

MOST COUNTY CHAMPIONSHIP HALF-CENTURIES 1996-2003			
Player	Scores 50+	No. of inns	Inns/50+ average
Mark Butcher	52	153	2.94
Adam Hollioake	49	159	3.24
Alistair Brown	48	179	3.73
Ian Ward	44	147	3.34
Graham Thorpe	32	89	2.78
Mark Ramprakash	23	60	2.61
Alec Stewart	21	76	3.62
Nadeem Shahid	18	100	5.55
Martin Bicknell	17	141	8.29
Jonathan Batty	15	113	7.53

County Championship Double-Centuries

Surrey batsmen amassed ten double-tons during the 1996-2003 glory years, with Ali Brown and Mark Butcher managing two apiece, and Mark Ramprakash a highly impressive three in his first three seasons with the county. Only four opposition batsmen - shown in the second of the two tables that follow - reached the magical 200 mark, with Ramprakash, when he was a Middlesex player, being one of those men. It is interesting to note that all of the opposition double-centuries came at either the start or end of a season - Bowler's came in the opening match of 1996; Ramprakash's was scored in the penultimate game of 1999 when Surrey had already secured the title; Smith's knock clinched the 1998 Championship for Leicestershire in the final match of the season; and Flower's was compiled in the last game of 2003 after Surrey's campaign had gone off the rails.

It is an indication of the batting talent in Surrey's ranks during their run of successful seasons in the Championship that they racked up 118 centuries to 64 by their opponents, and converted a much higher proportion of these into big hundreds - while opposing batsmen registered just a dozen scores of 150-plus between 1996 and 2003, Surrey's batsmen notched thirty-five individual scores of that magnitude.

COUNTY CHAMPIONSHIP DOUBLE CENTURIES BY SURREY BATSMEN 1996-2003

		Opponents	Venue	Season
295*	Alistair Brown	Leicestershire	Oakham School	2000
279*	Mark Ramprakash	Nottinghamshire	Whitgift School	2003
271*	Alec Stewart	Yorkshire	The Oval	1997
265	Alistair Brown	Middlesex	Lord's	1999
259	Mark Butcher	Leicestershire	Leicester	1999
230	Mark Butcher	Glamorgan	Cardiff	2001
222	Graham Thorpe	Glamorgan	The Oval	1997
218	Mark Ramprakash	Somerset	Taunton	2002
210*	Mark Ramprakash	Warwickshire	The Oval	2002
208	Adam Hollioake	Leicestershire	The Oval	2002

COUNTY CHAMPIONSHIP DOUBLE CENTURIES AGAINST SURREY 1996-2003

		For	Venue	Season
209*	Mark Ramprakash	Middlesex	Lord's	1999
207	Peter Bowler	Somerset	Taunton	1996
204	Ben Smith	Leicestershire	The Oval	1998
201*	Andy Flower	Essex	The Oval	2003

County Championship Wickets

The top four places in the table of leading wicket-takers are predictably filled by the four bowlers who were utterly dominant during the Championship-winning seasons of 1999 and 2000 in addition to playing leading roles in the 2002 triumph. The figures of Martin Bicknell and Saqlain Mushtaq would be outstanding in almost any era of the game and underline why Adam Hollioake often used to pair them in the attack when Surrey were under pressure or in desperate need of a wicket.

Ian Salisbury's statistics, in a country where conditions and pitches are far from conducive to wrist-spin bowling, are also very creditable indeed. Injuries and increasingly flat pitches made life difficult for him in the closing seasons of the period covered by this book but his partnership with the incredible Saqlain was a huge factor in many of the county's victories. In the same way, Alex Tudor was a superb foil to the admirable Bicknell, despite being frequently beset by injury problems.

The phenomenal success and longevity of the four main bowlers is underlined by the fact that Ben Hollioake was the only other man to capture a hundred Championship wickets, though James Ormond came close to reaching this milestone by claiming ninety-five victims during his first two seasons with the club.

MOST COUNTY CHAMPIONSHIP WICKETS 1996-2003		
Player	Wickets	Average
Martin Bicknell	451	22.56
Saqlain Mushtaq	356	19.91
Ian Salisbury	275	27.52
Alex Tudor	191	27.08
Ben Hollioake	101	32.96
James Ormond	95	33.08
Joey Benjamin	75	35.73
Brendon Julian	61	28.88
Chris Lewis	60	30.98
Azhar Mahmood	54	24.80

County Championship Five-Wicket Hauls

When it comes to five-wicket hauls, Saqlain Mushtaq predictably outstrips everyone else, having turned the trick thirty times in his seventy-two matches with the club between 1997 and 2003. It's a phenomenal performance, though the frequency with which he captured five wickets in an innings did drop off a little towards the end of the period as the off-spinner's form declined slightly and pitches around the country became more batsman-friendly.

During their glory years Surrey bowlers captured eighty-eight five-fors to the fifty-five managed by their opponents.

MOST COUNTY CHAMPIONSHIP FIVE-WICKET HAULS 1996-2003			
Player	No. of times 5 wkts/inns	No. of matches	No. of times 10 wkts/match
Saqlain Mushtaq	30	72	10
Martin Bicknell	17	114	2
Ian Salisbury	10	101	2
Alex Tudor	10	60	0
James Ormond	4	27	1
Brendon Julian	3	16	0

Best Bowling In A County Championship Innings

There is a little more competition for Saqlain when considering the instances of a Surrey bowler taking seven wickets in a Championship innings. Although the off-spinner still dominates the table with seven seven-plus hauls - six of which were picked up at The Oval - Martin Bicknell and Ian Salisbury each performed the feat three times, Alex Tudor managed it twice and Azhar Mahmood once. While Saqlain clearly appreciated the pitches in London SE11, Bicknell's liking for the tracks and conditions at his club ground in Guildford is demonstrated by the fact that all three of his best performances, statistically speaking, were recorded there. Looking at the wider picture, it is interesting to note that only three of Surrey's best bowling performances of the period came away from home, with The Oval being the venue on ten occasions, and Guildford - thanks to Bicknell - on three.

Opposition bowlers managed just six hauls of seven wickets in matches against Surrey between 1996 and 2003, with an even split between occurrences on Surrey and opposition soil.

BEST INNINGS FIGURES RECORDED BY SURREY BOWLERS IN THE COUNTY CHAMPIONSHIP 1996-2003

		Opponents	Venue	Season
9-47 *	Martin Bicknell	Leicestershire	Guildford	2000
8-60	Ian Salisbury	Somerset	The Oval	2000
8-61	Azhar Mahmood	Lancashire	The Oval	2002
8-65	Saqlain Mushtaq	Derbyshire	The Oval	1998
7-11	Saqlain Mushtaq	Derbyshire	The Oval	2000
7-19	Saqlain Mushtaq	Sussex	Hove	1999
7-30	Saqlain Mushtaq	Sussex	The Oval	1998
7-38	Saqlain Mushtaq	Durham	The Oval	1999
7-41	Saqlain Mushtaq	Worcestershire	The Oval	1998
7-48	Alex Tudor	Lancashire	The Oval	2000
7-58	Saqlain Mushtaq	Yorkshire	The Oval	2001
7-60	Martin Bicknell	Northamptonshire	Guildford	2001
7-65	Ian Salisbury	Glamorgan	Swansea	1998
7-72 +	Martin Bicknell	Leicestershire	Guildford	2000
7-77	Alex Tudor	Leicestershire	Leicester	1999
7-105	Ian Salisbury	Durham	The Oval	2000

* 2nd innings of match   + 1st innings of match

BEST INNINGS FIGURES RECORDED AGAINST SURREY IN THE COUNTY CHAMPIONSHIP 1996-2003

		For	Venue	Season
8-49	Mohammad Akram	Essex	The Oval	2003
8-63	Devon Malcolm	Leicestershire	Leicester	2001
7-34	Tim Munton	Derbyshire	Derby	2000
7-50	Gavin Hamilton	Yorkshire	Headingley	1998
7-93	Carl Hooper	Kent	The Oval	1998
7-110	Dougie Brown	Warwickshire	The Oval	2002

Best Bowling In A County Championship Match

Although the tables of ten-wicket match performances may, at first glance, appear to reveal nothing new - Saqlain dominates as a bowler and The Oval as a venue - there are a couple of points of interest.

Firstly, none of the fifteen ten-wicket performances by a Surrey bowler came at a venue north of Lord's! Given that twelve of these occurrences came from a spinner, I suppose one shouldn't be totally surprised that the south-east of the country, which tends to be drier and warmer, provided the venue on each occasion. Similarly, the three ten-wicket displays by opposition bowlers that occurred outside the home counties were all by seam bowlers.

Additionally, it is interesting to note how few ten-wicket performances came post-2000 - just five of the twenty-one occurrences in these tables were recorded in the last three years of the eight-year period under consideration. This could, of course, reflect that Surrey's bowling was in decline, but I suspect it was more to do with the significant improvement in the quality of pitches around the country as we entered the twenty-first century.

BEST MATCH FIGURES RECORDED BY SURREY BOWLERS IN THE COUNTY CHAMPIONSHIP 1996-2003				
		Opponents	Venue	Season
16-119	Martin Bicknell	Leicestershire	Guildford	2000
12-91	Ian Salisbury	Somerset	The Oval	2000
12-110	Saqlain Mushtaq	Durham	The Oval	1999
11-104	Saqlain Mushtaq	Sussex	The Oval	1998
11-104	Saqlain Mushtaq	Yorkshire	The Oval	2000
11-107	Saqlain Mushtaq	Derbyshire	The Oval	1998
11-117	Martin Bicknell	Glamorgan	The Oval	2001
11-154	Ian Salisbury	Durham	The Oval	2000
11-157	Saqlain Mushtaq	Worcestershire	The Oval	1998
11-180	Saqlain Mushtaq	Hampshire	The Oval	2002
10-97	Saqlain Mushtaq	Sussex	Hove	1999
10-116	Saqlain Mushtaq	Middlesex	Lord's	1997
10-128	Saqlain Mushtaq	Durham	The Oval	1997
10-135	Saqlain Mushtaq	Hampshire	Southampton	2000
10-178	James Ormond	Warwickshire	The Oval	2002

BEST MATCH FIGURES RECORDED AGAINST SURREY IN THE COUNTY CHAMPIONSHIP 1996-2003				
		For	Venue	Season
11-72	Gavin Hamilton	Yorkshire	Headingley	1998
10-119	Allan Donald	Warwickshire	Edgbaston	1997
10-142	Mohammad Akram	Essex	The Oval	2003
10-154	Muttiah Muralitharan	Lancashire	The Oval	1999
10-173	Gary Keedy	Lancashire	The Oval	1997
10-187	Devon Malcolm	Leicestershire	Leicester	2001

County Championship Catches (excluding wicketkeepers)

Catching statistics are often fairly worthless since dropped catches are never recorded - principally because it is often difficult to judge such things. Close-to-the-wicket catchers are always going to dominate this kind of list, especially when their team has had high-class bowlers. Ali Brown, Mark Butcher and Graham Thorpe picked up a large proportion of their catches in the slips off Martin Bicknell and Alex Tudor, while Adam Hollioake and Nadeem Shahid were outstanding fielders at bat-pad for the spinners.

MOST COUNTY CHAMPIONSHIP CATCHES 1996-2003		
Player	Catches	Matches
Alistair Brown	125	117
Adam Hollioake	111	107
Mark Butcher	99	93
Nadeem Shahid	68	61
Graham Thorpe	59	57
Ben Hollioake	58	65
Ian Salisbury	50	101
Ian Ward	47	88

It is perhaps a little surprising that there were only two instances of a Surrey outfielder claiming more than three catches in an innings between 1996 and 2003, though the first of these almost equalled a long-standing record. By claiming six catches as Kent were routed by Saqlain and Salisbury at The Oval in 1998, Graham Thorpe fell just one short of matching Micky Stewart's record of seven against Northamptonshire at Northampton in 1957.

MOST CATCHES IN A COUNTY CHAMPIONSHIP INNINGS 1996-2003				
Catches	Player	Opponents	Venue	Season
6	Graham Thorpe	Kent	The Oval	1998
4	Adam Hollioake	Somerset	The Oval	2000

NB - No outfielder took more than three catches in an innings against Surrey during the period in question.

The table for most catches in a match shows Thorpe, predictably enough, to be top of the pile again. His seven versus Kent again falls one short of the county record, which is eight by Tony Lock against Warwickshire at The Oval in 1957. Ali Brown's tally of five catches against Glamorgan in 1999 was augmented by a stumping during his spell as a stand-in for the injured Jon Batty.

MOST CATCHES IN A COUNTY CHAMPIONSHIP MATCH 1996-2003				
Catches	Player	Opponents	Venue	Season
7	Graham Thorpe	Kent	The Oval	1998
5	Adam Hollioake	Yorkshire	Middlesbrough	1996
5	Alistair Brown	Durham	The Oval	1999
5 *	Alistair Brown	Glamorgan	The Oval	1999
5	Adam Hollioake	Hampshire	The Oval	2000
5	Nadeem Shahid	Hampshire	The Oval	2002

* Includes 2 catches as stand-in wicketkeeper in 2nd innings

Yorkshire's David Byas, a high-class slip fielder, held five catches in the match at The Oval in 1997, and also managed to take two 'fours' against Surrey between 1996 and 2003 - the first for Yorkshire at Headingley in 2001 and the second for Lancashire at The Oval in 2002.

MOST CATCHES AGAINST SURREY IN A COUNTY CHAMPIONSHIP MATCH 1996-2003				
Catches	Player	Opponents	Venue	Season
5	David Byas	Yorkshire	The Oval	1997

County Championship Wicketkeepers' Dismissals
Surrey fielded just four specialist wicketkeepers in the County Championship during their glory years, with Jon Batty the regular gloveman for most of that time. It is interesting to see that the three principal keepers of the period all average almost exactly three dismissals per match, though Batty's stumping rate is much higher than that achieved by both Alec Stewart and the late Graham Kersey. This is easily explained by the lack of a top quality spinner in Surrey's ranks during the early years of the period under consideration - Kersey and Stewart were the club's wicketkeepers at this time, while Batty came into the side after Saqlain and Salisbury had become well established and were at the peak of their powers.

MOST DISMISSALS BY SURREY WICKETKEEPERS IN THE COUNTY CHAMPIONSHIP 1996-2003

Player	Total Dismissals	Catches + Stumpings	Matches *
Jonathan Batty	240	210 + 30	78
Alec Stewart	95	90 + 5	33
Graham Kersey	46	45 + 1	15
James Knott	9	8 + 1	5

* Only includes matches when keeping wicket

MOST DISMISSALS BY A SURREY WICKETKEEPER IN A COUNTY CHAMPIONSHIP INNINGS 1996-2003

	Player	Opponents	Venue	Season
6 (all ct)	Graham Kersey	Durham	Stockton-on-Tees	1996
5 (all ct)	Jonathan Batty	Northamptonshire	Northampton	1999
5 (4ct, 1st)	Jonathan Batty	Leicestershire	Oakham School	2000
5 (all ct)	Jonathan Batty	Northamptonshire	Guildford	2001
5 (all ct)	Jonathan Batty	Lancashire	Old Trafford	2002
5 (all ct)	Jonathan Batty	Leicestershire	The Oval	2002
5 (4ct, 1st)	Alec Stewart	Lancashire *	The Oval	2002
5 (all ct)	Alec Stewart	Lancashire +	The Oval	2002
5 (4ct, 1st)	Jonathan Batty	Kent	Canterbury	2003

* 1st innings of the match   + 2nd innings of the match

MOST DISMISSALS BY A WICKETKEEPER AGAINST SURREY IN A COUNTY CHAMPIONSHIP INNINGS 1996-2003

	Player	For	Venue	Season
6 (all ct)	Rob Turner	Somerset	Taunton	2001
5 (all ct)	Adrian Shaw	Glamorgan	The Oval	1997
5 (all ct)	Simon Guy	Yorkshire	Scarborough	2000
5 (4ct, 1st)	Chris Read	Nottinghamshire	Whitgift School	2003

MOST DISMISSALS BY A SURREY WICKETKEEPER IN A COUNTY CHAMPIONSHIP MATCH 1996-2003

	Player	Opponents	Venue	Season
10 (9ct, 1st)	Alec Stewart	Lancashire	The Oval	2002
9 (all ct)	Graham Kersey	Durham	Stockton-on-Tees	1996
8 (all ct)	Jonathan Batty	Northamptonshire	Guildford	2001
7 (all ct)	Jonathan Batty	Northamptonshire	Northampton	1999
7 (all ct)	Jonathan Batty	Durham	The Riverside	2000

MOST DISMISSALS BY A WICKETKEEPER AGAINST SURREY IN A COUNTY CHAMPIONSHIP MATCH 1996-2003

	Player	For	Venue	Season
9 (all ct)	Rob Turner	Somerset	Taunton	2001
7 (6ct, 1st)	Adrian Shaw	Glamorgan	The Oval	1997
7 (5ct, 2st)	Paul Nixon	Leicestershire	The Oval	1998
7 (all ct)	Mark Wallace	Glamorgan	The Oval	2001

(Empics/Surrey CCC)

NADEEM SHAHID

(Empics/Surrey CCC)

ALEC STEWART

(Empics/Surrey CCC)

GRAHAM THORPE

(Empics/Surrey CCC)

ALEX TUDOR

(Empics/Surrey CCC)

IAN WARD

(Empics/Surrey CCC)
ED GIDDINS

(Empics/Surrey CCC)
DAVID WARD

© www.cricket-heroes.net

BRENDON JULIAN

(Empics/Surrey CCC)

GRAHAM KERSEY

(Surrey Photo Library)
DAVE GILBERT

(Empics/Surrey CCC)
ALAN BUTCHER & KEITH MEDLYCOTT

With Or Without You - County Championship 'Key Men'

The following table attempts (and I use that word advisedly) to reveal Surrey's key players in the County Championship during the period covered by this book by looking at the team's results both with and without each individual player. So, taking Chris Lewis as an example:- Surrey won nine, drew nine and lost three of the Championship matches in which he played during the years he was with the club (1996-1997). Using a simple system of awarding two points for a win, one for a draw, and nothing for a defeat, that equates to a 64.29% success rate for Surrey in the matches he played. Similarly, the team won four, drew five and lost four of the matches in which he didn't play during that same period, which - using the same simple formula - equates to a 50.00% success rate. By subtracting the success rate figure for when he **didn't** play from the success rate figure for when he **did** play, we arrive at what we could call a 'success difference'. The higher the figure, the more significant the player was to the team, though I would stress that these statistics can only give a rough guideline, since Surrey's 'fringe' players often only got a chance to play when the team was lacking its international players and was, consequently, below full strength. I therefore think it would be wrong for me to comment on any individual's placing in the table.

Please note that the qualification rules were quite strict for this table, in order to produce the most reliable results - a player needed to have played for a minimum of three seasons or, if they played for only two, to have played in and missed at least a dozen matches.

Special thanks are due to Richard Arnold for his help with producing these figures.

SURREY'S KEY MEN IN THE COUNTY CHAMPIONSHIP 1996-2003									
		WITH PLAYER				WITHOUT PLAYER			
Player	Difference	W	D	L	%success	W	D	L	%success
Martin Bicknell	+29.00	58	44	12	70.18%	5	4	8	41.18%
Saqlain Mushtaq	+21.93	42	23	7	74.31%	13	18	11	52.38%
Ian Salisbury	+18.32	50	38	13	68.32%	5	3	5	50.00%
Azhar Mahmood	+16.39	8	4	1	76.92%	8	7	4	60.53%
Chris Lewis	+14.29	9	9	3	64.29%	4	5	4	50.00%
Jon Batty	+13.57	42	26	10	70.51%	13	15	8	56.94%
Ian Ward	+13.55	46	30	12	69.32%	9	11	6	55.77%
Mark Ramprakash	+11.22	16	17	4	66.22%	3	5	2	55.00%
Alistair Brown	+10.38	59	40	18	67.52%	4	8	2	57.14%
Mark Butcher	+10.14	47	35	11	69.35%	16	13	9	59.21%
Gary Butcher	+4.17	6	6	0	75.00%	18	15	3	70.83%
Graham Thorpe	+2.00	26	25	6	67.54%	37	23	14	65.54%
Adam Hollioake	-0.31	50	42	15	66.36%	13	6	5	66.67%
Darren Bicknell	-3.33	18	12	6	66.67%	7	7	1	70.00%
Alex Tudor	-4.14	27	23	10	64.17%	36	25	10	68.31%
Jason Ratcliffe	-5.83	24	12	10	65.22%	20	14	4	71.05%
Alec Stewart	-6.00	21	22	8	62.75%	42	26	12	68.75%
Nadeem Shahid	-6.18	29	19	13	63.11%	34	29	7	69.29%
Rupesh Amin	-6.20	7	3	4	60.71%	32	27	9	66.91%
Ben Hollioake	-8.98	30	22	13	63.08%	17	15	2	72.06%
Ed Giddins	-18.59	6	9	3	58.33%	7	6	0	76.92%
Joey Benjamin	-27.41	13	11	10	54.41%	22	10	1	81.82%
Rikki Clarke	-39.29	5	8	5	50.00%	11	3	0	89.29%
Qualification:- Three seasons/Two seasons with a minimum 12 games played & 12 games missed									

County Championship Captaincy Records

A study of the records of the players who captained Surrey in County Championship matches between 1996 and 2003 reveals that Adam Hollioake led the side in ninety-five of the 131 fixtures, winning almost half and losing only one in seven. Mark Butcher comes next in the list with fifteen games at the helm, eight of them in 1999 when Hollioake was absent with England's World Cup squad, and boasts a very impressive record of ten wins and just one defeat - if he can repeat that success rate in 2005 then Surrey will be back on the glory trail! Even when he was on the losing side, at Taunton in 1998, Butcher had the minor consolation of carrying his bat for 108, so it would appear that captaincy sits well with him.

COUNTY CHAMPIONSHIP CAPTAINCY RECORDS 1996-2003

ADAM HOLLIOAKE

Season	M	W	D	L
1996	7	4	2	1
1997	13	4	6	3
1998	15	9	2	4
1999	9	7	2	0
2000	16	9	5	2
2001	13	3	10	0
2002	9	5	2	2
2003	13	5	6	2
Total	95	46	35	14

MARK BUTCHER

Season	M	W	D	L
1998	2	1	0	1
1999	8	5	3	0
2002	4	3	1	0
2003	1	1	0	0
Total	15	10	4	1

ALEC STEWART

Season	M	W	D	L
1996	9	3	5	1
1997	1	0	0	1
2001	1	0	1	0
Total	11	3	6	2

CHRIS LEWIS

Season	M	W	D	L
1996	1	1	0	0
1997	3	1	1	1
Total	4	2	1	1

IAN WARD

Season	M	W	D	L
2002	3	2	1	0
2003	1	0	1	0
Total	4	2	2	0

MARTIN BICKNELL				
Season	M	W	D	L
2001	1	0	0	1
Total	1	0	0	1

IAN SALISBURY				
Season	M	W	D	L
2003	1	0	0	1
Total	1	0	0	1

LIMITED-OVERS CRICKET

Eight-Year Averages - Limited-Overs Batting

Mark Ramprakash completes an impressive double by repeating his County Championship feat of averaging over fifty and topping the list. Although averages in limited-overs cricket aren't an especially reliable guide to a player's performance because middle-order and lower middle-order batsmen often have to 'sacrifice' themselves in the pursuit of quick runs, this table proves that the top players do still tend to rise to the top over a period of time. Chris Lewis's value to Surrey in the one-day game is shown by his appearance in fourth place.

LIMITED-OVERS BATTING AVERAGES 1996-2003										
	M	I	NO	Runs	HS	Ave	100	50	ct	st
M.R. Ramprakash	52	51	11	2231	107*	55.78	4	18	14	-
G.P. Thorpe	93	87	17	3192	126*	45.60	4	20	49	-
A.J. Stewart	96	93	13	3277	160	40.96	5	23	100	18
C.C. Lewis	36	28	12	591	68*	36.94	0	2	19	-
A.D. Brown	178	175	6	5411	268	32.02	9	24	66	-
D.M. Ward	19	18	1	511	112	30.06	2	1	12	-
M.A. Butcher	102	99	13	2424	104	28.19	1	14	34	-
G.J. Batty	22	21	5	450	83*	28.13	0	3	6	-
D.J. Bicknell	30	29	5	666	62	27.75	0	3	10	-
I.J. Ward	125	118	12	2899	108	27.35	1	18	22	-
A.J. Hollioake	167	150	14	3623	117*	26.64	2	15	54	-
Azhar Mahmood	21	19	2	424	98	24.94	0	3	6	-
B.C. Hollioake	105	88	9	1967	98	24.90	0	10	32	-
R. Clarke	33	32	5	656	98*	24.30	0	4	11	-
Nadeem Shahid	93	87	15	1731	109*	24.04	1	8	26	-
J.D. Ratcliffe	77	61	9	1149	82	22.10	0	7	22	-
B.P. Julian	24	16	3	264	41	20.31	0	0	11	-
G.P. Butcher	17	16	4	241	37	20.08	0	0	2	-
M.P. Bicknell	146	82	39	789	57*	18.35	0	1	29	-
J.N. Batty	86	60	15	695	55*	15.44	0	1	90	15
I.D.K. Salisbury	91	58	16	549	34*	13.07	0	0	36	-
Saqlain Mushtaq	85	46	17	339	38*	11.69	0	0	16	-
A.J. Tudor	55	37	9	284	28	10.14	0	0	12	-
J.E. Benjamin	68	26	15	71	16*	6.45	0	0	10	-
T.J. Murtagh	23	16	7	54	14*	6.00	0	0	4	-
E.S.H. Giddins	46	20	10	37	13*	3.70	0	0	13	-
Qualification: 15 innings										

Eight-Year Averages - Limited-Overs Bowling
Chris Lewis follows his fourth spot in the batting list by heading the table of bowlers with fifty-six wickets at an excellent average of 19.16 runs apiece. He claimed three or four wickets in an innings on six occasions in his thirty-six appearances for Surrey, which represents a very good strike rate. Adam Hollioake's overall record with the ball is almost as good and achieved over a much longer period of time, with the figures below - 235 wickets in 825.4 overs - revealing that he took a wicket every 21 balls in limited-overs games for the county between 1996 and 2003.

LIMITED-OVERS BOWLING AVERAGES 1996-2003									
	O	M	Runs	Wkts	Ave	BB	5wi	3wi	Econ
C.C. Lewis	271.4	23	1073	56	19.16	4-21	-	6	3.95
A.J. Hollioake	825.4	21	4511	235	19.20	6-17	7	16	5.46
A.J. Tudor	397.3	40	1904	84	22.67	4-26	-	5	4.79
Azhar Mahmood	159.4	10	759	32	23.72	6-37	1	-	4.75
M.P. Bicknell	1142.0	126	4609	189	24.39	7-30	2	19	4.04
B.C. Hollioake	637.4	29	3187	121	26.34	5-10	1	14	5.00
Saqlain Mushtaq	667.2	39	2792	106	26.34	4-17	-	9	4.18
E.S.H. Giddins	353.5	34	1576	59	26.71	5-20	1	5	4.46
B.P. Julian	157.0	5	832	31	26.84	4-46	-	4	5.30
J.E. Benjamin	494.2	41	2053	72	28.51	4-19	-	4	4.15
J.D. Ratcliffe	223.2	9	984	33	29.82	4-44	-	2	4.41
T.J. Murtagh	191.2	11	963	31	31.06	4-31	-	3	5.03
I.D.K. Salisbury	588.0	19	2758	86	32.07	4-32	-	9	4.69
J. Ormond	179.3	11	898	24	37.42	3-46	-	3	5.00
G.J. Batty	119.3	6	591	15	39.40	4-36	-	-	4.95
R. Clarke	153.3	4	919	22	41.77	3-48	-	1	5.99
R.M. Pearson	143.4	2	762	18	42.33	3-33	-	2	5.30

Qualification: 15 wickets

Limited-Overs Appearances
Ali Brown's appearance record for Surrey in limited-overs matches between 1996 and 2003 is quite staggering. Discounting twelve games that were abandoned without a ball being bowled, he appeared in 178 (96.2%) of the 185 fixtures during that period. Adam Hollioake isn't far behind him, having been in the Surrey eleven for 167 of those games, while only four other men exceed the one-hundred appearance mark. Mark Butcher is, perhaps, the surprise 100-plus man, having been involved with England on a fairly regular basis and having also been omitted from the county's one-day team on a number of occasions in the past.

Although Alec Stewart and Graham Thorpe make it onto the 'leader board' for one-day appearances, having failed to make the Championship list, a large percentage of the matches in which they participated were in the Benson & Hedges Cup and Nat West/C&G Trophy, since England call-ups rarely impacted on these competitions. Fifty-five of Stewart's appearances were in the two cups, while the figure for Thorpe was forty-five.

Looking at each of the limited-overs competitions in isolation, Ali Brown turns out to have been the only ever-present player in both the Nat West/C&G Trophy and the Benson & Hedges Cup, having made a full twenty-five appearances in the former and the maximum thirty-six appearances (excluding games where there was no play) in the latter.

MOST LIMITED-OVERS APPEARANCES 1996-2003	
Player	Appearances
Alistair Brown	178
Adam Hollioake	167
Martin Bicknell	146
Ian Ward	125
Ben Hollioake	105
Mark Butcher	102
Alec Stewart	96
Nadeem Shahid	93
Graham Thorpe	93
Ian Salisbury	91

Limited-Overs Runs

There are no real surprises in the table of leading run-makers. Ali Brown and Adam Hollioake would be expected to fill the top two places since they missed very few matches during Surrey's glory years, while Alec Stewart and Graham Thorpe usually produced the goods when they were able to turn out for the county. Mark Ramprakash again does well to finish so high in the table after just three seasons with Surrey.

MOST LIMITED-OVERS RUNS 1996-2003		
Player	Runs	Average
Alistair Brown	5411	32.02
Adam Hollioake	3623	26.64
Alec Stewart	3277	40.96
Graham Thorpe	3192	45.60
Ian Ward	2899	27.35
Mark Butcher	2424	28.19
Mark Ramprakash	2231	55.78
Ben Hollioake	1967	24.90
Nadeem Shahid	1731	24.04
Jason Ratcliffe	1149	22.10

Limited-Overs Centuries... And Near Misses

It is no surprise whatsoever to see Ali Brown topping the limited-overs centurions list after accounting for nine of the twenty-nine tons recorded by Surrey batsmen between 1996 and 2003. Three batsmen - Mark Ramprakash, Alec Stewart and David Ward - can boast a better innings-per-century average than Brown, though Ward's average is rather unreliable since it is based on just eighteen innings.

Given the limited duration of a one-day innings, it is obviously a huge advantage, in terms of having time to make a century, for a batsman to bat in the top three of the order. It is, therefore, surprising to discover that Mark Butcher and Ian Ward each managed just one ton from around a hundred innings. While it is true to say that neither man was employed exclusively as an opener during the period under consideration, it would probably be fair to suggest that they opened often enough to have reached three figures on more than one occasion.

While Surrey batsmen were amassing their twenty-nine limited-overs centuries, opposition batsmen were managing to chalk up twenty-seven, with three men scoring two hundreds during this period - Rob Cunliffe (in five matches), Owais Shah (in eight) and Matthew Maynard (in nine). Twenty-three of the total number of fifty-six centuries were scored at The Oval, while five came at Hove and four were recorded at Guildford, Whitgift School, Taunton and Trent Bridge - all, significantly, good batting pitches for most or all of the period under examination.

Most interestingly, forty of these fifty-six hundreds were made by a batsman from the side batting first, with just sixteen centuries coming during a run chase. Clearly, the added pressure of chasing a target makes it a lot more difficult for a batsman to compile a century in limited-overs cricket. Looking at the breakdown for Surrey batsmen in isolation, the split is particularly dramatic - there were twenty-two first-innings hundreds scored, compared with just seven in the second half of a match. Then, delving a little deeper, it turns out that, quite incredibly, twenty of the first-half tons (i.e. 91%) led to a Surrey triumph, while five of the seven second-innings centuries (71%) brought victory to the men from London SE11. The breakdown for opposition batsmen is as follows:- First innings of the match - eighteen centuries, twelve wins (67%), one tie, five defeats; Second innings - nine centuries, four wins (44%), five defeats. We can see from these figures that Surrey centurions ended up on the winning side far more frequently than opposition centurions did.

When it comes to the near-miss nineties, Surrey batsmen have thirteen such scores to their credit, while opposing batsmen fell just short of the hundred mark on eight occasions. Ali Brown tops the Surrey list with three, followed by Alec Stewart, Ben Hollioake and Ian Ward with two apiece.

MOST CENTURIES BY SURREY BATSMEN IN LIMITED-OVERS MATCHES 1996-2003			
Player	100s	No. of inns	Inns/100 average
Alistair Brown	9	175	19.44
Alec Stewart	5	93	18.60
Mark Ramprakash	4	51	12.75
Graham Thorpe	4	87	21.75
David Ward	2	18	9.00
Adam Hollioake	2	150	75.00
Nadeem Shahid	1	87	87.00
Mark Butcher	1	99	99.00
Ian Ward	1	118	118.00

Limited-Overs Half-Centuries

An examination of the number of innings of fifty-plus scored by Surrey batsmen puts Brown on top again, though his average of one half-century every 5.3 innings falls some way short of the averages achieved by the next three men in the list, Alec Stewart, Graham Thorpe and Mark Ramprakash. This is not unexpected, however, since Brown's role was usually to get Surrey away to a rapid start and this, inevitably, led to a greater number of cheap dismissals, whereas the other three usually played a central anchoring role. Similarly, most of the other batsmen in this list would have had to sacrifice their wicket on many occasions, resulting in a higher innings-per-fifty average.

It is worth noting how dangerous Brown was once he passed fifty. His thirty-three scores in excess of fifty included nine tons, which represents a great conversion rate for one-day cricket.

MOST LIMITED-OVERS HALF-CENTURIES 1996-2003			
Player	Scores 50+	No. of inns	Inns/50+ average
Alistair Brown	33	175	5.30
Alec Stewart	28	93	3.32
Graham Thorpe	24	87	3.63
Mark Ramprakash	22	51	2.32
Ian Ward	19	118	6.21
Adam Hollioake	17	150	8.82
Mark Butcher	15	99	6.60
Ben Hollioake	10	88	8.80
Nadeem Shahid	9	87	9.67
Jason Ratcliffe	7	61	8.71

Limited-Overs Highest Scores

It's six out of ten for Ali Brown as he dominates the table of the highest individual innings of the period. Brown has the three highest Sunday/National League scores to his credit as well as the top NatWest/C&G Trophy innings, while Alec Stewart deprives him of the clean sweep, courtesy of his 160 against Hampshire in the Benson & Hedges Cup.

HIGHEST INDIVIDUAL INNINGS BY SURREY BATSMEN IN LIMITED-OVERS MATCHES 1996-2003					
		Opponents	Venue	Comp'n	Season
268	Alistair Brown	Glamorgan	The Oval	CGT	2002
203	Alistair Brown	Hampshire	Guildford	SL	1997
160	Alec Stewart	Hampshire	The Oval	BHC	1996
157*	Alistair Brown	Leicestershire	Leicester	SL	1997
130	Alistair Brown	Nottinghamshire	Trent Bridge	NL	2001
126*	Graham Thorpe	Nottinghamshire	Guildford	NL	2000
125*	Alec Stewart	Essex	The Oval	NWT	1996
117*	Alistair Brown	Sussex	Hove	BHC	1996
117*	Adam Hollioake	Sussex	Hove	CGT	2002
116	Alistair Brown	Warwickshire	Whitgift School	NL	2001

HIGHEST INDIVIDUAL INNINGS AGAINST SURREY IN LIMITED-OVERS MATCHES 1996-2003					
		For	Venue	Comp'n	Season
155*	Jacques Kallis	Glamorgan	Pontypridd	NL	1999
137*	Rob Cunliffe	Gloucestershire	The Oval	BHC	1996
135*	Andy Flintoff	Lancashire	The Oval	NWT	2000
132	Matthew Maynard	Glamorgan	The Oval	SL	1997
130	Simon Ecclestone	Somerset	Taunton	SL	1996
123	Robin Smith	Hampshire	The Oval	BHC	1996
120*	Darren Maddy	Leicestershire	Leicester	BHC	1998
119	Robert Croft	Glamorgan	The Oval	CGT	2002
117	Martin Speight	Sussex	Guildford	SL	1996
116*	David Byas	Yorkshire	The Oval	BHC	1996

Limited-Overs Wickets

By heading Surrey's limited-overs wicket-takers table, Adam Hollioake proves himself to have been quite possibly the foremost 'one-day specialist', in bowling terms, that the domestic game has ever seen. Although most counties have, or have had, bowlers who have been used more regularly, and have enjoyed greater success, in limited-overs cricket than in County Championship cricket, I doubt that anyone has more disparate figures over a period of time than Adam Hollioake. Between 1996 and 2003, the Surrey skipper took fifty-three Championship wickets at 43.45 runs apiece compared to his 235 one-day scalps at 19.20 each. His ability to out-think batsmen who were trying to score quick runs was second to none and yielded the rich harvest of wickets that he was never likely to achieve in four-day cricket when batsmen would usually be playing each ball on its merits.

Brother Ben's appearance at number three on the list might surprise a lot of people. He was, of course, a regular member of Surrey's limited-overs team for much of the time after making his debut in 1996 and I suppose it also reflects how he relished the challenges of the shorter form of the game. Similarly, I think it would be fair to say that Chris Lewis and Ed Giddins were more highly motivated by the limited-overs form of the game than they were by four-day cricket. Consequently, it is no surprise to see them in the top ten of this table, having claimed very creditable tallies of fifty-nine and fifty-six wickets respectively in just two seasons with the club.

Finally, it is worth noting how limited-overs cricket reduced the impact made by spin twins Saqlain Mushtaq and Ian Salisbury. Although their figures are still very respectable they don't bear comparison to their statistics in Championship cricket. There are many possible reasons for this, including the use of the seamer-friendly white ball; opposition batsmen adopting a more positive approach to spinners; the more defensive style of bowling required of spin bowlers in one-day cricket; and the inability, due to the restricted allocation of overs, to settle into a long spell.

MOST LIMITED-OVERS WICKETS 1996-2003		
Player	Wickets	Average
Adam Hollioake	235	19.20
Martin Bicknell	189	24.39
Ben Hollioake	121	26.34
Saqlain Mushtaq	106	26.34
Ian Salisbury	86	32.07
Alex Tudor	84	22.67
Joey Benjamin	72	28.51
Ed Giddins	59	26.71
Chris Lewis	56	19.16
Jason Ratcliffe	33	29.82

Limited-Overs Five-Wicket Hauls

Bearing in mind the restricted number of overs that any bowler can deliver in a one-day match, five-wicket hauls tend be quite hard to come by… unless you are Adam Hollioake, of course! Adam achieved the feat on no fewer than seven occasions while his side were in their pomp, while the rest of his bowlers managed it five times between them.

It's interesting to note that no Surrey bowler took a five-for in the Benson & Hedges Cup, despite the team's success in that competition, and that the only Nat West/C&G Trophy five-wicket bag came in the highest scoring game of all! The use of the more bowler-friendly white ball in the Sunday/National League probably explains why almost all of the best bowling analyses have been recorded in that competition.

The Oval clearly dominates as a venue on the Surrey list, which is perhaps a little surprising given its reputation for being one of the very best pitches in the country for all forms of cricket. It could perhaps be the case that a combination of the swinging, seaming white ball and the bouncy surfaces at The Oval has proved to be a lethal cocktail for visiting batsmen in Sunday/National League matches during the period in question.

Looking at the five-wicket hauls taken by opposition bowlers against Surrey, we finally find the presence of a spinner - Hampshire's Shaun Udal. Although it's true to say that spin bowlers tend to operate mostly in mid-innings in a defensive role, it seems incredible that there is only one instance of a five-wicket performance by a spinner in eight years of limited-overs matches involving a county that has had Saqlain Mushtaq and Ian Salisbury in its ranks.

FIVE-WICKET HAULS BY SURREY BOWLERS IN LIMITED-OVERS MATCHES 1996-2003					
		Opponents	Venue	Comp'n	Season
7-30	Martin Bicknell	Glamorgan	The Oval	NL	1999
6-17	Adam Hollioake	Kent	Canterbury	NL	2003
6-37	Azhar Mahmood	Essex	The Oval	NL	2003
5-10	Ben Hollioake	Derbyshire	The Oval	SL	1996
5-20	Ed Giddins	Sussex	The Oval	NL	2002
5-26	Martin Bicknell	Lancashire	The Oval	NL	2002
5-29	Adam Hollioake	Durham	Riverside	NL	2000
5-38	Adam Hollioake	Kent	Canterbury	SL	1997
5-43	Adam Hollioake	Hampshire	The Oval	NL	2002
5-44	Adam Hollioake	Sussex	Guildford	SL	1996
5-58	Adam Hollioake	Northamptonshire	The Oval	SL	1996
5-77	Adam Hollioake	Glamorgan	The Oval	CGT	2002

FIVE-WICKET HAULS AGAINST SURREY IN LIMITED-OVERS MATCHES 1996-2003					
		For	Venue	Comp'n	Season
7-16	Darren Thomas	Glamorgan	Swansea	SL	1998
6-25	Simon Renshaw	Hampshire	Southampton	BHC	1997
5-25	Darren Gough	Yorkshire	Headingley	SL	1998
5-30	Mike Smith	Gloucestershire	The Oval	NL	2002
5-40	Phillip DeFreitas	Leicestershire	The Oval	NL	2003
5-43	Shaun Udal	Hampshire	Southampton	SL	1998
5-54	Matthew Fleming	Kent	The Oval	BHC	1997

Limited-Overs Most Economical Bowlers

I wonder how many Surrey fans would have expected to find Chris Lewis at the top of this particular table? Although he was undoubtedly a fine bowler at the start and end of an innings during his two seasons with the club, there were times when he could be wild and expensive, as well as profligate with no-balls and wides. This list clearly demonstrates that the tight days greatly outnumbered the loose days, however, since his economy rate is excellent, especially when you take into account the periods of the innings when he did most of his bowling.

Although only an occasional bowler, Jason Ratcliffe enjoyed a couple of fine seasons with the ball in the National League - usually when bowling in tandem with Saqlain Mushtaq - and, as a result, earns fifth place in the table.

MOST ECONOMICAL SURREY BOWLERS IN LIMITED-OVERS MATCHES 1996-2003			
	Runs/ Over	Runs Conceded	Overs Bowled
Chris Lewis	3.95	1073	271.4
Martin Bicknell	4.04	4609	1142.0
Joey Benjamin	4.15	2053	494.2
Saqlain Mushtaq	4.18	2792	667.2
Jason Ratcliffe	4.41	984	223.2
Ed Giddins	4.46	1576	353.5
Ian Salisbury	4.69	2758	588.0
Azhar Mahmood	4.75	759	159.4
Qualification: 100 overs			

Limited-Overs Catches (excluding wicketkeepers)
Always one of the safest pairs of hands in the outfield, Ali Brown tops yet another of the limited-overs lists, with sixty-six catches taken between 1996 and 2003. Graham Thorpe, usually stationed at slip or in the fielding circle, boasts the best catching rate - better than a catch every other match - with forty-nine victims in his ninety-three appearances.

MOST LIMITED-OVERS CATCHES 1996-2003		
Player	Catches	Matches
Alistair Brown	66	178
Adam Hollioake	54	165
Graham Thorpe	49	93
Ian Salisbury	36	91
Mark Butcher	34	102
Ben Hollioake	32	105
Martin Bicknell	29	146
Nadeem Shahid	26	93

Thorpe's impressive catching stats are greatly helped by the four he took in the 1997 Benson & Hedges Cup semi-final, plus a further three instances of three catches in a match. The three in an innings feat was achieved on ten occasions by a Surrey fielder between 1996 and 2003.

MOST CATCHES IN A LIMITED-OVERS MATCH 1996-2003					
Catches	Player	Opponents	Venue	Comp'n	Season
4	Graham Thorpe	Leicestershire	The Oval	BHC	1997

NB - No outfielder took more than three catches in an innings against Surrey during the period in question, though there were six instances of a player managing three.

Limited-Overs Wicketkeepers' Dismissals
Statistically, there is nothing much to choose between the records of Alec Stewart and Jon Batty during Surrey's glory years, with each man having kept wicket in eighty-six of the 185 matches played and just seven dismissals separating the pair.

MOST DISMISSALS BY SURREY WICKETKEEPERS IN LIMITED-OVERS MATCHES 1996-2003			
Player	Total Dismissals	Catches + Stumpings	Matches *
Alec Stewart	111	93 + 18	86
Jonathan Batty	104	89 + 15	86
James Knott	11	11 + 0	6
Graham Kersey	8	8 + 0	7
* Only includes matches when keeping wicket			

In addition to the two instances, given below, of a Surrey wicketkeeper claiming five dismissals in a match, there were eight games in which the designated gloveman ended up with four victims. Jon Batty was the keeper on six of these occasions and Alec Stewart was behind the stumps for the other two. Karl Krikken of Derbyshire was the only man to perform the five-victims feat against Surrey, while five opposition keepers - Adrian Aymes, David Nash, Keith Piper, Chris Read and Steve Rhodes (debatably!) managed to record four dismissals in a match.

MOST DISMISSALS BY A SURREY WICKETKEEPER IN A LIMITED-OVERS MATCH 1996-2003					
	Player	Opponents	Venue	Comp'n	Season
5 (4ct, 1st)	Jonathan Batty	Gloucestershire	The Oval	NL	2001
5 (all ct)	Alec Stewart	Lancashire	The Oval	NL	2002

MOST DISMISSALS BY A WICKETKEEPER AGAINST SURREY IN A LIMITED-OVERS MATCH 1996-2003					
	Player	For	Venue	Comp'n	Season
5 (3ct, 2st)	Karl Krikken	Derbyshire	The Oval	SL	1998

With Or Without You - Limited-Overs 'Key Men'
The following table attempts to reveal Surrey's key players in limited-overs matches, in the same way as the table in the preceding County Championship section. Please see the description above that table, as this one is calculated in exactly the same way, and all the comments I made there also apply here.
Please note that the qualification rules were again quite strict for this table, in order to produce the most reliable results - a player needed to have played for a minimum of three seasons or, if they played for only two, to have played in and missed at least twenty matches.
Special thanks are again due to Richard Arnold for his help with producing these figures.

SURREY'S KEY MEN IN LIMITED-OVERS MATCHES 1996-2003

Player	Difference	WITH PLAYER				WITHOUT PLAYER			
		W	T	L	%success	W	T	L	%success
Alistair Brown	+48.64	109	1	64	62.93%	1	0	6	14.29%
Rikki Clarke	+34.01	25	0	7	78.13%	15	0	19	44.12%
Adam Hollioake	+24.61	103	1	59	63.50%	7	0	11	38.89%
Graham Thorpe	+17.80	63	0	27	70.00%	47	1	43	52.20%
Mark Ramprakash	+14.00	32	0	18	64.00%	8	0	8	50.00%
Azhar Mahmood	+9.53	15	0	6	71.43%	13	0	8	61.90%
Mark Butcher	+9.05	64	1	34	65.15%	46	0	36	56.10%
Martin Bicknell	+8.99	90	0	53	62.94%	20	1	17	53.95%
Darren Bicknell	+6.30	19	0	11	63.33%	36	1	27	57.03%
Saqlain Mushtaq	+3.39	50	0	33	60.24%	41	1	31	56.85%
James Ormond	+3.18	15	0	7	68.18%	13	0	7	65.00%
Alec Stewart	+2.23	59	0	36	62.11%	51	1	34	59.88%
Jonathan Batty	+2.11	49	1	33	59.64%	42	0	31	57.53%
Tim Murtagh	+0.40	14	0	9	60.87%	26	0	17	60.47%
Ian Salisbury	-3.15	51	0	38	57.30%	40	1	26	60.45%
Ben Hollioake	-4.25	60	0	43	58.25%	22	1	13	62.50%
Joey Benjamin	-4.92	38	0	28	57.58%	17	1	10	62.50%
Nadeem Shahid	-5.65	53	0	38	58.24%	57	1	32	63.89%
Jason Ratcliffe	-6.06	43	1	31	58.00%	41	0	23	64.06%
Ian Ward	-7.74	69	1	52	56.97%	22	0	12	64.71%
Alex Tudor	-7.83	30	0	24	55.56%	80	1	46	63.39%
Gareth Batty	-17.24	8	1	13	38.64%	38	0	30	55.88%

Qualification:- Three seasons/Two seasons with a minimum 20 games played & 20 games missed

Limited-Overs Captaincy Records

Adam Hollioake led Surrey in 147, or 79.5%, of the 185 limited-overs matches they played during their glory years, with eighty-nine (60.5%) of those games ending in victory for his side. Alec Stewart's nineteen matches in charge - eighteen of which were in 1996 - resulted in a win percentage of 73.7%, while Mark Butcher will certainly want to improve on his record of one win in eight matches at the helm during the 1999 and 2002 seasons. Butcher's poor results when captaining Surrey's one-day side are probably partly attributable to the fact that the man he was standing in for - Adam Hollioake - was a vital member of the team and would have been badly missed.

LIMITED-OVERS CAPTAINCY RECORDS 1996-2003
ADAM HOLLIOAKE

Season	M	W	L	T/A
1996	6	5	1	0
1997	22	14	7	1
1998	26	11	14	1
1999	15	7	7	1
2000	21	15	6	0
2001	24	12	11	1
2002	15	11	3	1
2003	18	14	4	0
Total	**147**	**89**	**53**	**5**

ALEC STEWART				
Season	M	W	L	A
1996	18	13	5	0
1997	1	1	0	0
Total	19	14	5	0

MARK BUTCHER				
Season	M	W	L	A
1999	5	1	4	0
2002	3	0	3	0
Total	8	1	7	0

IAN WARD				
Season	M	W	L	A
2002	6	3	3	0
Total	6	3	3	0

CHRIS LEWIS				
Season	M	W	L	A
1996	1	1	0	0
1997	2	2	0	0
Total	3	3	0	0

MARTIN BICKNELL				
Season	M	W	L	A
2001	1	0	1	0
Total	1	0	1	0

IAN SALISBURY				
Season	M	W	L	A
2002	1	0	1	0
Total	1	0	1	0

Successes And Failures - Surrey Players

It is quite amazing how often a particular batsman or bowler will always succeed against some teams yet fare poorly against others. This section examines the performances of individual Surrey players against all the other counties during the club's eight triumphant seasons and highlights those who were particularly successful when faced by certain opponents.

It goes without saying that the county's players couldn't all be successful all the time, so I have also compiled tables giving the statistics of those who had a particularly difficult time against certain other sides. In order to ensure that these tables include only the most consistently successful/unsuccessful players I have set fairly demanding qualification standards, equating to something like four County Championship games or five limited-overs matches.

County Championship Batting - Thorns In Their Side

No fewer than twenty-six Surrey batsmen boast an average in excess of fifty against one or other of the first-class counties between 1996 and 2003. Although there are a few cases where a big double-century has boosted the average, the imposition of a qualification of six completed innings (i.e. an innings that ended in the batsman's dismissal) ensures that no totally undeserving cases have crept in.

It is interesting to note the wide spread of counties featured in this list, with only Gloucestershire, Nottinghamshire and Worcestershire not represented. Since Surrey played very few games against Gloucestershire and Worcestershire during the period in question the absence of those counties is entirely predictable, but it's not so easy to understand why no individual batsman has a fifty-plus average against Nottinghamshire, especially when you consider that Surrey won five of the six fixtures played between the two counties. It probably just comes down to the fact that a number of those games were played on pitches that favoured the bowlers rather than the batsmen.

Hampshire, meanwhile feature four times in the table, with Graham Thorpe, Adam Hollioake, Mark Butcher and Ian Ward having all enjoyed themselves at the south coast county's expense. This goes some way towards explaining why Hampshire were perennial strugglers against the men from The Oval.

Turning our attention to individuals, it should be pointed out that Mark Ramprakash would have made more than three appearances on the list had he reached the qualifying mark against a number of counties - for example, he scored 554 runs against Warwickshire at an astonishing average of 138.50, but this was from only four completed innings. It then comes as quite a surprise to discover that this is not the most unfortunate case of a batsman boasting a fantastic average without being able to claim a place in the table. That 'honour' falls to Ali Brown, whose record against Northamptonshire during Surrey's glory years was quite amazing. In six innings, two of them undefeated, he scored four centuries and one fifty in racking up 588 runs at an average of 147.00.

Graham Thorpe was also rather partial to the Northamptonshire bowling, registering two tons and a half-century while amassing 408 runs from four completed innings, though he fared even better against Sussex. The south coast county's bowlers must have been sick of the sight of the England left-hander as he scored 499 runs in six innings, two of them unbeaten, at an average of 124.75, bagging three centuries and a fifty along the way.

SURREY BATSMEN AVERAGING OVER 50 v OTHER COUNTIES IN THE COUNTY CHAMPIONSHIP 1996-2003				
Player	Opponents	Average	Runs Scored	Comp'd Innings
Mark Ramprakash	Somerset	85.33	512	6
Adam Hollioake	Middlesex	76.17	457	6
Alistair Brown	Middlesex	76.00	532	7
Alec Stewart	Yorkshire	75.33	452	6
Adam Hollioake	Somerset	74.75	598	8
Mark Butcher	Glamorgan	74.00	444	6
Adam Hollioake	Northamptonshire	72.57	508	7
Graham Thorpe	Derbyshire	72.17	433	6
Mark Butcher	Durham	65.25	522	8
Adam Hollioake	Warwickshire	64.75	518	8
Adam Hollioake	Essex	62.83	377	6
Graham Thorpe	Hampshire	59.60	596	10
Adam Hollioake	Hampshire	59.56	536	9
Mark Butcher	Leicestershire	58.77	764	13
Mark Butcher	Hampshire	58.50	585	10
Alistair Brown	Glamorgan	58.13	465	8
Mark Butcher	Kent	55.33	664	12
Alistair Brown	Sussex	55.33	498	9
Jonathan Batty	Essex	55.14	386	7
Mark Ramprakash	Sussex	55.00	330	6
Ian Ward	Kent	54.36	598	11
Graham Thorpe	Somerset	53.83	323	6
Alistair Brown	Leicestershire	52.73	791	15
Ian Ward	Hampshire	52.44	472	9
Ian Ward	Leicestershire	50.60	506	10
Mark Ramprakash	Lancashire	50.29	352	7
Qualification: 6 completed innings				

County Championship Bowling - Thorns In Their Side

There are no fewer than thirty instances of a Surrey bowler with a sub-25 average against an opposition county during the period covered by this book, which clearly explains why the team was so dominant in the Championship. It's no surprise to see that Martin Bicknell and Saqlain Mushtaq dominate the list, with thirteen and twelve entries respectively, since they were the leading bowlers of the period, but their level of consistency is still quite incredible.

An examination of Bicknell's figures against the other seventeen counties reveals that he averaged between 17.71 and 27.59 runs per wicket against no fewer than fifteen of them, while his average of 30.14 when taking on Worcestershire was not entirely representative since he delivered only 70.4 overs. Just one county, therefore, got the better of him... as we will see later.

Saqlain's average exceeded twenty-five against only two teams - Essex and Gloucestershire - while his thirty-one Warwickshire scalps cost exactly twenty-five runs apiece. Essex batsmen restricted him to just four wickets at 37.25 from a sub-qualifying forty-nine overs, while Gloucestershire yielded seven victims to him at 25.43 from sixty-two overs. Northamptonshire, meanwhile, managed to steer well clear of the Pakistani spin king, facing just eight overs from him in the course of their six clashes with Surrey between 1997, when Saqlain arrived at The Oval, and 2001.

How Derbyshire must wish that the fixture lists had been as kind to them! To say that Saqlain was a thorn in their side is something of an understatement, since a phenomenal record of twenty-eight wickets at 9.36 runs apiece suggests that he didn't merely irritate them - he menaced and terrorised them.

As in the batting list, there are a couple of cases where a player has a very good record that doesn't quite meet the qualification standard - Ian Salisbury's sixteen Nottinghamshire wickets were taken in the course of just 88.3 overs at an average of 13.69, while Joey Benjamin managed to claim fifteen Durham scalps at 15.93 runs apiece in eighty-two overs.

SURREY BOWLERS AVERAGING UNDER 25 v OTHER COUNTIES IN THE COUNTY CHAMPIONSHIP 1996-2003				
Player	Opponents	Average	Wkts Taken	Runs Conceded
Saqlain Mushtaq	Derbyshire	9.36	28	262
Saqlain Mushtaq	Durham	14.56	25	364
Saqlain Mushtaq	Sussex	16.85	33	556
Saqlain Mushtaq	Middlesex	17.69	16	283
Martin Bicknell	Glamorgan	17.71	28	496
Ian Salisbury	Durham	17.75	16	284
Martin Bicknell	Kent	18.62	34	633
Saqlain Mushtaq	Yorkshire	19.16	32	613
Alex Tudor	Leicestershire	19.57	21	411
Martin Bicknell	Middlesex	19.66	29	570
Martin Bicknell	Derbyshire	20.31	26	528
Saqlain Mushtaq	Nottinghamshire	20.50	16	328
Saqlain Mushtaq	Kent	20.76	25	519
Saqlain Mushtaq	Glamorgan	20.94	17	356
Saqlain Mushtaq	Leicestershire	21.12	25	528
Martin Bicknell	Yorkshire	21.13	31	655
Martin Bicknell	Leicestershire	21.17	48	1016
Martin Bicknell	Hampshire	21.37	38	812
Saqlain Mushtaq	Hampshire	21.39	41	877
Martin Bicknell	Durham	21.74	23	500
Martin Bicknell	Warwickshire	21.86	29	634
Martin Bicknell	Gloucestershire	22.00	19	418
Martin Bicknell	Nottinghamshire	22.00	18	396
Ian Salisbury	Warwickshire	22.15	20	443
Alex Tudor	Northamptonshire	22.47	15	337
Martin Bicknell	Essex	23.08	26	600
Ian Salisbury	Somerset	24.36	39	950
Saqlain Mushtaq	Lancashire	24.57	21	516
Saqlain Mushtaq	Somerset	24.79	24	595
Martin Bicknell	Northamptonshire	24.88	25	622
Qualification: 100 overs bowled				

County Championship Batting - Surrey Players Who Struggled

Nadeem Shahid must have had nightmares when he saw a fixture against Kent looming, since he clearly never mastered their attack. Martin Saggers proved to be a particularly difficult opponent for him, claiming his wicket four times as he mustered just thirty-three runs in seven completed innings, one of which was a score of twenty.

Although Ben Hollioake had a surprisingly lean time against Surrey's whipping boys, Hampshire, the biggest shock in this table is surely the appearance of Alec Stewart in third place with an average of just nine from six completed innings against Glamorgan. I suppose this goes to show that even the best players have a bogey side.

These hoodoos can be beaten, however, as Ali Brown proved in 2004 when he completed his full set of first-class centuries against the other counties by scoring a brilliant ton on a turning pitch at Old Trafford. Between 1996 and 2003, Lancashire had been his least favourite opponents as he passed fifty just twice in the course of nineteen completed innings that yielded just 354 runs. Although he put the record straight in fine style at the end of 2004, that innings of 154 fell outside the sphere of this book.

Player	Opponents	Average	Runs Scored	Comp'd Innings
Nadeem Shahid	Kent	4.71	33	7
Ben Hollioake	Hampshire	6.50	39	6
Alec Stewart	Glamorgan	9.00	54	6
Martin Bicknell	Middlesex	11.29	79	7
Ben Hollioake	Lancashire	13.50	108	8
Nadeem Shahid	Gloucestershire	13.88	111	8
Jason Ratcliffe	Gloucestershire	16.00	128	8
Adam Hollioake	Durham	16.57	116	7
Ben Hollioake	Glamorgan	16.83	101	6
Nadeem Shahid	Essex	17.33	104	6
Alistair Brown	Lancashire	18.63	354	19
Darren Bicknell	Essex	19.17	115	6
Ian Ward	Essex	19.38	155	8

SURREY BATSMEN/ALL-ROUNDERS AVERAGING UNDER 20 v OTHER COUNTIES IN THE COUNTY CHAMPIONSHIP 1996-2003

Qualification: 6 completed innings

County Championship Batting - Surrey 'Bunnies'

There are surprisingly few cases of a Surrey batsman being regularly dismissed by the same bowler in Championship matches during the club's peak years. Although Gary Keedy got the better of Ali Brown on six occasions, I suspect that contests between the Lancashire left-arm spinner and the Surrey middle-order batsman were probably rather more evenly balanced than that figure suggests. The same would probably be true of battles between Ian Ward and Chris Silverwood, whereas Richard Johnson's achievement of claiming Brown's scalp on five occasions out of eight seems to be far more significant.

SURREY BATSMEN DISMISSED MORE THAN FOUR TIMES BY THE SAME BOWLER IN THE COUNTY CHAMPIONSHIP 1996-2003

Player	Bowler	County	Comp'd Inns *	% Total Dismissals
6 times				
Alistair Brown	Gary Keedy	Lancashire	14	42.86%
5 times				
Alistair Brown	Richard Johnson	Middx/Somerset	8	62.50%
Ian Ward	Chris Silverwood	Yorkshire	11	45.45%

* Only includes completed innings when relevant bowler played and bowled
Qualification: 7 completed innings

County Championship Bowling - Surrey Players Who Struggled

Martin Bicknell, like Ali Brown, had a pretty poor time of it against Lancashire while Surrey were in their pomp. He did, however, emulate his long-term team-mate by coming good against the men from Old Trafford in 2004, taking 8-159 in the course of the two matches between the sides. Given that the red rose county were Championship runners-up on four occasions during the period under investigation, it is not too surprising that Surrey's most prolific bowler and batsman found them to be their toughest opponents, though Bicknell's average of 38.94 is a surprising eleven points higher than his second-worst qualifying average of 27.59 against Somerset.

Of the other bowlers, Ian Salisbury clearly didn't enjoy matches against Leicestershire or Northamptonshire, while Alex Tudor's poor average against Somerset might be partly explained by the good batting tracks at Taunton. It is interesting to note that while Salisbury and Ben Hollioake found wickets very hard to come by when playing Leicestershire, Surrey's other front-line bowlers of the period - Alex Tudor (19.57), Saqlain Mushtaq (21.12) and Martin Bicknell (21.17) - all had exceptional records against the Foxes.

SURREY BOWLERS AVERAGING OVER 35 v OTHER COUNTIES IN THE COUNTY CHAMPIONSHIP 1996-2003				
Player	Opponents	Average	Wkts Taken	Runs Conceded
Ian Salisbury	Northamptonshire	64.00	7	448
Ben Hollioake	Leicestershire	56.43	7	395
Ian Salisbury	Leicestershire	50.33	12	604
Alex Tudor	Somerset	47.64	11	524
Ed Giddins	Kent	47.38	8	379
Martin Bicknell	Lancashire	38.94	18	701
Ian Salisbury	Middlesex	37.67	9	339

Qualification: 100 overs bowled

Limited-Overs Batting - Thorns In Their Side

Ali Brown, Alec Stewart and Graham Thorpe rather dominate the table of Surrey batsmen who have been thorns in the side of other counties in limited-overs cricket, with Brown's highly impressive average of 75.50 against Leicestershire leading the way. His tally of 453 runs against the Foxes includes two centuries and a fifty, whereas his total of 524 runs against Glamorgan leans rather heavily on a certain innings of 268!

SURREY BATSMEN AVERAGING OVER 40 v OTHER COUNTIES IN LIMITED-OVERS CRICKET 1996-2003				
Player	Opponents	Average	Runs Scored	Comp'd Inns
Alistair Brown	Leicestershire	75.50	453	6
Graham Thorpe	Kent	56.60	283	5
Graham Thorpe	Gloucestershire	56.14	393	7
Alec Stewart	Kent	54.00	270	5
Mark Butcher	Sussex	50.00	250	5
Adam Hollioake	Sussex	49.71	348	7
Alistair Brown	Glamorgan	47.64	524	11
Graham Thorpe	Somerset	47.60	238	5
Alistair Brown	Sussex	46.00	552	12
Alec Stewart	Somerset	41.50	249	6
Alec Stewart	Essex	40.67	244	6
Graham Thorpe	Warwickshire	40.67	244	6

Qualification: 5 completed innings

Limited-Overs Bowling - Thorns In Their Side

Adam Hollioake's value to Surrey as a bowler in limited-overs cricket is amply demonstrated by the following table. His consistency in the short-course form of the game matches that of Bicknell and Saqlain in four-day cricket, since he averaged between 12.30 and 28.67 runs per wicket against every county on the circuit. When playing against Kent, he not only took his wickets at a cost of just 12.30 runs each, he also claimed a victim every 13.67 deliveries, which is nothing short of remarkable over the course of eleven games, during which he bowled 61.3 overs. This strike-rate is only a little better than the wicket every 14.59 balls that he managed against Hampshire and shows just how deadly his variations were at the end of an innings. While talking about Hampshire, a glance at this table shows why they often struggled to post decent totals against Surrey - Martin Bicknell and the Hollioakes captured a combined total of fifty-eight wickets against them at the paltry average of 17.27 runs apiece.

SURREY BOWLERS AVERAGING UNDER 20 v OTHER COUNTIES IN LIMITED-OVERS CRICKET 1996-2003				
Player	Opponents	Average	Wkts Taken	Runs Conceded
Adam Hollioake	Kent	12.30	27	332
Adam Hollioake	Glamorgan	14.67	24	352
Ed Giddins	Sussex	15.67	12	188
Martin Bicknell	Yorkshire	16.53	15	248
Ben Hollioake	Hampshire	16.56	16	265
Adam Hollioake	Hampshire	16.95	22	373
Adam Hollioake	Essex	18.18	17	309
Martin Bicknell	Hampshire	18.20	20	364
Adam Hollioake	Leicestershire	18.21	14	255
Adam Hollioake	Durham	18.23	13	237
Adam Hollioake	Derbyshire	18.57	14	260
Saqlain Mushtaq	Derbyshire	19.38	8	155
Martin Bicknell	Glamorgan	19.42	19	369
Qualification: 40 overs bowled				

Limited-Overs Batting - Surrey Players Who Struggled

In addition to suffering a nightmare run of scores against Leicestershire (0, 8, 2, 1 and 0), it turns out that poor Nadeem Shahid fared no better against Kent in limited-overs matches than he did in Championship fixtures. While Martin Saggers was his bete noire in the four-day game, Andrew Symonds was his nemesis in one-day matches, claiming his wicket on three occasions. This table also reveals that Adam Hollioake never got to grips with the Yorkshire attack in nine attempts, though he was far from being the only Surrey batsman to have trouble with the Tykes - Ali Brown reached fifty just once in eleven innings, scoring 166 runs at an average of 15.09, while only Graham Thorpe and Mark Butcher averaged over thirty against the white rose county between 1996 and 2003.

SURREY BATSMEN/ALL-ROUNDERS AVERAGING UNDER 15 v OTHER COUNTIES IN LIMITED-OVERS CRICKET 1996-2003				
Player	Opponents	Average	Runs Scored	Comp'd Innings
Nadeem Shahid	Leicestershire	2.20	11	5
Ben Hollioake	Glamorgan	5.86	41	7
Nadeem Shahid	Kent	7.43	52	7
Jonathan Batty	Glamorgan	9.00	45	5
Adam Hollioake	Yorkshire	11.00	99	9
Jason Ratcliffe	Derbyshire	11.20	56	5
Ben Hollioake	Sussex	14.20	71	5
Qualification: 5 completed innings				

Limited-Overs Bowling - Surrey Players Who Struggled

Although he conceded runs against Leicestershire at a respectable rate of just 4.65 per over, Saqlain Mushtaq found Foxes' wickets extremely hard to come by in limited-overs matches, claiming just two at ninety-three runs apiece. It is even more of a shock to discover that the off-spinner also suffered a wicket drought against Sussex in the one-day game, since he reaped a rich harvest against the south coast county in Championship cricket.

While it is most surprising to find that Martin Bicknell's name also appears twice in this 'bottom six' - with Sussex proving to have been difficult opponents for him, too - things could have been worse for Surrey's two principal 'glory years' wicket-takers had the table been extended downwards by just a few points - Saqlain averaged 39-plus against Glamorgan and Yorkshire, while Bicknell averaged in excess of thirty-seven against Essex and Somerset.

SURREY BOWLERS AVERAGING OVER 40 v OTHER COUNTIES IN LIMITED-OVERS CRICKET 1996-2003				
Player	Opponents	Average	Wkts Taken	Runs Conceded
Saqlain Mushtaq	Leicestershire	93.00	2	186
Ben Hollioake	Kent	64.50	4	258
Ian Salisbury	Glamorgan	46.20	5	231
Martin Bicknell	Northamptonshire	44.86	7	314
Saqlain Mushtaq	Sussex	44.50	4	178
Martin Bicknell	Sussex	41.13	8	329
Qualification: 40 overs bowled				

Successes And Failures - Opposition Players

Although Surrey were indisputably the dominant force in county cricket between 1996 and 2003 there were, naturally enough, a number of opposition players who still managed to score plenty of runs and take a good number of wickets against them. I think it would be true to say that the best players tend to rise to the occasion when facing the most difficult opponents, so it's no surprise to see that it is, generally speaking, top-class performers who show up in the following tables.

Naturally, there were also quite a few players who struggled to make an impact against the nation's premier team. The inclusion of the statistics for those who had a tough time is intended to demonstrate the potency of the Surrey side rather than highlight the shortcomings of these players, many of whom were well respected names on the county scene at the time.

County Championship Batting - Thorns In Our Side

I'm sure it will come as no surprise to regular Surrey fans to discover that Stuart Law, the prolific Australian, tops all the batting tables. The Essex and Lancashire strokeplayer was always a highly dangerous opponent, amassing almost a thousand Championship runs at an average in excess of seventy. Eighteen visits to the crease yielded three centuries and four half-centuries for Law, with Messrs Bicknell, Saqlain and company only managing to dismiss him in single figures on two occasions.

Of the sixteen batsmen to average in excess of forty, only four - Mal Loye, Paul Nixon, Tony Penberthy and Ben Smith - have not played Test or one-day international cricket, while it is interesting to note that just four overseas players - Law, Darren Lehmann, Murray Goodwin and Andrew Symonds - make the grade.

\multicolumn{5}{c}{BATSMEN AVERAGING OVER 40 v SURREY IN THE COUNTY CHAMPIONSHIP 1996-2003}
Player	County	Average	Runs Scored	Comp'd Innings
Stuart Law	Essex/Lancs	70.29	984	14
Darren Lehmann	Yorkshire	59.78	538	9
Mark Ramprakash	Middlesex	56.43	395	7
Nick Knight	Warwickshire	56.00	560	10
Mal Loye	Northants/Lancs	54.38	435	8
Paul Nixon	Leics/Kent	53.08	637	12
John Morris	Durham	51.00	357	7
Murray Goodwin	Sussex	45.38	363	8
Matthew Maynard	Glamorgan	44.44	400	9
Chris Adams	Derbys/Sussex	43.43	608	14
Michael Vaughan	Yorkshire	42.60	426	10
Tony Penberthy	Northamptonshire	42.50	340	8
Ben Smith	Leicestershire	42.36	593	14
Andrew Symonds	Gloucs/Kent	42.09	463	11
John Crawley	Lancs/Hants	41.20	412	10
Warren Hegg	Lancashire	40.09	441	11

Qualification: 7 completed innings

In addition to heading the table of leading averages by a quite incredible 10.51 points, Stuart Law leads the runs aggregate table by 334 from his nearest challenger, Darren Maddy, who took guard against the Surrey attack on more occasions than any other batsman between 1996 and 2003. Although Maddy's tally of 650 runs looks impressive, his average of 30.95 is nothing to get excited about. This is because the centuries he took off the Surrey attack in 1997 and 2002 are more than balanced by ten single-figure scores, including three ducks recorded in the midst of a horrific sequence of scores in the 2000 and 2001 seasons. Those four Leicestershire versus Surrey clashes saw Maddy recording scores of 10, 0, 3, 0, 8, 6, 1 and 0, with Martin Bicknell dismissing him five times, including all four occasions when the pair went head-to-head during the 2000 campaign. Taking this disastrous sequence into account, an overall average of almost thirty-one suddenly looks very impressive! I will return to the history of Bicknell versus Maddy confrontations later in this section.

BATSMEN SCORING OVER 450 RUNS v SURREY IN THE COUNTY CHAMPIONSHIP 1996-2003				
Player	County	Runs Scored	Comp'd Innings	Average
Stuart Law	Essex/Lancs	984	14	70.29
Darren Maddy	Leicestershire	650	21	30.95
Paul Nixon	Leics/Kent	637	12	53.08
Chris Adams	Derbys/Sussex	608	14	43.43
Ben Smith	Leicestershire	593	14	42.36
David Fulton	Kent	582	17	34.24
Peter Bowler	Somerset	571	15	38.07
Michael Burns	Somerset	564	15	37.60
Nick Knight	Warwickshire	560	10	56.00
Darren Lehmann	Yorkshire	538	9	59.78
Aftab Habib	Leics/Essex	491	15	32.73
Iain Sutcliffe	Leics/Lancs	481	18	26.72
Ian Blackwell	Derbys/Somerset	474	12	39.50
Andrew Symonds	Gloucs/Kent	463	11	42.09

Ben Smith, like his erstwhile Leicestershire colleague, proved to be rather inconsistent when facing Surrey during their glory years, though his three centuries enable him to top the following 'tons' table alongside Stuart Law. While his Championship-clinching 204 at The Oval in 1998, an innings of 102 at Guildford in 2000, and a knock of 179 at Grace Road in 2001, produced a total of 485 runs, his remaining eleven visits to the crease against Surrey yielded just 108 runs in all. The century at Guildford was highly significant, since it was the only hundred conceded by the eventual County Champions of 2000.

A total of sixty-four Championship centuries were recorded against Surrey between 1996 and 2003, with just four of those tons being converted into a double century. The batsmen to join that exclusive club were Peter Bowler (207 for Somerset at Taunton in 1996); Ben Smith (as above); Mark Ramprakash (209* for Middlesex at Lord's in 1999); and Andy Flower (208* for Essex at The Oval in 2003).

BATSMEN SCORING MORE THAN ONE CENTURY v SURREY IN THE COUNTY CHAMPIONSHIP 1996-2003			
Player	County	No. of 100's	Seasons
Stuart Law	Essex/Lancs	3	1996, 2001, 2003
Ben Smith	Leicestershire	3	1998, 2000, 2001
David Fulton	Kent	2	1997, 2001
Paul Grayson	Essex	2	1997, 2001
Darren Lehmann	Yorkshire	2	1997, 2001
Darren Maddy	Leicestershire	2	1997, 2002
Mal Loye	Northants/Lancs	2	2001, 2003
Chris Adams	Derbys/Sussex	2	2002, 2003
Nick Knight	Warwickshire	2	2002, 2003
Andrew Symonds	Gloucs/Kent	2	2002, 2003
Matthew Wood	Somerset	2	Both 2002

Before moving on to the bowlers who enjoyed success against Surrey, it is worth pointing out a couple of batting curiosities.

David Nash must rate as Surrey's most irritating batting opponent of the period, since their bowlers couldn't find a way to dismiss him in either 1999 (25 not out and 56 not out at Lord's) or in 2003 (36 not out at Lord's and 96 not out at Guildford) when county cricket's London-based rivals next met in the County Championship. From six innings - just two of them completed - Nash totalled 238 runs, with 213 of these coming from those four successive undefeated knocks.

On a different theme, there are two opposition batsmen who really should be kicking themselves for consistently getting a start against Surrey without going on to reach a half-century - Will Kendall of Hampshire and Mark Chilton of Lancashire. Kendall's consistent sequence of 17, 9, 7, 41, 23, 15, 36, 36, 38 and 23 (245 runs at an average of 24.50) is mirrored pretty closely by Chilton's run of 15, 37, 30, 5, 26, 35, 13, 23, 28, 27 and 33 not out (272 runs at 27.20).

County Championship Bowling - Thorns In Our Side

Since Surrey boasted great strength and depth in batting during the period under investigation, it was understandable that very few opposition bowlers relished the prospect of pitting their skills against Adam Hollioake's team. Some did come out on top on a fairly consistent basis, however, with eight men who bowled in excess of a hundred overs managing to return an average below twenty-five runs per wicket. Gloucestershire's Mike Smith, though a very fine bowler in all forms of the game, was recognised more for his ability in the one-day format, so it is a trifle surprising to find him at the top of the list. The suspicion that Surrey's batsmen were often susceptible to left-arm seamers with the ability to swing the ball is underlined by Smith being joined in the top five by Ryan Sidebottom, then of Yorkshire. Additionally, Kevin Dean of Derbyshire, though failing to bowl sufficient overs to qualify for the table of top bowlers, took fourteen wickets at 12.57 in his three appearances against Surrey in 1997, 1998 and 2000, while Alan Mullally (20 wickets at 30.75) often proved to be a difficult opponent.

It is interesting to note that while none of the fastest bowlers of the period, Chris Silverwood apart, enjoyed regular success against Surrey, the skilful fast-medium swing and seam bowlers, like Gavin Hamilton, Martin Saggers and Peter Martin tended to thrive. Although this can be partially explained by the prevailing conditions and pitches around the country for much of the period in question, it may also have been because Surrey's fearsome batting line-up usually contained a higher proportion of dashing strokemakers than steady accumulators... and it would probably be fair to say that the former tend to struggle more against the moving ball than the latter.

It is also clear from the table of leading bowlers that the average county spinner rarely troubled the men from London SE11, since the only tweakers to feature in the list are the top-class operators of the time - Muralitharan, Warne and Tufnell. Surrey actually tended to play both Warne and Murali pretty well, yet these two all-time great spinners have still emerged with fine figures.

BOWLERS AVERAGING UNDER 30 v SURREY IN THE COUNTY CHAMPIONSHIP 1996-2003				
Player	County	Average	Wkts Taken	Runs Conceded
Mike Smith	Gloucestershire	16.13	24	387
Gavin Hamilton	Yorkshire	16.70	23	384
Muttiah Muralitharan	Lancs/Kent	17.00	24	408
Shane Warne	Hampshire	20.86	14	292
Ryan Sidebottom	Yorkshire	22.31	13	290
James Ormond	Leicestershire	23.00	15	345
Tim Munton	Warwicks/Derbys	23.23	13	302
Martin Saggers	Durham/Kent	23.57	28	660
Phil Tufnell	Middlesex	25.14	14	352
Peter Martin	Lancashire	25.65	23	590
Chris Silverwood	Yorkshire	26.76	29	776
David Millns	Leicestershire	26.92	12	323
Dominic Cork	Derbyshire	27.25	12	327
Richard Johnson	Middx/Somerset	27.41	22	603
Ashley Cowan	Essex	28.67	15	430
Ronnie Irani	Essex	28.69	16	459
Mark Ilott	Essex	28.74	19	546
Matthew Hoggard	Yorkshire	29.54	13	384
Qualification: 100 overs bowled				

The table of leading wicket-takers is rather interesting as it includes some of the bowlers who just failed to average under thirty runs per wicket, including the man who finished top of this particular tree, Gary Keedy. The Lancashire left-arm spinner delivered a total of 320.3 overs to Surrey batsmen in Championship cricket between 1996 and 2003 - more than anybody else - though Phillip DeFreitas, who stands sixth in the wicket-takers table, ran him close with 319.5 overs. Glen Chapple, whose wickets came at an even greater cost than DeFreitas's, sent down 306.4 overs to record the third heaviest workload, some forty-one overs ahead of Devon Malcolm.

BOWLERS TAKING 20 OR MORE WICKETS v SURREY IN THE COUNTY CHAMPIONSHIP 1996-2003				
Player	County	Wickets	Runs	Average
Gary Keedy	Lancashire	33	1006	30.48
Chris Silverwood	Yorkshire	29	776	26.76
Martin Saggers	Durham/Kent	28	660	23.57
Dougie Brown	Warwickshire	28	854	30.50
Devon Malcolm	Derbys/Northants/Leics	27	1018	37.70
Phillip DeFreitas	Derbys/Leics	25	1016	40.64
Mike Smith	Gloucestershire	24	387	16.13
Muttiah Muralitharan	Lancs/Kent	24	408	17.00
Gavin Hamilton	Yorkshire	23	384	16.70
Peter Martin	Lancashire	23	590	25.65
James Kirtley	Sussex	23	908	39.48
Glen Chapple	Lancashire	23	1069	46.48
Richard Johnson	Middx/Somerset	22	603	27.41
Alan Mullally	Leics/Hants	20	615	30.75
Andy Caddick	Somerset	20	642	32.10

Five-wicket hauls against Surrey in Championship cricket were comparatively rare during the eight years covered by this book, with just fifty-five occurrences recorded. Only two bowlers ended up with an eight-wicket haul - Devon Malcolm (8-63 for Leicestershire at Leicester, 2001) and Mohammad Akram (8-49 for Essex at The Oval, 2003) - while Carl Hooper, Gavin Hamilton, Tim Munton and Dougie Brown were the only men to capture seven scalps in an innings.

Chris Silverwood, who managed the five-wicket feat in successive seasons from 1997 to 1999, struggled a little thereafter, picking up just eleven more victims in seven innings during the four matches he played against Surrey in 2000 and 2002.

BOWLERS WITH MORE THAN ONE FIVE-WICKET HAUL v SURREY IN THE COUNTY CHAMPIONSHIP 1996-2003			
Player	County	No. of 5-wkt hauls	Seasons
Chris Silverwood	Yorkshire	3	1997, 1998, 1999
Gary Keedy	Lancashire	2	1997, 2002
Mike Smith	Gloucestershire	2	1998, 1999
Alan Mullally	Leics/Hants	2	1999, 2000
Muttiah Muralitharan	Lancs/Kent	2	1999, 2001
Shane Warne	Hampshire	2	Both 2000
Dougie Brown	Warwickshire	2	2002, 2003

County Championship Batting - Opposition Players Who Struggled

The batting tables below exclude bowlers, since they wouldn't have been expected to flourish against an attack as good as Surrey's. All specialist batsmen, all-rounders and wicketkeeper-batsmen were, however, fair game for this analysis, with a minimum of seven completed innings ensuring that those unfortunate enough to make this table had a reasonable chance to prove themselves.

Matthew Cassar, the Sydney-born Derbyshire all-rounder, heads the list after recording scores of 4, 9, 1, 4, 5, 4, 1 and 0 when confronted by the Surrey bowlers. He was far from alone in failing to come to terms with the wiles of Saqlain Mushtaq, as we will see later, but the Pakistani off-spinner was the man most responsible for Cassar recording such a disastrous sequence of scores. Nottinghamshire's Guy Welton, on the other hand, had no particular nemesis yet still found the going against Surrey to be very tough, as his scores of 7, 15, 4, 16, 0, 4, 0 and 0 suggest. Jimmy Daley of Durham meanwhile started his four games against Surrey with an unbeaten nineteen before scraping together just twenty-eight more runs from seven further innings, while Keith Dutch found that a switch of counties didn't help him when it came to scoring runs against Surrey - having made twenty-three runs from four knocks for Middlesex, he fared only slightly better with Somerset, notching forty-six runs from six innings for his new county.

Moving down the table, we find the established front-line batsmen - Dominic Ostler, Paul Collingwood, David Byas, Trevor Ward and company - who you would have expected to do better. While Surrey were in their pomp, however, you often felt that the reputation of their attack had some batsmen beaten almost before they had taken guard and, once a player had got into a bad run, Messrs Bicknell, Saqlain and friends were never likely to let him forget it. Some of the sequences suffered by these batsmen are quite remarkable. Hampshire's Jason Laney - a Bicknell 'bunny' if ever there was one - suffered a horrendous run of 2, 0, 0, 7, 0 and 0 between 1998 and 2000; Graham Lloyd recorded scores of 0, 1, 1 and 1 in the two Surrey versus Lancashire matches played in 2000; and Darren Stevens of Leicestershire bagged three successive ducks at one stage.

\multicolumn{5}{|c|}{BATSMEN/ALL-ROUNDERS AVERAGING UNDER 20 v SURREY IN THE COUNTY CHAMPIONSHIP 1996-2003}				
Player	County	Average	Runs Scored	Comp'd Innings
Matthew Cassar	Derbyshire	3.50	28	8
Guy Welton	Nottinghamshire	5.75	46	8
Jimmy Daley	Durham	6.71	47	7
Keith Dutch	Middx/Somerset	6.90	69	10
Karl Krikken	Derbyshire	9.00	63	7
Gavin Hamilton	Yorkshire	9.29	65	7
Dominic Ostler	Warwickshire	10.82	119	11
Glen Chapple	Lancashire	11.86	166	14
Matthew Keech	Hampshire	12.14	85	7
Jason Laney	Hampshire	12.57	176	14
Paul Collingwood	Durham	14.22	128	9
David Byas	Yorks/Lancs	15.25	244	16
Paul Weekes	Middlesex	15.38	123	8
Trevor Ward	Kent/Leics	16.71	234	14
Darren Stevens	Leicestershire	17.55	193	11
Graham Lloyd	Lancashire	17.57	246	14
Gary Fellows	Yorkshire	18.45	203	11
David Hemp	Warwicks/Glam	19.63	157	8
Jonathan Lewis	Durham	19.70	197	10
Martin Speight	Sussex/Durham	19.89	179	9

Qualification: 7 completed innings

County Championship Batting - Opposition 'Bunnies'

It happens quite regularly in cricket that a batsman has recurring problems when facing a certain bowler - at Test level, for example, Mike Atherton struggled consistently against Glen McGrath. Opening batsmen are, naturally, most susceptible to earning a 'bunny' tag, since they tend to start their innings against the same opening bowlers many times throughout their career, whereas batsmen lower down the order can arrive at the wicket with any member of the opposition attack bowling. It is not surprising, therefore, that Martin Bicknell, during his long career, has a number of opposition openers in his bag of 'bunnies'. Darren Maddy heads the list, having been dismissed by Bicknell no fewer than eleven times in Championship cricket between 1996 and 2003. Leicestershire went some way to solving this problem by moving Maddy down the order after their former England opener had fallen to Bicknell in all four Championship innings in 2000. By the time the second Leicestershire versus Surrey match of 2001 came around - after another dismissal at the hands of his nemesis in the first game - he was down to number six, where he was dismissed by Alex Tudor and Saqlain Mushtaq, and thereafter he found success at number three, scoring eighty-one and ninety-four in the first encounter of 2002 and an unbeaten 127 in the second, when Bicknell wasn't playing.

As the following table shows, a number of other openers - including Jason Laney, Darren Robinson and Yorkshire's Matthew Wood - had a particularly bad time against Bicknell during Surrey's glory years, though it was Glamorgan's Steve James who perhaps deserves the tag of 'Bicknell's ultimate bunny', having fallen to the Surrey swing king seven times in nine visits to the crease. It is interesting to note that on the other two occasions James was undone by leg-spin, with Ian Salisbury dismissing him in 1997 and Nadeem Shahid doing the trick in 1996, after the former Glamorgan skipper had notched the century that denied Surrey a crack at the Championship title.

After Bicknell had terrorised the top order, Saqlain Mushtaq would often come into the attack to deal with the middle- and lower-order, so it is understandable that his 'bunnies' tend to be those batting below number five in the order. Phillip DeFreitas was often a victim of bat-pad catches as he fell to the Surrey off-spinner on seven occasions, while the Somerset spinners, Ian Blackwell and Keith Dutch, found their fellow tweaker to be a particularly difficult opponent, with more than half of their dismissals coming at the hands of the Pakistani spin wizard.

On a list dominated by Bicknell and Saqlain, there are a few appearances by Alex Tudor and Ian Salisbury to break things up. While Salisbury confounded Piran Holloway almost every time he got a chance to bowl to the Somerset left-hander, and enjoyed some very good contests with Kent's Mark Ealham, Alex Tudor managed to gain a measure of revenge for his record-breaking 1998 battering by claiming Andrew Flintoff's scalp on no fewer than five occasions.

At the other end of the spectrum, there are those who have proved to be no one's 'bunny' - David Fulton was dismissed by no fewer than eleven different Surrey bowlers during the period under investigation, while David Byas found his wicket being taken by ten different opponents in the chocolate colours.

BATSMEN DISMISSED MORE THAN FOUR TIMES BY THE SAME SURREY BOWLER IN THE COUNTY CHAMPIONSHIP 1996-2003				
Player	County	Bowler	Comp'd Inns *	% Total Dismissals
11 times				
Darren Maddy	Leicestershire	Martin Bicknell	18	61.11%
7 times				
Steve James	Glamorgan	Martin Bicknell	9	77.78%
Phillip DeFreitas	Derbys/Leics	Saqlain Mushtaq	11	63.63%
Jason Laney	Hampshire	Martin Bicknell	14	50.00%
6 times				
Ian Blackwell	Derbys/Somerset	Saqlain Mushtaq	9	66.66%
Darren Robinson	Essex	Martin Bicknell	9	66.66%
Piran Holloway	Somerset	Ian Salisbury	11	54.54%
Matthew Wood	Yorkshire	Martin Bicknell	11	54.54%
Dougie Brown	Warwickshire	Saqlain Mushtaq	12	50.00%
Trevor Ward	Kent/Leics	Martin Bicknell	12	50.00%
Iain Sutcliffe	Leics/Lancs	Martin Bicknell	13	46.15%
Ben Smith	Leicestershire	Martin Bicknell	14	42.86%
5 times				
Adrian Aymes	Hampshire	Saqlain Mushtaq	7	71.43%
Matthew Cassar	Derbyshire	Saqlain Mushtaq	8	62.50%
Keith Dutch	Middx/Somerset	Saqlain Mushtaq	8	62.50%
Jamie Cox	Somerset	Martin Bicknell	10	50.00%
Mark Ealham	Kent	Ian Salisbury	10	50.00%
Will Kendall	Hampshire	Martin Bicknell	10	50.00%
Rob Key	Kent	Martin Bicknell	10	50.00%
Nick Knight	Warwickshire	Martin Bicknell	10	50.00%
Andy Flintoff	Lancashire	Alex Tudor	11	45.45%
Paul Grayson	Essex	Martin Bicknell	11	45.45%

* Only includes completed innings when relevant bowler played and bowled
Qualification: 7 completed innings

BATSMEN WITH HIGHEST %AGE OF DISMISSALS TO THE SAME SURREY BOWLER IN THE COUNTY CHAMPIONSHIP 1996-2003					
Player	County	Bowler	Times Out	Comp'd Inns *	% Total Dismissals
Steve James	Glamorgan	Martin Bicknell	7	9	77.78%
Adrian Aymes	Hampshire	Saqlain Mushtaq	5	7	71.43%
Ian Blackwell	Derbys/Somerset	Saqlain Mushtaq	6	9	66.66%
Darren Robinson	Essex	Martin Bicknell	6	9	66.66%
Phillip DeFreitas	Derbys/Leics	Saqlain Mushtaq	7	11	63.63%
Matthew Cassar	Derbyshire	Saqlain Mushtaq	5	8	62.50%
Keith Dutch	Middx/Somerset	Saqlain Mushtaq	5	8	62.50%
Darren Maddy	Leicestershire	Martin Bicknell	11	18	61.11%
Piran Holloway	Somerset	Ian Salisbury	6	11	54.54%
Matthew Wood	Yorkshire	Martin Bicknell	6	11	54.54%

* Only includes completed innings when relevant bowler played and bowled
Qualification: 7 completed innings

Defying Bicknell

Any Surrey supporter will tell you that Martin Bicknell and Saqlain Mushtaq were the side's most consistently deadly bowlers during their glory years, and this is underlined by the following quite amazing statistic - there wasn't a single batsman with seven or more County Championship dismissals against Surrey in the period 1996-2003 who didn't fall prey to either Bicknell or Saqlain at some point. I doubt that many pairs of bowlers could match that record.

Many batsmen avoided being dismissed by Saqlain because they batted at the top of the order and were back in the pavilion by the time he came on to bowl, making 'surviving Saqi' analysis fairly worthless. It's a different matter with Bicknell, though, since he was almost as likely to bowl at the middle- and lower-order as he was to bowl at the top three. Those who failed to succumb to his bowling in Championship cricket would probably have faced him at some point in the vast majority of their innings.

PLAYERS NOT DISMISSED BY MARTIN BICKNELL IN THE COUNTY CHAMPIONSHIP 1996-2003		
Player	County	Completed Innings *
Michael Burns	Somerset	13
Tony Cottey	Glam/Sussex	11
Mark Ealham	Kent	10
Adrian Aymes	Hampshire	9
Ronnie Irani	Essex	9
Richard Blakey	Yorkshire	8
Chris Silverwood	Yorkshire	8
Ashley Giles	Warwickshire	7
Murray Goodwin	Sussex	7
Warren Hegg	Lancashire	7
Mark Wagh	Warwickshire	7

* Only includes completed innings when Bicknell played and bowled.
NB - All players, including bowlers, were eligible for this analysis.
Qualification: 7 completed innings

County Championship Bowling - Opposition Players Who Struggled

It wasn't just the batsmen who had a tough time against Surrey during the county's domination of the Championship. The bowlers had their work cut out, too, when faced by such a strong and long batting line-up.

The following table lists all recognised regular bowlers from opposing counties who delivered in excess of a hundred overs and found their wickets costing them more than forty runs apiece. Despite the fact that the pitches at The Oval often offered some assistance to spin bowlers during the period under examination, almost half of the bottom fifteen are spinners, all of whom, James Middlebrook excepted, have represented England at international level. This is not unexpected since Surrey's batsmen always adopted a very aggressive approach when facing the opposition's slow bowlers and tended to dominate against all bar the very best practitioners of the art.

Although there are no overseas bowlers in the list, no fewer than eleven of the eighteen played for England, and a couple of the others came very close to international honours. That is a fair indication of how tough it was to bowl against Surrey during their glory days... even when they were without the likes of Alec Stewart, Graham Thorpe and Mark Butcher on international duty.

BOWLERS/ALL-ROUNDERS AVERAGING OVER 40 v SURREY IN THE COUNTY CHAMPIONSHIP 1996-2003				
Player	County	Average	Wkts Taken	Runs Conceded
David Masters	Kent/Leics	88.60	5	443
Jeremy Snape	Nthts/Gloucs/Leics	62.38	8	499
Dimitri Mascarenhas	Hampshire	61.75	8	494
Min Patel	Kent	58.67	12	704
Shaun Udal	Hampshire	57.93	14	811
Jason Lewry	Sussex	50.00	8	400
Robin Martin-Jenkins	Sussex	48.82	11	537
Ashley Giles	Warwickshire	48.13	8	385
Glen Chapple	Lancashire	46.48	23	1069
Robert Croft	Glamorgan	45.07	14	631
John Stephenson	Hants/Essex	44.75	12	537
Paul Taylor	Northamptonshire	44.55	11	490
Mark Ealham	Kent	42.60	15	639
Ian Blackwell	Derbys/Somerset	41.28	18	743
James Middlebrook	Yorks/Essex	41.20	10	412
Simon Brown	Durham	40.82	11	449
Phillip DeFreitas	Derbys/Leics	40.64	25	1016
Steffan Jones	Somerset	40.00	19	760
Qualification: 100 overs bowled				

Limited-Overs Batting - Thorns In Our Side

In the shortened form of the game, eleven batsmen managed to average over forty against Surrey, with Mal Loye topping the list by scoring an impressive 444 runs at an average of seventy-four. Loye is one of half-a-dozen men to feature in both the Championship and limited-overs lists of those averaging in excess of forty when facing Surrey between 1996 and 2003, the others being Nick Knight, Matthew Maynard, Stuart Law, Ben Smith and

Chris Adams. This represents a magnificent effort, given the strength of the attack they were up against.

It is interesting to note that it wasn't just the extravagant strokemakers who were successful against Surrey in the shortened form of the game, with players such as Bowler, Montgomerie and Darren Bicknell demonstrating the value of the steady opening batsman. Additionally, Stuart Law is the only overseas representative in the list, though this is partly explained by the fact that a number of top-class batsmen didn't complete enough innings to qualify. Michael Bevan, for example, was dismissed just once while compiling 201 runs from four visits to the crease with Sussex and Yorkshire, while Mike Hussey notched 263 runs for Northamptonshire but was only out three times. An English batsman with an even more impressive, but non-qualifying, record is Rob Cunliffe, who amassed 350 runs - courtesy of scores of 137 not out, 42, 113 and 58 - in his four one-day knocks against Surrey for Gloucestershire.

BATSMEN AVERAGING OVER 40 v SURREY IN LIMITED-OVERS MATCHES 1996-2003				
Player	County	Average	Runs Scored	Comp'd Innings
Mal Loye	Northamptonshire	74.00	444	6
Owais Shah	Middlesex	68.00	408	6
Nick Knight	Warwickshire	55.71	390	7
Peter Bowler	Somerset	52.13	417	8
Matthew Maynard	Glamorgan	48.56	437	9
Stuart Law	Essex/Lancs	48.38	387	8
Darren Maddy	Leicestershire	46.38	371	8
Ben Smith	Leicestershire	45.29	317	7
Richard Montgomerie	Northants/Sussex	44.20	442	10
Darren Bicknell	Nottinghamshire	41.00	205	5
Chris Adams	Derbys/Sussex	40.75	326	8
Qualification: 5 completed innings				

BATSMEN SCORING OVER 350 RUNS v SURREY IN LIMITED-OVERS MATCHES 1996-2003				
Player	County	Runs Scored	Comp'd Innings	Average
Mal Loye	Northamptonshire	444	6	74.00
Richard Montgomerie	Northants/Sussex	442	10	44.20
Matthew Maynard	Glamorgan	437	9	48.56
Peter Bowler	Somerset	417	8	52.13
Owais Shah	Middlesex	408	6	68.00
Jack Russell	Gloucestershire	393	11	35.73
Nick Knight	Warwickshire	390	7	55.71
Stuart Law	Essex/Lancs	387	8	48.38
Robin Smith	Hampshire	382	11	34.73

Limited-Overs Bowling - Thorns In Our Side

The table of leading bowlers throws up a few unexpected names, with Glamorgan's Owen Parkin and steady medium-pacers, such as Dimitri Mascarenhas, Tony Penberthy and Matthew Fleming, earning slots in the top ten behind the leading man, Dominic Cork. Parkin, in fact, emerges as the leading wicket-taker against Surrey in limited-overs matches, having claimed twenty scalps in just seven matches. The spinning fraternity again fares badly, with Shaun Udal their sole representative in the list of fifteen bowlers averaging under twenty-five.

A comparison of the table of the top limited-overs bowlers with that compiled for Championship cricket reveals that four men made it into both lists - Cork, Chris Silverwood, Ashley Cowan and Mike Smith.

It is interesting to see that the two Hampshire bowlers in this list enjoyed much greater success in one-day matches against Surrey than they did in Championship cricket - Dimitri Mascarenhas's limited-overs average of 17.47 is an enormous improvement on his Championship average of 61.75, while Shaun Udal's 22.00 in one-day cricket easily outstrips the 57.93 he managed in the four-day format.

BOWLERS AVERAGING UNDER 25 v SURREY IN LIMITED-OVERS MATCHES 1996-2003				
Player	County	Average	Wkts Taken	Runs Conceded
Dominic Cork	Derbyshire	15.58	12	187
Owen Parkin	Glamorgan	16.15	20	323
Chris Silverwood	Yorkshire	16.75	12	201
Dimitri Mascarenhas	Hampshire	17.47	15	262
Ashley Cowan	Essex	18.06	16	289
Andy Caddick	Somerset	18.13	15	272
Tony Penberthy	Northamptonshire	19.13	16	306
James Kirtley	Sussex	21.08	12	253
Matthew Fleming	Kent	21.44	16	343
Dougie Brown	Warwickshire	21.65	17	368
Shaun Udal	Hampshire	22.00	17	374
Billy Taylor	Sussex	23.10	10	231
Mike Smith	Gloucestershire	23.27	15	349
Craig White	Yorkshire	23.33	12	280
Kevin Dean	Derbyshire	24.38	13	317
Qualification: 50 overs bowled				

BOWLERS TAKING 15 OR MORE WICKETS v SURREY IN LIMITED-OVERS MATCHES 1996-2003				
Player	County	Wkts Taken	Runs Conceded	Average
Owen Parkin	Glamorgan	20	323	16.15
Dougie Brown	Warwickshire	17	368	21.65
Shaun Udal	Hampshire	17	374	22.00
Ashley Cowan	Essex	16	289	18.06
Tony Penberthy	Northamptonshire	16	306	19.13
Matthew Fleming	Kent	16	343	21.44
Dimitri Mascarenhas	Hampshire	15	262	17.47
Andy Caddick	Somerset	15	272	18.13

When it comes to containment, Dominic Cork completes the bowling double by coming out on top of the pile again... by 0.47 runs per over, which is a quite staggering margin. It is perhaps surprising to see regular new-ball bowlers filling most of the top places, given that they had to bowl with the harshest of the fielding restrictions in place during the first fifteen overs of the innings, though it has to be said that Cork, Angus Fraser, Andy Caddick, Chris Silverwood and James Kirtley are a pretty formidable hand of England bowlers.

The sole spinner to make the top dozen in the economy stakes is Essex's Paul Grayson, whose canny left-arm over-the-wicket style has often proved effective in the one-day game. Grayson certainly never troubled Surrey in Championship cricket, where his two wickets in the period covered by this book cost him 121.50 runs apiece!

BOWLERS CONCEDING UNDER 4.25 RUNS PER OVER v SURREY IN LIMITED-OVERS MATCHES 1996-2003						
Player	County	Runs/ Over	Runs Conceded	Overs Bowled	Wkts Taken	Average
Dominic Cork	Derbyshire	3.19	187	58.4	12	15.58
Angus Fraser	Middlesex	3.66	238	65.0	9	26.44
Andy Caddick	Somerset	3.78	272	72.0	15	18.13
Chris Silverwood	Yorkshire	3.87	201	52.0	12	16.75
James Kirtley	Sussex	4.03	253	62.5	12	21.08
Robin Martin-Jenkins	Sussex	4.07	410	100.5	12	34.17
Mark Robinson	Sussex	4.15	307	74.0	9	34.11
Ronnie Irani	Essex	4.18	294	70.2	11	26.73
Graham Rose	Somerset	4.19	222	53.0	5	44.40
Kevin Dean	Derbyshire	4.23	317	75.0	13	24.38
Paul Grayson	Essex	4.23	345	81.3	11	31.36
Qualification: 50 overs bowled						

Limited-Overs Batting - Opposition Players Who Struggled

Although Australia's Matthew Hayden was not yet fully established at international level when he played county cricket for Hampshire (1997) and Northamptonshire (1999-2000), he was already a fine player, so it comes as quite a shock to discover that he accumulated just thirty-three limited-overs runs against Surrey from five completed innings. He wasn't on his own, however, since there were other big-name players who also had a sub-20 average against the county between 1996 and 2003, namely Marcus Trescothick (17.80), John Crawley (18.40) and Vikram Solanki (19.17). That probably makes the other members of this 'bottom thirteen' table feel a little better, though clearly none of them set the world alight despite being either (a) a specialist batsman; (b) acknowledged as an all-rounder; or (c) a regular top-seven batsman or pinch-hitter in one-day matches. Even though they had plenty of opportunity to score runs and were, generally speaking, able to steer clear of the perils of sacrificing their wicket in the end-of-innings slog, these players failed to cause Surrey any problems.

Although no batsman features in both this table and the list of players averaging under twenty against Surrey in the Championship, there are, in fact, three unfortunates who failed to average twenty in either form of the game - Warwickshire's Dominic Ostler (10.82 in the Championship and 19.50 in limited-overs cricket), Jonathan Lewis of Durham (19.70 and 16.00) and Lancashire's Graham Lloyd (17.57 and 19.20).

BATSMEN/ALL-ROUNDERS AVERAGING UNDER 15 v SURREY IN LIMITED-OVERS MATCHES 1996-2003

Player	County	Average	Runs Scored	Comp'd Innings
Kevin Curran	Northamptonshire	5.00	25	5
Matthew Hayden	Hants/Northants	6.60	33	5
Dimitri Mascarenhas	Hampshire	6.88	55	8
Matthew Fleming	Kent	8.44	76	9
John Stephenson	Hants/Essex	9.45	104	11
Keith Newell	Sussex/Glam	9.50	57	6
Richard Blakey	Yorkshire	9.57	67	7
Robin Martin-Jenkins	Sussex	11.18	123	11
Dominic Hewson	Derbys/Gloucs	11.60	58	5
Neil Smith	Warwickshire	12.25	98	8
Tim Hancock	Gloucestershire	13.00	156	12
Paul Johnson	Nottinghamshire	13.00	91	7
Vince Wells	Leicestershire	14.50	87	6

Qualification: 5 completed innings

Limited-Overs Bowling - Opposition Players Who Struggled

Having taken just three wickets in fifty-three overs against Surrey at an average of 104.67, Glamorgan's Dean Cosker is clearly the most unsuccessful opposition bowler of the period, though Melvyn Betts (two for 226 from 44 overs) and the economical Ryan Sidebottom (one wicket for 138 from 39.3 overs) are fortunate to have bowled insufficient overs to qualify for the table that follows. It is rather surprising to see the former England men, Richard Johnson and Mark Ealham, in second and third place respectively, and interesting to note that the eleven bowlers averaging over forty are an almost equal mix of spinners, medium pacers and fast-medium opening bowlers.

BOWLERS AVERAGING OVER 40 v SURREY IN LIMITED-OVERS MATCHES 1996-2003

Player	County	Average	Wkts Taken	Runs Conceded
Dean Cosker	Glamorgan	104.67	3	314
Richard Johnson	Middx/Somerset	59.40	5	297
Mark Ealham	Kent	54.29	7	380
A.J. Harris	Derbys/Notts	52.60	5	263
Simon Cook	Middlesex	47.20	5	236
Graham Rose	Somerset	44.40	5	222
Richard Stemp	Yorks/Notts	42.00	7	294
Jon Dakin	Leics/Essex	41.25	8	330
Martyn Ball	Gloucestershire	40.82	11	449
Adrian Dale	Glamorgan	40.71	7	285
John Wood	Durham/Lancs	40.50	6	243

Qualification: 50 overs bowled

It is more surprising still to see Mark Ealham, often a fine containing bowler for England in limited-overs internationals, in seventh place in the table of the most expensive bowlers. Gloucestershire's Jon Lewis, now a much improved bowler, tops the list after taking a few hammerings - from Ali Brown in particular - in the early years of his career, while Jon Dakin has consistently struggled to contain the Surrey batsmen. Owen Parkin, the leading wicket-taker against the county during their glory years, has been extremely expensive in capturing his twenty scalps, and a quick look at the spread of averages in the right-hand column suggests that there is no relationship whatsoever between economy and wicket-taking in limited-overs cricket - you can still be expensive whether or not you are picking up wickets along the way!

For anyone wondering why Glamorgan's Darren Thomas - who returned the best figures against Surrey (7-16 at Swansea in 1998) and then conceded that world record-breaking 108 runs from nine overs in the C&G match at The Oval in 2002 - doesn't feature in either the best or worst bowling tables, it is simply because he failed to reach the qualification standard of fifty overs. Just for the record, his figures are:- 13 wickets at 20.23 from forty-one overs, with an economy rate of 6.29 runs per over.

BOWLERS CONCEDING OVER 5.50 RUNS PER OVER v SURREY IN LIMITED-OVERS MATCHES 1996-2003						
Player	County	Runs/Over	Runs Conceded	Overs Bowled	Wkts Taken	Average
Jonathan Lewis	Gloucestershire	5.99	431	72.0	13	33.15
Jon Dakin	Leics/Essex	5.95	330	55.3	8	41.25
Dean Cosker	Glamorgan	5.92	314	53.0	3	104.67
Owen Parkin	Glamorgan	5.77	323	56.0	20	16.15
Steffan Jones	Somerset	5.62	293	52.1	11	26.64
Ashley Cowan	Essex	5.61	289	51.3	16	18.06
Mark Ealham	Kent	5.59	380	68.0	7	54.29
Qualification: 50 overs bowled						

National Service

It is quite amazing to record that players contracted to Surrey won no fewer than 272 Test caps and 369 One-Day International caps during the club's glory years - a grand total of 641 appearances in international cricket by fifteen different players.

It was also very much to the club's credit that every England Test team between April 1996 and September 2003 featured at least one Surrey player - a quite remarkable record - while the national side played just thirteen One-Day Internationals without a Surrey man in their eleven. Nine of these games were in South Africa and Zimbabwe in the winter of 1999-2000, three were in the Nat West Series of 2003, and the other one in India in 2001-2002.

INTERNATIONAL APPEARANCES BY SURREY CONTRACTED PLAYERS 1996-2003			
	TESTS	ODIs	TOTAL
Alec Stewart	80	97	177
Mark Butcher	57	0	57
Graham Thorpe	52	57	109
Mark Ramprakash	10	5	15
Alex Tudor	10	3	13
Ian Salisbury	6	0	6
Chris Lewis	5	3	8
Ian Ward	5	0	5
Adam Hollioake	4	35	39
Ben Hollioake	2	20	22
Martin Bicknell	2	0	2
Alistair Brown	0	16	16
Rikki Clarke	0	7	7
ENGLAND CAPS	**233**	**243**	**476**
Saqlain Mushtaq	39	112	151
Azhar Mahmood	0	14	14
PAKISTAN CAPS	**39**	**126**	**165**
TOTAL CAPS	**272**	**369**	**641**

It is perhaps more significant to look at the figures for international matches played in Britain, however, since those were the games that took players away from the county side. This table reveals that Surrey players made a total of 267 international appearances on British soil during the club's glory years, which underlines how well the county did to be so successful between 1996 and 2003, and how strong their squad was to cope with so many absences and the constant disruption caused. For a number of reasons, it is impossible to quantify, just by looking at the figures in this table, exactly how many Surrey matches players missed because they were on international duty - for example, not every Test or ODI clashed with a county match; since the introduction of ECB Central Contracts in 2000, players have been 'rested by England' before and after international matches and series; plus, Saqlain Mushtaq missed Surrey games when playing for Pakistan overseas. Whatever the actual number, these calls clearly placed a large demand on the county's resources.

INTERNATIONAL APPEARANCES IN BRITAIN BY SURREY CONTRACTED PLAYERS 1996-2003			
	TESTS	ODIs	TOTAL
Alec Stewart	49	40	89
Mark Butcher	31	0	31
Graham Thorpe	30	23	53
Alex Tudor	7	3	10
Chris Lewis	5	3	8
Ian Ward	5	0	5
Mark Ramprakash	4	0	4
Ian Salisbury	3	0	3
Adam Hollioake	2	13	15
Ben Hollioake	2	7	9
Martin Bicknell	2	0	2
Alistair Brown	0	11	11
Rikki Clarke	0	7	7
ENGLAND CAPS	**140**	**107**	**247**
Saqlain Mushtaq	1	16	17
Azhar Mahmood	0	3	3
PAKISTAN CAPS	**1**	**19**	**20**
TOTAL CAPS	**141**	**126**	**267**

England played eighty-eight Tests during the period under investigation, with the number of Surrey players in the eleven varying between one, on five occasions, and five, on two occasions. As the following table shows, the county generally had two or three representatives in every Test between April 1996 and September 2003, with a combination of Alec Stewart, Graham Thorpe and Mark Butcher often playing together in the same side.

SURREY REPRESENTATION IN TESTS 1996-2003	
No. Of Surrey Players	Occurrences
5	2
4	9
3	38
2	34
1	5

The picture in ODIs is rather different, since England's limited-overs team tended to change with much greater frequency during the 134 matches that were contested during the relevant period. The norm here was for Surrey to supply either one or two players, though there were nine occasions, between 1996 and 1998, when four men made the line-up.

SURREY REPRESENTATION IN ODIs 1996-2003	
No. Of Surrey Players	Occurrences
4	9
3	20
2	55
1	37
0	13

14 Eight Of The Best

There is no doubt that between 1996 and 2003 Surrey played some of the most amazing and entertaining cricket in the club's long and distinguished history. Their opponents, both at team and individual level, also produced some wonderful performances and it would be true to say that the overall standard of county cricket improved as Surrey raised the bar in the County Championship, and Gloucestershire set very high standards in the limited-overs format.

Having been fortunate enough to witness the vast majority of Surrey matches during this period, I feel sufficiently well qualified to select my personal 'bests' in this book. Some of the gaps in my viewing knowledge from 1996 and 1997 were filled by debating the merits of various matches and performances with other supporters, who also offered valuable opinions on the short lists I drew up ahead of picking my final eights. My discussions with fans who had seen a lot of the matches played during Surrey's glory years made me fully appreciate that no two people could ever come up with exactly the same list of, say, the eight best innings, nor would it be at all easy to rank them from one to eight. I should therefore emphasise that the selections that follow are very much personal choices, listed in chronological order.

BEST MATCHES

Before looking at individual performances, I've chosen the matches that I most enjoyed between 1996 and 2003, with a Surrey victory not being a pre-requisite for selection, as you will see! It is interesting to note that no fewer than five of my Championship 'picks' and five of my limited-overs selections turned out to be games that took place at The Oval. I think this confirms the validity of the belief that good pitches produce excellent cricket and high-quality cricketers, and it is worth noting that my three other Championship choices were games played on equally fine surfaces at Cheltenham, Guildford and Canterbury.

COUNTY CHAMPIONSHIP MATCHES
Everyone will have a different opinion about what makes a great four-day match, but the things that I considered to be most important included:- high quality of play and performers on view; an interesting finish; a switching of the balance of power; dramatic moments; and memorable individual performances.

GLOUCESTERSHIRE v SURREY at CHELTENHAM in 1998
A bad game for Surrey, as the two-wicket defeat was largely instrumental in the club failing to win the 1998 title, but undeniably a terrific contest over three days on a good fast track. Included a top-class innings from Adam Hollioake; brilliant bowling by Walsh, Smith, Bicknell and Saqlain; a nail-biting conclusion at the end of a tense and tight third day; and a couple of incredible collapses as the balance of power swung back and forth.

SURREY v SOMERSET at THE OVAL in 1999
How often does a four-day game go right down to the wire after 418 overs of play? Not very often, of course, yet this one was completed from the penultimate ball, with the most dramatic backdrop of thunder and lightning that you could imagine. After a couple of days of old-fashioned 'connoisseurs cricket', featuring plenty of spin bowling and determined batting, the thrilling climax saw Surrey snatching an important win that convinced them it was going to be their year to win the title.

SURREY v LANCASHIRE at THE OVAL in 1999
Surrey's showdown with a Muttiah Muralitharan inspired Lancashire held everyone's interest from start to finish. The game featured two strong sides, packed with internationals, going head-to-head, with each enjoying periods of domination before the home side secured another vital victory on a tense final morning.

SURREY v HAMPSHIRE at GUILDFORD in 1999
This clash between the top two sides in the table produced one of the greatest comebacks in Surrey's history, thanks to outstanding second-innings performances from Graham Thorpe and Saqlain Mushtaq. It was the sort of game that you couldn't take your eyes off for a minute as runs flowed and wickets tumbled, with the eventual champions gradually sucking the confidence and belief out of their opponents. A fine advert for four-day cricket played on a good pitch.

SURREY v HAMPSHIRE at THE OVAL in 2000
A real cliff-hanger, with plenty of twists and turns in the plot, as the underdogs from Hampshire - inspired by the bowling of Warne and Mullally - came so close to sending Surrey to the bottom of the table. A vital win, therefore, since morale would surely have been badly damaged by a defeat.

SURREY v LANCASHIRE at THE OVAL in 2002
This was a marvellously competitive match that showed the improving quality of the county game in the first division. In addition to a most amazing Surrey fightback that led to a fascinating fourth-innings battle, this game included two magnificent innings - Flintoff's 137 and Ramprakash's 119 not out - and a couple of excellent bowling performances, from Chapple (5-65) and Azhar Mahmood (8-61)... then you can also throw in ten catches for wicketkeeper Stewart, several of them top-class.

SURREY v WARWICKSHIRE at THE OVAL in 2002
Adam Hollioake described this as one of the best games of cricket he'd ever played in, and it was easy to see why. It was a hard-fought match that saw Warwickshire fight back to win for the first time in their history after being forced to follow on. The game featured some outstanding individual performances, including fine bowling from Shaun Pollock (4-44) as Surrey chased 169 from thirty-four overs in an exciting final session; a superb 210 not out from Mark Ramprakash; and some excellent seam bowling from James Ormond (5-116 and 5-62) and the highly competitive Dougie Brown (7-110).

KENT v SURREY at CANTERBURY in 2002
This was a quite fantastic contest, during which fans of both sides ran the gamut of emotions from joy to despair. Outplayed for long periods of the game, the visitors looked to be beaten on a number of occasions before coming through in thrilling style to register the county's highest ever fourth-innings score to win a match. Ian Ward's supreme unbeaten 168 would have been of little value without Adam Hollioake's incredible counter-attacking 122 in the first innings and vice versa, while Andrew Symonds contributed a fine innings of 118 for Kent. The bowling of Saggers, Saqlain and Salisbury was also admirable, as was the batting of Saqlain and Ormond on a memorable final day.

LIMITED-OVERS MATCHES
Although I placed a far greater emphasis on exciting strokeplay, fine fielding, and the game having a tight finish, I felt the criteria for selecting the best limited-overs matches were broadly similar to those relating to four-day games. Whereas it had been quite easy to select my eight best Championship matches, this category proved much tougher to judge. After I had noted down four

obvious choices, I was left to select the other four from a list of around fifteen equally worthy matches. Instinct then took over to produce the following eight.

SURREY v GLOUCESTERSHIRE at THE OVAL (BENSON & HEDGES CUP) in 1996
A typically excellent Oval pitch produced a veritable run-fest, with Surrey successfully chasing down a very stiff target of 308 to win. The game featured several excellent knocks, most notably Rob Cunliffe's unbeaten 137 for Gloucestershire and Ali Brown's explosive eighty-two for Surrey, and had its fair share of twists and turns.

SURREY v WARWICKSHIRE at THE OVAL (SUNDAY LEAGUE) in 1996
This wasn't a classic match in terms of overall quality or crowd-pleasing strokeplay, but it was a tense, exciting must-win affair that kept everyone on the edge of their seats and Surrey in contention for that elusive first trophy since 1982.

SURREY v NORTHAMPTONSHIRE at THE OVAL (SUNDAY LEAGUE) in 1996
A vital game, featuring 471 runs and seventeen wickets in eighty overs, with shifts in the balance of power, a last ball finish and, most important of all, a Surrey victory that put the club on the brink of claiming the Sunday League title. What more could you want? Well, there was also a brilliant century from David Capel, a superb knock under the most intense pressure from Chris Lewis, and one of the best catches you will ever see from the aforementioned Surrey all-rounder.

YORKSHIRE v SURREY at HEADINGLEY (BENSON & HEDGES CUP) in 2000
This match had most of the features required to make a great one-day game, with the exception of big totals and stunning strokeplay. Those elements weren't missed too much, however, as we saw great batting from Alec Stewart; fine bowling from Matthew Hoggard; three dramatic collapses; two brave recoveries; some fine catches and direct-hit run outs as Surrey fought back; and a very tense finish as Adam Hollioake was forced to throw Jason Ratcliffe the ball for the last over. When 'Ratters' bowled Sidebottom a fine game was transformed into a great game for Surrey fans.

GLOUCESTERSHIRE v SURREY at BRISTOL (NATIONAL LEAGUE) in 2002
It was the unpredictable nature of this match from start to finish that persuaded me to include it in my final eight - you were never quite sure where the next twist in the tale was going to take it. Although the pitch was far from ideal for good limited-overs cricket, a number of players turned in excellent performances, with Ali Brown's fifty-four and Jon Lewis's 4-22 being the outstanding efforts. Spectators at the County Ground had the added bonus of witnessing Ed Giddins's career-best limited-overs score!

SURREY v GLAMORGAN at THE OVAL (C & G TROPHY) in 2002
This was the game that had everything, with records of all descriptions falling like ninepins, though it must be acknowledged that it was the visitors' breathtaking response to Surrey's 438-5 that made it an all-time great match. In addition to Ali Brown's 268, we had Robert Croft's sensational 119, plus a fine century from David Hemp and an excellent ninety-seven from Ian Ward, as no fewer than 867 runs were racked up for the loss of fifteen wickets in a hundred overs. The match featured twenty-eight sixes and eighty-seven fours, and the result was in the balance until Dean Cosker was bowled by the penultimate delivery. Who said that cricket was boring?!

DERBYSHIRE v SURREY at DERBY (NATIONAL LEAGUE) in 2002
This was an important promotion tussle that had more twists and turns than an Agatha Christie mystery. It featured several fine individual performances - most notably Rikki Clarke's unbeaten ninety-eight - collapses, recoveries and a very tight finish that had a dash of controversy about it as Ed Giddins survived a confident lbw shout with his side three runs short of victory.

SURREY v KENT at THE OVAL (NATIONAL LEAGUE) in 2003
This high-scoring encounter on a superb Oval strip saw 638 runs scored for the loss of fourteen wickets in ninety overs. The Lions looked to have put the game out of Kent's reach, thanks largely to a combination of Mark Ramprakash's sublime strokeplay and the powerful hitting of Azhar Mahmood, but the Spitfires made a great game of it as Ed Smith and Matt Walker blasted back in style, before falling just short in an exciting climax.

COUNTY CHAMPIONSHIP BATTING AND BOWLING

EIGHT OF THE BEST INNINGS BY SURREY BATSMEN
This was easily the hardest category to judge, since Surrey's team was packed with awesome batting talent throughout their glory years and there were a great many brilliant innings played. When trying to gauge the merits of an innings there are so many things to take into account, too, including the standard of the opposition bowlers; the condition of the pitch; the importance of the match; the state of the game; the quality of the strokeplay; and the technical excellence. I felt it was therefore nigh on impossible to come up with a definitive eight 'best' innings of the period, especially when it came to weighing up the relative merits of knocks played in totally different situations - for example, is an innings that saves a match from a position of great adversity any less meritorious than one that wins a match? Consequently, I decided to select eight innings that I felt were the best of their kind, which seemed entirely reasonable since this section is entitled 'Eight Of The Best', as opposed to 'The Eight Best'.

GRAHAM THORPE'S 222 v GLAMORGAN at THE OVAL in 1997
This was just about the ultimate match-saving innings. When Thorpe came to the crease in the second innings, Surrey were 9-2 and still trailing by 225 runs, yet by the time he was eighth out, some seven-and-a-quarter hours later, they were leading by 217. The Glamorgan bowlers were unable to find any chink in his armour and had been driven to distraction long before he holed out to long-on after registering his career-best score in a high-pressure situation.

DARREN BICKNELL'S 57 v KENT at TUNBRIDGE WELLS in 1999
I nominate this as the best 'bad wicket' innings of Surrey's glory years. You might feel that a score of fifty-seven doesn't deserve a place in this list, but there were a number of factors that persuaded me to include it. Quite apart from the fact that a wet, lush outfield probably robbed Bicknell of fifteen to twenty runs, this innings was certainly worth a lot more than its face value, given a pitch of steep bounce that made many strokes - especially of the cross-bat variety - no-go areas, as numerous batsmen in the match discovered to their cost. I therefore felt that Darren was the only Surrey batsman of the period who was capable of playing this innings, since it required phenomenal powers of self-denial and self-discipline over four-and-a-half hours' batting. It should also be noted that no other batsman was able to reach forty in the match and that this knock - against a decent Kent seam attack of Headley, Thompson, Fleming and Symonds - was a major factor in setting up an important Surrey victory.

MARK BUTCHER'S 259 v LEICESTERSHIRE at LEICESTER in 1999
This was my favourite 'leading from the front' innings of the period covered by this book. After Surrey had dismissed Leicestershire for 272, Butcher - captaining the side in Adam Hollioake's absence - batted beautifully right from the start of his innings, immediately putting the hosts on the back foot and giving his team an added psychological advantage. A good Foxes attack,

comprising Mullally, Kasprowicz, Lewis, Millns and Brimson, rarely got a ball past his broad bat, while the range and quality of his strokes were also extremely impressive.

ALI BROWN'S 295* v LEICESTERSHIRE at OAKHAM SCHOOL in 2000
For all-round excellence nothing could touch this superlative innings on a fast, bouncy track at Oakham School. Arriving in the middle with his side at 25-3 in a vital match, Brown took on and destroyed a fine Leicestershire attack - Ormond, DeFreitas, Lewis, Wells, Kumble and Maddy - to transform his side's fortunes and demoralise the oppostition to such a degree that they crumbled to defeat inside three days.

ADAM HOLLIOAKE'S 122* v KENT at CANTERBURY in 2002
For my money this was the finest of many counter-attacking innings played by Surrey batsmen between 1996 and 2003. With his side in desperate trouble at 59-5 in reply to Kent's 374 when he took guard, Hollioake scored a comparatively measured half-century from fifty-four balls before a volley of stunning strokes took him to a century from his next forty-one deliveries and on to a final 122 not out from 103 balls that enabled his team to avoid the follow on... and the rest is history. Without this amazing knock, Surrey would have been out of the match and we would have been denied all the heroics and drama that followed, including Ian Ward's brilliant unbeaten 168. Just for good measure, it should be noted that Hollioake was badly inconvenienced throughout his innings by two injuries he had picked up in the field, a badly bruised knee that inhibited his running, and a chipped finger!

IAN WARD'S 168* v KENT at CANTERBURY in 2002
This was, without question, the best match-winning fourth-innings knock played during Surrey's glory years. Although Ward was very modest about his innings after the game, everyone who witnessed it will forever remember this study in phenomenal concentration, grit and determination that ensured Adam Hollioake's unbeaten 122 in Surrey's first innings of the match hadn't been in vain. This classic eight-hour, 367-ball knock went a long way towards securing the 2002 title and showed why Surrey were so hard to beat at this time.

MARK RAMPRAKASH'S 279* v NOTTINGHAMSHIRE at WHITGIFT SCHOOL in 2003
I have selected this innings for its supreme technical excellence. Faced by a Nottinghamshire attack that had underperformed for most of the season yet still looked pretty impressive on paper - Smith, Shreck, Franks, Cairns and MacGill - Ramprakash batted quite beautifully throughout the first day to reach 191 by the close of play. It was hard to remember him putting a foot wrong and it was almost like watching a coaching video as every stroke, whether defensive or offensive, was executed immaculately. On the second day, Ramprakash went on to a career-best score, his 400-ball knock having been studded with forty fours and four sixes.

JON BATTY'S 154* v LANCASHIRE at OLD TRAFFORD in 2003
This might appear to be another slightly 'left field' selection, but I have included this innings because I regard it as the finest of the period in the face of overwhelming adversity. Quite apart from the fact that it was a near flawless knock - chanceless, full of terrific strokes, and a rare example of an opener carrying his bat - there were numerous other factors that added to its excellence. Surrey had come into this game with just one day's rest after spending almost two-and-a-half days in the field at Grace Road, watching a winning position being transformed into a demoralising draw that had enabled Sussex to go top of the table. All the players must have been physically tired and mentally drained, but especially Batty, who had been required to concentrate behind the stumps for seven of the final eight sessions of the match. It therefore required a display

of phenomenal fortitude and energy for the Surrey wicketkeeper to bat through the whole day against a very good Lancashire attack, while his team-mates wilted around him.

To give an indication of the outstanding quality in this category, the following excellent innings didn't quite make it, though I felt many of them were the second or third best in one or more of the 'innings categories' above:- Alec Stewart's 271* v Yorkshire at The Oval, 1997; Alec Stewart's 170 v Kent at Canterbury, 1997; Adam Hollioake's 112 v Gloucestershire at Cheltenham, 1998; Ali Brown's 110* v Essex at The Oval, 1999; Graham Thorpe's 164 v Hampshire at Guildford, 1999; Ali Brown's 140* v Yorkshire at The Oval, 2000; Mark Butcher's 145* v Glamorgan at The Oval, 2001; Martin Bicknell's 101* v Kent at Canterbury, 2001; Ali Brown's 177 v Sussex at The Oval, 2002; Nadeem Shahid's 150 v Sussex at The Oval, 2002; Mark Ramprakash's 119* v Lancashire at The Oval, 2002; Ali Brown's 188 v Kent at The Oval, 2002; Rikki Clarke's 127* v Lancashire at The Oval, 2003; Martin Bicknell's 141 v Essex at Chelmsford, 2003

A SELECTION OF THE BEST INNINGS AGAINST SURREY
Carl Hooper's 94 for Kent at The Oval in 1998 - A masterclass in how to play high-class spin bowling on a turning pitch.
Ben Smith's 204 for Leicestershire at The Oval in 1998 - Epic Championship-clinching innings that broke Surrey's hearts.
Nicky Peng's 98 for Durham at The Riverside in 2000 - Incredibly mature knock by a 17-year-old on his debut in bowler-friendly conditions. Scored more boundaries in his innings than the whole Surrey team managed in the entire match!
Andy Flintoff's 137 for Lancashire at The Oval in 2002 - An awesomely destructive innings, during which he dominated every member of a high-class attack with the exception of Ian Salisbury.
Brad Hodge's 157 for Leicestershire at Leicester in 2003 - A devastating exhibition of strokeplay that was crucial in saving the match for his side and killing off Surrey's Championship challenge.
Carl Hooper's 114 for Lancashire at Old Trafford in 2003 - A wonderful demonstration of how to manipulate the bowlers and field-settings during a last-wicket partnership.

EIGHT OF THE BEST BOWLING PERFORMANCES FOR SURREY
Given Surrey's success in Championship cricket, there was obviously plenty of competition in this category, though performances with the ball seemed to be harder to evaluate than those with the bat. The things I tried to take into account included:- the quality of the opposition batting line-up and the victims claimed; the modes of dismissal; the state of the pitch; the importance and state of the match; and the context of the match in the season. It was particularly hard to assess Saqlain Mushtaq's five-wicket hauls, since a lot of them came against weak batting line-ups and it all seemed just too easy for him! Needless to say, there were a lot of fine performances that didn't make the final eight, but I think the following selections were all pretty special.

SAQLAIN MUSHTAQ'S 7-41 v WORCESTERSHIRE at THE OVAL in 1998
This was a sensational performance after Adam Hollioake had placed a lot of faith in his bowlers by making a challenging declaration. Despite having already delivered sixty overs in the visitors' first innings, he appeared to be fresh and vibrant as he delivered another twenty-eight immaculate overs while working his way through a strong and long Worcestershire line-up to earn his side a thrilling victory.

IAN SALISBURY'S 7-65 v GLAMORGAN at SWANSEA in 1998
Knowing that the Swansea pitch had a reputation for assisting spinners, Surrey gambled by including Salisbury in their team, even though he was still struggling with a groin injury. Having deliberately kept him out of the action in the first innings, Adam Hollioake let him loose after twenty-seven overs of the second with Glamorgan going nicely at 119-2 and the game was immediately transformed. Salisbury claimed seven of the last eight wickets during a superb 30-over spell to set up a six-wicket win.

JOEY BENJAMIN'S 6-35 v DURHAM at THE RIVERSIDE in 1998
A magnificent do-or-die display by the veteran paceman towards the end of his career that, temporarily at least, resuscitated Surrey's 1998 Championship challenge. Joey rolled back the years and rose to the occasion during a marathon spell, moving the ball both ways in the air and off the pitch to claim six victims bowled, lbw or caught behind the wicket.

IAN SALISBURY'S 8-60 v SOMERSET at THE OVAL in 2000
This performance is not included simply because it was the leg-spinner's career-best. Although the pitch and match situation were both in his favour, Salisbury's control was immaculate and he included almost all of the classic leg-spinner's dismissals in this spell:- his leg-break brought him a stumping; a miscued drive to backward point; and a left-hander lbw when padding up. His googly produced a right-hander 'gated' on the drive; a right-hander lbw when padding up; a right-hander beaten by turn when offering a defensive stroke; and two right-handers caught bat-pad at silly point. This was a magnificent exhibition of the leg-spinner's art.

MARTIN BICKNELL'S 7-72 v LEICESTERSHIRE at GUILDFORD in 2000
Despite having to shoulder an extremely heavy workload on a very warm day in excellent batting conditions, he picked up seven good wickets and kept a fine Leicestershire team's total within bounds. Bicknell himself felt that he bowled better in this innings than in the second innings when he claimed 9-47.

MARTIN BICKNELL'S 9-47 v LEICESTERSHIRE at GUILDFORD in 2000
A more spectacular effort than his first-innings 7-72, this display set Surrey up for an important victory in the context of the 2000 Championship-winning season. As in the first innings, his wickets were earned by nagging accuracy and an ability to make the most of what little assistance was available to him in batsman-friendly conditions.

ALEX TUDOR'S 7-48 v LANCASHIRE at THE OVAL in 2000
This was a very big performance in an important match, with Tudor having barely recovered from a side strain. Since he was unable to bowl at full pace, he reined himself back slightly and produced a marvellously controlled display to knock Lancashire over for just 120. With the red rose county unable to recover from a 190-run first-innings deficit, Surrey's winning run towards the 2000 title continued.

AZHAR MAHMOOD'S 8-61 v LANCASHIRE at THE OVAL in 2002
A wonderful exhibition of swing and seam bowling earned him eight good scalps - all specialist batsmen or all-rounders - with each of them either caught behind off the outside edge, lbw or bowled. This performance came at a good time, too, since it enabled Surrey to overcome a first-innings deficit of 104 runs and beat their potential Championship rivals.

A SELECTION OF THE BEST BOWLING PERFORMANCES AGAINST SURREY
Allan Donald's 6-55 for Warwickshire at Edgbaston in 1997 - A display of awesome fast bowling that devastated Surrey's second innings to set up victory for his side.

Gavin Hamilton's 7-50 for Yorkshire at Headingley in 1998 - An almost flawless demonstration of fast-medium seam and swing bowling in helpful conditions

Muttiah Muralitharan's 6-87 for Lancashire at The Oval in 1999 - Sensational spin bowling from the Sri Lankan master of mystery, even though Surrey's batsmen played him better than most during his phenomenally successful period with Lancashire.

Shane Warne's 5-31 for Hampshire at The Oval in 2000 - Masterful spell that brought his side right back into the match after Alan Mullally had made early inroads.

Shaun Pollock's 4-44 for Warwickshire at The Oval in 2002 - Two fine spells, one at each end of Surrey's second innings, to first inspire and then finish off Warwickshire's amazing comeback in the second half of the match.

Mohammad Akram's 8-49 for Essex at The Oval in 2003 - Combined pace and swing to devastating effect to rout Surrey's below-strength batting line-up.

LIMITED-OVERS BATTING AND BOWLING

EIGHT OF THE BEST INNINGS BY SURREY BATSMEN

There were a lot of fine innings to choose from in this category, though I didn't find it too difficult to pick out eight. I still had to omit a few magnificent efforts, however, including Ben Hollioake's seventy-three in the 2001 Benson & Hedges Cup final and Alec Stewart's 160 against Hampshire in the same competition in 1996, but I felt the following eight selections were all exceptional in one way or another. As I sorted through all the possible innings for inclusion it became clear to me that Ali Brown could provide a pretty impressive top eight all on his own!

CHRIS LEWIS'S 63 v NORTHAMPTONSHIRE at THE OVAL (SUNDAY LEAGUE) in 1996
In many ways the most important innings of Surrey's glory years, since the match, and the club's chances of claiming their first trophy since 1982, were very much on the line when the England all-rounder came to the crease in indifferent light with his side five down and needing 135 runs from eighteen overs. By scoring sixty-three from just 47 balls under immense pressure, Lewis took his side to the brink of victory before being dismissed. Martin Bicknell held his nerve to finish the job, but success would have been impossible without this knock from 'Lewy'. One can but wonder what might have happened had Surrey lost this match and ended up without a trophy for a fourteenth consecutive season. Perhaps there would have been no glory years?

ALI BROWN'S 157* v LEICESTERSHIRE at LEICESTER (SUNDAY LEAGUE) in 1997
This was a simply amazing innings that gave everyone a taste of what was to come later in the season at Guildford. Given that the Foxes' attack of Alan Mullally, Gordon Parsons, Matthew Brimson, Jon Dakin, Neil Johnson and Vince Wells was pretty impressive, and that this knock was played in a pressure situation with very little support from his team-mates as Surrey chased 235 to win, it is easy to understand why many people feel this was a better innings than the 203 against Hampshire.

ALI BROWN'S 203 v HAMPSHIRE at GUILDFORD (SUNDAY LEAGUE) in 1997
Although some people were quick to point out that Hampshire's attack was rather bland, and that there was a short boundary on the Dapdune Wharf side of the ground, I don't think either of those things detract in any way from Brown's sensational performance. His achievement of scoring an individual double-century in just forty overs was quite remarkable, especially since he was the first to accomplish the feat in the Sunday League, beating the previous highest mark by an impressive twenty-seven runs.

332

BEN HOLLIOAKE'S 98 v KENT at LORD'S (BENSON & HEDGES CUP) in 1997
Rising to the occasion and loving every minute of the big showpiece final at Lord's, Ben played quite beautifully to ensure that there were no slip-ups as Surrey chased Kent's total of 212. A classy knock of stunning maturity that was full of lovely strokes.

ALEC STEWART'S 97* v YORKSHIRE at HEADINGLEY (BENSON & HEDGES CUP) in 2000
This was an absolutely vital innings that secured a rare victory at Headingley and took Surrey into the semi-finals of the competition. After losing four of his team-mates to Matthew Hoggard with the new ball, Stewart used all his experience to hold the innings together and paced his effort perfectly in order to ensure that a competitive total was posted.

ALI BROWN'S 268 v GLAMORGAN at THE OVAL (C & G TROPHY) in 2002
Simply the best limited-overs innings you could wish to see. This was a sporting achievement that didn't get anything like the media coverage it deserved. Beating the 28-year-old previous record by a massive forty-six runs represented a quantum leap, comparable to Bob Beamon's long jump at the Mexico Olympics of 1968, or perhaps a sprinter taking half a second off the 100 metres world record, yet comparatively little interest was shown by football-obsessed sports editors across the nation. It will be a major surprise if Brown's record doesn't stand for many many years.

ADAM HOLLIOAKE'S 117* v SUSSEX at HOVE (C & G TROPHY) in 2002
This innings was absolutely awesome in its power and brutality, as every member of Sussex's varied if unexceptional attack felt the weight of Hollioake's flashing blade, just two days after the emotional service at Southwark Cathedral. As with Brown's 268, it didn't lead to the huge victory that had been expected but it would seem a fair bet to assume that Surrey might have lost the match without it.

AZHAR MAHMOOD'S 98 v ESSEX at CHELMSFORD (NATIONAL LEAGUE) in 2003
This superb knock transformed the match and enabled Surrey to get their triumphant 2003 NCL campaign off to a winning start. The Lions were in desperate trouble at 82-6 in bowler-friendly conditions when Azhar arrived at the crease but, in partnership with Adam Hollioake, he managed to turn things around in dramatic style. A combination of sensible singles and scintillating strokeplay enabled the Pakistani all-rounder to make ninety-eight from just seventy-three balls as Surrey recovered to a match-winning total of 268-8.

A SELECTION OF THE BEST INNINGS AGAINST SURREY
Simon Ecclestone's 130 for Somerset at Taunton in the Sunday League in 1996 - A quite brilliant display of clean hitting by the tall left-hander.
David Byas's 116* for Yorkshire at The Oval in the Benson & Hedges Cup in 1996 - A classy and authoritative innings full of magnificent drives that quickly snuffed out Surrey's hopes of defending a disappointing total.
Martin Speight's 117 for Sussex at Guildford in the Sunday League in 1996 - His side were in trouble at 71-5 shortly after his arrival at the wicket, yet he still maintained a positive approach to play a dashing and inventive innings.
David Capel's 112 for Northamptonshire at The Oval in the Sunday League in 1996 - In a game that was vital for both sides this was a brilliant effort, full of fine strokeplay and controlled hitting.
Matthew Maynard's 132 for Glamorgan at The Oval in the Sunday League in 1997 - Surrey's bowling might have been a little below par on the day but this brutal and powerful 75-ball innings was still something special.

Jacques Kallis's 155* for Glamorgan at Pontypridd in the National League in 1999 - Although it is only fair to point out that Surrey's attack was missing a number of key bowlers, this was still a brilliantly constructed innings full of sublime strokeplay on his county debut.

Andy Flintoff's 135* for Lancashire at The Oval in the Benson & Hedges Cup in 2000 - Dominated all the bowlers with typically powerful hitting that rushed Lancashire to an easy victory.

Robert Croft's 119 for Glamorgan at The Oval in the C & G Trophy in 2002 - A magnificently brave and thrilling riposte to Ali Brown's 268 that inspired his side and boosted their belief that they could chase Surrey's 438-5.

EIGHT OF THE BEST PERFORMANCES BY SURREY BOWLERS

Limited-overs bowling performances are even more difficult to assess than Championship bowling performances, since the match situation often dictates whether a wicketless but economical spell is more valuable than an expensive stint that yields a few wickets or vice versa. Having decided that it was impossible to select the eight 'best' displays, I opted for eight varied performances that stood out for me for one reason or another. As with the limited-overs batting list, it would be possible to compile a pretty good 'eight of the best' list for Adam Hollioake alone.

BEN HOLLIOAKE'S 5-10 v DERBYSHIRE at THE OVAL (SUNDAY LEAGUE) in 1996
This amazingly mature display of seam and swing bowling by the 18-year-old on his fifth first-team appearance led Surrey to a 50-run victory. His victims included Chris Adams and Dominic Cork as he delivered eight immaculate overs.

CHRIS LEWIS'S 3-39 v KENT at LORD'S (BENSON & HEDGES CUP) in 1997
Lewis received plenty of unjustified bad press for being rather 'pumped up' for the final against Kent, but Surrey were more than happy with his performance. Having picked up the wicket of Matthew Fleming during a tight early spell, he then did exactly what his captain wanted him to do - remove the potentially dangerous Graham Cowdrey - when he was recalled to the attack later.

SAQLAIN MUSHTAQ'S 4-32 v SOMERSET at TAUNTON (NAT WEST TROPHY) in 1999
As the Somerset batsmen thrashed Surrey's six other bowlers around the park to reach a total of 315-8, Saqlain delivered ten superb overs. The word 'outstanding' was entirely appropriate.

MARTIN BICKNELL'S 7-30 v GLAMORGAN at THE OVAL (NATIONAL LEAGUE) in 1999
The Glamorgan batsmen had no answer as the master of swing took full advantage of favourable conditions to record the best figures by a Surrey bowler in limited-overs cricket.

ADAM HOLLIOAKE'S 5-77 v GLAMORGAN at THE OVAL (C & G TROPHY) in 2002
In the highest scoring limited-overs match ever played, it seemed that the only way to make any impression on the run-rate was to take wickets, which is exactly what the Surrey captain did. Without this cool-headed contribution from Hollioake, Ali Brown could well have ended up on the losing side!

ED GIDDINS'S 3-31 v GLOUCESTERSHIRE at LORD'S (BENSON & HEDGES CUP) in 2001
Alex Tudor takes a fair share of the credit for this selection, since it was his wonderfully tight opening spell that set Giddins up to capture the three key wickets of Kim Barnett, Ian Harvey and Matt Windows that went a long way towards winning the 2001 Benson & Hedges Cup.

AZHAR MAHMOOD'S 6-37 v ESSEX at THE OVAL (NATIONAL LEAGUE) in 2003
Essex were going well on 193-4 after thirty-eight overs when Azhar returned to the attack to produce some of the best end-of-innings bowling you could ever wish to see. With his magnificent inswinging yorkers very much to the fore, the Surrey all-rounder claimed 5-12 in sixteen deliveries to reduce the Eagles to 220 all out, some 20-30 runs fewer than they might have expected, and Surrey went on to win the match.

ADAM HOLLIOAKE'S 6-17 v KENT at CANTERBURY (NATIONAL LEAGUE) in 2003
With the wheels starting to fall off at the end of the 2003 season, Surrey needed some strong individual performances to stave off a late charge from Gloucestershire in the NCL. The Lions' skipper certainly came up with the goods at Canterbury, almost single-handedly reducing Kent from a reasonably strong position of 109-3 to 142 all out and ensuring that his side picked up a vital victory.

A SELECTION OF THE BEST PERFORMANCES BY OPPOSITION BOWLERS
Paul Strang's 2-27 for Kent at The Oval in the Benson & Hedges Cup in 1997 - A superb spell of leg-spin bowling that regained the initiative for his side after Surrey had made a flying start to their innings.
Darren Gough's 5-25 for Yorkshire at Headingley in the Sunday League in 1998 - A fast and deadly spell in gathering gloom, after a rejected appeal for a catch at the wicket against Graham Thorpe had really fired up the England paceman.
Darren Thomas's 7-16 for Glamorgan at Swansea in the Sunday League in 1998 - Good pace and superb use of reverse swing to rout the middle- and lower-order batting.
Paul Jarvis's 4-28 for Somerset at Guildford in the National League in 1999 - A match-winning performance, in terms of both economy and wicket-taking, in batsman-friendly conditions at the fast-scoring Woodbridge Road ground.
Shane Warne's 2-6 for Hampshire at The Oval in the Benson & Hedges Cup in 2000 - It might only have been a two-over spell in a ten-overs-a-side game, but the impact on the match was immense. In addition to claiming the scalps of Graham Thorpe and Adam Hollioake, he had Mark Butcher missed at the wicket.
Jon Lewis's 4-22 for Gloucestershire at Bristol in the National League in 2002 - A marvellous spell of fast-medium seam and swing bowling that totally transformed the match after Ali Brown and Ian Ward had given Surrey a racing start.

BEST CATCHES

EIGHT OF THE BEST CATCHES BY SURREY PLAYERS
There is clearly no need to differentiate between the two formats of the game where catches are concerned, though I was a little surprised that I was able to recall a lot more good catches in four-day cricket than in the limited-overs game. Despite spending a lot of time racking my brain and going through notes, scorecards, press cuttings and books, I may well have overlooked one or two special catches, but since all the following efforts came fairly readily to mind I think it's fair to say that they all warranted selection in any case. All catches were taken in the County Championship unless otherwise stated.

ALI BROWN at DEEP BACKWARD POINT to dismiss VINCE WELLS at THE OVAL in 1996 (SUNDAY LEAGUE)
An incredible feat of hand-eye co-ordination as Brown ran round the boundary to intercept Wells's fast-flying upper-cut high and one-handed to his left-hand side. On a day when Surrey held some fine catches to dismiss Leicestershire for forty-eight, this was the pick of the bunch.

CHRIS LEWIS at BACKWARD POINT to dismiss NEIL LENHAM at GUILDFORD in 1996
This was an absolutely superb one-handed effort high to his right-hand side, requiring amazing athleticism, as Lenham's sliced drive at Bicknell looked destined for the boundary.

CHRIS LEWIS at SHORT THIRD MAN to dismiss MAL LOYE at THE OVAL in 1996 (SUNDAY LEAGUE)
When Mal Loye got a thick top edge to his cut off Adam Hollioake, he must have felt sure that the ball would evade Chris Lewis at short third man, but he was wrong. After taking a couple of short quick steps to his right, the fielder put in a full-length dive that enabled him to grab the ball just before it hit the turf, bringing spectators all around the ground to their feet. Given the importance of the match, and the fact that Loye was past fifty and going well, it was a crucial catch, as well as being one of the finest you could ever hope to see.

MARK BUTCHER at BACKWARD SQUARE LEG to dismiss WARREN HEGG at THE OVAL in 2000
Warren Hegg's violent sweep at Ian Salisbury's legside full-toss looked destined for the boundary until Mark Butcher flew away to his right at backward square leg to pull in a fantastic one-handed catch.

IAN SALISBURY at GULLY to dismiss DAVID FULTON at THE OVAL in 2002
When Dave Fulton cut Ed Giddins backward of point he probably expected to collect four runs, but Ian Salisbury dived away low to his right-hand side to pluck a remarkable catch out of thin air.

RIKKI CLARKE at 3RD SLIP to dismiss DARREN LEHMANN at GUILDFORD in 2002
This was a truly breathtaking catch. With Lehmann aiming to leg, the ball flew away, fast and low off a leading edge, into the gap between third slip and gully. Clarke must have seen the ball very late, yet managed to put in a prodigious dive to his left to grasp the ball one-handed just a couple of inches off the deck.

NADEEM SHAHID at SHORT LEG to dismiss RICHARD MONTGOMERIE at HOVE in 2002
During Surrey's glory years, Nadeem Shahid and Adam Hollioake held a great many fine catches at short leg and silly point - more than enough to have their own 'Eight Of The Best' section - but the one that really stuck in my mind was this stunning reflex effort by Shahid off Ed Giddins. Since Montgomerie had middled his clip to leg perfectly, it was no wonder he was mortified to see the ball snapped up at short leg. While there might have been a little bit of luck involved here, the catch owed a great deal more to courage, skill and anticipation than good fortune.

JON BATTY to dismiss IAN BELL at EDGBASTON in 2002
Alec Stewart and Jon Batty were responsible for any number of great catches during the period covered by this book, but this one was the best in my opinion. Bell's outside edge from a Bicknell outswinger looked to be flying very low and on the bounce between first and second slip until Batty's extraordinary dive, with his right arm at full stretch, enabled him to intercept the ball just in the nick of time. A stupendous effort.

A SELECTION OF THE BEST CATCHES AGAINST SURREY
Graeme Hick at Deep Midwicket to dismiss Ali Brown at Worcester in 1997 (Sunday League) - A fantastic right-handed overhead catch on the midwicket boundary to remove Brown from the third ball of the match.

Jason Gallian at First Slip to dismiss Alec Stewart at The Oval in 1999 - On a day of fine catches, this incredible effort, with the ball travelling low and fast to the fielder's left, really took the breath away.

Martin Speight to Ben Hollioake at The Riverside in 2000 - This was a particularly impressive catch by the Durham keeper because Hollioake's inside edge not only required him to change direction but also to swoop low since the ball was heading downwards all the way off the bat.

Paul Collingwood at Square Leg to dismiss Adam Hollioake at The Riverside in 2000 - Hollioake's miscued hook looked sure to land safely in the space at square leg, but Collingwood sprinted in from the boundary, and put in a fine forward dive to take an astonishing catch just before the ball could hit the turf.

Mark Wallace to dismiss Mark Ramprakash at The Oval in 2001 - This was a brilliant full-length diving effort at full stretch in front of the slips by the young Glamorgan wicketkeeper.

15 Keys To Success

It goes without saying that a club needs a fine group of cricketers in order to have the kind of sustained success that Surrey enjoyed between 1996 and 2003. As well as having a core of four outstanding bowlers - Bicknell, Tudor, Saqlain and Salisbury - who played for the majority of the 'glory years', and were largely instrumental in the capture of the three Championship titles, the club boasted what was surely the biggest and best group of batsmen in its history. The wicketkeeping was also in very safe hands, with Alec Stewart, Jon Batty and Graham Kersey all high-class practitioners of their art. Surrey had good squads in the past, however, without managing to secure much silverware, which goes to prove that a great number of other components are required to make a successful team. In this short chapter I have attempted to pick out some of the things that I personally believe made the county so successful during the period covered by this book.

I have grouped the 'keys to success' into five categories, namely:-

* **Ideal Management**
* **Outstanding Captaincy**
* **Cultivation Of A Strong Team Ethic**
* **Culture Of Attack/Taking The Positive Option**
* **That Extra Edge**

* **Ideal Management**

I think it would be true to say that Dave Gilbert and Keith Medlycott were the right men at the right time for Surrey.

Back in 1996, there was a culture of under-achievement at the club, and - as the Chairman Of Cricket, Vic Dodds appreciated - the young Australian was the ideal man to introduce some new methods and instil a fresh competitive approach. He quickly made his mark and ingrained a winning mentality into the team. Given the quality of the players at the club, it was clear that breaking the cycle of failure with a trophy would almost certainly lead to further success.

When Gilbert decided to move on, the time was right for a different kind of Manager, and Keith Medlycott fitted the bill perfectly. He had an immensely strong squad at his disposal and, by acting largely as an organiser, he allowed his players to concentrate solely on their cricket, and was happy to remain something of a background figure, letting the players have the limelight. As a result, he worked well with a strong captain like Adam Hollioake and they formed a magnificent team. 'Medders' was also a great believer in keeping a settled side and always showed total faith in his players, fully understanding that players would have bad games or poor runs of form, and needed to be supported, rather than dropped from the team, on those occasions. This allowed his players to play their natural game and express themselves fully, without fear of getting dropped if they suffered a disappointing sequence of results.

* **Outstanding Captaincy**

Adam Hollioake will clearly go down in cricketing history as one of the great captains, and deservedly so. If you were to list all the qualities you would want in a captain/leader, Hollioake would score highly in just about every category. He was positive, aggressive, shrewd and totally unselfish, always putting the team's needs before his own, sometimes, I felt, to the detriment of his own game. I suspect his batting statistics - good though they were - might have been better had he not been captain. He was, surprisingly, something of a reluctant skipper, and it was an open secret that he tried to give up the leadership on a number of occasions... though he was always persuaded that it was best for the club that he continued. On the field, it was always clear who was in charge - he was certainly always in authority, though never authoritarian. His field placings were invariably always more aggressive than those set by other county captains, and he understood the value of taking wickets in the limited-overs game - when his seamers were on top in favourable conditions he would often post three slips, and if Saqlain Mushtaq was on a roll, with a new batsman at the crease, the skipper would often drop himself in at silly point.

* Cultivation Of A Strong Team Ethic
I think it was very much to Surrey's advantage that a large number of the players in the 'glory years' squad came up together through the club's junior ranks and the second team. In that situation, players tend to be more closely bonded, and know one another's strengths and weaknesses, both as cricketers and human beings, so much better. After growing up together like this, they probably knew instinctively how a team-mate would react to any given match situation, which is obviously advantageous. Then, of course, the bonding grew stronger as a consequence of the two terrible tragedies that struck the club.

The situations where the team ethic was best demonstrated were perhaps when the side was shorn of its international players. The record of the so-called 'weakened' side was phenomenal throughout the period covered by this book, as everyone pulled together to show the depth of talent at the club. Loyal squad men such as Nadeem Shahid and Jason Ratcliffe, and Jon Batty before he became a regular in the side, were invaluable to Surrey. They were often unfortunate to be dropped, in order to accommodate a returning international player, after having had a good match but, instead of sulking or looking to move on to another club where they would play regularly, they remained with Surrey, giving the squad its enviable strength in depth.

* Culture Of Attack/Taking The Positive Option
As stated in the section about Adam Hollioake's outstanding captaincy, Surrey were quick to attack whenever possible during their pomp, whatever the form of the game, and players were never criticised if they tried to play positively and failed as a result. This took away the 'fear factor' and made a positive approach the first option. There were many occasions when a strong counter-attacking policy got the team out of trouble, though there were, inevitably, also times when it didn't come off, and I think this explains why Surrey often went down by a large margin when they suffered a defeat. When the team was on top, the ability to score quickly was often crucial, since it gave their bowlers extra time in which to capture the twenty wickets generally required to win a Championship match. As pitches have got better, and wickets have become harder to come by, so the need to bat positively has increased.

* That Extra Edge
Surrey often possessed a vital extra edge over their opponents, and it was demonstrated most clearly by the depth of their batting. There were only a few matches between 1996 and 2003 where their line-up didn't possess effective batting down to at least number ten in the order, with a player as good as Martin Bicknell even batting at number eleven on a couple of occasions. The opposition always knew, therefore, that Surrey were capable of incredible recoveries and there were a great many examples of these during the glory years. It wasn't only when the team was struggling that the lower-order batting showed itself as a strength, however, as it had the ability to totally demoralise the opposition from good positions, too - the example that springs most readily to mind is the match against Nottinghamshire at Whitgift in 2003, where Surrey were already well placed when numbers ten and eleven went out to join Mark

Ramprakash at the crease. It was also significant that all of the four main bowlers possessed the ability to either block or attack, as the situation demanded.

The other principal area in which the side always seemed to have something extra to offer was the close fielding in front of the wicket to the spinners. Nadeem Shahid, Adam Hollioake, and occasionally Ian Ward, were superb at silly point and short leg, with their fearless nature and razor-sharp reflexes earning them many fine catches and making the job of Saqlain and Salisbury that much easier.

16 Nobody Loves A Winner

"I really hate Surrey," said the man sitting a couple of seats away to my right-hand side at the County Ground, Chelmsford a few seasons ago. Although I didn't know this gentleman, I didn't want to miss what seemed to be a good opportunity… "And why is that exactly?" I asked. Taken aback by the fact that a complete stranger had asked him to justify his statement, the man seemed rather lost for words before managing, rather incoherently, to mutter something about not liking the aggressive style of Adam Hollioake. It didn't surprise me that this man had been unable to come up with any good reason to dislike Surrey, since I have never managed to get a sensible answer out of anyone when I have asked them that question. Since Surrey were, arguably, the nation's leading team on each occasion I have popped the question, one can only assume that jealousy might be the simple reason. I don't ever recall hearing anyone say that they hate Derbyshire, for example, though I suppose the words might be uttered at Trent Bridge or the County Ground, Derby when Nottinghamshire take on their local East Midlands rivals. Additionally, I can't remember Surrey being particularly unpopular in the 1960s, the 1970s or the 1980s when their successes were few and far between. It may, of course, come down to that peculiar British 'sport' of hyping something up and then knocking it down, added to the not uncommon desire for neutrals to support the underdog. In many ways the latter instinct is laudable, though the former doesn't seem to have anything to commend it. If we put this, and simple jealousy, to one side, could there be any other good reasons why Surrey appeared to be so disliked during their period of success between 1996 and 2003?

I'm not sure where the view that Surrey aspired to be "the Manchester United of cricket" came from originally, but it was bandied about in the media for quite a while and I don't think it did the cricket team any favours. Associating a London-based cricket club with a northern-based football club that has a great many more detractors than fans in the capital was never likely to be helpful, but I think Surrey tried to distance themselves from it in any case, as the comparison was always liable to be used out of context. While there were definitely some similarities between the clubs, in terms of having a successful team and being good at developing their own young players, Surrey's detractors happily took it to refer to being a wealthy club who could sign up any players they wanted. If the men from London SE11 return to winning ways in 2005 then I don't suppose it will be long before they start being dubbed "the Chelsea of cricket". Even then, there are no sensible financial comparisons to be drawn, since no county cricket club is ever likely to fall into the 'wealthy' category - there are simply those who are better off than others. At the time of the "Manchester United link", Surrey were certainly not wealthy - a loss of £350,000 was declared in 1995-96, remember - yet Glamorgan's Matthew Maynard probably felt he was stating a true fact when he said "they have a lot of money at The Oval" in an interview with *The South Wales Evening Post* just before Surrey played at Swansea in 1998. Maynard was far from alone in believing that the club was fabulously well off.

So, what else could have upset people? The issues of sledging, over-appealing, and 'playing the game hard' seemed to crop up from time to time. As far as sledging is concerned, I wouldn't know which are the 'best' and 'worst' sides in the domestic game in that area, and I would assume that would be the case for 99% of cricket fans. These things aren't debated in public, and if a county gets censured for such conduct it usually happens behind closed doors, so I wouldn't know whether Surrey were ever guilty of over-the-top sledging. I would be fairly sure that facing the likes of Saqlain Mushtaq and Ian Salisbury with Adam Hollioake at silly point and Nadeem Shahid at short leg probably wasn't a lot of fun for a batsman, and I'm sure those two close fielders would have applied all the psychological pressure they could muster, but I couldn't say whether they ever overstepped the mark or if they were any 'worse' than close fielders from other teams. It would be true to say that the County Champions of 1999, 2000 and 2002 employed men around the bat more frequently than their opponents, simply because they had two fine spinners and were often on top, so there would certainly have been a greater cumulative effect in terms of psychological pressure when batsmen were facing Surrey. Similarly, the county's strength in the bowling department would have led to more appeals. It is inevitable that the better bowlers in the game beat the bat more often than those who are less talented, and, as a result, they are more likely to hit the pad or the outside edge, resulting in a greater number of appeals. With bowlers such as Bicknell, Saqlain and Salisbury having the ability to achieve more lateral movement than many of their opponents, you would therefore expect them to be 'asking the question' more times than lesser mortals. Having said that, I can quite honestly state that I don't recall Surrey being any 'better' or any 'worse' than the opposition when it came to appealing during the period covered by this book. If you asked me to name the player responsible for the greatest number of appeals per innings then I would certainly have to say Mushtaq Ahmed, even though he only played a total of three games for the club, but that wasn't too unexpected, since he is a fine and enthusiastic bowler who beats the bat on a regular basis. I remember well that the Sussex members and supporters were appalled by the number of appeals issuing forth from the little leg-spinner when he made his Surrey debut at Hove in 2002, yet they seemed much more relaxed about it all a year later when he was leading them to the Championship title! Most players are probably guilty of putting pressure on umpires from time to time, and I suspect that Surrey did their fair share of this, even if only in minor ways. At the end of matches where his team was in danger of being docked points for a slow over rate, Adam Hollioake could often be seen engaged in a serious debate with one or both of the umpires as he left the field, while I'd hazard a guess that Martin Bicknell is one of the best players on the county circuit at getting a ball changed if he finds that it doesn't swing - if he can't persuade the umpire that the ball is just a little bit out of shape at the first time of asking then he'll badger away until the official decides that he'll swap the ball for a quiet life! Surrey's players certainly wouldn't have been alone in trying to gain an edge here or there, however, and these are hardly serious 'crimes' in any case. The same applies to the charge that Adam Hollioake's team played hard. What else do you expect from professional players in any sport? Paul Weaver of *The Guardian* came out with some very good comments ahead of the top-of-the-table clash with Hampshire at Guildford in 1999, when he defended Surrey's approach to the game, writing:-

"*Surrey are loud, brash, confident and successful. In other words, they are a little bit 'Australian'. But while it is acceptable to bring in hired guns from Oz to strengthen county sides, a strange and persevering Englishness maintains a rather sniffy attitude about our own players displaying such dubious qualities.*

"*... So what if some complain that the team does swagger and sledge? Surely this is part of the aggression with which we want to invigorate the domestic game?*

"*... So what is it we really want? We cannot complain that too many of our cricketers inhabit the comfort zone of the county game, that they are soft, lazy and lacking dedication, and then turn puce with indignation when they display aggression and violate the Corinthian code.*

"*... But before we become enslaved to the current fashion of hating the Brown Hats we should ask ourselves what it is we really want from our cricketers. We have witnessed a lowering of the standard, despite lofty promises to raise it. But Surrey, at least, cannot be blamed.*"

Fortunately, Mr Weaver was not alone in having an enlightened viewpoint, since the broadcaster and former Hampshire captain, Mark Nicholas, came out with similar comments in his newspaper column before the same game, stating:-

"Surrey are such a dangerous team and, dare I say it, for I appear to be in a minority group on this one, an enjoyable one, too. I can live with the swagger, especially as it increasingly represents genuine self-confidence rather than the fabricated stuff borne of insecurity a few years back. If their opponents at Guildford don't win the Championship then I hope Surrey do. It would be good for the English game if a team of real talent with an approach based on attack and a team of two class spinners were to visit Buckingham Palace in the autumn... to accept the pot of gold from His Royal Highness."

Having then won the title later that summer, Adam Hollioake came up with a fine response when the question of 'playing the game hard' was raised during an interview, saying:-

"We have been honest enough to say 'Yeah, we play the game hard, we hold our hands up', but we don't disrespect our opponents off the field. I can't see where the discussion goes after that."

Where indeed? It was a very fair point, since it is clearly not a winning strategy in sport to give your opponents too much respect on the field of play, though it is a different matter once the game is over. It is important not to be a bad loser, in other words, and Surrey always seemed to be very generous in defeat during their glory years, at least when they were in the public eye, which is all I can comment on. Adam Hollioake and his team were generally prepared to give credit where it was due after being beaten, with the reaction after the heavy defeat at the hands of Durham at The Riverside in 2000 being particularly magnanimous. The Surrey captain had made a special effort to congratulate the 17-year-old Nicky Peng on his debut innings of ninety-eight, and when I spoke to the players and Keith Medlycott about that match for my book *"Doubling Up With Delight"* they were all quick to praise Durham's outstanding performance. It is therefore hard to see how neutrals could consider Surrey to be bad losers. So what about their reaction to winning? The words 'cocky' and 'arrogant' were used more than a few times over the years but, again, you have to say that most winning teams and individuals in sport tend to be very sure of their ability, so it's hard to be critical unless the arrogance is really overdone. It would also be very harsh to complain about triumphs being celebrated to the full, especially when you bear in mind that many of the Surrey players lost, not just one, but two good friends in tragic circumstances during their period of success. Those losses made them reassess their outlook on life and taught them that you should make the most of the good times when they come around.

I suppose the issue of points deductions for damp or poor pitches might have upset a few teams and their supporters, especially in 2000, when Derbyshire and Yorkshire were both involved in controversies when they played Surrey. It is no real surprise that the most successful team of the period was involved in more of these 'pitch battles' than anyone else, since they were the side that everyone wanted to beat, and that many counties felt they probably couldn't overcome on a good true wicket. The solution was to produce a substandard surface and then come up with a plausible reason for it, in the hope that the gap between the two teams could be narrowed by variable bounce or excessive seam movement. Supporters of the counties who were docked points were understandably upset and tried to blame Surrey, which was, of course, quite ludicrous. As the Surrey captain said after the fiasco at Derby:- *"I find it unbelievable that anyone can seriously think that Adam Hollioake is the person who deducts the points. At the end of the day, the teams who produce poor pitches need to take a long hard look at themselves - if they provide a good wicket then they can save themselves a lot of problems."* The situation at both Derby and Scarborough wasn't helped by the Pitch Liaison Officer talking to the Surrey players in full view of the general public, since this gave the impression that the visiting players were seeking him out in an attempt to persuade him to punish the home side when, in reality, he was approaching them to ask their opinions. A lot of trouble and bad feeling could have been avoided if these interviews had been conducted in private. Additionally, Surrey weren't helped by a misconception that they were preparing turning pitches at The Oval for Saqlain and Salisbury long after they had actually started to produce a fresh, if dry, surface for every Championship match. Opposition teams who weren't aware of this, felt that there was one rule for Surrey and a different rule for everyone else. I believe there were only two occasions between 1996 and 2003 when a second-hand wicket was used at The Oval, the last time being in 1998, yet Derek Pringle, the former Essex and England all-rounder turned journalist, was still writing about Surrey having played their home matches on used pitches when he summed up their 2000 Championship-winning season. That sort of incompetence didn't help matters at all.

One final area that might have caused some irritation in the shires was the selection of England squads and teams, since there was a perception that Surrey players were given preference over equally good players from other counties. It was difficult to argue with most selections, however, since the Oval-based man had usually been performing well in a very good and successful side and clearly warranted being given a chance in the national team. Selectorial bias was certainly not an issue, since there was no former or current Surrey man on the selection committee, so it was hard to see why any blame should be attached to the south London-based club for the panel's choices. Since England endured some lean times during Surrey's glory years, I did wonder whether it was possible that the club was damned by association, even if only subconsciously. Certainly in 2001, when the county supplied a large number of players to the national side during the Ashes series, it seemed quite plausible that the average cricket fan's view of Surrey might have been adversely coloured by England's 4-1 defeat.

As my 'friend' at Chelmsford discovered, it is hard to find a good reason for the antipathy towards Surrey that was rife during the glory years and still appears to exist to this day.

17 Doing It The Right Way

Even their harshest critics would surely have to admit that Surrey were a 'role model' county during their 1996-2003 glory years... and they continue to be so. It would be virtually impossible to criticise their approach in all of the following major areas:-
* **Developing young players for Surrey and England**
* **Putting England's needs first**
* **Producing good pitches**
* **International match ticketing/Ongoing ground development**
* **Sound financial strategy**

Developing young players for Surrey and England
Surrey have an enviable record of bringing young players through into their first team and developing them into players capable of representing England. Ever since I started following the county in the mid-1970s, younger players have, wherever possible, been given preference over older players of similar, or slightly greater, ability who still had a few years of good cricket left in them. Graham Roope, Monte Lynch, David Ward and Darren Bicknell were examples of those who either moved on to another county or retired after Surrey decided that they shouldn't be allowed to stand in the way of younger men. This might have seemed rather harsh, especially to the players concerned, but it represented sensible forward planning. The youngsters who benefited from this policy - and the excellent work of Alan Butcher as coach of the second team - have then been given as much responsibility as possible, within the framework and requirements of the team, in order to accelerate their development. The easy option with a young cricketer is to hide him down the batting order or bring him on to bowl at the easiest times in limited-overs matches, but Surrey have always tried to put their youngsters in challenging situations. Examples of this included Ben Hollioake batting at number three in one-day matches while he was still a teenager, and, in more recent times, Rikki Clarke being asked to bowl at either the start or end of National League and Twenty20 Cup matches. Inevitably, with so many international players at the club, a few good young players have been forced to move on, and a handful have carved out successful careers elsewhere, though Gareth Batty is the only one, so far, to progress to international level. Surrey certainly wanted to keep the off-spinning all-rounder, but he clearly had no chance of ousting Saqlain Mushtaq and Ian Salisbury in the short term and had to put his own career first.

In order to give their young players opportunities and to best serve the national side's interests, Surrey have, thus far, steered clear of signing players - EU passport holders or 'Kolpak' players - who are not eligible to play for England yet manage to avoid being classified as overseas registrations. Another misconception about Surrey between 1996 and 2003 was that they were always signing big-name players. There were actually just five major 'imports' during that period - Chris Lewis, Ian Salisbury, Ed Giddins, Mark Ramprakash and James Ormond - while the only other signings directly from another county were Richard Pearson, Micky Bell, Gary Butcher and Ben Scott. A total of nine players signed from other counties in eight years would compare very favourably with every other county in the country. Additionally, Surrey have only signed overseas players when absolutely necessary, having used just five during their glory years - Saqlain Mushtaq (seven seasons), Azhar Mahmood (two seasons), Brendon Julian (one season), Mushtaq Ahmed (three matches) and Franklyn Rose (three matches).

The county continues to place a great emphasis on the development of young players, having been one of the first in the country to establish an academy.

* Putting England's needs first
Much was made of Surrey omitting Graham Thorpe from their line-up at Canterbury in 2002 - against England's wishes - yet the county faced extentuating circumstances as they chased the Championship title and had no choice but to go with the eleven they selected. Since it was just about the only time that Surrey hadn't put the national team's requirements first, the criticism that was meted out to the club was most unjust. Unlike many of the other counties, Surrey have never made a fuss when players have been rested from matches by the ECB, and have always given their England men due consideration, with perhaps the best example of this coming after the failed 1999 World Cup campaign. While Surrey allowed their players time to recover from their disappointment, Nasser Hussain, Neil Fairbrother, Andrew Flintoff, Darren Gough and Angus Fraser were all pressed into NCL action by their counties the following day.

* Producing good pitches
The Oval pitches have been rated amongst the best in the country for many years, and the positions in the ECB's Table Of Merit between 1996 and 2003 are certainly worth recording:-
Four-day Pitches: 1996 - Equal 1st; 1997- 2nd; 1998 - 5th; 1999 - 3rd; 2000 - 1st; 2001 - 4th; 2002 - 4th; 2003 - 1st.
One-day Pitches: 1996 - 4th; 1997 - Equal 4th; 1998 - 3rd; 1999 - 14th; 2000 - 3rd; 2001 - 5th; 2002 - 2nd; 2003 - 1st.
Those ratings, which are for the first-class counties only, are quite exceptional and reflect great credit on the head groundsmen of the period, Paul Brind and Bill Gordon. While some counties ask their groundsman to produce something a bit 'sporty', Surrey merely request that the best possible pitch is prepared for every match, which is surely the most sensible policy, since it minimises any risk of problems and points deductions, as well as keeping things simple for the ground staff. That is quite aside from the fact that a good surface produces the best cricket and high-quality cricketers, providing the best environment for the development of young players. The evidence of the eight years covered by this book proves that a high proportion of the finest matches and performances have come at The Oval, while it is only the better players who have thrived there, since good pitches tend to reward excellence and prove to be a graveyard for mediocrity. Players and the spectators therefore get the best possible deal. Fortunately, many of the other counties appreciate that fact these days, with only a minority stuck in the 'dark ages' of producing 'sporty' tracks. While it is true that Surrey did use a few second-hand pitches in the late 1990s - which didn't affect their placing in the Table Of Merit too badly - they quickly appreciated the error of their ways. Since Saqlain Mushtaq and Ian Salisbury were able to spin the ball on just about any surface, there was no need to offer them any additional assistance.

* International match ticketing/Ongoing ground development
Surrey's record of marketing and selling all their tickets for international matches at The Oval is outstanding. While the majority of the other English Test venues struggle to fill their ground for all but the biggest games, there is always a capacity crowd at The Oval, which is very good news in terms of income for the ECB and, therefore, the other first-class counties. Recognising the need to raise the capacity in order to avoid turning away spectators wishing to purchase tickets, Surrey have built the new OCS Stand at the Vauxhall end. By boosting the ground's capacity by 4,000 seats, the club will be able to generate more revenue for the ECB and the domestic game.

* Sound financial strategy
The club will not overstretch itself financially, however, with further planned developments unlikely to begin until the OCS Stand has been fully paid for. Unlike the boom-and-bust sports of

football and rugby, county cricket clubs tend to be better run, with Surrey one of the leading examples of an organisation that operates within sensible budgets and works hard to maximise its income from sponsorship. This sound financial management has transformed the club's position since the troubled times at the start of the glory years in 1996, with the turnaround in that area having been every bit as impressive as the progress made on the field of play.

Acknowledgements

Many thanks to all of the following people who have assisted me, in ways both large and small, with the production of this book. Every contribution is very much appreciated.

PHOTOGRAPHS
Surrey CCC
Empics
PA
www.cricket-heroes.net
Peter Frost

STATISTICS
Richard Arnold

PROOFREADING/EDITING
Brian Gee
Sue Leach

OTHER
Johnny Grave, Surrey CCC
Sam Streatfeild, Surrey CCC
Marcus Hook of www.ovalworld-online.com
Mark Newson
Richard Spiller
Gary Sutton

Surrey C.C.C. Supporters' Club

Should you wish to become a member of the Surrey C.C.C. Supporters' Club
please write to:-
Chris Keene, 11 Limes Row, Farnborough, Kent, BR6 7BD
Membership rates for 2005:- Full Members £5, Senior Members £3, Junior Members £1
(Junior members - under 18 on 01/01/2005; Senior members - 60 or over on 01/01/2005)

The CHASE Ben Hollioake Fund

Should you wish to make a donation to The Ben Hollioake Fund
please contact:-
Karen Thurston, CHASE Ben Hollioake Fund Manager,
CHASE Children's Hospice Service, Loseley Park, Guildford, GU3 1HS.
Tel: 01483 454213   Fax: 01483 454214
E-mail: karen.thurston@chasecare.org.uk   Web: www.benhollioakefund.com

BBC London Internet Radio Coverage

Don't forget that you can hear live ball-by-ball coverage of every Surrey match on the internet during the summer. Just go to www.surreycricket.com and follow the links to the BBC London site. Or go direct to www.bbc.co.uk/london/sport/cricket

Sponsor-Subscribers

I would not have been able to publish *'Eight Of The Best'* without the support and financial backing of the following sponsor-subscribers. Many thanks to all of you.

Les Allen	Phil Garrard	Sue Leach	David P. Ratcliffe
Stuart Allen	Andrew Gasson	Jerry Lodge	Keith Rivers
Derek Annetts	Brian Gee	Chris Luff	Don Scott
Richard Arnold	Neil Gelder	The Rt. Hon.	Dave (Schenker)
Sarah Atkins	Peter Gent	John Major, CH	Schneider
Keith Bain	Mr Cary Gilbart-Smith	Thomas Manley	David Seymour
John Banfield	Stewart Gilham	Iain McConachie	Alec Sidebotham
Ian P. J. Barton	John Gough-Cooper	Don McKay	Cliff Simpson
Derek Beard	Ted Grant	Simon Mellish	Gordon Smith
Derek Biscoe	Michael Greensmith	Richard W. S. Miller	Rev. Arthur Stubbs
Peter Bourne	Chris Gudgeon	Ann Millington-Jones	Surrey C.C.C.
Michael Brecknell	John Hall	Steve Mills	Gary Sutton
Colin Brown	Roger M. Hancock	Doug Minde	John Taverner
Geoffrey Brown	Edward Handley	Peter Molyneux	Colin John Taylor
Lester Brown	Julian Harding	Paul Monaghan	Iain Taylor
Mark Church	Raymond Hart	David Murray	Jim Taylor
Tony Church	Jacinta Hassett-Brown	James Murray	Mike Thorn
Alan, Margaret	Barry Hatcher	Jim Murray	Steve Tyler
and Adrian Clifton	Kevin Henriques	Les Murrell	Eric W. Waldron
Brian Cowley	Geoff Hetherington	Ken Myers	Brian Walton
Ronald Cronin	Neil Hewitt	David North	Mary Ward
Michael Culham	Mark Hilton	Ray O'Leary	David Watts
Michael Cunnew	Marcus Hook	Michael N. O'Malley	Wouter Wilton
Alan Curtis	Roger Hudson	Mr M.J. Organ	Peter Withey
Tony Dey	Trevor Humphreys	Chris Payne	Mark Witts
Vic Dodds	Elliott Hurst	Wayne Pearce	Edwin Woodcock
Paul Edwards	Mike Hyde	John Per	Steve Wooding
Reg Elliott	Alan B. Jones	A.R. Pettley	Andy Wotton
Keith Evemy	Alan and Joyce Jones	Susan Pharo	
Paul Ferguson	Albert Jordan	Gary Phillips	
Christopher G. Finch	Chris Keene	Keith Porter	
Peter Franks	Barrie P. King	Mr. William	
(Shepperton)	Victor Klarfeld	A. Powell	David Sawyer
Jean Galsworthy	Dominic Lang	Alison Prater	(Author of 'A
Mark Gardiner	Charles Lehec	Lorna Price	Century Of Surrey
Dave Gardner MBE	Stephen Lilley	David Rankin	Stumpers')

If you would like to become a sponsor-subscriber for any future books about Surrey CCC that might be produced by Trevor Jones then please write to the author at **P.O. Box 882, Sutton, Surrey, SM2 5AW** or email him at **tj@sportingdeclarations.co.uk**

Other Books By Trevor Jones

The following books by Trevor Jones about Surrey County Cricket Club are still available and may be purchased directly from the publisher at the discounted prices detailed below.

Order from **Sporting Declarations Books, P.O. Box 882, SUTTON, SM2 5AW**.
Cheques/postal orders payable to *Sporting Declarations Books*, please.

Pursuing The Dream - My Season With Surrey C.C.C.

The ultimately doomed Championship challenge of 1998 forms the central plank of Trevor Jones's first book, a fan's diary of a season following his team around the country. The author's personal day-by-day account of the summer includes tales of the lighter moments of his season with Surrey. Received impressive critical acclaim, including a three-ball review in Wisden Cricket Monthly.

256 pages   Published April 1999
Hardback   0 9535307 0 1   Price - £8.99 (inc UK p&p)   Softback   0 9535307 1 X   Price - £4.99 (inc UK p&p)

The Dream Fulfilled - Surrey's 1999 County Championship Triumph

'The Dream Fulfilled' records Surrey's first County Championship triumph for twenty-eight years. Includes twenty-four pages of full-colour photos, run charts and official Surrey CCC scorebook extracts of significant innings/events, press quotes and views from the other counties. Highly acclaimed everywhere it was reviewed, this book will be treasured by Surrey fans for years to come.

376 pages, including 24 pages of full-colour photographs   Published April 2000
Hardback only   0 9535307 2 8   Price - £13.99 (inc UK p&p)

Doubling Up With Delight - Surrey's Twin Triumphs 2000

The in-depth story of Surrey's first-ever double-winning season when they added the National League Division Two title to a second successive County Championship victory. Run charts, scorebook extracts and twenty-four pages of colour photos are included in another essential volume for followers of Surrey.

312 pages, including 24 pages of full-colour photographs   Published April 2001
Softback only   0 9535307 3 6   Price - £12.99 (inc UK p&p)

268 - The Blow-By-Blow Account Of Ali's Amazing Onslaught

The definitive record of Ali Brown's world record-breaking innings of 268 in the remarkable C&G Trophy match at The Oval in 2002 when countless world, UK, competition, club and personal records fell.

80 pages, including 8 pages of full-colour photographs   Published November 2002
Softback only   0 9535307 4 4   Price - £6.99 (inc UK p&p)

From Tragedy To Triumph - Surrey's Bittersweet Championship Success 2002

The detailed and moving story of how Surrey bounced back from the tragic loss of Ben Hollioake to secure a third Championship title in four seasons. Includes the usual exclusive interviews with the players, run charts and twenty-four pages of colour photos.

376 pages, including 24 pages of full-colour photographs   Published April 2003
Softback only   0 9535307 5 2   Price - £13.99 (inc UK p&p)

Two In Blue - Surrey's Double-Winning 2003 Season

The detailed day-by-day account of an amazing season that saw Surrey win two limited-overs trophies and lead the Championship for the greater part of the summer until Sussex came up on the rails to clinch their first-ever title. Includes exclusive interviews with the players, and sixteen pages of colour photos.

368 pages, including 16 pages of full-colour photographs   Published April 2004
Softback only   0 9535307 6 0   Price - £13.99 (inc UK p&p)

Further information and a special multiple-purchase book deal can be found at
www.sportingdeclarations.co.uk

Comments can be directed to the author at   **tj@sportingdeclarations.co.uk**